Cointegration, Causality, and Forecasting

Clive W. J. Granger

Cointegration, Causality, and Forecasting

A Festschrift in Honour of Clive W. J. Granger

Edited by
ROBERT F. ENGLE
and
HALBERT WHITE

OXFORD
UNIVERSITY PRESS

OXFORD
UNIVERSITY PRESS

Great Clarendon Street, Oxford OX2 6DP

Oxford University Press is a department of the University of Oxford.
It furthers the University's objective of excellence in research, scholarship,
and education by publishing worldwide in

Oxford New York

Athens Auckland Bangkok Bogotá Buenos Aires Calcutta
Cape Town Chennai Dar es Salaam Delhi Florence Hong Kong Istanbul
Karachi Kuala Lumpur Madrid Melbourne Mexico City Mumbai
Nairobi Paris São Paulo Singapore Taipei Tokyo Toronto Warsaw

with associated companies in Berlin Ibadan

Oxford is a registered trade mark of Oxford University Press
in the UK and in certain other countries

Published in the United States
by Oxford University Press Inc., New York

© Oxford University Press 1999

The moral rights of the author have been asserted

Database right Oxford University Press (maker)

First published 1999

British Library Cataloguing in Publication Data
Data available

Library of Congress Cataloging in Publication Data
Data available

ISBN 0-19-829683-5

1 3 5 7 9 10 8 6 4 2

Typeset in Euclid and Avenir
by BookMan Services
Printed in Great Britain
on acid-free paper by
Biddles Ltd., Guildford and King's Lynn

Contents

1

A Comparison of Linear and Nonlinear Univariate Models for Forecasting Macroeconomic Time Series

JAMES H. STOCK AND MARK W. WATSON

1 Introduction

This paper is inspired by four themes that run through Clive Granger's extraordinary body of research on time series analysis and economic forecasting. First, it is plausible that the complicated forces that drive economic events introduce nonlinear dynamics into aggregate time series variables, so an important research program is modeling and exploiting these nonlinearities for forecasting (Granger, 1993; Granger and Teräsvirta, 1993; Granger, Teräsvirta, and Anderson, 1993; Granger and Lin, 1994; Teräsvirta *et al.* 1994). Second, a dominant feature of economic time series data is the considerable persistence, or long-range dependence, of those series (Granger, 1966), and the correct modeling of this persistence is a critical step in constructing reliable forecasts over medium- and long-term forecasting horizons (Granger and Newbold, 1977). Third, because time series models are simplifications of complicated processes that are imperfectly understood, combinations of forecasts from different models using different information might well outperform the forecasts produced by any particular model (Bates and Granger, 1969; Granger and Ramanathan, 1984). Fourth, time series models and forecasting methods, however appealing from a theoretical point of view, ultimately must be judged by their performance in real economic forecasting applications.

Inspired by these themes, we tackle five specific questions in the context of forecasting US macroeconomic time series. First, do nonlinear time series models produce forecasts that improve upon linear models in real time? Second, if there are benefits to using nonlinear models, are the benefits greatest for relatively tightly parameterized models or for more nonparametric approaches?

This research was supported in part by National Science Foundation grant SBR–9409629 and SBR–9730489. We benefited from comments on this work by Frank Diebold, Robin Lumsdaine, Serena Ng, Pierre Perron, Norm Swanson, Andreas Weigend, Richard Zeckhauser and members of the NECSI Time Series Working Group.

Third, can forecasts at the six month or one year horizon be improved by using preliminary evidence on the persistence of the time series to select the forecasting model? Fourth, do combination forecasts outperform forecasts based on a single method across a range of time series, and, if so, how heavily should these combination forecasts weight the currently best performing forecasting methods? Finally, are the gains from using these advanced methods over simple autoregressive forecasts large enough to justify their use?

We conduct an experiment designed to answer these questions. In this experiment, various forecasts are compared at the one, six and twelve month horizons for 215 monthly US economic time series. The experiment simulates real-time implementation of these methods, that is, all forecasts (including all parameter estimates, all model selection rules, all pretests, all forecast combining weights, etc.) are based exclusively on data through the date of each forecast. The parameter estimates, model selection statistics, pretests, and forecast combining weights for all models are updated each month, and these updated statistics are used to make that month's simulated out of sample forecasts.

The forecasts studied here are produced by 49 forecasting methods. We refer to these as *methods* because many of these forecasts are based not on a single estimated model but on results from multiple models that are subject to model selection criteria or pretests. We shall refer to the underlying individual models used by these forecasting methods as *primitive models*, of which there are a total of 105. For example, one of our forecasting methods is an autoregression in levels with a constant term and lag order selection based on the Akaike Information Criterion (AIC), with lag length ranging from zero to twelve; in our terminology this forecasting method selects among thirteen primitive models. The primitive models fall into four classes: autoregressions (AR), exponential smoothing (EX), artificial neural networks (ANN), and logistic smooth transition autoregressions (LSTAR). As an additional benchmark, a "no change" forecast was also considered.

We also consider various procedures to combine information from these 49 forecasting methods. We refer to these as *forecast pooling procedures*. Bates and Granger (1969), Granger and Newbold (1977), and Granger and Ramanathan (1984) demonstrated that averaging forecasts from different models can improve forecast performance when all the models are approximations. The pooling procedures considered here differ by the amount of weight placed on the model with the currently best performance, including weighting all the forecasts equally, weighting the forecasts in inverse proportion to their current mean squared error (MSE), using median forecasts, and placing all weight on the forecasting method that currently has the lowest simulated real-time MSE; this final pooling procedure is simulated real-time model selection by predictive least squares (PLS).

The forecasting methods used in this study have been chosen in part to facilitate comparison with other large-scale "horse races" among time series models. Makridakis *et al.* (1982) studied performance of univariate methods in many series, some of which were economic time series, and concluded that exponential smoothing was often successful. Meese and Geweke (1984) compared various linear models using 150 macroeconomic time series and found that AR models with lag lengths selected by the AIC generally worked well. Interestingly, they also found that linear combination forecasts did not appreciably improve forecast quality. More recently, in a model comparison exercise conducted under the auspices of the Santa Fe Institute, Weigend and Gershenfeld (1994) compared linear models with a large number of nonlinear models; although they detected nonlinear dynamics in several non-economic time series, the nonlinear forecasting models fared relatively poorly for the economic time series they considered (exchange rates). Swanson and White (1995, 1997) compared multivariate ANN models to linear vector autoregressions, and found that the vector autoregressions generally had lower MSEs than the ANN models in simulated real time (their models are all multivariate however so their study does not compare directly to the exercise here).[1] Relative to this literature, the contributions of our study include the use of a large number of macroeconomic time series, the use of a large number of nonlinear models, the investigation of unit root pretest methods, and an extensive investigation of forecast pooling procedures.

The remainder of this paper is organized as follows. The experimental design and forecasting models are given in Section 2. The data are described briefly in Section 3 and in more detail in the Appendix. The results are presented and discussed in Section 4, and conclusions are summarized in Section 5.

2 Forecasting Methods and Experimental Design

2.1 General Considerations

Forecasting models. All the models investigated in this experiment are of the form:

$$y_{t+h} = f_i(Z_t; \theta_{ih}) + u_{it+h}, \tag{2.1}$$

where y_t is the series being forecast, h is the forecast horizon, i indexes the forecasting model ($i = 1, ..., 105$), θ_{ih} is a vector of unknown parameters, u_{it} is an error term, and Z_t is a vector of predictor variables. In general, $Z_t = (y_t, ..., y_{t-p}, \Delta y_t, ..., \Delta y_{t-p}, 1, t)$, where p is the maximal lag lengths. Typically, individual forecasting models use only a subset of the elements of Z_t.

All forecasts are made fully recursively, that is, forecasts of y_{t+h} are made using information in time periods 1, 2, ..., t. For the forecast of y_{t+h}, the parameter vector θ_{ih} is estimated using the data $(y_1, y_2, ..., y_t)$. In all models, the parameter vector is estimated by minimizing the sum of squared residuals of the h-step ahead forecast, that is, the estimate of θ_{ih} at time period t, $\hat{\theta}_{iht}$, solves, $\min_{\theta_{ih}} \Sigma_{s=t_0}^t [y_{t+h} - f_i(Z_t; \theta_{ih})]^2$, where t_0 denotes the first observation used for estimation for that model.

Note that in general each forecasting method, applied to a particular series, has different parameter values at different horizons (that is, the h-period ahead forecast is *not* computed by iterating forward for h periods the one-period ahead forecasting model). This has costs and benefits. If the errors are Gaussian and the one-period ahead forecasting model is correctly specified, then estimating it at the one-period horizon and iterating forward is more efficient than estimating the h-period ahead model directly. On the other hand, to the extent that the models are mis-specified, estimating the h-period ahead model directly permits the method to mitigate the effects of the mis-specification at the horizon at hand. From a practical perspective, forecasting the h-period ahead model directly requires more computer time for parameter estimation, but it simplifies the computation of multistep forecasts from the nonlinear models.

The h-step ahead forecast and the forecast error are:

$$y_{t+h|t,ih} = f_i(Z_t; \hat{\theta}_{iht}) \tag{2.2}$$
$$e_{t+h,ih} = y_{t+h} - y_{t+h|t,ih}. \tag{2.3}$$

Forecast trimming. For our main results, all forecasts were automatically trimmed so that a forecasted change that exceeded in absolute value any change previously observed for that series was replaced by a no-change forecast. This adjustment was adopted to simulate the involvement of a human forecaster, who would be present in actual applications but is absent from our computerized experiment. Because the forecasts in this experiment are made automatically, some models could (and do) make extreme forecasts. Possible sources of these extreme forecasts include parameter breaks, errors arising from incorrect inclusion of deterministic trends, and difficulties arising from multiple local optima for the nonlinear models. In true real time, such "crazy" forecasts would be noticed and adjusted by human intervention. Accordingly, our forecast trimming algorithm can be thought of as a rule of thumb that a human forecaster might use in real time to detect and address such problems. Although we focus primarily on the trimmed forecasts, some results for the untrimmed forecasts are also presented for the purpose of comparison.

Startup and forecast periods. For each series, there are three separate periods: a startup period over which initial estimates of the model are produced; an intermediate period over which forecasts are produced by the 105 primitive models and 49 forecasting methods, but not by the pooling procedures; and the simulated real-time forecast period over which recursive forecasts are produced by all models, methods, and pooling procedures. Let T_0 be the date of the first observation used in this study. Then the startup estimation period is $T_0 + 14$ to T_1, where $T_1 = T_0 + 134$ and the first 13 observations are used for initial conditions as needed. Thus 120 observations are used for the startup estimation period. The intermediate period is T_1 to $T_2 - 1$, where $T_2 = T_1 + 24$. The forecast period is T_2 to T_3, where T_3 is the date of the final observation (1996:12) minus the forecast horizon h.

All forecast performance results reported in the tables are from the simulated real-time forecast period, T_2 to T_3 (inclusive). For most series, the initial observation date is 1959:1, in which case $T_0 = 1959:1$, $T_1 = 1971:3$, $T_2 = 1973:3$, and $T_3 = 1996:12 - h$.

2.2 Forecasting Models and Methods

The forecasting methods are listed in Table 1.

Autoregressive (AR) models. Results are reported for 18 different autoregressive forecasting methods. These differ in their treatment of lag lengths (3 variants); in whether a constant, or a constant and a time trend, were included (2 variants); and in their treatment of persistence in the form of large autoregressive roots (3 variants).

Three alternative treatments of lag lengths were considered: a fixed lag length of 4; lag length determination by the BIC ($0 \leq p \leq 12$); and lag length determination by the AIC ($0 \leq p \leq 12$).

The possibility of persistence in the time series was handled by considering three alternatives. In the first, the autoregression was specified in levels, that is, y_{t+h} was forecast using $y_t, ..., y_{t-p+1}$ with no restrictions on the coefficients. In the second, a unit root was imposed, so that the dependent variable was $y_{t+h} - y_t$ and the predictors were $\Delta y_t, ..., \Delta y_{t-p+1}$.

The third approach was to use a recursive unit root pretest to select between the levels or first differences specification. Theoretical and Monte Carlo evidence suggests that forecasting performance can be improved by using a unit root pretest rather than always using levels or always using differences, see for example Campbell and Perron (1991), Stock (1996), and Diebold and Kilian (1997). The unit root pretesting approach is widely used in practice, and many unit root tests statistics are available for this purpose. In a Monte Carlo study of unit root pretest autoregressive forecasts at moderate to long horizons, Stock (1996) compared several different pretest methods at various significance levels, and found that the best forecast performance across different values of the largest autoregressive root was obtained using the Elliott–Rothenberg–Stock (1996) DF-GLS test with a small significance level. We therefore computed the unit root pretest using the DF-GLS$^\mu$ statistic for the

Table 1. Summary of forecasting methods

Code	Description
A. Linear Methods	
AR(p, u, d)	Autoregressive methods
	p = number of lags = 4, A (AIC, $0 \leq p \leq 12$), or B (BIC, $0 \leq p \leq 12$)
	u = method of handling possible unit root
	= L (levels), D (differences), or P (unit root pretest:
	DF-GLS$^\mu$ if $d = C$, DF-GLS$^\tau$ if $d = T$)
	d = deterministic components included
	= C (constant only) or T (constant and linear time trend)
EX1	Single exponential smoothing
EX2	Double exponential smoothing
EXP	DF-GLS$^\mu$ pretest between EX1 and EX2
B. Nonlinear Methods	
NN(p, u, n_1, n_2)	Artificial Neural Net methods
	p = number of lags = 3, A (AIC, $p = 1$, 3), or B (BIC, $p = 1$, 3)
	(same number of lags in each hidden unit)
	u = L (levels), D (differences), or P (DF-GLS$^\mu$ unit root pretest)
	n_1 = number of hidden units in first hidden layer
	= 2, A (AIC, $1 \leq n_1 \leq 3$), or B (BIC, $1 \leq n_1 \leq 3$)
	n_2 = number of hidden units in second hidden layer
	= 0 (only one hidden layer), 1 or 2
LS(p, u, ξ)	LSTAR methods
	p = number of lags = 3, A (AIC, $p = 1$, 3, 6), or B (BIC, $p = 1$, 3, 6)
	u = L (levels), D (differences), or P (DF-GLS$^\mu$ unit root pretest)
	ξ = switching variable
	= L ($\xi_t = y_t$), D ($\xi_t = \Delta y_t$), M (either L or D depending on unit
	root pretest), D6 ($\xi_t = y_t - y_{t-6}$), A (AIC over $\xi_t = \{y_t, y_{t-2},$
	$y_{t-5}, y_t - y_{t-6}$, and $y_t - y_{t-12}\}$ if levels specification, or $\xi_t = \{\Delta y_t,$
	$\Delta y_{t-2}, \Delta y_{t-5}, y_t - y_{t-6}$, and $y_t - y_{t-12}\}$ if differences specification),
	or B (BIC, same set as AIC)
C. No Change	
NOCHANGE	$y_{t+h\mid t} = y_t$
D. Pooling Procedures	
C(ω, TW, Group)	Linear combination forecasts
	ω = exponent in (2.9) = $\{0, 1, 5\}$ (0 is equal weighting)
	TW = number of observations in rolling window to compute MSEs
	= REC (recursive—all past forecasts used), 120, 60
	Group = A, B, A–C
Med(Group)	Median combination forecasts
	Group = A, B, A–C
PLS(TW, Group)	Predictive least squares combination forecasts
	TW = REC, 120, 60
	Group = A, B, A–C, or PM (all Primitive Methods)
E. Pooled Over All Groups	
PLS(TW, A–D)	Predictive least squares combination forecasts over groups A–D
	TW = REC, 120, 60

selection between models that included a constant term only. For selection between models that included a linear time trend under the levels alternative, the DF-GLS[7] statistic was used.[2]

In all, a total of 52 primitive autoregressive models were estimated (2 specifications of deterministic terms, 13 lag choices, in either levels or differences). The 18 forecasting methods based on these 52 primitive models include recursive model selection using information criteria and/or recursive unit root pretests, as detailed in Table 1.

For some of the results, it is useful to normalize the performance of the models by comparison to a benchmark method. Throughout, we use a simple autoregression as the benchmark method, specifically, an AR(4) (fixed lag length) in levels with a constant term.

Exponential Smoothing (EX). Two primitive exponential smoothing models are considered. Single or simple exponential smoothing forecasts are given by:

$$y_{t+h|t} = \alpha y_{t+h-1|t-1} + (1-\alpha)y_t. \tag{2.4}$$

Double exponential smoothing forecasts are given by:

$$f_t = \alpha_1(f_{t-1} + g_{t-1}) + (1-\alpha_1)y_t, \tag{2.5a}$$
$$g_t = \alpha_2 g_{t-1} + (1-\alpha_2)(f_t - f_{t-1}), \tag{2.5b}$$

where the forecast is $y_{t+h|t} = f_t + h g_t$. The parameters α in (2.4) and (α_1, α_2) in (2.5) are estimated by recursive nonlinear least squares for each horizon (cf. Tiao and Xu, 1993).

Single exponential smoothing is conventionally intended for use with nontrending series and double exponential smoothing is conventionally intended for trending series. We therefore considered a unit root pretest version of these two, in which the single exponential smoothing forecast was used if the recursive DF-GLS$^\mu$ pretest (described above) rejected the null of a unit root, otherwise the double exponential smoothing forecast was used. The three forecasting methods based on these two primitive models therefore include the I(0) specification (2.4), the I(1) specification (2.5), and the specification selected by a recursive unit root pretest.

Artificial neural networks (ANN).[3] Neural network models with one and two hidden layers were considered. The single layer feedforward neural network models have the form:

$$\nu_{t+h} = \beta_0' \zeta_t + \sum_{i=1}^{n_1} \gamma_{1i} g(\beta_{1i}' \zeta_t) + u_{t+h}, \tag{2.6}$$

where $g(z)$ is the logistic function, $g(z) = 1/(1 + e^z)$. When y_t is modeled in levels, $\nu_{t+h} = y_{t+h}$ and $\zeta_t = (1, y_t, y_{t-1}, ..., y_{t-p+1})$. When y_t is modeled in first differences, $\nu_{t+h} = y_{t+h} - y_t$ and $\zeta_t = (1, \Delta y_t, \Delta y_{t-1}, ..., \Delta y_{t-p+1})$. The neural network models with two hidden layers have the form:

$$\nu_{t+h} = \beta_0'\zeta_t + \sum_{j=1}^{n_2} \gamma_{2j} g\left[\sum_{i=1}^{n_1} \beta_{2ji} g(\beta_{1i}'\zeta_t)\right] + u_{t+h}. \tag{2.7}$$

Note that all the neural nets are forced to include a linear component. We will refer to (2.6) as having n_1 hidden units, and to (2.7) as having n_1 and n_2 hidden units, plus a linear component. Alternatively, (2.6) could be thought of as having $n_1 + 1$ hidden units, with one of the hidden units forced to be linear.

The variants of (2.6) and (2.7) that are considered include different lag lengths p; the number of hidden units; and specification in levels and differences. The choices for single hidden layer ANNs are $n_1 = \{1, 2, 3\}$, $p = \{1, 3\}$, and levels/differences specification, for a total of 12 primitive models. (The restricted lag length choice of $p = \{1, 3\}$ was used to reduce computational requirements.) The choices for ANNs with two hidden layers are $n_1 = 2$, $n_2 = \{1, 2\}$, $p = \{1, 3\}$, and levels/differences specification, comprising 8 primitive models. The 15 forecasting methods based on these 20 primitive models include recursive model selection using information criteria and/or recursive unit root pretests, as detailed in Table 1.

In all ANN models, coefficients were estimated by recursive nonlinear least squares. For these models, multiple local minima are an important concern, so the objective function was minimized by an algorithm developed for this application. The algorithm uses a combination of random search methods and local Gauss–Newton optimization. The algorithm and its performance are discussed in the Appendix.

Logistic smooth transition autoregressions (LSTAR).[4] The LSTAR models have the form:

$$\nu_{t+h} = \alpha'\zeta_t + d_t\beta'\zeta_t + u_{t+h}, \tag{2.8}$$

where ν_{t+h} and ζ_t are defined following (2.7) and $d_t = 1/(1 + \exp[\gamma_0 + \gamma_1\xi_t])$, where ξ_t is a function of current and past y_t and is the variable used to define the smooth threshold.

The variants of the LSTAR models differ by the variable used to define the threshold; the specification in levels or differences or unit root pretest; and the lag length p. For models specified in levels, the following five alternatives were used for the threshold variable: $\xi_t = y_t$; $\xi_t = y_{t-2}$; $\xi_t = y_{t-5}$; $\xi_t = y_t - y_{t-6}$; and $\xi_t = y_t - y_{t-12}$. For models specified in first differences, the following five alternatives were used for the threshold variable: $\xi_t = \Delta y_t$; $\xi_t = \Delta y_{t-2}$; $\xi_t = \Delta y_{t-5}$; $\xi_t = y_t - y_{t-6}$; and $\xi_t = y_t - y_{t-12}$. In each case, lag lengths of $p = \{1, 3, 6\}$ were considered, for a total of 30 primitive models (15 in levels, 15 in differences). The 12 forecasting methods based on these 30 primitive models include recursive model selection using information criteria and/or recursive unit root pretests, as detailed in Table 1.

The parameters α, β and γ were estimated using the optimizer described in the Appendix.

No change forecast. The no change forecast is $y_{t+h|t} = y_t$.

2.3 Forecast Pooling Procedures

Linear combination forecasts. Pooled forecasts were computed as weighted averages of the forecasts produced by the 49 forecasting methods. These combination forecasts have the form:

$$\sum_{i=1}^{M} \kappa_{iht} y_{t+h|t,ih}, \text{ where } \kappa_{iht} = (1/\text{MSE}_{iht})^\omega / \sum_{j=1}^{M} (1/\text{MSE}_{jht})^\omega, \tag{2.9}$$

where i runs over the M methods and $\{\kappa_{iht}\}$ are the weights. The weighting schemes differ in the choice of ω, how the MSE is computed, and the sets of methods that are combined. The simplest scheme places equal weight on all the forecasts, which corresponds to setting $\omega = 0$ (in which case the MSE does not enter). As ω is increased, an increasing amount of emphasis is placed on those models that have been performing relatively well.

As shown by Bates and Granger (1969), if forecast error variances are finite then the optimal linear weighting scheme under quadratic loss involves the entire covariance matrix of forecast errors (see Granger and Newbold, 1977). With the large number of forecasts at hand, this scheme is impractical and would be unreliable because of the large number of covariances that would need to be estimated. Instead, we follow Bates and Granger's (1969) suggestion and drop the covariance term from our weighting expressions. Accordingly, the weights on the constituent forecasts are inversely proportional to their out-of-sample MSE, raised to the power ω. The weights with $\omega = 1$ correspond to Bates and Granger's (1969) suggestion. We also explore the possibility that more weight should be placed on the best performing models than would be indicated by inverse MSE weights, and this is achieved by considering $\omega > 1$. If $\omega \neq 0$ the weights $\{\kappa_{iht}\}$ differ from series to series.

Bates and Granger (1969) also stress that the relative performance of different models can change over time. This suggests computing MSEs over rolling windows. The MSEs were therefore computed in three ways: over 60 and 120 period rolling windows (more precisely, over the past $\min(t - T_1 + 1, 60)$ or $\min(t - T_1 + 1, 120)$ periods, respectively), and recursively (over the past $t - T_1 + 1$ periods).

The averages were computed over three different sets of forecasts: the linear

methods (AR and EX); the nonlinear methods (ANN and LSTAR); and all
the methods discussed above (linear, nonlinear, and no change). Note that the
equal-weighted combinations do not depend on the rolling window; these are
denoted as C(0, REC, Group) in Table 1 for the different groups.

Median combination forecasts. If forecast errors are non-Gaussian then linear
combinations are no longer optimal. We therefore consider combination forecasts constructed as the median from a group of methods. In practice this
guards against placing weight on forecasts that are badly wrong for method-
specific reasons such as parameter breaks or parameter estimates achieving
local but not global optima. The medians were computed over three different
sets of forecasts: linear (AR and EX); nonlinear (ANN and LSTAR); and all
the methods discussed above (linear, nonlinear, and no change). This median
forecasts can be thought of as a consensus forecasts obtained by a vote of a
panel of experts, where each expert (forecasting method) gets one vote: the
consensus forecast is achieved when half the experts are on each side of the
forecast.

Predictive least squares (PLS) forecasts. An alternative approach to pooling
forecast information is to select the model that has produced the best forecasts
(as measured by the lowest out-of-sample MSE) up to the forecast date. This
constitutes selection across these models by predictive least squares. The PLS
forecasts differ by the period over which the PLS criterion is computed and
the sets of models for which it is computed.

The periods for which the PLS forecast were computed are the same as for
the combination forecasts, specifically, over the past $\min(t - T_1 + 1, 60)$ periods;
over the past $\min(t - T_1 + 1, 120)$ periods; and over the past $t - T_1 + 1$ periods.

The PLS forecasts were computed for five sets of models: all 49 models listed
in Table 1 under the categories AR, EX, ANN, LSTAR, NOCHANGE; all
linear models listed in Table 1 (AR and EX); all nonlinear models listed in
Table 1 (ANN and LSTAR); all 105 primitive models; and all 49 methods plus
the 36 linear combination, median, and PLS pooling forecasts. The purpose
of examining this final group is to see whether the potential optimality of pooled
forecasts could have been ascertained empirically in (simulated) real time.

3 Data

The data are monthly US macroeconomic time series. The 215 series fall into
the following general categories: production (including personal income), employment and unemployment, wages (hours and earnings), construction (including housing starts), trade (wholesale and retail), inventories, orders, money
and credit, stock returns, stock market dividends and volume, interest rates,
exchange rates, producer price inflation, consumer price inflation, consump-

tion, and miscellaneous (e.g. consumer confidence). In general, seasonally adjusted versions of these data were used for those series that, when unadjusted, have seasonal patterns. Non-seasonally adjusted data were generally used for inflation, interest rates, stock market variables, and exchange rates.

Some of these series were subjected to preliminary transformations. The series in dollars, real quantities and price deflators were transformed to their logarithms. Most other series (interest rates, the unemployment rate, exchange rates, etc.) were left in their native units.

In general, the first date used is either the first date for which the series is available or 1959:1, whichever is later. The exception to this rule is exchange rates; because exchange rates are essentially flat in the fixed exchange rate period, following Meese and Rogoff (1983) the first observation used for exchange rates is 1973:1.

A complete list of the series, their sources, the initial observation date used, whether the series were seasonally adjusted at the source, and the transformation used are given in the Appendix.

4 Results

4.1 Description of Tables

Table 2 contains statistics summarizing the performance of each forecasting method, relative to the benchmark method (an AR(4) specified with a constant term in levels). For each series, forecast method and horizon, the mean square of the $T_3 - T_2 + 1$ simulated out-of-sample forecast errors was computed; for forecasting method i, denote this $\text{MSE}_{ij,h}$, $j = 1, ..., 215$ and $h = 1$, 6, 12. The relative mean square forecast error of the ith forecasting method is $\text{MSE}_{ij,h}/\text{MSE}_{1j,h}$, where $i = 1$ corresponds to the benchmark AR(4) forecast. Table 2 contains the averages and empirical quantiles of the distribution (across series) of this relative MSE, for each of 49 AR, EX, no change, ANN, and LSTAR methods listed in Table 1, and for various pooled forecasts. If, for example, the median of this distribution exceeds one for a candidate forecasting model and horizon, then for at least half the series the benchmark method had a lower simulated out-of-sample MSE at that horizon than the candidate forecasting model.

Table 3 compares forecasting methods by presenting the fraction of series for which each forecasting method is either best or among the top five. The forecasts compared in this table consist of the 49 methods in groups A–C in Table 1 and the pooling procedures that use the full recursive sample ("REC"). For example, at horizon $h = 12$, for 5 percent of the series, the AR(4, L, C) method (which is the benchmark method used in Table 2) had the lowest simulated out-of-sample MSE of all the forecasting methods; for 20 percent of the series, its MSE was among the lowest five.

James H. Stock and Mark W. Watson

Table 2. Mean and percentiles of relative MSEs of various forecasting methods

relative MSE = MSE of method i/MSE of benchmark model
benchmark model = AR(4, L, C) (AR(4) in levels with a constant term)
For each forecast, the first row corresponds to one-step ahead forecasts; the second row,
to 6-step ahead forecasts; the third row, to 12-step ahead forecasts.

Method	Mean	2%	10%	25%	50%	75%	90%	98%
AR(4, L, C)	1.00	1.00	1.00	1.00	1.00	1.00	1.00	1.00
	1.00	1.00	1.00	1.00	1.00	1.00	1.00	1.00
	1.00	1.00	1.00	1.00	1.00	1.00	1.00	1.00
AR(4, L, T)	1.02	0.96	0.99	1.00	1.01	1.03	1.04	1.10
	1.10	0.78	0.88	0.99	1.08	1.17	1.27	1.56
	1.26	0.44	0.77	1.02	1.19	1.38	1.76	2.55
AR(4, D, C)	1.00	0.90	0.95	0.98	1.00	1.02	1.04	1.08
	0.98	0.59	0.77	0.90	0.97	1.05	1.17	1.36
	0.99	0.35	0.64	0.81	0.94	1.15	1.36	1.76
AR(4, D, T)	1.01	0.95	0.97	0.99	1.01	1.02	1.04	1.09
	1.06	0.74	0.89	0.99	1.03	1.11	1.25	1.46
	1.15	0.52	0.83	0.97	1.06	1.18	1.42	1.89
AR(4, P, C)	1.00	0.90	0.95	0.98	1.00	1.01	1.03	1.07
	0.98	0.59	0.77	0.91	0.97	1.05	1.15	1.34
	0.98	0.35	0.64	0.81	0.94	1.11	1.33	1.76
AR(4, P, T)	1.00	0.90	0.95	0.98	1.00	1.02	1.04	1.07
	0.98	0.59	0.77	0.91	0.97	1.06	1.16	1.34
	0.99	0.35	0.64	0.81	0.95	1.14	1.36	1.76
AR(A, L, C)	1.02	0.83	0.95	1.00	1.02	1.04	1.07	1.14
	1.00	0.61	0.86	0.99	1.01	1.06	1.13	1.24
	0.98	0.63	0.87	0.98	1.00	1.02	1.08	1.18
AR(A, L, T)	1.03	0.85	0.96	1.00	1.04	1.06	1.10	1.16
	1.12	0.66	0.81	0.96	1.10	1.25	1.37	1.82
	1.29	0.45	0.75	0.95	1.20	1.41	1.82	3.13
AR(A, D, C)	1.01	0.77	0.94	0.98	1.02	1.05	1.09	1.15
	0.97	0.43	0.72	0.88	0.99	1.09	1.18	1.42
	0.98	0.33	0.58	0.83	0.95	1.15	1.36	1.74
AR(A, D, T)	1.03	0.84	0.96	1.00	1.03	1.06	1.10	1.17
	1.07	0.60	0.80	0.96	1.06	1.16	1.31	1.53
	1.16	0.46	0.72	0.96	1.07	1.23	1.49	1.97
AR(A, P, C)	1.01	0.77	0.94	0.98	1.02	1.05	1.08	1.15
	0.97	0.43	0.72	0.89	0.99	1.09	1.15	1.40
	0.97	0.33	0.58	0.83	0.95	1.13	1.35	1.74
AR(A, P, T)	1.02	0.77	0.94	0.98	1.02	1.05	1.09	1.15
	0.98	0.43	0.72	0.89	0.99	1.09	1.18	1.41
	0.98	0.33	0.58	0.83	0.95	1.15	1.35	1.74
AR(B, L, C)	1.01	0.91	0.97	0.99	1.01	1.02	1.04	1.12
	0.99	0.68	0.87	0.98	1.01	1.03	1.07	1.20
	0.99	0.71	0.93	0.99	1.00	1.02	1.05	1.11
AR(B, L, T)	1.02	0.93	0.97	1.00	1.02	1.05	1.08	1.14
	1.11	0.67	0.83	0.96	1.09	1.23	1.36	1.67
	1.27	0.48	0.75	0.98	1.20	1.42	1.74	2.99
AR(B, D, C)	1.00	0.83	0.94	0.98	1.01	1.03	1.07	1.13
	0.97	0.43	0.73	0.90	0.98	1.07	1.17	1.42
	0.99	0.33	0.58	0.83	0.94	1.15	1.37	1.66

Table 2. (*cont.*)

Method	Mean	2%	10%	25%	50%	75%	90%	98%
AR(B, D, T)	1.02	0.89	0.96	1.00	1.02	1.04	1.08	1.14
	1.06	0.64	0.79	0.99	1.05	1.12	1.26	1.57
	1.16	0.62	0.76	0.99	1.07	1.19	1.43	1.93
AR(B, P, C)	1.00	0.83	0.94	0.98	1.00	1.03	1.06	1.12
	0.96	0.43	0.73	0.90	0.98	1.07	1.16	1.36
	0.98	0.33	0.58	0.83	0.94	1.14	1.31	1.66
AR(B, P, T)	1.00	0.83	0.94	0.98	1.01	1.03	1.07	1.13
	0.97	0.43	0.73	0.90	0.99	1.08	1.16	1.36
	0.99	0.33	0.58	0.83	0.95	1.15	1.36	1.66
EX1	1.73	0.90	0.98	1.01	1.09	1.47	2.82	8.42
	2.12	0.81	0.90	0.97	1.20	1.78	4.61	11.47
	1.83	0.69	0.81	0.95	1.17	1.87	3.02	9.18
EX2	1.06	0.82	0.94	1.00	1.04	1.10	1.18	1.37
	1.16	0.37	0.76	0.94	1.11	1.32	1.64	2.30
	1.26	0.30	0.63	0.91	1.15	1.47	2.14	3.02
EX3	1.06	0.82	0.94	1.00	1.04	1.09	1.18	1.37
	1.15	0.37	0.76	0.94	1.11	1.30	1.55	2.30
	1.23	0.30	0.63	0.91	1.14	1.40	1.92	2.79
NN(3, L, 2, 0)	1.03	0.80	0.91	0.96	1.01	1.08	1.16	1.53
	1.29	0.57	0.92	1.00	1.12	1.32	1.84	3.19
	1.42	0.51	0.81	1.02	1.20	1.51	2.16	4.19
NN(3, D, 2, 0)	0.99	0.83	0.89	0.95	1.00	1.03	1.07	1.24
	0.99	0.63	0.78	0.89	0.98	1.08	1.20	1.63
	1.02	0.35	0.64	0.80	0.95	1.17	1.43	2.35
NN(3, P, 2, 0)	0.99	0.84	0.90	0.95	0.99	1.02	1.07	1.24
	0.99	0.63	0.78	0.89	0.98	1.06	1.18	1.63
	1.01	0.35	0.64	0.81	0.95	1.15	1.35	2.35
NN(3, L, 2, 1)	0.99	0.80	0.89	0.95	1.00	1.03	1.09	1.18
	1.07	0.45	0.79	0.95	1.05	1.16	1.34	1.70
	1.12	0.30	0.60	0.91	1.09	1.24	1.57	2.54
NN(3, D, 2, 1)	0.99	0.83	0.91	0.95	0.99	1.03	1.07	1.21
	1.00	0.63	0.77	0.89	0.98	1.08	1.22	1.64
	1.02	0.35	0.64	0.82	0.95	1.18	1.45	2.31
NN(3, P, 2, 1)	0.99	0.83	0.91	0.95	0.99	1.03	1.07	1.16
	0.99	0.63	0.77	0.89	0.98	1.07	1.19	1.64
	1.01	0.35	0.64	0.82	0.95	1.16	1.38	2.31
NN(3, L, 2, 2)	0.99	0.77	0.88	0.95	1.00	1.04	1.10	1.22
	1.09	0.46	0.80	0.96	1.07	1.19	1.38	1.84
	1.22	0.33	0.73	0.97	1.15	1.39	1.87	2.56
NN(3, D, 2, 2)	1.01	0.85	0.91	0.95	1.00	1.04	1.08	1.24
	1.00	0.62	0.78	0.88	0.99	1.07	1.23	1.61
	1.02	0.35	0.63	0.81	0.97	1.18	1.44	2.31
NN(3, P, 2, 2)	1.01	0.85	0.90	0.95	1.00	1.04	1.08	1.23
	0.99	0.62	0.78	0.88	0.99	1.07	1.19	1.61
	1.01	0.35	0.63	0.81	0.97	1.16	1.36	2.31
NN(A, L, A, 0)	1.03	0.81	0.92	0.96	1.02	1.08	1.16	1.26
	1.32	0.47	0.94	1.02	1.16	1.45	1.91	3.19
	1.50	0.59	0.88	1.05	1.30	1.64	2.16	3.59

Table 2. (*cont.*)

Method	Mean	2%	10%	25%	50%	75%	90%	98%
NN(A, D, A, 0)	1.02	0.84	0.91	0.95	1.00	1.05	1.10	1.31
	1.00	0.62	0.77	0.89	0.98	1.10	1.24	1.64
	1.03	0.37	0.63	0.81	0.96	1.17	1.44	2.32
NN(A, P, A, 0)	1.01	0.82	0.91	0.95	1.00	1.04	1.10	1.24
	1.00	0.62	0.77	0.89	0.98	1.08	1.20	1.64
	1.02	0.37	0.63	0.83	0.96	1.16	1.37	2.32
NN(B, L, B, 0)	1.03	0.83	0.94	0.98	1.02	1.07	1.16	1.24
	1.31	0.56	0.95	1.04	1.15	1.45	1.83	2.92
	1.49	0.59	0.95	1.06	1.31	1.65	2.15	3.29
NN(B, D, B, 0)	1.02	0.87	0.93	0.96	1.01	1.05	1.10	1.19
	1.01	0.64	0.80	0.92	0.98	1.10	1.24	1.56
	1.03	0.37	0.65	0.83	0.95	1.18	1.41	2.22
NN(B, P, B, 0)	1.02	0.87	0.93	0.96	1.01	1.05	1.10	1.18
	1.00	0.64	0.80	0.92	0.98	1.08	1.18	1.56
	1.02	0.37	0.65	0.83	0.96	1.16	1.38	2.22
LS(3, L, L)	1.07	0.91	0.98	1.01	1.05	1.10	1.17	1.31
	1.24	0.80	1.00	1.06	1.15	1.34	1.72	2.00
	1.34	0.56	0.92	1.07	1.19	1.45	1.95	2.89
LS(3, D, D)	1.06	0.90	0.95	1.00	1.04	1.09	1.16	1.38
	1.04	0.69	0.82	0.93	1.02	1.11	1.26	1.60
	1.05	0.40	0.67	0.84	0.98	1.20	1.44	2.21
LS(3, P, P)	1.05	0.90	0.96	1.00	1.04	1.08	1.15	1.33
	1.03	0.69	0.82	0.93	1.02	1.11	1.22	1.60
	1.04	0.40	0.67	0.85	0.98	1.18	1.41	2.21
LS(3, L, D6)	1.04	0.93	0.97	1.00	1.03	1.07	1.12	1.25
	1.09	0.75	0.92	1.00	1.06	1.14	1.28	1.52
	1.10	0.74	0.92	1.01	1.06	1.16	1.26	1.61
LS(3, D, D6)	1.03	0.85	0.95	0.99	1.02	1.06	1.11	1.27
	1.01	0.52	0.72	0.91	1.00	1.12	1.24	1.46
	1.04	0.34	0.60	0.83	0.96	1.20	1.45	1.99
LS(3, P, D6)	1.03	0.85	0.95	0.99	1.02	1.06	1.11	1.24
	1.00	0.52	0.72	0.91	1.00	1.11	1.22	1.42
	1.03	0.34	0.60	0.84	0.96	1.17	1.45	1.99
LS(A, L, A)	1.13	0.92	0.98	1.04	1.08	1.18	1.33	1.68
	1.42	0.77	0.96	1.11	1.29	1.57	2.10	2.99
	1.47	0.73	0.92	1.12	1.34	1.70	2.13	3.27
LS(A, D, A)	1.11	0.83	0.97	1.01	1.08	1.16	1.29	1.72
	1.07	0.47	0.80	0.95	1.06	1.18	1.35	1.61
	1.06	0.31	0.60	0.82	1.00	1.25	1.56	2.35
LS(A, P, A)	1.11	0.83	0.97	1.01	1.07	1.16	1.29	1.61
	1.07	0.47	0.80	0.96	1.06	1.17	1.33	1.58
	1.05	0.31	0.60	0.83	1.00	1.24	1.57	2.36
LS(B, L, B)	1.11	0.89	0.97	1.02	1.07	1.15	1.27	1.70
	1.41	0.74	0.96	1.11	1.26	1.59	1.97	3.02
	1.46	0.72	0.90	1.11	1.32	1.71	2.09	3.19
LS(B, D, B)	1.07	0.81	0.96	1.00	1.05	1.11	1.19	1.46
	1.04	0.47	0.77	0.92	1.03	1.15	1.31	1.61
	1.06	0.31	0.60	0.84	0.99	1.20	1.52	2.31

Table 2. (*cont.*)

Method	Mean	2%	10%	25%	50%	75%	90%	98%
LS(B, P, B)	1.06	0.81	0.96	1.00	1.04	1.11	1.19	1.44
	1.03	0.47	0.77	0.92	1.03	1.15	1.29	1.61
	1.05	0.31	0.60	0.84	0.99	1.19	1.52	2.31
NOCHANGE	1.76	0.89	0.99	1.04	1.12	1.49	2.82	8.42
	2.14	0.81	0.90	1.00	1.22	1.78	4.61	11.47
	1.83	0.69	0.82	0.97	1.21	1.77	2.93	9.18
C(0, REC, A–C)	0.95	0.79	0.87	0.93	0.96	0.98	1.00	1.01
	0.89	0.42	0.69	0.85	0.92	0.97	1.03	1.12
	0.87	0.27	0.56	0.78	0.89	1.00	1.08	1.32
C(0, REC, A)	0.98	0.81	0.91	0.96	0.99	1.01	1.02	1.06
	0.92	0.46	0.68	0.88	0.96	1.01	1.08	1.15
	0.90	0.37	0.57	0.81	0.93	1.05	1.16	1.33
C(0, REC, B)	0.94	0.79	0.86	0.92	0.95	0.97	1.00	1.05
	0.90	0.45	0.72	0.85	0.92	0.99	1.04	1.13
	0.88	0.28	0.59	0.79	0.89	1.00	1.08	1.35
C(1, REC, A–C)	0.95	0.76	0.88	0.93	0.96	0.98	1.00	1.01
	0.89	0.43	0.69	0.85	0.92	0.98	1.03	1.11
	0.87	0.34	0.59	0.78	0.90	1.01	1.08	1.34
C(1, REC, A)	0.98	0.82	0.91	0.97	0.99	1.01	1.02	1.05
	0.93	0.48	0.71	0.90	0.96	1.01	1.08	1.15
	0.91	0.43	0.57	0.81	0.94	1.07	1.15	1.40
C(1, REC, B)	0.94	0.79	0.86	0.92	0.95	0.97	1.00	1.05
	0.89	0.44	0.70	0.85	0.91	0.99	1.04	1.14
	0.87	0.32	0.60	0.79	0.89	1.00	1.11	1.38
C(1, 60, A–C)	0.95	0.75	0.88	0.93	0.96	0.98	1.00	1.01
	0.89	0.42	0.68	0.85	0.93	0.98	1.03	1.12
	0.88	0.31	0.58	0.78	0.91	1.03	1.10	1.34
C(1, 120, A–C)	0.95	0.76	0.88	0.93	0.96	0.98	1.00	1.01
	0.89	0.43	0.69	0.85	0.92	0.98	1.03	1.11
	0.87	0.34	0.58	0.78	0.90	1.01	1.09	1.34
C(5, 60, A–C)	0.94	0.74	0.88	0.93	0.96	0.98	1.00	1.02
	0.91	0.41	0.64	0.85	0.94	1.01	1.07	1.15
	0.97	0.28	0.60	0.82	0.98	1.12	1.30	1.49
C(5, 120, A–C)	0.95	0.74	0.88	0.93	0.96	0.98	1.00	1.01
	0.89	0.43	0.68	0.85	0.93	0.99	1.04	1.11
	0.91	0.35	0.59	0.80	0.92	1.04	1.16	1.41
C(5, REC, A–C)	0.95	0.74	0.88	0.93	0.96	0.98	1.00	1.01
	0.90	0.42	0.69	0.85	0.93	0.99	1.04	1.11
	0.91	0.35	0.61	0.80	0.92	1.04	1.14	1.40
C(1, 60, A)	0.98	0.82	0.91	0.97	0.99	1.01	1.02	1.05
	0.93	0.47	0.71	0.90	0.96	1.01	1.08	1.15
	0.92	0.37	0.57	0.81	0.95	1.07	1.17	1.40
C(1, 120, A)	0.98	0.82	0.91	0.97	0.99	1.01	1.02	1.05
	0.93	0.48	0.71	0.90	0.96	1.01	1.08	1.15
	0.91	0.43	0.57	0.80	0.94	1.05	1.15	1.40
C(5, 60, A)	0.98	0.81	0.92	0.97	0.99	1.01	1.02	1.04
	0.94	0.48	0.73	0.90	0.98	1.03	1.08	1.18
	0.98	0.40	0.64	0.87	1.01	1.14	1.27	1.50

Table 2. (*cont.*)

Method	Mean	2%	10%	25%	50%	75%	90%	98%
C(5, 120, A)	0.98	0.82	0.91	0.97	1.00	1.01	1.02	1.04
	0.93	0.51	0.72	0.89	0.97	1.01	1.07	1.16
	0.93	0.43	0.60	0.82	0.96	1.06	1.14	1.52
C(5, REC, A)	0.98	0.82	0.91	0.97	1.00	1.01	1.02	1.04
	0.93	0.52	0.72	0.89	0.97	1.02	1.07	1.16
	0.93	0.42	0.61	0.82	0.96	1.06	1.16	1.52
C(1, 60, B)	0.94	0.79	0.86	0.92	0.95	0.97	1.00	1.05
	0.89	0.45	0.69	0.85	0.92	0.99	1.04	1.13
	0.88	0.31	0.59	0.79	0.91	1.03	1.10	1.38
C(1, 120, B)	0.94	0.79	0.86	0.92	0.95	0.97	1.00	1.05
	0.89	0.44	0.69	0.84	0.91	0.99	1.04	1.14
	0.87	0.32	0.58	0.79	0.88	1.00	1.10	1.38
C(5, 60, B)	0.94	0.78	0.86	0.92	0.95	0.97	1.00	1.06
	0.91	0.45	0.69	0.85	0.94	1.01	1.07	1.26
	0.97	0.28	0.60	0.80	0.96	1.13	1.31	1.56
C(5, 120, B)	0.94	0.77	0.86	0.92	0.95	0.97	1.00	1.04
	0.90	0.41	0.69	0.86	0.92	0.99	1.05	1.18
	0.91	0.32	0.59	0.79	0.91	1.06	1.16	1.50
C(5, REC, B)	0.94	0.77	0.86	0.92	0.95	0.97	1.00	1.04
	0.90	0.41	0.72	0.86	0.92	0.99	1.05	1.17
	0.92	0.32	0.60	0.78	0.91	1.06	1.17	1.52
PLS(REC, PM)	1.02	0.79	0.92	0.98	1.02	1.07	1.12	1.26
	1.05	0.48	0.74	0.95	1.05	1.16	1.35	1.55
	1.14	0.38	0.65	0.91	1.09	1.33	1.59	2.32
PLS(REC, A–C)	1.01	0.77	0.90	0.97	1.02	1.05	1.11	1.21
	1.03	0.47	0.75	0.93	1.03	1.15	1.27	1.50
	1.10	0.35	0.65	0.88	1.07	1.24	1.51	2.15
PLS(REC, A)	1.00	0.81	0.94	0.99	1.01	1.03	1.06	1.12
	1.01	0.49	0.75	0.94	1.03	1.10	1.21	1.36
	1.05	0.48	0.65	0.92	1.04	1.19	1.38	1.92
PLS(REC, B)	1.01	0.77	0.92	0.97	1.01	1.05	1.11	1.27
	1.04	0.50	0.81	0.94	1.04	1.14	1.31	1.61
	1.08	0.34	0.64	0.88	1.02	1.22	1.51	2.44
PLS(REC, A–D)	1.00	0.78	0.91	0.95	1.00	1.04	1.10	1.17
	1.05	0.42	0.77	0.93	1.06	1.16	1.32	1.62
	1.13	0.38	0.63	0.87	1.12	1.33	1.59	2.05
PLS(60, PM)	1.01	0.76	0.90	0.97	1.01	1.07	1.13	1.21
	1.11	0.40	0.76	0.96	1.11	1.28	1.43	1.74
	1.23	0.37	0.63	0.94	1.23	1.46	1.73	2.29
PLS(120, PM)	1.02	0.77	0.91	0.97	1.02	1.07	1.11	1.26
	1.06	0.45	0.75	0.94	1.07	1.19	1.32	1.55
	1.17	0.39	0.68	0.93	1.12	1.33	1.59	2.40
PLS(60, A–C)	1.01	0.73	0.91	0.96	1.01	1.06	1.11	1.30
	1.08	0.39	0.71	0.95	1.10	1.23	1.40	1.56
	1.18	0.33	0.65	0.88	1.16	1.45	1.69	2.19
PLS(120, A–C)	1.01	0.77	0.90	0.96	1.01	1.05	1.10	1.21
	1.04	0.42	0.75	0.93	1.05	1.18	1.32	1.47
	1.12	0.34	0.65	0.90	1.10	1.27	1.54	2.39

Table 2. (*cont.*)

Method	Mean	2%	10%	25%	50%	75%	90%	98%
PLS(60, A)	1.01	0.77	0.95	0.99	1.02	1.04	1.07	1.11
	1.06	0.47	0.79	0.96	1.07	1.19	1.28	1.48
	1.12	0.43	0.65	0.92	1.11	1.34	1.51	1.73
PLS(120, A)	1.00	0.79	0.94	0.99	1.01	1.03	1.06	1.13
	1.02	0.50	0.75	0.94	1.03	1.12	1.23	1.36
	1.05	0.44	0.64	0.89	1.05	1.19	1.41	1.91
PLS(60, B)	1.01	0.78	0.92	0.96	1.01	1.06	1.12	1.28
	1.09	0.41	0.78	0.98	1.08	1.22	1.38	1.68
	1.16	0.33	0.70	0.90	1.13	1.38	1.64	2.22
PLS(120, B)	1.01	0.78	0.92	0.96	1.01	1.05	1.10	1.23
	1.05	0.47	0.80	0.94	1.05	1.16	1.30	1.58
	1.09	0.34	0.64	0.87	1.06	1.22	1.60	2.16
PLS(60, A–D)	1.00	0.75	0.90	0.96	1.00	1.05	1.10	1.31
	1.09	0.40	0.78	0.95	1.08	1.23	1.42	1.74
	1.21	0.37	0.67	0.90	1.21	1.48	1.71	2.21
PLS(120, A–D)	1.00	0.78	0.91	0.95	1.01	1.05	1.10	1.17
	1.05	0.42	0.74	0.94	1.06	1.18	1.32	1.62
	1.12	0.38	0.63	0.88	1.12	1.35	1.60	2.02
MED(A–C)	0.96	0.81	0.90	0.94	0.97	0.99	1.00	1.02
	0.91	0.44	0.71	0.87	0.94	0.99	1.05	1.15
	0.90	0.32	0.58	0.79	0.91	1.05	1.16	1.49
MED(A)	0.99	0.82	0.93	0.97	1.00	1.01	1.03	1.07
	0.94	0.44	0.73	0.89	0.97	1.03	1.11	1.19
	0.94	0.37	0.59	0.83	0.93	1.11	1.22	1.54
MED(B)	0.95	0.80	0.89	0.93	0.96	0.99	1.01	1.05
	0.92	0.46	0.74	0.85	0.93	0.99	1.07	1.26
	0.92	0.31	0.58	0.79	0.90	1.05	1.23	1.57

A natural question to ask in this comparison is which forecasting method is best overall. The answer to this question depends, among other things, on the attitude towards risk of the forecaster, that is, on the forecaster's loss function. Table 4 therefore reports rankings of the different methods for different loss functions. The loss functions are all of the form:

$$\text{Loss}_{i,h} = (1/215)\sum_{\text{series }\{y\}} (T_3 - T_2 + 1)^{-1} \sum_{i=T_2}^{T_3} |(y_{t+h} - \hat{y}_{t+h|t,ih})/\sigma_h|^p, \qquad (4.1)$$

where σ_h is the estimated standard deviation of $y_{t+h} - y_t$.[5]

4.2 Highlights of the Results

Unit root pretests. Among the 215 series, a 5 percent DF-GLS$^\mu$ unit root test rejects the null in 13.5 percent of the series, and a 5 percent DF-GLS$^\tau$ test rejects the null in 10.2 percent of the series, using the full sample and six lags.

Table 3. Summary of rankings of various methods
Entries are fraction of series for which the indicated method performs in the top N

Method	1 step ahead		6 steps ahead		12 steps ahead	
	$N = 1$	5	$N = 1$	5	$N = 1$	5
AR(4, L, C)	0.00	0.03	0.04	0.10	0.05	0.20
AR(4, L, T)	0.00	0.02	0.00	0.06	0.00	0.07
AR(4, D, C)	0.00	0.03	0.00	0.03	0.00	0.03
AR(4, D, T)	0.00	0.00	0.00	0.01	0.01	0.04
AR(4, P, C)	0.00	0.02	0.00	0.03	0.00	0.03
AR(4, P, T)	0.00	0.03	0.01	0.03	0.00	0.03
AR(A, L, C)	0.01	0.03	0.04	0.11	0.02	0.14
AR(A, L, T)	0.01	0.01	0.04	0.06	0.04	0.07
AR(A, D, C)	0.00	0.04	0.00	0.06	0.01	0.07
AR(A, D, T)	0.01	0.02	0.00	0.02	0.01	0.03
AR(A, P, C)	0.00	0.04	0.01	0.07	0.02	0.07
AR(A, P, T)	0.01	0.05	0.01	0.06	0.01	0.07
AR(B, L, C)	0.00	0.03	0.00	0.11	0.03	0.16
AR(B, L, T)	0.00	0.01	0.01	0.07	0.02	0.07
AR(B, D, C)	0.00	0.03	0.00	0.04	0.00	0.04
AR(B, D, T)	0.00	0.01	0.01	0.02	0.00	0.02
AR(B, P, C)	0.00	0.01	0.00	0.03	0.00	0.03
AR(B, P, T)	0.01	0.03	0.00	0.04	0.00	0.03
EX1	0.03	0.06	0.04	0.12	0.05	0.13
EX2	0.01	0.03	0.00	0.05	0.01	0.06
EX3	0.00	0.03	0.04	0.06	0.03	0.07
NN(3, L, 2, 0)	0.05	0.17	0.01	0.07	0.01	0.08
NN(3, D, 2, 0)	0.02	0.13	0.00	0.06	0.00	0.05
NN(3, P, 2, 0)	0.05	0.13	0.00	0.07	0.00	0.04
NN(3, L, 2, 1)	0.02	0.18	0.07	0.15	0.05	0.12
NN(3, D, 2, 1)	0.02	0.09	0.00	0.05	0.00	0.05
NN(3, P, 2, 1)	0.03	0.13	0.01	0.06	0.01	0.05
NN(3, L, 2, 2)	0.06	0.19	0.04	0.13	0.02	0.08
NN(3, D, 2, 2)	0.00	0.12	0.01	0.08	0.01	0.04
NN(3, P, 2, 2)	0.01	0.12	0.00	0.07	0.00	0.04
NN(A, L, A, 0)	0.06	0.15	0.02	0.06	0.01	0.06
NN(A, D, A, 0)	0.05	0.12	0.04	0.08	0.05	0.09
NN(A, P, A, 0)	0.01	0.10	0.00	0.07	0.00	0.08
NN(B, L, B, 0)	0.00	0.07	0.01	0.05	0.01	0.03
NN(B, D, B, 0)	0.01	0.06	0.00	0.04	0.00	0.02
NN(B, P, B, 0)	0.01	0.06	0.00	0.04	0.00	0.02
LS(3, L, L)	0.00	0.03	0.00	0.03	0.01	0.04
LS(3, D, D)	0.00	0.00	0.00	0.02	0.00	0.02
LS(3, P, P)	0.00	0.01	0.01	0.02	0.00	0.02
LS(3, L, D6)	0.00	0.02	0.02	0.06	0.02	0.08
LS(3, D, D6)	0.01	0.04	0.01	0.05	0.00	0.06
LS(3, P, D6)	0.00	0.04	0.02	0.07	0.01	0.07
LS(A, L, A)	0.00	0.02	0.00	0.02	0.01	0.04
LS(A, D, A)	0.01	0.01	0.00	0.02	0.02	0.06

Table 3. (*cont.*)

Method	1 step ahead		6 steps ahead		12 steps ahead	
	N = 1	5	N = 1	5	N = 1	5
LS(A, P, A)	0.00	0.02	0.00	0.01	0.00	0.06
LS(B, L, B)	0.00	0.02	0.01	0.04	0.01	0.04
LS(B, D, B)	0.00	0.01	0.00	0.04	0.01	0.05
LS(B, P, B)	0.00	0.02	0.00	0.03	0.00	0.06
NOCHANGE	0.00	0.02	0.03	0.09	0.04	0.11
C(0, REC, A–C)	0.04	0.34	0.06	0.33	0.04	0.34
C(0, REC, A)	0.01	0.05	0.03	0.16	0.03	0.11
C(0, REC, B)	0.10	0.51	0.09	0.32	0.13	0.30
C(1, REC, A–C)	0.02	0.27	0.01	0.33	0.00	0.23
C(1, REC, A)	0.00	0.03	0.00	0.07	0.01	0.07
C(1, REC, B)	0.13	0.53	0.05	0.34	0.03	0.33
MED(A–C)	0.01	0.10	0.04	0.17	0.04	0.11
MED(A)	0.01	0.02	0.00	0.05	0.00	0.03
MED(B)	0.08	0.27	0.07	0.23	0.07	0.22
PLS(REC, PM)	0.00	0.04	0.01	0.05	0.01	0.06
PLS(REC, A–C)	0.00	0.06	0.00	0.04	0.00	0.05
PLS(REC, A)	0.00	0.03	0.00	0.06	0.00	0.06
PLS(REC, B)	0.00	0.04	0.01	0.06	0.01	0.04
PLS(REC, A–D)	0.01	0.06	0.00	0.07	0.00	0.03

When the DF-GLS unit root pretest is employed recursively with a critical value that depends on the sample size (see note 2), it generally improves forecast performance at all horizons as measured by mean or median relative MSEs in Table 2. The improvement is largest for EX methods. Among AR methods, this improvement is most pronounced when the levels specification includes a time trend. The improvement for ANN and LSTAR methods is small at $h = 1$ but increases with the forecast horizon. Evidently the AR methods in levels with time trends and the ANN and LSTAR methods in levels can produce forecasts which are quite poor, especially at the longer horizons, and pretesting to identify situations in which a unit root can be imposed reduces the frequency of extreme errors.

AIC- and BIC-based model selection. The performance of automatic lag length selection methods depends on the family of models being used, and it does not seem possible to reach general conclusions. Among autoregressions, on average automatic order selection yields only marginal improvements over the benchmark imposition of 4 lags. Comparison of the relative MSEs in Table 2 for autoregressive methods using AIC and BIC lag length choice indicates that

Table 4. Rankings of various methods, combined over all series, for different loss functions: Trimmed forecasts

Cost function = $E|e_t|^\rho$, e_t = forecast error

Rank	1 step ahead			6 steps ahead			12 steps ahead		
	$\rho = 1.0$	2.0	3.0	$\rho = 1.0$	2.0	3.0	$\rho = 1.0$	2.0	3.0
1	C(1, REC, B)	C(1, REC, B)	C(1, REC, B)	C(0, REC, A–C)	C(0, REC, A–C)	C(0, REC, A–C)	C(0, REC, A–C)	C(0, REC, A–C)	C(0, REC, A, C)
2	C(0, REC, B)	C(0, REC, B)	C(0, REC, B)	C(1, REC, B)	C(1, REC, B)	C(1, REC, B)	C(1, REC, B)	C(1, REC, B)	C(0, REC, B)
3	C(0, REC, A–C)	C(1, REC, A–C)	C(1, REC, A–C)	C(1, REC, B)	C(1, REC, B)	C(0, REC, B)	C(1, REC, B)	C(0, REC, B)	C(1, REC, B)
4	C(1, REC, A–C)	C(0, REC, A–C)	C(0, REC, A–C)	C(0, REC, B)	C(0, REC, B)	C(1, REC, A–C)	C(1, REC, A–C)	C(1, REC, A–C)	C(1, REC, A–C)
5	MED(B)	MED(B)	MED(B)	MED(A–C)	MED(A–C)	MED(A–C)	MED(A–C)	MED(A–C)	MED(A–C)
6	MED(A–C)	MED(A–C)	MED(A–C)	C(0, REC, A)	MED(B)	MED(B)	C(0, REC, A)	C(0, REC, A)	C(0, REC, A)
7	C(0, REC, A)	C(0, REC, A)	NN(3, L, 2, 1)	MED(B)	C(0, REC, A)	C(0, REC, A)	MED(B)	MED(B)	MED(B)
8	C(1, REC, A)	C(1, REC, A)	NN(3, L, 2, 2)	C(1, REC, A)	C(1, REC, A)	C(1, REC, A)	C(1, REC, A)	C(1, REC, A)	C(1, REC, A)
9	MED(A)	NN(3, L, 2, 1)	C(0, REC, A)	MED(A)	MED(A)	MED(A)	MED(A)	MED(A)	MED(A)
10	PLS(REC, A–D)	NN(3, P, 2, 0)	C(1, REC, A)	AR(B, P, C)	AR(B, P, C)	AR(B, P, C)	AR(A, P, C)	AR(A, P, C)	AR(A, D, C)
11	NN(3, P, 2, 0)	MED(A)	NN(3, P, 2, 0)	AR(A, P, C)	AR(A, P, C)	AR(B, P, T)	AR(A, D, C)	AR(A, D, C)	AR(A, P, C)
12	NN(3, P, 2, 1)	NN(3, L, 2, 2)	NN(3, D, 2, 0)	AR(B, P, T)	AR(B, P, T)	AR(B, D, C)	AR(A, P, T)	AR(A, P, T)	AR(A, P, T)
13	NN(3, D, 2, 0)	NN(3, D, 2, 0)	NN(3, P, 2, 1)	AR(A, D, C)	AR(B, D, C)	AR(A, P, C)	AR(B, P, C)	AR(B, P, C)	AR(B, P, C)
14	NN(3, D, 2, 1)	NN(3, P, 2, 1)	MED(A)	AR(B, D, C)	AR(A, D, C)	AR(A, D, C)	AR(B, D, C)	AR(B, D, C)	AR(B, D, C)
15	AR(4, P, C)	NN(3, D, 2, 1)	NN(3, D, 2, 1)	AR(A, P, T)	AR(A, P, T)	AR(A, P, T)	AR(B, P, T)	AR(B, P, T)	AR(B, P, T)
16	AR(4, D, C)	AR(4, P, C)	AR(4, P, C)	AR(4, P, C)	AR(4, P, C)	AR(4, D, C)	AR(4, P, C)	AR(4, P, C)	AR(4, P, C)
17	AR(4, P, T)	AR(4, P, T)	AR(4, P, T)	AR(4, D, C)	AR(4, D, C)	AR(4, P, T)	AR(4, D, C)	AR(4, D, C)	AR(4, D, C)
18	NN(3, P, 2, 2)	AR(4, D, C)	AR(4, D, C)	AR(4, P, T)	AR(4, P, T)	NN(3, P, 2, 0)	AR(4, P, T)	AR(4, P, T)	AR(4, P, T)
19	NN(3, L, 2, 1)	PLS(REC, A–D)	AR(4, D, C)	NN(3, P, 2, 0)	NN(3, P, 2, 0)	NN(3, P, 2, 1)	LS(3, P, D6)	LS(3, P, D6)	LS(3, P, D6)
20	PLS(REC, A)	AR(4, L, C)	PLS(REC, A–D)	LS(3, P, D6)	LS(3, P, D6)	NN(3, P, 2, 1)	NN(3, P, 2, 0)	NN(3, P, 2, 0)	LS(3, D, D6)
21	AR(B, P, C)	PLS(REC, A)	AR(B, P, C)	NN(3, P, 2, 2)	NN(3, P, 2, 2)	NN(3, D, 2, 0)	NN(3, D, 2, 0)	NN(3, D, 2, 0)	NN(3, P, 2, 0)
22	NN(3, L, 2, 2)	AR(B, P, C)	AR(B, L, C)	NN(3, P, 2, 1)	NN(3, P, 2, 1)	NN(3, D, 2, 1)	NN(3, D, 2, 1)	NN(3, P, 2, 2)	NN(B, D, B, 0)
23	AR(B, D, C)	AR(B, P, T)	AR(B, P, T)	LS(3, D, D6)	LS(3, D, D6)	NN(3, P, 2, 2)	NN(3, P, 2, 2)	NN(3, P, 2, 1)	NN(B, P, B, 0)
24	AR(B, P, T)	AR(B, D, C)	NN(A, L, A, 0)	AR(B, L, C)	LS(3, P, D6)	LS(3, P, D6)	LS(3, P, D6)	NN(A, P, A, 0)	NN(3, D, 2, 0)
25	AR(4, L, C)	AR(B, L, C)	AR(B, D, C)	PLS(REC, A)	AR(B, L, C)	AR(B, L, C)	NN(3, D, 2, 2)	NN(3, D, 2, 1)	NN(3, P, 2, 1)
26	NN(A, P, A, 0)	PLS(REC, A–C)	AR(4, L, T)	NN(3, D, 2, 0)	NN(A, P, A, 0)	NN(3, D, 2, 2)	NN(3, D, 2, 1)	NN(3, D, 2, 1)	NN(3, D, 2, 1)
27	NN(3, D, 2, 2)	AR(4, D, T)	AR(4, D, T)	NN(3, D, 2, 2)	NN(3, D, 2, 2)	PLS(REC, A)	NN(A, D, A, 0)	NN(3, D, 2, 2)	NN(3, D, 2, 2)
28	PLS(REC, A–C)	PLS(REC, B)	PLS(REC, A–D)	AR(A, L, C)	LS(3, D, D6)	NN(A, P, A, 0)	LS(B, P, B)	NN(B, P, B, 0)	NN(3, P, 2, 2)
29	NN(A, D, A, 0)	NN(3, P, 2, 2)	AR(A, L, C)	NN(A, D, A, 0)	NN(A, D, A, 0)	AR(4, L, C)	NN(B, P, B, 0)	NN(A, D, A, 0)	NN(3, D, 2, 2)
30	AR(B, L, C)	AR(A, P, C)	AR(B, L, T)	PLS(REC, A)	PLS(REC, A)	LS(3, D, D6)	LS(3, D, D6)	NN(B, D, B, 0)	NN(A, P, A, 0)
31	PLS(REC, B)	AR(4, L, T)	AR(B, D, T)	LS(B, P, B)	NN(B, P, B, 0)	NN(A, D, A, 0)	LS(B, D, B)	LS(B, P, B)	LS(B, P, B)

Table 4. (*cont.*)

Rank	1 step ahead			6 steps ahead			12 steps ahead		
	$\rho = 1.0$	2.0	3.0	$\rho = 1.0$	2.0	3.0	$\rho = 1.0$	2.0	3.0
32	NN(B, P, B, 0)	AR(A, D, C)	AR(A, P, C)	NN(B, P, B, 0)	AR(A, L, C)	NN(B, P, B, 0)	NN(B, D, B, 0)	LS(B, D, B)	NN(A, D, A, 0)
33	NN(B, D, B, 0)	AR(A, L, C)	NN(B, L, B, 0)	NN(A, D, A, 0)	AR(4, L, C)	NN(B, D, B, 0)	LS(A, P, A)	LS(A, P, A)	LS(A, P, A)
34	AR(A, P, C)	AR(A, P, T)	PLS(REC, A-C)	LS(B, D, B)	AR(A, L, C)	AR(A, L, C)	LS(A, D, A)	LS(A, D, A)	LS(A, D, A)
35	AR(A, D, C)	NN(A, L, A, 0)	NN(3, L, 2, 0)	NN(B, D, B, 0)	LS(B, D, B)	PLS(REC, A-C)	AR(A, L, C)	AR(A, L, C)	AR(A, L, C)
36	PLS(REC, PM)	AR(B, D, T)	AR(A, D, C)	PLS(REC, A-C)	LS(B, D, B)	LS(3, P, P)	LS(3, P, P)	LS(3, P, P)	LS(3, P, P)
37	AR(A, P, T)	NN(3, D, 2, 2)	AR(A, P, T)	AR(4, L, C)	PLS(REC, A-C)	AR(4, D, T)	AR(B, L, C)	AR(B, L, C)	LS(3, D, D)
38	AR(4, D, T)	NN(A, P, A, 0)	PLS(REC, B)	LS(A, P, A)	LS(3, P, P)	LS(B, P, B)	LS(3, D, D)	LS(3, D, D)	PLS(REC, A)
39	AR(A, L, C)	PLS(REC, PM)	PLS(REC, PM)	PLS(REC, B)	LS(3, D, D)	LS(B, D, B)	PLS(REC, B)	PLS(REC, A)	AR(B, L, C)
40	LS(3, P, D6)	NN(B, P, B, 0)	AR(A, L, T)	LS(3, P, P)	PLS(REC, B)	AR(B, D, T)	PLS(REC, A)	PLS(REC, B)	PLS(REC, A-D)
41	LS(3, D, D6)	AR(B, L, T)	LS(3, P, D6)	LS(A, D, A)	PLS(REC, PM)	LS(3, D, D)	PLS(REC, A-C)	PLS(REC, A-C)	PLS(REC, B)
42	AR(B, D, T)	NN(A, L, A, 0)	AR(A, D, T)	LS(3, D, D)	AR(B, D, T)	PLS(REC, B)	PLS(REC, A-D)	PLS(REC, A-C)	PLS(REC, A-C)
43	AR(4, L, T)	NN(B, D, B, 0)	LS(3, D, D6)	PLS(REC, A-D)	PLS(REC, A-D)	PLS(REC, PM)	AR(4, L, C)	AR(4, L, C)	NN(3, L, 2, 1)
44	NN(A, L, A, 0)	NN(3, L, 2, 0)	LS(3, L, D6)	PLS(REC, PM)	PLS(REC, PM)	PLS(REC, A-D)	PLS(REC, PM)	NN(3, L, 2, 1)	PLS(REC, PM)
45	AR(A, D, T)	LS(3, P, D6)	EX3	AR(B, D, T)	AR(4, D, T)	AR(A, D, T)	NN(3, L, 2, 1)	PLS(REC, PM)	AR(4, L, C)
46	NN(3, L, 2, 0)	NN(B, L, B, 0)	EX2	AR(A, D, T)	LS(A, D, A)	NN(3, L, 2, 1)	LS(3, L, D6)	AR(A, D, T)	AR(A, D, T)
47	AR(B, L, T)	LS(3, D, D6)	LS(3, L, L)	AR(4, D, T)	LS(A, P, A)	AR(4, L, T)	AR(A, D, T)	EX3	EX3
48	LS(3, P, P)	AR(A, D, T)	LS(3, L, L)	NN(3, L, 2, 1)	NN(3, L, 2, 1)	NN(3, L, 2, 2)	LS(3, L, D6)	EX3	EX2
49	LS(3, L, D6)	AR(A, L, T)	NN(B, P, 2, 2)	LS(3, L, D6)	NN(3, L, 2, 2)	LS(A, D, A)	AR(B, D, T)	AR(B, D, T)	AR(B, D, T)
50	NN(B, L, B, 0)	LS(3, L, D6)	LS(3, P, P)	NN(3, L, 2, 2)	LS(3, L, D6)	AR(B, L, T)	AR(4, D, T)	LS(3, L, D6)	AR(4, D, T)
51	LS(3, D, D)	EX3	NN(B, D, B, 0)	EX3	AR(4, L, T)	LS(A, P, A)	LS(3, L, D6)	EX2	LS(3, L, D6)
52	LS(B, P, B)	LS(3, P, P)	NN(A, P, A, 0)	EX2	AR(B, L, T)	LS(3, L, D6)	EX2	NN(3, L, 2, 2)	NN(3, L, 2, 2)
53	LS(B, D, B)	EX2	LS(3, D, D)	AR(B, L, T)	EX3	AR(A, L, T)	NN(3, L, 2, 2)	AR(B, L, T)	AR(A, L, T)
54	AR(A, L, T)	LS(3, D, D)	NN(3, D, 2, 2)	AR(4, L, T)	AR(A, L, T)	EX3	AR(B, L, T)	AR(4, L, T)	AR(B, L, T)
55	EX3	LS(B, P, B)	LS(B, P, B)	AR(A, L, T)	EX2	EX2	AR(4, L, T)	AR(4, L, T)	AR(4, D, T)
56	EX2	LS(3, L, L)	NN(A, D, A, 0)	NN(3, L, 2, 0)	LS(3, L, L)	LS(3, L, L)	NN(3, L, 2, 0)	LS(3, L, 2, 0)	LS(3, L, L)
57	LS(A, P, A)	LS(B, D, B)	LS(B, D, B)	LS(3, L, L)	NN(3, L, 2, 0)	NN(B, L, B, 0)	LS(3, L, L)	LS(3, L, L)	NN(3, L, 2, 0)
58	LS(3, L, L)	LS(B, L, B)	LS(B, L, B)	NN(A, L, A, 0)	NN(A, L, A, 0)	NN(A, L, A, 0)	NN(B, L, B, 0)	NN(B, L, B, 0)	LS(B, L, B)
59	LS(A, D, A)	LS(A, P, A)	LS(A, P, A)	NN(B, L, B, 0)	NN(B, L, B, 0)	NN(3, L, 2, 0)	NN(A, L, A, 0)	LS(B, L, B)	NN(B, L, B, 0)
60	LS(B, L, B)	LS(A, D, A)	LS(A, D, A)	LS(B, L, B)	LS(B, L, B)	LS(B, L, B)	LS(B, L, B)	NN(A, L, A, 0)	LS(A, L, A)
61	LS(A, L, A)	LS(A, L, A)	LS(A, L, A)	LS(A, L, A)	LS(A, L, A)	LS(A, L, A)	LS(A, L, A)	LS(A, L, A)	NN(A, L, A, 0)
62	EX1	EX1	EX1	EX1	EX1	EX1	NOCHANGE	NOCHANGE	NOCHANGE
63	NOCHANGE	NOCHANGE	NOCHANGE	NOCHANGE	NOCHANGE	NOCHANGE	EX1	EX1	EX1

BIC lag choice yields slightly lower average MSE than AIC-based methods. Among ANNs, average forecast performance was slightly better using BIC than AIC, and the worst AIC-based forecasts were worse than the worst BIC-based forecasts. Among LSTARs, neither the AIC nor the BIC methods have mean, median, or 10 percent and 90 percent percentile relative MSEs as good as some of the fixed methods (in particular the LS(3, D, D6) and LS(3, P, D6) methods).

On average, the MSE improvement over the benchmark method from using data-based model selection methods are modest. For example, adopting BIC lag selection and unit root pretesting in an autoregression with a constant produces a median relative MSE of 1.00 for $h = 1$, 0.98 for $h = 6$, and 0.94 for $h = 12$. However, for some series, large MSE gains are possible, relative to the benchmark forecast. For example, in 2 percent of series, MSE reductions of two-thirds were achieved at the 12 month horizon by introducing BIC lag selection and unit root pretests to the benchmark method. Comparison of the AR(4, L, C), AR(B, L, C), AR(4, P, C), and AR(B, P, C) results in Table 2 shows that most of these gains are achieved by the unit root pretest rather than BIC lag selection.

Performance of simple methods. The simplest methods performed poorly relative to the benchmark AR(4, L, C) method. For example, for approximately three-fourths of series, the no change forecast was worse than the benchmark forecast at all three horizons (Table 2). The exponential smoothing method EX1 went badly wrong for some series, and on average all exponential smoothing methods have relative MSEs exceeding one at all horizons.

ANN methods. Generally speaking, some ANN methods performed well at the one-month horizon but no ANN methods performed as well as autoregressions at the six and twelve month horizons. First consider the results for the one month horizon. Based on the $\rho = 2$ results in Table 4, for $h = 1$ the best ANN model is NN(3, L, 2, 1) and the best AR model is AR(4, P, C). At $h = 1$, ANN methods are best for 40 percent of the individual series (Table 3). Comparison of the $h = 1$ entries in Table 2 for these models reveals that, for the ANN methods, the relative MSE performance measure has heavier tails than for the AR methods: the successes and failures across series are more pronounced. However, these methods have the same median and approximately the same mean. On average the forecasting gains from using the ANN models over the AR models at $h = 1$ are small or negligible from the perspective of mean square error loss. Thus while it is intriguing that ANN methods rank highly at short horizons, their edge in performance over autoregressive models is slim.

The relative performance of the ANN methods deteriorates as the forecast horizon increases. For the twelve month horizon, the worst ANN forecasts are considerably worse than the worst AR forecasts, with all ANN methods having relative MSEs exceeding 2 for at least 2 percent of the series. At these longer horizons, the ANN methods specified in levels perform particularly poorly. This generally poor performance of feedforward ANN methods for economic data, relative to linear models, is consistent with the findings in Swanson and White (1995, 1997) and Weigend and Gershenfeld (1994).

LSTAR methods. Although the LSTAR methods were rarely best for any series, in some cases they provided average MSE improvements, relative to the benchmark method. The best-performing LSTAR methods were the LS(3, D, D6) and its pretest variant LS(3, P, D6). Although both have mean relative MSEs of at least one, their median relative MSEs are less than one at the twelve month horizon (Table 2). The LSTAR methods generally performed worse than the ANN methods.

Forecast pooling. One of the striking features in Tables 2–4 is the strong performance of various forecast pooling procedures. Simple average forecasts, forecasts weighted by inverse MSEs, and the median forecasts outperform the benchmark method. Indeed, based on the loss function comparisons in Table 4, the most attractive forecast at the six and twelve month horizons for $\rho = 1$, 2 or 3 is the simple average of the forecasts from all methods, and this is nearly the best at the one month horizon as well. Among the various weighting schemes, simple averaging and weighting by inverse MSEs produce similar performance. Performance, as measured by mean relative MSE, deteriorates as ω increases, especially at long horizons. In fact, performance of the PLS forecasts, which are the limit as $\omega \to \infty$ of the weighted average forecasts, is worse than all weighted average forecasts and the median forecast for all horizons and all ρ. As measured by average relative MSEs, the PLS forecasts are never better than the benchmark forecast. Use of a shortened window (60 or 120 months) seems to have little effect on the combination forecasts based on inverse MSE weights.

For $h = 6$ and $h = 12$, the pooling procedures that combine forecasts from all 49 methods have a slight edge over these procedures applied to only the linear, or only the nonlinear, methods. Indeed, for one-third of the series at all three horizons, the equal-weighted linear combination forecast that averages the forecasts from all 49 methods produces forecasts that are among the top five in Table 3 at all horizons. For one-fourth of the series, at all horizons a linear combination procedure produces the best forecast.

Sensitivity to forecaster attitudes towards risk. Rankings are provided in Table 4 for three loss functions: mean absolute error loss ($\rho = 1$), quadratic loss ($\rho = 2$), and cubic absolute error loss ($\rho = 3$). Mean absolute error loss characterizes a forecaster who is equally concerned about small and large errors; cubic loss most heavily penalizes large errors.

The rankings among the various methods are surprisingly insensitive to the choice of risk parameter ρ. Linear combination procedures minimize average loss for all three loss functions and, given h, the best combination method does not depend on ρ. For a given horizon, the identity of the best individual method usually does not depend on ρ (the exception is $h = 1$, $\rho = 2$).

Table 4 establishes a clear ranking of classes of models and procedures. At the six and twelve month horizons, combination forecasts are first, followed by AR forecasts, followed by ANN forecasts, followed by LSTAR forecasts, followed by EX and no change. At the one month horizon, combination forecasts are first, followed (in order) by ANN, AR, LSTAR, EX, and no change. If pooling procedures are excluded, the best method at the six and twelve month horizon is an autoregression based on a unit root pretest, a data-dependent lag length, and a constant. At the one month horizon, an AR(4) with a unit root pretest is the best linear method, but it is slightly outperformed by several ANN methods, in particular NN(3, L, 2, 1).

Effect of forecast trimming. All results discussed so far are based on trimmed forecasts. The results for some methods are very different when the forecasts are not trimmed. The effects of trimming are most important for the nonlinear methods, which for some series at some dates produce forecasts that err by an order of magnitude. The trimming also considerably improves AR forecasts in levels with a time trend.

For comparison purposes, the rankings for the various forecasting methods based on the untrimmed forecasts are given in Table 5. The differences between the rankings based on the trimmed (Table 4) and untrimmed (Table 5) forecasts are attributable to the relatively few extremely large forecast errors made by the nonlinear methods and, to a lesser degree, by the AR methods in levels with time trends. Because of these outliers, the median pooled forecasts are optimal for the untrimmed forecasts, and because the large errors are most frequent in the nonlinear methods, the linear combination forecasts perform well only when computed over just the linear methods.

The rankings of the individual methods change somewhat for the untrimmed forecasts. Autoregressive methods are now best at all horizons for all ρ. Autoregressive methods work well if the series is specified in levels with a constant, in first differences with a constant and/or time trend, or if a pretest is used, but they work poorly for the levels/time trend specification. Exponential smoothing and no change methods rank relatively higher because they produce fewer extreme errors. Among nonlinear methods for $\rho = 2$, the best ranking at any horizon is for NN(3, P, 2, 1), which is fifteenth for $h = 6$.

Nonlinearities across categories of series. The relative performance of linear and nonlinear methods for different groups of series is explored in Table 6 for the trimmed forecasts. The first three columns compare the relative performance of a linear method, AR(B, P, C), to two nonlinear methods,

Table 5. Rankings of various methods, combined over all series, for different loss functions: Untrimmed forecasts

Cost function = $E|e_t|^\rho$, e_t = forecast error

Rank	1 step ahead			6 steps ahead			12 steps ahead		
	$\rho = 1.0$	2.0	3.0	$\rho = 1.0$	2.0	3.0	$\rho = 1.0$	2.0	3.0
1	MED(B)	MED(B)	MED(B)	MED(A–C)	MED(A–C)	MED(A–C)	MED(A–C)	MED(A–C)	MED(A–C)
2	MED(A–C)	MED(A–C)	MED(A–C)	C(0, REC, A)	MED(B)	MED(B)	C(0, REC, A)	C(0, REC, A)	C(0, REC, A)
3	C(0, REC, A)	C(0, REC, A)	C(0, REC, A)	MED(B)	C(0, REC, A)	C(0, REC, A)	MED(B)	MED(B)	MED(B)
4	C(1, REC, A)	C(1, REC, A)	C(1, REC, A)	C(1, REC, A)	C(1, REC, A)	C(1, REC, A)	C(1, REC, A)	C(1, REC, A)	C(1, REC, A)
5	MED(A)	MED(A)	MED(A)	MED(A)	MED(A)	MED(A)	MED(A)	MED(A)	MED(A)
6	AR(4, P, C)	AR(4, P, C)	AR(4, P, C)	AR(B, P, C)	AR(B, P, C)	AR(B, P, C)	AR(A, P, C)	AR(A, D, C)	AR(A, D, C)
7	AR(4, D, C)	AR(4, P, T)	AR(4, P, T)	AR(A, P, C)	AR(A, P, T)	AR(B, P, T)	AR(A, D, C)	AR(A, D, C)	AR(A, P, C)
8	AR(4, P, T)	AR(4, D, C)	AR(4, L, C)	AR(B, P, T)	AR(B, P, T)	AR(B, D, C)	AR(A, P, T)	AR(A, P, T)	AR(A, P, T)
9	PLS(REC, A)	AR(4, L, C)	AR(4, D, C)	AR(A, D, C)	AR(B, D, C)	AR(A, P, C)	AR(B, P, C)	AR(B, P, C)	AR(B, P, C)
10	NN(3, D, 2, 1)	PLS(REC, A)	PLS(REC, A)	AR(B, D, C)	AR(A, P, C)	AR(A, D, C)	AR(B, P, T)	AR(B, D, C)	AR(B, D, C)
11	NN(3, P, 2, 1)	AR(B, P, C)	AR(B, P, C)	AR(4, P, C)	AR(4, P, C)	AR(A, P, T)	AR(4, P, C)	AR(B, P, T)	AR(B, P, T)
12	AR(B, P, C)	AR(B, D, C)	AR(B, L, C)	AR(4, D, C)	AR(4, D, C)	AR(4, P, C)	AR(4, D, C)	AR(4, P, C)	AR(4, P, C)
13	AR(B, D, C)	AR(B, L, C)	AR(B, P, T)	AR(4, P, T)	AR(4, P, T)	AR(4, D, C)	AR(4, P, T)	AR(4, D, C)	AR(4, D, C)
14	AR(4, L, C)	AR(4, D, T)	AR(B, D, C)	PLS(REC, A)	NN(3, P, 2, 1)	AR(4, P, T)	AR(A, L, C)	AR(4, P, T)	AR(4, P, T)
15	AR(B, P, T)	AR(A, P, C)	AR(4, L, T)	AR(B, L, C)	AR(B, L, C)	AR(A, L, C)	NN(3, P, 2, 1)	AR(A, L, C)	AR(A, L, C)
16	AR(B, L, C)	AR(A, P, T)	AR(B, D, C)	AR(A, L, C)	PLS(REC, A)	PLS(REC, A)	NN(3, D, 2, 1)	NN(3, P, 2, 1)	NN(3, P, 2, 1)
17	NN(3, P, 2, 2)	AR(A, D, C)	AR(A, A, C)	NN(3, P, 2, 1)	NN(3, D, 2, 1)	NN(3, P, 2, 1)	AR(B, L, C)	NN(3, D, 2, 1)	NN(3, D, 2, 1)
18	AR(A, D, C)	AR(B, D, T)	AR(B, D, T)	NN(3, D, 2, 1)	AR(4, L, C)	AR(B, L, C)	PLS(REC, A)	AR(B, L, C)	AR(B, L, C)
19	AR(A, P, T)	AR(B, L, T)	AR(B, D, T)	AR(4, L, C)	NN(3, D, 2, 1)	NN(3, D, 2, 1)	PLS(REC, A)	PLS(REC, A)	PLS(REC, A)
20	AR(A, P, T)	AR(A, P, T)	AR(A, P, T)	AR(4, L, C)	AR(4, L, C)	AR(A, L, C)	AR(4, L, C)	AR(4, L, C)	AR(4, L, C)
21	AR(4, D, T)	PLS(REC, A–C)	AR(A, A, C)	AR(B, D, T)	AR(B, D, T)	AR(4, D, T)	PLS(REC, A–C)	PLS(REC, A–C)	PLS(REC, A–C)
22	PLS(REC, A–C)	AR(A, D, T)	AR(A, D, T)	AR(A, D, T)	AR(4, D, T)	AR(B, D, T)	AR(A, D, T)	AR(A, D, T)	AR(A, D, T)
23	NN(3, D, 2, 2)	AR(A, L, T)	AR(A, L, T)	PLS(REC, A–C)	AR(A, D, T)	AR(A, D, T)	AR(B, D, T)	AR(B, D, T)	AR(B, D, T)
24	AR(A, L, C)	EX3	AR(A, D, T)	PLS(REC, PM)	AR(4, L, T)	AR(4, L, T)	AR(A, D, T)	AR(4, D, T)	AR(4, D, T)
25	AR(B, D, T)	EX2	EX3	LS(3, L, 2, 1)	AR(B, L, T)	AR(B, L, T)	EX3	EX3	EX3
26	AR(4, L, T)	NN(3, D, 2, 1)	EX2	AR(4, L, T)	EX3	AR(A, L, T)	EX2	EX2	EX2
27	AR(A, D, T)	NN(3, P, 2, 1)	EX1	PLS(REC, B)	AR(A, L, T)	EX3	AR(B, L, T)	AR(B, L, T)	AR(B, L, T)
28	AR(B, L, T)	NN(3, P, 2, 2)	NOCHANGE	EX2	EX2	EX2	AR(A, L, T)	AR(A, L, T)	AR(A, L, T)
29	AR(A, L, T)	NN(3, D, 2, 2)	NN(3, D, 2, 1)	LS(3, L, D6)	NN(3, L, 2, 1)	NN(3, L, 2, 1)	LS(3, L, D6)	AR(4, L, T)	AR(4, L, T)
30	EX3	EX3	NN(3, P, 2, 1)	AR(4, L, T)	LS(3, L, D6)	EX1	LS(3, P, D6)	NOCHANGE	NOCHANGE
31	EX2	PLS(REC, A–C)	NN(3, D, 2, 2)	EX1	EX1	NOCHANGE	AR(B, L, T)	EX1	EX1

Table 5. (cont.)

Rank	1 step ahead			6 steps ahead			12 steps ahead		
	ρ = 1.0	2.0	3.0	ρ = 1.0	2.0	3.0	ρ = 1.0	2.0	3.0
32	LS(3, P, D6)	EX1	NN(3, P, 2, 2)	AR(B, L, T)	NOCHANGE	LS(3, L, D6)	AR(A, L, T)	LS(3, L, L)	LS(3, L, L)
33	NN(3, L, 2, 1)	NOCHANGE	PLS(REC, A-C)	NN(3, P, 2, 0)	LS(3, L, L)	LS(B, L, B)	AR(4, L, T)	NN(3, P, 2, 2)	NN(3, P, 2, 2)
34	EX1	LS(3, P, D6)	LS(3, P, D6)	AR(A, L, T)	LS(B, L, B)	LS(3, L, L)	LS(A, D, A)	NN(3, D, 2, 2)	NN(3, D, 2, 2)
35	NOCHANGE	NN(3, L, 2, 1)	NN(3, L, 2, 1)	NN(3, D, 2, 0)	LS(A, L, A)	LS(A, L, A)	LS(B, P, B)	NN(3, L, 2, 2)	NN(3, L, 2, 2)
36	NN(3, L, 2, 2)	NN(3, L, 2, 2)	NN(3, L, 2, 2)	LS(3, L, L)	PLS(REC, A-C)	PLS(REC, A-C)	LS(B, D, B)	LS(B, L, B)	LS(B, L, B)
37	LS(3, D, D6)	LS(3, D, D6)	LS(3, D, D6)	LS(3, P, P)	PLS(REC, B)	PLS(REC, B)	LS(3, D, D6)	LS(3, L, D6)	LS(3, L, D6)
38	LS(3, P, P)	LS(3, P, P)	LS(3, P, P)	LS(3, D, D)	PLS(REC, PM)	PLS(REC, PM)	LS(3, L, 2, 2)	LS(3, P, D6)	LS(3, P, P)
39	LS(3, D, D)	LS(3, D, D)	LS(3, D, D)	LS(B, L, B)	NN(3, P, 2, 0)	NN(3, P, 2, 0)	LS(3, L, L)	LS(A, D, A)	LS(3, D, D)
40	LS(B, P, B)	LS(B, P, B)	LS(B, P, B)	LS(A, L, A)	NN(3, D, 2, 0)	NN(3, D, 2, 0)	LS(3, L, L)	LS(B, D, B)	LS(3, P, D6)
41	LS(B, D, B)	LS(B, D, B)	LS(B, D, B)	EX1	LS(3, P, P)	LS(3, P, P)	LS(3, P, P)	LS(B, P, B)	LS(A, D, A)
42	LS(3, L, D6)	LS(3, L, D6)	LS(3, L, D6)	NOCHANGE	LS(3, D, D)	LS(3, D, D)	NOCHANGE	LS(A, L, A)	LS(B, D, B)
43	PLS(REC, B)	PLS(REC, B)	PLS(REC, B)	LS(B, P, B)	LS(B, P, B)	LS(B, P, B)	EX1	LS(3, P, P)	LS(B, P, B)
44	LS(3, L, L)	LS(3, L, L)	LS(3, L, L)	LS(B, D, B)	LS(A, P, A)	LS(A, P, A)	LS(B, L, B)	LS(3, D, D)	LS(A, L, A)
45	LS(B, L, B)	LS(B, L, B)	LS(B, L, B)	LS(A, D, A)	LS(B, D, B)	LS(B, D, B)	LS(A, L, A)	LS(3, D, D6)	LS(3, D, D6)
46	LS(A, L, A)	LS(A, L, A)	LS(A, L, A)	LS(A, P, A)	LS(A, D, A)	LS(A, D, A)	LS(A, P, A)	LS(A, P, A)	LS(A, P, A)
47	LS(A, P, A)	LS(A, P, A)	LS(A, P, A)	NN(3, P, 2, 2)	NN(3, L, 2, 2)	NN(3, L, 2, 2)	NN(3, L, 2, 1)	NN(3, L, 2, 1)	NN(3, L, 2, 1)
48	LS(A, D, A)	LS(A, D, A)	LS(A, D, A)	NN(3, D, 2, 2)	NN(3, P, 2, 2)	NN(3, P, 2, 2)	NN(B, P, B, 0)	NN(B, P, B, 0)	NN(B, P, B, 0)
49	NN(B, P, B, 0)	NN(B, D, B, 0)	NN(B, D, B, 0)	NN(3, L, 2, 2)	NN(3, D, 2, 2)	NN(3, D, 2, 2)	PLS(REC, B)	PLS(REC, B)	PLS(REC, B)
50	NN(B, D, B, 0)	NN(B, P, B, 0)	NN(B, P, B, 0)	LS(3, P, D6)	LS(3, P, D6)	LS(3, P, D6)	NN(B, D, B, 0)	NN(B, D, B, 0)	NN(B, D, B, 0)
51	PLS(REC, A-D)	PLS(REC, A-D)	PLS(REC, A-D)	LS(3, D, D6)	LS(3, D, D6)	LS(3, D, D6)	NN(A, P, A, 0)	NN(A, P, A, 0)	NN(A, P, A, 0)
52	PLS(REC, PM)	PLS(REC, PM)	PLS(REC, PM)	NN(A, P, A, 0)	NN(A, P, A, 0)	NN(A, P, A, 0)	NN(A, D, A, 0)	NN(A, D, A, 0)	NN(A, D, A, 0)
53	NN(3, L, 2, 0)	NN(3, L, 2, 0)	NN(B, L, B, 0)	NN(A, D, A, 0)	NN(A, D, A, 0)	NN(A, D, A, 0)	NN(3, D, 2, 0)	NN(3, D, 2, 0)	NN(3, D, 2, 0)
54	NN(B, L, B, 0)	C(1, REC, B)	C(1, REC, A-C)	PLS(REC, A-D)	PLS(REC, A-D)	PLS(REC, A-D)	NN(3, D, 2, 0)	NN(3, P, 2, 0)	NN(3, P, 2, 0)
55	NN(A, L, A, 0)	NN(B, L, B, 0)	C(0, REC, B)	NN(B, D, B, 0)	NN(B, D, B, 0)	NN(B, D, B, 0)	PLS(REC, A-D)	PLS(REC, A-D)	PLS(REC, A-D)
56	C(0, REC, A-C)	C(0, REC, A-C)	C(1, REC, B)	NN(B, P, B, 0)	NN(B, P, B, 0)	NN(B, P, B, 0)	PLS(REC, PM)	PLS(REC, PM)	PLS(REC, PM)
57	C(1, REC, A-C)	C(1, REC, A-C)	C(0, REC, A-C)	NN(B, L, B, 0)	NN(B, L, B, 0)	C(0, REC, A-C)	NN(B, L, B, 0)	NN(B, L, B, 0)	C(1, REC, A-C)
58	C(0, REC, B)	NN(A, L, A, 0)	NN(A, L, A, 0)	NN(3, L, 2, 0)	NN(3, L, 2, 0)	C(1, REC, A-C)	NN(3, L, 2, 0)	NN(3, L, 2, 0)	NN(A, L, A, 0)
59	C(1, REC, B)	C(1, REC, B)	NN(3, P, 2, 0)	C(1, REC, A-C)	C(1, REC, A-C)	C(1, REC, B)	C(1, REC, A-C)	C(1, REC, A-C)	C(1, REC, A-C)
60	NN(3, D, 2, 0)	C(0, REC, B)	NN(A, P, 2, 0)	C(1, REC, B)	C(1, REC, B)	NN(B, L, B, 0)	C(1, REC, B)	C(1, REC, B)	C(0, REC, B)
61	NN(3, P, 2, 0)	NN(3, D, 2, 0)	NN(3, D, 2, 0)	C(0, REC, A-C)	C(0, REC, A-C)	NN(3, L, 2, 0)	C(0, REC, B)	C(1, REC, B)	C(0, REC, B)
62	NN(A, P, A, 0)	NN(A, P, A, 0)	NN(3, L, 2, 0)	C(0, REC, B)	C(0, REC, B)	C(0, REC, A-C)	C(0, REC, B)	C(0, REC, B)	NN(B, L, B, 0)
63	NN(A, D, A, 0)	NN(A, D, A, 0)	NN(A, D, A, 0)	NN(A, L, A, 0)	NN(A, L, A, 0)	NN(A, L, A, 0)	NN(A, L, A, 0)	NN(A, L, A, 0)	NN(3, L, 2, 0)

Table 6. Forecasting performance broken down by category of series

Numbers in parentheses are the number of time series in each category
For each forecast, the first row corresponds to one-step ahead forecasts; the second row, to 6-step ahead forecasts; the third row, to 12-step ahead forecasts.

Category	Individual Methods			Pooling Procedures	
	Linear	Nonlinear		Linear	Nonlinear
	AR(B, P, C)	NN(B, P, B, 0)	LS(B, P, B)	C(1, REC, A)	C(1, REC, B)
Production	0.54	0.25	0.21	0.08	0.92
(24)	0.38	0.29	0.33	0.21	0.79
	0.33	0.21	0.46	0.38	0.63
Employment	0.52	0.21	0.28	0.17	0.83
(29)	0.48	0.48	0.03	0.21	0.79
	0.28	0.41	0.31	0.17	0.83
Wages	0.57	0.00	0.43	0.43	0.57
(7)	0.71	0.00	0.29	0.29	0.71
	0.43	0.00	0.57	0.29	0.71
Construction	0.57	0.29	0.14	0.19	0.81
(21)	0.29	0.38	0.33	0.05	0.95
	0.48	0.29	0.24	0.14	0.86
Trade	0.60	0.30	0.10	0.00	1.00
(10)	0.60	0.30	0.10	0.50	0.50
	0.90	0.10	0.00	0.40	0.60
Inventories	0.50	0.50	0.00	0.30	0.70
(10)	0.60	0.30	0.10	0.30	0.70
	0.50	0.20	0.30	0.40	0.60
Orders	0.64	0.29	0.07	0.07	0.93
(14)	0.57	0.29	0.14	0.29	0.71
	0.57	0.36	0.07	0.29	0.71
Money & Credit	0.43	0.48	0.09	0.13	0.87
(21)	0.39	0.30	0.30	0.57	0.43
	0.52	0.39	0.09	0.39	0.61
Stock Prices	0.36	0.55	0.09	0.00	1.00
(11)	0.64	0.18	0.18	0.55	0.45
	0.55	0.27	0.18	0.82	0.18
Interest Rates	0.18	0.73	0.09	0.00	1.00
(11)	0.18	0.64	0.18	0.00	1.00
	0.45	0.45	0.09	0.45	0.55
Exchange Rates	0.17	0.50	0.33	0.33	0.67
(6)	1.00	0.00	0.00	0.33	0.67
	0.33	0.50	0.17	0.17	0.83
Producer Prices	0.31	0.44	0.25	0.19	0.81
(16)	0.69	0.25	0.06	0.50	0.50
	0.63	0.25	0.13	0.44	0.56
Consumer Prices	0.38	0.50	0.13	0.19	0.81
(16)	0.69	0.00	0.31	0.63	0.38
	0.31	0.25	0.44	0.44	0.56
Consumption	0.40	0.40	0.20	0.00	1.00
(5)	0.40	0.40	0.20	0.40	0.60
	0.40	0.00	0.60	0.80	0.20
Miscellaneous	0.50	0.21	0.29	0.21	0.79
(14)	0.57	0.29	0.14	0.50	0.50
	0.50	0.36	0.14	0.57	0.43

Notes: Comparisons are for trimmed forecasts. For each row, the entries in the first three columns sum to 1.00, as do the entries in the final two columns, up to rounding error.

ANN(B, P, B, 0) and LS(B, P, B), by reporting the fraction of times that the column forecasting method is best among these three methods for the category of series specified in that row, by horizon. These three methods are automatic methods and were chosen for comparability: they all entail a recursive unit root pretest, recursive BIC lag length selection, and, for the nonlinear methods, recursive BIC-selected nonlinear parameterization. The final two columns provide a similar comparison, computed for the two linear combination forecasts respectively based on the linear and nonlinear methods (in both cases, weights are recursive inverse MSE).

The results suggest that the importance of nonlinearities differs across horizons and series. At $h = 1$, the nonlinear methods have the greatest relative success for interest rates and exchange rates, and have the least success for trade and orders. Combinations of the nonlinear forecasts are better than combinations of linear forecasts at $h = 1$ for most categories, notably so for stock prices, trade, and consumption. At the twelve month horizon, nonlinear methods work best for production, employment, exchange rates, and consumer prices. Exchange rates are interesting because the combination of nonlinear forecasts outperforms the combination of linear forecasts for five of the six exchange rates at $h = 12$. This is in some contrast to previous studies which have found limited ability of nonlinear methods to forecast exchange rates (Brooks, 1997). Consistent with the previous findings, the LSTAR methods generally are not the best (although they are for wages); of the nonlinear methods, the ANN forecasts are first more often.

5 Discussion and Conclusions

The LSTAR and ANN models must be viewed as these models *cum* the optimizers with which they were fit. The optimizers are designed to achieve local optima and, by random searching, to compare several local optima and to select the best. However, the evidence presented in the Appendix indicates that the resulting sequence of recursively estimated local optima are not, in general, global optima, and moreover different repetitions of the optimizer using different randomly drawn starting parameter values produce different sequences of local optima and thus different sequences of forecast errors. At first blush, this sounds like an important deficiency in this study, but in fact this is not obvious because improvements in the in-sample objective function seem not to correspond to better out-of-sample forecasts. In fact, the evidence in the Appendix suggests that improving the in-sample objective function over the value obtained using our algorithms on average neither improves nor worsens out-of-sample forecast performance. Thus, it is not clear that using an optimizer that more reliably achieved higher in-sample fits would necessarily improve the out-of-sample performance. These issues appear to be most pronounced for ANN models in levels and least pronounced for LSTAR models in differences. One interpretation of this is that the highly nonlinear ANN models can overfit these data at the global optimum, and more reliable out-of-sample forecasts are produced when "sensible" local optima are used. This makes us reluctant to endorse ANN models, even for the application in which they perform best in this study, one month ahead forecasting.

Another issue is whether our use of seasonally adjusted data might favor nonlinear methods. It is known that seasonal adjustment procedures are nonlinear filters, and Ghysels, Granger and Siklos (1996) showed that for Census X-11 these nonlinearities are sufficiently important that they can be detected with nontrivial power using various tests for nonlinearities. This suggests that some of the forecast MSE reduction of nonlinear methods is attributable to seasonal adjustment. It should be borne in mind that, were this the case, its implications are not self-evident. On the one hand, to the extent that we are interested in empirical evidence of nonlinear dynamics to guide theoretical macroeconomic modeling, then it is important to know if these nonlinearities are spuriously introduced by seasonal adjustment. On the other hand, if our interest is in forecasting seasonally adjusted series, the source of the nonlinearity is of only academic interest and the relevant question is which forecasting method best handles this nonlinearity. In any event, because the nonlinear models performed relatively poorly at the six and twelve month horizon, and made only slight improvements over linear models at the one month horizon, spurious nonlinearity from seasonal adjustment seems not to be an important practical consideration for forecasting, at least on average over these series.

Some additional caveats are also in order. Although a large number of methods have been considered, we have only considered two classes of nonlinear methods, and within artificial neural networks we have only considered feedforward neural nets. It is possible that other nonlinear methods, for example feedforward neural nets with more lags or recurrent neural nets, could perform better than those considered here. Also, these results are subject to sampling error. Although the design has carefully adhered to a recursive (simulated real-time) structure, because there are many forecasting methods considered, the estimated performance of the best-performing single method for these data arguably overstates the population counterpart of this performance measure. This criticism is less likely to be a concern, however, for the combination forecasts. Finally, it is unlikely that the best performing forecasts could have been identified as such in real time. When PLS was applied to all forecasts (including all the combination forecasts), the resulting PLS forecasts performed considerably worse than the best combination forecast, and indeed on average it performed worse than the benchmark method as measured by its mean relative MSE.

Bearing these comments in mind, we turn to the implications of this forecasting experiment for the five questions raised in the introduction.

First, although some of the nonlinear forecasts improve upon the linear forecasts for some series, most of the nonlinear forecasting methods produce worse
forecasts than the linear methods. Overall, AR methods have lower average
loss than the LSTAR or ANN methods at the six and twelve month horizons.
The ANN methods have lower average loss at the one month horizon than
the AR methods, but the improvement is small and is only present after trimming the outlier forecasts.

Second, perhaps surprisingly the nonlinear models that perform the best
are not necessarily the most tightly parameterized. Generally speaking the
ANN models have more nonlinear parameters than the LSTAR models, yet
the ANN models outperform the LSTAR models. Evidently the nonlinearities
exploited by the ANN models go beyond the switching or threshold effects
captured by the LSTAR specifications.

Third, forecasts at all horizons are improved by unit root pretests. Severe
forecast errors are made in nonlinear models specified in levels and in linear
models in levels with time trends, and these errors are reduced substantially
by choosing a differences or levels specification based on a preliminary test
for a unit root.

Fourth, pooled forecasts were found to outperform the forecasts from any
single method. The pooled forecasts that performed best combined the forecasts from all methods. Interestingly, although individual nonlinear methods
performed poorly, the median nonlinear forecast outperformed all individual
methods at all horizons, as did the averages of the nonlinear forecasts after
trimming. The pooling procedures that place weight on all forecasting methods
(whether equal weighting, inverse MSE weighting, or median) proved most
reliable, while those that emphasized the recently best performing methods
(especially PLS) proved least reliable. At the twelve month horizon, the mean
relative MSE of the pooled forecast computed by simple averaging of all 49
methods is .87, and the 2 percent percentile relative MSE is .27. There was
little effect (positive or negative) of using a reduced or rolling sample for computing the combination weights. We find these gains from combining forecasts
to be surprising. Bates and Granger's (1969) motivation for combining forecasts is that each forecast draws on a different information set, so that the
information embodied in the combined forecast is greater than the information
in any individual forecast. Here, however, all forecasts are univariate, and in
this sense the information sets of the forecasts are the same. These issues are
further explored in Chan, Stock, and Watson (1998).

Fifth, although the combination forecasts require considerable programming
and computation time to produce, the gains might well be worth this cost. If,
however, a macroeconomic forecaster is restricted to using a single method,
then, for the family of loss functions considered here, he or she would be well
advised to use an autoregression with a unit root pretest and data-dependent
lag length selection.

Appendix

A.1 Nonlinear Optimization Methods

The ANN, exponential smoothing, and LSTAR models are nonlinear in the parameters. This Appendix describes the optimization methods used to minimize the least squares objective functions for the models.

Exponential Smoothing. The parameters of the exponential smoothing models were estimated using a Gauss–Newton optimizer. The parameters at date T_1 were estimated using 200 iterations of the optimizer from a starting value of 0.5. These estimates were updated in subsequent time periods using two iterations of the optimizer.

LSTAR models. The parameters of the LSTAR models were estimated using a modified random search algorithm. The initial parameter estimates at date T_1 were obtained as follows. The LSTAR models can be organized into families of models that have natural nestings, from least complicated (fewest parameters) to most complicated. For example, one such family is, in increasing order of complexity, {LS(1, L, L), LS(3, L, L), LS(6, L, L)}. For each family, the most restrictive version of the model was estimated first. For this most restrictive version the objective function was evaluated using 5,000 random draws of the parameter vector. The parameter vectors corresponding to the four smallest values of the objective function were then used as initial values for 250 Gauss–Newton iterations, and the minimizer was chosen from the resulting set of parameters. This parameter vector together with 1,000 additional random draws was used to evaluate the objective function associated with the next most complicated model in the family; the parameter vectors associated with the two smallest values of the function were used to initialize 100 Gauss–Newton iterations. This procedure was repeated for each larger model in the nesting sequence.

At subsequent dates ($T_1 < t \leq T_3$), with probability .99 the parameter values for each model were updated by taking three Gauss–Newton steps, using the parameter estimates from the previous date as starting values. With probability .01 the parameters were updated by using the minimum of these results and results obtained by completely reoptimizing from a set of 500 randomly selected initial parameter values (using the same method as at time T_1).

ANN models. ANN objective functions typically have multiple local minima. When the previous algorithm was applied to ANN models, local minima were obtained, and many of these local minima produced poor out of sample forecasts. A different algorithm was therefore used to fit the ANN models.

The algorithm used for the ANN models has two stages, a preprocessing phase and a recursive estimation phase. In the preprocessing phase, the objective function for each model was intensively minimized at three dates, T_1, T_3, and $T_{\mathrm{mid}} = (T_1 + T_3)/2$. For a model with one hidden unit the algorithm is: (i) fit an AR(p) with a constant or time trend, in levels or differences as appropriate, for the desired horizon, and save the residuals $\hat{u}_t^{(0)} = y_t - \hat{\beta}_0' \zeta_{t-h}$; (ii) using 10 randomly selected initial conditions for the nonlinear parameter vector β_{11} in the first hidden unit, compute 50 Gauss–Newton iterations on the objective function $\sum_t [\hat{u}_t^{(0)} - \gamma_{11} g(\beta_{11}' \zeta_t)]^2$, and retain the best of the resulting 10 sets of values of β_{11}; (iii) perform 15 Gauss–Seidel iterations over the full model. Each Gauss–Seidel iteration involves (iiia) fixing β_{11} and estimating β_0 and γ_{11} by OLS; (iiib) given the resulting values of β_0, reestimating β_{11} and γ_{11} by 10 Gauss–Newton iterations. At each Gauss–Newton step only updated values of β_{11} that improved the objective function were retained so that each step of this algorithm is guaranteed not to increase the objective function.

For models with $n_1 > 1$ hidden units and a single layer, the same procedure was used, except that (i) was omitted, (ii) used the residuals from the model with $n_1 - 1$ hidden units, and in (iii) the Gauss–Seidel steps moved sequentially over each hidden unit, estimating β_{1i} holding β_{1j} fixed, $j \neq i$, etc.

For models with two hidden units, this algorithm was used, with the modification that the nonlinear parameters $\{\beta_{2ji}, \beta_{1i}\}$ were estimated jointly by Gauss–Newton, given $\{\beta_0, \gamma_{2j}\}$, then given $\{\beta_{2ji}, \beta_{1i}\}$, $\{\beta_0, \gamma_{2j}\}$ were estimated by OLS, etc.

In the recursive estimation phase, for $t = T_1, \ldots, T_3$, in each time period a single Gauss–Seidel iteration (with one nested Gauss–Newton step) was used to update the parameters, with the initial estimates at $t = T_1$ obtained from the initial estimation phase. The objective function was also evaluated for the parameter values obtained in the initial phase for T_1, T_{mid} and T_3. If at date t either of these three produced a lower objective function value than the recursively updated parameters, the Gauss–Seidel step for date t was recomputed using the T_1, T_{mid} or T_3 parameter vector (as appropriate) as the initialization, and the resulting new parameter vector was retained as the recursive estimate and as the initial parameter vector for the Gauss–Seidel step at $t + 1$.

Performance of Algorithms. Several checks were performed on these algorithms to assess their performance. These checks entailed examining the performance of the optimizers (and variants on these optimizers) for different series and different models.

One such check, which examined four series (mdu, fygm3, hsbr, ivmtq) and four models, is discussed here. In this experiment, the optimizer described above was run 25 times for each model/series combination. This produced 25 series of recursive forecasts. The time series of optimized parameter values, and thus the time series of recursive forecasts, differ from one trial to the next solely because of different random draws of the starting values for the parameters. The four models investigated in this experiment are two LSTAR and two ANN models using both levels and differences of the data (LS(3, L, Δy_{t-2}), LS(3, D, Δy_{t-2}), NN(3, L, 0), and NN(3, D, 0)). For the purpose of this paper, the appropriate measure for assessing whether these algorithms converge to a common optimum is neither the value of the in-sample objective function nor the values of the estimated parameters, but rather the path of recursive forecast errors produced. If the same sequence of forecasts is produced by each trial, then for the purposes of this project the algorithms effectively converge to the same value, which can reasonably be taken to be the optimum.

The results for six month ahead forecasts are summarized in Table A1. The entries are summary statistics of the distribution of relative MSEs of the sequence of simulated out of sample forecast errors across the 25 trials; as in Table 2, the relative MSEs are standardized by the MSE of the AR(4, L, C). Shown in the final row of each block are results from forecasts constructed from more computationally intensive maximization algorithms. In the case of the LSTAR model increasing computation by a factor of 50 led to results that consistently achieved what appears to be the global optimum.[6] In the case of the ANN models, experiments suggested that there was little hope of consistently achieving a global optimum for each time period even with a significant increase in computational resources. In this case we simply computed a sequence of forecasts from the 25 trials by recursively choosing the forecast with the best in-sample fit: that is, at each date, the current objective functions of the 25 trials are compared, and the parameter values associated with the currently best of these in-sample objective functions is used to produce the forecast at that date. This sequence of forecasts will by construction have the lowest sequence of in-sample objective functions and in this sense is the closest to the global optimum.

The results in Table A1 suggest several conclusions. For some series and models, the trials resulted in essentially identical results (for example, ivmtq and LS(3, D, Δy_{t-2})), while in other cases there was considerable variation across the trials (mdu and NN(3, L, 0)). In general, the distribution of relative MSEs is tighter for LSTAR models than for ANN models, and is tighter in first differences than in levels. Strikingly, the relative MSE of the forecast based on the global optimum (LSTAR models) does about as well as a randomly selected forecast from the original group of 25: among the eight LSTAR cases in Table A1, the global optimum produces forecast MSEs that are greater than the median of the 25 trials in four cases and are less than or equal to the median in four cases. The same is true for the forecasts based on the recursive best fit for the ANN models. Evidently, among these model/series combinations, the parameters with the best in-sample fits do not in general provide the best out of sample forecasts. Rather, the forecasts with the lowest out of sample MSEs typically are obtained from in-sample fits that are at local but not global optima.

These findings are consistent with those from other checks we performed.

Table A1. Distribution of relative MSES of 6-month ahead forecasts across 25 optimization trials for selected series and models

Model	Series			
	mdu	fygm3	hsbr	ivmtq
LS(3, L, Δy_{t-2})				
Minimum	1.24	1.06	1.05	1.18
1st Quartile	1.30	1.10	1.06	1.18
Median	1.42	1.18	1.06	1.19
3rd Quartile	1.43	1.20	1.07	1.20
Maximum	2.41	1.43	1.16	1.27
In-Sample Optimum	1.76	1.35	1.20	1.18
LS(3, D, Δy_{t-2})				
Minimum	0.99	0.99	1.10	1.01
1st Quartile	1.00	1.03	1.12	1.01
Median	1.00	1.21	1.16	1.01
3rd Quartile	1.01	1.22	1.19	1.01
Maximum	1.02	1.27	1.19	1.01
In-Sample Optimum	0.99	1.12	1.17	1.01
NN(3, L, 2, 0)				
Minimum	1.71	0.91	0.97	1.62
1st Quartile	2.38	0.99	1.00	1.80
Median	2.46	1.07	1.04	1.93
3rd Quartile	2.77	1.16	1.05	1.97
Maximum	3.24	1.32	1.11	2.37
Rec. Best In-Sample	2.56	1.18	1.02	1.85
NN(3, D, 2, 0)				
Minimum	0.92	0.98	1.05	1.01
1st Quartile	0.97	1.07	1.13	1.03
Median	1.00	1.12	1.15	1.04
3rd Quartile	1.04	1.21	1.19	1.06
Maximum	1.10	1.30	1.24	1.09
Rec. Best In-Sample	1.01	1.09	1.18	1.07

Notes: Entries are summaries of the distribution of relative MSEs of recursive forecasts, where the benchmark MSE is the AR(4, L, C) model. "In-Sample Optimum" refers to forecasts constructed from parameters that achieve the global recursively calculated in-sample MSE. "Rec. Best In-Sample" refers to the simulated real time forecast error produced using the sequence of parameter values that, date by date, have the best in-sample fit selected from the 25 optimized parameter values in the different trials.

For many series, this indicates that there was a significant likelihood that these algorithms would not locate a global optimum over some fraction of the sample period. The probability of achieving a local and not global maximum appeared to be higher for the ANN models than for the LSTAR models and higher for series modeled in levels than in first differences. Finally, achieving a better in-sample value of the objective function does not necessarily imply producing forecasts with better out-of-sample performance.

A.2 Data Description

This Appendix lists the time series used. The data were obtained from the DRI BASIC Economics Database (creation date 9/97). The format for each series is its DRI BASIC mnemonic; a brief description; and the first date used (in brackets). A series that was preliminarily transformed by taking its logarithm is denoted by "log" in parentheses; otherwise, the series was used without preliminary transformation.

Abbreviations: sa = seasonally adjusted; saar = seasonally adjusted at an annual rate; nsa = not seasonally adjusted.

IP	industrial production: total index (1992 = 100, sa) [1959:1] (log)
IPP	industrial production: products, total (1992 = 100, sa) [1959:1] (log)
IPF	industrial production: final products (1992 = 100, sa) [1959:1] (log)
IPC	industrial production: consumer goods (1992 = 100, sa) [1959:1] (log)
IPCD	industrial production: durable consumer goods (1992 = 100, sa) [1959:1] (log)
IPCN	industrial production: nondurable consumer goods (1992 = 100, sa) [1959:1] (log)
IPE	industrial production: business equipment (1992 = 100, sa) [1959:1] (log)
IPI	industrial production: intermediate products (1992 = 100, sa) [1959:1] (log)
IPM	industrial production: materials (1992 = 100, sa) [1959:1] (log)
IPMD	industrial production: durable goods materials (1992 = 100, sa) [1959:1] (log)
IPMND	industrial production: nondurable goods materials (1992 = 100, sa) [1959:1] (log)
IPMFG	industrial production: manufacturing (1992 = 100, sa) [1959:1] (log)
IPD	industrial production: durable manufacturing (1992 = 100, sa) [1959:1] (log)
IPN	industrial production: nondurable manufacturing (1992 = 100, sa) [1959:1] (log)
IPMIN	industrial production: mining (1992 = 100, sa) [1959:1] (log)
IPUT	industrial production: utilities (1992 = 100, sa) [1959:1] (log)
IPX	capacity util rate: total industry (% of capacity, sa)(frb) [1967:1]
IPXMCA	capacity util rate: manufacturing, total (% of capacity, sa)(frb) [1959:1]
IPXDCA	capacity util rate: durable mfg (% of capacity, sa)(frb) [1967:1]
IPXNCA	capacity util rate: nondurable mfg (% of capacity, sa)(frb) [1967:1]
IPXMIN	capacity util rate: mining (% of capacity, sa)(frb) [1967:1]
IPXUT	capacity util rate: utilities (% of capacity, sa)(frb) [1967:1]
LHEL	index of help-wanted advertising in newspapers (1967 = 100; sa) [1959:1]
LHELX	employment: ratio; help-wanted ads: no. unemployed clf [1959:1]

LHEM	civilian labor force: employed, total (thous., sa) [1959:1] (log)
LHNAG	civilian labor force: employed, nonagric.industries (thous., sa) [1959:1] (log)
LHUR	unemployment rate: all workers, 16 years & over (%, sa) [1959:1]
LHU680	unemploy. by duration: average (mean) duration in weeks (sa) [1959:1]
LHU5	unemploy. by duration: persons unempl. less than 5 wks (thous., sa) [1959:1] (log)
LHU14	unemploy. by duration: persons unempl. 5 to 14 wks (thous., sa) [1959:1] (log)
LHU15	unemploy. by duration: persons unempl. 15 wks + (thous., sa) [1959:1] (log)
LHU26	unemploy. by duration: persons unempl. 15 to 26 wks (thous., sa) [1959:1] (log)
LHU27	unemploy. by duration: persons unempl. 27 wks + (thous, sa) [1959:1] (log)
LHCH	average hours of work per week (household data)(sa) [1959:1]
LPNAG	employees on nonag. payrolls: total (thous., sa) [1959:1] (log)
LP	employees on nonag. payrolls: total, private (thous, sa) [1959:1] (log)
LPGD	employees on nonag. payrolls: goods-producing (thous., sa) [1959:1] (log)
LPMI	employees on nonag. payrolls: mining (thous., sa) [1959:1] (log)
LPCC	employees on nonag. payrolls: contract construction (thous., sa) [1959:1] (log)
LPEM	employees on nonag. payrolls: manufacturing (thous., sa) [1959:1] (log)
LPED	employees on nonag. payrolls: durable goods (thous., sa) [1959:1] (log)
LPEN	employees on nonag. payrolls: nondurable goods (thous., sa) [1959:1] (log)
LPSP	employees on nonag. payrolls: service-producing (thous., sa) [1959:1] (log)
LPTU	employees on nonag. payrolls: trans. & public utilities (thous., sa) [1959:1] (log)
LPT	employees on nonag. payrolls: wholesale & retail trade (thous., sa) [1959:1] (log)
LPFR	employees on nonag. payrolls: finance, insur.&real estate (thous., sa) [1959:1] (log)
LPS	employees on nonag. payrolls: services (thous., sa) [1959:1] (log)
LPGOV	employees on nonag. payrolls: government (thous., sa) [1959:1] (log)
LW	avg. weekly hrs. of prod. wkrs.: total private (sa) [1964:1]
LPHRM	avg. weekly hrs. of production wkrs.: manufacturing (sa) [1959:1]
LPMOSA	avg. weekly hrs. of production wkrs.: mfg., overtime hrs. (sa)[1959:1]
LEH	avg. hr earnings of prod wkrs: total private nonagric ($, sa) [1964:1] (log)
LEHCC	avg. hr earnings of constr wkrs: construction ($, sa) [1959:1] (log)
LEHM	avg. hr earnings of prod wkrs: manufacturing ($, sa) [1959:1] (log)
LEHTU	avg. hr earnings of nonsupv wkrs: trans & public util ($, sa) [1964:1] (log)
LEHTT	avg. hr earnings of prod wkrs: wholesale & retail trade (sa) [1964:1] (log)
LEHFR	avg. hr earnings of nonsupv wkrs: finance, insur., real est ($, sa) [1964:1] (log)
LEHS	avg. hr earnings of nonsupv wkrs: services ($, sa) [1964:1] (log)

HSFR	housing starts: nonfarm(1947–58); total farm&nonfarm(1959–)(thous., sa) [1959:1] (log)
HSNE	housing starts: northeast (thous.u.)s.a. [1959:1] (log)
HSMW	housing starts: midwest(thous.u.)s.a. [1959:1] (log)
HSSOU	housing starts: south (thous.u.)s.a. [1959:1] (log)
HSWST	housing starts: west (thous.u.)s.a. [1959:1] (log)
HSBR	housing authorized: total new priv. housing units (thous., saar) [1959:1] (log)
HSBNE	houses authorized by build. permits: northeast(thou.u.)s.a [1960:1] (log)
HSBMW	houses authorized by build. permits: midwest(thou.u.)s.a. [1960:1] (log)
HSBSOU	houses authorized by build. permits: south(thou.u.)s.a. [1960:1] (log)
HSBWST	houses authorized by build. permits: west(thou.u.)s.a. [1960:1] (log)
HNS	new one-family houses sold during month (thous, saar) [1963:1] (log)
HNSNE	one-family houses sold: northeast(thou.u., s.a.) [1973:1] (log)
HNSMW	one-family houses sold: midwest(thou.u., s.a.) [1973:1] (log)
HNSSOU	one-family houses sold: south(thou.u., s.a.) [1973:1] (log)
HNSWST	one-family houses sold: west(thou.u., s.a.) [1973:1] (log)
HNR	new one-family houses, month's supply @ current sales rate (ratio) [1963:1]
HMOB	mobile homes: manufacturers' shipments (thous.of units, saar) [1959:1] (log)
CONTC	construct.put in place: total priv & public 1987$ (mil$, saar) [1964:1] (log)
CONPC	construct.put in place: total private 1987$ (mil$, saar) [1964:1] (log)
CONQC	construct.put in place: public construction 87$ (mil$, saar) [1964:1] (log)
CONDO9	construct.contracts: comm'l & indus.bldgs (mil.sq.ft.floor sp.; sa) [1959:1] (log)
MSMTQ	manufacturing & trade: total (mil of chained 1992 dollars)(sa) [1959:1] (log)
MSMQ	manufacturing & trade: manufacturing; total (mil of chained 1992 dollars)(sa) [1959:1] (log)
MSDQ	manufacturing & trade: mfg; durable goods (mil of chained 1992 dollars)(sa) [1959:1] (log)
MSNQ	manufact. & trade: mfg; nondurable goods (mil of chained 1992 dollars)(sa) [1959:1] (log)
WTQ	merchant wholesalers: total (mil of chained 1992 dollars)(sa) [1959:1] (log)
WTDQ	merchant wholesalers: durable goods total (mil of chained 1992 dollars)(sa) [1959:1] (log)
WTNQ	merchant wholesalers: nondurable goods (mil of chained 1992 dollars)(sa) [1959:1] (log)
RTQ	retail trade: total (mil of chained 1992 dollars)(sa) [1959:1] (log)
RTDQ	retail trade: durable goods total (mil.87$)(s.a.) [1959:1] (log)
RTNQ	retail trade: nondurable goods (mil of 1992 dollars)(sa) [1959:1] (log)
IVMTQ	manufacturing & trade inventories: total (mil of chained 1992)(sa) [1959:1] (log)

IVMFGQ   inventories, business, mfg (mil of chained 1992 dollars, sa) [1959:1] (log)
IVMFDQ   inventories, business durables (mil of chained 1992 dollars, sa)
          [1959:1] (log)
IVMFNQ   inventories, business, nondurables (mil of chained 1992 dollars, sa)
          [1959:1] (log)
IVWRQ   manufacturing & trade inv: merchant wholesalers (mil of chained
          1992 dollars)(sa) [1959:1] (log)
IVRRQ   manufacturing & trade inv: retail trade (mil of chained 1992
          dollars)(sa) [1959:1] (log)
IVSRQ   ratio for mfg & trade: inventory/sales (chained 1992 dollars, sa)
          [1959:1]
IVSRMQ   ratio for mfg & trade: mfg; inventory/sales (87$)(s.a.) [1959:1]
IVSRWQ   ratio for mfg & trade: wholesaler; inventory/sales (87$)(s.a.) [1959:1]
IVSRRQ   ratio for mfg & trade: retail trade; inventory/sales (87$)(s.a.) [1959:1]
PMI   purchasing managers' index (sa) [1959:1]
PMP   napm production index (percent) [1959:1]
PMNO   napm new orders index (percent) [1959:1]
PMDEL   napm vendor deliveries index (percent) [1959:1]
PMNV   napm inventories index (percent) [1959:1]
PMEMP   napm employment index (percent) [1959:1]
PMCP   napm commodity prices index (percent) [1959:1]
MOCMQ   new orders (net)—consumer goods & materials, 1992 dollars (bci)
          [1959:1] (log)
MDOQ   new orders, durable goods industries, 1992 dollars (bci) [1959:1] (log)
MSONDQ   new orders, nondefense capital goods, in 1992 dollars (bci) [1959:1]
          (log)
MO   mfg new orders: all manufacturing industries, total (mil$, sa) [1959:1]
          (log)
MOWU   mfg new orders: mfg industries with unfilled orders (mil$, sa) [1959:1]
          (log)
MDO   mfg new orders: durable goods industries, total (mil$, sa) [1959:1]
          (log)
MDUWU   mfg new orders: durable goods industries with unfilled orders (mil$,
          sa) [1959:1] (log)
MNO   mfg new orders: nondurable goods industries, total (mil$, sa) [1959:1]
          (log)
MNOU   mfg new orders: nondurable gds ind.with unfilled orders (mil$, sa)
          [1959:1] (log)
MU   mfg unfilled orders: all manufacturing industries, total (mil$, sa)
          [1959:1] (log)
MDU   mfg unfilled orders: durable goods industries, total (mil$, sa) [1959:1]
          (log)
MNU   mfg unfilled orders: nondurable goods industries, total (mil$, sa)
          [1959:1] (log)
MPCON   contracts & orders for plant & equipment (bil$, sa) [1959:1] (log)
MPCONQ   contracts & orders for plant & equipment in 1992 dollars (bci)
          [1959:1] (log)
FM1   money stock: m1(curr, trav.cks, dem dep, other ck'able dep)(bil$, sa)
          [1959:1] (log)

FM2	money stock: m2(m1 + o'nite rps, euro$, g/p&b/d mmmfs&sav&sm time dep (bil$, sa) [1959:1] (log)
FM3	money stock: m3(m2 + lg time dep, term rp's&inst only mmmfs)(bil$, sa) [1959:1] (log)
FML	money stock: l(m3 + other liquid assets) (bil$, sa) [1959:1] (log)
FM2DQ	money supply—m2 in 1992 dollars (bci) [1959:1] (log)
FMFBA	monetary base, adj. for reserve requirement changes(mil$, sa) [1959:1] (log)
FMBASE	monetary base, adj. for reserve req chgs(frb of st.louis)(bil$, sa) [1959:1] (log)
FMRRA	depository inst reserves: total, adj for reserve req chgs(mil$, sa) [1959:1] (log)
FMRNBA	depository inst reserves: nonborrowed, adj res req chgs(mil$, sa) [1959:1] (log)
FMRNBC	depository inst reserves: nonborrow + ext cr, adj res req cgs(mil$, sa) [1959:1] (log)
FMFBA	monetary base, adj for reserve requirement changes(mil$, sa) [1959:1] (log)
FCLS	loans & sec @ all coml banks: total (bil$, sa) [1973:1] (log)
FCSGV	loans & sec @ all coml banks: US govt. securities (bil$, sa) [1973:1] (log)
FCLRE	loans & sec @ all coml banks: real estate loans (bil$, sa) [1973:1] (log)
FCLIN	loans & sec @ all coml banks: loans to individuals (bil$, sa) [1973:1] (log)
FCLNBF	loans & sec @ all coml banks: loans to nonbank fin. inst (bil$, sa) [1973:1] (log)
FCLNQ	commercial & industrial loans oustanding in 1992 dollars (bci) [1959:1] (log)
FCLBMC	wkly rp lg com'l banks:net change com'l & indus loans (bil$, saar) [1959:1]
CCI30M	consumer instal.loans: delinquency rate, 30 days & over, (%, sa) [1959:1]
CCINT	net change in consumer instal cr: total (mil$, sa) [1975:1]
CCINV	net change in consumer instal cr: automobile (mil$, sa) [1975:1]
FSNCOM	nyse common stock price index: composite (12/31/65 = 50) [1959:1] (log)
FSNIN	nyse common stock price index: industrial (12/31/65 = 50) [1966:1] (log)
FSNTR	nyse common stock price index: transportation (12/31/65 = 50) [1966:1] (log)
FSNUT	nyse common stock price index: utility (12/31/65 = 50) [1966:1] (log)
FSNFI	nyse common stock price index: finance (12/31/65 = 50) [1966:1] (log)
FSPCOM	s&p's common stock price index: composite (1941–43 = 10) [1959:1] (log)
FSPIN	s&p's common stock price index: industrials (1941–43 = 10) [1959:1] (log)
FSPCAP	s&p's common stock price index: capital goods (1941–43 = 10) [1959:1] (log)
FSPTR	s&p's common stock price index: transportation (1970 = 10) [1970:1] (log)

FSPUT	s&p's common stock price index: utilities (1941–43 = 10) [1959:1] (log)
FSPFI	s&p's common stock price index: financial (1970 = 10) [1970:1] (log)
FSDXP	s&p's composite common stock: dividend yield (% per annum) [1959:1] (log)
FSPXE	s&p's composite common stock: price–earnings ratio (%, nsa) [1959:1] (log)
FSNVV3	nyse mkt composition: reptd share vol by size, 5000 + shrs, % [1959:1] (log)
FYFF	interest rate: federal funds (effective) (% per annum, nsa) [1959:1]
FYCP	interest rate: commercial paper, 6-month (% per annum, nsa) [1959:1]
FYGM3	interest rate: US treasury bills, sec mkt, 3-mo.(% per ann, nsa) [1959:1]
FYGM6	interest rate: US treasury bills, sec mkt, 6-mo. (% per ann, nsa) [1959:1]
FYGT1	interest rate: US treasury const maturities, 1-yr. (% per ann, nsa) [1959:1]
FYGT5	interest rate: US treasury const maturities, 5-yr. (% per ann, nsa) [1959:1]
FYGT10	interest rate: US treasury const maturities, 10-yr. (% per ann, nsa) [1959:1]
FYAAAC	bond yield: moody's aaa corporate (% per annum) [1959:1]
FYBAAC	bond yield: moody's baa corporate (% per annum) [1959:1]
FWAFIT	weighted avg foreign interest rate(%, sa) [1959:1]
FYFHA	secondary market yields on fha mortgages (% per annum) [1959:1]
EXRUS	united states; effective exchange rate(merm)(index no.) [1973:1] (log)
EXRGER	foreign exchange rate: germany (deutsche mark per US$) [1973:1] (log)
EXRSW	foreign exchange rate: switzerland (swiss franc per US$) [1973:1] (log)
EXRJAN	foreign exchange rate: japan (yen per US$) [1973:1] (log)
EXRUK	foreign exchange rate: united kingdom (cents per pound) [1973:1] (log)
EXRCAN	foreign exchange rate: canada (canadian $ per US$) [1973:1] (log)
HHSNTN	u. of mich. index of consumer expectations (bcd–83) [1959:1]
F6EDM	US mdse exports: [1964:1] (log)
FTMC6	US mdse imports: crude materials & fuels (mil$, nsa) [1964:1] (log)
FTMM6	US mdse imports: manufactured goods (mil$, nsa) [1964:1] (log)
PWFSA	producer price index: finished goods (82 = 100, sa) [1959:1] (log)
PWFCSA	producer price index: finished consumer goods (82 = 100, sa) [1959:1] (log)
PWIMSA	producer price index: intermed mat. supplies & components (82 = 100, sa) [1959:1] (log)
PWCMSA	producer price index: crude materials (82 = 100, sa) [1959:1] (log)
PWFXSA	producer price index: finished goods, excl. foods (82 = 100, sa) [1967:1] (log)
PW160A	producer price index: crude materials less energy (82 = 100, sa) [1974:1] (log)
PW150A	producer price index: crude nonfood mat less energy (82 = 100, sa) [1974:1] (log)

PW561	producer price index: crude petroleum (82 = 100, nsa) [1959:1] (log)
PWCM	producer price index: construction materials (82 = 100, nsa) [1959:1] (log)
PWXFA	producer price index: all commodities ex. farm prod (82 = 100, nsa) [1959:1] (log)
PSM99Q	index of sensitive materials prices (1990 = 100)(bci–99a) [1959:1] (log)
PUNEW	cpi-u: all items (82–84 = 100, sa) [1959:1] (log)
PU81	cpi-u: food & beverages (82–84 = 100, sa) [1967:1] (log)
PUH	cpi-u: housing (82–84 = 100, sa) [1967:1] (log)
PU83	cpi-u: apparel & upkeep (82–84 = 100, sa) [1959:1] (log)
PU84	cpi-u: transportation (82–84 = 100, sa) [1959:1] (log)
PU85	cpi-u: medical care (82–84 = 100, sa) [1959:1] (log)
PUC	cpi-u: commodities (82–84 = 100, sa) [1959:1] (log)
PUCD	cpi-u: durables (82–84 = 100, sa) [1959:1] (log)
PUS	cpi-u: services (82–84 = 100, sa) [1959:1] (log)
PUXF	cpi-u: all items less food (82–84 = 100, sa) [1959:1] (log)
PUXHS	cpi-u: all items less shelter (82–84 = 100, sa) [1959:1] (log)
PUXM	cpi-u: all items less medical care (82–84 = 100, sa) [1959:1] (log)
PSCCOM	spot market price index:bls & crb: all commodities (67 = 100, nsa) [1959:1] (log)
PSCFOO	spot market price index:bls & crb: foodstuffs (67 = 100, nsa) [1959:1] (log)
PSCMAT	spot market price index:bls & crb: raw industrials (67 = 100, nsa) [1959:1] (log)
PZFR	prices received by farmers: all farm products (1977 = 100, nsa) [1975:1] (log)
PCGOLD	commodities price:gold, london noon fix, avg of daily rate, $ per oz [1975:1] (log)
GMDC	pce, impl pr defl: pce (1987 = 100) [1959:1] (log)
GMDCD	pce, impl pr defl: pce; durables (1987 = 100) [1959:1] (log)
GMDCN	pce, impl pr defl: pce; nondurables (1987 = 100) [1959:1] (log)
GMDCS	pce, impl pr defl: pce; services (1987 = 100) [1959:1] (log)
GMPYQ	personal income (chained) (series #52) (bil 92$, saar) [1959:1] (log)
GMYXPQ	personal income less transfer payments (chained) (#51) (bil 92$, saar) [1959:1] (log)
GMCQ	personal consumption expend (chained): total (bil 92$, saar) [1959:1] (log)
GMCDQ	personal consumption expend (chained): total durables (bil 92$, saar) [1959:1] (log)
GMCNQ	personal consumption expend (chained): nondurables (bil 92$, saar) [1959:1] (log)
GMCSQ	personal consumption expend (chained): services (bil 92$, saar) [1959:1] (log)
GMCANQ	personal cons expend (chained): new cars (bil 92$, saar) (log)

Notes

1. It should be emphasized that, like the experiment reported in this paper, these studies are simulated real-time exercises, not a comparison of true real-time forecasts. True real-time forecasts are based on preliminary data and often contain significant judgmental adjustments; see for example McNees (1986, 1990) and the surveys in Granger and Newbold (1977, ch. 8.4 and 1986, ch. 9.4). Although true out-of-sample MSEs would differ from those reported here, the simulated real-time nature of this experiment provides a controlled environment for comparing and ranking different forecasting methods.
2. A fixed lag length of six was used to compute the unit root test statistics. The unit root pretests were computed and applied recursively, that is, the forecast of y_{t+h} using data through time t were computed using the model selected at time t by the unit root pretest computed using data through time t. The critical values for the unit root tests were chosen so that the pretest constituted a consistent rule for selecting between the I(0) and I(1) specification. Specifically, for the DF-GLS$^{\mu}$ test, the critical value was $\ln(120/t) - 1.95$, and for the DF-GLS$^{\tau}$ test the critical value was $\ln(120/t) - 2.89$. When $t = 120$, these correspond to 5 percent significance level unit root pretests, with lower significance levels as the sample size increases.
3. See Swanson and White (1995, 1997) for discussion of ANN models in economics; for a monograph treatment, see Masters (1994).
4. See Granger and Teräsvirta (1993) for an exposition of the threshold autoregression and smooth transition autoregression family of models, including LSTAR models.
5. Other loss functions are possible, for example, the forecaster might have asymmetric loss, cf. Granger (1969) and Diebold and Christofferson (1997). Under nonquadratic loss, least squares forecasts are not optimal, but considering alternative estimation methods is beyond the scope of this paper.
6. The basic algorithm described above was augmented at each date t by 1,000 randomly selected trial values of the parameters. The four sets of parameters that yielded the smallest SSR together with the optimum at date $t - 1$ were each used as initial values for 250 Gauss–Newton iterations. Finally, the parameter values associated with the resulting smallest SSR was used to construct the forecasts and carried forward as initial condition for date $t + 1$. Experiments indicated that this algorithm yielded essentially identical function values in repeated trials, suggesting that it achieved a global optimum.

References

Bates, J. M. and C. W. J. Granger (1969), "The Combination of Forecasts," *Operations Research Quarterly*, 20: 451–68.

Brooks, C. (1997), "Linear and Non-linear (Non-)Forecastability of High-Frequency Exchange Rates," *Journal of Forecasting*, 16: 125–45.

Campbell, J. Y. and P. Perron (1991), "Pitfalls and Opportunities: What Macro-economists Should Know about Unit Roots," *NBER Macroeconomics Annual*, 20.

Chan, L., J. H. Stock, and M. W. Watson (1998), "A Dynamic Factor Model Framework for Forecast Combination," manuscript, Harvard University.

Diebold, F. X. and P. F. Christoffersen (1997), "Optimal Prediction under Asymmetric Loss," *Econometric Theory*, 13: 808–17.

Diebold, F. X. and L. Kilian (1997), "Unit Roots and Forecasting: To Difference or Not To Difference?" manuscript, University of Pennsylvania.

Diebold, F. X. and P. Pauly (1990), "The Use of Prior Information in Forecast Combination," *International Journal of Forecasting*, 6: 503–8.

Elliott, G., T. J. Rothenberg, and J. H. Stock (1996), "Efficient Tests for an Autoregressive Unit Root," *Econometrica*, 64: 813–36.

Ghysels, E., C. W. J. Granger, and P. L. Siklos (1996), "Is Seasonal Adjustment a Linear or Nonlinear Data Filtering Process?" *Journal of Business and Economic Statistics*, 14: 374–86.

Granger, C. W. J. (1966), "The Typical Spectral Shape of an Economic Variable," *Econometrica*, 34: 150–61.

Granger, C. W. J. (1969), "Prediction with a Generalized Cost of Error Function," *Operational Research Quarterly*, 20: 199–207.

Granger, C. W. J. (1993), "Strategies for Modelling Nonlinear Time Series Relationships," *Economic Record*, 60: 233–8.

Granger, C. W. J. and J.-L. Lin (1994), "Forecasting from Non-Linear Models in Practice," *Journal of Forecasting*, 13: 1–10.

Granger, C. W. J. and P. Newbold (1977), *Forecasting Economic Time Series*. New York: Academic Press.

Granger, C. W. J. and P. Newbold (1986), *Forecasting Economic Time Series*, 2nd edn. New York: Academic Press.

Granger, C. W. J. and R. Ramanathan (1984), "Improved Methods of Combining Forecasting," *Journal of Forecasting*, 3: 197–204.

Granger, C. W. J. and T. Teräsvirta (1993), *Modelling Non-linear Economic Relationships*. Oxford: Oxford University Press.

Granger, C. W. J., T. Teräsvirta, and H. M. Anderson (1993), "Modeling Nonlinearity over the Business Cycle," ch. 8 in J. H. Stock and M. W. Watson (eds.), *Business Cycles, Indicators, and Forecasting*. Chicago: University of Chicago Press for the NBER, pp. 311–27.

McNees, S. K. (1986), "Forecasting Accuracy of Alternative Techniques: A Comparison of U.S. Macroeconomic Forecasts," *Journal of Business and Economic Statistics*, 4: 5–24.

McNees, S. K. (1990), "The Role of Judgment in Macroeconomic Forecasting Accuracy," *International Journal of Forecasting*, 6: 287–299.

Makridakis, S., A. Anderson, R. Carbonne, R. Fildes, M. Hibon, R. Lewandowski, J. Newton, E. Parzen, and R. Winkler (1982), "The Accuracy of Extrapolation (Time Series) Methods: Results of a Forecasting Competition," *Journal of Forecasting*, 1: 111–53.

Masters, T. (1994), *Signal and Image Processing with Neural Networks*. New York: John Wiley and Sons.

Meese, R. and J. Geweke (1984), "A Comparison of Autoregressive Univariate Forecasting Procedures for Macroeconomic Time Series," *Journal of Business and Economic Statistics*, 2: 191–200.

Meese, R. and K. Rogoff (1983), "Empirical Exchange Rate Models of the Seventies: Do They Fit out of Sample?" *Journal of International Economics*, 14: 3–24.

Stock, J. H. (1996), "VAR, Error Correction and Pretest Forecasts at Long Horizons," *Oxford Bulletin of Economics and Statistics*, 58/4: 685–701; reprinted in A. Banerjee and D. F. Hendry (eds.), *The Econometrics of Economic Policy.* Oxford: Basil Blackwell, 1997, pp. 115–32.

Swanson, N. R. and H. White (1995), "A Model Selection Approach to Assessing the Information in the Term Structure Using Linear Models and Artificial Neural Networks," *Journal of Business and Economic Statistics*, 13: 265–75.

Swanson, N. R. and H. White (1997), "A Model Selection Approach to Real-Time Macroeconomic Forecasting Using Linear Models and Artificial Neural Networks," *Review of Economics and Statistics*, 79: 540–50.

Teräsvirta, T., D. Tjostheim, and C. W. J. Granger (1994), "Aspects of Modelling Nonlinear Time Series," ch. 48 in R. Engle and D. McFadden (eds.), *Handbook of Econometrics*, vol. 4. Amsterdam: Elsevier, pp. 2919–60.

Tiao, G. C. and D. Xu (1993), "Robustness of Maximum Likelihood Estimates for Multi-Step Predictions: The Exponential Smoothing Case," *Biometrika*, 80: 623–41.

Weigend, A. S. and N. A. Gershenfeld (1994), *Time Series Prediction: Forecasting the Future and Understanding the Past.* Reading, MA: Addison-Wesley for the Santa Fe Institute.

2
A Multivariate Time Series Analysis of the Data Revision Process for Industrial Production and the Composite Leading Indicator

NORMAN R. SWANSON, ERIC GHYSELS, AND MYLES CALLAN

1 Introduction

In this paper we introduce and examine a real-time dataset consisting of all releases of seasonally adjusted and unadjusted US industrial production, and the US composite leading indicator. This is done by forming various forecasting models for the revision processes of our variables. Although forecasting is clearly an area of research which Clive Granger holds dear, the topic of real-time data may not appear to be an appropriate topic with which to pay tribute to the work of Clive Granger. However, the subject is one to which Oscar Morgenstern—one of Clive's earliest collaborators—devoted an entire monograph. Further, Oskar Morgenstern's importance in Clive's early academic development, and Clive's great respect for him, should not go unnoticed. To illustrate this point, consider that it was Morgenstern who invited Clive, upon receiving the prestigious Harkness Scholarship of the Commonwealth Fund, to join a time series research project at Princeton University. While at Princeton, Clive began his work on spectral analysis, leading to one of his first monographs (see Granger and Hatanaka, 1964), and also resulting in at least one of his many seminal contributions to the analysis of time series data (i.e. Granger, 1969).[1]

Today, Morgenstern would most likely write a somewhat different monograph. For example, he would likely examine preliminary data with many of the time series techniques and tools which Clive and many of his collaborators have developed over the last four decades. These might include careful examination of the integratedness properties of the revision process (see e.g. Granger

The authors are grateful to two anonymous referees and the editors for useful comments, and to Greg Orlosky and Scott Briggs for excellent research assistance. Swanson thanks the National Science Foundation (Grant No. SBR-9730102) and the Research and Graduate Studies Office at Pennsylvania State University for research support.

and Newbold, 1974; Granger and Ding, 1996; Granger and Ermini, 1993; Granger and Hallman, 1991; Granger and Swanson, 1997), cointegration analysis (see e.g. Granger, 1983, 1986; Engle and Granger, 1987; Granger and Gonzalo, 1995; Granger and Lee, 1990; Granger and Swanson, 1996; Granger and Weiss, 1983), causal analysis (see e.g. Granger, 1969, 1980, 1988; Granger and Lin, 1995; Swanson and Granger, 1997), and forecasting experimentation (see e.g. Granger, 1992, 1996; Bates and Granger, 1969; Granger and Nelson, 1979), for example. At this juncture, our goal is not to produce such a monograph. We offer only a modest attempt to reflect again on the issue of preliminary data releases which is so important in many regards, and which has perhaps not yet received as much attention as it deserves. Of course, this subject has not been completely ignored since the publication of Morgenstern (1963). A very limited number of recent articles in this area (from which many other important references can be obtained) are: Boschen and Grossman (1982), Conrad and Corrado (1979), Ghysels (1982), Hamilton and Perez-Quiros (1996), Harvey *et al.* (1993), Kavajecz and Collins (1995), Keane and Runkle (1990), Koenig and Emery (1994), Mankiw and Shapiro (1986), Mankiw *et al.* (1984), Maravall and Pierce (1986), Mariano and Tanizaki (1995), Patterson (1995), Pierce (1981), Swanson (1996), and Swanson and White (1995, 1997a, b).

There are many examples in applied economics which illustrate the need to take a closer look at questions pertaining to the quality of preliminary data releases. For example, many econometric forecasting models are routinely constructed using "currently available" data. In the USA, data are often downloaded from CITIBASE, and used without giving too much thought to the "timing" of the data. However, it is well known that many CITIBASE series are formed by combining various different "vintages" of economic data (e.g. preliminary data and data which have been revised a number of times).[2] Along the same lines, consider that it is most often preliminary data which are used by policymakers while, *post mortem*, their actions are scrutinized based on the use of revised data.[3] Further, forecasters typically use a mixture of revised and preliminary data in real time settings, and their predictions are initially appraised against preliminary releases. *Ex post* or *in-sample* benchmarking of forecasting performance, however, is usually based on final figures. One natural question which arises in these types of scenarios is: "Which vintages of data are used and/or should be used by policy setters and forecasters, and are these data the same as those that are usually used in the construction of standard econometric models and forecasts?" While we do not attempt to provide an answer to this question, we hope that our forecasting evidence illustrates the potential importance of such questions.

In our analysis, we classify economic data into three categories:

(1) *Preliminary*, *First Reported*, or *Unrevised* Data. These types of data consist of the first reported datum for each variable at each point in time. Thus, a series of this type has had no revisions to any observations at any point

in time. Swanson and White (1997a, b) use unrevised data to construct real-time or *ex ante* forecasts of a group of macroeconomic variables, and find that professional forecasts (which are necessarily real-time) are sometimes dominated by econometric models, based of a number of model selection criteria such as mean square forecast error and directional change forecasting ability.

(2) *Partially Revised* or *Real-Time* Data. These types of data are difficult to collect, as they are made up of a full vector of observations at each point in time for each variable. For example, if constructing a real-time dataset for money, say M2, then for January 1990 a complete sequence of data, from say 1959 to January 1990 must be collected. Furthermore, the data must be collected as if one were in January 1990, so that no revisions of any kind made after January 1990 are incorporated into the dataset at time January 1990. Then, a whole new sequence of data from 1959 to February 1990 is collected, representing all of the information which was available in February of 1990, and thus including unrevised figures for February 1990, "once" revised figures for January 1990, and so on. This procedure is continued for each observational period in the sample. This real-time data collection strategy ensures that "future information" due to the use of information which is temporally antecedent to the date under consideration is not (accidentally) used in the construction of revised data. Also, this type of data avoids many of the types of problems associated with seasonal revisions, benchmark revisions, and definitional changes, for example, and can be thought of as truly real-time in the sense that it is the dataset which is available to real-time forecasters and policy-setters at any given point in time. As an illustration of the potential for problems of this sort to arise, note that when dealing with seasonally adjusted data, it is has been observed by Pierce (1981) that revisions are mostly due to the adjustment process, as it involves two-sided filters. But these two-sided filters necessarily involve a mixing of data vintages (e.g. future data seep into the revised values of past data), and as such it is clearly difficult to ensure the future information does not enter into the revision process. For more on the features of the most commonly used X-11 seasonal adjustment procedure, see for instance Ghysels, Granger and Siklos (1996) among others. In this paper, we focus on real-time datasets, examining the revision process across more than three decades for our series.[4] One of the real-time datasets which we examine in this paper is an updated version of the real-time CLI dataset used by Diebold and Rudebusch (1991) in their analysis of the forecasting ability of the CLI for fully revised industrial production.

(3) *Fully Revised* or *Final* Data. It is quite possible that true "final" data will never be available for many economic series. This is because benchmark and definitional changes are ongoing and may continue into the indefinite future, for instance. In practice, by final data we usually mean the revision of a data observation after which no more revisions will be made. This is the type of data that academics often have in mind when conducting economic

time series studies, perhaps simply because they are data which are not subject
to revision, and it is felt that if one could adequately forecast a "final revised"
figure, then there is no need for further modeling. However, these data are
clearly not easy to obtain, as data are generally subject to revision for indefinite
lengths of time. Indeed, most datasets which are constructed by applied economists clearly consist of a mixture of preliminary data, partially revised data,
and final revised data. In the following, we consider real-time data, where
$X_{t+i}(t)$ refers to the $t + i$th release date of data pertaining to calendar date t,
and X is the growth rate of the original series.

Our primary aim in this paper is to underscore this potential shortcoming of
dataset construction by examining real-time datasets, noting their time series
characteristics, and examining univariate and multivariate regression models
of the data revision process. This approach allows us to assess whether there
are predictable patterns in the data revision process. We indeed find that this
is the case. For example, our findings based on regressions which include both
IP and the CLI suggest that multivariate information "matters" in the revision
process. In particular, previously available IP revisions are useful for explaining
CPI revisions, suggesting that releases of CPI do not fully incorporate newly
available IP data. In addition, real-time forecasting experiments suggest that
there is useful univariate as well as multivariate information in the revision
processes of IP and the CLI. Given these sorts of findings, we suggest that
there is a need for careful examination of real-time data when asking a variety
of standard questions, including: "Are two variables Granger causal for one
another?" and "Is variable x useful for constructing forecasts of variable y, in
a real-time forecasting scenario, say, such as that faced by policy makers in
Washington as well as decision makers on Wall street?"

The rest of the paper is organized as follows. In Section 2, we examine basic
statistical properties of our data, including integratedness, cointegratedness,
and autoregressive behavior. In Section 3 we perform a series of regression and
ex ante forecasting experiments in order to ascertain whether or not revisions
to our industrial production series are useful for forecasting revisions to the
composite leading indicator, and vice versa, thereby examining the "efficiency"
of data revision within the context of providing optimal forecasts of "fully
revised" data. The fourth section concludes and makes recommendations for
future research.

2 The Data

The three variables for which we collect real-time data are US seasonally adjusted industrial production (1950:4 to 1996:2), unadjusted industrial produc-

tion (1950:4 to 1996:2), and the composite leading indicator (1968:10 to 1996:2). A typical months' release of data for these variables comprises of a first, or preliminary, release for the previous month, and four to six months of revisions to data previously released. In addition, more comprehensive benchmark and base-year revisions occur from time to time for each of the variables.

Turning first to our industrial production data, the following details are perhaps worth noting. The seasonally adjusted industrial production and unadjusted industrial production series are compiled by the Federal Reserve Board. The main source for seasonally adjusted industrial production data is the *Federal Reserve Bulletin*. For unadjusted industrial production data we use the *Federal Reserve Bulletin* for data up to 1959:12, and the *Survey of Current Business* for data after 1959:12. Additional data for each series are obtained from Federal Reserve monthly statistical releases.[5] Also, for three of the major (benchmark) revisions to the variables, the Federal Reserve Board released separate publications—(1) Industrial Production 1957–59 Base, (2) Industrial Production 1971, and (3) 1976 Revision. Since 1980, benchmark revisions to both industrial production series have occurred approximately every two years, while prior to 1980 such revisions were less frequent. Benchmark revisions to industrial production usually result in updates of around two years of previously available data, and occur five times during our sample period: December 1953, December 1959, July 1971, July 1985, and April 1990.[6] These five base year revisions incorporate re-weighting of, and changes to the components of the index. For both series there are three missing entries due to two major revisions, they are 1953:11, 12 and 1985:03. We replaced each missing observation with the first available data for that period (which in each case is a second release).

Our other variable, the composite leading indicator was compiled by the Department of Commerce until 1994:12. It is currently released by The Conference Board. Our CLI dataset up until 1988:12 was made available to us by Glenn Rudebusch (see e.g. Diebold and Rudebusch, 1991). We augment this dataset by including data from the *Business Consumers Digest*, up to 1990:12, and the *Survey of Current Business*, from 1991:1 to 1994:12. Benchmark revisions to the CLI occur every 12–18 months, and are revisions to the whole series. These revisions incorporate changes in methodology for computing the index, updated statistical factors, and historical revisions in component data. Base year revisions to the CLI occur three times—August 1970, January 1989, and October 1993.[7] For our analysis, we examine revisions of monthly growth rates, and hence data not rebased. This approach allows us to avoid problems associated with level shifts in our CLI series. We address what might be called "variance shifts" by examining subsamples of our datasets.

3 Basic Statistics and Data Analysis

In our examination of the real-time datasets discussed above, we examine revisions to the data process. In particular, we consider what we shall call fixed width revisions, which are defined as $X_{t+i}(t) - X_{t+i-1}(t)$, where X is the growth rate of the original levels data, formed by taking log differences. Here, the subscript refers to the release date of the data, and the bracketed index denotes the date to which the release pertains. Thus, by varying the index, i, while keeping t fixed, we examine various different "releases" of data for a given time period, for example. We also consider what we call increasing width revisions, which are defined as $X_{t+i}(t) - X_t(t)$.[8] The increasing width revisions represent the accumulated fixed width revisions, and for $i = 24$ we obtain the difference between what we will here call the "final" datum, and the first available datum. Our examination of this type of data allows us to assess whether or not there is significant systematic bias in accumulated revisions, when there is no significant systematic bias in individual revisions. One reason why such information is of interest is that we can then ascertain whether there is significant bias in the difference between first and final releases of our variables.

Tables 1a–2b contain summary statistics for fixed and increasing width revisions of unadjusted and seasonally adjusted industrial production and the CLI, for the entire datasets (Tables 1a–1b) and for a smaller sample from 1975:10–1996:2 (Tables 2a–2b).[9] We consider revisions over horizons $i = 1$, ..., 12, 18, and 24. Each table contains three panels corresponding to our three variables. The first panel pertains to seasonally adjusted IP. We report the mean, variance, skewness and kurtosis for both the fixed and increasing width revisions. We observe that the mean of fixed length revisions is significantly different from zero at a 95 percent level of confidence, for $i = 1, 3$, and 6. This suggests that there is systematic bias in revisions of adjusted industrial production, which could be used to increase the accuracy of preliminary releases.[10] Interestingly, this feature also characterizes unadjusted IP and, to a lesser

---

Notes to Tables 1–3

* denotes a mean value that is significantly different from zero based on a 95% confidence interval constructed using a heteroskedasticity and autocorrelation consistent variance estimator. The statistics reported refer to all revisions, including those that occur during benchmark updates. Fixed width revisions are constructed as $(X_{t+i}(t) - X_{t+i-1}(t))$ (or $\Delta X_{t+i}(t)$). Increasing width revisions are constructed as $(X_{t+i}(t-2) - X_t(t))$, which is equivalent to the cumulated revisions obtained by summing the fixed width revisions across i. Where X is the growth rate, per month, of either IP or CLI. In these definitions, the subscript refers to the release date of the data, while the bracketed index denotes the date to which the release pertains. For example, the "$i = 2$" rows in the table correspond to $(X_{t+2}(t) - X_{t+1}(t))$ for the fixed width revisions. In this case, the second release for the period t is subtracted from the third release for period t. For increasing width revisions, "$i = 2$" rows correspond to $(X_{t+2}(t) - X_t(t))$, so that the first release (or first available data) is subtracted from the third release for the period t.

Table 1a. Real-time dataset summary statistics for all revisions

	Fixed width revisions				Increasing width revisions			
	Mean	Variance	Skewness	Kurtosis	Mean	Variance	Skewness	Kurtosis
Seasonally adjusted industrial production: 1950:4–1996:2								
i = 1	−0.035*	0.111	−0.351	10.03	−0.035*	0.111	−0.351	10.03
i = 2	−0.004	0.064	0.651	10.35	−0.039*	0.180	−0.587	8.154
i = 3	−0.023*	0.025	2.337	61.19	−0.062*	0.209	0.149	9.214
i = 4	−0.006	0.045	−11.83	281.3	−0.069*	0.260	−1.058	17.69
i = 5	0.008	0.015	9.974	137.2	−0.061*	0.273	−0.905	16.54
i = 6	−0.008*	0.010	−6.340	77.32	−0.069*	0.279	−0.946	15.92
i = 7	−0.004	0.006	−17.22	357.0	−0.073*	0.279	−0.939	15.87
i = 8	0.008	0.018	13.27	144.3	−0.069	0.572	0.569	26.77
i = 9	−0.004	0.014	−13.21	142.5	−0.068	0.909	−0.136	25.88
i = 10	−0.002	0.005	−4.277	66.08	−0.070	0.913	−0.134	25.59
i = 11	0.004	0.009	10.28	198.3	−0.066	0.923	−0.138	25.87
i = 12	−0.004	0.007	−10.01	160.2	−0.071	0.933	−0.133	25.08
i = 18	0.001	0.013	5.038	194.5	−0.079	0.933	−0.127	24.10
i = 24	−0.003	0.005	−3.273	77.14	−0.087	0.937	−0.119	24.82
Seasonally unadjusted industrial production: 1950:4–1996:2								
i = 1	−0.036*	0.207	−0.192	6.270	−0.036*	0.207	−0.192	6.270
i = 2	−0.033*	0.100	0.015	5.678	−0.069*	0.308	−0.027	4.833
i = 3	−0.022*	0.059	−6.039	90.40	−0.091*	0.357	0.147	4.830
i = 4	−0.001	0.042	10.76	180.2	−0.092*	0.369	0.134	4.756
i = 5	0.003	0.006	2.740	75.95	−0.090*	0.373	0.128	4.682
i = 6	−0.002	0.014	−4.674	110.7	−0.092*	0.378	0.164	4.642
i = 7	0.001	0.011	1.417	124.4	−0.091*	0.386	0.175	4.639
i = 8	0.000	0.003	−0.571	115.9	−0.091*	0.389	0.162	4.602
i = 9	0.001	0.007	−1.902	146.9	−0.091*	0.400	0.098	4.547
i = 10	−0.001	0.009	−3.839	86.11	−0.091*	0.401	0.085	4.495
i = 11	−0.002	0.013	−1.829	132.3	−0.093*	0.417	0.118	4.401
i = 12	−0.003	0.007	−4.137	105.9	−0.096*	0.424	0.085	4.384
i = 18	0.003	0.016	8.574	213.8	−0.104*	0.574	−0.009	7.672
i = 24	−0.002	0.007	−2.805	124.4	−0.105*	0.616	−0.113	7.369
Composite leading indicator: 1968:10–1996:2								
i = 1	−0.017	0.270	0.713	6.869	−0.017	0.270	0.713	6.869
i = 2	−0.028*	0.047	−0.280	6.245	−0.045	0.286	0.378	5.417
i = 3	0.004	0.021	0.247	7.563	−0.041	0.313	0.520	6.032
i = 4	−0.014	0.021	0.045	11.49	−0.055	0.308	0.626	6.441
i = 5	0.002	0.012	−0.400	9.019	−0.052	0.306	0.649	6.393
i = 6	0.012	0.023	6.995	85.01	−0.041	0.332	0.694	6.065
i = 7	0.009*	0.009	2.598	23.95	−0.032	0.332	0.755	6.316
i = 8	0.004	0.036	8.637	124.6	−0.028	0.361	0.717	5.753
i = 9	0.001	0.030	7.917	123.1	−0.027	0.373	0.677	5.290
i = 10	0.007	0.027	8.939	126.1	−0.020	0.379	0.591	5.073
i = 11	0.022*	0.025	6.174	74.77	0.002	0.377	0.540	4.915
i = 12	0.004	0.014	12.38	204.3	0.005	0.371	0.514	4.820
i = 18	0.006	0.009	6.787	106.3	0.031	0.412	1.065	7.081
i = 24	−0.012*	0.010	−8.556	83.96	0.026	0.436	0.958	6.767

Notes: See notes to Tables 1–3 opposite.

Table 1b. Real-time dataset summary statistics for non-benchmark revisions

	Fixed width revisions				Increasing width revisions			
	Mean	Variance	Skewness	Kurtosis	Mean	Variance	Skewness	Kurtosis
Seasonally adjusted industrial production: 1950:4–1996:2								
i = 1	−0.035*	0.109	−0.388	10.32	−0.035*	0.109	−0.388	10.32
i = 2	−0.005	0.061	0.612	10.86	−0.039*	0.176	−0.661	8.351
i = 3	−0.027*	0.017	−2.599	25.20	−0.066*	0.190	−0.398	7.237
i = 4	−0.003	0.005	−3.698	53.93	−0.069*	0.196	−0.524	7.498
i = 5	0.004	0.007	11.73	19.90	−0.065*	0.201	−0.430	7.509
i = 6	−0.004	0.005	−4.879	94.27	−0.070*	0.210	−0.503	7.308
i = 7	0.000	0.001	−2.656	60.25	−0.070*	0.210	−0.501	7.304
i = 8	0.006	0.085	3.313	45.66	−0.063	0.553	0.304	48.38
i = 9	−0.008	0.085	−3.306	45.44	−0.071	0.886	0.379	25.01
i = 10	0.002	0.003	−0.614	91.16	−0.070	0.886	0.377	25.00
i = 11	0.001	0.001	−1.017	95.55	−0.069	0.888	0.376	25.88
i = 12	−0.002	0.002	−8.476	128.9	−0.070	0.890	0.378	25.70
i = 18	−0.001	0.001	−8.747	135.0	−0.073	0.896	0.380	25.25
i = 24	0.000	0.001	7.080	160.7	−0.073	0.900	0.380	25.99
Seasonally unadjusted industrial production: 1950:4–1996:2								
i = 1	−0.030	0.201	−0.199	6.523	−0.030*	0.201	−0.199	6.523
i = 2	−0.036*	0.095	−0.127	5.514	−0.066*	0.297	−0.042	5.028
i = 3	−0.012	0.030	0.623	12.37	−0.078*	0.328	0.333	4.575
i = 4	−0.007*	0.007	−5.952	58.08	−0.085*	0.326	0.232	4.446
i = 5	0.002	0.004	1.956	124.3	−0.083*	0.329	0.233	4.404
i = 6	0.000	0.006	2.759	103.0	−0.083*	0.327	0.259	4.413
i = 7	0.000	0.003	−3.981	188.1	−0.083*	0.335	0.164	4.610
i = 8	−0.002	0.001	−14.83	279.5	−0.085*	0.338	0.150	4.598
i = 9	0.001	0.001	16.24	341.7	−0.084*	0.340	0.145	4.567
i = 10	−0.001	0.003	−9.935	173.4	−0.086*	0.336	0.124	4.585
i = 11	0.001	0.002	11.57	243.6	−0.084*	0.339	0.127	4.545
i = 12	−0.001	0.001	−6.245	208.8	−0.085*	0.341	0.121	4.516
i = 18	−0.001	0.000	−15.13	288.9	−0.088*	0.347	0.124	4.416
i = 24	−0.001	0.000	−17.48	317.0	−0.088*	0.348	0.124	4.377
Composite leading indicator: 1968:10–1996:2								
i = 1	−0.011	0.251	0.916	7.234	−0.011	0.251	0.916	7.234
i = 2	−0.027*	0.044	−0.403	6.669	−0.039	0.269	0.534	5.491
i = 3	0.000	0.017	−0.077	7.530	−0.038	0.281	0.503	5.500
i = 4	−0.010	0.018	0.185	13.29	−0.049	0.276	0.576	5.697
i = 5	0.007	0.010	0.102	10.15	−0.042	0.279	0.721	5.930
i = 6	0.001	0.008	0.324	12.75	−0.040	0.282	0.563	5.383
i = 7	0.005	0.005	1.001	8.341	−0.035	0.281	0.589	5.619
i = 8	−0.006	0.011	0.841	33.85	−0.041	0.293	0.453	5.107
i = 9	−0.006	0.010	−2.380	24.81	−0.047	0.301	0.412	5.044
i = 10	−0.005	0.007	−1.431	12.87	−0.052	0.296	0.274	4.619
i = 11	0.016*	0.008	2.647	21.27	−0.037	0.291	0.220	4.521
i = 12	−0.001	0.001	−11.28	191.0	−0.037	0.290	0.221	4.541
i = 18	0.000	0.000	−3.153	77.63	−0.036	0.296	0.206	4.408
i = 24	−0.002	0.001	−15.09	256.1	−0.040	0.299	0.211	4.357

Notes: See notes to Tables 1–3 on p. 50. The statistics reported refer to all revisions *excluding* those that occur during benchmark updates.

Table 2a. Real-time dataset summary statistics for all revisions: 1975:10–1996:2

	Fixed width revisions				Increasing width revisions			
	Mean	Variance	Skewness	Kurtosis	Mean	Variance	Skewness	Kurtosis
Seasonally adjusted industrial production								
i = 1	−0.023*	0.032	0.142	2.927	−0.023*	0.032	0.142	2.927
i = 2	−0.022*	0.025	−0.250	3.515	−0.045*	0.074	−0.105	3.068
i = 3	−0.026*	0.008	−0.217	4.376	−0.071*	0.090	0.027	3.163
i = 4	0.003*	0.001	1.841	28.56	−0.068*	0.093	0.014	3.214
i = 5	0.002	0.002	5.465	56.96	−0.066*	0.095	0.088	3.365
i = 6	−0.006	0.002	−6.099	58.09	−0.071*	0.100	0.020	3.406
i = 7	−0.004*	0.002	−4.489	35.08	−0.076*	0.103	−0.005	3.414
i = 8	0.005	0.002	6.637	57.87	−0.071*	0.110	0.114	3.461
i = 9	−0.005	0.003	−5.620	49.17	−0.075*	0.111	0.146	3.402
i = 10	0.006*	0.003	6.631	58.17	−0.069*	0.113	0.114	3.320
i = 11	0.009	0.004	6.987	49.45	−0.060*	0.126	0.229	4.535
i = 12	−0.002	0.002	−4.217	43.08	−0.061*	0.130	0.288	4.438
i = 18	−0.002	0.001	−2.938	48.66	−0.065*	0.156	0.270	4.333
i = 24	0.002	0.006	0.679	47.06	−0.071*	0.148	−0.036	3.484
Seasonally unadjusted industrial production								
i = 1	−0.009	0.066	−0.017	3.376	−0.009	0.066	−0.017	3.376
i = 2	−0.033*	0.063	0.253	6.619	−0.042*	0.157	−0.199	3.572
i = 3	−0.026*	0.027	−3.743	40.58	−0.068*	0.194	−0.103	3.435
i = 4	−0.004	0.006	−5.328	51.94	−0.073*	0.207	−0.190	3.691
i = 5	0.001	0.002	1.493	37.85	−0.072*	0.211	−0.163	3.681
i = 6	0.002	0.007	2.234	72.16	−0.070*	0.231	−0.035	3.817
i = 7	−0.003	0.002	−5.008	72.89	−0.073*	0.236	−0.064	3.753
i = 8	0.003	0.001	5.477	61.11	−0.070*	0.238	−0.070	3.701
i = 9	0.001	0.001	4.609	59.94	−0.069*	0.239	−0.073	3.685
i = 10	0.006	0.004	9.524	111.4	−0.063*	0.246	−0.042	3.627
i = 11	0.001	0.002	0.500	44.30	−0.062*	0.248	−0.006	3.642
i = 12	−0.001	0.005	−2.497	55.85	−0.063*	0.256	−0.041	3.511
i = 18	0.005	0.005	9.910	108.7	−0.060*	0.317	0.031	3.531
i = 24	0.001	0.008	1.614	103.3	−0.062*	0.332	0.027	3.327
Composite leading indicator								
i = 1	−0.057*	0.132	−0.113	4.495	−0.057*	0.132	−0.113	4.495
i = 2	−0.001	0.032	0.072	6.459	−0.057*	0.161	−0.017	4.952
i = 3	0.016*	0.018	0.073	8.608	−0.041	0.175	−0.020	4.853
i = 4	−0.013	0.019	0.260	14.39	−0.053	0.164	0.148	4.941
i = 5	0.001	0.009	0.120	9.639	−0.053	0.162	0.156	4.635
i = 6	0.011*	0.010	3.274	27.52	−0.041	0.183	0.328	4.817
i = 7	0.009	0.008	3.420	34.90	−0.033	0.177	0.446	4.973
i = 8	−0.007	0.011	−1.672	22.01	−0.039	0.189	0.365	5.011
i = 9	−0.004	0.007	−1.806	15.49	−0.043	0.199	0.286	5.093
i = 10	0.004	0.009	2.950	26.51	−0.039	0.206	0.234	5.104
i = 11	0.019*	0.014	1.704	26.32	−0.020	0.211	0.296	4.856
i = 12	−0.005	0.003	−5.664	52.44	−0.025	0.210	0.289	4.879
i = 18	−0.002	0.003	−8.998	128.7	−0.020	0.212	0.216	4.538
i = 24	−0.005	0.003	−7.182	72.97	−0.025	0.239	−0.072	4.819

Notes: See notes to Tables 1–3 on p. 50.

Norman R. Swanson, Eric Ghysels, and Myles Callan

Table 2b. Real-time dataset summary statistics for non-benchmark revisions:
1975:10–1996:2

	Fixed width revisions				Increasing width revisions			
	Mean	Variance	Skewness	Kurtosis	Mean	Variance	Skewness	Kurtosis
Seasonally adjusted industrial production								
$i = 1$	−0.020*	0.032	0.123	3.003	−0.020*	0.032	0.123	3.003
$i = 2$	−0.022*	0.024	−0.207	3.552	−0.043*	0.072	−0.112	3.207
$i = 3$	−0.025*	0.007	0.040	3.751	−0.068*	0.089	−0.002	3.167
$i = 4$	0.003*	0.001	3.492	40.41	−0.065*	0.092	0.003	3.195
$i = 5$	0.002	0.002	6.145 ·	65.58	−0.063*	0.095	0.077	3.341
$i = 6$	−0.004	0.002	−6.929	71.34	−0.067*	0.100	−0.016	3.353
$i = 7$	−0.002	0.001	−3.651	43.24	−0.069*	0.100	−0.007	3.318
$i = 8$	0.001	0.001	6.493	69.23	−0.067*	0.103	0.044	3.377
$i = 9$	−0.003	0.002	−7.037	76.05	−0.071*	0.105	0.063	3.332
$i = 10$	0.006	0.002	8.016	73.65	−0.065*	0.106	0.034	3.262
$i = 11$	0.003	0.001	2.136	70.96	−0.062*	0.108	0.016	3.195
$i = 12$	−0.002	0.001	−5.958	68.96	−0.064*	0.111	−0.004	3.197
$i = 18$	−0.003	0.001	−6.094	64.63	−0.066*	0.117	−0.044	3.145
$i = 24$	0.002	0.003	5.625	82.38	−0.064*	0.124	−0.090	2.941
Seasonally unadjusted industrial production								
$i = 1$	−0.005	0.063	0.026	3.509	−0.005	0.063	0.026	3.509
$i = 2$	−0.038*	0.054	−0.435	3.970	−0.043*	0.147	−0.297	3.614
$i = 3$	−0.022*	0.016	0.272	4.787	−0.065*	0.179	−0.067	3.379
$i = 4$	0.003	0.002	1.861	44.55	−0.062*	0.182	−0.077	3.579
$i = 5$	0.002	0.001	4.817	61.65	−0.060*	0.184	−0.048	3.643
$i = 6$	0.002	0.002	3.585	74.34	−0.058*	0.191	−0.006	3.662
$i = 7$	−0.003*	0.001	−8.220	76.34	−0.061*	0.194	−0.013	3.630
$i = 8$	0.000	0.000	−1.716	110.3	−0.061*	0.194	−0.013	3.609
$i = 9$	0.000	0.000	3.490	77.54	−0.061*	0.194	−0.012	3.621
$i = 10$	0.002	0.001	7.917	85.33	−0.059*	0.195	−0.006	3.637
$i = 11$	0.002	0.001	7.401	96.57	−0.057*	0.196	0.020	3.676
$i = 12$	−0.001	0.002	−5.228	129.3	−0.058*	0.200	−0.021	3.650
$i = 18$	−0.001*	0.000	−12.30	182.3	−0.059*	0.212	−0.013	3.741
$i = 24$	−0.001	0.000	−11.53	138.9	−0.060*	0.212	−0.027	3.661
Composite leading indicator								
$i = 1$	−0.058*	0.126	−0.119	4.720	−0.058*	0.126	−0.119	4.720
$i = 2$	0.001	0.030	0.120	6.937	−0.057*	0.156	0.034	5.171
$i = 3$	0.015*	0.015	0.107	9.819	−0.042	0.167	0.036	5.181
$i = 4$	−0.011*	0.017	0.477	16.96	−0.053	0.157	0.094	5.313
$i = 5$	0.005	0.007	0.879	10.32	−0.048	0.154	0.167	5.040
$i = 6$	0.004	0.006	0.599	16.26	−0.044	0.165	0.258	5.154
$i = 7$	0.006	0.004	1.009	8.814	−0.038	0.163	0.291	5.321
$i = 8$	−0.009*	0.007	−3.222	23.36	−0.047	0.174	0.185	5.128
$i = 9$	−0.006	0.006	−2.564	19.34	−0.052	0.183	0.074	5.070
$i = 10$	−0.004	0.004	−0.814	11.78	−0.056	0.186	0.076	5.310
$i = 11$	0.008*	0.007	3.410	27.06	−0.038	0.184	0.176	5.322
$i = 12$	−0.001	0.001	−9.695	141.5	−0.039	0.183	0.174	5.365
$i = 18$	0.000	0.000	−2.714	57.62	−0.038	0.190	0.148	5.062
$i = 24$	−0.002	0.001	−12.97	189.6	−0.042	0.194	0.148	4.968

Notes: See notes to Table 1b.

extent, the CLI. This result holds for our full sample periods (Table 1a–1b), as well as for the smaller sample period (Table 2a–2b), which we use in our "efficiency" tests described in the next section. Notice also that the results in Tables 1a and 2a show some clear departures from normality as both the skewness and kurtosis statistics usually differ from the values associated with the Gaussian distribution, but only for the fixed revision case.

Perhaps not surprisingly, nonzero mean revisions also arise for increasing width revisions. Indeed, we expect that fixed length revision mean bias associated with lower values of i leads to mean bias for subsequent values of i, when examining increasing width revisions. Interestingly, the number of significant nonzero means is much greater for the columns associated with increasing width revisions than for those associated with fixed widths. For example, based on increasing revisions with $i = 24$, the difference between the "final" and initial releases display significant mean bias for a number of variables and sample periods (see Tables 1a–2b). In these cases, a correction could be made to all releases of the variables, prior to their final release, which improves the accuracy of all of our preliminary data.

An important caveat to the above discussion is that the summary statistics for our data series reported in Tables 1a and 2a are reported for the entire data series. Hence, no effort has been made to assess the impact of benchmark revisions on the findings, for example. In an effort to address this issue, we also include two additional tables (Tables 1b and 2b) which contain summary statistics based on datasets from which observations associated with benchmark revisions have been removed. Interestingly, the patterns of significant revision biases are essentially the same as those reported above, although bias estimates are generally lower, as might be expected given that we have removed observations which might be viewed as outliers. Another feature of our datasets which is worth mentioning is that major revision points are usually associated with base year and benchmark revisions. For IP, benchmark revisions occurred on 1953:11, 1959:12, 1967:10, 1971:8, 1976:7, 1985:6, 1990:3, 1994:1, 1997:1, and 1997:11, while base-year revisions occurred on 1953:11, 1959:12, 1962:10, 1971:8, 1985:6, 1990:3, and 1997:1. For the CLI, benchmark revisions occurred on 1973:9, 1975:4, 1975:10, 1979:2, 1983:1, 1993:9, and 1996:10, while base-year revisions occurred on 1968:12, 1970:7, 1976:10, 1988:12, and 1993:9. Casual examination of these dates, however, suggests that there are no obvious links between major revisions of IP and major revisions of CLI.

The statistics reported in Tables 1b and 2b are complemented by a set of figures displaying the data without benchmark revisions (see Figures 1 to 3). Each figure shows plots of the first, second, sixth, and twelfth fixed width revisions, as well as the first, second, eighteenth, and twenty-fourth increasing width revisions. We notice some common patterns in Figures 1 and 2 (Industrial Production). First, there appears to be much more variability in first revisions than in later revisions. This finding corresponds to the results

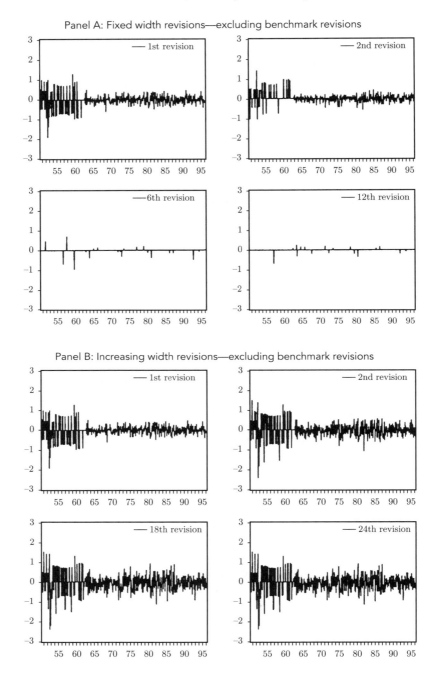

Figure 1. Seasonally adjusted industrial production (sample period: 1950:4–1996:2)
Notes: See notes to Tables 1–3 on p. 50.

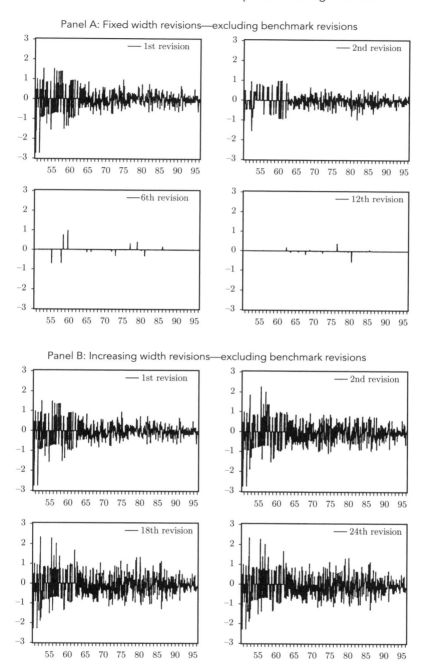

Figure 2. Seasonally unadjusted industrial production (1950:4–1996:2)
Notes: See notes to Tables 1–3 on p. 50.

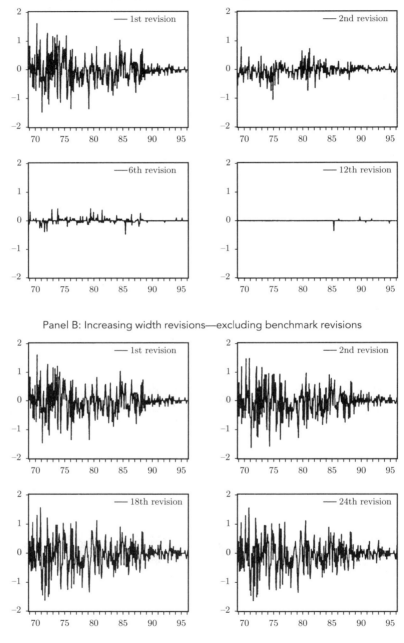

Figure 3. Composite leading indicator (sample period: 1968:10–1996:2)
Notes: See notes to Tables 1–3 on p. 50.

presented in Tables 1a and 1b, where we primarily find significant mean bias for fixed length revisions constructed using small values of i. This finding does not impact on our results concerning increasing length revisions, though, as in these cases even small errors accumulate over time. Indeed, the increasing width revisions plotted in Figures 1 and 2 are not only highly variable but are also frequently nonzero, regardless of the value of i. Second, the revision patterns are somewhat similar, with most outliers occurring in the same time periods, regardless of whether the data have been seasonally adjusted or not. This might be viewed as somewhat surprising, given that seasonally adjusted data are contaminated by future information "leakage" caused by the use of two-sided moving average filters (see above discussion). On the other hand, the result makes sense given that benchmark revisions which tend to drive the outliers do not follow a seasonal pattern. Figure 3 contains plots of CLI revisions. Overall the features of these data are similar to those of the IP series, and there is no obvious structural break, although there is an apparent decrease in fixed revision variability associated not only with 1st revisions versus 2nd revisions, say, but also with increasing calendar time for any given revision series. Next, we turn to an examination of the predictability of our variables using information in past revisions. Any evidence of this type of predictability which we find will be taken as evidence that the revision process is "inefficient." Thus our use of the word of efficiency is used only in the context of predictability.

4 Efficiency of Data Revisions

The main question we are concerned with in this section is whether there are predictable patterns in the revision process. We attempt to answer this question by constructing various different regressions and by examining the autocorrelation functions of the variable. Before turning to our regression results, consider the autocorrelation functions plotted in Figures 4 and 5. Each figure consists of four three-dimensional plots. On one axis we display the order of the autocorrelations, while the other axis corresponds to different values of i. Thus, each row of autocorrelation bars, corresponding to the revision index, is based on the examination of an individual revision time series, i.e. $\rho[(X_{t+i}(t) - X_{t+i-1}(t)), (X_{t-j+i}(t-j) - X_{t-j+i-1}(t-j))]$ for fixed width revisions, and $\rho[(X_{t+i}(t) - X_t(t)), (X_{t-j+i}(t-j) - X_{t-j}(t-j))]$ for increasing width revisions, where ρ denotes the autocorrelation, i is the revision index, and j is the lag order. We first discuss the results appearing in Figure 4, which are based on an examination of seasonally adjusted and unadjusted Industrial Production. The left two panels correspond to fixed width, while the right two panels are for increasing width revisions. We note two features of importance. First, the autocorrelations in the seasonally adjusted data are rather similar in magni-

Norman R. Swanson, Eric Ghysels, and Myles Callan

Panel A: IP (seasonally adjusted)—fixed width revisions

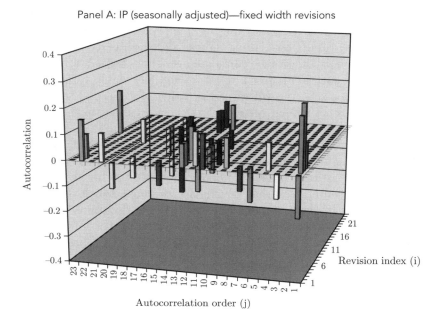

Panel C: IP (unadjusted)—fixed width revisions

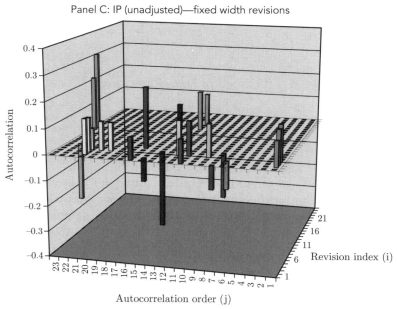

Figure 4. Autocorrelation functions for industrial production

Notes: The sample period is 1950:4–1996:2. The revision index (i), 1 to 24, on the horizontal axis corresponds to the "i" index in Table 1a, 1 representing the "first available revision," 2 representing the second, and so on. The autocorrelation order is j in $\rho(X_t, X_{t-j})$. Only significant autocorrelations are plotted, based on a confidence interval of $\pm 2n^{1/2}$.

Panel B: IP (seasonally adjusted)—increasing width revisions

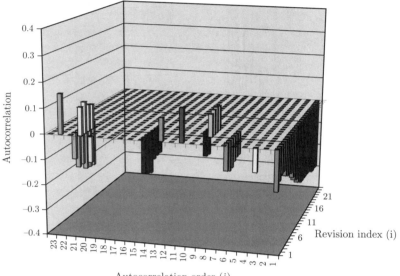

Panel D: IP (unadjusted)—increasing width revisions

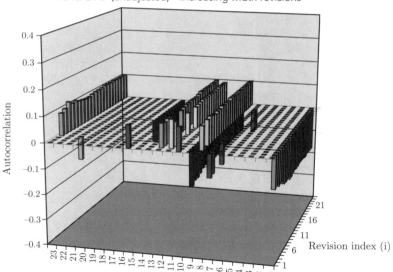

Figure 4. (*cont.*)

Norman R. Swanson, Eric Ghysels, and Myles Callan

Panel A: Fixed width revisions (1968:10–1996:2)

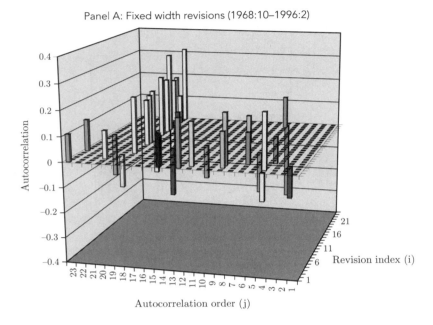

Panel C: Fixed width revisions (1975:10–1996:2)

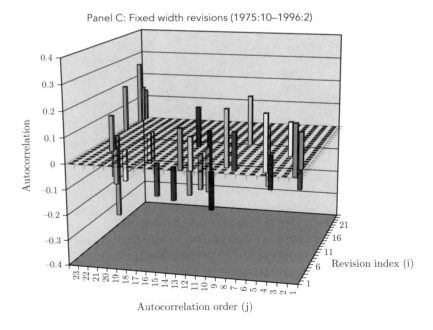

Figure 5. Autocorrelation functions for the composite leading indicator

Notes: See notes to Figure 4.

Panel B: Increasing width revisions (1968:10–1996:2)

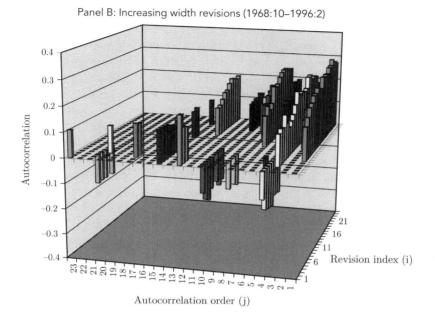

Panel D: Increasing width revisions (1975:10–1996:2)

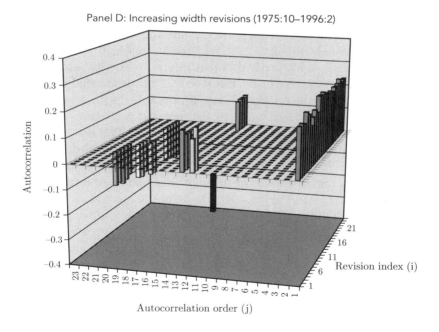

Figure 5. (*cont.*)

tude to those associated with unadjusted data, although there are *more* fixed width autocorrelations which are significantly different from zero when adjusted data are examined. Second, there is much more persistence in the increasing width revisions. The second feature is consistent with the accumulation of errors in increasing width revisions, while the first feature provides weak evidence in support of a hypothesis of increasing autocorrelation associated with the use of two-sided seasonal adjustment filters (i.e. a hypothesis that there is information leakage when seasonally adjusted data are revised). In summary, though, the incidence of nonzero autocorrelations in this first casual examination of autocorrelation functions suggests that past revisions may be useful for predicting future revisions, and hence future releases of the actual data. Thus, the revision process may be inefficient. Even cursory examination of Figure 5 suggests that these findings also apply to the CLI revisions data. Moreover, it is interesting to note that the CLI autocorrelation functions are similar in the upper and lower panels, suggesting that our shorter sample has prediction patterns similar to our longer sample.

In order to investigate the statistical significance of any predictable patterns in our data, we began by running a number of autoregressions. In particular, we ran autoregressions based on all of the data series plotted in Figures 4 and 5 (i.e. $i = 1, ..., 24$), and with lags selected based on the Schwarz Information Criterion. The regressions are formed by projecting jth revisions of data pertaining to time t onto the jth revisions pertaining to time $t - i$, $i = 1, ..., 24$. Tables 3a–3b contain our findings for the full and shorter sample periods, where results are only tabulated for regressions in which at least one explanatory variable is significantly different from zero at a 90 percent level of confidence.[11] Our overall conclusion based on this univariate analysis is clearly that the inefficiency in the revision process is primarily due to mean bias (note the number of significant constants in the reported regressions), with little information in autoregressive variables being relevant. This can be seen most clearly by examining the results contained in Table 3b. In addition, note that reported adjusted R^2 values are quite small, suggesting that there is little predictive content, at least when we attempt to explain a first revision today with a first revision yesterday, say, as is done in the regressions.

In order to further examine the issue of efficiency in a univariate context, we consider regressions involving different vintages of revisions of the same variable, for a fixed time period. Hence, instead of running autoregressions with time period $t - i$, $i = 1, ..., 24$, used to construct the explanatory variables, we fix $i = 0$, and the regressions are thus formed by projecting jth revisions of data pertaining to time t onto $(j - i)$th revisions pertaining to time t, $i = 1, ..., 24$, where the number of regressors in each regression is constrained by the condition that $j > i$. This condition is needed in order to ensure that present and/or future information is not used in and of the explanatory variables. Tables 4a–4b contain our findings, where again only coefficients significantly

Table 3a. Autoregressions for fixed width revisions: entire sample

$$\Delta X_{t+j}(t) = c + \sum_i \beta_i (\Delta X_{t+j+i}(t+i)) + \varepsilon_t,\ i = 1, 2, ..., 24 \text{ for each } j = 0, 1, ..., 23$$

Dependent variable	Lags	Significant coefficients			$\bar{R}^2$	D.W.
Seasonally adjusted industrial production: 1950:4–1996:2						
$\Delta X_t(t)$	5	c (0.044)	β_4 (0.090)		0.052	1.99
$\Delta X_{t+1}(t)$	6	β_1 (0.194)			0.087	1.99
$\Delta X_{t+2}(t)$	5	c (0.019)	β_1 (0.187)		0.029	1.98
$\Delta X_{t+4}(t)$	3	β_3 (0.216)			0.041	2.00
$\Delta X_{t+5}(t)$	3	c (0.006)	β_3 (0.162)		0.038	1.99
$\Delta X_{t+12}(t)$	3	c (0.005)			−0.002	2.00
Seasonally unadjusted industrial production: 1950:4–1996:2						
$\Delta X_t(t)$	16	β_7 (−0.097)	β_8 (0.096)	β_{10} (0.074)		
		β_{11} (0.088)	β_{15} (0.096)		0.051	2.02
$\Delta X_{t+1}(t)$	1	c (0.027)	β_1 (0.106)		0.025	1.98
$\Delta X_{t+2}(t)$	1	c (0.021)	β_1 (0.084)		0.017	2.00
$\Delta X_{t+6}(t)$	3	β_4 (0.197)			0.034	2.00
Composite leading indicator: 1968:10–1996:2						
$\Delta X_{t+1}(t)$	8	β_4 (0.214)	β_7 (0.122)	β_8 (0.107)	0.080	2.01
$\Delta X_{t+3}(t)$	1	c (0.136)			0.088	1.98
$\Delta X_{t+6}(t)$	1	c (−0.009)			−0.001	1.99
$\Delta X_{t+10}(t)$	1	c (−0.023)			0.034	1.99
$\Delta X_{t+22}(t)$	1	β_6 (−0.317)			0.083	2.00
$\Delta X_{t+23}(t)$	1	c (0.012)			0.084	2.00

Notes: See notes to Tables 1–3 on p. 50 for definitions of the dependent variable. Regression lag orders are chosen using the Schwarz Information Criterion, and only coefficients which are significant at a 90% level of confidence are tabulated.

different from zero at a 90 percent level of confidence are reported. We find that future revisions (e.g. $X_{t+j}(t) - X_{t+j-1}(t)$), can often be predicted from past revisions when j is small, regardless of which sample period is used. For instance, for the CLI (small sample, see Table 4b) various coefficients associated with regressions, where the dependent variable is $X_{t+j}(t) - X_{t+j-1}(t)$ for $j = 2$, 4, 6, 8, 9, 10, 20, 21, and 22, are significant. Such predictable patterns also occur, but to a lesser extent, for revisions in unadjusted and adjusted IP. Thus, while our autoregressions reported in Tables 3a–3b show that inefficiencies often appear through mean biases when examining individual revision vintages (allowing t to vary), our results in Tables 4a–4b suggest that inefficiencies also occur *between* different vintages (for fixed t).

Given these findings, it should also be of interest to assess whether information in lags of one of our variables is useful for predicting revisions in other variables. We first address this question by running multivariate regressions of the type reported on in Table 5. In all, 16 regressions—with up to 23 explanatory variables in each—were run, and, as above, those with significant

Table 3b. Autoregressions for fixed width revisions: 1975:10–1996:2

$$\Delta X_{t+j}(t) = c + \sum_i \beta_i (\Delta X_{t+j+i}(t+i)) + \varepsilon_t, \; i = 1, 2, ..., 24 \text{ for each } j = 0, 1, ..., 23$$

Dependent variable	Lags	Significant coefficients			$\bar{R}^2$	D.W.
Seasonally adjusted industrial production						
$\Delta X_t(t)$	1	c (0.022)			0.053	2.00
$\Delta X_{t+1}(t)$	1	c (0.020)			−0.002	1.98
$\Delta X_{t+2}(t)$	1	c (0.019)	β_1 (0.211)		0.054	1.95
$\Delta X_{t+3}(t)$	4	c (−0.004)			−0.003	1.99
$\Delta X_{t+4}(t)$	1	c (0.005)			−0.003	2.00
$\Delta X_{t+5}(t)$	1	c (−0.005)			−0.004	2.00
$\Delta X_{t+12}(t)$	1	c (−0.001)	β_{10} (−0.216)		0.017	2.00
Seasonally unadjusted industrial production						
$\Delta X_{t+1}(t)$	5	c (0.032)	β_4 (−0.173)		0.093	2.00
$\Delta X_{t+2}(t)$	2	c (0.027)	β_1 (0.149)	β_2 (−0.106)	0.021	1.98
$\Delta X_{t+3}(t)$	1	c (0.036)			−0.039	2.00
Composite leading indicator						
$\Delta X_t(t)$	10	c (0.048)	β_1 (0.306)	β_3 (−0.140)		
		β_9 (−0.166)	β_{10} (−0.174)		0.012	2.02
$\Delta X_{t+2}(t)$	1	c (0.016)			0.041	1.96
$\Delta X_{t+3}(t)$	1	β_1 (0.140)			0.030	1.97
$\Delta X_{t+10}(t)$	1	c (−0.018)	β_1 (−0.111)		0.061	2.00

Notes: See notes to Table 3a.

coefficients are reported on in the table. In all regressions, the dependent variable is the first revision of a given variable, say $Y_{t+1}(t) - Y_t(t)$. Panel A of the table contains regression results based on fixed width revisions, while Panel B contains results for increasing width revisions. In the fixed width regressions, the explanatory variables are first revisions available during previous time periods, $X_{t-i+1}(t-i) - X_{t-i}(t-i)$, for $i = 1, ..., 24$. In the increasing width regressions, the explanatory variables are accumulated revisions available at time t regarding previous periods' data (i.e. $X_t(t-i) - X_{t-i}(t-i)$, for $i = 1, ..., 24$). The first column in the table lists the dependent variable, while the second shows the independent variable. The third column lists the significant coefficients from each regression. The results are interesting for a number of reasons. First, there are a number of significant regressors in our regressions, suggesting that multivariate information may "matter" in the revision process, particularly in increasing width revision cases. In addition, note the relatively high $\bar{R}^2$ values for some of the regressions. Second, the usefulness of previously available IP revisions for explaining CLI revisions suggests that releases of the composite leading indicator do not fully incorporate newly available IP data. For example, we might expect a one period lag in the transfer (across government agencies) of updated IP information to the CLI. However, we find that information available prior to time $t - 1$ is useful for predicting

Table 4a. Efficiency of revisions based on univariate regressions: entire sample

$$\Delta X_{t+j}(t) = c + \sum_i \beta_i (\Delta X_{t+i}(t)) + \varepsilon_t, \ i = j-1, j-2, ..., 0 \text{ for each } j = 1, 2, ..., 23$$

Dependent variable	Significant coefficients					$\bar{R}^2$	D.W.
Seasonally adjusted industrial production: 1950:4–1996:2							
$\Delta X_{t+2}(t)$	c	(0.023)				0.002	1.82
$\Delta X_{t+3}(t)$	β_3	(0.072)				0.012	2.03
$\Delta X_{t+5}(t)$	c	(0.008)				−0.002	2.01
$\Delta X_{t+7}(t)$	β_3	(0.496)	β_6	(0.580)		0.093	1.96
$\Delta X_{t+8}(t)$	β_3	(0.564)				0.071	2.00
Seasonally unadjusted industrial production: 1950:4–1996:2							
$\Delta X_{t+1}(t)$	c	(0.032)				−0.001	1.97
$\Delta X_{t+2}(t)$	c	(−0.034)	β_1	(−0.085)		0.010	1.90
$\Delta X_{t+3}(t)$	c	(0.036)	β_1	(−0.075)		0.028	2.04
$\Delta X_{t+6}(t)$	β_4	(−0.151)	β_5	(−0.035)		0.086	1.99
$\Delta X_{t+15}(t)$	β_1	(0.050)	β_3	(−0.084)		0.028	2.02
$\Delta X_{t+22}(t)$	β_1	(−0.134)				0.037	2.00
Composite leading indicator: 1968:10–1996:2							
$\Delta X_t(t)$	c	(0.028)	β_1	(−0.056)	β_2 (−0.036)	0.015	2.07
$\Delta X_{t+3}(t)$	c	(0.015)	β_1	(−0.096)	β_2 (−0.036)	0.019	1.89
$\Delta X_{t+4}(t)$	β_2	(−0.116)	β_3	(−0.076)		0.037	2.09
$\Delta X_{t+5}(t)$	β_1	(−0.148)				0.008	2.05
$\Delta X_{t+6}(t)$	c	(−0.010)	β_4	(−0.081)		0.015	2.06
$\Delta X_{t+7}(t)$	β_5	(−0.180)	β_5	(−0.117)		0.022	1.97
$\Delta X_{t+9}(t)$	β_1	(−0.111)	β_6	(−0.226)	β_7 (−0.108)	0.033	1.86
$\Delta X_{t+10}(t)$	c	(−0.022)				−0.002	2.07
$\Delta X_{t+15}(t)$	β_6	(−0.082)				0.046	1.99
$\Delta X_{t+22}(t)$	β_6	(−0.353)				0.091	2.00
$\Delta X_{t+23}(t)$	c	(0.008)	β_{16}	(−0.308)	β_{18} (−0.098)	0.162	1.97

Notes: See notes to Table 3a, and discussion in the text.

CLI revisions in 2 CLI regressions. This multivariate result is rather significant, as it casts some doubt on the accuracy of early CLI releases. In addition, note that this result is not affected by the use of our shorter sample period. Finally, it is worth pointing out that CLI revisions may be useful for predicting IP revisions, although the relationship appears weaker than that from IP to CLI revisions.

In order to shed additional light on the above findings, we also report on a different variety of multivariate regression (see Table 6). In these regressions, previous updates of the CLI are used to model current updates of IP, for example. The most surprising result from this table is that past revisions of a particular calendar date for CLI are useful for predicting the current IP revision for the same calendar date, in many cases. In addition, there appears to be causality from IP to CLI, but the linkages are weaker than for the CLI to IP case. Thus, our earlier conclusions based on an examination of the results

Table 4b. Efficiency of revisions based on univariate regressions: 1975:10–1996:2
$\Delta X_{t+j}(t) = c + \sum_i \beta_i(\Delta X_{t+i}(t)) + \varepsilon_t$, $i = j - 1, j - 2, ..., 0$ for each $j = 1, 2, ..., 23$

Dependent variable	Significant coefficients			$\bar{R}^2$	D.W.
Seasonally adjusted industrial production					
$\Delta X_{t+1}(t)$	c (0.016)	β_2 (0.262)		0.085	1.86
$\Delta X_{t+2}(t)$	c (0.024)	β_2 (0.089)		0.026	1.87
$\Delta X_{t+4}(t)$	c (−0.039)	β_2 (0.213)		0.006	2.01
$\Delta X_{t+9}(t)$	c (−0.063)			−0.003	2.02
Seasonally unadjusted industrial production					
$\Delta X_{t+2}(t)$	c (0.031)	β_7 (0.215)		0.044	1.84
$\Delta X_{t+3}(t)$	c (0.025)			0.001	1.84
$\Delta X_{t+5}(t)$	β_1 (−0.038)	β_4 (0.036)		0.041	2.87
$\Delta X_{t+6}(t)$	β_1 (−0.500)	β_4 (0.062)		0.062	2.02
Composite leading indicator					
$\Delta X_{t+2}(t)$	c (−0.016)			0.004	2.14
$\Delta X_{t+4}(t)$	β_1 (−0.105)	β_2 (−0.185)		0.072	1.98
$\Delta X_{t+6}(t)$	β_2 (−0.130)	β_4 (−0.113)	β_6 (−0.031)	0.035	1.98
$\Delta X_{t+8}(t)$	β_4 (−0.100)	β_6 (−0.076)		0.016	2.04
$\Delta X_{t+9}(t)$	β_3 (0.207)			0.026	1.94
$\Delta X_{t+10}(t)$	c (−0.017)	β_3 (−0.215)		0.040	2.07
$\Delta X_{t+20}(t)$	β_8 (−0.130)	β_{12} (0.213)		0.091	2.00
$\Delta X_{t+21}(t)$	β_{12} (0.322)			0.040	1.98
$\Delta X_{t+22}(t)$	β_8 (−0.239)	β_{10} (−0.186)		0.112	2.00

Notes: See notes to Table 4a, and discussion in the text.

in Table 5 remain intact when a different variety of multivariate regression is run. In summary, our multivariate analysis appears to point to a number of potentially interesting types of inefficiencies inherent to the revision process which are not readily apparent when univariate data are examined.

In the spirit of much of Clive Granger's work on out-of-sample forecasting, we close our discussion of the data revision process with an examination of the relevance of our regression findings within the context of a real-time forecasting experiment. In particular, for a variety of the univariate and multivariate fixed width regressions reported on in Tables 3a–3b and 5 we construct a sequence of 1-step ahead forecasts based on regressions formulated using increasing samples of data with coefficients re-estimated at each point in time (model specifications were fixed beforehand using the SIC). A representative sample of our findings is reported in Figure 6. Of particular note is that the out-of-sample R^2 values (see e.g. Swanson and White, 1995, for further explanation of out-of-sample R^2 values) based on all of the reported experiments (where the *ex ante* period is 1992:1–1996:2) are greater than zero, with many values greater than 0.10. In addition, the highest R^2 values are associated with experiments based on univariate models.

Table 5. Efficiency of revisions based on multivariate regressions I

A. *Fixed width revisions:* $\Delta Y_t(t) = c + \sum_i \beta_i (\Delta X_{t-i}(t-i)) + \varepsilon_t,\ i = 1, 2, ..., 23$

Dependent variable	Independent variable	Significant coefficients			$\bar{R}^2$	D.W.
Sample period: 1968:10–1996:2						
CLI	Adjusted IP	None			−0.003	1.84
CLI	Unadjusted IP	β_{10} (0.290)	β_{11} (0.183)	β_{15} (0.245)		
		β_{18} (−0.274)			0.076	1.86
Adjusted IP	CLI	c (0.016)	β_1 (−0.029)		0.004	2.01
Unadjusted IP	CLI	β_4 (0.054)	β_{13} (−0.061)	β_{15} (0.094)		
		β_{18} (−0.074)			0.039	2.02
Sample period: 1975:10–1996:2						
CLI	Adjusted IP	c (0.055)	β_1 (0.042)	β_8 (0.529)		
		β_9 (0.267)	β_{11} (−0.356)		0.111	1.91
CLI	Unadjusted IP	c (0.055)	β_1 (−0.190)	β_8 (0.315)		
		β_9 (0.159)	β_{11} (−0.248)		0.098	1.92
Adjusted IP	CLI	c (0.028)	β_1 (−0.106)		0.042	2.04
Unadjusted IP	CLI	β_1 (−0.017)			0.051	1.98

B. *Increasing width revisions:* $\Delta Y_t(t) = c + \sum_i \beta_i (X_t(t-i) - X_{t-i}(t-i)) + \varepsilon_t,\ i = 1, 2, ..., 23$

Dependent variable	Independent variable	Significant coefficients			$\bar{R}^2$	D.W.
Sample period: 1968:10–1996:2						
CLI	Adjusted IP	β_4 (−0.204)			0.007	1.85
CLI	Unadjusted IP	β_3 (−0.118)			0.010	1.82
Adjusted IP	CLI	c (0.016)	β_2 (−0.029)		0.004	2.01
Unadjusted IP	CLI	β_{13} (−0.063)			0.017	2.04
Sample period: 1975:10–1996:2						
CLI	Adjusted IP	β_1 (−0.194)	β_8 (0.269)	β_9 (0.154)		
		β_{11} (−0.171)			0.103	1.81
CLI	Unadjusted IP	c (0.044)	β_1 (−0.194)	β_8 (0.179)		
		β_9 (0.084)	β_{11} (−0.135)		0.106	1.83
Adjusted IP	CLI	c (0.028)	β_1 (−0.106)		0.042	2.04
Unadjusted IP	CLI	β_1 (−0.164)			0.051	1.98

Notes: See notes to Table 3a. Y in the regression equation is the dependent variable given in the first column of the table, whereas X corresponds to the independent variable used in each regression. In all regressions, 24 exogenous variables are used. In the fixed width regressions, these are all first available revisions, available from $t-1$ to $t-24$. In the increasing width regressions, the regressors used are: $X_t(t-1) - X_{t-1}(t-1)$, $X_t(t-2) - X_{t-2}(t-2)$, ..., $X_t(t-24) - X_{t-24}(t-24)$, so that increasing width revisions are used as the availability of the information becomes more distant.

Table 6. Efficiency of revisions based on multivariate regressions II

$$\Delta Y_{t+j}(t) = c + \sum_i \beta_i (\Delta X_{t+i}(t)) + \varepsilon_t, \; i = j-1, j-2, ..., 0 \text{ for each } j = 1, 2, ..., 23$$

Sample period: 1975:10–1996:2

Dependent variable	Significant coefficients			$\bar{R}^2$	D.W.
(i) $Y = CLI$, $X = $ Seasonally adjusted industrial production					
$\Delta Y_{t+2}(t)$	β_1 (−0.129)			0.019	2.12
$\Delta Y_{t+5}(t)$	c (−0.011)			−0.003	2.01
$\Delta Y_{t+7}(t)$	β_1 (0.352)			0.015	1.97
$\Delta Y_{t+11}(t)$	c (0.005)	β_6 (0.309)	β_{10} (0.076)	0.080	2.02
$\Delta Y_{t+20}(t)$	β_6 (0.276)			0.027	1.98
$\Delta Y_{t+21}(t)$	β_4 (−0.854)	β_6 (−0.554)		0.131	2.02
$\Delta Y_{t+23}(t)$	β_{16} (0.118)	β_{17} (−0.331)		0.071	1.87
(ii) $Y = CLI$, $X = $ Seasonally unadjusted industrial production					
$\Delta Y_{t+2}(t)$	β_1 (−0.102)			0.032	2.10
$\Delta Y_{t+4}(t)$	β_2 (0.064)			0.011	1.90
$\Delta Y_{t+6}(t)$	β_1 (0.309)			0.031	2.02
$\Delta Y_{t+9}(t)$	β_4 (0.309)	β_5 (−0.408)	β_6 (−0.296)	0.154	2.01
$\Delta Y_{t+10}(t)$	c (−0.018)	β_4 (−0.854)	β_6 (−0.554)	0.131	2.02
$\Delta Y_{t+15}(t)$	β_6 (−0.223)			0.055	2.00
(iii) $Y = $ Seasonally adjusted industrial production, $X = CLI$					
$\Delta Y_{t+1}(t)$	c (0.025)	β_1 (−0.050)		0.009	1.93
$\Delta Y_{t+4}(t)$	β_3 (0.041)			0.023	2.00
$\Delta Y_{t+5}(t)$	β_2 (0.051)			0.013	1.98
$\Delta Y_{t+6}(t)$	c (0.004)	β_3 (−0.048)		0.012	2.06
$\Delta Y_{t+9}(t)$	c (−0.006)			−0.004	2.03
$\Delta Y_{t+11}(t)$	β_2 (−0.049)			0.004	1.96
$\Delta Y_{t+12}(t)$	β_3 (−0.080)			0.035	2.02
$\Delta Y_{t+14}(t)$	β_2 (−0.221)			0.026	2.07
$\Delta Y_{t+15}(t)$	β_2 (0.129)			0.015	2.00
$\Delta Y_{t+16}(t)$	β_2 (−0.236)			0.013	2.00
$\Delta Y_{t+20}(t)$	β_2 (−0.726)	β_7 (−0.197)		0.209	2.02
$\Delta Y_{t+21}(t)$	β_7 (−0.136)			0.049	2.00
$\Delta Y_{t+22}(t)$	β_2 (−0.168)			0.009	1.72
$\Delta Y_{t+23}(t)$	β_2 (−0.198)			0.007	2.00
(iv) $Y = $ Seasonally unadjusted industrial production, $X = CLI$					
$\Delta Y_{t+1}(t)$	c (0.038)	β_2 (−0.072)		0.014	1.88
$\Delta Y_{t+2}(t)$	c (0.026)			−0.003	1.83
$\Delta Y_{t+5}(t)$	β_3 (−0.072)			0.013	1.98
$\Delta Y_{t+6}(t)$	β_5 (0.036)			0.012	1.86
$\Delta Y_{t+8}(t)$	β_2 (−0.035)	β_4 (−0.040)		0.010	2.01
$\Delta Y_{t+16}(t)$	β_2 (0.209)			0.012	2.01
$\Delta Y_{t+17}(t)$	β_2 (0.414)			0.124	2.01
$\Delta Y_{t+18}(t)$	c (0.004)	β_2 (−0.064)		0.002	2.03
$\Delta Y_{t+20}(t)$	β_2 (0.401)			0.328	1.98

Notes: See notes to Table 3a, and discussion in the text. All regressions are based on fixed width revisions.

Fixed width revisions   *Increasing width revisions*

Panel A: Forecast of CLI using past CLI

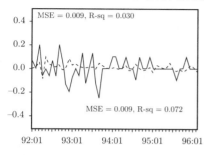 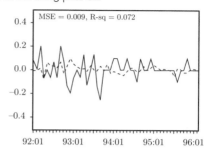

Panel B: Forecast of seasonally adjusted IP using past seasonally adjusted IP

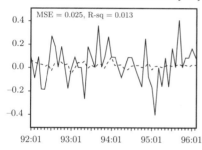 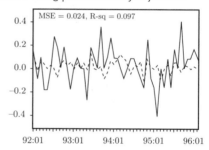

Panel C: Forecast of seasonally adjusted IP using past CLI

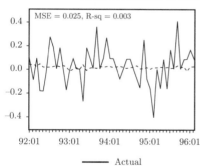 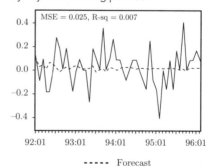

———— Actual   - - - - - Forecast

Figure 6. 1-step ahead forecasting experiments

Notes: The forecast period is 1992:1–1996:2. The regressions of real-time revisions used to derive the forecasts are of the form given in Table 5. The parameters in the forecast regression are re-estimated before each new 1-step ahead forecast is constructed. The R-squared reported is the out-of-sample R-squared.

5 Conclusions and Recommendations

In this paper we have undertaken a multivariate time series analysis of the data revision process for industrial production (IP) and the composite leading indicator (CLI). We offer the following conclusions. First, there appears to be mean bias in the revision process for both seasonally adjusted and unadjusted IP, and for the CLI. This type of inefficiency is interesting, because merely adding constants to preliminary releases can correct such systematic bias. Second, based on univariate autoregressive models we find some evidence that past revisions of our variables have predictive content for current and future revisions. This in turn suggests that past revisions can be used to improve upon our estimates (or preliminary releases) of final data. Third, we present findings based on multivariate regressions which suggest that multivariate information "matters" in the revision process. For example, previously available IP revisions are useful for explaining CLI revisions, suggesting that releases of CLI do not fully incorporate newly available IP data. In addition, real-time forecasting experiments suggest that there is useful univariate as well as multivariate information in the revision processes of IP and the CLI.

This work represents a starting point, and many issues remain to be explored, both theoretical and empirical. From a theoretical perspective, for example, it is of interest to characterize the data revision process within the context of a macroeconomic model of policy decision making. From an empirical perspective, it is of interest to assess whether knowledge of the revision process be used in a real-time context to improve economic forecasts of fully revised data. Also, within a multivariate real-time data context, many questions concerning Granger causality and model specification remain unanswered. Finally, it remains to assess whether the types of inefficiencies which we find in this paper characterize real-time data in general, or are specific to our datasets.

Notes

1. Further details of Clive's early research appear in the *Econometric Theory* interview of Clive Granger by Peter Phillips (1997).
2. There are various exceptions to this practice. For example, Fair and Shiller (1990) acknowledge the issue of data revision quite explicitly, although they do not address it in their analysis.
3. One of the few explicit treatments of data errors and its transmission into policy decisions is Maravall and Pierce (1986).
4. Sargent (1989) is one of the few examples where revision process errors (in his case, "final" data errors) is treated explicitly, examining how they affect the estimation of econometric models.

5. Federal Reserve releases for industrial production are referred to as G.12.3 for dates up to 1990:4, and G.17 thereafter. These releases are typically published on the fifteenth of each month and contain the preliminary data for the previous month, as well as revisions to data for earlier months.

6. Details of the base year changes are available in the relevant *Federal Reserve Bulletin*, see e.g. pp. 1247–79, December 1953; pp. 1451–66 and pp. 552–73, July 1971; pp. 447–97, July 1985; and pp. 187–204, April 1990.

7. See *Business Conditions Digest*, p. iii, August 1970, and the *Survey of Current Business*, pp. 23–7, January 1989, and pp. 44–52, October 1993, for details of the revision.

8. All time series formed in our analysis were tested for nonstationarity using augmented Dickey–Fuller tests with an intercept, and with the number of lagged dependent variables used in the regressions chosen by starting with 20 lags, and decreasing the number of lags used until the last included lag had a coefficient significantly different from zero at a 95 percent level of confidence. In all cases, the I(1) null hypothesis was rejected at a 5 percent significance level.

9. The smaller sample period was selected because in late 1975 there appears to be a "variance shift" in the CLI and in IP (see Figures 1–3). In addition, it is worth noting that there was a 25 percent level shift in the CLI in late 1975. However, this level shift does not affect our data, as we are looking at growth rate revisions.

10. Our mean bias tests implicitly assume a null hypothesis that the mean of the revision error is zero. Whether or not a rejection of this null leads to the conclusion that preliminary releases could and should be adjusted depends to some extent on the loss function of the agency using the data releases. In addition, the agency producing the initial releases may not want to adjust these releases until "hard" evidence is available.

11. The values in parentheses are the numerical values of the significant coefficient estimates. All estimates are based on OLS and are evaluated using HAC standard error estimates. For illustrative purposes, Durbin–Watson statistics are reported for all regressions, even though they suffer from reduced power and are biased towards 2 in our context.

References

Bates, J. and C. W. J. Granger (1969), "The Combination of Forecasts," *Operational Research Quarterly*, 20: 451–68.

Boschen, J. F. and H. I. Grossman (1982), "Tests of Equilibrium Macroeconomics Using Contemporaneous Monetary Data," *Journal of Monetary Economics*, 10: 309–33.

Conrad, W. and C. Corrado (1979), "Application of the Kalman Filter to Revisions in Monthly Retail Sales Estimates," *Journal of Economic Dynamics and Control*, 1: 177–198.

Diebold, F. X. and G. D. Rudebusch (1991), "Forecasting Output with the Composite Leading Index: A Real Time Analysis," *Journal of the American Statistical Association*, 603–10.

Engle, R. F. and C. W. J. Granger (1987), "Co-integration and Error Correction: Representation, Estimation, and Testing," *Econometrica*, 55: 251–76.

Fair, R. C. and R. J. Shiller (1990), "Comparing Information in Forecasts from Econometric Models," *American Economic Review*, 80: 375–89.

Ghysels, E. (1982), "Tijdreeksanalyse en Fouten in BNP–Cijfers—Een Theoretische Korrektie en Herinterpretatie," *Cahiers Economiques de Bruxelles*, 96: 489–95.

Ghysels, E., C. W. J. Granger, and P. Siklos (1996), "Is Seasonal Adjustment a Linear or Nonlinear Data-Filtering Transformation?" *Journal of Business and Economic Statistics*, 14: 374–86.

Granger, C. W. J. (1969), "Investigating Causal Relations by Econometric Models and Cross Spectral Methods," *Econometrica*, 37: 428–38.

Granger, C. W. J. (1980), "Testing for Causality, a Personal Viewpoint," *Journal of Economic Dynamics and Control*, 2: 329–52.

Granger, C. W. J. (1983), "Co-integrated Variables and Error-Correcting Models," Discussion Paper 83–13, University of California, San Diego.

Granger, C. W. J. (1986), Developments in the Study of Co-integrated Economic Variables, Oxford Bulletin of Economics and Statistics, 48, 213–228.

Granger, C. W. J. (1988), "Some Recent Developments in a Concept of Causality," *Journal of Econometrics*, 39: 199–211.

Granger, C. W. J. (1992), "Forecasting Stock Market Prices: Lessons for Forecasters," *International Journal of Forecasting*, 8: 3–13.

Granger, C. W. J. (1996), "Can We Improve the Perceived Quality of Economic Forecasts?" *Journal of Applied Econometrics*, 11: 455–73.

Granger, C. W. J. and Z. Ding (1996), "Varieties of Long Memory Models," *Journal of Econometrics*, 73: 61–77.

Granger, C. W. J. and L. Ermini (1993), "Some Generalizations of the Algebra of I(1) Processes," *Journal of Econometrics*, 58: 369–84.

Granger, C. W. J. and J. Gonzalo (1995), "Estimation of Common Long Memory Components in Cointegrated Systems," *Journal of Business and Economic Statistics*, 13: 27–35.

Granger, C. W. J. and J. Hallman (1991), "Nonlinear Transformations of Integrated Time Series," *Journal of Time Series Analysis*, 12: 207–24.

Granger, C. W. J. and M. Hatanaka (1964), *Spectral Analysis of Economic Time Series.* Princeton: Princeton University Press.

Granger, C. W. J. and T.-H. Lee (1990), "Multicointegration," in G. F. Rhodes and T. B. Fomby (eds.), *Advances in Econometrics: Co-Integration, Spurious Regressions and Unit Roots.* Greenwich, CT: JAI Press.

Granger, C. W. J. and J.-L. Lin (1995), "Causality in the Long Run," *Econometric Theory*, 11: 530–6.

Granger, C. W. J. and H. L. Nelson (1979), "Experience with Using the Box–Cox Transformation when Forecasting Economic Time Series," *Journal of Econometrics*, 9: 57–69.

Granger, C. W. J. and P. Newbold (1974), "Spurious Regressions in Econometrics," *Journal of Econometrics*, 2: 111–20.

Granger, C. W. J. and N. R. Swanson (1996), "Further Developments in the Study of Cointegrated Economic Variables," *Oxford Bulletin of Economics and Statistics*, 58: 537–53.

Granger, C. W. J. and N. R. Swanson (1997), "An Introduction to Stochastic Unit Root Processes," *Journal of Econometrics*, 80: 35–62.

Granger, C. W. J. and A. A. Weiss (1983), "Time Series Analysis of Error-Correction Models," in S. Karlin, T. Amemiya, and L. A. Goodman (eds.), *Studies in Econo-*

metrics, Time Series and Multivariate Statistics, in honor of T. W. Anderson. Academic Press.

Hamilton, J. D. and G. Perez-Quiros (1996), "What Do the Leading Indicators Lead?" *Journal of Business*, 69: 27–49.

Harvey, A. C., C. R. McKenzie, D. P. C. Blake and M. J. Desai (1993), "Irregular Data Revisions," in A. Zellner (ed.), *Applied Time Series Analysis of Economic Data*. Bureau of the Census, pp. 329–47.

Kavajecz, K. A. and S. Collins (1995), "Rationality of Preliminary Money Estimates," *Review of Economic Studies*, 62: 32–41.

Keane, M. P. and D. E. Runkle (1990), "Testing the Rationality of Price Forecasts," *American Economic Review*, 80: 714–35.

Koenig, E. F. and K. M. Emery (1994), "Why the Composite Index of Leading Indicators Does Not Lead," *Contemporary Economic Policy*, 12: 52–66.

Mankiw, N. G. and M. D. Shapiro (1986), "News or Noise: An Analysis of GNP Revisions," *Survey of Current Business*, 66: 20–5.

Mankiw, N. G., D. E. Runkle, and M. D. Shapiro (1984), "Are Preliminary Announcements of the Money Stock Rational Forecasts?" *Journal of Monetary Economics*, 14: 15–27.

Maravall, A. and D. Pierce (1986), "The Transmission of Data Noise into Policy Noise in U.S. Monetary Control," *Econometrica*, 54: 961–79.

Mariano, R. S. and Tanizaki, H. (1995), "Prediction of Final Data with Use of Preliminary and/or Revised Data," *Journal of Forecasting*, forthcoming.

Morgenstern, O. (1963), *On the Accuracy of Economic Observations*, 2nd edn. Princeton: Princeton University Press.

Patterson, K. D. (1995), "An Integrated Model of the Data Measurement and Data Generation Process with an Application to Consumers' Expenditure," *Economic Journal*, 105: 54–76.

Phillips, P. C. B. (1997), "*ET* Interview: Clive Granger," *Econometric Theory*, 13: 253–305.

Pierce, D. A. (1981), "Sources of Error in Economic Time Series," *Journal of Econometrics*, 17: 305–21.

Sargent, T. J. (1989), "Two Models of Measurements and the Investment Accelerator," *Journal of Political Economy*, 97: 251–87.

Swanson, N. R. (1996), "Forecasting Using First-Available versus Fully Revised Economic Time-Series Data," *Studies in Nonlinear Dynamics and Econometrics*, 1: 47–64.

Swanson, N. R. and C. W. J. Granger (1997), "Impulse Response Functions Based on Causal Approach to Residual Orthogonalization in Vector Autoregressions," *Journal of the American Statistical Association*, 92: 357–67.

Swanson, N. R. and H. White (1995), "A Model Selection Approach to Assessing the Information in the Term Structure Using Linear Models and Artificial Neural Networks," *Journal of Business and Economic Statistics*, 13: 265–75.

Swanson, N. R. and H. White (1997a), "A Model Selection Approach to Real-Time Macroeconomic Forecasting Using Linear Models and Artificial Neural Networks," *Review of Economics and Statistics*, 79: 540–50.

Swanson, N. R. and H. White (1997b), "Forecasting Economic Time Series Using Flexible versus Fixed Specification and Linear Versus Nonlinear Econometric Models," *International Journal of Forecasting*, 13: 439–61.

3
Evaluating Density Forecasts of Inflation: The Survey of Professional Forecasters

FRANCIS X. DIEBOLD, ANTHONY S. TAY,
AND KENNETH F. WALLIS

1 Introduction

Economic decision makers routinely rely on forecasts to assist their decisions. Until recently, most forecasts were provided only in the form of point forecasts, although forecasters sometimes attached measures of uncertainty, such as standard errors or mean absolute errors, to their forecasts. Recently, the trend has been to accompany point forecasts with a more complete description of the uncertainty of the forecasts, such as explicit interval or density forecasts. An interval forecast indicates the likely range of outcomes by specifying the probability that the actual outcome will fall within a stated interval. The probability may be fixed, at say 0.95, and the associated interval may then vary over time, or the interval may be fixed, as a closed or open interval, and the forecast probability presented, as in the statement that "our estimate of the probability that inflation next year will be below 2.5 percent is p." A density forecast is stated explicitly as a density or probability distribution. This may be presented analytically, as in "we estimate that next year's inflation rate is normally distributed around an expected value of 2 percent with a standard deviation of 1 percent," or it may be presented numerically, as when a histogram is reported.

Density forecasts were rarely seen until recently but are becoming more common. In finance, practical implementation of recent theoretical developments has dramatically increased the demand for density forecasts; the boom-

Dean Croushore and Tom Stark provided valuable assistance and advice, and an anonymous referee provided helpful comments. We thank the National Science Foundation, the Sloan Foundation, the University of Pennsylvania Research Foundation, the National University of Singapore and the Economic and Social Research Council for support. Our collaboration was initiated at the 1997 UC San Diego Conference on Financial Econometrics organized by Rob Engle, Clive Granger and Gloria Gonzalez-Rivera.

ing field of financial risk management, for example, is effectively dedicated to providing density forecasts of changes in portfolio value, as revealed by a broad reading of literature such as J.P. Morgan (1996). There is also a growing literature on extracting density forecasts from options prices, which includes Aït-Sahalia and Lo (1998) and Söderlind and Svensson (1997). In macroeconomics, there has also been increased discussion of density forecasts recently, in response to criticism of the lack of transparency of traditional forecasting practice, and to demands for acknowledgment of forecast uncertainty in order to better inform the discussion of economic policy. Macroeconomic density forecasts are the subject of this article.

In the USA the Survey of Professional Forecasters has, since its introduction in 1968, asked respondents to provide density forecasts of inflation and growth. In the early days of the survey these received little attention, with the notable exception of Zarnowitz and Lambros (1987); more recently the distributions, averaged over respondents, have featured in the public release of survey results. In the UK the history is much shorter. In November 1995 the National Institute of Economic and Social Research began to augment its long-established macroeconomic point forecasts with estimates of the probability of the government's inflation target being met and of there being a fall in GDP. This was extended in February 1996 to a complete probability distribution of inflation and growth forecasts. In the same month the Bank of England launched the presentation of an estimated probability distribution of possible outcomes surrounding its conditional projections of inflation. In November 1996 the Treasury's Panel of Independent Forecasters, following repeated suggestions by one of the present authors, reported its individual members' density forecasts for growth and inflation, using the same questions as the US Survey of Professional Forecasters. Our success was short-lived, however, as the new Chancellor of the Exchequer dissolved the panel shortly after taking office in May 1997.

The production and publication of any kind of forecast subsequently requires an evaluation of its quality. For point forecasts, there is a large literature on the *ex post* evaluation of *ex ante* forecasts, and a range of techniques has been developed, recently surveyed by Wallis (1995) and Diebold and Lopez (1996). The evaluation of interval forecasts has a much newer literature (Christoffersen, 1998), as does the evaluation of density forecasts. In this article we use the methods of Diebold, Gunther, and Tay (1998), augmented with resampling procedures, to evaluate the density forecasts of inflation contained in the Survey of Professional Forecasters. Forecasts of inflation are of intrinsic interest, especially in the monetary policy regime of inflation targeting that is common to many OECD economies, and it is also of interest to demonstrate the use of new tools for forecast evaluation and their applicability even in very small samples. As with most of the forecast evaluation literature we pay no attention to the construction of the forecast, and consider only the assessment of its adequacy, after the fact. That is, because little is known about the construction of the density forecasts reported by the survey respondents, we concentrate on the outputs, not the inputs. The density forecast could be based on a formal statistical or econometric model, an ARCH model for a single financial time series or a large-scale macroeconometric model for aggregate macroeconomic variables, for example, or it could be based on more subjective approaches, blending the forecaster's judgment informally with a model-based forecast or using expert elicitation methods.

The remainder of this article is organized as follows. In Section 2 we present a brief description of the Survey of Professional Forecasters, its advantages and disadvantages, leading to our selection of the series of first-quarter current-year mean density forecasts of inflation for evaluation. In Section 3 we develop our evaluation methods, based on the series of probability integral transforms of realized inflation with respect to the forecast densities and the null hypothesis that this is a series of independent uniformly distributed random variables. We present the results in Section 4, and we conclude in Section 5.

2 The Survey of Professional Forecasters

The Survey of Professional Forecasters (SPF) is the oldest quarterly survey of macroeconomic forecasters in the USA. The survey was begun in 1968 as a joint project by the Business and Economic Statistics Section of the American Statistical Association (ASA) and the National Bureau of Economic Research (NBER) and was originally known as the ASA–NBER survey. Zarnowitz (1969) describes the original objectives of the survey, and Zarnowitz and Braun (1993) provide an assessment of its achievements over its first 22 years. In June 1990 the Federal Reserve Bank of Philadelphia, in cooperation with the NBER, assumed responsibility for the survey, at which time it became known as the Survey of Professional Forecasters (see Croushore, 1993).

The survey is mailed four times a year, the day after the first release of the National Income and Product Accounts data for the preceding quarter. Most of the questions ask for point forecasts, for a range of variables and forecast horizons. In addition, however, density forecasts are requested for aggregate output and inflation. The output question was unfortunately switched from nominal to real in the early 1980s, thereby rendering historical evaluation of the output forecasts more difficult, whereas the inflation question has no such defect and provides a more homogeneous sample. Thus we focus on the density forecasts of inflation. Each forecaster is asked to attach a probability to each of a number of intervals, or bins, in which inflation might fall, in the current year and in the next year. The definition of inflation is annual, year over year. The probabilities are averaged over respondents, and for each bin the SPF reports the mean probability that inflation will fall in that bin, in the current year and in the next year. The report on the survey results that was previously published in the *NBER Reporter* and the *American Statistician* did not always refer to the density forecasts, and sometimes combined bins, but means for all the bins in the density forecasts have been included in the Philadelphia Fed's press release since 1990, and the complete results dating from 1968 are currently available on their Web page (http://www.phil.frb.org/econ/spf/ spfpage.html). This mean probability distribution is typically viewed as a representative forecaster and is our own focus of attention. The mean forecast was the only one available to analysts and commentators in real time.

There are a number of complications, including:

(a) The number of respondents over which the mean is taken varies over time, with a low of 14 and a high of 65.

(b) The number of bins and their ranges have changed over time. From 1968:4 to 1981:2 there were 15 bins, from 1981:3 to 1991:4 there were 6 bins, and from 1992:1 onward there are 10 bins.

(c) The base year of the price indexes has changed. For surveys on or before 1975:4, the base year is 1958, from 1976:1 to 1985:4 the base year is 1972, and from 1986:1 to 1991:4 the base year is 1982. Beginning in 1992:1, the base year is 1987.

(d) The price index used to define inflation in the survey has changed over time. From 1968:4 to 1991:4 the SPF asked about inflation as assessed via the implicit GNP deflator, and from 1992:1 to 1995:4 it asked about inflation as assessed via the implicit GDP deflator. Presently the SPF asks about inflation as assessed via the chain-weighted GDP price index.

(e) The forecast periods to which the SPF questions refer have changed over time. Prior to 1981:3, the SPF asked about inflation only in the current year, whereas it subsequently asked about inflation in the current year and the following year. Errors occurred in 1985:1, 1986:1 and 1990:1, when the first annual forecast was requested for the previous year and the second forecast for the current year, as opposed to the current and the following year.

Most of the complications (e.g., a, b, c and d) are minor and inconsequential. Complication (e), on the other hand, places very real constraints on what can be done with the data. It is apparent, however, that the series of first-quarter current-year forecasts represents an unbroken sample of annual three-quarter ahead inflation density forecasts, with non-overlapping innovations. (If the information set consists only of data up to the final quarter of the preceding year, then this is a conventional annual series of one-step-ahead forecasts; it is likely, however, that information on the current year available in its first few weeks is also used in constructing forecasts.) The sample runs from 1969 to 1996, for a total of 28 annual observations (densities), which form the basis of our examination of inflation density forecast adequacy.

3 Evaluating Inflation Density Forecasts

We evaluate the forecasts using the methodology proposed by Diebold, Gunther, and Tay (1998), the essence of which is consideration of the series of probability integral transforms of realized inflation $\{y_t\}_{t=1}^{28}$ with respect to the forecast densities $\{p_t(y_t)\}_{t=1}^{28}$. That is, we consider the series:

$$\{z_t\}_{t=1}^{28} = \left[\int_{-\infty}^{y_t} p_t(u)du \right]_{t=1}^{28}.$$

Diebold, Gunther, and Tay (1998) show that if the density forecasts are optimal (in a sense that they make precise), then $\{z_t\}_{t=1}^{28} \overset{iid}{\sim} U(0, 1)$. The basic idea is to check whether the realizations y_t come from the forecast densities $p_t(y_t)$ by using the standard statistical result that, for a random sample from a given density, the probability integral transforms of the observations with respect to the density are iid $U(0, 1)$, extended to allow for potentially time-varying densities. In a forecasting context, independence corresponds to the usual notion of the efficient use of an information set, which implies the independence of a sequence of one-step-ahead errors. For our inflation density forecasts, an "error" is an incorrect estimate of the probability that inflation will fall within a given bin; a correct estimate of the tail area probability, for example, implies that we observe the same relative frequency of correspondingly extreme forecast errors, in the usual sense of the discrepancy between point forecast and actual outcome for inflation.

Formal tests of density forecast optimality face the difficulty that the relevant null hypothesis—iid uniformity of z—is a joint hypothesis. For example, the classical test of fit based on Kolmogorov's D_n-statistic, the maximum absolute difference between the empirical cumulative density function (c.d.f.) and the hypothetical (uniform) c.d.f., rests on an assumption of random sampling. The test is usually referred to as the Kolmogorov–Smirnov test, following Smirnov's tabulation of the limiting distribution of D_n and introduction of one-sided statistics, while other authors have provided finite-sample tables (see Stuart and Ord, 1991, §30.37). Little is known, however, about the impact on the distribution of D_n of departures from independence; thus test outcomes in either direction may be unreliable whenever the data are not generated by random sampling. More generally the test is not constructive, in that if rejection occurs, the test itself provides no guidance as to *why*.

More revealing methods of exploratory data analysis are therefore needed to supplement formal tests. To assess unconditional uniformity we use the obvious graphical tools, estimates of the density and c.d.f. We estimate the density with a simple histogram, which allows straightforward imposition of the constraint that z has support on the unit interval, in contrast to more sophisticated procedures such as kernel density estimates with the standard kernel functions. To assess whether z is iid, we again use the obvious graphical tool, the correlogram. Because we are interested not only in linear dependence but also in other forms of nonlinear dependence such as conditional hetero-skedasticity, we examine both the correlogram of $(z - \bar{z})$ and the correlogram of $(z - \bar{z})^2$.

It is useful to place confidence intervals on the estimated histogram and correlograms, in order to help guide the assessment. There are several complications, however. In order to separate fully the desired U(0, 1) and iid properties of z, we would like to construct confidence intervals for histogram bin heights that condition on uniformity but that are robust to dependence of unknown form. Similarly, we would like to construct confidence intervals for the autocorrelations that condition on independence but that are robust to non-uniformity. In addition, the SPF sample size is small, so we would like to use methods tailored to the specific sample size.

Unfortunately, we know of no asymptotic, let alone finite-sample, method for constructing serial-correlation-robust confidence intervals for histogram bin heights under the U(0, 1) hypothesis. Thus we compute histogram bin height intervals under the stronger iid U(0, 1) assumption, in which case we can also compute the intervals tailored to the exact SPF sample size, by exploiting the binomial structure. For example, for a 5-bin histogram formed from 28 observations, the number of observations falling in any bin is distributed binomial $(28, 5/28)$ under the iid U(0, 1) hypothesis. (This formulation relates to each individual bin height when the other four bins are combined, and the intervals should not be interpreted jointly.)

To assess the significance of the autocorrelations, we construct finite-sample confidence intervals that condition on independence but that are robust to deviations from uniformity by sampling with replacement from the observed z series and building up the distribution of the sample autocorrelations. The sampling scheme preserves the unconditional distribution of z while destroying any serial correlation that might be present.

Two practical issues arise in the construction of the z series. The first concerns the fact that the forecasts are recorded as discrete probability distributions, not continuous densities, and so we use a piecewise linear approximation to the c.d.f. For example, suppose the forecast probability for $y < 4$ is 0.4 and the forecast probability for $4 \leq y < 5$ is 0.3. If the realization of y is 4.6, then we compute z as $0.4 + 0.6(0.3) = 0.58$. Further, the two end bins are open; they give the probabilities of y falling above or below certain levels. When a realization falls in one of the end bins, to apply the piecewise linear approximation we assume that the end bins have the same width as all the other bins. This occurs for only three observations, and in each case the realized inflation rate is very close to the interior boundary of the end bin.

The second issue is how to measure realized inflation: whether to use real-time or final-revised data, and for which inflation concept. As regards the use of real-time vs. final-revised data, we take the view that forecasters try to forecast the "true" inflation rates, the best estimates of which are the final revised values. Thus we use the most recently revised values as our series for realized inflation. Regarding the inflation concept, we noted earlier that the price index used to define inflation in the survey has changed over time from the implicit GNP deflator to the implicit GDP deflator to the chain-weighted price index. Accordingly, we measure realized inflation as the final revised value of the inflation concept about which the survey respondents were asked. From 1969 to 1991 we use the percentage change in the implicit GNP deflator, from 1992 to 1995 we use the percentage change in the implicit GDP deflator, and for 1996 we use the percentage change in the chain-weighted price index.

Two previous studies of the SPF inflation density forecasts merit discussion. Zarnowitz and Lambros (1987) use the survey results to draw the important distinction between uncertainty, as indicated by the spread of the probability distribution of possible outcomes, and disagreement, as indicated by the dispersion of respondents' (point) forecasts: consensus among forecasters need not imply a high degree of confidence about the commonly predicted outcome. Zarnowitz and Lambros find that the variance of the point forecasts tends to understate uncertainty as measured by the variance of the density forecasts. The former varies much more over time than the latter, although the measures of consensus and certainty (or the lack thereof) are positively correlated. Zarnowitz and Lambros also find that expectations of higher inflation are associated with greater uncertainty. Throughout their paper, however, they summarize the individual density forecasts by their means and standard deviations prior to averaging over respondents; thus they use only part of the information in the density forecasts.

McNees and Fine (1996) evaluate the individual inflation density forecasts of a sample of 34 forecasters who responded to the survey on at least 10 occasions. They proceed by calculating the implied 50 percent and 90 percent prediction intervals, and test whether the actual coverage—the proportion of occasions on which the outcome fell within the interval—corresponds to the claimed coverage, 50 percent or 90 percent as appropriate, using the binomial distribution. Again, only part of the information in the density forecasts is used. Moreover, even in the more limited framework of interval forecast evaluation, the McNees–Fine procedure examines only *unconditional* coverage, whereas in the presence of dynamics it is important to examine *conditional* coverage, as in Christoffersen (1998). Put differently, in the language of density forecast evaluation, McNees and Fine implicitly *assume* that z is iid in order to invoke the binomial distribution; they test only whether z is unconditionally $U(0, 1)$.

4 Results

We show the basic data on realized inflation and "box-and-whisker" plots representing the density forecasts in Figure 1. The bottom and top of the box are the 25 percent and 75 percent points, the interior line is the median, the bottom whisker is the 10 percent point, and the top whisker is the 90 percent point. The box-and-whisker plots point to a number of features of the forecasts and their relationship to the realizations. First, comparing forecasts and realizations, similar patterns to those observed by Zarnowitz and Braun (1993, 30–1) in the distribution of individual point forecasts for the period 1968:4–1990:1 can be seen: "in 1973–74, a period of supply shocks and deepening recession, inflation rose sharply and was greatly underestimated. . . . The same tendency to underpredict also prevailed in 1976–80, although in somewhat weaker form. . . . In between, during the recovery of 1975–76, inflation decreased markedly and was mostly overestimated. Another, much longer disinflation occurred in 1981–85. . . . Here again most forecasters are observed to overpredict inflation. . . . Finally, in 1986–89, inflation . . . was generally well predicted," and this has been maintained up to the end of our present sample, when the errors, although persistently of the same sign, are relatively small. There is also evidence of adaptation: although inflation is *unexpectedly* high when it initially turns high, and *unexpectedly* low when it initially falls, forecasters do eventually catch up.

Second, the data seem to accord with the claim that the level and uncertainty of inflation are positively correlated, as suggested by Friedman (1977). Although this hypothesis has typically been verified by relating the variability of inflation to its actual level, in a forecasting context the relevant hypothesis is that expectations of high inflation are associated with increased uncertainty, and this is verified for a shorter sample of these data by Zarnowitz and Lambros (1987), using different techniques, as noted above. In Figure 1 the forecasts for 1975 and 1980 immediately catch the eye, with two of the largest values of the interdecile range—the distance between the whiskers—corresponding to two of the highest median forecasts. Overall there is a strongly significant positive association between these measures; the coefficient in a regression of the interdecile range on the median forecast has a p-value of 0.0198 (with allowance made for positive residual autocorrelation, discussed below). On the other hand the forecasts for 1986 and 1987 are outliers: these give the two largest values of the interdecile range, at relatively low median forecasts (and yet lower realizations). Perhaps this reflects genuine uncertainty about the impact of the fall in the world price of oil, or simply indicates sampling problems, because the number of survey respondents was falling through the late 1980s, prior to revival of the survey by the Philadelphia Fed.

Third, there has been a gradual tightening of the forecast densities since

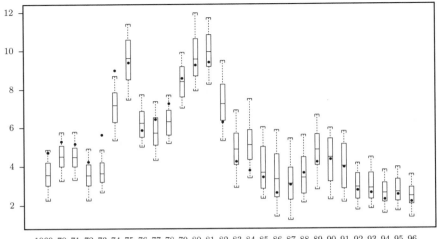

Figure 1. Inflation forecasts and realizations

Notes: The density forecasts are represented by box-and-whisker plots. The boxes represent the inter-quartile range of the forecasts, and the inner line represents the median; the tails represent the 10th and 90th percentiles. We represent inflation realizations with •.

the late 1980s, perhaps due to a reduction of perceived likely supply and demand shocks, an increase in central bank credibility, a reduction in uncertainty associated with the lower level of inflation, or some combination of these. The distributions nevertheless seem to be still too dispersed, because most of the realizations over this period fall squarely in the middle of the forecast densities.

Next, we compute the z series by integrating the forecast densities up to the realized inflation rate, period by period, and we plot the result in Figure 2, in which large values correspond to unexpectedly high values of realized inflation, and conversely. Even at this simple graphical level, deviations of z from iid uniformity are apparent, as z appears serially correlated. In the first half of the sample, for example, z tends to be mostly above its average, whereas in the second half of the sample it appears that the representative forecaster overestimated the uncertainty of inflation, because most of the values of z cluster around 0.4, and they vary little compared to the first half of the sample. This is the counterpart to the observation in Figure 1 that most of the recent realizations are near the middle of the forecast densities, a result that diverges from Chatfield (1993) and the literature he cites, which often finds that forecasters are overconfident, in that their interval forecasts are too *tight*, not too wide.

To proceed more systematically, we examine the distributional and autocorrelation properties of z. We show the histogram and empirical c.d.f. of z in

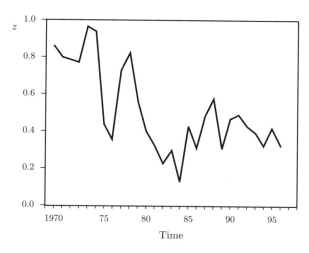

Figure 2. Time series plot of z

Figure 3, together with finite-sample 95 percent confidence intervals calculated by simulation under the assumption of iid uniformity. The unavoidably wide intervals reflect the small sample size.

The empirical c.d.f. lies within the 95 percent confidence interval. Kolmogorov's D_n-statistic has a value of 0.2275, which is less than the 5 percent critical value of 0.24993 given for this sample size by Miller (1956), although little is known about the impact of departures from randomness on the performance of this test, as noted above. In the histogram two bins lie outside their individual 95 percent confidence intervals. The chi-square goodness-of-fit statistic has a value of 10.21, which exceeds the simulated 5 percent critical value for this sample size of 9.14 (the corresponding asymptotic chi-square (4) value is 9.49), although the above caveat again applies.

Two features of the data stand out in both panels of Figure 3. First, too few realizations fall in the left tail of the forecast densities to accord with the probability forecasts, resulting in an empirical c.d.f. that lies substantially below the 45-degree line in the lower part of its range, and a significantly small leftmost histogram bin. This reflects the fact that many of the inflation surprises in the sample came in the 1970s, when inflation tended to be unexpectedly *high*; episodes of unexpectedly low inflation are rarer than the survey respondents think. Second, the middle histogram bin is significantly too high and the empirical c.d.f. lies above the 45-degree line in this range, both indicating too many realizations in the middle of the forecast densities, an already-noted phenomenon driven primarily by the events of the late 1980s and 1990s. The observations from the first half of the sample are shaded in the histogram and are seen to be more uniformly distributed, except again for the lowest

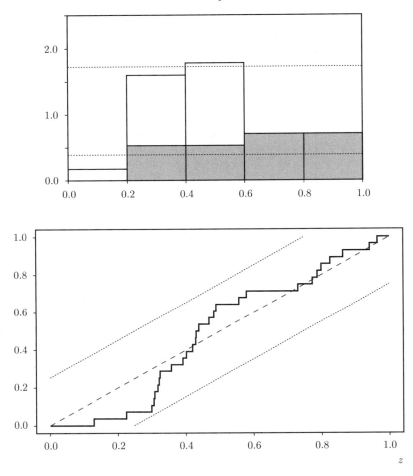

Figure 3. Histogram and empirical cumulative density function of z

Notes: In the top panel, dashed lines represent 95% confidence intervals for individual bin heights under the hypothesis that z is iid U(0, 1). The shaded region corresponds to the first fourteen z observations. In the bottom panel, we superimpose on the empirical c.d.f. a U(0, 1) c.d.f., together with 95% confidence intervals under the hypothesis that z is iid U(0, 1). See text for details.

values, illustrating once more the different characteristics of the two sub-periods.

We show the correlograms of $(z - \bar{z})$ and $(z - \bar{z})^2$ in Figure 4, together with finite-sample 95 percent confidence intervals for the autocorrelations computed by simulation under the assumption that z is iid but not necessarily U(0, 1). The first correlogram clearly indicates serial correlation in z itself. The first sample autocorrelation, in particular, is large and highly statistically significant, and most of the remaining sample autocorrelations are positive and significant as well. A Ljung–Box test on the first five sample autocorrelations

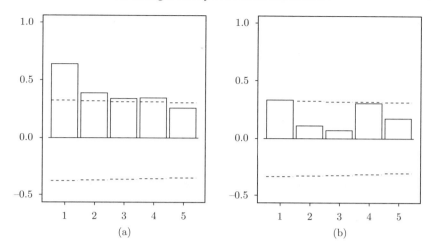

Figure 4. Sample autocorrelation functions of $(z - \bar{z})$ and $(z - \bar{z})^2$

Note: The dashed lines indicate 95% confidence intervals computed under the hypothesis that $\{z_t\}_{t=1}^m \sim$ iid. See text for details.

of $(z - \bar{z})$ rejects the white noise hypothesis at the 1 percent level, using simulated finite-sample critical values computed in the same way as for the correlogram confidence intervals.

Several explanations come to mind, one being the possibility that forecasters are more adaptive than rational, noted above. The inflation series itself is highly persistent, and the forecast densities might not be expected to change rapidly; hence forecasters might use a more-than-optimal amount of extrapolation. Forecast errors are often autocorrelated due to information lags: if a forecast for time $t + 1$ made at time t is based on an information set dated $t - 1$, then it is in effect a two-step-ahead forecast and so, even if optimal, its errors will exhibit an MA(1) correlation structure. The present forecasts are made at the beginning of the year, at which time forecasters have data on the previous year, albeit liable to revision. Because the forecast relates to the current year it is close to a genuine one-step-ahead forecast, and the impact of data revisions is unlikely to be sufficient to cause substantial autocorrelation in forecast errors. An examination of the autocorrelations of z based on preliminary inflation figures supports the later claim; a Ljung–Box test on the first five sample autocorrelations, again using simulated critical values, also rejects the iid hypothesis at the 1 percent level. In any event, the autocorrelations at higher lags in Figure 4 are not suggestive of a moving average structure. It is not clear precisely what kinds of autocorrelation in z might be expected once the density forecasts depart from optimality, but here also there is evidence of too much persistence.

It is also possible that serial correlation in z may be due to the departure or inclusion over time of forecasters who tend to be systematically optimistic or pessimistic. There is no way to check whether this is indeed the case without examining the survey returns of individual respondents, but the problem is likely to be pertinent only if the number of respondents is small. As it turns out, the number of respondents was greater than twenty in all years but four. Furthermore, Figures 2 and 3 suggest that any systematic inclusion of optimistic forecasters would have been in the early years of the sample, but that is the period when the survey enjoyed the greatest number of respondents.

It is interesting to note that although $(z - \bar{z})$ appears serially correlated, there is little evidence of serial correlation in $(z - \bar{z})^2$. Serial correlation in $(z - \bar{z})^2$ would suggest that the inflation density forecasts tend to miss heteroskedasticity in realized inflation. Hence the serial dependence in z appears to be associated with dynamics in the conditional mean of inflation neglected by the density forecasts, not with neglected dynamics in the conditional variance of inflation.

5 Conclusion

Our overall conclusion is that the density forecasts of inflation reported in the Survey of Professional Forecasters are not optimal—the probability integral transforms of the realizations with respect to the forecast densities are nonuniform and autocorrelated. Formal hypothesis tests more clearly support the autocorrelation part of this joint rejection, because here our resampling procedures produce tests that are robust to non-uniformity. The impact of this autocorrelation on the behavior of goodness-of-fit tests is not known, and our rejection of uniformity rests to a greater extent on descriptive methods. In general the density forecasts overestimate the probability that inflation will fall substantially below the point forecast, because there are too few observations in the left tail of the z density: negative inflation surprises occur less often than these forecasters expect. In the more recent data this tendency extends to both tails of the z density, and surprises of either sign occur less often than expected. In the 1990s the forecasters were more uncertain than they should have been, perhaps because they did not recognize, at least to a sufficient degree, that expectations of lower inflation are associated with lower uncertainty. This conclusion was already documented by Zarnowitz and Lambros (1987), and is endorsed here.

We have treated the mean density forecast as a collective forecast, although the sample over which the mean is taken varies in size and composition over time, and so it would be interesting to repeat the analysis for individual forecasters. One of the original aims of the survey was to keep a comprehensive record of forecasts so that forecast evaluation could be conducted on a "broader, more objective and systematic basis" (Zarnowitz, 1969), and we have clearly benefited from the archive that has been accumulated. On the other hand a little scrutiny reveals the difficulties in extending our analysis to individual forecasters, again because the survey's coverage varies, with high turnover of participants; hence only a relatively short series of forecasts is available for most individuals. The number of forecasts might be increased by adding the second, third and fourth quarter forecasts and even, in most of the recent years of the survey, also including forecasts for the following year as well as the current year. However, the pattern of the optimal evolution of density forecasts in such situations is not immediately apparent. For point forecasts, tests of the optimality of a sequence of fixed-event forecasts are based on the independence of successive forecast revisions (Clements, 1997), and the counterpart for density forecasts awaits further research. In the meantime, the evaluation methods for a conventional series of density forecasts employed in the present application are commended for wider use as such series accumulate.

References

Aït-Sahalia, Y. and Lo, A. W. (1998), "Nonparametric Estimation of State-Price Densities Implicit in Financial Asset Prices," *Journal of Finance*, 53: 499–547.

Chatfield, C. (1993), "Calculating Interval Forecasts," *Journal of Business and Economic Statistics*, 11: 121–35.

Christoffersen, P. F. (1998), "Evaluating Interval Forecasts," *International Economic Review*, 39: 841–62.

Clements, M. P. (1997), "Evaluating the Rationality of Fixed-Event Forecasts," *Journal of Forecasting*, 16: 225–39.

Croushore, D. (1993), "The Survey of Professional Forecasters," *Business Review*, Federal Reserve Bank of Philadelphia, November/December: 3–15.

Diebold, F. X. and Lopez, J. A. (1996), "Forecast Evaluation and Combination," in G. S. Maddala and C. R. Rao (eds.), *Handbook of Statistics 14: Statistical Methods in Finance*, pp. 241–68. Amsterdam: North-Holland.

Diebold, F. X., Gunther, T. A. and Tay, A. S. (1998), "Evaluating Density Forecasts with Applications to Financial Risk Management," *International Economic Review*, 39: 863–83.

Friedman, M. (1977), "Nobel Lecture: Inflation and Unemployment," *Journal of Political Economy*, 85: 451–72.

J.P. Morgan (1996), "RiskMetrics: Technical Document," 4th edn., New York.

McNees, S. K. and Fine, L. K. (1996), "Forecast Uncertainty: Can It Be Measured?" paper presented at the Conference on Expectations in Economics, Federal Reserve Bank of Philadelphia, October, 1996.

Miller, L. H. (1956), "Table of Percentage Points of Kolmogorov Statistics," *Journal of the American Statistical Association*, 51: 111–21.

Söderlind, P. and Svensson, L. E. O. (1997), "New Techniques to Extract Market Expectations from Financial Instruments," *Journal of Monetary Economics*, 40: 383–429.

Stuart, A. and Ord, J. K. (1991), *Kendall's Advanced Theory of Statistics*, 5th edn., vol. 2. London: Edward Arnold.

Wallis, K. F. (1995), "Large-Scale Macroeconometric Modeling," in M. H. Pesaran and M. R. Wickens (eds.), *Handbook of Applied Econometrics*, pp. 312–55. Oxford: Blackwell.

Zarnowitz, V. (1969), "The New ASA–NBER Survey of Forecasts by Economic Statisticians," *American Statistician*, 23: 12–16.

Zarnowitz, V. and Braun, P. (1993), "Twenty-Two Years of the NBER–ASA Quarterly Economic Outlook Surveys: Aspects and Comparisons of Forecasting Performance," in J. H. Stock and M. W. Watson (eds.), *Business Cycles, Indicators, and Forecasting* (NBER Studies in Business Cycles, vol. 28), pp. 11–84. Chicago: University of Chicago Press.

Zarnowitz, V. and Lambros, L. A. (1987), "Consensus and Uncertainty in Economic Prediction," *Journal of Political Economy*, 95: 591–621.

4
Ranking Competing Multi-Step Forecasts

PAUL NEWBOLD, DAVID I. HARVEY,
AND STEPHEN J. LEYBOURNE

1 Introduction

Early research on methodology for the evaluation of forecasts was analyzed
by Granger and Newbold (1973), who proposed alternative approaches. These
authors argued that a set of forecasts is most reasonably assessed through
comparison with competing forecasts. This comparison could be achieved
through mean squared errors of forecasts at specific horizons, though other
economic loss functions such as mean absolute error or mean absolute percentage error could equally well be applied. Diebold and Mariano (1995) and
Harvey *et al.* (1997) discuss tests of the null hypothesis of equality of performance of two competing forecasts. A second possibility, advocated by Granger
and Newbold, is based on the idea of combining forecasts, introduced by Bates
and Granger (1969). If the optimal weight that should be attached to a particular forecast in a composite predictor which is a weighted average of the forecast
and its competitor is one, that forecast is said to be conditionally efficient
with respect to the competitor. Chong and Hendry (1986) then say that the
forecast encompasses its competitor. Harvey *et al.* (1998) discuss formal hypothesis tests for forecast encompassing.

Although tests for forecast encompassing are often applied, by far the most
common approach in practice to forecast evaluation is through the comparison
of mean squared errors, or similar statistics based on other economic loss measures, for alternative forecasts at several horizons. However, in an important
contribution to the theory of forecast evaluation, Clements and Hendry (1993)
strongly criticize this approach, and propose an alternative. These authors are
uncomfortable with a methodology that could conclude, for example, that,
while one forecaster or forecasting model is best at prediction six months ahead,
a competitor is better at prediction two years ahead. They prefer an approach
that would yield a single ranking of forecasters based on predictions at all
horizons of interest. Clements and Hendry also note that, beyond one-step-
ahead, mean squared error comparisons are not invariant to isomorphic trans-

formations. For example, ranking reversals can occur if the quantity of interest is future period-to-period change in a variable rather than its future level.

Let e_{T+h} denote the error in an h-steps prediction made at time T, and assume stationarity. Then, the mean squared forecast error is:

$$\text{MSFE}(h) = E(e_{T+h}^2).$$

Assume that interest is in forecasts at all horizons up to h and let $E'_{T,h} = (e_{T+1}, ..., e_{T+h})$. Then, Clements and Hendry propose comparison of forecast performances through the generalized forecast error second moment (GFESM), defined as:

$$\text{GFESM}(h) = \left| E(E_{T,h} E'_{T,h}) \right|. \tag{1}$$

They extend this concept to prediction of several variables at several horizons, but in this paper we shall restrict our attention to a single variable. Of course, once the maximum horizon h of interest is specified, GFESM delivers a single quantity measure for each forecaster. Moreover, it is straightforward to show that the quantity (1) is invariant to isomorphic transformations.

These properties are appealing, but do not alone constitute a theoretical foundation for the adoption of GFESM. Clements and Hendry briefly illustrate that, in particular circumstances, such a foundation is available through predictive likelihood. It is worth developing this point in some detail. This is most naturally achieved in a framework where independent replications of the forecast-generating mechanism are feasible, as would be the case in a simulation study. Indeed, such a study of Engle and Yoo (1987) partially motivated the work of Clements and Hendry. Assume that, in each replication, two single sets of competing forecasts for all horizons up to h are computed. Denote these forecasts (f_{1k}, f_{2k}), and the corresponding true values y_k, $k = 1, ..., h$. Further assume that it is possible to specify the true values as:

$$y_k = g_k(f_{1k}, f_{2k}, \beta_k) + e_k; \quad k = 1, ..., h, \tag{2}$$

where the functions $g_k(.)$ are continuous in the parameters β_k, and these functions are such that there are values of β_k so that $g_k(f_{1k}, f_{2k}, \beta_k) = f_{jk}$, $j = 1, 2$. Of course, the usual weighted average used in the combination of forecasts satisfies these requirements. It will further be assumed that the error terms e_k in (2) are independent of (f_{1k}, f_{2k}), and are jointly normally distributed with zero mean and $h \times h$ covariance matrix Ω. Then, in obvious vector notation, the h equations in (2) can be written

$$y = g(.) + e. \tag{3}$$

At each replication of the simulation experiment a single h-vector of observations of the variables in (3) is observed. Using the subscript i to denote the ith replicate, and assuming n replications, the log likelihood function under our assumptions is:

$$\ln L(\beta, \Omega | y) = const - \frac{n}{2} \ln(|\Omega|) - \frac{1}{2} \sum_{i=1}^{n} [y_i - g_i(.)]' \Omega^{-1} [y_i - g_i(.)],$$

so that the concentrated log likelihood is:

$$\ln L_c(\beta | y) = const - \frac{n}{2} \ln(|\hat{\Omega}(\beta)|), \tag{4}$$

where

$$\hat{\Omega}(\beta) = n^{-1} \sum_{i=1}^{n} [y_i - g_i(.)][y_i - g_i(.)]'.$$

Now, we have assumed existence of (β_1, β_2) such that $g(.; \beta_j) = f_j$, $j = 1, 2$. Then, it follows from (4) that we might say that β_1 is "more likely than" β_2 if $|\hat{\Omega}(\beta_1)| < |\hat{\Omega}(\beta_2)|$. We could then argue that the likelihood criterion prefers the forecasts f_1 to f_2 if

$$\left| n^{-1} \sum_{i=1}^{n} (y_i - f_{1i})(y_i - f_{1i})' \right| < \left| n^{-1} \sum_{i=1}^{n} (y_i - f_{2i})(y_i - f_{2i})' \right|.$$

Notice that the probability limits of the statistics in this expression are simply the GFESMs, defined in (1), for the two forecasts. It follows that, given a sufficiently large number n of replications, the likelihood principle will deliver with probability arbitrarily close to one preference for the forecasts for which GFESM is smaller.

The assumptions required to generate this result are quite restrictive, and could certainly be somewhat relaxed. However, the requirement for independent replications seems quite crucial, and does not correspond to the situation in a typical forecast evaluation exercise. There, we would have a single "hold-out sample," say y_{T+j}, $j = 1, ..., m$, allowing the calculation of a series of k-step forecast errors, $k = 1, ..., h$. However, there is then no unique way of writing down the joint distribution of the y_{T+j}, given forecasts at all horizons. Nevertheless, it will be possible to consistently estimate GFESM, and we could retain the likelihood justification by appealing to a "thought experiment" where independent replications are possible. It could then be argued that, if GFESM is a sensible quantity to estimate in the thought experiment, it is equally sensible to estimate it in the real world. Given the assumptions behind the specification (3), the likelihood justification for GFESM is particularly convincing when one forecast encompasses the other at all horizons of interest. Indeed, the above argument demonstrates that GFESM will then prefer the superior forecast. However, further exploration is desirable in non-encompassing cases, as could occur when both forecasts are based on models that are incorrectly or not fully specified in some substantive way, which one would expect to be the case in many practical applications.

Clements and Hendry (1993) was published with commentary from twelve discussants, to which the authors replied (see also Armstrong and Fildes, 1995). While it is not possible here to adequately summarize that commentary, it is perhaps fair to say that the general reaction was skeptical. It was not widely accepted that preferences for different forecasters at different horizons was undesirable, or that the property of ranking preservation under isomorphic transformations was important in practice. A telling criticism was the failure of GFESM beyond one-step-ahead to correspond to any simple economic loss function. Our own view is that, could it be well-justified, a single criterion applicable to a spectrum of forecast horizons has obvious attractions. We have seen that the likelihood principle provides such justification in a limited range of circumstances.

In the next section we extend that range, considering the case where competing forecasts are generated from misspecified models. To preserve some realism, we shall assume that the parameters of those models are calibrated to yield one-step forecasts with the smallest expected squared errors. In that framework we ask two questions:

1. Does the GFESM ranking depend on the choice of h?
2. Is it possible for one forecaster to be preferred by $\text{MSFE}(k)$ for all $k = 1, ..., h$, but for another forecaster to be preferred by $\text{GFESM}(h)$?

We show through a simple example that the answer to both questions is "yes". This is disturbing, as each question is important. In practical applications, the choice of h is somewhat arbitrary, so that it is only through such arbitrary choice that GFESM delivers a unique ranking. Second, the actual levels of a series are often precisely the quantities of interest to a decision maker. For example, it would be difficult to recommend a sales forecasting model on the basis of GFESM if some other model achieved superior sales forecasts at all horizons of interest. In Section 3 of the paper, we retain the reliance on a single criterion, seeking one that has the desirable invariance properties of GFESM, but not its undesirable ranking reversal properties. This is only possible if indeterminate rankings are permitted. The paper is concluded in Section 4.

2 GFESM and Ranking Reversals

We now show that it is possible to find a reasonably realistic example in which GFESM ranking depends on the choice of h, and GFESM(h) can prefer a forecasting model that is mean squared error-dominated at all horizons up to h.

Let the time series y_t be generated by the stationary and invertible ARMA(1, 1) model

$$y_t = \phi y_{t-1} + \varepsilon_t - \theta \varepsilon_{t-1}, \tag{5}$$

where ε_t is zero-mean white noise with variance σ^2. We consider forecasts from two misspecified models; a first order autoregression,

$$y_t = \alpha y_{t-1} + \eta_t, \tag{6}$$

and a first order moving average,

$$y_t = u_t - \beta u_{t-1}, \tag{7}$$

where η_t and u_t are incorrectly taken to be white noise in generating forecasts. It is sufficient for our purposes to consider forecasts up to two-steps-ahead. To keep the example somewhat realistic, we assume that α in (6) and β in (7) are chosen to minimize the respective expected squared one-step forecast errors. Equivalently, these values are the probability limits of the estimators when the two models are estimated by least squares. Here, and throughout, we abstract from issues of both in-sample parameter estimation, and tests based on evaluation criteria, discussed by West (1996).

In the case of an assumed first order autoregression, then, we take α as the first autocorrelation of y_t, so from the properties of (5):

$$\alpha = (1 + \theta^2 - 2\phi\theta)^{-1}(1 - \phi\theta)(\phi - \theta).$$

Forecasts of y_{T+1} and y_{T+2}, made at time T are then:

$$\hat{y}_{T+1} = \alpha y_T; \quad \hat{y}_{T+2} = \alpha^2 y_T,$$

with, from (5), errors

$$e_{T+1} = (\phi - \alpha)y_T + \varepsilon_{T+1} - \theta\varepsilon_T;$$
$$e_{T+2} = (\phi^2 - \alpha^2)y_T + \varepsilon_{T+2} + (\phi - \theta)\varepsilon_{T+1} - \phi\theta\varepsilon_T.$$

Straightforward but tedious algebra, based on the properties of the model (5), then yields:

$$\mathrm{MSFE}_{AR}(1) = \mathrm{GFESM}_{AR}(1) = \sigma^2(1 + p_2^{-1}\theta^2 p_1^2), \tag{8}$$

where

$$p_1 = \phi - \theta; \quad p_2 = 1 + \theta^2 - 2\phi\theta. \tag{9}$$

Also,

$$\mathrm{MSFE}_{AR}(2) = \sigma^2[(\phi^2 - p_2^{-2}p_1^2 p_3^2)^2 p_4^{-1} p_2 + 1 + p_1^2 + \phi^2\theta^2$$
$$- 2\phi\theta(\phi^2 - p_2^{-2}p_1^2 p_3^2)], \tag{10}$$

and

$$\mathrm{GFESM}_{AR}(2) = \sigma^4\{1 + p_2^{-1}\theta^2 p_1^2[(\phi^2 - p_2^{-2}p_1^2 p_3^2)^2 p_4^{-1} p_2 + 1 + p_1^2 + \phi^2\theta^2$$
$$- 2\phi\theta(\phi^2 - p_2^{-2}p_1^2 p_3^2)] - (p_1 + p_2^{-1}\phi\theta^2 p_1^2)^2\}, \tag{11}$$

where

$$p_3 = 1 - \phi\theta; \quad p_4 = 1 - \phi^2. \tag{12}$$

Turning now to the moving average forecast generator (7), β is chosen to minimize the variance of $(1 - \beta L)^{-1} y_t$, where L is the lag operator. Thus, from (5), we require the value of β for which the variance of Z_t is a minimum, where Z_t is generated by the ARMA(2, 1) process $(1 - \phi L)(1 - \beta L)Z_t = (1 - \theta L)\varepsilon_t$. Then, we require β to minimize

$$V = p_4^{-1}(1 - \beta\phi - \beta^2 + \beta^3\phi)^{-1}[p_2 + \beta(\phi - 2\theta + \phi\theta^2)]; \quad -1 < \beta < 1.$$

In practice, for any given pair of parameter values (ϕ, θ), it is straightforward to find the corresponding β numerically. Forecasts of y_{T+1} and y_{T+2} made at time T on the basis of the assumed first order moving average specification are then:

$$\hat{y}_{T+1} = -\beta u_T = -\beta(1 - \beta L)^{-1} y_T; \quad \hat{y}_{T+2} = 0,$$

with, using (5), errors

$$e_{T+1} = y_{T+1} + \beta(1 - \beta L)^{-1} y_T; \quad e_{T+2} = \phi^2 y_T + \varepsilon_{T+2} + (\phi - \theta)\varepsilon_{T+1} - \phi\theta\varepsilon_T.$$

Then, after tedious algebra we find:

$$\mathrm{MSFE}_{MA}(1) = \mathrm{GFESM}_{MA}(1) = \sigma^2[p_4(1 - \beta\phi - \beta^2 + \beta^3\phi)]^{-1}$$
$$\times [p_2 + \beta(\phi - 2\theta + \phi\theta^2)]; \tag{13}$$
$$\mathrm{MSFE}_{MA}(2) = \sigma^2 p_4^{-1} p_2, \tag{14}$$

and

$$\mathrm{GFESM}_{MA}(2) = \sigma^4 \{ p_4^{-2}(1 - \beta\phi - \beta^2 + \beta^3\phi)^{-1} p_2[p_2 + \beta(\phi - 2\theta + \phi\theta^2)]$$
$$- [p_4^{-1}(1 - \beta\phi)^{-1} p_1 p_3]^2 \}, \tag{15}$$

where the p_j are given in (9) and (12).

As a practical matter, further analytic progress with expressions (8), (10), (11), and (13)–(15) is infeasible. However, it is straightforward to compute their relative values for any pair of parameters (ϕ, θ). Of course, ratios of corresponding expressions for the autoregressive and moving average forecast generators do not involve the innovation variance σ^2. Figure 1 shows for a quadrant of the parameter surface those regions where one or other of the misspecified forecasting models—AR(1) or MA(1)—is preferred according to MSFE(1), MSFE(2), or GFESM(2). The figure reports results only for positive θ as results for $(\phi, -\theta)$ are identical to those for $(-\phi, \theta)$. Also, results for ϕ and θ both positive are omitted, as these do not display the GFESM ranking reversals in which we are interested. (In this case AR(1) is preferred by both GFESM(1) and GFESM(2) if and only if $\phi > \theta$.) The information in Figure 1 is sufficient to allow us to answer "yes" to the two questions posed in the previous section. The shaded area shows a region in which the AR(1) predictor (6) is preferred by GFESM(1) while the MA(1) predictor (7) is preferred by GFESM(2). Moreover, in this region, although GFESM(2) would select the

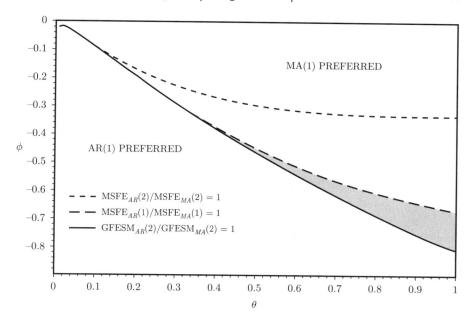

Figure 1. MSFE and GFESM comparisons of AR(1) and MA(1) predictors for an
ARMA(1, 1) generating model

Notes: Regions above each line are where the MA(1) predictor is preferred by that criterion; regions below each line are where the AR(1) predictor is preferred.

Shaded area is region where GFESM(1) (=MSFE(1)) and GFESM(2) rankings differ. In this region the GFESM(2) ranking differs from both the MSFE(1) and MSFE(2) rankings.

MA(1) predictor, the AR(1) predictor delivers smaller expected squared forecast errors for both one-step-ahead and two-steps-ahead forecasts.

3 An Invariant Criterion without Ranking Reversals

The Clements/Hendry critique that mean squared forecast error rankings are not invariant to isomorphic transformations suggests we consider the prediction of all linear combinations of future values of a variable. Granger and Newbold (1986) discuss the prediction of linear functions of variables. Suppose at time T we require to forecast $\sum_{k=1}^{h} d_k y_{T+k}$, and denote by $E'_{T,h} = (e_{T+1}, ..., e_{T+h})$ the vector of forecast errors. Then, we might say that one forecaster dominates another, in mean squared error sense, if there is no linear combination for which inferior forecasts are produced, and there is at least one linear combination for which superior forecasts are produced. Define the second moment matrix of forecast errors as:

$$\Phi_h = E(E_{T,h} E'_{T,h}),$$

so that, as in (1), GFESM is the determinant of Φ_h. Then, we would say that forecaster 1 is preferred to forecaster 2 if

$$d'\Phi_{1h}d \leq d'\Phi_{2h}d, \quad \forall d \neq 0, \tag{16}$$

where the inequality is strict for at least one vector $d' = (d_1, ..., d_h)$. In that case, we say that forecaster 1 dominates by the generalized mean squared forecast error matrix (GMSFEM) criterion (compare with Clements and Hendry, 1993, p. 630). Writing (16) as:

$$d'(\Phi_{1h} - \Phi_{2h})d \leq 0, \quad \forall d \neq 0, \tag{17}$$

the implication is that forecaster 1 dominates if no eigenvalue of $(\Phi_{1h} - \Phi_{2h})$ is positive, and at least one is negative. Obviously, dominance of forecaster 2 can be defined in the same way, and equally obviously there will be circumstances in which the criterion fails to determine a ranking. Thus we see that while, in common with GFESM, the GMSFEM criterion is invariant to isomorphic transformations and *can* yield an unambiguous ranking for any given h, it is not guaranteed to do so.

The GMSFEM criterion, in common with GFESM, requires the specification of a maximum contemplated forecast horizon h. GMSFEM dominance is a very stringent requirement, the degree of stringency increasing with h. For example, if one set of forecasts dominates another through GMSFEM(h), those forecasts necessarily dominate according to any criterion that is a linear function of MSFE(j), $j = 1, ..., h$, with positive weights, though the converse is not necessarily true. The price of this stringency is a region of indeterminacy, in which no forecast will dominate according to GMSFEM, so that in that sense its adoption does not resolve the difficulties associated with GFESM identified in the previous section. We do not regard such indeterminacy as necessarily a bad thing. Indeed, it is a virtue in a world in which the relative effectiveness of a forecaster depends strongly on the prediction horizon. Our view is that, while GMSFEM dominance represents a strong positive statement about the relative quality of a forecaster, GFESM dominance may not.

It is also true that, if forecaster 1 dominates forecaster 2 by GMSFEM(h), forecaster 2 cannot be preferred by GFESM(h). This follows since, if the matrix A is positive definite, and B is some positive semi-definite matrix, $|A + B| \geq |A|$. In our notation, let $B = \Phi_{2h} - \Phi_{1h}$, which is positive semi-definite by GMSFEM dominance of forecaster 1. Also, let $A = \Phi_{1h}$, which, as a covariance matrix must be positive definite, or singular, in which case GFESM is not defined. In the former case, we have $|\Phi_{2h}| \geq |\Phi_{1h}|$, as required. Furthermore, for GMSFEM we can answer "no" to the questions asked of GFESM in Section 1. It is clearly not possible to get GMSFEM ranking reversals for different values of h, though it is possible for the criterion to be indeterminate for a higher value of h while yielding a definite conclusion for a lower value. This result follows since the set of quantities on the left-hand side of (17) for a smaller h is a subset of the corresponding set for a larger h. Also, if one forecaster is preferred by MSFE(k) for any k, a competitor cannot be preferred by GMSFEM(h) for any $h \geq k$. This follows by letting the vector d in (17) have kth element one, with all other elements zero. Of course, the arguments of this and the previous paragraph imply that GMSFEM indeterminacy regions will be larger than corresponding GFESM ranking reversal regions, such as that illustrated in Figure 1.

Figure 2 shows the outcomes of GMSFEM(2) comparisons for the example of the previous section. In this simple example, the criterion does frequently yield a preference for one forecast generator or the other. There are two situations in which indeterminate cases arise. First, in all cases where GFESM produces ranking reversals, GMSFEM is, as already noted, indeterminate. The same is true for pairs of parameter values (ϕ, θ) that are close to this region. Second, and again unsurprisingly, indeterminism arises when there is cancellation or near-cancellation in the autoregressive and moving average operators in the generating model (5), though, as θ approaches one, greater deviations from near-cancellation yield this outcome.

Given autocorrelation in forecast errors beyond one-step-ahead, it would be extremely difficult to devise a formal test for GMSFEM dominance. However, sample estimates of the matrices $(\Phi_{1h} - \Phi_{2h})$ of (17) are readily calculated, and

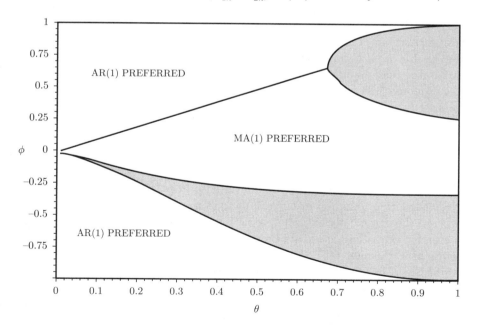

Figure 2. GMSFEM(2) comparisons of AR(1) and MA(1) predictors for an ARMA(1, 1) generating model

Note: Shaded area is region of indeterminacy for GMSFEM(2).

it would be potentially interesting to know if GMSFEM dominance occurred on average in a sample. Practical experience is necessary in order to estimate how often the criterion is likely to yield a definite ranking. Of course, the chief drawback to the criterion is the requirement that (17) holds for *all* values of d, however irrelevant are the corresponding linear combinations of future observations to the forecaster. It is the scope of this requirement that is likely to generate indeterminacy in practice. Nevertheless, many different linear combinations may be important in applications. Clements and Hendry stress the requirement to predict changes. By contrast, in sales forecasting for example, it is important to predict well the sum of the next few observations. Naturally, if only a single specific linear combination is of interest, evaluation should be based only on the prediction of that quantity. A further potential drawback to GMSFEM is that it would be very difficult to account for this criterion when estimating a model from sample data—a strategy that Granger (1993) urged should be associated with forecast evaluation criteria.

4 Summary

The GFESM criterion, introduced by Clements and Hendry (1993), has three potentially attractive attributes. It delivers a single ranking in the comparison of competing multi-step-ahead forecasts, rankings are invariant to isomorphic transformations of future observations, and a predictive likelihood justification is available in particular circumstances. However, this criterion also has three attributes that might be considered unattractive. It does not correspond to any economic loss function, ranking reversals are possible when the maximum forecast horizon considered is increased, and it can prefer forecasts that are mean squared error-dominated at all contemplated horizons.

By contrast, the GMSFEM criterion at least partially retains the attractive attributes of GFESM, without possessing the unattractive attributes. GMSFEM *can* deliver an unambiguous ranking of competing multi-step-ahead forecasts. However, the ranking could be indeterminate in particular applications. By its construction, rankings are invariant to isomorphic transformations. Moreover, to the extent to which the predictive likelihood justification of GFESM is seen as compelling, it should be noted that, if a forecaster is preferred to a competitor through GFESM, the competitor cannot be preferred through GMSFEM. The GMSFEM criterion is motivated through mean squared error loss, and, as we have seen, ranking reversals of the sort to which GFESM is subject are not possible. Incorporation of further forecasts at longer horizons cannot reverse GMSFEM rankings, though this could induce indeterminacy where previously one forecaster was preferred. Moreover, if a forecaster is best at all contemplated horizons, that forecaster cannot be inferior through GMSFEM.

In this paper we have concentrated on the prediction of a single variable at specific horizons. Clements and Hendry (1993) developed GFESM to incorporate also the prediction of several variables. It is clear that GMSFEM dominance can also be defined for this broader problem. However, whether it is prudent or practical to do so is problematic. This expansion would be likely to considerably increase the probability of indeterminate rankings. Moreover, it would not be at all surprising to learn that a particular forecaster was relatively more successful in the prediction of some sectors of an economy than others. The construction of a single measure that did not reveal this fact could amount to discarding important information of value to both forecasters and decision makers.

References

Armstrong, J. S. and Fildes, R. (1995). "Correspondence on the selection of error measures for comparisons among forecasting methods (with reply)," *Journal of Forecasting*, 14: 67–75.

Bates, J. M. and Granger, C. W. J. (1969). "The combination of forecasts," *Operational Research Quarterly*, 20: 451–68.

Chong, Y. Y. and Hendry, D. F. (1986). "Econometric evaluation of linear macroeconomic models," *Review of Economic Studies*, 53: 671–90.

Clements, M. P. and Hendry, D. F. (1993). "On the limitations of comparing mean square forecast errors (with discussion)," *Journal of Forecasting*, 12: 617–76.

Diebold, F. X. and Mariano, R. S. (1995). "Comparing predictive accuracy," *Journal of Business and Economic Statistics*, 13: 253–63.

Engle, R. F. and Yoo, B. S. (1987). "Forecasting and testing in cointegrated systems," *Journal of Econometrics*, 35: 143–59.

Granger, C. W. J. (1993). "On the limitations of comparing mean square forecast errors: Comment," *Journal of Forecasting*, 12: 651–2.

Granger, C. W. J. and Newbold, P. (1973). "Some comments on the evaluation of economic forecasts," *Applied Economics*, 5: 35–47.

Granger, C. W. J. and Newbold, P. (1986). *Forecasting Economic Time Series*, 2nd edn. Orlando, FL: Academic Press.

Harvey, D. I., Leybourne, S. J. and Newbold, P. (1997). "Testing the equality of prediction mean squared errors," *International Journal of Forecasting*, 13: 281–91.

Harvey, D. I., Leybourne, S. J. and Newbold, P. (1998). "Tests for forecast encompassing," *Journal of Business and Economic Statistics*, 16: 254–9.

West, K. D. (1996). "Asymptotic inference about predictive ability," *Econometrica*, 64: 1067–84.

5
The Pervasiveness of Granger Causality in Econometrics

DAVID F. HENDRY AND GRAYHAM E. MIZON

1 Introduction

Granger (1969), which defined the concept of Granger causality, is one of the most influential papers in econometrics: it had been cited on more than 850 occasions at the time of writing. We are delighted to contribute a chapter reviewing its role to a volume in honor of Clive. The concept of causality has intrigued philosophers for millennia, and both statisticians and economists have attempted to test for its existence, as it is particularly important if one is interested in testing theories or conducting policy analysis. Any paper that proposes a definition of the concept of causality is bound to attract considerable attention—and not a little controversy: see the many papers cited in Granger (1980).

Our aim is neither to justify nor criticize the notion that Granger proposed: rather, we seek to analyze the consequences of its appearance in numerous areas of econometrics, since Granger causality is both pervasive, and important, in econometric modeling. At first sight, this may seem unsurprising, but many of its effects do not in fact depend on the role that Granger causality was initially designed to play, namely testing for actual causality. Moreover, finding Granger causality in an empirical model does not necessarily entail "causal links"—in the sense of genuine influences in the real world—nor does the empirical absence of Granger causality entail no link. These results, established below, might be thought to vitiate the value of the notion. However, the importance of Granger causality often rests on its presence within the data set under analysis, as it can have a marked impact on empirical modeling in general, and inference in particular, even when this just reflects an inappro-

Financial support from the UK Economic and Social Research Council under grant R000233447, and the EUI Research Council grant *Econometric Modeling of Economic Time Series*, is gratefully acknowledged. We are indebted to Marianne Sensier for her invaluable research assistance, and to an anonymous referee, Rob Engle and Hal White for their comments on an earlier version of the paper.

priate reduction, that is, indirect feedbacks due to using limited information: several sections illustrate this phenomenon. Nevertheless, a number of economic theories, such as the formulation of the permanent-income hypothesis in Hall (1978), or arbitrage theories of asset prices, preclude Granger causality (as initially formulated), making it an important hypothesis to test in many instances, and perhaps suggesting it should not be prevalent in economics. Conversely, general-equilibrium theories would suggest the opposite. We conclude that the case for the practical importance of Granger causality needs to be evaluated. This is particularly so because there are two directions in which such causality might operate, with very different consequences, namely from a non-modeled variable to a variable of interest, and vice versa. Both directions are analyzed below.

Our paper investigates ten aspects of econometric modeling in which Granger causality plays an important role, namely: marginalizing models with respect to unwanted variables (Section 3); conditioning on variables to be treated as "exogenous" (Section 4); the distributions of estimators and test statistics (Section 5); inference via simulation (such as simulated likelihood, Section 6); cointegration analyses (Section 7); encompassing (Section 8); *ex ante* forecasting (Section 9); policy analyses (Section 10); dynamic simulation (Section 11); and impulse response analyses (Section 12).

In the remainder of this section, we introduce our notation, record the original definition of Granger causality, and comment on some forms of its empirical application to testing "causality". We distinguish between the data-generation process (DGP) within which causality does or does not hold, and an econometric model thereof based on a restricted information set.

1.1 Notation

Let $(\Omega, \mathcal{F}, \mathsf{P}(\cdot))$ denote the probability space supporting the vector of N real random variables $\mathbf{w}_t$. We only consider discrete time processes. At each point in time $t \in \mathcal{T}$, the joint density $\mathsf{D}_{\mathsf{W}_t}(\mathbf{w}_t|\mathcal{F}_{t-1})$ of $\mathbf{w}_t$ characterizes the economy under analysis, with sample space Ω and event space $\mathcal{F}_{t-1}$. We assume that this density exists, but the analysis could be conducted at the level of the (cumulative) distribution $\mathsf{P}(\cdot)$. We also assume that this DGP can be represented as a vector stochastic process, with sufficient continuity to make it meaningful to postulate d parameters $\boldsymbol{\delta} \in \mathcal{D}^d \subseteq \mathbb{R}^d$ which do not depend on $\mathcal{F}_{t-1}$ at any t. We do not restrict the parameters to be constant over time, nor exclude transient parameters. Given the prevalent use of congruential random-number generators in simulating stochastic processes, which are high-dimensional deterministic chaotic processes, we doubt that assuming $\{\mathbf{w}_t\}$ to be a stochastic process is overly restrictive.

Denote the history of the stochastic process $\{\mathbf{w}_t\}$ up to time $(t-1)$ by the notation $\mathbf{W}_{t-1} = (\mathbf{W}_0, \mathbf{w}_1, ..., \mathbf{w}_{t-1}) = (\mathbf{W}_0, \mathbf{W}_{t-1}^1)$, where $\mathbf{W}_0$ is the set of initial conditions. Then, for a sample period $t = 1, ..., T$, the DGP is denoted $D_W(\mathbf{W}_T^1|\mathbf{W}_0, \boldsymbol{\delta})$, and is sequentially factorized as:

$$D_W(\mathbf{W}_T^1 \mid \mathbf{W}_0, \boldsymbol{\delta}) = \prod_{t=1}^{T} D_{w_t}(\mathbf{w}_t \mid \mathbf{W}_{t-1}, \boldsymbol{\kappa}_t), \tag{1}$$

where $\mathbf{g}(\boldsymbol{\delta}) = (\boldsymbol{\kappa}_1 \, ... \, \boldsymbol{\kappa}_T)$ for a 1–1 function $\mathbf{g}(\cdot)$, so that the $\boldsymbol{\kappa}_t$ may be non-constant over time due to regime shifts and structural breaks—see Hendry and Mizon (1998a, b) for discussion of the distinction between these parameter changes.

1.2 Granger Causality

If, in the universe of information, deleting the history of one set of variables does not alter the joint distribution of any of the remaining variables, then the omitted variables were defined by Granger (1969) not to cause the remaining variables. To formalize this notion, partition $\mathbf{w}_t$ into the two sets $\mathbf{w}_{1,t}$ and $\mathbf{w}_{2,t}$ where $\mathbf{w}_t' = (\mathbf{w}_{1,t}', \mathbf{w}_{2,t}')$, and correspondingly factorize $D_{w_t}(\mathbf{w}_t|\mathbf{W}_{t-1}, \boldsymbol{\kappa}_t)$ as:

$$D_{w_t}(\mathbf{w}_t \mid \mathbf{W}_{t-1}, \boldsymbol{\kappa}_t) = D_{w_{1,t}|w_{2,t}}(\mathbf{w}_{1,t} \mid \mathbf{w}_{2,t}\mathbf{W}_{t-1}, \boldsymbol{\kappa}_t) \, D_{w_{2,t}}(\mathbf{w}_{2,t} \mid \mathbf{W}_{t-1}, \boldsymbol{\kappa}_{2,t}) \tag{2}$$

where $\boldsymbol{\kappa}_t' = (\boldsymbol{\kappa}_{1,t}', \boldsymbol{\kappa}_{2,t}')$ is appropriately specified *ab initio* to sustain this conditional-marginal factorization. Similarly, partition $\mathbf{W}_{t-1}$ into $\mathbf{W}_{1,t-1}$ and $\mathbf{W}_{2,t-1}$. Then:

Definition 1. *If the density* $D_{w_{2,t}}(\cdot)$ *does not depend on* $\mathbf{W}_{1,t-1}$, *so that:*

$$D_{w_{2,t}}(\mathbf{w}_{2,t} \mid \mathbf{W}_{t-1}, \cdot) = D_{w_{2,t}}(\mathbf{w}_{2,t} \mid \mathbf{W}_{2,t-1}, \cdot), \tag{3}$$

then $\mathbf{w}_1$ *does not Granger cause* $\mathbf{w}_2$.

Thus, the absence of feedback from one set of variables to another in the DGP is captured in the concept of Granger non-causality.

Independently of whether the original notion of Granger causality characterizes "cause," there are many possibilities for mistakes in applying Granger causality empirically. First, Granger causality does not explicitly involve parameters, and this has been criticized as a serious lacuna (see e.g., Engle, Hendry, and Richard, 1983). Secondly, Granger causality in a model does not entail its existence in the DGP: the effects detected may be proxies, falsely suggesting the importance of cross-lagged values. Conversely, Granger causation in the DGP need not be reflected in a model thereof—Hendry (1997) shows that when models are misspecified and the DGP is non-constant, extrapolative models (based on lagged own values alone) can out-forecast econometric equations (i.e., the causal effects can be camouflaged by structural breaks), but equally, the relevant variables may be omitted: Section 2 establishes these results.

Further, the definition is non-operational as it relates to the universe of information, such that, when removing variables entails no loss of information, then they are Granger non-causal of the variables that remain. In practice, many authors have applied the idea to eliminating variables from a small set, as in bivariate modeling for example. Without the untenable assumption that the small set of variables selected is indeed the universe of relevant information, nothing about "causality" in the DGP can be deduced from the empirical evidence. The sequence of model changes in Sims (1972) to Sims (1980) reveals the problems with that logic. Indeed, in the limit, such an approach is tantamount to deducing a lack of cause from a lack of simple correlation. Hence the universe of information plays a key role in detecting "genuine Granger causality."

Finally, as formalized here, Granger causality is a phenomenon that is specific to each point in time, and could change over time: for example, the interest rate might Granger cause the exchange rate in a floating regime, but not under a fixed peg. The possibility that there are changes in Granger causality in the DGP over time can confound empirical tests. In the interest rate–exchange rate nexus, even after a peg is in place, regressing exchange rates on past interest rates and its own lags, for a sufficiently fine time division, may detect apparent Granger causality from their earlier links, despite the current non-existence of a link (see Richard, 1980, for modeling changes in causality between regimes).

These potentially serious difficulties with the concept of Granger cause do not imply it is valueless. Indeed, we demonstrate below that its role is pervasive even when Granger causality is simply reflecting a reduction phenomenon, i.e., the presence or absence of feedbacks in a limited dataset, irrespective of whether or not they are "genuine DGP causes". Its presence often has a marked impact on modeling in general and inference in particular, and the paper focuses on ten aspects of econometric modeling in which this occurs.

1.3 The Econometric Model

An econometric model $f_x(\cdot)$ for $n < N$ variables $\mathbf{x}_t$ implicitly derived from $\mathbf{w}_t$ by aggregation and transformation is denoted by:

$$f_X(\mathbf{X}_T^1 \mid \mathbf{X}_0, \boldsymbol{\theta}) = \prod_{t=1}^{T} f_x(\mathbf{x}_t \mid \mathbf{X}_{t-1}, \boldsymbol{\theta}) \text{ where } \boldsymbol{\theta} = (\theta_1, ..., \theta_k)' \in \boldsymbol{\Theta} \subseteq \mathbb{R}^k \qquad (4)$$

when $f_x(\mathbf{x}_t | \mathbf{X}_{t-1}, \boldsymbol{\theta})$ is the postulated sequential joint density at time t. We assume that $k < d$ and $\boldsymbol{\theta}$ represents the constant parameters postulated by the modeler, so any time-dependent effects have been reparameterized accordingly (as in a "structural time series model" re-represented as an ARIMA process: see Harvey, 1993).

From the theory of reduction (see, *inter alia*, Hendry, 1995a; Mizon, 1995), there exists a "local DGP" $D_{x_t}(\mathbf{x}_t | \mathbf{X}_{t-1}, \boldsymbol{\zeta})$ derived from $D_{w_t}(\mathbf{w}_t | \cdot)$ by reduction.

Section 3 considers the role of Granger non-causality in precisely that reduction. In general, $f_x(\cdot) \neq D_{x_t}(\cdot)$, and this divergence has to be taken into account when making inferences about $\boldsymbol{\theta}$.

As noted above, empirical tests for Granger causality are based on reductions within $f_x(\mathbf{x}_t | \mathbf{X}_{t-1}, \cdot)$ (see Granger, 1969). Let $\mathbf{x}_t$ be partitioned as $\mathbf{x}'_t = (\mathbf{y}'_t : \mathbf{z}'_t)$ where $\mathbf{y}_t$ is $n_1 \times 1$ and $\mathbf{z}_t$ is $n_2 \times 1$ with $n = n_1 + n_2$, and partition $\mathbf{X}_{t-1}$ accordingly as $(\mathbf{Y}_{t-1}, \mathbf{Z}_{t-1})$. To factorize $f_x(\mathbf{x}_t | \mathbf{X}_{t-1}, \boldsymbol{\theta})$, we first transform the original model parameters $\boldsymbol{\theta} \in \Theta$ to the set $\boldsymbol{\phi} \in \Phi$ given by:

$$\phi = \mathbf{h}(\boldsymbol{\theta}) \text{ where } \phi \in \Phi \text{ and } \boldsymbol{\theta} \in \Theta, \tag{5}$$

such that $\mathbf{h}(\cdot)$ defines a 1–1 reparameterization of θs into ϕs designed to sustain the partition $\boldsymbol{\phi}' = (\boldsymbol{\phi}'_1 : \boldsymbol{\phi}'_2)$, where $\boldsymbol{\phi}_i$ has k_i elements ($k_1 + k_2 = k$), corresponding to the factorization of the joint density into a conditional density and a marginal density as:

$$f_x(\mathbf{x}_t \mid \mathbf{X}_{t-1}, \boldsymbol{\theta}) = f_{y|z}(\mathbf{y}_t \mid \mathbf{z}_t, \mathbf{X}_{t-1}, \phi_1) f_z(\mathbf{z}_t \mid \mathbf{X}_{t-1}, \phi_2). \tag{6}$$

Section 4 considers the role of Granger non-causality in this conditioning reduction. Prior to that we define empirical Granger causality with respect to the information set generated by $\{\mathbf{x}_t\}$:

Definition 2. *If the density* $f_z(\cdot)$ *does not depend on* $\mathbf{Y}_{t-1}$, *so that:*

$$f_z(\mathbf{z}_t \mid \mathbf{X}_{t-1}, \cdot) = f_z(\mathbf{z}_t \mid \mathbf{Z}_{t-1}, \mathbf{X}_0, \cdot), \tag{7}$$

then $\mathbf{y}$ *does not empirically Granger cause* $\mathbf{z}$.

Thus, the absence of feedback from one set of variables to another in the context of a model is captured in the concept of *empirical* Granger non-causality, which we denote by its acronym EGNC. We now consider the implications of EGNC in econometric modeling.

2 Granger Causality and Empirical Granger Causality

The fundamental results for empirical modeling are that empirical Granger causality does not entail Granger causality; and Granger causality does not imply empirical Granger causality. We establish these by simple counter examples, each of which refutes the claim that the former does entail the latter.

Consider two independent processes, y_t and z_t:

$$\begin{pmatrix} y_t \\ z_t \end{pmatrix} \sim \mathsf{IN}_2 \left[\begin{pmatrix} \mu_y \\ \mu_z \end{pmatrix}, \begin{pmatrix} \sigma_y^2 & 0 \\ 0 & \sigma_z^2 \end{pmatrix} \right] \text{ for } t < T_b.$$

However, at time T_b, there is a mean shift in the $\{z_t\}$ process from μ_z to μ_z^* (see Clements and Hendry, 1998, on the important role of deterministic shifts in forecast failure). Also, ℓ-periods later, a shift from μ_y to μ_y^* occurs, unrelated in source, sign, or magnitude to that which affected z_t. Let $\delta_z = \mu_z^* - \mu_z$, and $\delta_y = \mu_y^* - \mu_y$, then over the whole sample, when $1_{\{t \geq T_b\}}$ denotes the indicator function (zero unless $t \geq T_b$, in which case it is unity):

$$\begin{pmatrix} y_t \\ z_t \end{pmatrix} \sim \text{IN}_2 \left[\begin{pmatrix} \mu_y + \delta_y 1_{\{t \geq T_b + \ell\}} \\ \mu_z + \delta_z 1_{\{t \geq T_b\}} \end{pmatrix}, \begin{pmatrix} \sigma_y^2 & 0 \\ 0 & \sigma_z^2 \end{pmatrix} \right]. \tag{8}$$

The timing of such structural breaks would be included in the universe of information, so dropping the information on $\{z_t\}$ would not affect the distribution of y_t, as (2) shows. Empirically, however, in finite samples of size $T > T_b + \ell$, $z_{t-\ell}$ will have a break at the same time as that in y_t. Consider applying least-squares estimation to the following model with $n_z \geq \ell$, when the break indicator is not included:

$$y_t = \alpha_0 + \sum_{i=1}^{n_y} \alpha_i y_{t-i} + \sum_{j=1}^{n_z} \beta_j z_{t-j} + u_t. \tag{9}$$

Provided $T_b > \ell$ (to allow lags), since:

$$y_t - \mu_y - \frac{\delta_y}{\delta_z}(z_{t-\ell} - \mu_z) = \delta_y 1_{\{t \geq T_b + \ell\}} + v_{y,t} - \frac{\delta_y}{\delta_z}(\delta_z 1_{\{t-\ell \geq T_b\}} + v_{z,t})$$

$$= v_{y,t} - \frac{\delta_y}{\delta_z} v_{z,t}, \tag{10}$$

then for sufficiently large breaks, $\hat{\beta}_\ell \simeq \delta_y/\delta_z$ will be statistically significant empirically even when lagged ys are included in (9). Indeed, from (8), for $\tau = (T_b - 1)/(T - \ell)$:

$$\mathsf{E}\left[(T - \ell)^{-1} \sum_{t=\ell+1}^{T} (y_t - \bar{y})^2\right] = \mathsf{MSE}[\{y_t\}] = \sigma_y^2 + \tau(1 - \tau)\delta_y^2,$$

when $\mathsf{MSE}[\{y_t\}]$ denotes the expected mean square error over $\ell + 1$, ..., T, whereas from (10), the corresponding average of the conditional MSE over $\{z_t\}$ is:

$$\mathsf{MSE}[\{y_t\}|\{z_{t-\ell}\}] = \sigma_y^2 + \sigma_z^2 \delta_y^2 / \delta_z^2,$$

so:

$$\mathsf{MSE}[\{y_t\}|\{z_{t-\ell}\}] < \mathsf{MSE}[\{y_t\}] \text{ when } \sigma_z^2 < \tau(1 - \tau)\delta_z^2.$$

This is an example of spurious intertemporal co-breaking (see Hendry, 1995c). The converse follows along similar lines. Let:

$$\begin{pmatrix} y_t \\ z_t \end{pmatrix} \sim \text{IN}_2 \left[\begin{pmatrix} \mu_y + \delta_y 1_{\{t \geq T_b + \ell\}} + \rho z_{t-1} \\ \mu_z \end{pmatrix}, \begin{pmatrix} \sigma_y^2 & 0 \\ 0 & \sigma_z^2 \end{pmatrix} \right]. \tag{11}$$

Now, for a sufficiently large break, estimation of (9) will deliver a near unit root in the $\{y_t\}$ component (see e.g. Hendry and Neale, 1991), and insignificant estimates of the effects of the $\{z_t\}$ components, jointly and marginally, even when ρ would have been highly significant in the absence of a break. These results are easily verified by Monte Carlo. Of course, the resulting models would fail a variety of mis-specification tests, but as the survey by Allen and Fildes (1998) notes, such testing remains remarkably rare in empirical econometrics. Despite this apparently adverse result, EGNC remains of considerable empirical importance, as the remaining sections demonstrate.

3 Marginalization

The n variables in the econometric model are a transformed subset $\mathbf{x}_t$ of $\mathbf{w}_t$. We first investigate the role of Granger non-causality in determining the validity of the resulting econometric model, which occurs when there is no loss of information from the reduction. Map from $\mathbf{w}_t$ to $\boldsymbol{\xi}_t$ by an information-preserving transform $\mathbf{a}(\cdot)$ so that $\boldsymbol{\xi}_t = \mathbf{a}(\mathbf{w}_t) = (\mathbf{x}_t, \boldsymbol{\xi}_{2,t})$: $\mathbf{a}(\cdot)$ need not be 1–1 if, for example, signs must be recorded as well as magnitudes after a quadratic transform. The parameter $\boldsymbol{\kappa}_t$ is transformed to $\boldsymbol{\lambda}_t$ where $\boldsymbol{\lambda}_t' = (\boldsymbol{\lambda}_{1,t}', \boldsymbol{\lambda}_{2,t}')$, so that the resulting density can be factorized as:

$$\mathsf{D}_{\mathbf{w}_t}(\mathbf{w}_t \mid \mathbf{W}_{t-1}, \boldsymbol{\kappa}_t) = \mathsf{D}_{\xi_{2,t}|\mathbf{x}_t}(\boldsymbol{\xi}_{2,t} \mid \mathbf{x}_t, \mathbf{W}_{t-1}, \boldsymbol{\lambda}_{1,t}) \mathsf{D}_{\mathbf{x}_t}(\mathbf{x}_t \mid \mathbf{W}_{t-1}, \boldsymbol{\lambda}_{2,t}). \tag{12}$$

Notice that we wish to eliminate the $\boldsymbol{\xi}_{2,t}$, so these are in the conditional model, focusing attention on the marginal model $\mathsf{D}_{\mathbf{x}_t}(\cdot)$, which is all that is retained.

The conditions for valid marginalization discussed in Hendry (1995a) require that:

$$\mathsf{D}_{\mathbf{x}_t}(\mathbf{x}_t \mid \mathbf{W}_{t-1}, \boldsymbol{\lambda}_{2,t}) = \mathsf{D}_{\mathbf{x}_t}(\mathbf{x}_t \mid \mathbf{X}_{t-1}, \mathbf{W}_0, \boldsymbol{\lambda}_{2,t}), \tag{13}$$

so that $\boldsymbol{\xi}_2$ does not Granger cause $\mathbf{x}$, in addition to conditions determining that the parameters of interest in the analysis (denoted $\boldsymbol{\mu}$, a vector of $q \leq k$ elements) are a function of $\boldsymbol{\lambda}_{2,t}$, and that $\boldsymbol{\lambda}_{1,t}$ and $\boldsymbol{\lambda}_{2,t}$ are variation free. Otherwise, lagged $\boldsymbol{\xi}_2$ are potentially important omitted explanatory variables, and if so, when $\boldsymbol{\lambda}_{1,t}$ is non-constant, so will be the coefficients of $\mathsf{D}_{\mathbf{x}_t}(\mathbf{x}_t|\mathbf{X}_{t-1}, \mathbf{W}_0, \cdot)$ in (13) even when $\boldsymbol{\lambda}_{2,t}$ in (12) is constant (see e.g., Hendry and Doornik, 1997).

Thus, Granger causality in the original sense of Granger (1969) plays a fundamental role in econometric modeling by sustaining the elimination of lagged values of variables that are to be excluded from the analysis. This holds irrespective of the philosophical "causality" status ascribed to the concept. However, we note that the conditions for valid marginalization are features of the DGP and as such are untestable, though they can be indirectly tested via tests for EGNC in econometric models. Further, Granger non-causality of $\boldsymbol{\xi}_2$ for $\mathbf{x}$ is necessary, but not sufficient, to sustain inference without loss of relevant information in the marginal distribution. For example, (13) may be a valid reduction given $\lambda_{2,t}$, but μ may not be a function of $\lambda_{2,t}$ so the analysis does not deliver the parameters of interest. This criticism has nothing to do with the role that Granger causality aims to play, but is important in clarifying its precise role.

4 Conditioning

In the preceding section, factorizations involved both conditional and marginal densities, but we focused only on the latter. We now turn attention to the former, and consider the role of EGNC in conditioning, when the conditional model is the focus of an investigator's interest. Thus, we assume that $D_{\mathbf{x}_t}(\mathbf{x}_t|\mathbf{X}_{t-1}, \mathbf{W}_0, \lambda_{2,t})$ in (13) is a valid reduction, and consider modeling $\mathbf{y}_t$ conditional on $\mathbf{z}_t$ where, as above, $\mathbf{x}'_t = (\mathbf{y}'_t : \mathbf{z}'_t)$. The potential drawback of doing so is a loss of information. Weak exogeneity of the conditioning variables for the parameters of interest, as defined in Engle $et\ al.$ (1983), is the requirement for conditional estimation not to result in any loss of information, assessed via the econometric model $f_{\mathbf{x}}(\cdot)$.

Reconsider the factorization of $f_{\mathbf{x}}(\mathbf{x}_t|\mathbf{X}_{t-1}, \boldsymbol{\theta})$ in (6), where $f_{\mathbf{y}|\mathbf{z}}(\mathbf{y}_t|\mathbf{z}_t, \mathbf{X}_{t-1}, \boldsymbol{\phi}_1)$ is to be retained, and the marginal model $f_{\mathbf{z}}(\mathbf{z}_t|\mathbf{X}_{t-1}, \boldsymbol{\phi}_2)$ discarded (i.e., $\mathbf{z}_t$ is not modeled). Then:

Definition 3. $\mathbf{z}_t$ *is weakly exogenous for* μ *iff:*
   (i) $\mu = \mathbf{f}(\boldsymbol{\phi}_1)$ *alone; and:*
   (ii) $\boldsymbol{\phi}_1$ *and* $\boldsymbol{\phi}_2$ *are variation free:* $\Phi = \Phi_1 \times \Phi_2$.

These conditions ensure that μ can be learned without loss of information from the parameters $\boldsymbol{\phi}_1$ of the conditional model alone, so $\mathbf{z}_t$ does not need to be modeled (Ericsson, Hendry, and Mizon, 1998, discuss the information losses deriving from different forms of failure of these weak exogeneity conditions). Weak exogeneity, therefore, justifies discarding the marginal model, which is not dependent on the presence or absence of feedback, and does not directly involve EGNC, although some authors have mistakenly viewed EGNC as sufficient to deem variables "exogenous" (see e.g., Sims, 1972; Geweke, 1978, 1984).

Conversely, the fact that $\mathbf{z}_t$ is weakly exogenous for μ does not imply that $\mathbf{z}_t$ causes $\mathbf{y}_t$ in any sense: for example, an irrelevant but autonomous (self-caused) variable will be weakly exogenous even though it does not enter the conditional density. Engle $et\ al.$ (1983) also stressed that a variable $\mathbf{z}_t$ may be absent from the conditional density (in that it has zero coefficients in any model of that density), yet not be weakly exogenous.

The joint occurrence of weak exogeneity and Granger non-causality of the modeled variables for the non-modeled was defined by Engle $et\ al.$ (1983) to be strong exogeneity, and is the requirement for "full-sample" conditioning. This necessitates the additional condition that the marginal model $f_z(\mathbf{z}_t|\mathbf{X}_{t-1},\, \boldsymbol{\phi}_2)$ can be expressed as in (7). Then, as is well known, under strong exogeneity, using (4) and (6):

$$f_X(\mathbf{X}_T^1 \mid \mathbf{X}_0, \boldsymbol{\theta}) = \prod_{t=1}^{T} f_{y|z}(\mathbf{y}_t \mid \mathbf{z}_t, \mathbf{X}_{t-1}, \boldsymbol{\phi}_1)\, f_z(\mathbf{z}_t \mid \mathbf{Z}_{t-1}, \mathbf{X}_0, \boldsymbol{\phi}_2)$$
$$= f_{Y|Z}(\mathbf{Y}_T^1 \mid \mathbf{Z}_T^1, \mathbf{X}_0, \boldsymbol{\phi}_1) f_Z(\mathbf{Z}_T^1 \mid \mathbf{X}_0, \boldsymbol{\phi}_2), \tag{14}$$

so that $f_{Y|Z}(\mathbf{Y}_T^1|\mathbf{Z}_T^1, \mathbf{X}_0,\, \boldsymbol{\phi}_1)$ can be analyzed without loss of information. As the next section shows, EGNC importantly affects the distributions underlying estimation and inference. It also affects the validity of in-sample dynamic simulation as Section 11 discusses.

5 Distributions of Estimators and Test Statistics

The presence or absence of EGNC is well known to affect the distributions of test statistics and estimators. The classic example is when testing for residual serial correlation after regression estimation. When all the regressors are strongly exogenous, the Durbin–Watson statistic (DW) is a powerful test, with correct size under the null; however, when a lagged-dependent variable is present, DW has the wrong size, and low rejection frequency at conventional critical values (see Durbin, 1970). More generally, if any regressor is Granger caused by the dependent variable, then the residual serial correlations are "flattened" compared to those of the original errors on the equation, again biasing the DW statistic towards non-rejection (see e.g., Hendry, 1975). Moreover, the resulting parameter estimates are inconsistent (see e.g., Hendry, 1979).

To illustrate, consider the p-variable linear regression model:

$$y_t = \boldsymbol{\beta}'\mathbf{z}_t + u_t \text{ where } u_t = \rho u_{t-1} + \epsilon_t, \tag{15}$$

when $|\rho| < 1$, $\epsilon_t \sim \mathsf{IN}[0, \sigma_\epsilon^2]$ with $\mathsf{E}[\mathbf{z}_t\epsilon_t]= \mathbf{0}$, so:

$$y_t = \boldsymbol{\beta}'\mathbf{z}_t + \rho y_{t-1} - \rho\boldsymbol{\beta}'\mathbf{z}_{t-1} + \epsilon_t. \tag{16}$$

This is the basic COMFAC (common factor in the dynamics) model in Sargan (1964, 1980). We restrict the $\{\mathbf{z}_t\}$ process to be stationary and generated by:

$$\mathbf{z}_t = \boldsymbol{\pi}_{21}y_{t-1} + \boldsymbol{\nu}_t, \tag{17}$$

with $\boldsymbol{\nu}_t \sim \mathsf{IN}_k[\mathbf{0}, \boldsymbol{\Omega}]$, such that $\boldsymbol{\nu}$ is independent of y, and so:

$$\mathsf{E}[\mathbf{z}_t y_{t-1}] = \boldsymbol{\pi}_{21}m_{yy} \neq \mathbf{0},$$
$$\mathsf{E}[\mathbf{z}_t\mathbf{z}_t'] = \mathsf{E}[(\boldsymbol{\pi}_{21}y_{t-1} + \boldsymbol{\nu}_t)(\boldsymbol{\pi}_{21}y_{t-1} + \boldsymbol{\nu}_t)'] = \boldsymbol{\pi}_{21}\boldsymbol{\pi}_{21}'m_{yy} + \boldsymbol{\Omega} = \mathbf{M}_{zz}, \tag{18}$$

and:

$$\mathsf{E}[\mathbf{z}_t\mathbf{z}_{t-1}'] = \mathsf{E}[(\boldsymbol{\pi}_{21}y_{t-1} + \boldsymbol{\nu}_t)(\boldsymbol{\pi}_{21}y_{t-2} + \boldsymbol{\nu}_{t-1})'] = \boldsymbol{\pi}_{21}\boldsymbol{\pi}_{21}'m_{yy_1} + \boldsymbol{\pi}_{21}\boldsymbol{\beta}'\boldsymbol{\Omega},$$

when $\mathsf{E}[y_t^2]= m_{yy}$ and $\mathsf{E}[y_ty_{t-1}]= m_{yy_1}$. Let $\gamma = \beta'\pi_{21}$ and $e_t = \beta'\nu_t$, where for stationarity, $|\gamma| < 1$. Then, for $\rho \neq 0$:

$$\mathsf{E}[\mathbf{z}_tu_t]= \rho\mathsf{E}[\mathbf{z}_tu_{t-1}] = \rho\mathsf{E}[\mathbf{z}_t(y_{t-1} - \mathbf{z}_{t-1}'\beta)]$$
$$= \rho\pi_{21}(m_{yy} - \gamma m_{yy_1} - \beta'\Omega\beta) = \phi \neq \mathbf{0}.$$

Hence, from (17) and (18), estimating (15) by least squares, ignoring the autocorrelation:

$$\plim_{T\to\infty}\left(\widehat{\beta} - \beta\right) = \plim_{T\to\infty}\left[T^{-1}\sum_{t=1}^{T}\mathbf{z}_t\mathbf{z}_t'\right]^{-1}\left[T^{-1}\sum_{t=1}^{T}\mathbf{z}_tu_t\right] = \mathbf{M}_{zz}^{-1}\phi = \psi \neq \mathbf{0}.$$

Consequently, the estimator is inconsistent when $\rho\pi_{21} \neq \mathbf{0}$. Thus, the violation of EGNC is important here. For example, when $p = 1$, $T = 100$, $\beta = 1$, $\rho = -0.8$, and $\pi_{21} = 0.8$, with $\sigma_\epsilon^2 = 0.01$ and $\omega_{11} = 0.04$, then $\psi = -0.09$, and essentially all $\widehat{\beta} < \beta$.

Further, the residual autocorrelation is "flattened" since (in large samples):

$$\widehat{u}_t = y_t - \widehat{\beta}'\mathbf{z}_t = u_t - \left(\widehat{\beta} - \beta\right)'\mathbf{z}_t \simeq u_t - \psi'\mathbf{z}_t,$$

so:

$$\widehat{u}_t \simeq \rho u_{t-1} + \epsilon_t - \psi'\mathbf{z}_t \simeq \rho\widehat{u}_{t-1} + \epsilon_t - \psi'\mathbf{z}_t^\dagger,$$

where $\mathbf{z}_t^\dagger = \mathbf{z}_t - \rho\mathbf{z}_{t-1}$. In effect, there is an omitted moving-average component when $\rho\pi_{21} \neq \mathbf{0}$, of the opposite sign to the residual autoregression. We return to the potential impact of EGNC on estimation and inference in the context of cointegrated processes in Section 7 below.

6 Inference via Simulation

The estimation of dynamic latent-variables models by simulating the underlying latent processes has become increasingly common, with the method of simulated moments (MSM) being particularly popular (see e.g., McFadden, 1989; Pakes and Pollard, 1989). The likelihood functions of such models tend to be analytically intractable, since marginalizing with respect to latent variables requires high-dimensional integration. However, Monte Carlo simulation can be used to compute integrals as the expectations (means) of equivalent stochastic problems (see e.g., Hendry, 1984), so marginalization can be achieved numerically by simulation to obtain the likelihood for the observables. Although the distributions of latent variables conditional on observables are generally unknown, an importance function can be used as a random-number generator (see e.g., Geweke, 1988). As we will show, EGNC is important for the feasibility of some approaches. We first consider simulated likelihood functions, then turn to MSM, before commenting on indirect inference and boot-strap methods.

6.1 Simulated Likelihood Functions

First, some background and notation, in a setting where there are no unmodeled variables (see Hendry and Richard, 1991). Let $\mathbf{y}_t$ denote the vector of n observ-able random variables at time t, and $\mathbf{s}_t$ the vector of m unobservable variables. Let $f_{Y,S}(\mathbf{Y}, \mathbf{S}|\boldsymbol{\theta})$ for $\boldsymbol{\theta} \in \Theta \subseteq \mathbb{R}^k$ be a model of the joint density of $\mathbf{Y}$ and $\mathbf{S} \in S$ for a sample of size T. Initial conditions are assumed known or included in $\mathbf{S}$, depending on the context. The likelihood function $L(\boldsymbol{\theta}|\mathbf{Y})$ which we wish to compute, and perhaps maximize, is:

$$L(\boldsymbol{\theta}; \mathbf{Y}) \propto f_Y(\mathbf{Y} \mid \boldsymbol{\theta}) = \int \cdots \int_S f_{Y,S}(\mathbf{Y}, \mathbf{S} \mid \boldsymbol{\theta}) d\mathbf{S}, \tag{19}$$

where the dimension of integration depends on that of $\mathbf{S}$. To estimate $\boldsymbol{\theta}$ by Monte Carlo methods requires factorizing $f_{Y,S}(\mathbf{Y}, \mathbf{S}|\boldsymbol{\theta})$ into the product of the importance function $g_Y(\mathbf{S}|\boldsymbol{\theta})$ from which samples of $\{\mathbf{s}_t\}$ can be drawn at ran-dom, and a remainder function $f(\mathbf{Y}, \mathbf{S}|\boldsymbol{\theta})$ defined in (20) below. The observed matrix $\mathbf{Y}$ is treated as a fixed constant, although the choice of $g_Y(\cdot)$ may depend on the observed values. Thus, factorize $f_{Y,S}(\mathbf{Y}, \mathbf{S}|\boldsymbol{\theta})$ as:

$$f_{Y,S}(\mathbf{Y}, \mathbf{S} \mid \boldsymbol{\theta}) = f(\mathbf{Y}, \mathbf{S} \mid \boldsymbol{\theta}) g_Y(\mathbf{S} \mid \boldsymbol{\theta}). \tag{20}$$

Consequently, from (19) and (20):

$$L(\boldsymbol{\theta}; \mathbf{Y}) \propto \int \cdots \int_S f(\mathbf{Y}, \mathbf{S} \mid \boldsymbol{\theta}) g_Y(\mathbf{S} \mid \boldsymbol{\theta}) d\mathbf{S} = \mathsf{E}_g[f(\mathbf{Y}, \mathbf{S} \mid \boldsymbol{\theta})]. \tag{21}$$

The importance function $g_Y(\cdot)$, while specifically designed to enable the evalu-ation of this integral, must have the properties of a density, namely $\int \cdots \int_{S} g_Y(\mathbf{S}|\boldsymbol{\theta}) d\mathbf{S} = 1$ and $g_Y(\cdot) \geq \forall \boldsymbol{\theta} \in \Theta$ and $\mathbf{S} \in S$. Hence the integral in (21) is the integral of $f(\mathbf{Y}, \mathbf{S}|\boldsymbol{\theta})$ with respect to $g_Y(\cdot)$, that is $\mathsf{E}_g[\cdot]$. In turn, $\mathsf{E}_g[\cdot]$ can be estimated by Monte Carlo simulation using the mean of M random samples of $\mathbf{S}$ drawn from $g_Y(\mathbf{S}|\boldsymbol{\theta})$:

$$\widehat{\mathsf{E}_g}[f(\mathbf{Y}, \mathbf{S} \mid \boldsymbol{\theta})] = \frac{1}{M} \sum_{i=1}^{M} f(\mathbf{Y}, \mathbf{S}_i \mid \boldsymbol{\theta}).$$

A practical simulant requires explicit formulae for $f(\mathbf{Y}, \mathbf{S}|\boldsymbol{\theta})$ and $g_Y(\cdot)$. One basis for the selection of $f(\mathbf{Y}, \mathbf{S}|\boldsymbol{\theta})$ and $g_Y(\cdot)$ that arises naturally in the context of dynamic latent variables (DLV) models, which are inherently sequential, is the sequential conditional factorization of $f_{Y,S}(\mathbf{Y}, \mathbf{S}|\boldsymbol{\theta})$:

$$f_{Y,S}(\mathbf{Y}, \mathbf{S} \mid \boldsymbol{\theta}) = \prod_{t=1}^{T} f_{y|s}(\mathbf{y}_t \mid \mathbf{s}_t, \mathbf{X}_{t-1}, \phi_1) f_s(\mathbf{s}_t \mid \mathbf{X}_{t-1}, \phi_2), \tag{22}$$

where $\mathbf{X}_{t-1} = (\mathbf{Y}_{t-1}, \mathbf{S}_{t-1})$. Then, a natural choice for $g_Y(\cdot)$ is the second factor:

$$g_Y(\mathbf{S} \mid \boldsymbol{\theta}) = \prod_{t=1}^{T} \mathsf{f}_s(\mathbf{s}_t \mid \mathbf{X}_{t-1}, \phi_2),\tag{23}$$

and hence:

$$f(\mathbf{Y}, \mathbf{S} \mid \boldsymbol{\theta}) = \prod_{t=1}^{T} \mathsf{f}_{\mathsf{y}|\mathsf{s}}(\mathbf{y}_t \mid \mathbf{s}_t, \mathbf{X}_{t-1}, \phi_1).\tag{24}$$

At each time t, it must be possible to draw from the latent process $\{\mathbf{s}_t | \mathbf{X}_{t-1}, \phi_2\}$, given $\mathbf{X}_{t-1}$ and an admissible value of $\boldsymbol{\theta}$; repeating over different $\boldsymbol{\theta}$ generates $\mathsf{L}(\boldsymbol{\theta}|\mathbf{Y})$ from (19). This can be made as precise as desired by choosing a sufficiently large M.

With this sequential conditional factorization, $\mathbf{Y}$ (as opposed to $\mathbf{Y}_{t-1}$ at each t) is not being held fixed in the generation of $\mathbf{S}$. Monte Carlo sampling variability is introduced into the generation of $f(\mathbf{Y}, \mathbf{S}|\boldsymbol{\theta})$ by the dependence of $\mathbf{y}_t$ on $\mathbf{S}_{t-1}$. These problems disappear in the special case with EGNC from $\mathbf{s}$ to $\mathbf{y}$, since there then exists a full-sample factorization (rather than a sequential factorization). In particular with EGNC from $\mathbf{s}$ to $\mathbf{y}$:

$$\mathsf{f}_Y(\mathbf{Y} \mid \boldsymbol{\theta}) = \prod_{t=1}^{T} \mathsf{f}_y(\mathbf{y}_t \mid \mathbf{X}_{t-1}, \varphi_1) = \prod_{t=1}^{T} \mathsf{f}_y(\mathbf{y}_t \mid \mathbf{Y}_{t-1}, \varphi_1),\tag{25}$$

so that:

$$\mathsf{f}_{Y,S}(\mathbf{Y}, \mathbf{S} \mid \boldsymbol{\theta}) = \mathsf{f}_{S|Y}(\mathbf{S} \mid \mathbf{Y}, \boldsymbol{\theta})\mathsf{f}_Y(\mathbf{Y} \mid \boldsymbol{\theta}),$$

with

$$\mathsf{f}_{S|Y}(\mathbf{S} \mid \mathbf{Y}, \boldsymbol{\theta}) = \prod_{t=1}^{T} \mathsf{f}_{s|y}(\mathbf{s}_t \mid \mathbf{y}_t, \mathbf{X}_{t-1}, \varphi_2).\tag{26}$$

In the absence of considerations associated with acceleration or variance reduction techniques, aiming to minimize the sampling variance of the residual function $f(\cdot)$ favors this full-sample factorization since the Monte Carlo sampling variance of $f(\mathbf{Y}, \mathbf{S})$ is zero. Some examples are given in Hendry and Richard (1991).

We now consider the complications arising from the presence of unmodeled variables, where again EGNC plays an important role.

6.2 Exogeneity Issues

Simulation treating exogenous variables as fixed in repeated samples requires that the latter be strongly exogenous, and hence both weakly exogenous and not Granger-caused by the latent variables. Let $\mathbf{z}_t$ denote the vector of variables weakly exogenous for the parameters of interest, and $\mathbf{X}_{t-1}^{\dagger} = (\mathbf{S}_{t-1}, \mathbf{Z}_{t-1}, \mathbf{Y}_{t-1})$ be the lagged values of all relevant variables. The symbol $\perp$ denotes independence in probability, or conditional independence when followed by the conditioning operator $|$. To validate likelihood simulation conditional on the matrix $\mathbf{Z}$ of weakly exogenous variables, we require:

$$\mathbf{z}_t \perp \mathbf{S}_{t-1} \mid \mathbf{Z}_{t-1}, \mathbf{Y}_{t-1}, \tag{27}$$

which implies that $f_z(\mathbf{z}_t | \mathbf{X}_{t-1}^{\dagger}, \cdot) = f_z(\mathbf{z}_t | \mathbf{Z}_{t-1}, \mathbf{Y}_{t-1}, \cdot)$. Since:

$$f_{y,z}(\mathbf{y}_t, \mathbf{z}_t \mid \mathbf{X}_{t-1}^{\dagger}, \cdot) = \int f_{y,s|z}(\mathbf{y}_t, \mathbf{s}_t \mid \mathbf{z}_t, \mathbf{X}_{t-1}^{\dagger}, \cdot) f_z(\mathbf{z}_t \mid \mathbf{X}_{t-1}^{\dagger}, \cdot) d\mathbf{s}_t, \tag{28}$$

the conditional likelihood function is:

$$L(\boldsymbol{\theta}; \mathbf{Y} \mid \mathbf{Z}) = \int \cdots \int \left[\prod_{t=1}^{T} f_{y,s|z}(\mathbf{y}_t, \mathbf{s}_t \mid \mathbf{z}_t, \mathbf{X}_{t-1}^{\dagger}, \cdot) \right] d\mathbf{S} \tag{29}$$

since $\mathbf{z}_t$ does not depend on the latent variables, so factors out of the integral in (28), thus yielding (29), and thereby reducing the problem to (22). Hence, when $\mathbf{z}_t$ is weakly exogenous for $\boldsymbol{\mu}$, there will be no loss of information in estimating $\boldsymbol{\theta}$ (and so $\boldsymbol{\mu}$) using a simulated likelihood function for (29).

Comparing (29) with the first term in (22) shows that under condition (27), the exogenous variables are kept fixed at their observed values in the evaluation of (29). If assumption (27) did not hold, then the exogenous process must be included in the integral in (28) and the derivation of a conditional likelihood as in (29) is not possible. The alternative of not conditioning on $\mathbf{z}_t$ requires formulating an auxiliary model of the $\mathbf{z}_t$ process as a function of the latent variables and observables, which may not be well specified, and further increases the dimensionality of the parameter space. Thus, when EGNC is present as in (27), a more robust and simpler problem results. Related considerations apply to the MSM approach.

6.3 Method of Simulated Moments

The generalized method of moments (GMM: see Hansen, 1982) estimation procedure chooses $\widetilde{\boldsymbol{\theta}}$ to minimize:

$$\left[\sum_{t=1}^{T} \mathbf{h}(\mathbf{y}_t, \mathbf{z}_t, \mathbf{X}_{t-1}; \widetilde{\boldsymbol{\theta}}) \right]' \boldsymbol{\Omega} \left[\sum_{t=1}^{T} \mathbf{h}(\mathbf{y}_t, \mathbf{z}_t, \mathbf{X}_{t-1}; \widetilde{\boldsymbol{\theta}}) \right] \tag{30}$$

when $T^{-1}\sum_{t=1}^{T} \mathbf{h}(\mathbf{y}_t, \mathbf{z}_t, \mathbf{X}_{t-1}; \widetilde{\boldsymbol{\theta}})$ is the empirical counterpart of the $q \geq k$ moment conditions:

$$\mathbf{H}(\boldsymbol{\theta}) = \mathsf{E}_{y|z}[\mathbf{h}(\mathbf{y}_t, \mathbf{z}_t, \mathbf{X}_{t-1}; \boldsymbol{\theta})] = \mathbf{0} \quad \forall t \tag{31}$$

and $\boldsymbol{\Omega}$ is a non-negative definite symmetric $q \times q$ matrix. Let $\boldsymbol{\theta}_p$ denote the population value of $\boldsymbol{\theta}$, then the statistical formulation of an econometric model often suggests choosing an $\mathbf{h}(\cdot)$ for which the moment conditions in (31) are satisfied at $\boldsymbol{\theta} = \boldsymbol{\theta}_p$: examples include orthogonality conditions and score vectors. Alternatively, $\mathbf{h}(\cdot)$ can be any function such that a point estimate, $\widehat{\mathbf{H}}$, is available for $\mathbf{H}(\boldsymbol{\theta})$. In cases where there is no closed form for $\mathbf{h}(\cdot)$, or when $\mathbf{h}(\cdot)$ is a function of latent variables, the moments in (31) are estimated via simulation thus leading to the method of simulated moments (MSM).

Consider first, for simplicity, the case in which there are latent variables $\mathbf{s}_t$ but no exogenous variables $\mathbf{z}_t$. Then, since random-number generators are often available for the sequential distribution of $\{\mathbf{y}_t\}$ and $\{\mathbf{s}_t\}$, which enable random samples to be drawn from the joint distribution (e.g., Gibbs resampling as in Geman and Geman, 1984), integrals like:

$$\mathbf{H}(\boldsymbol{\theta}) = \int \dots \int_{\mathcal{S},\mathcal{Y}} \mathbf{h}(\mathbf{Y},\mathbf{S};\boldsymbol{\theta})\, \mathsf{f}_{Y,S}(\mathbf{Y},\mathbf{S};\boldsymbol{\theta})\mathrm{d}\mathbf{S}\mathrm{d}\mathbf{Y}, \qquad (32)$$

can be estimated by simulation for a range of dynamic models. MSM uses simulation techniques to evaluate $\mathbf{H}(\boldsymbol{\theta})$ for different $\boldsymbol{\theta}$, and then takes as the estimator of $\boldsymbol{\theta}$ the value of $\boldsymbol{\theta}$ that minimizes the distance between the estimate $\widehat{\mathbf{H}}$ and the predicted value $\mathbf{H}(\boldsymbol{\theta}_p)$ (see Lerman and Manski, 1981; Pakes, 1986; Hajivassiliou, 1989; McFadden, 1989; Hajivassiliou and McFadden, 1989: for theoretical analyses of the properties of these simulation estimators, see Andrews, 1989; Duffie and Singleton, 1989; Pakes and Pollard, 1989). To apply MSM to dynamic models with exogenous variables $\mathbf{z}_t$, when both the latent and the observable endogenous variables are subject to simulation, assumption (27) has to be replaced by the stronger condition that:

$$\mathbf{z}_t \perp (\mathbf{S}_{t-1}, \mathbf{Y}_{t-1}) \mid \mathbf{Z}_{t-1}. \qquad (33)$$

Thus, two EGNC conditions are needed, precluding feedback from either the latent or observed processes onto the non-modeled variables, as well as the earlier conditions for weak exogeneity. If that feedback exists, but is ignored, inference is likely to be distorted; if it is taken into account, a more complex and higher dimensional analysis is involved, perhaps contaminated by inappropriate modeling of the $\mathbf{z}_t$: in both cases EGNC is a considerable help.

We also note briefly that similar considerations apply to indirect inference (see Gouriéroux, Montfort, and Renault, 1993) when it is applied to dynamic models with weakly exogenous variables, namely EGNC from the endogenous variables $\mathbf{y}_t$ to the weakly exogenous variables $\mathbf{z}_t$ is required. Indeed, Gouriéroux and Montfort (1995) in their chapter on indirect inference only consider the case in which EGNC applies. Equally, when bootstrap methods (see Efron, 1979; Efron and Tibshirani, 1993; Young, 1994) are applied, for example, to linear regression models using re-sampling from the regressand and (weakly) exogenous regressor observations, EGNC from the regressand to the regressors is required for valid bootstrapping, so conditioning variables must be strongly exogenous.

7 Cointegration

Cointegration is, of course, another of Clive Granger's seminal contributions (see Granger, 1981), but its entry here is only in relation to EGNC. In an I(1) integrated–cointegrated system, Engle and Granger (1987) show that at least one direction of Granger causality is entailed by cointegration: also see Granger (1986). This implication follows because the cointegrating combination must enter at least one equation to be well defined, and so the lagged values of the other variables in the cointegrating vector must enter that equation. We draw on many results in this extensive literature (see, *inter alia*, Stock, 1987; Phillips and Durlauf, 1986; Phillips and Loretan, 1991), but refer specifically to Banerjee *et al.* (1993) and Johansen (1995) as convenient sources.

Consider the following n-dimensional closed linear system:

$$\mathbf{x}_t = \sum_{i=1}^{s} \mathbf{\Pi}_i \mathbf{x}_{t-i} + \boldsymbol{\delta} + \boldsymbol{\varepsilon}_t \quad \text{with} \quad \boldsymbol{\varepsilon}_t \sim \mathsf{IN}_n[\mathbf{0}, \boldsymbol{\Sigma}]. \tag{34}$$

Then, from the Granger representation theorem for cointegrated processes, when there are r $(1 \leq r \leq n)$ cointegrating relationships, (34) can be rewritten as:

$$\Delta \mathbf{x}_t = \sum_{i=1}^{s-1} \mathbf{\Gamma}_i \Delta \mathbf{x}_{t-i} + \boldsymbol{\alpha} \boldsymbol{\beta}' \mathbf{x}_{t-1} + \boldsymbol{\delta} + \boldsymbol{\varepsilon}_t, \tag{35}$$

where $\boldsymbol{\alpha}$ and $\boldsymbol{\beta}$ are $n \times r$ of rank r such that $\boldsymbol{\alpha}\boldsymbol{\beta}' = \sum_{i=1}^{s} \mathbf{\Pi}_i - \mathbf{I}_n$ and $\mathbf{\Gamma}_i = -\sum_{j=i+1}^{s} \mathbf{\Pi}_j$. Confining attention to $\mathbf{x}_t \sim$ I(1), it follows that $\boldsymbol{\beta}'\mathbf{x}_t$ and $\Delta \mathbf{x}_t$ are I(0), so that the latter has a Wold (1938) representation:

$$\Delta \mathbf{x}_t = \mathbf{C}(L)(\boldsymbol{\varepsilon}_t + \boldsymbol{\delta}) = [\mathbf{C}(1) + \Delta \mathbf{C} * (L)](\boldsymbol{\varepsilon}_t + \boldsymbol{\delta}), \tag{36}$$

when:

$$\mathbf{C}(1) = \boldsymbol{\beta}_{\perp} (\boldsymbol{\alpha}'_{\perp} \mathbf{\Gamma} \boldsymbol{\beta}_{\perp})^{-1} \boldsymbol{\alpha}'_{\perp} \quad \text{with} \quad \mathbf{\Gamma} = \sum_{i=1}^{s-1} \mathbf{\Gamma}_i - \mathbf{I}_n, \tag{37}$$

where $\boldsymbol{\alpha}_{\perp}$ and $\boldsymbol{\beta}_{\perp}$ are the orthogonal complements of $\boldsymbol{\alpha}$ and $\boldsymbol{\beta}$ respectively, so that:

$$\boldsymbol{\beta}' \mathbf{C}(1) = \mathbf{0} \quad \text{and} \quad \mathbf{C}(1)\boldsymbol{\alpha} = \mathbf{0}. \tag{38}$$

The necessary and sufficient condition for $\mathbf{x}_t$ not to be I(2) is $rank(\boldsymbol{\alpha}'_{\perp} \mathbf{\Gamma} \boldsymbol{\beta}_{\perp}) = n - r$. We assume this holds.

There are two potential sources for Granger causality in (35). First, if off-diagonal elements of any $\mathbf{\Gamma}_i$ are non-zero, then lagged differences of some variables empirically Granger cause other differences. Secondly, from (35) and $rank(\boldsymbol{\alpha}) = r$, when any columns of $\boldsymbol{\beta}$ have more than one nonzero element, some lagged levels empirically Granger cause others. Although both of these operate through I(0) links, their consequences for estimation and inference are not necessarily the same as we next discuss.

7.1 Granger Causality in a Cointegrated System

To focus on the central theme of the role of EGNC, we consider a simple bivariate model for the I(1) vector $\mathbf{x}_t = (y_t : z_t)'$ from Hendry (1995b):

$$y_t = \beta z_t + \epsilon_{1,t}$$
$$\Delta z_t = \lambda \Delta y_{t-1} + \rho(y_{t-1} - \beta z_{t-1}) + \epsilon_{2,t} \tag{39}$$

where $\epsilon_t = (\epsilon_{1,t} : \epsilon_{2,t})' \sim \mathsf{IN}_2[\mathbf{0}, \boldsymbol{\Sigma}]$ (error variances are normalized at unity for simplicity, and γ denotes the covariance of $\epsilon_{1,t}$ with $\epsilon_{2,t}$). The parameter of interest is β, which determines the cointegration of y with z, and hence that z Granger causes y. The two other possible sources of Granger causality are $\lambda \neq 0$ for feedbacks of Δy onto Δz, and $\rho \neq 0$, for levels feedbacks. The latter automatically also determines a failure of weak exogeneity of z_t for β, as that parameter of interest then enters the marginal distribution for z_t; the former does so when $\gamma\lambda \neq 0$.

Letting $\mathcal{I}_{t-1}$ denote available information, the conditional expectation of y_t given $(z_t, \mathcal{I}_{t-1})$ is:

$$\mathsf{E}[y_t \mid z_t, \mathcal{I}_{t-1}] = \beta z_t + \gamma \Delta z_t - \gamma\rho(y_{t-1} - \beta z_{t-1}) - \gamma\lambda \Delta y_{t-1}. \tag{40}$$

When $\gamma = 0$, (40) coincides with the first equation of (39), but inference can be distorted if $\rho \neq 0$, whereas when weak exogeneity holds ($\rho = \gamma\lambda = 0$), no serious difficulties arise from Granger causality due to $\lambda \neq 0$. When $\gamma \neq 0$, the first equation of (39) suffers from "simultaneity bias" (z_t and $\epsilon_{1,t}$ are correlated), but when there is no Granger causality from y to z (i.e., $\rho = 0$) or Δy to Δz ($\lambda = 0$), the conditional expectation:

$$\mathsf{E}[y_t \mid z_t, \mathcal{I}_{t-1}] = \beta z_t + \gamma \Delta z_t, \tag{41}$$

remains valid, and OLS applied to (41) is superconsistent and asymptotically median unbiased for β. We now contrast the impact of these two aspects of Granger causality on the limiting distribution of the OLS estimator of β in the first equation of (39).

7.2 Limiting Distributions

First consider the case in which Δy is EGNC for Δz ($\lambda = 0$), but $\gamma \neq 0$ and $\rho \neq 0$. From the results in Phillips (1986, 1987), the limiting distribution of $T(\hat{\beta} - \beta)$ using OLS is:

$$\left[\int_0^1 B_2(r)^2\,\mathrm{d}r\right]^{-1}$$

$$\times\left[\left[\frac{(1-\gamma^2)^{\frac{1}{2}}}{\omega_{22}}\right]\int_0^1 B_2(r)\mathrm{d}B_1(r)+\left[\frac{(\gamma+\rho)}{\omega_{22}}\right]\int_0^1 B_2(r)\mathrm{d}B_2(r)+\frac{\gamma}{\omega_{22}}\right], \quad (42)$$

where $\omega_{22}=1+2\gamma\rho+\rho^2$, and $B_1(r)$ and $B_2(r)$ are independent standardized Wiener processes, such that:

$$DF_\alpha = \left[\int_0^1 B_2(r)^2\,\mathrm{d}r\right]^{-1}\int_0^1 B_2(r)\mathrm{d}B_2(r) = \left[\int_0^1 B_2(r)^2\,\mathrm{d}r\right]^{-1}\tfrac{1}{2}(\chi^2(1)-1) \quad (43)$$

is the Dickey and Fuller (1979, 1981) $T(\hat\alpha-1)$ distribution for testing for a unit root in the univariate marginal process for $\{z_t\}$, and conditional on $\int_0^1 B_2(r)$:

$$\left[\int_0^1 B_2(r)^2\,\mathrm{d}r\right]^{-1}\int_0^1 B_2(r)\mathrm{d}B_1(r) \sim \mathsf{N}\left[0,\left[\int_0^1 B_2(r)^2\,\mathrm{d}r\right]^{-1}\right].$$

Thus, (42) is a mixture of the normal and Dickey–Fuller distributions. For sufficiently large $\rho>0$, the last term will impart a negative shift to the distribution (conversely for negative ρ). The terms in $\omega_{22}^{-1}[\frac{1}{2}(\gamma+\rho)(\chi^2(1)-1)+\gamma]$ partially offset each other, so having both a failure of weak exogeneity and simultaneity could induce less distortion than either alone. Nevertheless, the limiting distribution is non-central when $\rho\neq0$, whereas it is central for $\rho=\gamma=0$ (OLS in (41) is central for $\gamma\neq0$). Hence, even when Δy is EGNC for Δz the presence or absence of GC from y to z has a major effect on the limiting distribution of the OLS estimator of β.

Turning to the case in which Δy does EGC Δz ($\lambda\neq0$), the limiting distribution of $T(\hat\beta-\beta)$ is:

$$(1-\beta\lambda)\left[\int_0^1 B_2(r)^2\,\mathrm{d}r\right]^{-1}$$

$$\times\left[(1-\gamma^2)^{\frac{1}{2}}\int_0^1 B_2(r)\mathrm{d}B_1(r)+\gamma\left(\int_0^1 B_2(r)\mathrm{d}B_2(r)+(1-\beta\lambda)\right)\right]. \quad (44)$$

Thus, for $\gamma=0$, despite the fact that y Granger causes z, since $B_1(r)$ and $B_2(r)$ are independent Wiener processes, the distribution of the OLS estimator is a mixture of normals, centered on zero. The violation of strong exogeneity, when weak exogeneity is maintained, does not seriously affect inference in this unit-root model, and conditional on $B_2(r)$:

$$T(\hat\beta-\beta) \sim \mathsf{N}\left[0,(1-\beta\lambda)^2\left[\int_0^1 B_2(r)^2\,\mathrm{d}r\right]^{-1}\right]. \quad (45)$$

However, when $\lambda\gamma\neq0$, weak exogeneity is violated and the limiting distribution of $T(\widehat{\beta} - \beta)$ is a mixture of a conditionally-normal and a Dickey–Fuller distribution in (44), with a non-centrality when $\gamma \neq 0$, although the last two terms could partially offset each other.

7.3 Inference

Consider testing hypotheses of the form $H_0 : \beta = \beta^*$, using the error-variance estimator:

$$\widehat{\sigma}_1^2 = T^{-1} \sum_{t=1}^{T} (y_t - \widehat{\beta} z_t)^2. \tag{46}$$

First, when $\lambda = 0$, the t-test of $H_0 : \beta = \beta^*$ based on $t_{\beta=\beta^*} = (\widehat{\beta} - \beta^*)/SE[\widehat{\beta}]$ is well behaved under the null provided $\rho = \gamma = 0$:

$$t_{\beta=\beta^*} = \left(T^{-2} \sum_{t=1}^{T} z_t^2 \right)^{-\frac{1}{2}} \left(\frac{T(\widehat{\beta} - \beta^*)}{\widehat{\sigma}_1} \right) \Rightarrow N[0,1]. \tag{47}$$

Such tests have the correct size asymptotically. However, if either $\gamma \neq 0$, or $\rho \neq 0$, the bias in the limiting distribution of $T(\widehat{\beta} - \beta)$ affects inference even asymptotically. For example, when $\lambda = \gamma = 0$ but $\rho \neq 0$:

$$t_{\beta=\beta^*} \Rightarrow (1 + \rho^2)^{-1}(N[0,1] + \rho DF_t), \tag{48}$$

where DF_t is the Dickey–Fuller "t" distribution:

$$DF_t = \left(\int_0^1 B_2(r)^2 \, dr \right)^{-\frac{1}{2}} \int_0^1 B_2(r) dB_2(r), \tag{49}$$

so the distribution in (48) is non-normal, and conventional hypothesis tests will not have the correct size. Even though (41) coincides with the first equation of (39) in this case, Monte Carlo evidence shows that substantial over rejection can occur when (47) is incorrectly assumed to hold (see Hendry, 1995b).

When $\lambda \neq 0$ but $\rho = \gamma = 0$ from (45), t-tests of H_0 will be asymptotically $N[0, 1]$ so no distortion of inference arises from Granger causality alone, albeit that non-centrality reappears when $\gamma \neq 0$ as well, inducing a violation of weak exogeneity.

8 Encompassing

The analysis in Govaerts, Hendry, and Richard (1994) reveals the important role of Granger causality in the construction of various encompassing statistics. Here we show how the need to model the process for the conditioning variable can result in invalid inference if incorrectly accomplished. First, a model M_1

encompasses a rival model M_2 if M_1 can explain the results obtained by M_2 (see Hendry and Richard, 1989). A Wald encompassing test (WET) checks if a statistic of interest to M_2 coincides with an estimator of its predicted value under M_1 (see Mizon and Richard, 1986).

For parametric dynamic models M_1 and M_2 of a common variable y_t, when there are no exogenous variables, let $\alpha \in \mathcal{A} \subseteq \mathbb{R}^{n_1}$ and $\delta \in \mathcal{D} \subseteq \mathbb{R}^{n_2}$ be their parameters, with estimators $\widehat{\alpha}_T$ and $\widehat{\delta}_T$. Let $\widehat{M}_1 = (M_1, \widehat{\alpha}_T)$ and $\widehat{M}_2 = (M_2, \widehat{\delta}_T)$ denote the estimated models. Then in stationary processes, $\widehat{M}_1$ asymptotically encompasses $\widehat{M}_2$ (denoted by $\widehat{M}_1 \mathcal{E} \widehat{M}_2$) if and only if there exists a function λ such that:

$$\widehat{\delta}_T = \lambda(\widehat{\alpha}_T) + o_p\left(T^{-\frac{1}{2}}\right),$$

M_1 almost surely. Wald encompassing tests (WETs), introduced by Mizon and Richard (1986), use pseudo-true values to examine whether or not the encompassing difference $\sqrt{T}(\widehat{\delta}_T - \lambda(\widehat{\alpha}_T))$ is significant on M_1.

When the competing models include weakly-exogenous variables, the sampling distribution of $\widehat{\delta}_T$ on M_1 depends on the properties of the exogenous process. Let M_c denote a sequential model for the weakly exogenous variables z_t, with density function $f_z(z_t|X_{t-1}, \tau)$, where $x'_t = (y_t : z'_t)$ and $\tau \in \mathcal{T}$. Letting $\widehat{M}_i^c = (\widehat{M}_i, \widehat{M}_c)$ for $i = 1, 2$, then $\widehat{M}_1$ encompasses $\widehat{M}_2$ given $\widehat{M}_c$ if and only if $\widehat{M}_1^c \mathcal{E} \widehat{M}_2^c$ relative to $\widehat{\delta}_T$. The analysis of the choice of regressor problem in Mizon and Richard (1986) only considered cases where z_t was strongly exogenous, so that y_t did not Granger cause z_t.

Let $\widetilde{\alpha}$ denote a consistent estimator of α under M_1 and $\widetilde{\phi}$ a statistic of interest in M_2. The pseudo-true value ϕ_α of $\widetilde{\phi}$ under M_1 is:

$$\phi_\alpha = \underset{M_1 : T \to \infty}{\text{plim}} \ \widetilde{\phi}.$$

Let $\widetilde{\Delta}_\phi = \widetilde{\phi} - \phi_{\widetilde{\alpha}}$ denote the estimated encompassing difference relative to $\widetilde{\phi}$, of dimension n_3. The limiting distribution of $\sqrt{T}\widetilde{\Delta}_\phi$ on M_1 is:

$$\sqrt{T}\,\widetilde{\Delta}_\phi \ \underset{\widetilde{M}_1}{\sim} \ N_{n_3}[\mathbf{0}, \mathbf{V}_\alpha],$$

where $\widetilde{M}_1$ denotes "is asymptotically distributed on M_1 as." Using the estimated variance $\widehat{\mathbf{V}}_\alpha$, a WET statistic with respect to $\widetilde{\phi}$ is given by:

$$\eta_W(\widetilde{\phi}) = T\widetilde{\Delta}'_\phi \ \widehat{\mathbf{V}}_\alpha^+ \widetilde{\Delta}_\phi \ \underset{\widetilde{M}_1}{\sim} \ \chi^2(p),$$

where $p \leq n_3$ is the rank of $\widehat{\mathbf{V}}_\alpha$, and the superscript $^+$ denotes the Moore–Penrose inverse. Once Granger causality from y_t to z_t is allowed, care is required in formulating the completing model as the following example illustrates.

Consider the two rival models:

$$M_1 : y_t = \beta z_t + \epsilon_{1,t}$$
$$M_2 : y_t = \gamma y_{t-1} + \epsilon_{2,t},$$

where both modelers claim that $\epsilon_{i,t} \sim \text{IN}[0, \sigma_i^2]$. To construct the Wald encompassing test of M_1 against M_2, we first postulate an auxiliary model that is appropriate, which Govaerts et $al.$ (1994) call the realizable projection model, and prove is the minimal completing model:

$$\text{M}_c^m : z_t = \delta y_{t-1} + u_t \quad \text{where} \quad u_t \sim \text{IN}[0, \omega^2]. \tag{50}$$

If we switch the rival models:

$$\text{M}_1^* : y_t = \beta y_{t-1} + \epsilon_{1,t}$$
$$\text{M}_2^* : y_t = \gamma z_t + \epsilon_{2,t},$$

where the $\epsilon_{i,t}$ are as before, then the completing model remains M_c^m. Govaerts et $al.$ (1994) show that the WET has the same non-centrality as the F-statistic for testing for the reduction to M_1^* of the minimal nesting model for M_1^* and M_2^*.

However, the use of other completing models may generate WET statistics that lose efficiency. For example, consider:

$$\text{M}_c : z_t = u_t,$$

which ignores the possibility of Granger causality, and thereby treats the $\{z_t\}$ process as fixed in repeated samples relative to $\{y_t\}$. If the DGP is $(\text{M}_1, \text{M}_c^m)$, then the WET will tend to reject, even though M_1 is a valid model for y_t when an appropriate specification for $\{z_t\}$ is used. Such an outcome demonstrates the dangers of falsely imposing EGNC on completing models. Similar implications hold for Monte Carlo encompassing tests, where drawings given $\{z_t\}$ will not deliver the correct distribution when EGNC is violated.

9 Forecasting

As most economic policy analyses undertake conditional forecasting of the path of y_t both before and after proposed policy interventions, we consider forecasting y_t conditional on a set of policy variables z_t, as well as jointly with z_t. These analyses could be preceded by joint or conditional estimation, and may assume strong, or only weak, exogeneity of the policy variables for the parameters of the econometric system.

Forecasting y_t and z_t jointly from a system $f_x(x_t | X_{t-1}, \theta)$ (such as (34) in the I(0) case or (35) in the cointegrated I(1) case), will be efficient provided that the system is congruent and encompassing, and its parameters θ remain constant in the forecast period. If the $\{x_t\}$ process is interdependent, in that there is Granger causality amongst the variables, system forecasting will be more efficient than subsystem: in particular, when z Granger causes y, system forecasting of y_t will be more efficient than autoregressive.

However, when there is a policy intervention in the forecast period, θ need not remain constant. If the intervention is known and affects ϕ_2 only, this information can be used in generating the forecasts from the system. Alternatively, conditional forecasting of $\mathbf{y}_t$ given $\mathbf{z}_t$ is a common practice in such a setting, because modeling the past behavior of policy variables in $f_z(\cdot)$ is often difficult. Efficient forecasting of $\mathbf{y}_t$ conditional on $\mathbf{z}_t$ requires that:

(1) the conditional model $f_{y|z}(\mathbf{y}_t|\mathbf{z}_t, \mathbf{X}_{t-1}, \phi_1)$ is congruent and encompassing;
(2) ϕ_1 remains constant in the forecast period;
(3) the predicted values $\widehat{\mathbf{z}}_t$; of $\mathbf{z}_t$ (for $t > T$) are available; and:
(4) $\mathbf{y}$ does not Granger cause $\mathbf{z}$ in the DGP with a lag shorter than the forecast horizon.

These conditions ensure the equivalence of conditional forecasting to system forecasting, and efficiency relative to autoregressive forecasting of $\mathbf{y}_t$ when $\mathbf{z}$ Granger causes $\mathbf{y}$, which is the basis of the approach in Granger and Deutsch (1992). Although system estimation is efficient, conditional estimation is often used in such cases, and is appropriate when $\mathbf{z}_t$ is weakly exogenous for the parameters of interest $\boldsymbol{\mu}$. Hence $\mathbf{z}_t$ must be strongly exogenous for $\boldsymbol{\mu}$ if conditional estimation followed by conditional forecasting is to be valid.

When policy rules depend on $\mathbf{X}_{t-1}^1$, Granger non-causality from $\mathbf{y}$ to $\mathbf{z}$ will not be valid, and conditional forecasts may be misleading howsoever parameters are estimated (e.g., the rule depends on correcting deviations from long-run equilibria determined by the private sector: see Section 7). Such an outcome could occur if a fixed set of values is used for a policy variable within an econometric model, but feedback from $\mathbf{y}$ to $\mathbf{z}$ occurs over the forecast horizon when the policy is implemented. This suggests testing for both weak exogeneity and EGNC, as well as invariance, to sustain estimation conditional on policy variables, then forecasting jointly using the policy rule that will be implemented in reality (rather than conditionally on preassigned values for the policy variables). Thus, Granger causality is important in efficient forecasting of dependent variables, and its presence or absence is critical in policy analysis as we now discuss.

10 Policy Analysis

The objective of economic policy is taken to be shifting the mean of some or all the target variables $\mathbf{y}_t$ in the DGP $D_{x_t}(\mathbf{x}_t|\mathbf{X}_{t-1}, \boldsymbol{\zeta})$ to a desired value. This is to be achieved by changing the value of the instruments $\mathbf{z}_t$. The value of the policy instruments $\mathbf{z}_t$ can be changed according to a policy rule, or as a result of implementing a regime shift. In the former case, the parameter ζ_2 of the marginal distribution of $\mathbf{z}_t$—$D_{z_t}(\mathbf{z}_t|\mathbf{X}_{t-1}, \zeta_2)$—remains constant, whereas a regime shift arises when ζ_2 changes. The partial response matrix $(\partial \mathbf{y}_t/\partial \mathbf{z}_t')_{|\zeta_1}$ in the DGP would be invaluable for assessing what changes in $\mathbf{z}$ are required to achieve the desired values for $\mathbf{y}$, but as the DGP is unknown, this assessment is typically undertaken using an econometric model. Hendry and Mizon (1998a) discuss these issues for policy analysis using closed econometric models, and Hendry and Mizon (1998b) for open models conditioned on $\mathbf{z}_t$.

Whether the policy being considered is implemented via a policy rule or constitutes a regime shift, the analysis of it using an econometric model will only be useful if linkages exist between the targets and the instruments. Consequently, a well-specified model of policy links is needed (see e.g., Granger and Deutsch, 1992). Although contemporaneous causality between $\mathbf{y}_t$ and $\mathbf{z}_t$ can be important, policy responses are often delayed so that Granger causality is important for the feasibility of economic policy and EGC critical for empirical analysis of policy. We now indicate the role of EGNC in economic policy analysis.

Apply the partition $\mathbf{x}_t = (\mathbf{y}_t' : \mathbf{z}_t')'$, with the corresponding partition of the parameters, to (35), so the VEqCM with one lag becomes:

$$\begin{pmatrix} \Delta \mathbf{y}_t \\ \Delta \mathbf{z}_t \end{pmatrix} = \begin{pmatrix} \boldsymbol{\alpha}_{11} & \boldsymbol{\alpha}_{12} \\ \boldsymbol{\alpha}_{21} & \boldsymbol{\alpha}_{22} \end{pmatrix} \begin{pmatrix} \boldsymbol{\beta}_{11}' & \boldsymbol{\beta}_{12}' \\ \boldsymbol{\beta}_{21}' & \boldsymbol{\beta}_{22}' \end{pmatrix} \begin{pmatrix} \mathbf{y}_{t-1} \\ \mathbf{z}_{t-1} \end{pmatrix} + \begin{pmatrix} \boldsymbol{\delta}_1 \\ \boldsymbol{\delta}_2 \end{pmatrix} + \begin{pmatrix} \boldsymbol{\Gamma}_{11} & \boldsymbol{\Gamma}_{12} \\ \boldsymbol{\Gamma}_{21} & \boldsymbol{\Gamma}_{22} \end{pmatrix} \begin{pmatrix} \Delta \mathbf{y}_{t-1} \\ \Delta \mathbf{z}_{t-1} \end{pmatrix} + \begin{pmatrix} \boldsymbol{\epsilon}_{1,t} \\ \boldsymbol{\epsilon}_{2,t} \end{pmatrix}. \quad (51)$$

In (51), the dimensions of $\boldsymbol{\beta}_{11}$ and $\boldsymbol{\beta}_{12}$ are $n_1 \times r_1$ and $n_1 \times r_2$ respectively, and $\boldsymbol{\beta}_{21}$ and $\boldsymbol{\beta}_{22}$ are $n_2 \times r_1$ and $n_2 \times r_2$ respectively, where $r_1 + r_2 = r$: $\boldsymbol{\alpha}$ is partitioned conformably. With this notation, we give conditions for empirical Granger non-causality between $\mathbf{y}_t$ and $\mathbf{z}_t$.

Lemma 1. *There will be EGNC from the target variables* $\mathbf{y}_t$ *to the instruments* $\mathbf{z}_t$ *if and only if* $\boldsymbol{\Gamma}_{21} = \mathbf{0}$ *and* $(\boldsymbol{\alpha}_{21}\boldsymbol{\beta}_{11}' + \boldsymbol{\alpha}_{22}\boldsymbol{\beta}_{21}') = \mathbf{0}$.

These conditions are unlikely to be satisfied in practice since the values of target variables resulting from past policy usually influence the choice of instrument values: for example, recent past inflation and excess demand are likely to influence the tightness of monetary and fiscal policy.

Of more importance for economic policy is that changes to the instruments $\mathbf{z}_t$ affect the targets $\mathbf{y}_t$.

Lemma 2. *There will be EGNC from the policy instruments* $\mathbf{z}_t$ *to the targets* $\mathbf{y}_t$ *if and only if* $\boldsymbol{\Gamma}_{12} = \mathbf{0}$ *and* $(\boldsymbol{\alpha}_{11}\boldsymbol{\beta}_{12}' + \boldsymbol{\alpha}_{12}\boldsymbol{\beta}_{22}') = \mathbf{0}$.

$\boldsymbol{\Gamma}_{12} \neq \mathbf{0}$ ensures a short-run impact, and $(\boldsymbol{\alpha}_{11}\boldsymbol{\beta}_{12}' + \boldsymbol{\alpha}_{12}\boldsymbol{\beta}_{22}') \neq \mathbf{0}$ a permanent effect: tests of such conditions are considered by Mosconi and Giannini (1992) and Toda and Phillips (1993). Without causality in the DGP between the instruments and targets, policy is unlikely to be effective, although if empirical links indirectly reflect causation—perhaps intermediated by an omitted variable that policy influences and which influences targets—then policy will affect targets despite the absence of direct causation. However, the outcome will be as anticipated only if all the parameters involved have the appropriate signs and magnitudes, and remain constant. These conditions for Granger (non-)

causality, relevant for assessing the feasibility of economic policy, are features of the DGP of $\mathbf{y}_t$ and $\mathbf{z}_t$. Nevertheless, EGNC is important in assessing the effectiveness of economic policy analysis using econometric models.

11 Dynamic Simulation

Here we note the critique in Hendry and Richard (1982) concerning in-sample dynamic simulation as a model evaluation, or selection, technique, when the non-modeled variables are Granger caused by the modeled. The analytics follow directly from Section 4. There, "full-sample" conditioning required EGNC of the modeled variables for the non-modeled, so that:

$$\mathsf{f}_X(\mathbf{X}_T^1 \mid \mathbf{X}_0, \boldsymbol{\theta}) = \mathsf{f}_{Y|Z}(\mathbf{Y}_T^1 \mid \mathbf{Z}_T^1, \mathbf{X}_0, \boldsymbol{\phi}_1)\mathsf{f}_Z(\mathbf{Z}_T^1 \mid \mathbf{X}_0, \boldsymbol{\phi}_2). \tag{52}$$

Otherwise, $\mathsf{f}_{Y|Z}(\mathbf{Y}_T^1|\mathbf{Z}_T^1, \mathbf{X}_0, \boldsymbol{\phi}_1)$ cannot be analyzed without loss of information. In-sample dynamic simulation necessitates knowledge of $\mathbf{Z}_T^1$, so will be potentially misleading when (52) is invalid. In many contexts this is obvious; consider analyzing price inflation conditional on the exchange rate and wage inflation— the answers delivered about how well the model tracks the data tell us little about its validity, or adequacy, or about economic policy. Further critiques and results are provided in Chong and Hendry (1986) and Pagan (1989).

12 Impulse Response Analysis

Another commonly applied tool in the analysis of macroeconomic policy is impulse response analysis (see e.g., Lütkepohl, 1991; Runkle, 1987; Sims, 1980). We now show that Granger causality, and more particularly EGNC, are major determinants of the forms that such responses take.

Reconsider the model in equations (34) and (35) of Section 7. The solution of (36) for $\mathbf{x}_t$ is:

$$\mathbf{x}_t = \mathbf{K}_{\beta\perp}\mathbf{x}_0 + \mathbf{C}(1)\sum_{i=1}^{t}(\boldsymbol{\varepsilon}_i + \boldsymbol{\delta}) + \mathbf{C}^*(L)(\boldsymbol{\varepsilon}_t + \boldsymbol{\delta}) \tag{53}$$

with $\mathbf{K}_{\beta\perp} = \boldsymbol{\beta}_\perp(\boldsymbol{\beta}'_\perp\boldsymbol{\beta}_\perp)^{-1}\boldsymbol{\beta}'_\perp$. Note that $\mathbf{K}_{\beta\perp} = \mathbf{0}$ and $\mathbf{C}(1) = \mathbf{0}$ when $r = n$ so that $\mathbf{x}_t \sim \mathsf{I}(0)$. Letting $\mathsf{E}[\Delta\mathbf{x}_t] = \boldsymbol{\gamma}$ such that $\boldsymbol{\beta}'\boldsymbol{\gamma} = \mathbf{0}$, then $\mathsf{E}[\boldsymbol{\beta}'\mathbf{x}_t] = \boldsymbol{\psi}$ allows the re-definition of the vector of constants $\boldsymbol{\delta} = -\boldsymbol{\Gamma}\boldsymbol{\gamma} - \boldsymbol{\alpha}\boldsymbol{\psi}$, such that (35) can be re-written in terms of variables with zero means as:

$$(\Delta\mathbf{x}_t - \boldsymbol{\gamma}) = \sum_{i=1}^{s-1}\boldsymbol{\Gamma}_i(\Delta\mathbf{x}_{t-1} - \boldsymbol{\gamma}) + \boldsymbol{\alpha}(\boldsymbol{\beta}'\mathbf{x}_{t-1} - \boldsymbol{\psi}) + \boldsymbol{\varepsilon}_t. \tag{54}$$

This in turn yields alternative expressions for (36) and (53) respectively:

$$\Delta \mathbf{x}_t = \mathbf{C}(1)(\boldsymbol{\varepsilon}_t - \boldsymbol{\Gamma}\boldsymbol{\gamma}) + \mathbf{C}*(L)\Delta(\boldsymbol{\varepsilon}_t - \boldsymbol{\Gamma}\boldsymbol{\gamma} - \boldsymbol{\alpha}\boldsymbol{\psi}) \tag{55}$$

as $\mathbf{C}(1)\boldsymbol{\alpha} = \mathbf{0}$, and:

$$\mathbf{x}_t = \mathbf{K}_{\beta\perp}\mathbf{x}_0 + \mathbf{C}(1)\sum_{i=1}^{t}(\boldsymbol{\varepsilon}_i - \boldsymbol{\Gamma}\boldsymbol{\gamma}) + \mathbf{C}*(L)(\boldsymbol{\varepsilon}_t - \boldsymbol{\Gamma}\boldsymbol{\gamma}) - \mathbf{C}*(1)\boldsymbol{\alpha}\boldsymbol{\psi} \tag{56}$$

Given these moving-average representations for $\Delta\mathbf{x}_t$ and $\mathbf{x}_t$, it is now possible to derive the h-period unit impulse response matrices:

$$\frac{\partial \Delta\mathbf{x}_{t+h}}{\partial \boldsymbol{\varepsilon}_t'} = \mathbf{C}_h^* - \mathbf{C}_{h+1}^* \quad \forall h > 0 \quad \text{and} \quad \frac{\partial \Delta\mathbf{x}_t}{\partial \boldsymbol{\varepsilon}_t'} = \mathbf{C}(1) + \mathbf{C}_0^* = \mathbf{I}_n, \tag{57}$$

since $\mathbf{C}(L) = \mathbf{C}(1) + \mathbf{C}^*(L)\Delta$ so that $\mathbf{C}(0) = \mathbf{C}(1) + \mathbf{C}_0^* = \mathbf{I}_n$ for identification, and:

$$\frac{\partial \mathbf{x}_{t+h}}{\partial \boldsymbol{\varepsilon}_t'} = \mathbf{C}(1) + \mathbf{C}_h^* \quad \forall h \geq 0. \tag{58}$$

Noting that $\det \mathbf{C}^*(z) = \mathbf{0}$ has all its roots outside the unit circle:

$$\frac{\partial \Delta\mathbf{x}_{t+h}}{\partial \boldsymbol{\varepsilon}_t'} \to \mathbf{0} \quad \text{and} \quad \frac{\partial \mathbf{x}_{t+h}}{\partial \boldsymbol{\varepsilon}_t'} \to \mathbf{C}(1) \quad \text{as} \quad h \to \infty.$$

This follows since $\mathbf{x}_t \sim \mathrm{I}(1)$ so that there is persistence in the $\mathbf{x}_t$ process, but since $\mathbf{C}(1)$ has rank $(n-r)$ there is an attribution problem: the attribution of this persistence to $(n-r)$ particular elements of $\mathbf{x}_t$ or $(n-r)$ linear combinations of them is arbitrary—but see the discussion below of a special case of EGNC that solves this problem. However, there are r linear combinations of $\mathbf{x}_t$ that do not exhibit persistence, the cointegrated combinations $\boldsymbol{\beta}'\mathbf{x}_t$ for which the h-period impulse responses are:

$$\frac{\partial \boldsymbol{\beta}'\mathbf{x}_{t+h}}{\partial \boldsymbol{\varepsilon}_t'} = \boldsymbol{\beta}'(\mathbf{C}(1) + \mathbf{C}_h^*) = \boldsymbol{\beta}'\mathbf{C}_h^* \quad \forall h \geq 0, \tag{59}$$

with

$$\frac{\partial \boldsymbol{\beta}'\mathbf{x}_{t+h}}{\partial \boldsymbol{\varepsilon}_t'} \to 0 \quad \text{as} \quad h \to \infty.$$

The commonly used standard-error and orthogonalized impulses yield the following response matrices:

$$\frac{\partial \Delta\mathbf{x}_{t+h}}{\partial \boldsymbol{\varepsilon}_t^{+'}} = (\mathbf{C}_h^* - \mathbf{C}_{h+1}^*)\mathbf{Q} \quad \forall h > 0 \quad \text{and} \quad \frac{\partial \Delta\mathbf{x}_t}{\partial \boldsymbol{\varepsilon}_t^{+'}} = \mathbf{Q} \tag{60}$$

and:

$$\frac{\partial \mathbf{x}_{t+h}}{\partial \boldsymbol{\varepsilon}_t^{+'}} = (\mathbf{C}(1) + \mathbf{C}_h^*)\mathbf{Q} \quad \forall h \geq 0, \tag{61}$$

with $\mathbf{Q} = diag(\sqrt{\sigma_{11}}, \sqrt{\sigma_{22}}, ..., \sqrt{\sigma_{nn}})$ for the standard error impulses, and $\mathbf{Q} = (\mathbf{P}')^{-1}$ for the orthogonalized impulses with $\mathbf{\Sigma}^{-1} = \mathbf{PP}'$, where $\varepsilon_t^+ = \mathbf{Q}'\varepsilon_t$.

To see the role of EGNC in determining the properties of responses in co-integrated systems, consider the partition of $\mathbf{x}_t'$ into $(\mathbf{y}_t', \mathbf{z}_t')$ with corresponding partitions of (34):

$$\begin{pmatrix} \Delta\mathbf{y}_t \\ \Delta\mathbf{z}_t \end{pmatrix} = \begin{pmatrix} \boldsymbol{\alpha}_1 \\ \boldsymbol{\alpha}_2 \end{pmatrix} \begin{pmatrix} \boldsymbol{\beta}_1' & \boldsymbol{\beta}_2' \end{pmatrix} \begin{pmatrix} \mathbf{y}_{t-1} \\ \mathbf{z}_{t-1} \end{pmatrix} + \sum_{i=1}^{s-1} \begin{pmatrix} \boldsymbol{\Gamma}_{11,i} & \boldsymbol{\Gamma}_{12,i} \\ \boldsymbol{\Gamma}_{21,i} & \boldsymbol{\Gamma}_{22,i} \end{pmatrix} \begin{pmatrix} \Delta\mathbf{y}_{t-1} \\ \Delta\mathbf{z}_{t-1} \end{pmatrix} + \begin{pmatrix} \boldsymbol{\epsilon}_{1,t} \\ \boldsymbol{\epsilon}_{2,t} \end{pmatrix}. \tag{62}$$

The conditions $\boldsymbol{\alpha}_2 = \mathbf{0}$ and $\boldsymbol{\Gamma}_{21,i} = \mathbf{0}\ \forall i$ ensure that there is no Granger causality from $\mathbf{y}$ to $\mathbf{z}$. When all elements of $\mathbf{x}_t$ are $\mathrm{I}(1)$, so that every column of $\boldsymbol{\beta}$ involves more than one variable, there has to be Granger causality in the system: $rank(\boldsymbol{\alpha}) = r$ implies that the minimum number of GC relations is r, and the assumption that all elements of $\mathbf{x}_t$ are $\mathrm{I}(1)$ means that the maximum number is $(n-1)$. When $\boldsymbol{\alpha}_2 = \mathbf{0}$ (so $\mathbf{z}_t$ is weakly exogenous for $\boldsymbol{\beta}$), the rank condition on $\boldsymbol{\alpha}$ also implies that the $n_1 \times r$ matrix $\boldsymbol{\alpha}_1$ must have $n_1 \geq r$, and that it has the form $\boldsymbol{\alpha}_1' = (\boldsymbol{\alpha}_r' : \boldsymbol{\alpha}_{\bar{r}}')$ with the $r \times r$ matrix $\boldsymbol{\alpha}_r$ non-singular without loss of generality. Thus:

$$\boldsymbol{\alpha}_\perp = \left[\begin{pmatrix} \mathbf{0} \\ \mathbf{I}_{n-r} \end{pmatrix} - \begin{pmatrix} \mathbf{I}_r \\ \mathbf{0} \end{pmatrix} (\boldsymbol{\alpha}_r)^{-1} \boldsymbol{\alpha}_{\bar{r}}' \right].$$

Hence, when $\boldsymbol{\alpha}_2 = \mathbf{0}$ and $n_1 = r$ (i.e, $\boldsymbol{\alpha}_\perp' = (\mathbf{0} : \mathbf{I}_{n-r})$), the "common trends" are $\boldsymbol{\alpha}_\perp' \sum_{i=1}^t \boldsymbol{\epsilon}_i = \sum_{i=1}^t \boldsymbol{\epsilon}_{2,i}$, so the $\mathbf{z}_t$ contain the "common trends," and this special case of EGNC (in which only $\boldsymbol{\alpha}_2 = \mathbf{0}$) provides a solution to the attribution problem. More generally, even when there is EGNC from $\mathbf{y}$ to $\mathbf{z}$ via $\boldsymbol{\alpha}_2 \neq \mathbf{0}$, the form of $\boldsymbol{\alpha}_\perp$ entails that the "common trends" will be linear combinations of $\sum_{i=1}^t \boldsymbol{\epsilon}_{1i}$ and $\sum_{i=1}^t \boldsymbol{\epsilon}_{2,i}$.

To illustrate the role of EGNC in impulse response analysis, we reconsider the bivariate example in Section 7.1. As noted in the Appendix of Hendry (1995b), (39) has a VARMA(1, 2) representation in $\Delta\mathbf{x}_t$:

$$\Delta\mathbf{x}_t = \boldsymbol{\Upsilon}\Delta\mathbf{x}_{t-1} + \boldsymbol{\Xi}_0\boldsymbol{\epsilon}_t + \boldsymbol{\Xi}_1\boldsymbol{\epsilon}_{t-1} + \boldsymbol{\Xi}_2\boldsymbol{\epsilon}_{t-2}, \tag{63}$$

with $\boldsymbol{\Upsilon} = \beta\lambda\mathbf{I}_2$ and:

$$\boldsymbol{\Xi}_0 = \begin{pmatrix} 1 & \beta \\ 0 & 1 \end{pmatrix}, \ \boldsymbol{\Xi}_1 = \begin{pmatrix} \beta\lambda - 1 & 0 \\ \lambda + \rho & 0 \end{pmatrix}, \ \text{and } \boldsymbol{\Xi}_2 = \begin{pmatrix} 0 & 0 \\ -\lambda & 0 \end{pmatrix}. \tag{64}$$

Provided $|\beta\lambda| < 1$ and $\beta\lambda \neq 0$ the Wold representation for $\Delta\mathbf{x}_t$ is:

$$\Delta\mathbf{x}_t = \sum_{i=0}^{\infty} \boldsymbol{\Upsilon}^i [\boldsymbol{\Xi}_0\boldsymbol{\epsilon}_{t-i} + \boldsymbol{\Xi}_1\boldsymbol{\epsilon}_{t-1-i} + \boldsymbol{\Xi}_2\boldsymbol{\epsilon}_{t-2-i}]. \tag{65}$$

Cases in which $\beta\lambda = 0$ are considered below. From (65) the unit impulse responses for $\Delta\mathbf{x}_t$ are:

$$
\boxed{
\begin{aligned}
\frac{\partial \Delta \mathbf{x}_{t+h}}{\partial \boldsymbol{\epsilon}_t'} &= \boldsymbol{\Xi}_0 & h &= 0 \\
&= \boldsymbol{\Upsilon} \boldsymbol{\Xi}_0 + \boldsymbol{\Xi}_1 & h &= 1 \\
&= \boldsymbol{\Upsilon}^{h-2}[\boldsymbol{\Upsilon}^2 \boldsymbol{\Xi}_0 + \boldsymbol{\Upsilon} \boldsymbol{\Xi}_1 + \boldsymbol{\Xi}_2] & h &\geq 2
\end{aligned}
}
$$

and so $(\partial \Delta \mathbf{x}_{t+h}/\partial \boldsymbol{\epsilon}_t') \to \mathbf{0}$ as $h \to \infty$ since $|\beta \lambda| < 1$. Using (56) yields:

$$
\mathbf{x}_t = \mathbf{K}_{\beta \perp} \mathbf{x}_0 + \mathbf{C}(1) \sum_{i=1}^{t} \boldsymbol{\varepsilon}_i + \mathbf{C}^*(L) \boldsymbol{\varepsilon}_t,
$$

with:

$$
\mathbf{K}_{\beta \perp} = \frac{1}{1+\beta^2}\begin{pmatrix} \beta^2 & \beta \\ \beta & 1 \end{pmatrix} \quad \text{and} \quad \mathbf{C}(1) = \frac{1}{1-\beta \lambda}\begin{pmatrix} \beta \rho & \beta \\ \rho & 1 \end{pmatrix},
$$

so $\mathbf{C}(1)$ is singular as required for a cointegrated system, and as both $\mathbf{K}_{\beta \perp}$ and $\mathbf{C}(1)$ are annihilated when pre-multiplied by the cointegrating vector $\boldsymbol{\beta}' = (1, -\beta)$, then $\boldsymbol{\beta}' \mathbf{x}_t = \mathbf{C}^*(L) \boldsymbol{\epsilon}_t \sim \mathsf{I}(0)$. Letting:

$$
\mathbf{C}^*(L) = \mathbf{C}_0^* + \mathbf{C}_1^* \cdots \mathbf{C}_h^* + \cdots \quad \text{where} \quad \mathbf{C}_i^* = \begin{pmatrix} C_{11,i}^* & C_{12,i}^* \\ C_{21,i}^* & C_{22,i}^* \end{pmatrix},
$$

for $i = 0, 1, 2, \ldots$, then $\partial \mathbf{x}_{t+h}/\partial \boldsymbol{\epsilon}_t'$ can be written as:

$$
\begin{pmatrix} \dfrac{\partial y_{t+h}}{\partial \epsilon_{1,t}} & \dfrac{\partial y_{t+h}}{\partial \epsilon_{2,t}} \\ \dfrac{\partial z_{t+h}}{\partial \epsilon_{1,t}} & \dfrac{\partial z_{t+h}}{\partial \epsilon_{2,t}} \end{pmatrix} = \mathbf{C}_h^* + \frac{1}{1-\beta \lambda}\begin{pmatrix} \beta \rho & \beta \\ \rho & 1 \end{pmatrix}, \tag{66}
$$

so that, as expected, $\partial \mathbf{x}_{t+h}/\partial \boldsymbol{\epsilon}_t' \to \mathbf{C}(1)$ as $h \to \infty$. We now consider the effect on the unit impulse responses $(\partial \Delta \mathbf{x}_{t+h}/\partial \boldsymbol{\epsilon}_t')$ and $(\partial \mathbf{x}_{t+h}/\partial \boldsymbol{\epsilon}_t')$ of different Granger causality conditions.

- y is EGNC for z ($\rho = 0$):

$$
\frac{\partial \Delta \mathbf{x}_{t+h}}{\partial \boldsymbol{\epsilon}_t'} = \begin{pmatrix} \dfrac{\partial \Delta y_{t+h}}{\partial \epsilon_{1,t}} & \dfrac{\partial \Delta y_{t+h}}{\partial \epsilon_{2,t}} \\ \dfrac{\partial \Delta z_{t+h}}{\partial \epsilon_{1,t}} & \dfrac{\partial \Delta z_{t+h}}{\partial \epsilon_{2,t}} \end{pmatrix} = (\beta \lambda)^{h-2}\begin{pmatrix} \beta \lambda(\beta \lambda - 1) & \beta(\beta \lambda)^2 \\ \lambda(\beta \lambda - 1) & (\beta \lambda)^2 \end{pmatrix} \quad h \geq 2,
$$

and $\partial \mathbf{x}_{t+h}/\partial \boldsymbol{\epsilon}_t'$ is given by (66) evaluated at $\rho = 0$. Thus, as $h \to \infty$, $\partial \Delta \mathbf{x}_{t+h}/\partial \boldsymbol{\epsilon}_t' \to \mathbf{0}$, and:

$$
\frac{\partial \mathbf{x}_{t+h}}{\partial \boldsymbol{\epsilon}_t'} \to \begin{pmatrix} 0 & \frac{\beta}{1-\beta \lambda} \\ 0 & \frac{\beta}{1-\beta \lambda} \end{pmatrix}.
$$

The major change in these responses relative to the general case is the absence of a "persistent" effect of a shock to $\epsilon_{1,t}$ on either y_t or z_t.

Considerable simplification arises in the remaining cases, which we summarize in (67) for the responses to $\partial \Delta \mathbf{x}_{t+h}/\partial \boldsymbol{\epsilon}_t'$ ($\mathbf{0}$ for $h > 2$):

h	$\lambda = 0$	$\lambda = \rho = 0$	$\beta = 0$
0	$\begin{pmatrix} 1 & \beta \\ 0 & 1 \end{pmatrix}$	$\begin{pmatrix} 1 & \beta \\ 0 & 1 \end{pmatrix}$	$\begin{pmatrix} 1 & 0 \\ 0 & 1 \end{pmatrix}$
1	$\begin{pmatrix} (\beta\rho - 1) & 0 \\ \rho & 0 \end{pmatrix}$	$\begin{pmatrix} -1 & 0 \\ 0 & 0 \end{pmatrix}$	$\begin{pmatrix} -1 & 0 \\ (\lambda + \rho) & 0 \end{pmatrix}$
2	$\mathbf{0}$	$\mathbf{0}$	$\begin{pmatrix} 0 & 0 \\ -\lambda & 0 \end{pmatrix}$

$$(67)$$

and in (68) for $\partial \mathbf{x}_{t+h}/\partial \boldsymbol{\epsilon}_t'$:

h	$\lambda = 0$	$\lambda = \rho = 0$	$\beta = 0$
0	$\begin{pmatrix} 1 & \beta \\ 0 & 1 \end{pmatrix}$	$\begin{pmatrix} 1 & \beta \\ 0 & 1 \end{pmatrix}$	$\begin{pmatrix} 1 & 0 \\ -\rho & 1 \end{pmatrix}$
1	$\begin{pmatrix} \beta\rho & \beta \\ \rho & 1 \end{pmatrix}$	$\begin{pmatrix} 0 & \beta \\ 0 & 1 \end{pmatrix}$	$\begin{pmatrix} 0 & 0 \\ \rho & (1+\lambda) \end{pmatrix}$
> 1	$\begin{pmatrix} \beta\rho & \beta \\ \rho & 1 \end{pmatrix}$	$\begin{pmatrix} 0 & \beta \\ 0 & 1 \end{pmatrix}$	$\begin{pmatrix} 0 & 0 \\ \rho & 1 \end{pmatrix}$

$$(68)$$

- Δy is EGNC for Δz ($\lambda = 0$). Here:

$$\begin{pmatrix} \Delta y_t \\ \Delta z_t \end{pmatrix} = \begin{pmatrix} 1 & \beta \\ 0 & 1 \end{pmatrix} \begin{pmatrix} \epsilon_{1,t} \\ \epsilon_{2,t} \end{pmatrix} + \begin{pmatrix} (\beta\rho - 1) & 0 \\ \rho & 0 \end{pmatrix} \begin{pmatrix} \epsilon_{1,t-1} \\ \epsilon_{2,t-1} \end{pmatrix}, \tag{69}$$

and:

$$\begin{pmatrix} y_t \\ z_t \end{pmatrix} = \frac{1}{1+\beta^2} \begin{pmatrix} \beta^2 & \beta \\ \beta & 1 \end{pmatrix} \begin{pmatrix} y_0 \\ z_0 \end{pmatrix} + \begin{pmatrix} \beta\rho & \beta \\ \rho & 1 \end{pmatrix} \begin{pmatrix} \sum_{i=1}^{t} \epsilon_{1,i} \\ \sum_{i=1}^{t} \epsilon_{2,i} \end{pmatrix} + \begin{pmatrix} (1-\beta\rho)\epsilon_{1,t} \\ -\rho\epsilon_{1,t} \end{pmatrix}. \tag{70}$$

The results in (67) and (68) follow directly from (69) and (70) respectively. Using (37), and:

$$\mathbf{C}(1) = \begin{pmatrix} \beta\rho & \beta \\ \rho & 1 \end{pmatrix} = \begin{pmatrix} \beta \\ 1 \end{pmatrix} (\rho \quad 1), \tag{71}$$

the "common trend" takes the form $\rho \sum_{i=1}^{t} \epsilon_{1,i} + \sum_{i=1}^{t} \epsilon_{2,i}$.

- Complete EGNC from y to z ($\lambda = \rho = 0$). Since cointegration requires Granger causality in at least one direction, it will only exist in this case if z Granger causes y ($\beta \neq 0$). Even further simplifications arise in this case, obtained by setting $\rho = 0$ in (69) and (70) respectively. Using (37) and (71), for $\lambda = \rho = 0$, the "common trend" takes the form $\sum_{i=1}^{t} \epsilon_{2,i}$. This case provides an illustration of the "common trend" being the weakly exogenous variable alone, when the number of endogenous variables n_1 is equal to the number of cointegrating and Granger causal relations.

- Complete EGNC from z to y ($\beta = 0$). In terms of EGNC, this is the opposite of the previous case, and yields equally simplified—but very different— impulse responses. Cointegration is possible since there is GC from y to z ($\rho \neq 0$), but the cointegrating vector simplifies to $(1, 0)$, so that the system is unbalanced with $y_t \sim \mathrm{I}(0)$ and $z_t \sim \mathrm{I}(1)$. The impulse responses follow from:

$$\begin{pmatrix} \Delta y_t \\ \Delta z_t \end{pmatrix} = \begin{pmatrix} \epsilon_{1,t} \\ \epsilon_{2,t} \end{pmatrix} + \begin{pmatrix} -1 & 0 \\ (\lambda + \rho) & 0 \end{pmatrix} \begin{pmatrix} \epsilon_{1,t-1} \\ \epsilon_{2,t-1} \end{pmatrix} + \begin{pmatrix} 0 & 0 \\ -\lambda & 0 \end{pmatrix} \begin{pmatrix} \epsilon_{1,t-2} \\ \epsilon_{2,t-2} \end{pmatrix},$$

and:

$$\begin{pmatrix} y_t \\ z_t \end{pmatrix} = \begin{pmatrix} 0 \\ z_0 \end{pmatrix} + \begin{pmatrix} 0 \\ \rho \sum_{i=1}^{t} \epsilon_{1,i} + \sum_{i=1}^{t} \epsilon_{2,i} \end{pmatrix} + \begin{pmatrix} \epsilon_{1,t} \\ -\rho\epsilon_{1,t} + \lambda\epsilon_{2,t-1} \end{pmatrix}.$$

Now using (37) and (71) for $\beta = 0$, the "common trend" has the form $\rho\sum_{i=1}^{t}\epsilon_{1,i} + \sum_{i=1}^{t}\epsilon_{2,i}$ as in the case with $\lambda = 0$.

- Complete absence of Granger causality ($\beta = \lambda = \rho = 0$). In terms of Granger causality, this is the simplest case, and can be obtained as a simplification of either of the last two cases. This system is now unbalanced with y_t white noise and so $\mathrm{I}(0)$, and z_t an $\mathrm{I}(1)$ random walk. The impulse response matrices take their simplest form in this case, and achieve their long-run values after at most one period.

This analysis in the bivariate cointegrated system (39) of the effect various forms of EGNC have on unit impulse responses has demonstrated that there can be major differences. For example, whenever there is EGNC from z to y ($\beta = 0$) or EGNC from Δy to Δz ($\lambda = 0$) the impulse responses $\partial\Delta\mathbf{x}_{t+h}/\partial\boldsymbol{\epsilon}_t'$ and $\partial\mathbf{x}_{t+h}/\partial\boldsymbol{\epsilon}_t'$ approach their long-run values very rapidly—after one or two periods. This reflects the important role that $\beta\lambda$ plays in the autoregressive dynamics of the system—see (63) and (64). On the other hand, although $\partial y_{t+h}/\partial\epsilon_{1,t}$ and $\partial z_{t+h}/\partial\epsilon_{1,t}$ both tend to zero as $h \to \infty$ when z_t is weakly exogenous for (β, σ_1), the speed with which this effect of EGNC (namely EGNC y to z) is achieved depends on the magnitude of $\beta\lambda$ and hence on the absence of EGNC from z to y and EGNC from Δy to Δz.

Finally, Ericsson *et al.* (1998) use the conditional/marginal factorization of (34) to show that the absence of Granger causality from $\mathbf{y}$ to $\mathbf{z}$ is a sufficient condition for system impulse responses to be the same as conditional-model impulse responses.

13 Conclusions

On some constructions of the concept, "Granger causality" has nothing to do with "causality." Nonetheless, Granger causality retains a major role in econometric modeling. We have demonstrated its central position in the areas of modeling, estimation, inference, simulation, forecasting, and policy. In several of these settings, what matters is the presence or absence of Granger causality in the data generation process. That would be consistent with its interpretation as a form of "causality." In other settings, all that is needed is the presence or absence of Granger causality empirically. Thus, finding lagged feedbacks in a modeling exercise can be sufficient to render some approaches hazardous even if there is no "genuine causality" in the DGP directly between the variables. We have shown that finite-sample tests for EGNC can deliver spurious outcomes when variables have deterministic breaks, so "spurious" causality can occur when the relevant variables have no links.

The direction of Granger causality important to modeling can be either from the non-modeled to the modeled variables, or the converse. Either or both can influence the distributions of estimators and tests, and hence the validity of inferences about parameter values, forecasts, or policy recommendations. Thus, we conclude that Granger causality is pervasive in econometrics, and deserves to be a separate construct in the econometrician's cognitive toolkit. It is a striking example of the numerous important contributions that Clive has made during his illustrious career.

References

Allen, P. G., and Fildes, R. A. (1998). "Econometric forecasting strategies and techniques." Mimeo, University of Massachusetts. Forthcoming in J. S. Armstrong (ed.), *Principles of Forecasting.* Kluwer Academic Press.

Andrews, D. W. K. (1989). "An empirical process central limit theorem for dependent non-identically distributed random variables." Cowles Foundation discussion paper 907, Yale University.

Banerjee, A., Dolado, J. J., Galbraith, J. W., and Hendry, D. F. (1993). *Co-integration, Error Correction and the Econometric Analysis of Non-Stationary Data.* Oxford: Oxford University Press.

Chong, Y. Y., and Hendry, D. F. (1986). "Econometric evaluation of linear macroeconomic models." *Review of Economic Studies*, 53: 671–90. Reprinted in C. W. J. Granger (ed.) (1990), *Modelling Economic Series.* Oxford: Clarendon Press.

Clements, M. P., and Hendry, D. F. (1998). *Forecasting Non-stationary Economic Time Series: The Zeuthen Lectures on Economic Forecasting.* Cambridge, MA: MIT Press. Forthcoming.

Dickey, D. A., and Fuller, W. A. (1979). "Distribution of the estimators for autoregressive time series with a unit root." *Journal of the American Statistical Association*, 74: 427–31.

Dickey, D. A., and Fuller, W. A. (1981). "Likelihood ratio statistics for autoregressive time series with a unit root." *Econometrica*, 49: 1057–72.

Duffie, D., and Singleton, K. J. (1989). "Simulated moments estimation of Markov models of asset prices." Mimeo, Stanford University.

Durbin, J. (1970). "Testing for serial correlation in least squares regression when some of the regressors are lagged dependent variables." *Econometrica*, 38: 410–21.

Efron, B. (1979). "Bootstrap methods: another look at the jackknife." *Annals of Statistics*, 7: 1–26.

Efron, B., and Tibshirani, R. J. (1993). *An Introduction to the Bootstrap*. London: Chapman and Hall.

Engle, R. F., and Granger, C. W. J. (1987). "Cointegration and error correction: representation, estimation and testing." *Econometrica*, 55: 251–76.

Engle, R. F., Hendry, D. F., and Richard, J.-F. (1983). "Exogeneity." *Econometrica*, 51: 277–304. Reprinted in D. F. Hendry (1993), *Econometrics: Alchemy or Science?* Oxford: Blackwell Publishers.

Ericsson, N. R., Hendry, D. F., and Mizon, G. E. (1998). "Exogeneity, cointegration and economic policy analysis." *Journal of Business and Economic Statistics*, 16: 370–87.

Geman, S., and Geman, D. (1984). "Stochastic relaxation, Gibbs distributions and the Bayesian restoration of images." *IEEE Transactions on Pattern Analysis and Machine Intelligence*, 6: 721–41.

Geweke, J. B. (1978). "Testing the exogeneity specification in the complete dynamic simultaneous equations model." *Journal of Econometrics*, 7: 163–85.

Geweke, J. B. (1984). "Inference and causality in economic time series models." In Griliches and Intriligator (1984), ch. 19.

Geweke, J. B. (1988). "Acceleration methods for Monte Carlo integration in Bayesian inference." In *Proceedings of the 20th Symposium on the Interface: Computing Science and Statistics*.

Gouriéroux, C., and Monfort, A. (1995). *Simulation Based Econometric Methods*. Oxford: Oxford University Press.

Gouriéroux, C., Monfort, A., and Renault, E. (1993). "Indirect inference." *Journal of Applied Econometrics*, 8: 85–118.

Govaerts, B., Hendry, D. F, and Richard, J.-F. (1994). "Encompassing in stationary linear dynamic models." *Journal of Econometrics*, 63, 245–70.

Granger, C. W. J. (1969). "Investigating causal relations by econometric models and cross-spectral methods." *Econometrica*, 37: 424–38.

Granger, C. W. J. (1980). "Testing for causality: a personal viewpoint." *Journal of Economic Dynamics and Control*, 2: 329–52.

Granger, C. W. J. (1981). "Some properties of time series data and their use in econometric model specification." *Journal of Econometrics*, 16: 121–30.

Granger, C. W. J. (1986). "Developments in the study of cointegrated economic variables." *Oxford Bulletin of Economics and Statistics*, 48: 213–28.

Granger, C. W. J., and Deutsch, M. (1992). "Comments on the evaluation of policy models." *Journal of Policy Modeling*, 14: 497–516.

Griliches, Z., and Intriligator, M. D. (eds.) (1984). *Handbook of Econometrics*, vols. 2–3. Amsterdam: North-Holland.

Hajivassiliou, V. A. (1989). "Macroeconomic shocks in an aggregate disequilibrium model." Mimeo, Yale University.

Hajivassiliou, V. A., and McFadden, D. L. (1989). "The method of simulated scores for the estimation of LDV models with an application to the problem of external debt crisis." Mimeo, Yale University.

Hall, R. E. (1978). "Stochastic implications of the life-cycle permanent income hypothesis: evidence." *Journal of Political Economy*, 86, 971–87.

Hansen, L. P. (1982). "Large sample properties of generalized method of moments estimators." *Econometrica*, 50: 1027–54.

Harvey, A. C. (1993). *Time Series Models*, 2nd edn. Hemel Hempstead: Harvester Wheatsheaf.

Hendry, D. F. (1975). "The consequences of mis-specification of dynamic structure, autocorrelation and simultaneity in a simple model with an application to the demand for imports." In G. A. Renton (ed.), *Modelling the Economy*, ch. 11. London: Heinemann Educational Books.

Hendry, D. F. (1979). "The behaviour of inconsistent instrumental variables estimators in dynamic systems with autocorrelated errors." *Journal of Econometrics*, 9: 295–314.

Hendry, D. F. (1984). "Monte Carlo experimentation in econometrics," in Griliches and Intriligator (1984), ch. 16.

Hendry, D. F. (1995a). *Dynamic Econometrics*. Oxford: Oxford University Press.

Hendry, D. F. (1995b). "On the interactions of unit roots and exogeneity." *Econometric Reviews*, 14: 383–419.

Hendry, D. F. (1995c). "A theory of co-breaking." Mimeo, Nuffield College, University of Oxford.

Hendry, D. F. (1997). "The econometrics of macro-economic forecasting." *Economic Journal*, 107: 1330–57.

Hendry, D. F., and Doornik, J. A. (1997). "The implications for econometric modelling of forecast failure." *Scottish Journal of Political Economy*, 44: 437–61. Special Issue.

Hendry, D. F., and Mizon, G. E. (1998a). "Exogeneity, causality, and co-breaking in economic policy analysis of a small econometric model of money in the UK." *Empirical Economics*, 23: 267–94.

Hendry, D. F., and Mizon, G. E. (1998b). "On selecting policy analysis models by forecast accuracy." Mimeo, Nuffield College, University of Oxford.

Hendry, D. F, and Neale, A. J. (1991). "A Monte Carlo study of the effects of structural breaks on tests for unit roots." In P. Hackl and A. H. Westlund (eds.), *Economic Structural Change, Analysis and Forecasting*, pp. 95–119. Berlin: Springer-Verlag.

Hendry, D. F, and Richard, J.-F. (1982). "On the formulation of empirical models in dynamic econometrics." *Journal of Econometrics*, 20: 3–33. Reprinted in C. W. J. Granger (ed.) (1990), *Modelling Economic Series*. Oxford: Clarendon Press and in D. F. Hendry (1993), *Econometrics: Alchemy or Science?* Oxford: Blackwell Publishers.

Hendry, D. F., and Richard, J.-F. (1989). "Recent developments in the theory of encompassing." In B. Cornet and H. Tulkens (eds.), *Contributions to Operations Research and Economics. The XXth Anniversary of CORE*, pp. 393–440. Cambridge, MA: MIT Press.

Hendry, D. F., and Richard, J.-F. (1991). "Likelihood evaluation for dynamic latent variables models." In H. M. Amman, D. A. Belsley, and L. F. Pau (eds.), *Computational Economics and Econometrics*, ch. 1. Dordrecht: Kluwer.

Johansen, S. (1995). Likelihood-Based Inference in Cointegrated Vector Autoregressive Models. Oxford: Oxford University Press.

Lerman, S., and Manski, C. (1981). "On the use of simulated frequencies to approximate choice probabilities." In C. Manski and D. McFadden (eds.), *Structural Analysis of Discrete Data with Econometric Applications.* Cambridge, MA: MIT Press.

Liitkepohi, H. (1991). *Introduction to Multiple Time Series Analysis.* New York: Springer-Verlag.

McFadden, D. L. (1989). "A method of simulated moments for estimation of discrete response models without numerical integration." *Econometrica*, 57: 995–1026.

Mizon, G. E. (1995). "Progressive modelling of macroeconomic time series: the LSE methodology." In K. D. Hoover (ed.), *Macroeconometrics: Developments, Tensions and Prospects*, pp. 107–169. Dordrecht: Kluwer Academic Press.

Mizon, G. E., and Richard, J.-F. (1986). "The encompassing principle and its application to non-nested hypothesis tests." *Econometrica*, 54, 657–78.

Mosconi, R., and Giannini, C. (1992). "Non-causality in cointegrated systems: representation, estimation and testing." *Oxford Bulletin of Economics and Statistics*, 54: 399–417.

Pagan, A. R. (1989). "On the role of simulation in the statistical evaluation of econometric models." *Journal of Econometrics*, 40: 125–139.

Pakes, A. (1986). "Patents as options: some estimates of the value of holding European patent stocks." *Econometrica*, 54, 755–74.

Pakes, A., and Pollard, D. (1989). "Simulation and the asymptotics of optimization estimation." *Econometrica*, 57: 1027–1058.

Phillips, P. C. B. (1986). "Understanding spurious regressions in econometrics." *Journal of Econometrics*, 33: 311–40.

Phillips, P. C. B. (1987). "Time series regression with a unit root." *Econometrica*, 55: 277–301.

Phillips, P. C. B., and Durlauf, S. N. (1986). "Multiple time series regression with integrated processes." *Review of Economic Studies*, 53, 473–95.

Phillips, P. C. B., and Loretan, M. (1991). "Estimating long-run economic equilibria." *Review of Economic Studies*, 58: 407–36.

Richard, J.-F. (1980). "Models with several regimes and changes in exogeneity." *Review of Economic Studies*, 47: 1–20.

Runkle, D. E. (1987). "Vector autoregressions and reality." *Journal of Business and Economic Statistics*, 5: 437–42.

Sargan, J. D. (1964). "Wages and prices in the United Kingdom: a study in econometric methodology (with discussion)." In P. E. Hart, G. Mills, and J. K. Whitaker (eds.), *Econometric Analysis for National Economic Planning*, vol. 16 of *Colston Papers*, pp. 25–63. London: Butterworth Co. Reprinted in D. F. Hendry and K. F. Wallis (eds.) (1984), *Econometrics and Quantitative Economics*, pp. 275–314. Oxford: Basil Blackwell, and in J. D. Sargan (1988), *Contributions to Econometrics*, vol. 1, pp. 124–69. Cambridge: Cambridge University Press.

Sargan, J. D. (1980). "Some tests of dynamic specification for a single equation." *Econometrica*, 48, 879–97. Reprinted in J. D. Sargan (1988), *Contributions to Econometrics*, vol. 1, pp. 191–212. Cambridge: Cambridge University Press.

Sims, C. A. (1972). "Money, income and causality." *American Economic Review*, 62: 540–52.

Sims, C. A. (1980). "Macroeconomics and reality." *Econometrica*, 48: 1–48. Reprinted in C. W. J. Granger (ed.) (1990), *Modelling Economic Series*. Oxford: Clarendon Press.

Stock, J. H. (1987). "Asymptotic properties of least squares estimators of cointegrating vectors." *Econometrica*, 55: 1035–56.

Toda, H. Y., and Phillips, P. C. B. (1993). "Vector autoregressions and causality." *Econometrica*, 61: 1367–93.

Wold, H. O. A. (1938). *A Study in the Analysis of Stationary Time Series*. Stockholm: Almqvist and Wicksell.

Young, G. A. (1994). "Bootstrap: more than a stab in the dark?" *Statistical Science*, 9: 382–415.

6
A Class of Tests for Integration and Cointegration

JAMES H. STOCK

1 Introduction

The intellectual architecture of cointegration analysis constitutes a watershed accomplishment of time series econometrics in the 1980s. As of 1980, econometricians confronted several apparently conflicting pieces of evidence about long run relations among time series. It was recognized that many macroeconomic time series exhibit trend-like behavior and have considerable persistence. Granger (1966) expressed this as the series having much of their spectral power at low frequencies, and Nelson and Plosser (1982) argued that this persistence was captured by modeling the series as having a unit autoregressive root (being integrated of order one). But how to model multiple time series in levels remained unclear. On the one hand, regressions involving highly persistent, unrelated series can produce spuriously large correlations and thus can incorrectly appear to be related (Yule, 1926; Granger and Newbold, 1974). On the other hand, the view that all levels relations are spurious seemed too severe: some "great ratios," such as the share of consumption in income, appeared stable even though the variables themselves were growing (Kosobud and Klein, 1961), and these great ratios, when incorporated as regressors in otherwise standard "first differences" specifications, can have statistically significant coefficients and can be economically large (Davidson, Hendry, Srba, and Yeo, 1978). The achievement of cointegration analysis, as developed by Granger (1983, 1986), Granger and Weiss (1983), and Engle and Granger (1987), was to provide a unified framework in which to understand and to reconcile the apparent conflict between spurious regressions and economically meaningful long-run relations. Moreover, this early work provided probability models of levels relations which were sufficiently well articulated to form a foundation for the development and analysis of new tools for statistical inference in poten-

The author thanks Don Andrews, Frank Diebold, Bruce Hansen, Jerry Hausman, Danny Quah, Mark Watson, and Jeff Wooldridge for helpful suggestions, and Robin Lumsdaine for research assistance. This paper is a May 1990 revision of a March 1988 paper by the same title, edited for this Festschrift. This work was supported in part by National Science Foundation grant SES-86-18984.

tially cointegrated systems. Among the issues stressed in this early work is the importance of correctly specifying the orders of integration of the component series and testing for possible cointegration among the series, that is, of the construction of powerful and reliable tests for integration and cointegration.[1]

This paper introduces a class of statistics that can be used to test for integration or cointegration in time series data. Many of the existing tests for integration and cointegration are motivated by considering the problem of testing whether an autoregressive root equals one against the alternative that it is not equal to one; see, for example, Dickey and Fuller (1979), Phillips (1987), and Phillips and Perron (1988) for tests for integration, and Engle and Granger (1987), Phillips and Ouliaris (1990), and Stock and Watson (1988) for tests for cointegration. In contrast, statistics in the proposed class test directly the implication that an integrated process has a growing variance, that is, has an order in probability of $T^{1/2}$ (is $O_p(T^{1/2})$).

To motivate these statistics, let y_t, $t = 1, ..., T$, be a univariate integrated process with zero drift, $s_{\Delta y}(0)$ be the spectral density of $\Delta y_t \equiv y_t - y_{t-1}$ at frequency zero, $[\cdot]$ denote the greatest lesser integer function, $=>$ denote weak convergence on $D[0, 1]$, and define $v_T^*(\lambda) = (2\pi s_{\Delta y}(0) T)^{-1/2} y_{[T\lambda]}$ for $0 \le \lambda \le 1$. Then, under general conditions, $v_T^* => W$, where W is standard Brownian motion on $[0, 1]$. The scaling factor $T^{-1/2}$ is consequence of y_t being I(1). In contrast, if y_t is I(0), y_t is $O_p(1)$.

These observations suggest developing test statistics based on the implication that an I(1) process is $O_p(T^{1/2})$ whereas an I(0) process is $O_p(1)$. The approach pursued in this paper is to consider the class of tests constructed using continuous functionals $g: D[0, 1] \to \Re^1$, such that the distribution of $g(W)$ has arbitrarily small mass in a small neighborhood of $g(0)$. Heuristically, if y_t is I(0), then by the continuous mapping theorem $g(v_T^*)$ will converge to $g(0)$. This suggests that $g(v_T^*)$ could be used to construct a test of the I(1) null that is consistent against the I(0) alternative. If $s_{\Delta y}(0)$ is suitably estimated, it will have an asymptotic null distribution that does not depend on any nuisance parameters. This approach readily handles general trend specifications, including both the leading cases of demeaning or polynomial detrending as well as more general trend specifications. The details are provided in Section 2.

In addition to suggesting new test statistics, this class of tests provides a unifying framework for many previously proposed tests. It therefore provides a simple way to generalize results for existing tests to different types of trends, for example. Although not all tests for a unit root fit into this framework, three that do are examined in Section 3. These are a modified version of Sargan and Bhargava's (1983) uniformly most powerful (UMP) and Bhargava's (1986) locally most powerful invariant (MPI) tests in the first order case; the Phillips (1987) and Phillips–Perron (1988) Z_α statistic; and Lo's (1991) generalization of Mandelbrot's (1975) rescaled range ("R/S") statistic.

Section 4 extends the results of Section 2 to tests for cointegration. These tests build on Engle and Granger's (1987) suggestion by replacing y_t with the residual from a contemporaneous regression of the level of one element of a detrended multivariate time series on the levels of the other elements. The technical arguments in this section draw on results of Phillips and Ouliaris (1990). Like the univariate tests, these are developed for general trends.

Section 5 considers issues of consistency. Section 6 presents the results of a Monte Carlo experiment that compares selected new $g(\cdot)$ tests with several previously proposed tests. The experimental design includes several models estimated for postwar US data. Section 7 concludes.

2 Tests for Integration

Suppose that, under the null hypothesis, the univariate time series variable y_t can be written as the sum of a purely deterministic component $d_t(\beta)$ and a component that is integrated of order one:

$$y_t = d_t(\beta) + \sum_{s=1}^{t} u_s, \quad t = 1, ..., T. \tag{2.1}$$

The finite dimensional parameter vector β is estimated by $\hat{\beta}$. Let $\omega = 2\pi s_u(0)$, where $s_u(0)$ is the spectral density of u_t at frequency zero, let $\nu_T(\lambda) = T^{-\frac{1}{2}} \sum_{s=1}^{[T\lambda]} u_s$, and let $D_T(\lambda; \beta) = d_{[T\lambda]}(\beta)$. The two processes ν_T and $D_T(\cdot; \beta)$ are assumed to satisfy:

Assumption 1. The following hold jointly:

(a) $\nu_T => \sqrt{\omega} W$, where $0 < \omega < \infty$, and
(b) $T^{-\frac{1}{2}}\{D_T(\cdot; \hat{\beta}) - D_T(\cdot; \beta)\} => \sqrt{\omega} D$, where $D \in D[0, 1]$ has a distribution that does not depend on β or on the nuisance parameters describing the distribution of $\{u_t\}$.

This covers many special cases of practical interest. Consider first the partial sum process ν_T. For most of what follows, the general Assumption 1(a) will suffice, although at times it is convenient to consider the special case in which u_t is the linear process,

$$u_t = c(L)\epsilon_t, \quad \sum_{j=0}^{\infty} j|c_j| < \infty, \quad c(1) \neq 0 \tag{2.2}$$

where ϵ_t is a martingale difference sequence with $E[\epsilon_t^2|\epsilon_{t-1}, \epsilon_{t-2}, ...] = \sigma^2$ and $\sup_t E[|\epsilon_t|^{2+\delta}|\epsilon_{t-1}, \epsilon_{t-2}, ...] < \infty$ for some $\delta > 0$. The one-summability of $c(L)$, along with these moment conditions, implies Assumption 1(a) (where $\omega = c(1)^2\sigma^2$) using a standard functional central limit theorem (e.g., Chan and Wei, 1988, theorem 2.2; Hall and Heyde, 1980, theorem 4.1).[2]

Assumption 1(b) is satisfied by a wide variety of trend functions. To establish notation, some important special cases follow.

A. *Constant.* In this case $d_t(\beta) = \beta_0$. A natural estimator of β_0 is $\hat{\beta}_0 = \bar{y} \equiv T^{-1}\sum_{t=1}^{T} y_t$; the demeaned series is

$$y_t^\mu = y_t - \bar{y}. \tag{2.3a}$$

B. *Linear time trend.* For reasons discussed below, it is convenient to normalize the known parts of the trend specification to be bounded. Thus the linear trend is written $d_t(\beta) = \beta_0 + \beta_1(t/T)$. If the unknown parameters β_0 and β_1 are estimated by the ordinary least squares (OLS) estimators $(\hat{\beta}_0, \hat{\beta}_1)$, then the detrended series is

$$y_t^\tau = y_t - \hat{\beta}_0 - \hat{\beta}_1(t/T). \tag{2.3b}$$

Bhargava (1986) derives an alternative detrending procedure for his locally MPI tests in the first order Gaussian case with drift; his estimators are $\tilde{\beta}_0 = \bar{y} - (T+1)/(2(T-1))(y_T - y_1)$ and $\tilde{\beta}_1 = (T/(T-1))(y_T - y_1)$. The detrended series is

$$y_t^B = y_t - \tilde{\beta}_0 - \tilde{\beta}_1(t/T). \tag{2.3c}$$

C. *General trends that are linear in* β. This framework nests the more general time trend $d_t(\beta) = \beta'x_t$, where x_t is a $J \times 1$ vector of known deterministic terms. Let $\tau_T(\lambda) = x_{[T\lambda]}$ and assume that:

$$\tau_T \to \tau, \quad \tau_i \in D[0,1], \quad i = 1,...,J, \quad \text{where} \quad M = \int_0^1 \tau(s)\tau(s)'\mathrm{d}s \tag{2.4}$$

is nonsingular and $\sup_{\lambda\in[0,1]}|\tau_{iT}(\lambda)| \leq \bar{\tau}$ for all T, $i = 1, ..., J$.

A natural estimator of β is the OLS estimator $\hat{\beta} = (\sum_{t=1}^{T}x_t x_t')^{-1}\sum_{t=1}^{T}x_t y_t$. The normalization $|\tau_{iT}(\lambda)| \leq \bar{\tau}$ obtains by selecting the proper scaling factor, which can be done without loss of generality. In this normalization the true coefficient might depend on T, e.g. a trend γt with γ fixed is rewritten as $\beta_1(t/T)$, where $\beta_1 = \gamma T$. This complicates the interpretation of the coefficients but simplifies treatment of the projections, the latter being of interest here. This is clarified by two examples.

C(i). *Polynomial time trends.* In this case, $d_t(\beta) = \sum_{j=0}^{J-1}\beta_j(t/T)^j$, so that $\tau_T(\lambda) = (1, [T\lambda]/T, ..., ([T\lambda]/T)^{J-1})'$. Evidently $\tau_T \to \tau = (1, \lambda, ..., \lambda^{J-1})'$; direct calculation indicates that M is nonsingular, with $M_{ij} = 1/(i+j-1)$.

C(ii). *Segmented time trend.* Perron (1989) has proposed tests for a unit root against the alternative hypothesis that the deterministic component of the series contains a segmented trend. An example is the "mean shift" model,

$$d_t(\beta) = \beta_0 + \beta_1 \mathbf{1}(t > [T\lambda_0]) + \beta_2(t/T), \quad 0 < \lambda_0 < 1,$$

where $\mathbf{1}(\cdot)$ denotes the indicator function. In this model the intercept term increases from β_0 to $\beta_0 + \beta_1$ after a fraction λ_0 of the sample has passed; generalizations to other shifts or breaks in the trend are discussed in Perron (1989).

In the mean shift model, $\tau_T(\lambda) = (1, \mathbf{1}([T\lambda] > [T\lambda_0]), [T\lambda]/T)$, and (2.4) is satisfied with $\tau(\lambda) = (1, \mathbf{1}(\lambda > \lambda_0), \lambda)$.

The limiting representations in Assumption 1 depend on ω. To eliminate this dependence, assume for now that there is a consistent estimator for ω:

Assumption 2. Under the null hypothesis $\hat{\omega} \xrightarrow{p} \omega$.

A variety of such estimators exist; an autoregressive estimator is considered in Section 4.

Define v_T^d to be the scaled stochastic process formed using the detrended series:

$$v_T^d(\lambda) \equiv (T\hat{\omega})^{-\frac{1}{2}} \{ y_{[T\lambda]} - d_{[T\lambda]}(\hat{\beta}) \}. \tag{2.5}$$

If Assumptions 1 and 2 hold, then

$$v_T^d => V^d \tag{2.6}$$

where V^d is the stochastic process $V^d = W - D$.

In general, Assumption 1 must be verified for the form of detrending and the null stochastic process at hand. The condition in Assumption 1(b) is demonstrated here for the leading cases. Let $v_T(\lambda) = (T\hat{\omega})^{-\frac{1}{2}} y_{[T\lambda]}$, $v_T^\mu(\lambda) = (T\hat{\omega})^{-\frac{1}{2}} y_{[T\lambda]}^\mu$, $v_T^\tau(\lambda) = (T\hat{\omega})^{-\frac{1}{2}} y_{[T\lambda]}^\tau$, and $v_T^B(\lambda) = (T\hat{\omega})^{-\frac{1}{2}} y_{[T\lambda]}^B$. We have:

Theorem 1. Assume that Assumptions 1(a) and 2 hold.
(a) If $d_t(\beta) = 0$, then $v_T => W$;
(b) If $d_t(\beta) = \beta_0$, then $v_T^\mu => V^\mu$, where $V^\mu(\lambda) = W(\lambda) - \int_0^1 W(s) ds$;
(c) If $d_t(\beta) = \beta_0 + \beta_1 t$, then $v_T^\tau => V^\tau$ and $v_T^B => V^B$, where $V^\tau(\lambda) = W(\lambda) - a_1(\lambda)\int_0^1 W(s) ds - a_2(\lambda)\int_0^1 s W(s) ds$ and $V^B(\lambda) = W(\lambda) - (\lambda - \frac{1}{2}) W(1) - \int_0^1 W(s) ds$, where $a_1(\lambda) = 4 - 6\lambda$ and $a_2(\lambda) = -6 + 12\lambda$.
(d) For general trends that are linear in β, if (2.4) holds and β is estimated by OLS, then $v_T^d => V^d$, where $V^d(\lambda) = W(\lambda) - \{\int_0^1 W(s)\tau(s)' ds M^{-1}\}\tau(\lambda)$.

Proofs of theorems are in Appendix A.

Theorem 1 provides expressions for V^d, the limiting detrended process, in the leading cases. The processes V^μ and V^τ, derived in Park and Phillips (1988, 1989) and Stock and Watson (1988), have natural Hilbert space interpretations as the continuous time analogues of the discrete time detrended processes; for a discussion, see Park and Phillips (1988, 1989). To simplify notation the result (d) is presented explicitly only for the OLS estimator. However, it generalizes directly to other estimators of β that are linear in y_t as long as the weights satisfy a condition analogous to (2.4).

It follows from (2.6) and the Continuous Mapping Theorem (e.g. Hall and Heyde, 1980, theorem A.3) that if $g(\cdot)$ is a continuous function from $D[0, 1]$ to $\mathfrak{R}^1$, then

$$g(v_T^d) => g(V^d) \tag{2.7}$$

Theorem 1 implies that this holds for each of the leading cases.

The asymptotic representations (2.6) and (2.7) form the basis for the proposed class of tests of integration. Specifically, let $G^d = \{g : D[0, 1] \to \mathfrak{R}^1\}$ be the collection of functionals that satisfy:

(a) g is continuous;   (2.8)
(b) $\exists\, c_\alpha, |c_\alpha| < \infty$, such that $\Pr[g(V^d) \leq c_\alpha] = \alpha$ for all α, $0 < \alpha < 1$;
(c) $g(0) < c_\alpha$ for all α, $0 < \alpha < 1$.

Several remarks are in order.

(a) The family G^d provides a natural class of test statistics for the null hypothesis that $y_t - d_t(\beta)$ is I(1) against the alternative that it is I(0). Under the null, $g(v_T^d)$ has an asymptotic distribution on the real line, with critical values c_α that depend on the functional g. Under a fixed stationary alternative, $y_t - d_t(\beta)$ is $O_p(1)$. This suggests constructing tests of level α of the form, reject if $g(v_T^d) \leq c_\alpha$. (The use of the left tail as the rejection region is without loss of generality, since the $g(\cdot)$ can be replaced by $-g(\cdot)$.) Conditions for consistency, including choice of $\hat{\omega}$, are discussed in Section 5.

(b) This approach to constructing tests suggests working backwards from the desired asymptotic representations to the actual test statistic. For example, suppose one wished to develop a unit root test with a χ_1^2 asymptotic null distribution. Because W (and in general V^d) has Gaussian marginals, it is simple to write down continuous functionals of these processes with χ_1^2 distributions. For example, $W(1)^2$ and $V^d(1)^2$ have distributions that are multiples of a χ_1^2, so $g(v_T^d) = v_T^d(1)^2/E(V^d(1)^2)$ provides a unit root test statistic that has a χ_1^2 distribution. Kahn and Ogaki's (1988) J_T test statistic is of this form: $J_T = g(v_T) + o_p(1)$, where $g(f) = f(1)^2$, so that J_T has an asymptotic χ_1^2 distribution.

(c) Other examples of existing tests that fall into this framework are a modification of the Sargan–Bhargava (1983) and Bhargava (1986) tests, the Phillips Perron Z_α statistic, and Lo's (1991) modification of Mandelbrot's (1975) R/S statistic. These are discussed in more detail in the next section.

(d) Condition (2.8)(b) indexes G^d by the type of detrending. In general the type of detrending restricts the functionals g that can be used to construct consistent tests. For example, consider $g(f) = \{\int_0^1 sf(s)\,ds\}^2$. From Theorem 1, $g(V^\mu) = \{\int_{s=0}^1 s(W(s) - \int_{r=0}^1 W(r)\,dr)\,ds\}^2 = \{\int_0^1 (s-\frac{1}{2})W(s)\,ds\}^2$, which is distributed as a constant times a χ_1^2. Because g is also continuous, g $\in G^\mu$. However, straightforward algebra shows that $g(V^\tau) = 0$ a.s., so $g \notin G^\tau$. This result has a simple interpretation in light of the discussion of V^τ following Theorem 1: because V^τ can be thought of as detrended Brownian motion, its Hilbert space projection against a linear trend is zero.

(e) The definition of G^d might seem so broad as to include all consistent unit root tests, but this is not so; the class refers only to continuous functionals of v_T. An example of a test not in this class is Park and Choi's (1988) $J(p, q)$ statistic (also see Park, 1990). To be concrete, suppose that $d_t = 0$, so the

$J(0, 1)$ statistic is appropriate; this is $J(0, 1) = T^{-1}\sum_{t=1}^{T}y_t^2/T^{-1}\sum_{t=1}^{T}(y_t - \bar{y})^2 - 1 => \{\int_0^1 W(s)^2 ds/(\int_0^1 W(s)\,ds)^2 - 1\}^{-1}$. The asymptotic representation suggests considering the functional, $g(f) = \{\int_0^1 f^2/(\int_0^1 f)^2 - 1\}^{-1}$. However, this functional is not continuous at $f = 0$.[3] This is not just a technicality: when $v_T => 0$ under the alternative, g must be continuous at 0 to ensure consistency.

The reason that the J statistic does not fall into this class yet is consistent in that it exploits a different property to obtain consistency. The G class exploits the different orders in probability of the underlying time series, while the J statistic exploits the relative differences in rates of convergence of sums of $\Delta^{-d}u_t$ and $(\Delta^{-d}u_t)^2$ for $d = -1, 0, 1$, where u_t is I(0).

(f) The fact that the form of the $g(\cdot)$ functional does not depend on the type of detrending (subject to remark (d) above) emphasizes that the steps of eliminating the deterministic components and testing for unit roots are conceptually distinct. This is sometimes obscured in procedures in which detrending and testing are performed in the same step. It is also evident that detrending a series when it is not required does not change the asymptotic size of the tests (although it can adversely affect power), because D does not depend on β. In contrast, failing to detrend a series that contains a trend typically leads to a loss of consistency and an incorrect asymptotic size.

3 Relation to Previously Proposed Tests for Integration

This section shows that several previously proposed tests for integration can be expressed, or are closely related to, $g(\cdot)$ tests. The main result is that there are simple $g(\cdot)$ statistics that are asymptotically equivalent to Sargan and Bhargava's (1983) and Bhargava's (1986), where the asymptotic equivalence occurs both under the null and under a local alternative. It is also shown that the Phillips–Perron Z_α statistic can be cast as a $g(\cdot)$ statistic, as can Lo's (1991) modification of Mandelbrot's (1975) R/S statistic.

3.1 The Sargan–Bhargava and Bhargava Tests

Sargan and Bhargava (1983) considered the problem of testing for integration in the first order Markov model with i.i.d. Gaussian errors:

$$y_t = \beta_0 + \sum_{s=1}^{t}\rho^{t-s}\epsilon_s, \quad \epsilon_s \text{ i.i.d. } N(0,\sigma^2), \quad t = 1,...,T, \tag{3.1}$$

where $(\rho, \beta_0, \sigma^2)$ are unknown parameters. They showed that the statistic

$$R = \sum_{t=2}^{T}(\Delta y_t)^2 / \sum_{t=1}^{T}(y_t^\mu)^2 \tag{3.2}$$

provides the basis for a test of the random walk null ($\rho = 1$) against the stationary alternative ($|\rho| < 1$). (Note that R is the Durbin–Watson statistic for a regression of y_t against a constant.) Similarly, in the case of a time trend, Bhargava (1986) considered the maintained model,

$$y_t = \beta_0 + \beta_1 t + \sum_{s=1}^{t} \rho^{t-s} \epsilon_s, \quad \epsilon_s \text{ i.i.d. } N(0, \sigma^2), \quad t = 1, \ldots, T, \tag{3.3}$$

where $(\rho, \beta_0, \beta_1, \sigma^2)$ are unknown; he showed that

$$R = \sum_{t=2}^{T} (\Delta y_t^B)^2 \Big/ \sum_{t=1}^{T} (y_t^B)^2 \tag{3.4}$$

can be used to construct a test of $\rho = 1$ against $|\rho| < 1$, which he claimed to be MPI in the neighborhood of $\rho = 1$, where y_t^B is given in (2.3c).

Sargan–Bhargava and Bhargava did not provide asymptotic distribution theory for their tests. However, it obtains as a direct consequence of Theorem 1.

Corollary 1.1. Assume that y_t is generated by (2.1). Then

(a) $T^{-1} R^{-1} => m \int_0^1 V^\mu(s)^2 ds$

(b) $T^{-1} R_2^{-1} => m \int_0^1 V^B(s)^2 ds$

where $m = \omega / \text{var}(\Delta y_t)$.

Thus the asymptotic null distribution of the R and R_2 statistics depends on the nuisance parameters through the spectral density of Δy_t at the origin. However, there is a simple $g(\cdot)$ statistic that is essentially the same as the R and R_2 statistic, but which provides the basis for an asymptotically similar test under the null model (2.1). Let

$$g_{SB}(f) = \int_0^1 f(s)^2 \, ds, \tag{3.5}$$

so that $g_{SB}(v_T^\mu) = T^{-1} \sum_{t=1}^{T} (v_t^\mu)^2 = T^{-2} \sum_{t=1}^{T} (y_t^\mu)^2 / \hat\omega$ and $g_{SB}(v_T^B) = T^{-1} \sum_{t=1}^{T} (v_t^B)^2 = T^{-2} \sum_{t=1}^{T} (y_t^B)^2 / \hat\omega$. Thus $g_{SB}(v_T^\mu)$ and $g_{SB}(v_T^B)$ are respectively $T^{-1} R^{-1}$ and $T^{-1} R_2^{-1}$, except that $\hat\omega$ appears in the denominator rather than $T^{-1} \sum_{t=2}^{T} (\Delta y_t)^2$. It follows from Theorems 1 and 2 that, if Assumptions 1 and 2 hold and $\omega = \text{var}(\Delta y_t)$ (as is implied by (3.1) with $\rho = 1$), then $g_{SB}(v_T^\mu)$ and $g_{SB}(v_T^B)$ respectively are asymptotically equivalent to the Sargan–Bhargava and Bhargava tests under the null hypothesis.

The primary merit of the R and R_2 statistics is Sargan–Bhargava's and Bhargava's claims of finite sample optimality properties under (3.1) and (3.3). It is therefore of interest to compare the power of R and R_2 to that of the $g_{SB}(\cdot)$ statistics. This can be done by deriving a representation for these statistics under a local alternative, that is, under an alternative that approaches the unit root null as the sample size increases. Since the Sargan–Bhargava and Bhargava exact tests assume a first order model, suppose that y_t is generated by

$$y_t = \rho_T y_{t-1} + \epsilon_t, \quad t = 1, \ldots, T, \quad \epsilon_t \text{ i.i.d. } (0, \sigma_\epsilon^2), \tag{3.6}$$

where $E|\epsilon_t|^4 < \infty$. As the local alternative, adopt Phillips' (1987) formulation, so that $\rho_T = e^{c/T}$ where c is a constant (also see Cavanagh, 1985; Chan and Wei, 1987). Following Phillips (1987) and Phillips and Perron (1988), define $W_c(\lambda) = \int_{s=0}^{\lambda} e^{(\lambda-s)c} dW(s)$.

Computation of the $g(\cdot)$ statistics requires selecting a specific estimator of ω. For this discussion, suppose that ω is estimated by an average of sample covariances:

$$\tilde{w} = \{T^{-1} \sum_{t=2}^{T} \hat{u}_t^2 + 2 \sum_{j=1}^{\ell} T^{-1} \sum_{t=j+2}^{T} \hat{u}_t \hat{u}_{t-j}\}, \tag{3.7}$$

where $\hat{u}_t = y_t^{\mu} - \hat{\rho} y_{t-1}^{\mu}$, where $\hat{\rho} = \sum_{t=2}^{T} y_t^{\mu} y_{t-1}^{\mu} / \sum_{t=2}^{T} (y_{t-1}^{\mu})^2$. Note that, as is pointed out in Phillips and Ouliaris (1990) and Stock and Watson (1988), it is important to use the estimated $\hat{\rho}$ rather than the null value $\rho = 1$ in constructing $\hat{\omega}$ to ensure that the resulting test is consistent.

The next result uses Theorem 6.2 of Phillips and Perron (1988) to provide a limiting representation for the $g(\cdot)$, R, and R_2 statistics under this local alternative.

Theorem 2. Let y_t be generated by (3.6), and let the estimator $\tilde{\omega}$ in (3.7) be used to construct v_T^{μ} and v_T^{B}, where $\ell \to \infty$ as $T \to \infty$ and $\ell = o(T^{1/4})$. Then:

(a) $g_{SB}(v_T^{\mu}) => \int_0^1 V_c^{\mu}(s)^2 ds$,

(b) $g_{SB}(v_T^{B}) => \int_0^1 V_c^{B}(s)^2 ds$,

(c) $T^{-1}R^{-1} => \int_0^1 V_c^{\mu}(s)^2 ds$, and

(d) $T^{-1}R_2^{-1} => \int_0^1 V_c^{B}(s)^2 ds$,

where $V_c^{\mu}(\lambda) = W_c(\lambda) - \int_0^1 W_c(s) ds$ and $V_c^{B}(\lambda) = W_c(\lambda) - (\lambda - \frac{1}{2}) W_c(1) - \int_0^1 W_c(s) ds$.

In summary the $g_{SB}(\cdot)$ statistics have asymptotic null distributions that do not depend on the nuisance parameters for general I(1) processes; Theorem 2 implies that, for the AR(1) case, they have the same local asymptotic representations and therefore the same local power as the original Sargan–Bhargava and Bhargava statistics.

3.2 The Phillips and Phillips–Perron Tests

The Z_α statistics proposed by Phillips (1987) and Phillips and Perron (1988) also are closely related to a $g(\cdot)$ statistic. Assume here that $d_t(\beta) = 0$ and $y_0 = 0$, so that their statistic is

$$Z_\alpha = T(\hat{\rho} - 1) - \frac{1}{2} \{\tilde{\omega} - T^{-1} \sum_{t=1}^{T} (y_t - \hat{\rho} y_{t-1})^2\} / T^{-2} \sum_{t=1}^{T} y_{t-1}^2, \tag{3.8}$$

where $\tilde{\omega}$ and $\hat{\rho}$ are defined in and following (3.7), respectively. Because $\sum_{t=1}^{T} y_{t-1} \Delta y_t = \frac{1}{2}\{y_T^2 - \sum_{t=1}^{T}(\Delta y_t)^2\}$ (where $y_0 = 0$), (3.8) can be rearranged to yield

$$Z_\alpha = \tfrac{1}{2}\{\tilde{v}_T(1)^2 - 1\}/T^{-1}\sum_{t=1}^{T-1}\tilde{v}_T(t/T)^2 - \tfrac{1}{2}T(\hat{\rho}-1)^2, \qquad (3.9)$$

where $\tilde{v}_T(\lambda) = (T\tilde{\omega})^{-\frac{1}{2}}y_{[T\lambda]}$. Thus the Z_α statistic can be rewritten as $Z_\alpha = g_z(\tilde{v}_T) - \tfrac{1}{2}T(\hat{\rho}-1)^2$, where:

$$g_z(f) = \tfrac{1}{2}\{f(1)^2 - 1\}/\int_0^1 f(s)^2 \, ds. \qquad (3.10)$$

Under the null and the local alternative (3.6), $T(\hat{\rho}-1)^2 \overset{p}{\to} 0$ so $Z_\alpha - g_z(\tilde{v}_T) \overset{p}{\to} 0$, so in this case Z_α and $g_z(\tilde{v}_T)$ are asymptotically equivalent. Tests formed using $g_z(f)$ in (3.10) will be referred to below as modified Z_α (MZ_α) tests. In addition, g_z is the functional associated with the Dickey–Fuller root test in the first order model.

3.3 The R/S Statistic

Mandelbrot (1975) proposed the "rescaled range," or "range over standard deviation" (R/S), statistic to detect fractionally differenced processes. Mandelbrot's motivation is essentially that used here: the order in probability of a fractionally differenced process is other than $T^{\frac{1}{2}}$ (the order depends on the fractional differencing parameter). Suppose here that $d_t(\beta) = \beta_0$. Then the R/S statistic is,

$$\tilde{Q}_T = T^{-\frac{1}{2}}(\max_{1 \leq t \leq T} y_t - \min_{1 \leq t \leq T} y_t)/(T^{-1}\sum_{t=2}^{T}\Delta y_t^2)^{\frac{1}{2}}.$$

Because $\sup_{\lambda \in [0,1]} f(\lambda) - \inf_{\lambda \in [0,1]} f(\lambda)$ is continuous, it follows from Assumption 1 that $\tilde{Q}_T \Rightarrow \sqrt{m}\{\sup_{\lambda \in [0,1]} W(\lambda) - \inf_{\lambda \in [0,1]} W(\lambda)\}$, where $m = \omega/\mathrm{var}(\Delta y_t)$. As do the Sargan–Bhargava and Bhargava statistics, the asymptotic distribution of $\tilde{Q}_T$ depends on the nuisance parameter m.

Lo (1991) suggested eliminating this dependence on m by considering a modification of the R/S statistic:

$$Q_T = (T\hat{\omega})^{-\frac{1}{2}}(\max_{1 \leq t \leq T} y_t - \min_{1 \leq t \leq T} y_t). \qquad (3.11)$$

Evidently this is a g-statistic: $Q_T = g_{RS}(v_T)$, where $g_{RS}(f) = \sup_{\lambda \in [0,1]} f(\lambda) - \inf_{\lambda \in [0,1]} f(\lambda)$. Under Assumptions 1 and 2, $g_{RS}(v_T) \Rightarrow g_{RS}(W)$.

4 Testing for Cointegration

Engle and Granger (1987) proposed testing for whether a multivariate time series is cointegrated of order $(1, 1)$ by regressing one of the individual series on the remaining series and testing for a unit root in the residual. The reasoning behind this procedure is that, if the multivariate series are individually integrated and are not jointly cointegrated, then any linear combination of the series will be integrated; if, however, the series are cointegrated, then the linear combination formed by the cointegrating vector will be stationary. Since the OLS estimator of the cointegrating vector is consistent (Stock, 1987), the residuals from a levels cointegrating regression can proxy for this linear combination.

Engle and Yoo (1987) derived the asymptotic distribution of the Dickey–Fuller (1979) $\hat{\tau}_{\mu}$ t-statistic, computed using the residuals from a levels regression, under the null hypothesis that the constituent time series are independent random walks. Phillips and Ouliaris (1990) derived the asymptotic distributions of this and other residual-based cointegration test statistics under more general conditions. Their approach is used here to generalize the univariate $g(\cdot)$ tests to residual-based tests for cointegration.

Let Y_t be a $n \times 1$ time series variable generated by the multivariate counterpart of (2.1):

$$Y_t = d_t(\beta) + \sum_{s=1}^{t} U_s, \quad t = 1, \ldots, T, \tag{4.1}$$

where $d_t(\beta)$ and U_t are $n \times 1$ deterministic and stochastic terms, respectively. The parameter vector β is typically unknown and is estimated by $\hat{\beta}$. The assumption made on $\{d_t(\hat{\beta}), U_t\}$ in the multivariate case is analogous to Assumptions 1(a) and 1(b). Let $\nu_T^d(\lambda; \hat{\beta}) = T^{-1/2}\{Y_{[T\lambda]} - d_{[T\lambda]}(\hat{\beta})\}$. Then:

Assumption 3. $\nu_T^d(\cdot, \hat{\beta}) \Rightarrow B^d$, where B^d is an $n \times 1$ Gaussian process on $D[0, 1]$ with mean 0 and $E\{B^d(\lambda) B^d(\lambda)'\} = \Omega f(\lambda)$, where f is a scalar function on $[0, 1]$ that does not depend on β or the distribution of $\{U_t\}$, and where Ω is $n \times n$.

Because Ω can be factored as $\Omega = HH'$, Assumption 3 implies that

$$\nu_T^d(\cdot, \hat{\beta}) \Rightarrow HV^d, \tag{4.2}$$

where V^d is a $n \times 1$ Gaussian process with $E(V^d(\lambda) V^d(\lambda)') = f(\lambda)I_n$, so the distribution of V^d does not depend on β or on the nuisance parameters describing the distribution of $\{U_t\}$.

Like Assumption 1, Assumption 3 is satisfied under general conditions on U_t. For example, if $U_t = C(L)\epsilon_t$, where $C(L)$ is 1-summable and ϵ_t is an $n \times 1$ martingale difference sequence satisfying multivariate extensions of the moment conditions stated after (2.2), then Assumption 3 follows from Chan and Wei (1988), Theorem 2.2, with $\Omega = C(1)\Sigma_\epsilon C(1)'$, where $\Sigma_\epsilon = E\epsilon_t\epsilon_t'$. As is discussed below, the assumption is also satisfied by a large number of estimated trend specifications.

Under the null hypothesis, Y_t is not cointegrated. It is assumed here that interest is in testing whether Ω has full versus reduced rank; β is treated as a nuisance parameter. (An alternative, not pursued here, would be to consider cointegration that involves the trend terms as well.) Thus it is natural to consider residual-based tests in which the series are initially detrended.

Partition Y_t^d as $[Y_{1t}^d | Y_{2t}^d]'$, where $Y_t^d = Y_t - d_t(\hat{\beta})$ and Y_{1t}^d is a scalar process. Suppose that the cointegrating vector α is estimated by regressing Y_{1t}^d on Y_{2t}^d:

$$\hat{\alpha}^d = \begin{bmatrix} 1 \\ -(\sum Y_{2t}^d Y_{2t}^{d\prime})^{-1} (\sum Y_{2t}^d Y_{1t}^d) \end{bmatrix}.$$

The residuals are $\hat{z}_t^d = \hat{\alpha}^{d\prime} Y_t^d$. Let

$$\tilde{\omega}_z = \{T^{-1} \sum_{t=2}^{T} \tilde{u}_t^2 + 2 \sum_{j=1}^{\ell} T^{-1} \sum_{t=j+2}^{T} \tilde{u}_t \tilde{u}_{t-j}\}, \tag{4.3}$$

where $\tilde{u}_t = \hat{z}_t - \tilde{\rho} \hat{z}_{t-1}$, with $\tilde{\rho} = \sum_{t=2}^{T} \hat{z}_t \hat{z}_{t-1} / \sum_{t=2}^{T} \hat{z}_{t-1}^2$.

The strategy is to apply the univariate $g(\cdot)$ tests to the residuals $\hat{z}_t^d$. The standardized detrended residuals are:

$$\hat{v}_T^d(\lambda) = (T \tilde{\omega}_z)^{-\frac{1}{2}} \hat{z}_{[T\lambda]}^d. \tag{4.4}$$

To handle the leading special cases, analogously to Section 2 adopt the notation $\hat{v}_T$, $\hat{v}_T^\mu$, $\hat{v}_T^\tau$, and $\hat{v}_T^B$. As in the univariate case, these standardized residuals have limiting representations in terms of functionals of Brownian motion. Let W denote standard $n \times 1$ Brownian motion, and partition the $n \times 1$ stochastic processes V, W, etc. conformably with Y_t. The following theorem summarizes results for the leading cases.

Theorem 3. Assume that Assumption 3 holds, that Ω has full rank, and that $\sup_t E(U_{it})^4 < \infty$, $i = 1, ..., n$. Then $\hat{v}_T^d => (\tilde{\alpha}^{d\prime} \tilde{\alpha}^d)^{-\frac{1}{2}} \tilde{\alpha}^{d\prime} V^d$, where

$$\tilde{\alpha}^d = [1 | -(\int_0^1 V_1^d(s) V_2^d(s)' ds)(\int_0^1 V_2^d(s) V_2^d(s)' ds)^{-1}]'.$$

In the leading special cases, this result holds with:

(a) for $d_t(\beta) = 0$, $V^d = W$;

(b) for $d_t(\beta) = \beta_0$, $V^\mu(\lambda) = W(\lambda) - \int_0^1 W(s) ds$;

(c) for $d_t(\beta) = \beta_0 + \beta_1 t$, $V^\tau(\lambda) = W(\lambda) - a_1(\lambda) \int_0^1 W(s) ds - a_2(\lambda) \int_0^1 s W(s) ds$
and $V^B(\lambda) = W(\lambda) - (\lambda - \frac{1}{2}) W(1) - \int_0^1 W(s) ds$, where $a_1(\lambda) = 4 - 6\lambda$
and $a_2(\lambda) = -6 + 12\lambda$.

Theorem 3 states that, under the null hypothesis of no cointegration, the residuals from the levels regressions have an asymptotic distribution that is the same as the indicated functionals of multivariate Brownian motion.

The multivariate version of trends that are linear in β is $d_t(\beta) = \beta x_t$, where β is $n \times J$ and x_t is $J \times 1$. The OLS estimator is $\hat{\beta} = (\sum_{t=1}^{T} Y_t x_t')(\sum_{t=1}^{T} x_t x_t')^{-1}$. If $\tau_T(\lambda) = x_{[T\lambda]}$ satisfies (2.4), a direct calculation as in the proof of Theorem 1(d) shows that $v_T^d(\cdot, \hat{\beta}) => H V^d$, where $V^d(\lambda) = W(\lambda) - \{\int_0^1 W(s) \tau(s)' ds M^{-1}\} \tau$.

Thus, like the leading cases addressed in Theorem 4, this more general trend specification satisfies Assumption 3 and (4.2).

As in the univariate case, if $g(\cdot)$ is continuous, then $g(\hat{v}_T^d) => g(V^d)$. Because the limiting representations in Theorem 3 do not depend on any nuisance parameters other than n, this can form the basis for constructing tests with critical values that can be tabulated as a function of n. This therefore generalizes Phillips and Ouliaris's (1990) results for selected residual-based tests for cointegration to the entire family of tests defined by G^d.

As a specific example, consider the modification of the Sargan–Bhargava statistic formed using (3.5):

$$g_{SB}(\hat{v}_T) = T^{-2} \sum_{t=1}^{T} \hat{z}_t^2 / \tilde{\omega} => \tilde{\alpha}' \{ \int_0^1 V(s)V(s)' ds \} \tilde{\alpha} / (\tilde{\alpha}' \tilde{\alpha}). \tag{4.5}$$

This statistic is related to the $\hat{P}_u$ statistic proposed by Phillips and Ouliaris (1990); the difference is that, in (4.5), the cointegrating residuals are scaled by $\tilde{\omega}$, while in the $\hat{P}_u$ statistic these residuals are scaled by an estimate of the conditional variance of Y_{1t} given Y_{2t} constructed using an estimate of the spectral density matrix $S_{\Delta Y}(0)$.

5 Consistency

This section examines the consistency of univariate g-tests against I(0) alternatives both in general and in some special cases. The general consistency result is given in the following theorem. Recall that, in the notation of Section 2, $D_T(\lambda, \beta) \equiv d_{[T\lambda]}(\beta)$ and, for trends that are linear in β, $d_t(\beta) = \beta' x_t$, with $\tau_T(\lambda) \equiv x_{[T\lambda]}$.

Theorem 4. Assume that $y_t = d_t(\beta) + w_t$, where $\sup_t E|w_t|^{2+\delta} < \infty$ for some $\delta > 0$, and that one of the following holds:

(a) $T^{-\frac{1}{2}} \{ D_T(\cdot, \hat{\beta}) - D_T(\cdot, \beta) \} => 0$; or

(b) $D_T(\lambda, \beta) = \beta' \tau_T(\lambda)$, where τ_T satisfies (2.4) and β is estimated by OLS. If $\hat{\omega} \xrightarrow{p} k \neq 0$, then $g(v_T^d)$ is consistent for all $g \in G^d$.

This provides sufficient conditions for the consistency of all $g \in G^d$. However, some $g \in G^d$ will be consistent under weaker conditions, and rate results can be obtained for specific tests if different conditions are assumed. In addition, this theorem assumes that $\hat{\omega}$ has a nonzero limit under the alternative, something that must be shown on an estimator-by-estimator basis.

We therefore examine the consistency of four specific $g(\cdot)$ tests, constructed using an autoregressive estimator of ω, in the case that $d_t(\beta) = 0$. The four functionals are:

$$g_1(f) = \int_0^1 |f(s)|^r ds, \tag{5.1a}$$

$$g_2(f) = \int_0^1 \ln|f(s)|\,ds, \tag{5.1b}$$

$$g_3(f) = [\int_0^1 s^r f(s)\,ds]^2, \tag{5.1c}$$

$$g_{RS}(f) = \sup_{\lambda\in[0,1]} f(s) - \inf_{\lambda\in[0,1]} f(s), \tag{5.1d}$$

where $f(s)$ is a function on the unit interval.

The g_1 functional is examined because, for $r=2$, it leads to the generalization of the Sargan–Bhargava and Bhargava statistics. As mentioned in Section 2, the g_3 functional has the useful property that, in the univariate context, its distribution is a constant times a χ_1^2. (Note however that for $n>1$ the distribution of g_3 is not χ^2, but rather involves the random processes in Theorem 3.) The g_{RS} functional leads to Lo's (1991) modification (3.11) of the R/S statistic. The g_2 statistic is included to demonstrate the variety of conditions that lead to consistency of $g(\cdot)$ tests.

The calculated test statistics are the sample analogs of (5.1):

$$g_1(v_T) = T^{-1}\sum_{t=1}^T |v_t|^r, \tag{5.2a}$$

$$g_2(v_T) = T^{-1}\sum_{t=1}^T \ln|v_t|, \tag{5.2b}$$

$$g_3(v_T) = \{T^{-1}\sum_{t=1}^T (t/T)^r v_t\}^2, \tag{5.2c}$$

$$g_{RS}(v_T) = \max_{1\le t\le T} v_t - \min_{1\le t\le T} v_t = Q_T. \tag{5.2d}$$

Here, ω is estimated by a sequence of autoregressive spectral density estimators. That is, let $\hat{a}(1)$ be the OLS estimator of $a(1)$ in the regression,

$$\Delta y_t = \beta_0 + \beta_1 y_{t-1} + a(L)\Delta y_{t-1} + e_t, \tag{5.3}$$

where $a(L)$ is a lag polynomial of length p and e_t is the regression error. The autoregressive spectral density estimator is $\hat{\omega} = \hat{\sigma}_e^2/(1-\hat{a}(1))^2$.

Were y_{t-1} not in the regression (5.3), $\hat{\omega}$ would be the autoregressive spectral density estimator considered by Berk (1974), who proved its consistency under general conditions on $c(L)$ in (2.2) for $p\to\infty$ and $p=o(T^{1/3})$. Said and Dickey (1984) extended this result to the regression coefficients of (5.3); the consistency of $\hat{\omega}$ under the null is an implication of their Theorem 6.1. Thus $\hat{\omega}$ satisfies Assumption 2.

The properties of the univariate tests are investigated under the alternative that y_t is a stationary linear process with nonzero mean:

$$y_t = \beta_0 + w_t, \text{ where } w_t = b(L)\epsilon_t, \ \epsilon_t \text{ i.i.d. } (0,\sigma_\epsilon^2), \ E\epsilon_t^4 < \infty, \tag{5.4}$$

$$\text{where } 0 < \left|b(e^{i\omega})\right|^2 < \infty \ \forall\omega\in(-\pi,\pi], \ \sum_{j=0}^\infty |b_j| < \infty,$$

$$\text{and } \sum_{j=0}^\infty j|d_j| < \infty, \text{ where } d(z) = b(z)^{-1}.$$

In general $\hat{\omega}$ converges to a nonzero constant under this alternative:

Lemma 1. Suppose that y_t is generated by (5.4), $p\to\infty$, $p=o(T^{1/3})$, $p^{1/2}\sum_{k=p+1}^\infty |d_k|\to 0$, and $\sum_{j=0}^\infty (j-1)d_j \ne 0$. Then $\hat{\omega} \xrightarrow{p} \sigma_\epsilon^2/(\sum_{j=0}^\infty (j-1)d_j)^2 \equiv \kappa$.

The next theorem provides rates of consistency against (5.4).

Theorem 5. Assume that the conditions of Lemma 1 hold.

(a) If $E(\epsilon_t^{2r}) < \infty$, then $(T^{\frac{1}{2}r}/\ln T)g_1(v_T) \xrightarrow{p} 0$ for all $r > 0$.

(b) If $E(\ln|y_t|)^2 < \infty$, then $g_2(v_T) + (\frac{1}{2} - \delta)\ln T \xrightarrow{p} -\infty$ for all $\delta > 0$.

(c) $Tg_3(v_T) \xrightarrow{p} \beta_0^2/\kappa(1 + r)^2$ for all $r \geq 0$.

(d) If $\epsilon_j = 0$, $j \leq 0$, and if there exist nonstochastic sequences $\{a_T, b_T\}$ such that $b_T + a_T\max_{1 \leq t \leq T}|\epsilon_t| \xrightarrow{d} \epsilon^*$, where ϵ^* has a distribution on the real line, then $g_{RS}(v_T) = O_p(\max(|b_T|, 1)/\sqrt{T}a_T)$.

Two remarks are in order.

(a) The rates at which the statistics converge under the alternative is strikingly different. Indeed, the rate of convergence of the test $g_1(\cdot)$ can be made arbitrarily large; the cost of a faster rate is an increased number of moments of ϵ_t assumed to exist under the alternative. It is instructive to compare these to other rate results in the literature. In particular, Phillips and Ouliaris (1990) show that the Z_α statistic has a rate of T under the fixed alternative, whereas the Dickey–Fuller t-statistic has a rate of $T^{\frac{1}{2}}$. All else equal, these results suggest that the Z_α, MZ_α, and the modified Sargan–Bhargava statistics might be expected to exhibit better power against I(0) alternatives than the Dickey–Fuller t-statistic.

(b) The rate of convergence of the R/S statistic depends on the rate of convergence of the extreme order statistics of $\{\epsilon_t\}$. In general, if $b_T + a_T\max_{1 \leq t \leq T}|\epsilon_t|$ has a limiting distribution, then it will be of the Fréchet, Weibull, or Gumbel form; the sequences $\{a_T, b_T\}$, if they exist, depend on the distribution of $\{\epsilon_t\}$ (Reiss, 1989, p. 152). For example, if $\{\epsilon_t\}$ are i.i.d. $N(0, \sigma^2)$, then $a_T = (2\ln T)^{\frac{1}{2}}$ and $b_T = -2\ln T$. Thus, for Gaussian ϵ_t, $Q_T = O_p((2\ln T)^{\frac{1}{2}}/\sqrt{T})$ under H_1. It can also be shown that $v_T \Rightarrow 0$ under the conditions of Theorem 5(d). Thus these conditions are sufficient to show the consistency not just of the R/S test, but of all g-statistics. In this sense, the treatment of the R/S statistic in theorem 5 relies on the strongest conditions for consistency.

6 Monte Carlo Results

This section presents the results of a Monte Carlo study of several of the tests discussed in the previous sections. The design includes two types of models: stylized models found elsewhere in the literature, included here to permit comparisons across studies, and empirical models based on postwar US time series data. The motivation for using the empirical models is that, to make recommendations for empirical practice, it is important to study the finite sample behavior of the statistics in probability models typical of those found in applications.

6.1 Univariate Tests

The experiment examines the behavior of seven tests for a unit root under eight different probability models (data generating processes). The leading case in practice is an I(1) null with unknown drift versus the alternative that the process is stationary around a linear time trend; see, for example, the extensive discussion in Christiano and Eichenbaum (1989). Thus the Monte Carlo experiment focuses on the linear trend case, $d_t(\beta) = \beta_0 + \beta_1(t/T)$.

Of the seven unit root tests, five are $g(\cdot)$ tests discussed above, of which four are new, and two are standard tests. These two are the Dickey–Fuller t-statistic and the Phillips–Perron Z_α statistic. These statistics have been studied extensively elsewhere and therefore provide a basis for comparison of these results with Monte Carlo examinations of other tests. The unit root tests considered are:

1. The modified Sargan–Bhargava (MSB) statistic, based on the functional

$$g_{MSB}(f) = \{\int_0^1 f(s)^2 \, \mathrm{d}s\}^{\frac{1}{2}}; \tag{6.1}$$

2. The Dickey–Fuller t-statistic (DF_τ);
3. The Phillips–Perron Z_α statistic given in (3.8);
4. The modified Phillips–Perron Z_α statistic (MZ_α), $g_z(v_T^\tau)$, where $g_z(f) = \frac{1}{2}(f(1)^2 - 1)/\int_0^1 f(s)^2 ds$;
5. The modified R/S statistic Q_t given in (3.11);
6. The g_2 statistic in (5.2b), in which $g_2(f) = \int_0^1 \ln|f(s)| \, ds$;
7. The g_3 statistic in (5.2c) with $r = 2$, so that $g_3(f) = \{\int_0^1 s^2 f(s) \, ds\}^2$.

The MSB statistic (6.1) is evaluated using v_T^B, while the MZ_α, R/S, g_2, and g_3 statistics are evaluated using v_T^τ; for these tests, the spectral density was estimated by the autoregressive spectral estimator $\hat\omega$ defined following (5.3), with 4 lags ($T = 100$) and 5 lags ($T = 200$). The DF_τ autoregression was evaluated with 4 lags ($T = 100$) and 5 lags ($T = 200$). The Z_α statistic was evaluated using $\ell = 4$ ($T = 100$) and $\ell = 5$ ($T = 200$).

Asymptotic critical values for the $g(\cdot)$ tests were computed by Monte Carlo simulation using a standard Gaussian random walk of length $T = 500$. Critical values for the univariate DF_τ and Z_α statistics were taken from Fuller (1976, pp. 373 and 371, respectively). As a reference, asymptotic critical values for the MSB statistic are provided in Table 1.

Of the eight probability models considered, the first three are standard and provide a basis for comparison against other results in the literature (in particular Schwert, 1989). These take the form:

$$(1 - \rho L)y_t = u_t, \quad u_t = \epsilon_t + \theta\epsilon_{t-1}, \quad \epsilon_t \text{ i.i.d. } N(0,1), \quad t = 1,\dots,T, \tag{6.2}$$

where $\theta = 0$ (model 1), $\theta = 0.5$ (model 2), and $\theta = -0.5$ (model 3).

The remaining probability models were estimated using five quarterly US

Table 1. Asymptotic critical percentiles for the univariate
MSB statistic

Percentile	Demeaned	Detrended
.025	0.17405	0.15250
.05	0.19144	0.16449
.10	0.21426	0.18050
.20	0.24894	0.20415
.30	0.27957	0.22418
.50	0.34302	0.26235
.70	0.42787	0.30843
.80	0.49094	0.34229
.90	0.58267	0.39049
.95	0.66777	0.43341
.975	0.74723	0.47113

Notes: The MSB statistic is $g_{\text{MSB}}(v_T^\mu)$ (demeaned) and $g_{\text{MSB}}(v_T^B)$ (detrended), where $g_{\text{MSB}}(f) = \{\int_0^1 f(s)^2 ds\}^{\frac{1}{2}}$ and where v_T^μ and v_T^B are defined in Section 2. Based on 20,000 Monte Carlo replications with $T = 500$.

time series over the period 1948:I to 1988:IV. The series were selected using two criteria: first, that the series either has been examined in the literature for its unit root properties or is closely related to series that have been so studied; and second, it has a spectral shape that is representative of those found in postwar US data. The evaluation of the second criterion drew on Stock and Watson (1990), in which various time series properties of 163 monthly US time series, including plots of their spectra, are cataloged.

The five series chosen are: model 4: the real money supply (M2), in logarithms; model 5: the inventory to sales ratio for manufacturing and trade (IVT82); model 6: the number of new business incorporations, in logarithms (INC); model 7: the 90-day US Treasury bill rate (FYGM3); and model 8: total real personal income less transfer payments (GMYXP8). The data (and mnemonics) are from the CITIBASE database. Most empirical macroeconomic research uses quarterly series, often quarterly averages of monthly values, so these monthly series were aggregated to the quarterly level before transformations or estimation.

The empirical models were obtained by estimating

$$a(L)(1 - \rho L)y_t = \beta_0 + \epsilon_t, \tag{6.3}$$

where $a(L)$ has order 6 and, for estimation, $\rho = 1$ is imposed.[4] A natural way to assess the fit of these models is to consider the qualitative adequacy of their approximations in the frequency domain. To this end, the spectra of these series, estimated using the AR(6) approximation (solid line) and using a smoothed periodogram with a Fejer kernel with bandwidth 10 (dashed line) are graphed in Figures 1–5. In each case, there appears to be no qualitatively

James H. Stock

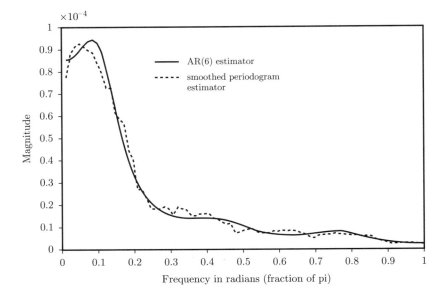

Figure 1. Real money supply (M2), USA, 1948:I–1988:IV:
estimated spectral density (growth rates)

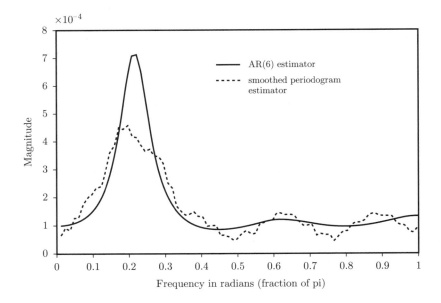

Figure 2. Inventory to sales ratio, manufacturing and trade, USA, 1948:I–1988:IV:
estimated spectral density (changes)

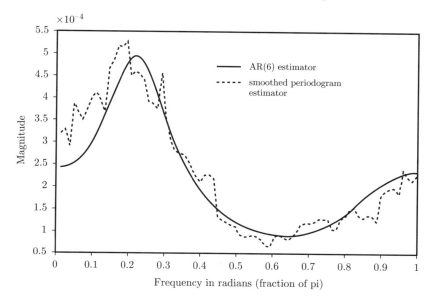

Figure 3. Number of new business incorporations, 1948:I–1988:IV: estimated spectral density (growth rates)

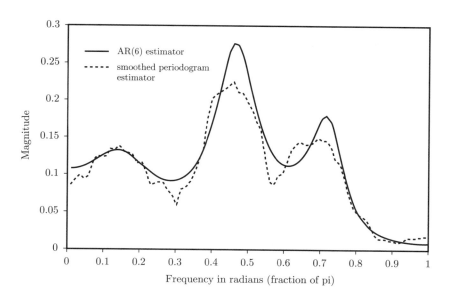

Figure 4. 90-day Treasury bill rate, USA, 1948:I–1988:IV: estimated spectral density (changes)

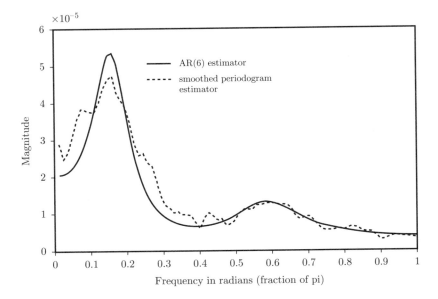

Figure 5. Total real personal income less transfer payments, USA, 1948:I–1988:IV: estimated spectral density (growth rates)

important feature of the spectrum missed by the AR(6) estimates. One notable feature is that although the 90-day Treasury bill rate and new business incorporations exhibit substantial high frequency power, none of the spectra increase sharply with frequency. This is typical of the 163 series in Stock and Watson (1990). In only a few cases, such as import and export figures, are the series dominated by their high frequency movements. Even in these cases, however, aggregation to the quarterly level substantially reduces the high frequency component. The estimated parameters are provided in Appendix B.

Because these models are based on autoregressive approximations, there is the possibility that the performance of autoregression-based tests will be overstated because the model approximation error is slight. For each series, the calculations were therefore repeated using an ARMA(1, 5) model, $(1 - \rho L)y_t^\tau = b(L)\epsilon_t$ with ρ and $b(L)$ estimated by maximum likelihood. By varying ρ in simulations (keeping $b(L)$ fixed), this model is capable of generating data under both the null and the alternative.

For each of the eight models, the tests were studied using Gaussian errors under the null ($\rho = 1$) and under three alternatives: for $T = 100$, $\rho = .95, .90$, and .80; for $T = 200$, $\rho = .975, .95$, and .90. These choices of ρ permit examining the predicted stability of the power function under the local alternative $\rho_T = e^{c/T} = 1 + c/T + o(c/T)$.

6.2 Cointegration Tests

The test statistics examined in the univariate experiments were also examined using four bivariate models, except that the g_3 statistic was evaluated using $r = 1$ in (5.1c), i.e. $g_3(f) = \{\int_0^1 sf(s)\,ds\}^2$. The test statistics were computed as described for the univariate tests, except using the cointegrating residuals based on demeaned series. The choice was made to demean rather than detrend for comparability with earlier studies. Critical values for the DF_τ ("ADF" in Engle and Granger, 1987; Phillips and Ouliaris, 1990) and Z_α tests were taken from Phillips and Ouliaris (1990); for the other statistics, they were computed by Monte Carlo simulation using the asymptotic representations of these statistics with 5,000 Monte Carlo replications.

The simulation examined four models. The first three are bivariate extensions of the univariate model (6.2), namely,

$$y_{1t} = \tfrac{1}{2}\sum_{s=1}^{t} u_{1t} + \tfrac{1}{2}\sum_{s=1}^{t} \rho^{t-s} u_{2t}, \quad y_{2t} = \tfrac{1}{2}\sum_{s=1}^{t} u_{1t} - \tfrac{1}{2}\sum_{s=1}^{t} \rho^{t-s} u_{2t}, \tag{6.4}$$

where $u_t = \epsilon_t + \theta\epsilon_{t-1}$, $t = 1, ..., T$, with ϵ_t i.i.d. $N(0, I_2)$ and $\theta = 0$ (model 1), 0.5 (model 2), and –0.5 (model 3). Under the alternative, $\rho < 1$, the cointegrating vector is $(1\ {-}1)$ and $z_t = \rho z_{t-1} + u_{2t}$. This simple model provides a useful starting point: because z_t is generated by the same process under the alternative in (6.4) as is y_t in the stationary univariate case in (6.2), the differences in size and power between the univariate and bivariate tests can largely be attributed to random variations of the estimated cointegrating vector and to the different types of detrending, rather than to differences in the specification of nuisance parameters.

The experiment also examined an empirical model (model 4) of the form:

$$\Delta y_t = \mu_1 + u_{1t}, \tag{6.5}$$
$$(1 - \rho L)z_t = \mu_2 + u_{2t},$$

where $U_t = (u_{1t}\ u_{2t})'$ was approximated by a VAR(6). The model was estimated with y_{1t} and y_{2t} respectively being inventories (IVMT82) and sales (MT82) in manufacturing and trade, aggregated from the monthly to the quarterly level, in logarithms, from 1952:I to 1988:IV. The motivation for choosing this pair is that the inventory-to-sales ratio was one of the series examined in the previous Monte Carlo simulation. The cointegrating vector $(1\ {-}1)$ was imposed in estimation, and the possibility of cointegration was admitted in estimation by specifying the right-hand side of the z_t equation in (6.5) in terms of z_{t-1} and lags of Δz_{t-1}, with the dependent variable being z_{t-1}.

In all four models, the pseudo-data were generated using $T = 200$, Gaussian errors, and zero drift ($\mu_1 = \mu_2 = 0$ in (6.5)). Under the null of no cointegration, $\rho = 1$; the alternatives were $\rho = .95, .9$, and $.85$.

6.3 Results and Discussion

The univariate results are summarized in Tables 2–4. For each model, the first row gives the size of the test based on the asymptotic critical value. Because the size typically differs from the asymptotic level, the reported power is size-

Table 2. Size and power of tests for integration, detrended statistics, $T = 100$
Rejection probabilities for tests with asymptotic level 5%

Model	ρ	MSB	DF_τ	Z_α	MZ_α	R/S	g_2	g_3
		Test statistic						
1	1.00	.081	.070	.062	.084	.157	.083	.054
	.95	.164	.070	.102	.162	.153	.144	.093
	.90	.306	.128	.235	.308	.274	.275	.143
	.80	.574	.309	.669	.572	.477	.524	.236
2	1.00	.075	.062	.009	.072	.174	.076	.053
	.95	.168	.072	.081	.163	.158	.144	.089
	.90	.308	.123	.159	.306	.272	.272	.126
	.80	.564	.282	.374	.564	.478	.503	.211
3	1.00	.043	.082	.802	.042	.055	.043	.063
	.95	.170	.074	.091	.170	.162	.158	.087
	.90	.327	.149	.198	.329	.298	.304	.139
	.80	.606	.441	.491	.628	.571	.595	.259
4	1.00	.028	.105	.008	.029	.187	.037	.052
	.95	.231	.071	.080	.260	.231	.222	.070
	.90	.487	.117	.168	.524	.466	.436	.123
	.80	.737	.210	.359	.760	.662	.679	.201
5	1.00	.168	.203	.072	.171	.257	.167	.090
	.95	.181	.079	.082	.175	.171	.166	.086
	.90	.384	.165	.147	.380	.359	.352	.150
	.80	.781	.476	.335	.773	.733	.736	.313
6	1.00	.003	.074	.018	.003	.026	.009	.055
	.95	.253	.083	.071	.284	.258	.242	.073
	.90	.580	.151	.157	.607	.560	.526	.126
	.80	.874	.373	.402	.891	.814	.838	.251
7	1.00	.047	.046	.065	.046	.099	.047	.054
	.95	.160	.072	.103	.165	.145	.146	.085
	.90	.297	.119	.223	.305	.249	.275	.128
	.80	.532	.272	.621	.532	.417	.478	.209
8	1.00	.042	.223	.079	.037	.174	.054	.069
	.95	.048	.041	.036	.068	.052	.066	.023
	.90	.465	.128	.128	.555	.478	.474	.081
	.80	.915	.350	.434	.942	.903	.894	.291

Notes: The pseudo-data were generated using (6.2) (models 1–3) and (6.3) (models 4–8). The first row for each model (with $\rho = 1$) presents size, based on the asymptotic critical values; the remaining rows present the size-adjusted power. The MSB statistic was evaluated using v_T^B, the remaining g-statistics and Z_α using v_T^τ, and $(1, t)$ were included as regressors in the DF_τ autoregression. The asymptotic critical values were computed by Monte Carlo simulation. The results are based on 5,000 Monte Carlo replications.

Table 3. Size and power of tests for integration, detrended statistics, $T = 200$
Rejection probabilities for tests with asymptotic level 5%

Model	ρ	Test statistic						
		MSB	DF_τ	Z_α	MZ_α	R/S	g_2	g_3
1	1.00	.060	.060	.072	.058	.085	.062	.064
	.975	.141	.084	.093	.143	.140	.134	.068
	.95	.302	.155	.210	.307	.272	.273	.100
	.90	.681	.436	.651	.689	.592	.608	.165
2	1.00	.047	.052	.025	.049	.095	.047	.055
	.975	.148	.073	.089	.143	.134	.136	.069
	.95	.310	.138	.205	.318	.273	.286	.107
	.90	.683	.399	.561	.687	.572	.620	.187
3	1.00	.032	.080	.721	.025	.020	.027	.061
	.975	.165	.078	.100	.165	.154	.158	.071
	.95	.348	.163	.238	.360	.319	.336	.109
	.90	.727	.509	.699	.769	.670	.727	.190
4	1.00	.053	.103	.033	.052	.165	.059	.062
	.975	.091	.068	.067	.109	.098	.095	.045
	.95	.321	.148	.184	.375	.324	.302	.091
	.90	.727	.367	.521	.773	.684	.666	.175
5	1.00	.157	.200	.243	.158	.178	.147	.070
	.975	.185	.097	.102	.181	.179	.172	.077
	.95	.408	.202	.220	.403	.373	.371	.135
	.90	.843	.600	.592	.849	.785	.807	.234
6	1.00	.018	.073	.065	.018	.032	.020	.056
	.975	.078	.079	.056	.092	.085	.093	.047
	.95	.334	.168	.179	.385	.343	.337	.090
	.90	.813	.473	.559	.862	.785	.791	.199
7	1.00	.032	.043	.095	.027	.046	.031	.057
	.975	.149	.078	.102	.158	.151	.141	.074
	.95	.322	.153	.233	.334	.300	.288	.108
	.90	.682	.412	.669	.699	.584	.628	.184
8	1.00	.107	.214	.189	.113	.199	.110	.060
	.975	.002	.033	.006	.003	.001	.008	.005
	.95	.052	.143	.070	.126	.051	.154	.032
	.90	.683	.516	.501	.848	.729	.801	.167

Notes: See the notes to Table 2.

adjusted: the power was computed using the critical values that produce 5 percent rejections under the null hypothesis for the indicated number of observations for the given model. This size-adjusted power is reported in the remaining three rows for each model.

In model 1, all the statistics have sizes close to their 5 percent level, even for $T = 100$ (except for the R/S statistic). The size results for the DF_τ and Z_α statistics for models 2 and 3 are similar to those that have appeared elsewhere, with the size of the DF_τ statistic being stable but the size of the

Table 4. Size and power of tests for integration, ARMA(1, 5) models,
detrended statistics, $T = 200$
Rejection probabilities for tests with asymptotic level 5%

Model	ρ	Test statistic						
		MSB	DF_τ	Z_α	MZ_α	R/S	g_2	g_3
4	1.00	.076	.068	.023	.079	.188	.078	.060
	.975	.159	.079	.090	.161	.150	.149	.077
	.95	.308	.134	.183	.312	.273	.277	.102
	.90	.618	.327	.468	.619	.501	.550	.168
5	1.00	.023	.037	.016	.022	.060	.029	.051
	.975	.151	.070	.086	.157	.151	.138	.079
	.95	.307	.124	.172	.313	.284	.269	.124
	.90	.637	.320	.420	.625	.526	.554	.188
6	1.00	.089	.079	.019	.093	.175	.092	.057
	.975	.150	.079	.094	.162	.154	.145	.075
	.95	.308	.144	.184	.316	.279	.274	.118
	.90	.638	.362	.467	.642	.542	.573	.186
7	1.00	.190	.149	.032	.208	.345	.187	.065
	.975	.169	.083	.091	.168	.162	.149	.078
	.95	.343	.158	.208	.336	.303	.304	.119
	.90	.665	.399	.585	.667	.568	.610	.202
8	1.00	.079	.076	.022	.088	.209	.089	.057
	.975	.152	.073	.090	.154	.147	.131	.076
	.95	.308	.135	.186	.310	.283	.253	.110
	.90	.633	.338	.504	.625	.537	.535	.180

Notes: The data were generated according to estimated ARMA(1, 5) models described in the text.
See the notes to Table 2.

Z_α statistic changing substantially with θ. The tradeoff between this stability of the size and the size-adjusted power is evident in these models, with the Z_α statistic having better power than DF_τ. Interestingly, in models 1–3 the MZ_α statistic has power properties comparable to the Z_α statistic, but has size that is closer to the level. Indeed, the MZ_α statistic has essentially the same size as the MSB statistic under model 1, the case in which the MSB statistic is asymptotically equivalent to Bhargava's exact test. The g_2 statistic also exhibits good power, better than DF_τ and almost as good as MZ_α, and stable size in these simple models.

The size distortions in models 2 and 3 are not in the same direction for all the statistics. In particular, the size of the MZ_α statistic in model 3 is substantially below its level, while the opposite is true for the Z_α statistic. Because the main difference between these statistics is the spectral estimator at frequency zero, this emphasizes its key role in determining the sampling properties of the statistics.

The results for the empirically derived models differ from those for the simpler models and warrant several observations. First, the size distortions for the DF_τ statistic are as large as for the Z_α statistic (models 5 and 8). Second, the size distortions, while substantial, are not nearly as severe as in model 3. A possible explanation is that none of the models exhibit spectra with the preponderance of power at high frequencies. However, this possibility was admitted by estimating relatively long autoregressions on potentially overdifferenced series. To the extent that these series are typical of those used in empirical analyses, this negative MA problem might not be as severe in practice as might be suggested by the results for model 3.

Third, the R/S statistic exhibits substantial size distortions, even for $T = 200$ and even for models in which the other statistics do not exhibit this problem. This suggests that the sampling distribution of the finite-sample extreme order statistic in series with complicated dependence is not well-approximated by its asymptotic limit.

Fourth, although the size results for the AR and ARMA simulations typically differ, the size performance for the autoregressions-based tests is not clearly better in the AR simulations. The implication, reinforced by the results for models 2 and 3, is that specification bias is not key in determining the sampling distribution of the spectral density estimator. However, the size distortion of the Z_α statistic is substantially less when the ARMA model is used; in this case, the Z_α statistic (which uses 5 lags for $T = 200$) is correctly specified.

Fifth, the size-adjusted power of the autoregressive tests is reduced when the data are generated according to the MA specification. However, the overall ranking of the powers is largely unaffected, with the Dickey–Fuller t-statistic having lower power than the MSB, Z_α, or MZ_α statistics. This is consistent with the theoretical predictions of Theorem 4 (and related results in the literature) that indicate relatively faster rates of convergence for these statistics under the null.

Sixth, the MSB statistic performs well. Aside from the g_3 statistic (which has the best size performance and by far the worst power), the MSB statistic has the least size distortion, followed by g_2. The power of the MSB statistic is also quite good. For example, in models 5 and 6, its power against $\rho = .9$ with $T = 200$ exceeds 80 percent in the AR simulations. The power also compares well to the power of Bhargava's MPI R_2 statistic in the first order model (model 1). For example, the power of the R_2 test was separately computed to be .76 for $\rho = .9$ and $T = 200$, while the MZ_α and MSB statistics respectively have power .68 and .69. In several models, MZ_α performs as well as MSB.

The cointegration results are summarized in Table 5. The most powerful tests are the Z_α, MZ_α, and MSB tests. The univariate size difficulties of the Z_α statistic are mirrored in bivariate model 3. For the models considered here, only the DF_τ and g_3 statistics have size consistently close to their level, and the power of the g_3 statistic is so low as to eliminate it as a serious contender. For all tests, in models 1–3 the power is lower than in the corresponding uni-

Table 5. Size and power of cointegration tests, demeaned statistics, $n = 2$, $T = 200$
Rejection probabilities for tests with asymptotic level 5%

Model	ρ	Test statistic						
		MSB	DF_τ	Z_α	MZ_α	R/S	g_2	g_3
1	1.00	.115	.052	.069	.104	.157	.112	.064
	.95	.180	.127	.192	.179	.154	.170	.055
	.90	.426	.329	.553	.433	.338	.392	.081
	.85	.669	.583	.878	.673	.530	.620	.112
2	1.00	.124	.054	.024	.110	.185	.121	.066
	.95	.160	.121	.154	.162	.152	.163	.061
	.90	.388	.305	.413	.391	.322	.380	.090
	.85	.620	.556	.684	.621	.509	.593	.115
3	1.00	.070	.050	.663	.059	.060	.068	.060
	.95	.143	.119	.184	.147	.133	.146	.062
	.90	.358	.336	.579	.365	.317	.351	.072
	.85	.564	.599	.901	.574	.481	.553	.083
4	1.00	.127	.078	.056	.112	.148	.126	.068
	.95	.108	.113	.077	.110	.093	.103	.080
	.90	.173	.193	.100	.174	.147	.165	.105
	.85	.251	.298	.124	.253	.206	.243	.138

Notes: The pseudo-data were generated using (6.4) (models 1–3) and (6.5) (model 4). The first row for each model (with $\rho = 1$) presents size, based on the asymptotic critical values; the remaining rows present the size-adjusted power. All statistics were evaluated using the residuals from cointegrating regressions of y_{1t}^μ on y_{2t}^μ. For the MSB, MZ_α, R/S, g_2, and g_3 tests, these residuals were standardized by an autoregressive estimate of the spectral density with 5 lags. The asymptotic critical values were computed by Monte Carlo simulation. The results are based on 5,000 Monte Carlo replications.

variate case. A striking feature of model 4 is that the power of all of the tests is very low, much lower than in the stylized models 1–3, although the size distortion is no more severe than under the base model 1. Despite the limited nature of these results, they suggest that these tests can exhibit low power and substantial size distortions, indicating room for further work.

7 Summary and Conclusions

The statistics developed here provide a new class of tests for integration and cointegration. The idea behind these tests is simple: that an integrated process grows at rate $T^{1/2}$, whereas a stationary process does not. This formulation also provides a unifying framework for many previous tests found in the literature and extends to general trend processes.

Once the class of tests is formulated, a natural question is which member of the class will have the greatest power against a specific model, and whether the finite-sample properties of the test are satisfactory. Although it is possible to obtain general results for some processes, such as local-to-unit root processes, and to characterize the rate of convergence of specific members of the class under a fixed alternative, such results provide only a partial answer to the question of determining the optimal test in this class. The approach taken here has been to investigate size and power numerically. The main novelty of the Monte Carlo simulations is the use of empirical models to generate the pseudo-data. In the univariate case, these models are representative of a broad set of US time series, and include series that have substantial power at high frequencies.

While the Monte Carlo results examine only a limited number of tests, they nonetheless provide several conclusions for empirical practice. First, the MSB and MZ_α tests have good power properties, relative to the other tests. The size of both tests is also reasonably well controlled. Second, the size distortions of the Z_α statistic suggested elsewhere might be overstated in terms of their practical importance: in the empirical models, both in their AR and MA formulation, the size distortions are less than in the stylized pure MA(1) models (but see Schwert, 1989, for an argument for using more extreme MA representations). Third, simulations using the empirical models suggest that the size distortion for the Dickey–Fuller t-statistic can be more severe than is suggested by simulations based on the simple MA(1) models; in addition, the size-adjusted power of the Dickey–Fuller statistics is typically substantially lower than that of several of the other statistics. Fourth, the modified R/S statistic has consistently poor size properties.

The main conclusion from the more limited Monte Carlo analysis of the residual-based cointegration tests is that, of those studied, none performs particularly well. Although the size of some of the tests, for example the Dickey–Fuller t-statistic, is close to its asymptotic level, the power of all of the tests is poor in the one empirical model examined.

Appendix A: Proofs of Theorems

Proof of Theorem 1. (a)–(c). The results follow from Assumption 1 and Theorem 2.2 of Chan and Wei (1988) after straightforward calculations. The calculations for $y^\tau_{[T\lambda]}$ are given in the proof of Theorem 5.1 of Stock and Watson (1988).

(d). Write

$$T^{-\frac{1}{2}}\{D_T(\lambda;\hat{\beta}) - D_T(\lambda;\beta)\} = \{(T^{-1}\sum_{t=1}^{T}x_t x_t')^{-1}(T^{-\frac{3}{2}}\sum_{t=1}^{T}x_t\sum_{s=1}^{t}u_s)\}'\tau_T([T\lambda]/T).$$

It follows from (2.4) that $T^{-1}\sum_{t=1}^{T}x_t x_t' \to M$ and $T^{-3/2}\sum_{t=1}^{T}x_t\sum_{s=1}^{t}u_s \Rightarrow \sqrt{\omega}\int_0^1\tau(s)W(s)ds$, so $T^{-\frac{1}{2}}\{D_T(\lambda;\hat{\beta}) - D_T(\lambda;\beta)\} \Rightarrow \sqrt{\omega}\{M^{-1}\int_0^1\tau(s)W(s)ds\}'\tau(\lambda)$.

Because τ and M do not depend on unknown parameters, Assumption 1(b) is satisfied. It follows that $v_T^d => W - \beta^{*\prime}\tau$, where $\beta^* = M^{-1}\int_0^1 \tau(s)\,W(s)\,ds$. ∎

Proof of Theorem 2. The results (a) and (b) follow from Theorem 6.2 of Phillips and Perron (1988), since under the local alternative $T^{1/2}(\hat{\rho} - \rho_T) \xrightarrow{p} 0$. The results (c) and (d) follow by direct calculation, noting that $T(\rho_T - 1) \rightarrow c$. ∎

Proof of Theorem 3. Consider the terms $T^{-1/2}\hat{\alpha}^{d\prime}Y_t^d$ and $\tilde{\omega}_z$ separately. First, following Phillips and Ouliaris (1990), partition H conformably with Y_t so that

$$H = \begin{bmatrix} h_{11} & H_{12} \\ 0 & H_{22} \end{bmatrix} = \begin{bmatrix} H_1 \\ H_2 \end{bmatrix},$$

where h_{11} is a scalar. Then $T^{-1/2}\hat{\alpha}'Y_{[T\lambda]}^d$ can be written as:

$$
\begin{aligned}
T^{-\frac{1}{2}}\hat{\alpha}'Y_{[T\lambda]}^d &= [1 \mid -(\sum Y_{1t}^d Y_{2t}^{d\prime})(\sum Y_{2t}^d Y_{2t}^{d\prime})^{-1}](T^{-\frac{1}{2}}Y_{[T\lambda]}^d) \\
&=> [1 \mid -(\int H_1 V^d V_2^{d\prime} H_{22}')(\int H_{22} V_2^d V_2^{d\prime} H_{22}')^{-1}]\begin{bmatrix} h_{11} & H_{12} \\ 0 & H_{22} \end{bmatrix}V^d(\lambda) \\
&= [h_{11} \mid H_{12} - H_1(\int V^d V_2^{d\prime})(\int V_2^d V_2^{d\prime})^{-1}]V^d(\lambda) \\
&= [h_{11} \mid H_{12} - h_{11}(\int V_1^d V_2^{d\prime})(\int V_2^d V_2^{d\prime})^{-1} - H_{12}]V^d(\lambda) \\
&= h_{11}\tilde{\alpha}^{d\prime}V^d(\lambda) \qquad\qquad (A.1)
\end{aligned}
$$

where $\tilde{\alpha}^{d\prime} = [1 \mid -(\int V_1^d V_2^{d\prime})(\int V_2^d V_2^{d\prime})^{-1}]$, and, to simplify notation, $\int V_1^d V_2^{d\prime}$ represents $\int_0^1 V_1^d(s)\,V_2^d(s)'\,ds$, etc.

Next consider $\tilde{\omega}_z$ and let $\alpha^{*d} = [1 \mid -H_1 \int V^d V_2^{d\prime})(\int V_2^d V_2^{d\prime})^{-1}H_{22}^{-1}]$. Then

$$
\begin{aligned}
\tilde{\omega}_z &= \sum_{j=-\ell}^{\ell} T^{-1}\sum_{t=j+2}^{T}(\hat{z}_t^d - \tilde{\rho}\hat{z}_{t-1}^d)(\hat{z}_{t-j}^d - \tilde{\rho}\hat{z}_{t-j-1}^d) \\
&= \hat{\alpha}^{d\prime}\left[\sum_{j=-\ell}^{\ell}T^{-1}\sum_{t=j+2}^{T}(Y_t^d - \tilde{\rho}Y_{t-1}^d)(Y_{t-j}^d - \tilde{\rho}Y_{t-j-1}^d)'\right]\hat{\alpha}^d \\
&=> \alpha^{*d\prime}\Omega\alpha^{*d}.
\end{aligned}
$$

The argument that the term in brackets converges to Ω is made in Phillips and Ouliaris (1990), proof of Theorem 4.1(a). It relies on $\ell \rightarrow \infty$, $\ell = o(T^{1/4})$, and $\tilde{\rho} - 1 = o_p(1)$; see Phillips and Ouliaris (1990) for the details. Using $\Omega = HH'$ and (A.1), one obtains:

$$\tilde{\omega}_z => \alpha^{*d\prime}\Omega\alpha^{*d} = \alpha^{*d\prime}HH'\alpha^{*d} = h_{11}^2\tilde{\alpha}^{d\prime}\tilde{\alpha}^d. \qquad\qquad (A.2)$$

It follows from (A.1) and (A.2) that $(T\tilde{\omega}_z)^{-1/2}\hat{\alpha}^{d\prime}Y_{[T\lambda]}^d => (\tilde{\alpha}^{d\prime}\tilde{\alpha}^d)^{-1/2}\tilde{\alpha}^{d\prime}V^d(\lambda)$.

(a), (b), (c). The proof of (a) is immediate with $Y_t^d = Y_t$, $V^d = W$, etc. To prove (b) and (c) it only needs to be shown that $D_T(\lambda; \hat{\beta})$ is such that (A3) is satisfied. This follows by direct calculation. For example, $T^{-1/2}(Y_{[T\lambda]}^\mu - T^{-1}\sum_{t=1}^{T}Y_t) => B(\lambda) - \int_0^1 B(s)\,ds \equiv B^\mu(\lambda)$, where B has covariance matrix Ω

$= 2\pi S_U(0)$; this can be factored as $B^\mu = HV^\mu$, where V^μ is as given in the statement of the theorem. ∎

Proof of Theorem 4. (a) Write $v_T^d(\lambda) = (T\hat\omega)^{-\frac12}\{y_{[T\lambda]} - d_{[T\lambda]}(\hat\beta)\} = (T\hat\omega)^{-\frac12}\{y_{[T\lambda]}$
$- d_{[T\lambda]}(\beta)\} - (T\hat\omega)^{-\frac12}\{D_T(\lambda, \hat\beta) - D_T(\lambda, \beta)\}$.

By assumption, $\hat\omega \xrightarrow{p} k > 0$ and $T^{-\frac12}\{D_T(\cdot, \hat\beta) - D_T(\cdot, \beta)\} => 0$. Thus the result follows if $(T\hat\omega)^{-\frac12}w_T^d => 0$, where $w_T^d(\lambda) \equiv y_{[T\lambda]} - d_{[T\lambda]}(\beta) = w_{[T\lambda]}$.

To show that $(T\hat\omega)^{-\frac12}w_T^d => 0$, it is convenient to work in the restriction of $D[0, 1]$ to $C[0, 1]$, with the metric $\rho_C(f_1, f_2) = \sup_{\lambda\in[0,1]}|f_1(\lambda) - f_2(\lambda)|$ (see Hall and Heyde, 1980). Let $w_0 = 0$ and define the interpolation of $w_{[T\lambda]}$ to be $w_T^\dagger(\lambda) = \{w_{[T\lambda]} + (T\lambda - [T\lambda])(w_{[T\lambda]+1} - w_{[T\lambda]})\}/(T\hat\omega)^{\frac12}$ so that $w_T^\dagger(\lambda) \in C[0, 1]$. Note that $\max_{1\le t\le T}|w_t| = \sup_{\lambda\in[0,1]}|w_T^\dagger(\lambda)|$. Then, for all $\epsilon > 0$,

$$\Pr[\rho_C(w_T^\dagger, 0) > \epsilon] = \Pr[\sup_{0\le\lambda\le1}\left|w_T^\dagger(\lambda)\right| > \epsilon]$$
$$= \Pr[\max_{1\le t\le T}\left|w_t/(T\hat\omega)^{\frac12}\right| > \epsilon]$$
$$\le \mathrm{E}\{\max_{1\le t\le T}\left|w_t\right|/\{(T\hat\omega)^{\frac12}\epsilon\}\}^{2+\delta}$$
$$\le T^{-\frac12\delta}\epsilon^{-(2+\delta)}T^{-1}\sum_{t=1}^{T}E\{\left|w_t\right|^{2+\delta}\hat\omega^{-(1+\frac12\delta)}\},$$

which tends to zero under the assumptions $\hat\omega \xrightarrow{p} k \ne 0$ and $\sup_t E|w_t|^{2+\delta} < \infty$. Thus $w_T^\dagger => 0$ so $v_T^d => 0$. Because g is continuous at 0, $g(v_T^d) => g(0)$, so in particular, by the definition of G^d, $\Pr[g(v_T^d) < c_\alpha] \to \Pr[g(0) < c_\alpha] = 1$ for all α.

(b) Write $D_T(\lambda, \hat\beta) - D_T(\lambda, \beta) = \tau_T(\lambda)'(\hat\beta - \beta)$. By assumption, $\tau_T \to \tau$, where $\sup_{\lambda\in[0,1]}|\tau_i(\lambda)| \le \bar\tau$, $i = 1, ..., J$. Thus $D_T(\lambda, \hat\beta) - D_T(\lambda, \beta) => 0$ if $\hat\beta - \beta \xrightarrow{p} 0$. But this follows from noting first that $T^{-1}\sum x_t x_t' \to M$, where M is nonsingular by assumption; and second that:

$$\mathrm{E}\,T^{-2}\sum_{t=1}^{T}\sum_{s=1}^{T}x_t x_s' w_t w_s \le \bar\tau^2 T^{-1}\sum_{u=-\infty}^{\infty}\left|\mathrm{cov}(w_t, w_{t-u})\right| < \infty.$$

With this result and Chebyshev's inequality, $\hat\beta - \beta \xrightarrow{p} 0$, so $D_T(\lambda, \hat\beta) - D_T(\lambda, \beta) => 0$, so condition (i) in the statement of the theorem is satisfied. ∎

Proof of Lemma 1. Under (5.4), y_t has the autoregressive representation, $d(L)y_t = \beta_0 d(1) + \epsilon_t$, or $y_t = \beta_0 d(1) + \delta(L)y_{t-1} + \epsilon_t$. Thus:

$$\Delta y_t = \beta_0 d(1) + (\delta(1) - 1)y_{t-1} + \delta*(L)\Delta y_{t-1} + \epsilon_t, \tag{A.3}$$

where $d_0 = 1$, $\delta(L) = L^{-1}(1 - d(L))$ and $\delta_j^* = -\sum_{i=j+1}^{\infty}\delta_i$. Thus (A.3) is the population regression, the parameters of which are estimated by the sequence of pth order autoregressions (5.3). The stated assumptions satisfy the conditions of Berk's (1974) Theorem 1 for the ℓ_1-consistency of $\hat\delta(z)$. Thus the OLS estimator of a linear combination of these parameters will be consistent. Thus $\hat\omega \xrightarrow{p} \sigma_\epsilon^2/(1 - \delta*(1))^2$. By direct calculation, $\delta*(1) = \sum_{j=0}^{\infty}(-\sum_{i=j+1}^{\infty}\delta_i) = 1$

$-\sum_{j=0}^{\infty}(1-j)\,d_j$. Thus $\hat{\omega}\xrightarrow{p}\sigma_\epsilon^2/[\sum_{j=0}^{\infty}(j-1)\,d_j]^2\equiv\kappa$, where $\sum_{j=0}^{\infty}(j-1)\,d_j$ is nonzero by assumption. ∎

Proof of Theorem 5. (a) $(T^{1/2 r}/\ln T)g_1(v_T)=T^{-1}\sum_{t=1}^{T}T^{1/2 r}|(T\hat{\omega})^{-1/2}y_t|^r/\ln T=\hat{\omega}^{-1/2 r}(T^{-1}\sum_{t=1}^{T}|y_t|^r)/\ln T$.

By Lemma 1, $\hat{\omega}^{1/2 r}\xrightarrow{p}\kappa^{1/2 r}$. By Chebyschev's inequality, it therefore suffices to show that $E(T^{-1}\sum_{t=1}^{T}|y_t|^r/\ln T)^2\to 0$. Now:

$$E(T^{-1}\sum_{t=1}^{T}\bigl|y_t\bigr|^r/\ln T)^2=T^{-2}\sum_{t=1}^{T}\sum_{s=1}^{T}E\bigl|\beta_0+w_t\bigr|^r\bigl|\beta_0+w_s\bigr|^r/(\ln T)^2,$$

which converges to zero if $E|w_tw_s|^r\le c<\infty$ for all t, s. Now:

$$
\begin{aligned}
E\bigl|w_tw_s\bigr|^r &\le Ew_t^{2r}=E(b(L)\epsilon_t)^{2r}\\
&\le\sum_{j_1=0}^{\infty}\cdots\sum_{j_{2r}=0}^{\infty}\bigl|b_{j_1}\bigr|\cdots\bigl|b_{j_{2r}}\bigr|E\bigl(\bigl|\epsilon_{t-j_1}\bigr|\cdots\bigl|\epsilon_{t-j_{2r}}\bigr|\bigr)\\
&\le(\sum_{j=0}^{\infty}\bigl|b_j\bigr|)^{2r}E(\epsilon_t^{2r}),
\end{aligned}
$$

for all t, whence the result follows.

(b) $\Pr[g_2(v_T)+(1/2-\delta)\ln T>c]=\Pr[T^{-1}\sum_{t=1}^{T}\ln|y_t|+1/2\ln\hat{\omega}>c+\delta\ln T]\le E\{T^{-1}\sum_{t=1}^{T}\ln|y_t|+1/2\ln\hat{\omega}\}^2/(c+\delta\ln T)^2$.

Because $\ln\hat{\omega}\xrightarrow{p}\ln\kappa$, the final expression tends to 0 for any fixed c, $|c|<\infty$, if $E(T^{-1}\sum_{t=1}^{T}\ln|y_t|)^2$ is bounded. But $E(T^{-1}\sum_{t=1}^{T}\ln|y_t|)^2\le E(\ln|y_t|)^2$, which is finite by assumption, so $\Pr[g_2(v_T)+(1/2-\delta)\ln T>c]\to 0$ for all $\delta>0$, $|c|<\infty$.

(c) $Tg_3(v_T)=T\{T^{-1}\sum(t/T)^r y_t/[T\hat{\omega}]^{1/2}\}^2=\{T^{-1}\sum(t/T)y_t\}^2/\hat{\omega}$. The result follows from $T^{-1}\sum(t/T)^r y_t\xrightarrow{p}\beta_0/(1+r)$.

(d) $g_{RS}(v_T)=(T\hat{\omega})^{-1/2}\{\max_{1\le t\le T}(\beta_0+w_t)-\min_{1\le t\le T}(\beta_0+w_t)\}$
$$
\begin{aligned}
&\le 2(T\hat{\omega})^{-1/2}\max_{1\le t\le T}|w_t|\\
&\le 2(T\hat{\omega})^{-1/2}\max_{1\le t\le T}(\sum_{j=0}^{t-1}|b_j||\epsilon_{t-j}|)\\
&\le(2\hat{\omega}^{-1/2}\sum_{j=0}^{\infty}|b_j|)\,T^{-1/2}\max_{1\le t\le T}|\epsilon_t|.
\end{aligned}
$$

Let $\hat{q}\equiv 2\hat{\omega}^{-1/2}\sum_{j=0}^{\infty}|b_j|$ and $|\epsilon|_{(T)}\equiv\max_{1\le t\le T}|\epsilon_t|$. Then:

$$
\begin{aligned}
a_T T^{1/2}/\max(|b_T|,1))g_{RS}(v_T)&\le\hat{q}(a_T/\max(|b_T|,1))\{(b_T+a_T|\epsilon|_{(T)})/a_T-b_T/a_T\}\\
&=\hat{q}(b_T+a_T|\epsilon|_{(T)})/\max(|b_T|,1)-\hat{q}b_T/\max(|b_T|,1)\equiv\Psi_T.
\end{aligned}
$$

If $\max(|b_T|,1)\to\infty$, then $\Psi_T\xrightarrow{p}2\sum_{j=0}^{\infty}|b_j|/\kappa=O(1)$. If $\max(|b_T|,1)\to 1$, then $\Psi_T=>(2\sum_{j=0}^{\infty}|b_j|/\kappa)(\epsilon^*+\lim_{T\to\infty}b_T)=O_p(1)$. In either case, $(a_T T^{1/2}/\max(|b_T|,1))g_{RS}(v_T)=O_p(1)$. ∎

Appendix B: Parameter Values for Univariate Empirical Models

Table B.1. Parameter values for autoregressive models

$$\Delta y_t = \mu + \sum_{j=1}^{6} a_j \Delta y_{t-j} + \epsilon_t, \text{var}(\epsilon_t) = \sigma^2$$

	FM2D82	IVT82	INC	FYGM3	GMYXP8
μ	.00258	.00014	.01161	.03745	.00604
a_1	.67637	.20533	.23772	.38856	.41444
a_2	−.08429	.07999	.17634	−.50840	−.01607
a_3	.15530	−.09785	−.23341	.42858	.19326
a_4	−.12098	−.15694	−.04855	−.28511	−.09893
a_5	.13364	−.18534	.00143	.28979	−.14897
a_6	−.13687	−.02694	−.02781	−.20488	−.05931
σ^2	.00871	.02996	.03466	.72906	.00810

Table B.2. Parameter values for moving average models

$$y_t = \rho y_{t-1} + \sum_{j=1}^{5} b_j \epsilon_{t-j}, \text{var}(\epsilon_t) = \sigma^2$$

	FM2D82	IVT82	INC	FYGM3	GMYXP8
μ	−.01259	−.00119	−.00403	−.06702	.00293
ρ	.94752	.70443	.83050	.82045	.91451
b_1	.69039	.44577	.35072	.51793	.44412
b_2	.38310	.42911	.37087	−.28322	.22312
b_3	.32080	.13251	−.00319	.23636	.34864
b_4	.16604	.03387	−.03071	.36649	.28337
b_5	.11714	−.17188	−.00009	−.08113	.12500
σ^2	.00870	.02897	.03373	.70532	.00804

Notes: The mnemonics refer to the Citibase name of the series; the series and transformations are discussed in the text. The moving average parameters were estimated by maximum likelihood using detrended series.

Notes

1. My personal introduction to these issues came when John Geweke asked me to discuss some paper by Granger on modeling time series in levels (Granger, 1983) at the winter meetings of the Econometric Society in December 1983. I was a first year assistant professor and this was my first opportunity to be a discussant. In that discussion I showed that if two variables are cointegrated of order (1,1) in Granger's (1983) terminology, if they have a bivariate finite order moving average representation in first differences, and if there are sufficiently many moments, then the estimator of the cointegrating coefficients will be consistent at rate T. Professor Granger approached me afterward and encouraged me to write up my notes. The result was eventually published (Stock, 1987), and I have always been grateful for his intellectual generosity, encouragement, and support.

2. Alternative conditions under which Assumption 1(a) is satisfied are provided by Herrndorf (1984) (also see Phillips, 1987; Ethier and Kurtz, 1986).

3. To see this, let $f_1(\lambda) = \frac{1}{2}\lambda\delta$, $f_2(\lambda) = \frac{1}{2}\delta$, so $f_1, f_2 \in C[0, 1]$. Under the sup norm, $\rho_C(f_1, f_2) = \sup_{\lambda \in [0,1]}|f_1(\lambda) - f_2(\lambda)|$, both f_1 and f_2 are in a δ-neighborhood of 0. But $g(f_1) = 3$ and $g(f_2) = \infty$, so there is no open δ-neighborhood of 0 that maps into an arbitrarily small ϵ-neighborhood.

4. The first differences were used to produce null models that would err on the side of inducing substantial power at high frequencies, a situation in which unit root tests have performed poorly (see Schwert, 1989). The same AR(6) approximation was used for all series in part because of its theoretical justification (Berk, 1974), in part because the objective here is not to develop optimal forecasting models of these particular series but rather to have a conveniently parameterized set of time series models with representative spectra.

References

Berk, K. N. (1974), "Consistent Autoregressive Spectral Estimates." *Annals of Statistics*, 2: 489–502.

Bhargava, A. (1986), "On the Theory of Testing for Unit Roots in Observed Time Series." *Review of Economic Studies*, 53: 369–384.

Cavanagh, C. L. (1985), "Roots Local to Unity." Mimeograph, Harvard University.

Chan, N. H. and C. Z. Wei (1987), "Asymptotic Inference for Nearly Nonstationary AR(1) Processes." *Annals of Statistics*, 15: 1050–63.

Chan, N. H. and C. Z. Wei (1988), "Limiting Distributions of Least Squares Estimates of Unstable Autoregressive Processes." *Annals of Statistics*, 16: 367–401.

Christiano, L. C. and M. Eichenbaum (1989), "Unit Roots in GNP: Do We Know and Do We Care?" *Carnegie–Rochester Conference Series on Public Policy*.

Davidson, J. E. H., D. F. Hendry, F. Srba, and S. Yeo (1978), "Econometric Modelling of the Aggregate Time-Series Relationship Between Consumer's Expenditure and Income in the United Kingdom." *Economic Journal*, 86: 661–92.

Dickey, D. A. and W. A. Fuller (1979), "Distribution of the Estimators for Autoregressive Time Series With a Unit Root." *Journal of the American Statistical Association*, 74: 427–31.

Engle, R. F. and C. W. J. Granger (1987), "Dynamic Model Specification with Equilibrium Constraints: Co-Integration and Error-Correction." *Econometrica*, 55: 251–76.

Engle, R. F., and B. S. Yoo (1987), "Forecasting and Testing in Co-integrated Systems." *Journal of Econometrics*, 35: 143–59.

Ethier, S. N. and T. G. Kurtz (1986), *Markov Processes*. New York: Wiley.

Fuller, W. A. (1976), *Introduction to Statistical Time Series*. New York: Wiley.

Granger, C. W. J. (1966), "The Typical Spectral Shape of an Economic Variable," *Econometrica*, 34: 150–61.

Granger, C. W. J. (1983), "Co-integrated Variables and Error Correcting Models," UCSD Discussion Paper number 83–13a.

Granger, C. W. J. (1986), "Developments in the Study of Co-integrated Economic Variables." *Oxford Bulletin of Economics and Statistics*, 48: 213–28.

Granger, C. W. J. and P. Newbold (1974), "Spurious Regressions in Econometrics." *Journal of Econometrics*, 2: 111–20.

Granger, C. W. J. and A. Weiss (1983), "Time Series Analysis of Error-Correction Models." In S. Karlin, T. Amemiya, and L. A. Goodman (eds.), *Studies in Econo-*

metrics, Time Series and Multivariate Statistics, in honor of T. W. Anderson. Academic Press.

Hall, P. and C. C. Heyde (1980), *Martingale Limit Theory and its Applications.* New York: Academic Press.

Herrndorf, N. (1984), "A Functional Central Limit Theorem for Weakly Dependent Sequences of Random Variables." *Annals of Probability*, 12: 141–53.

Kahn, J. A. and M. Ogaki (1988), "A Chi-Square Test for a Unit Root." University of Rochester, Discussion Paper no. 212.

Kosobud, R. and L. Klein (1961), "Some Econometrics of Growth: Great Ratios of Economics." *Quarterly Journal of Economics* 25 (May): 173–98.

Lo, A. (1991), "Long Term Memory in Stock Market Prices." *Econometrica*, 59: 1279–1314.

Mandelbrot, B. (1975), "Limit Theorems on the Self-Normalized Range for Weakly and Strongly Dependent Processes." *Z. Wahrscheinlichkeitstheorie verw. Gebiete*, 31: 271–85.

Nelson, C. and C. Plosser (1982), "Trends and Random Walks in Macroeconomic Time Series." *Journal of Monetary Economics*, 10: 139–62.

Park, J. Y. (1990), "Testing for Unit Roots and Cointegration by Variable Addition." In G. F. Rhodes and T. B. Fomby (eds.), *Advances in Econometrics: Co-Integration, Spurious Regressions and Unit Roots.* Greenwich, CT: JAI Press.

Park, J. Y. and B. Choi (1988), "A New Approach to Testing for a Unit Root." CAE Working Paper no. 88–23, Cornell University.

Perron, P. (1989), "The Great Crash, the Oil Price Shock, and the Unit Root Hypothesis." *Econometrica*, 57: 1361–1402.

Phillips, P. C. B. (1987), "Time Series Regression with a Unit Root." *Econometrica*, 55: 277–302.

Phillips, P. C. B. and S. Ouliaris (1990), "Asymptotic Properties of Residual-Based Tests for Cointegration." *Econometrica*, 58: 165–94.

Phillips, P. C. B. and P. Perron (1988), "Testing for a Unit Root in Time Series Regression." *Biometrika*, 75: 335–46.

Reiss, R. D. (1989), *Approximate Distributions of Order Statistics.* New York: Springer-Verlag.

Said, S. E. and D. A. Dickey (1984), "Testing for Unit Roots in Autoregressive-Moving Average Models of Unknown Order." *Biometrika*, 71: 599–607.

Sargan, J. D. and A. Bhargava (1983), "Testing for Residuals from Least Squares Regression for Being Generated by the Gaussian Random Walk." *Econometrica*, 51: 153–74.

Schwert, W. G. (1989), "Tests for Unit Roots: A Monte Carlo Investigation." *Journal of Business and Economic Statistics*, 7: 147–59.

Stock, J. H. (1987), "Asymptotic Properties of Least Squares Estimators of Cointegrating Vectors." *Econometrica*, 55: 1035–56.

Stock, J. H. and M. W. Watson (1988), "Testing for Common Trends." *Journal of the American Statistical Association*, 83: 1097–1107.

Stock, J. H. and M. W. Watson (1990). "Business Cycle Properties of Selected U.S. Economic Time Series." Mimeograph, Harvard University.

Yule, G. U. (1926), "Why Do We Sometimes Get Nonsense Correlations Between Time Series?" *Journal of the Royal Statistical Society B*, 89: 1–64.

7

Order Selection in Testing for the Cointegrating Rank of a VAR Process

HELMUT LÜTKEPOHL AND PENTTI SAIKKONEN

1 Introduction

Following the invention of cointegration by Granger (1981, 1986) and Engle and Granger (1987), time series econometrics has changed considerably. In multiple time series analysis investigating the cointegration properties at an early stage of the analysis has become standard practice by now. For this purpose, Johansen's (1988, 1991, 1995) likelihood ratio (LR) tests are used frequently (see also Reinsel and Ahn, 1992). In that approach a vector autoregressive (VAR) process or error correction model (ECM) of some finite order is usually fitted to the data and the tests are then performed conditionally on the order being the true one. In some studies it was found, however, that the choice of the lag order or truncation lag can have an important impact on the outcome of unit root and cointegration tests (see, e.g., Schwert, 1989, Ng and Perron, 1995, Agiagloglou and Newbold, 1996, for unit root tests in univariate time series and Reimers, 1992, and Haug, 1996, for cointegration tests in vector processes). Therefore it is of interest to investigate the relation between the choice of truncation lag and the properties of the resulting cointegration tests based on a model with a prespecified order.

In practice, the VAR or ECM order is usually chosen by some criterion based on the available data. In particular, the order is chosen so that the residuals appear to be white noise under some data dependent criterion. The cointegration tests are then performed conditionally on the order obtained in this way. Therefore, a proper overall assessment of the properties of cointegration tests has to take into account the data dependent choice of the order or truncation lag of the underlying model. Also assuming that the true data generation process (DGP) is in fact of finite order may be too limited for cap-

We thank Christian Müller and Kirstin Hubrich for helping with the computations and two anonymous referees for comments. The Deutsche Forschungsgemeinschaft, SFB 373, provided financial support. Part of this research was done while the second author was visiting the Institute of Statistics and Econometrics at the Humboldt University in Berlin.

turing all situations of relevance for applied work. This has been acknowledged in the univariate case for unit root tests by Said and Dickey (1984), Hall (1994) and Ng and Perron (1995) who investigate the asymptotic properties of augmented Dickey–Fuller unit root tests for a number of different rules for choosing the truncation lag. They find that the tests maintain their asymptotic properties for quite general DGPs if the truncation lag is chosen by a suitable deterministic rule or by one of the standard lag order selection criteria. For a deterministic rule a similar result was obtained by Saikkonen and Luukkonen (1997) (henceforth SL) for LR cointegration tests.

In this study we will extend these results to data dependent rules for choosing the truncation lag in multivariate models. In particular, it will be shown that if the DGP is in fact a finite order VAR process then any one of the consistent model selection criteria may be used prior to testing for cointegration. The asymptotic properties of the LR tests for the cointegrating rank will in that case be the same as if the true order were known. Furthermore, if the true DGP is an infinite order process similar results are shown to hold. We also report some simulation results to illustrate the small sample problems related to choosing the truncation lag prior to testing for cointegration.

The structure of this study is as follows. In the next section the standard LR approach for testing for the cointegrating rank is presented formally. The model assumptions used for our purposes are presented in Section 3. In Section 4 results for choosing the VAR order in some deterministic fashion are summarized and in Section 5 the consequences of a data dependent order choice are explored. In Sections 2–4 we operate under the unrealistic assumption that the DGP has no deterministic terms. This is done for convenience in order to simplify the exposition. In Section 6 the extension to the case where the DGP has a nonzero mean term is discussed. Simulation results are reported in Section 7 and Section 8 concludes. Most proofs of our theoretical results are given in the Appendix.

The following notation is used throughout. The vector $y_t = (y_{1t}, ..., y_{nt})'$ denotes an observable n-dimensional set of time series variables. The sample size is signified by T, the symbol K is reserved for the lag order or truncation lag of an ECM and $N = T - K - 1$ is the effective sample size used for estimation and testing. The differencing operator is denoted by Δ, that is, $\Delta y_t = y_t - y_{t-1}$. The symbol $I(d)$ is used to denote a process which is integrated of order d, that is, it is stationary (or asymptotically stationary) after differencing d times while it is still nonstationary after differencing just $d - 1$ times. The symbol $\overset{p}{\to}$ signifies convergence in probability and $O(\cdot)$, $o(\cdot)$, $O_p(\cdot)$ and $o_p(\cdot)$ are the usual symbols for the order of convergence and convergence in probability, respectively, of a sequence. We abbreviate "independently, identically distributed" in the usual way by i.i.d.. The normal distribution with mean (vector) μ and variance (covariance matrix) Σ is denoted by $N(\mu, \Sigma)$. Moreover, I_n denotes the $(n \times n)$ identity matrix. If A is an $(n \times m)$ matrix we let

$A_\perp$ stand for its orthogonal complement. As a general convention, a sum is defined to be zero if the lower bound of the summation index exceeds the upper bound.

2 Cointegration Tests

Given a system of n variables $y_t = (y_{1t}, ..., y_{nt})'$, the number of linearly independent cointegrating relations among them is usually determined by considering the rank of the matrix Π in the error correction form

$$\Delta y_t = \Pi y_{t-1} + \sum_{j=1}^{K} \Gamma_j \Delta y_{t-j} + e_t. \tag{2.1}$$

This is usually done by testing either one of the following two pairs of hypotheses:

$$H_0(r_0) : \text{rk}(\Pi) = r_0 \quad \text{vs.} \quad H_1(r_0) : \text{rk}(\Pi) > r_0, \tag{2.2}$$

or

$$H_0(r_0) : \text{rk}(\Pi) = r_0 \quad \text{vs.} \quad \bar{H}_1(r_0) : \text{rk}(\Pi) = r_0 + 1. \tag{2.3}$$

Assuming that the error term e_t in (2.1) is Gaussian white noise, the corresponding likelihood ratio statistics as derived by Johansen (1988) and Reinsel and Ahn (1992) may be obtained as follows. For a sample $y_1, ..., y_T$, define $z_t' = (\Delta y_{t-1}', ..., \Delta y_{t-K}')$ and, using $N = T - K - 1$,

$$M_T = N^{-1} \left[\sum_{t=K+2}^{T} y_{t-1} y_{t-1}' - \sum_{t=K+2}^{T} y_{t-1} z_t' \left(\sum_{t=K+2}^{T} z_t z_t' \right)^{-1} \sum_{t=K+2}^{T} z_t y_{t-1}' \right]. \tag{2.4}$$

Denoting the least squares (LS) residuals from model (2.1) by $\tilde{e}_t$, define

$$\tilde{\Sigma} = N^{-1} \sum_{t=K+2}^{T} \tilde{e}_t \tilde{e}_t'. \tag{2.5}$$

Moreover, let $\tilde{\Pi}$ be the LS estimator of Π from (2.1). Denoting by $\tilde{\lambda}_1 \geq \cdots \geq \tilde{\lambda}_n$ the ordered generalized eigenvalues obtained as solutions of

$$\det(\tilde{\Pi} M_T \tilde{\Pi}' - \lambda \tilde{\Sigma}) = 0, \tag{2.6}$$

Johansen's trace statistic for testing the pair of hypotheses (2.2) is given by

$$LR_{trace}(r_0) = N \sum_{j=r_0+1}^{n} \log(1 + \tilde{\lambda}_j), \tag{2.7}$$

and the so-called maximum eigenvalue statistic for testing (2.3) is given by

$$LR_{max}(r_0) = N \log(1 + \tilde{\lambda}_{r_0+1}). \tag{2.8}$$

The null distributions of these two test statistics are nonstandard and critical values have been tabulated, e.g., by Johansen (1988, 1995).

In practice it is usually assumed that the maximum lag K in the ECM (2.1) is chosen appropriately which means that it has to be chosen in such a way that the test statistics have the correct asymptotic null distributions. Usually some data-driven procedure is used for choosing K. In the following we will show that under quite general assumptions, the usual model selection criteria may be used for that purpose without affecting the asymptotic properties of the test statistics. In the next section we will spell out the precise assumptions for the data generation process (DGP) which are used in the theoretical analysis. It will be seen that K does not have to be the "true" lag length or order. In fact, the DGP may have an infinite order VAR representation.

As mentioned in the introduction, in practice there will often be deterministic terms in the ECM (2.1) such as an intercept, seasonal dummies or a linear trend term. To simplify the theoretical analysis we will begin by assuming that no such terms are present. In Section 6 we will comment on the consequences of a nonzero mean term. It will be argued that our results can be extended in a straightforward manner to that case.

3 Model Assumptions

We use the general framework of Saikkonen (1992) and Saikkonen and Lütkepohl (1996) and partition y_t as

$$y_t = \begin{bmatrix} y_{1t} \\ y_{2t} \end{bmatrix}, \quad t = 1,\ldots,T, \tag{3.1}$$

where y_{it} is $(n_i \times 1)$, $i = 1, 2$, and $n_1 + n_2 = n$. We assume that the DGP is of the following form:

$$y_{1t} = A y_{2t} + u_{1t}, \tag{3.2a}$$
$$\Delta y_{2t} = u_{2t}. \tag{3.2b}$$

Here $u_t = [u_{1t}', u_{2t}']'$ is a strictly stationary process with $E(u_t) = 0$, positive definite covariance matrix $\Sigma_u = E(u_t u_t')$ and continuous spectral density matrix which is positive definite at zero frequency. These assumptions imply that y_{2t} is $I(1)$ and not cointegrated while y_{1t} and y_{2t} are cointegrated. Without affecting the subsequent results the initial vector y_0 is assumed to be any random vector with a fixed probability distribution.

It is well-known that the model (3.2a)/(3.2b) may be written in triangular error correction form

$$\Delta y_t = J\Theta' y_{t-1} + v_t, \tag{3.3}$$

where $J' = [-I_{n_1} : 0]$, $\Theta' = [I_{n_1} : -A]$, and $v_t = [v'_{1t}, v'_{2t}]'$ is a nonsingular linear transformation of u_t given by:

$$v_t = \begin{bmatrix} I_{n_1} & A \\ 0 & I_{n_2} \end{bmatrix} u_t$$

(see, e.g., Phillips, 1991, and Saikkonen, 1992). The process v_t (and hence u_t) is assumed to have an infinite order VAR representation

$$\sum_{j=0}^{\infty} G_j v_{t-j} = \varepsilon_t, \quad G_0 = I_n, \tag{3.4}$$

where ε_t is a sequence of continuous i.i.d. $(0, \Sigma)$ random vectors with Σ being positive definite. It is also assumed that the ε_t have finite fourth moments and that the $(n \times n)$ coefficient matrices G_j satisfy the summability condition

$$\sum_{j=0}^{\infty} j^a \left\| G_j \right\| < \infty \quad \text{for some } a \geq 1. \tag{3.5}$$

This condition restricts the temporal dependence of the process v_t. It is satisfied for all $a \geq 1$ in the important special case where v_t is a vector autoregressive moving average (VARMA) process. Condition (3.5) also implies that the process v_t and, hence, y_t can be approximated by a finite order autoregression. Specifically, using (3.3) and (3.4) it can be shown that

$$\Delta y_t = \Pi y_{t-1} + \sum_{j=1}^{K} \Gamma_j \Delta y_{t-j} + e_t, \quad t = K+2, K+3,\ldots \tag{3.6}$$

where

$$e_t = \varepsilon_t - \sum_{j=K+1}^{\infty} G_j v_{t-j}.$$

Thus, the model can be brought in the form of our starting model (2.1). Now the error term is not white noise, though, if some of the G_j are nonzero for $j > K$. Note, however, that our assumptions do not rule out finite order VAR models.

Due to the cointegration assumption, the coefficient matrix Π has reduced rank and, hence, the structure:

$$\Pi = \Phi \Theta' = -\sum_{j=0}^{K} G_j J \Theta', \tag{3.7}$$

where the second equality defines the $(n \times n_1)$ matrix Φ which is of full column rank (at least for K large enough). Details of the derivation of (3.6) and (3.7) can be found in Saikkonen (1992) and Saikkonen and Lütkepohl (1996) and are not repeated here. We note, however, that the coefficient matrices Γ_j $(j =$

$1, ..., K$) are functions of Θ, G_j ($j = 1, 2, ...$) and K and they form an absolutely summable sequence.

In Section 2 we have argued that the (approximate) ECM (3.6) forms a basis for cointegration testing procedures. It may be worth noting that the cointegration tests do not require knowledge on which components of y_t belong to y_{1t} and y_{2t}. In fact, for them it is sufficient to know that the components of y_t can in principle be divided into the two groups, possibly after a suitable linear transformation. The application of the tests does require a suitable choice of the truncation lag or order of truncation, K, however. It is intuitively clear that K should be so large that $G_j \approx 0$, $j > K$, because then we approximately have $e_t \approx \varepsilon_t$. In particular, to be able to prove useful asymptotic results, one has to assume that the order of truncation increases with the sample size at a suitable rate. Since it is clear that consistent estimators and tests cannot be obtained if the order of truncation increases too fast compared with the sample size, the following technical assumption is commonly used in the literature which considers approximating an infinite order model by a finite order VAR or ECM (e.g., SL; Lewis and Reinsel, 1985; Lütkepohl and Poskitt, 1996; Saikkonen and Lütkepohl, 1995, 1996; Lütkepohl and Saikkonen, 1997).

Assumption 1. K is chosen as a function of T such that $K \to \infty$ and $K^3/T \to 0$ as $T \to \infty$.

Assumption 1 specifies an upper bound for the rate at which the value of K is allowed to tend to infinity with the sample size. In most of the aforementioned related literature a lower bound for the lag order is also imposed. Recently Ng and Perron (1995) showed, however, that the limiting distribution of the univariate unit root tests of Said and Dickey (1984) may be obtained under Assumption 1 without imposing a lower bound condition for the lag length. Ng and Perron (1995) also showed that choosing the order of truncation on the basis of conventional model selection criteria, like AIC or SC (see Lütkepohl, 1991, chs. 4 and 11), yields $K = O_p(\log T)$, a choice which is consistent with Assumption 1. In the next sections results similar to those of Ng and Perron (1995) are obtained for the multivariate case.

4 Results with Deterministic Choice of the Truncation Lag

SL show that the LR tests for the cointegrating rank of a system remain valid for processes without deterministic trend if the lag order is chosen according to Assumption 1. We will summarize their result here because it is the basis for studying the consequences of using data dependent rules for the lag order. It is assumed that the tests of the cointegrating rank are based on the estimated version of (3.6):

$$\Delta y_t = \tilde{\Pi} y_{t-1} + \tilde{\Gamma} z_t + \tilde{\varepsilon}_t, \quad t = K + 2, ..., T, \tag{4.1}$$

where $z_t = [\Delta y'_{t-1}, ..., \Delta y'_{t-K}]'$, as in (2.4), and $\tilde{\Pi}$ and $\tilde{\Gamma} = [\tilde{\Gamma}_1 : \cdots : \tilde{\Gamma}_K]$ are the ordinary least squares (OLS) estimators of the coefficient matrices Π and $\Gamma = [\Gamma_1 : \cdots : \Gamma_K]$, respectively. Moreover, the $\tilde{\varepsilon}_t$ are the OLS residuals. The following theorem states that the LR tests for the cointegrating rank maintain their usual asymptotic properties if the truncation lag is chosen according to some rule which satisfies Assumption 1.

Theorem 4.1. If the truncation lag is chosen as prescribed in Assumption 1 then LR_{trace} and LR_{max} have the same limiting distribution under the null hypothesis as in the case where the true VAR order is known and finite.

A detailed proof of this result for the test statistic LR_{trace} may be found in SL. The arguments used there may be adapted to prove the theorem also for LR_{max}.

5 Results with Data-Dependent Choice of the VAR Order

In this section we shall study the data-dependent selection of the order of truncation in the unrestricted approximate ECM (3.6). It is assumed that the order of truncation is chosen by minimizing the criterion:

$$\log\left|\tilde{\Sigma}_K\right| + (K+1)C_T / T, \quad K \le K_T = o(T^{\frac{1}{3}}), \quad C_T > n^2, \quad C_T / T \to 0, \quad (5.1)$$

where $\tilde{\Sigma}_K$ equals our previous $\tilde{\Sigma}$. The sequences K_T and C_T have to be prescribed. The former provides an upper bound for the considered values of K. Unless otherwise stated it will be assumed that $K_T \to \infty$ so that K_T satisfies the upper bound condition in Assumption 1. This assumption is needed for the results to be proved in the following. The sequence C_T determines the considered criterion. If $C_T = 2n^2$ then (5.1) yields the familiar Akaike information criterion, AIC, choosing $C_T = 2n^2 \log \log T$ gives the Hannan–Quinn criterion, HQ, and if $C_T = n^2 \log T$ then another popular criterion, often referred to as SC, is obtained (see, e.g., Lütkepohl, 1991, ch. 4). We write $\tilde{K}$ for the value that minimizes (5.1).

We now wish to derive the asymptotic properties of the LR tests based on a model with lag order $\tilde{K}$. For this purpose we first consider the infeasible least squares regression

$$\Delta y_t = \hat{\Phi} u_{1,t-1} + \hat{\Gamma} z_t + \hat{\varepsilon}_{Kt}, \quad t = K+2,...,T, \quad (5.2)$$

and define the associated residual covariance matrix by

$$\hat{\Sigma}_K = N^{-1} \sum_{t=K+2}^{T} \hat{\varepsilon}_{Kt}\hat{\varepsilon}'_{Kt}.$$

The following lemma shows that in (5.1) the covariance matrix estimator $\tilde{\Sigma}_K$

can be replaced by $\hat{\Sigma}_K$ without affecting the asymptotic behavior of the criterion. A proof is given in the appendix.

Lemma 5.1. Suppose that y_t $(t = 1, ..., T)$ is generated by (3.3) and (3.4) and that condition (3.5) holds for some $a > 1$. Suppose further that K_T in (5.1) satisfies Assumption 1. Then, uniformly in $K \leq K_T$, $\tilde{\Sigma}_K = \hat{\Sigma}_K + o_p(K_T/T)$.

Lemma 5.1 is a multivariate extension of Lemma 4.2 of Ng and Perron (1995). These authors show that the error term is $o_p(T^{-1/2})$. An examination of the error term reveals, however, that the error is even of order $o_p(K_T/T)$. This property of the error term is actually of importance because the penalty term $(K + 1) C_T/T$ in the criterion (5.1) is typically of a smaller order than $T^{-1/2}$. Clearly, if one wishes to replace the estimator $\tilde{\Sigma}_K$ by $\hat{\Sigma}_K$ without affecting the asymptotic behavior of the criterion, the error can be at most $o_p(K_T C_T/T)$.

It is easy to see that equation (5.2) can be reparameterized as a regression of Δy_t on $u_{t-1}, ..., u_{t-K}, u_{1,t-K-1}$ (see (A.1) in the Appendix). As far as the minimization of (5.1) is concerned, one can here also replace the regressand by u_t because $\Delta y_{1t} = A u_{2t} + \Delta u_{1t}$ and $\Delta y_{2t} = u_{2t}$. Thus, Lemma 5.1 implies that asymptotic properties of a minimizer of (5.1) can be studied by using the stationary process u_t (or v_t). In the stationary case these properties have been studied extensively, as the monograph of Hannan and Deistler (1988) shows. Although the results in Hannan and Deistler (1988) are formulated without the regressor $u_{1,t-K-1}$ it is clear that this has no effect on the main conclusions. Thus, from Lemma 5.1 and Theorem 7.4.7(b) of Hannan and Deistler (1988) we can, for instance, conclude that, if the order of truncation is chosen by minimizing the AIC or SC criterion, we have $\tilde{K} = O_p(\log T)$ if u_t (or v_t) has a finite order VARMA representation which satisfies suitable conditions. For the details of this result see the discussion by Hannan and Deistler (1988, p. 334).

We shall not provide a detailed discussion of the asymptotic behavior of a minimizer of (5.1) but only prove the following theorem in the Appendix.

Theorem 5.1. Under the conditions of Lemma 5.1 the following results hold.

(a) If (3.4) is not a finite order autoregression then $\tilde{K} \to \infty$ in probability.

(b) If (3.4) is an autoregression of a finite order $K_0 \leq K_T$ and $C_T \to \infty$ then $\tilde{K} \xrightarrow{p} K_0$.

The first result of Theorem 5.1 shows that choosing the value of K by conventional model selection criteria is consistent with the upper bound condition in Assumption 1. The following theorem shows that choosing the VAR order by a criterion of the form (5.1) leaves the asymptotic null distributions of the test statistics for the cointegrating rank unchanged. Again, a proof is provided in the Appendix.

Theorem 5.2. If the assumptions of Lemma 5.1 are satisfied, then LR_{trace} and LR_{max}, computed on the basis of a model with lag order $\tilde{K}$, have the same limiting distributions under the null hypothesis as in the case where the true VAR order is known and finite.

Our results also remain valid for the tests proposed by Horvath and Watson (1995). These authors consider LR and Wald tests under the assumption that some cointegrating relations are prespecified. Since the limiting distributions of these tests follow from asymptotic properties of sample moments similar to those in the test statistic LR_{trace} it is straightforward to use the auxiliary results in the appendix to show that Theorem 5.2 holds for the Horvath–Watson tests as well.

Ng and Perron (1995) also consider a sequential testing procedure for choosing the lag order which can be extended to the multivariate case. For this purpose consider the model (3.6) and suppose that K not only satisfies Assumption 1 but also the lower bound condition

$$T^{\frac{1}{2}} \sum_{j=K+1}^{\infty} \left\| G_j \right\| = o(1).$$

Let W_K be the Wald test of Saikkonen and Lütkepohl (1996, theorem 4) for the null hypothesis $\Gamma_K = 0$. Then, using arguments similar to those in the proof of Lemma 5.1 of Ng and Perron (1995) it can be seen that $W_K \xrightarrow{d} \chi^2_{K^2}$. Hence, we have an analog of Lemma 5.1 of Ng and Perron (1995) and therefore we can repeat the arguments in the proof of Lemma 5.2 of that paper to obtain a testing strategy based on the null hypotheses $\Gamma_K = 0$, $\Gamma_{K-1} = 0$, ... We will not consider this strategy in the following because in the lag selection context the Wald tests are known to have undesirable small sample properties in multivariate models even in the stationary case (see Lütkepohl, 1991, ch. 4).

6 Models with an Intercept

The results of the previous sections can be extended to models with intercept terms in the cointegrating relations. In this case (3.2a) becomes:

$$y_{1t} = \mu + A y_{2t} + u_{1t}, \tag{3.2a$'$}$$

while (3.2b) remains as before. This implies that instead of (3.6) we have:

$$\Delta y_t = \nu + \Pi y_{t-1} + \sum_{j=1}^{K} \Gamma_j \Delta y_{t-j} + e_t^*, \quad t = K+2, K+3,\ldots \tag{3.6$'$}$$

where $\nu = -\Phi\mu$ and Π has the structure (3.7). Of course, we now have to add intercept terms to the least squares regressions. However, in the same way as in Saikkonen (1992) all the results proved in Sections 4 and 5 still hold provided appropriate modifications are made in their presentation. Details of these modifications are discussed in Saikkonen (1992, section 5) and are not repeated here. Modifications required in the proofs are briefly discussed in the Appendix. In the next section some small sample results are obtained by simulations.

7 Simulation Results

For unit root tests in the context of univariate time series Ng and Perron (1995) and Agiagloglou and Newbold (1996) found that the ADF tests lose power if the lag length is overspecified. Also some size distortion was observed if the lag length is underspecified. Since LR cointegration tests are the corresponding tests in the multivariate case one may expect that they have similar small sample properties. Because in practice the cointegrating rank is usually determined by testing $H(0) : \mathrm{rk}(\Pi) = 0$, $H(1) : \mathrm{rk}(\Pi) = 1$, etc. sequentially until the null hypothesis is rejected for the first time, one would expect that too few cointegration relations are found if a large lag length is chosen. Previous simulation studies which have also considered this aspect of testing for cointegration are Reimers (1992), Cheung and Lai (1993), Yap and Reinsel (1995), Haug (1996) and SL among others. In all these studies it was confirmed that the lag order choice has a substantial impact on the outcome of cointegration tests in samples of the size commonly used in macroeconometric studies.

In particular, Reimers found that choosing an unnecessarily large lag order results in size distortions and power reductions. In his simulation study the empirical size does not necessarily decline with increasing lag length. In contrast, the rejection rate in some cases exceeded the nominal one substantially when the lag order was overspecified. In his experiment the SC criterion worked best for choosing the VAR order prior to using LR tests for the cointegrating rank. This may be a consequence of the specific processes used. In particular, he considered only VAR processes of orders 1 and 2 (ECMs of order $K = 0$ and 1). Clearly, for low order processes parsimonious criteria such as SC may have an advantage over more lavish criteria such as AIC.

Cheung and Lai (1993) investigated the impact of the lag length on the size of LR cointegration tests in a bivariate setting and found that underspecifying the true lag length can lead to massive size distortions while overspecifying the lag order may be less problematic. Severe size problems were also found for infinite order processes. Similar conclusions were also reached by Haug (1996) for bivariate processes and Yap and Reinsel (1995) and SL for three-dimensional processes. In fact, Haug (1996, p. 113) concludes that "the study of Ng and Perron should be extended to cointegration tests because the experiments with various lag lengths . . . indicate that additional lags decrease size distortions dramatically, however, the loss in power may also be large." Following this proposal we have performed a Monte Carlo experiment which focuses on the specific impact of the lag length on size and power of LR tests for the cointegrating rank.

In most of the aforementioned studies the properties of the tests for specific null hypotheses are investigated whereas in practice the aforementioned sequential procedure is commonly used. We will therefore investigate the properties of the sequential procedure which tests $H(0) : \mathrm{rk}(\Pi) = 0$, $H(1) : \mathrm{rk}(\Pi) = 1$, etc. and terminates when the null hypothesis is rejected for the first time. We will use the DGPs from SL and focus our study on the following questions: What is the impact of the lag order on the distribution of the cointegrating ranks determined by the LR tests? If the lag length is chosen by some model selection criterion, what is the impact of the model selection criterion on the properties of the LR tests? In the previous sections we have seen that asymptotically the choice of the lag length has no impact on the LR tests for the cointegrating rank provided the simple condition for the upper bound of the lag order in Assumption 1 is observed. Of course, the situation may be quite different in small samples.

Although our DGPs have zero mean, we will only present results for tests which allow for a nonzero mean term. The reason is that assuming a zero mean is rather unusual in practice. For simplicity we focus on LR_{trace}. Critical values are taken from Johansen and Juselius (1990, table A.2).

As mentioned earlier, our simulations are based on the DGPs used in SL. The first one is a VAR(2) process which has an EC representation of order $K_0 = 1$,

$$\Delta y_t = P^{-1} \left(\begin{bmatrix} \lambda_1 & 0 & 0 \\ 0 & \lambda_2 & 0 \\ 0 & 0 & \lambda_3 \end{bmatrix} - I_3 \right) P y_{t-1}$$
$$+ \begin{bmatrix} -0.080 & 0.224 & -0.152 \\ 0.177 & 0.046 & -0.254 \\ 0.000 & -0.102 & 0.129 \end{bmatrix} \Delta y_{t-1} + \varepsilon_t \tag{7.1}$$

with $\varepsilon_t \sim$ i.i.d. $N(0, \Sigma)$. Here

$$P = \begin{bmatrix} -0.29 & -0.47 & -0.57 \\ -0.01 & -0.85 & 1.00 \\ -0.75 & 1.39 & -0.55 \end{bmatrix} \text{ and } \Sigma = \begin{bmatrix} 0.47 & 0.20 & 0.18 \\ 0.20 & 0.32 & 0.27 \\ 0.18 & 0.27 & 0.30 \end{bmatrix}.$$

The second DGP is a mixed VARMA process which was also used by Yap and Reinsel (1995),

$$\Delta y_t = P^{-1} \left(\begin{bmatrix} \lambda_1 & 0 & 0 \\ 0 & \lambda_2 & 0 \\ 0 & 0 & \lambda_3 \end{bmatrix} - I_3 \right) P y_{t-1} + \varepsilon_t$$
$$- P_\theta \begin{bmatrix} 0.297 & 0 & 0 \\ 0 & -0.202 & 0 \\ 0 & 0 & \lambda_\theta \end{bmatrix} P_\theta^{-1} \varepsilon_{t-1}, \tag{7.2}$$

where P and ε_t are as in (7.1) and

$$P_\theta = \begin{bmatrix} -0.816 & -0.657 & -0.822 \\ -0.624 & -0.785 & 0.566 \\ -0.488 & 0.475 & 0.174 \end{bmatrix}.$$

Yap and Reinsel (1995) also considered a process very similar to (7.1) in their Monte Carlo experiment. Using the two processes (7.1) and (7.2) allows us to obtain results for finite order as well as infinite order VAR processes. We have chosen three-dimensional processes because, given the empirical studies reported in the literature, this dimension may be regarded as moderate. In any case, it turned out to be large enough to study important features related to variations in the cointegrating rank. The values of the λ_i, $i = 1, 2, 3$, determine the cointegration properties of the processes. More precisely, the number of λ_i with absolute value less than one is just the cointegrating rank of the system. The precise values used in the simulations will be given later when we discuss the results. The size of λ_θ determines to some extent how well the mixed VARMA process can be approximated by a low order pure VAR model. A λ_θ close to zero ensures that a low order VAR provides a good approximation because the other eigenvalues of the MA coefficient matrix are also small (0.297 and –0.202). A large λ_θ value, on the other hand, requires a larger VAR order for a good approximation. To ensure invertibility of the MA part, $|\lambda_\theta|$ has to be less than one. We have chosen $\lambda_\theta = 0$ and $\lambda_\theta = \pm 0.5$ in the simulations and report some of the results in the following.

The number of replications is 1,000 and we have used sample sizes of $T = 100$ and $T = 200$. The effective sample size used in a specific situation depends on the VAR order, of course, as in the theoretical derivations of the previous sections. The maximal orders K_T are chosen to be $K_{100} = 4$ and $K_{200} = 5$, that is, K_T is the largest integer which is smaller than $T^{1/3}$. In (5.1) K_T is required to be of smaller order than $T^{1/3}$. This, however, is only an asymptotic condition. In principle this does not mean that the order cannot be greater than $T^{1/3}$ for any given finite T. The maximal lag lengths used here turn out to be sufficient to study the implications of a relatively large and potentially over-specified lag order.

In Table 1 some of the results for samples of size $T = 100$ obtained for the pure VAR process (7.1) are given. It is obvious from the table that the choice of the lag order has an impact on both the size and the power of the co-integration tests. For the DGP with cointegrating rank $r = 0$, the impact of the lag order on the size of the test is seen most easily. In this case the empirical size is grossly distorted if the test is based on a zero order ECM and hence, the order is underspecified. Instead of the nominal 5 percent the actual rejection rate of $H(0) : \text{rk}(\Pi) = 0$ is almost five times as large. On the other hand, the rejection rate also tends to increase with the lag order if the latter is overspecified. For an increasing lag order the sampling uncertainty increases

Table 1. Frequency distributions of cointegrating ranks selected for VAR DGP with order $K_0 = 1$ based on sample size 100

Rank	Lag order K					AIC	HQ	SC
	0	1	2	3	4			
Characteristics of DGP: $r = 0$, $\lambda_1 = \lambda_2 = \lambda_3 = 1$								
0	0.768	0.909	0.887	0.861	0.844	0.869	0.839	0.779
1	0.215	0.080	0.103	0.131	0.141	0.118	0.146	0.204
2	0.013	0.010	0.009	0.007	0.013	0.011	0.011	0.013
3	0.004	0.001	0.001	0.001	0.002	0.002	0.004	0.004
Characteristics of DGP: $r = 1$, $\lambda_1 = \lambda_2 = 1$, $\lambda_3 = 0.9$								
0	0.005	0.368	0.446	0.499	0.520	0.305	0.177	0.028
1	0.921	0.574	0.489	0.434	0.407	0.625	0.748	0.897
2	0.070	0.052	0.058	0.061	0.067	0.063	0.069	0.070
3	0.004	0.006	0.007	0.006	0.006	0.007	0.006	0.005
Characteristics of DGP: $r = 1$, $\lambda_1 = \lambda_2 = 1$, $\lambda_3 = 0.7$								
0	0.000	0.010	0.096	0.241	0.322	0.011	0.005	0.001
1	0.932	0.925	0.818	0.669	0.586	0.909	0.912	0.928
2	0.060	0.057	0.075	0.079	0.087	0.073	0.075	0.063
3	0.008	0.008	0.011	0.011	0.005	0.007	0.008	0.008
Characteristics of DGP: $r = 2$, $\lambda_1 = 1$, $\lambda_2 = \lambda_3 = 0.9$								
0	0.000	0.024	0.106	0.202	0.293	0.027	0.020	0.010
1	0.650	0.837	0.759	0.681	0.592	0.817	0.778	0.684
2	0.324	0.127	0.121	0.105	0.096	0.146	0.189	0.282
3	0.026	0.012	0.014	0.012	0.019	0.010	0.013	0.024
Characteristics of DGP: $r = 2$, $\lambda_1 = 1$, $\lambda_2 = \lambda_3 = 0.8$								
0	0.000	0.000	0.001	0.052	0.145	0.002	0.000	0.000
1	0.264	0.693	0.738	0.731	0.678	0.678	0.645	0.478
2	0.676	0.280	0.237	0.193	0.155	0.292	0.324	0.479
3	0.060	0.027	0.024	0.024	0.022	0.028	0.031	0.043
Characteristics of DGP: $r = 2$, $\lambda_1 = 1$, $\lambda_2 = \lambda_3 = 0.6$								
0	0.000	0.000	0.000	0.000	0.036	0.001	0.000	0.000
1	0.000	0.230	0.380	0.520	0.587	0.236	0.227	0.221
2	0.926	0.732	0.583	0.436	0.344	0.724	0.735	0.737
3	0.074	0.038	0.037	0.044	0.033	0.039	0.038	0.042
Characteristics of DGP: $r = 3$, $\lambda_1 = \lambda_2 = \lambda_3 = 0.9$								
0	0.472	0.509	0.545	0.564	0.590	0.486	0.460	0.443
1	0.393	0.336	0.317	0.312	0.306	0.357	0.381	0.407
2	0.099	0.120	0.112	0.097	0.084	0.121	0.122	0.111
3	0.036	0.035	0.026	0.027	0.020	0.036	0.037	0.039

which affects the performance of the LR test for the cointegrating rank. Note, however, that even for the true lag order $K = 1$ the actual rejection rate of the true null hypothesis $\mathrm{rk}(\Pi) = 0$ exceeds the nominal 5 percent considerably in this case. When $r > 0$, the power of the LR test is much better for an underspecified lag length than for an overspecified order. Of course, the former result is a reflection of the massive size distortion for an underspecified lag order. The power deteriorates with increasing lag order K. In other words, too small a rank is chosen with an increasing probability if K increases. Generally the choice of the cointegrating rank is more diverse if the lag order is increased and the true rank is greater than one.

For the present process, using order selection criteria such as AIC, HQ or SC amounts to choosing an order around the true lag order of $K_0 = 1$ with a high probability and consequently, selecting the lag length with any one of these criteria overall results in a better performance of the LR tests for the cointegrating rank than for a deterministically chosen order of about $T^{1/3}$. Although the choice of the selection criterion has some impact on the outcome of the cointegration tests, none of the criteria is generally superior to its competitors. In particular, none of the model selection criteria leads to generally superior performance of the cointegration tests. Note, however, that the tests do not find the correct rank with much certainty if the rank is greater than one, say, and λ_2, λ_3 are not clearly distinct from 1. With a sample size of $T = 100$, which is the order of magnitude often encountered in macroeconometric studies with quarterly data, it is obviously difficult for the LR test to find the correct rank if that is greater than one, even under the present artificial conditions. Still it may be worth investing some effort in choosing a reasonable lag order.

We have repeated this experiment with samples of size $T = 200$ and also for other λ_i values. The results are not shown because they are qualitatively similar to those for $T = 100$ although the reliability of the tests in finding the true cointegrating rank improves if $T = 200$ and a small VAR order is used. For instance, if model selection criteria are employed, a true rank of one is found in more than 90 percent of the replications. However, even with 200 observations there is a good chance that a true rank of 2 or 3 is not found. Generally the performance of the LR tests in terms of power and size deteriorates for increasing VAR order.

In Table 2 some results for VARMA processes are given. The sample size underlying the table is $T = 100$. Because the characteristics of the MA part now determine which lag order is necessary for a good approximation of the DGP it is not surprising that the frequency distributions of the cointegrating ranks selected now also depend on the MA characteristics. Using a very small lag order may result in a quite poor performance of the LR tests both in terms of size and power. In addition, the performance of the LR tests again deteriorates eventually for increasing lag length. Using the proportion of correct choices of the cointegrating rank as a criterion, it is clearly helpful to apply order selection criteria. However, even with this device a choice of a correct rank $r > 1$ is not very likely.

As can be seen in Table 3, the situation improves slightly for samples of size $T = 200$. Even then the success rate is not impressive, though. Note also

Table 2. Frequency distributions of cointegrating ranks selected for VARMA DGP
based on sample size 100

Rank	Lag order K					AIC	HQ	SC
	0	1	2	3	4			
Characteristics of DGP: $r = 0$, $\lambda_1 = \lambda_2 = \lambda_3 = 1$, $\lambda_\theta = 0$								
0	0.627	0.864	0.875	0.871	0.845	0.792	0.687	0.633
1	0.349	0.124	0.112	0.117	0.137	0.190	0.289	0.343
2	0.020	0.011	0.013	0.010	0.016	0.017	0.021	0.020
3	0.004	0.001	0.000	0.002	0.002	0.001	0.003	0.004
Characteristics of DGP: $r = 0$, $\lambda_1 = \lambda_2 = \lambda_3 = 1$, $\lambda_\theta = -0.5$								
0	0.614	0.853	0.869	0.868	0.849	0.826	0.762	0.664
1	0.353	0.133	0.119	0.118	0.129	0.158	0.218	0.306
2	0.025	0.013	0.012	0.012	0.020	0.015	0.016	0.023
3	0.008	0.001	0.000	0.002	0.002	0.001	0.004	0.007
Characteristics of DGP: $r = 1$, $\lambda_1 = \lambda_2 = 1$, $\lambda_3 = 0.9$, $\lambda_\theta = 0$								
0	0.043	0.311	0.328	0.411	0.462	0.250	0.173	0.070
1	0.606	0.586	0.590	0.499	0.458	0.573	0.562	0.595
2	0.323	0.087	0.076	0.083	0.072	0.156	0.243	0.308
3	0.028	0.016	0.006	0.007	0.008	0.021	0.022	0.027
Characteristics of DGP: $r = 1$, $\lambda_1 = \lambda_2 = 1$, $\lambda_3 = 0.9$, $\lambda_\theta = -0.5$								
0	0.038	0.101	0.201	0.284	0.367	0.107	0.083	0.060
1	0.547	0.776	0.689	0.606	0.537	0.739	0.696	0.597
2	0.366	0.107	0.099	0.101	0.085	0.135	0.197	0.303
3	0.049	0.016	0.011	0.009	0.011	0.019	0.024	0.040
Characteristics of DGP: $r = 2$, $\lambda_1 = 1$, $\lambda_2 = \lambda_3 = 0.8$, $\lambda_\theta = 0$								
0	0.000	0.002	0.007	0.053	0.126	0.001	0.000	0.000
1	0.567	0.595	0.660	0.663	0.633	0.577	0.560	0.562
2	0.418	0.378	0.308	0.251	0.218	0.398	0.420	0.420
3	0.015	0.025	0.025	0.033	0.023	0.024	0.020	0.018
Characteristics of DGP: $r = 2$, $\lambda_1 = 1$, $\lambda_2 = \lambda_3 = 0.8$, $\lambda_\theta = -0.5$								
0	0.000	0.001	0.010	0.050	0.137	0.004	0.000	0.000
1	0.875	0.511	0.702	0.663	0.630	0.564	0.628	0.811
2	0.117	0.462	0.261	0.259	0.212	0.409	0.347	0.173
3	0.008	0.026	0.027	0.028	0.021	0.023	0.025	0.016

that the model selection criteria do not necessarily find the optimal lag order for the purposes of testing for the cointegrating rank. For instance, in Table 3 for a DGP with $r = 1$ and $\lambda_1 = \lambda_2 = 1$, $\lambda_3 = 0.9$, $\lambda_\theta = -0.5$, the correct rank is found by the testing procedure in 92.4 percent of the replications if $K = 2$, whereas less than 90 percent correct decisions on the cointegrating rank are made if any of the order selection criteria is used. In most cases, however, using model selection criteria results in correct decisions with a probability close to the best one obtained with any one fixed order. Hence, on the basis of this limited evidence using model selection criteria seems to be a good idea.

Table 3. Frequency distributions of cointegrating ranks selected for VARMA DGP based on sample size 200

Rank	Lag order K						AIC	HQ	SC
	0	1	2	3	4	5			
Characteristics of DGP: $r = 0,\ \lambda_1 = \lambda_2 = \lambda_3 = 1,\ \lambda_\theta = 0$									
0	0.588	0.884	0.915	0.910	0.900	0.893	0.886	0.852	0.705
1	0.386	0.107	0.077	0.084	0.088	0.098	0.104	0.137	0.273
2	0.023	0.008	0.007	0.005	0.011	0.007	0.009	0.009	0.018
3	0.003	0.001	0.001	0.001	0.001	0.002	0.001	0.002	0.004
Characteristics of DGP: $r = 0,\ \lambda_1 = \lambda_2 = \lambda_3 = 1,\ \lambda_\theta = -0.5$									
0	0.560	0.876	0.914	0.910	0.894	0.888	0.886	0.874	0.833
1	0.421	0.116	0.078	0.084	0.095	0.104	0.104	0.118	0.159
2	0.016	0.008	0.007	0.006	0.010	0.006	0.010	0.008	0.008
3	0.003	0.000	0.001	0.000	0.001	0.002	0.000	0.000	0.000
Characteristics of DGP: $r = 1,\ \lambda_1 = \lambda_2 = 1,\ \lambda_3 = 0.9,\ \lambda_\theta = 0$									
0	0.000	0.010	0.013	0.029	0.060	0.132	0.012	0.010	0.005
1	0.637	0.876	0.914	0.894	0.863	0.788	0.884	0.857	0.752
2	0.338	0.099	0.064	0.067	0.069	0.070	0.094	0.119	0.227
3	0.025	0.015	0.009	0.010	0.008	0.010	0.010	0.014	0.016
Characteristics of DGP: $r = 1,\ \lambda_1 = \lambda_2 = 1,\ \lambda_3 = 0.9,\ \lambda_\theta = -0.5$									
0	0.000	0.000	0.003	0.011	0.022	0.054	0.002	0.000	0.000
1	0.571	0.890	0.924	0.911	0.895	0.862	0.897	0.889	0.853
2	0.379	0.095	0.064	0.070	0.074	0.076	0.089	0.096	0.127
3	0.050	0.015	0.009	0.008	0.009	0.008	0.012	0.015	0.020
Characteristics of DGP: $r = 2,\ \lambda_1 = 1,\ \lambda_2 = \lambda_3 = 0.8,\ \lambda_\theta = 0$									
0	0.000	0.000	0.000	0.000	0.000	0.001	0.000	0.000	0.000
1	0.033	0.062	0.110	0.180	0.256	0.300	0.073	0.048	0.036
2	0.937	0.903	0.855	0.777	0.697	0.651	0.890	0.917	0.931
3	0.030	0.035	0.035	0.043	0.047	0.048	0.037	0.035	0.033
Characteristics of DGP: $r = 2,\ \lambda_1 = 1,\ \lambda_2 = \lambda_3 = 0.8,\ \lambda_\theta = -0.5$									
0	0.000	0.000	0.000	0.000	0.000	0.001	0.000	0.000	0.000
1	0.408	0.030	0.169	0.191	0.281	0.337	0.075	0.041	0.194
2	0.564	0.936	0.796	0.767	0.674	0.617	0.889	0.925	0.773
3	0.028	0.034	0.035	0.042	0.045	0.045	0.036	0.034	0.033

In most cases AIC and HQ have a slight advantage over the very parsimonious SC criterion. This is in line with simulation results by Agiagloglou and Newbold (1996) for univariate unit root tests but contrasts with findings by Reimers (1992). Of course, it is not clear that the proportion of correct choices of the cointegrating rank is necessarily the best performance criterion here. Therefore the full frequency distributions of the selected ranks are given in the tables. Obviously the frequency distributions tend to be more concentrated on small ranks if the lag order increases.

As mentioned earlier, we have also used other Monte Carlo designs. They led to qualitatively similar results and are therefore not shown in order to save space. The general conclusion from the simulations is that the choice of the lag order has a massive impact on the cointegrating rank determined in the usual sequential manner on the basis of LR tests. Choosing too small an order as well as overspecifying the order both lead to size distortions and loss in power. Unfortunately, it turns out that even for the simple processes considered in our simulation experiment a correct cointegrating rank greater than one is not found very often for samples of the size typically available in macro-econometric studies.

8 Conclusions

In this study we have investigated the impact of the choice of the lag order on tests for the number of cointegrating relations in a VAR or ECM framework. It is found that the asymptotic distribution of LR tests for the cointegrating rank remains unchanged if the true DGP is of finite order and a consistent model selection criterion is used for choosing the lag order. In fact, the asymptotic distribution of the LR tests remains even valid if the true VAR order is infinite as, for instance, in VARMA processes. In other words, from an asymptotic point of view, the common practice of choosing the lag order with one of the model selection criteria is justified.

Using simulations we found that the small sample properties of the cointegration tests are dependent on the choice of the lag length. Choosing a very small lag length which results in a poor approximation of the true DGP may equally well result in major size distortions and reduced power of the tests as a large lag length which introduces substantial sampling uncertainty into the estimated model. Generally, increasing the lag length eventually results in size and power erosions. Therefore, choosing the lag length with order selection criteria which tend to find a balance between a good approximation of the DGP and an efficient use of the sample information seems to be a good strategy for applied work.

Our simulation results are exclusively based on three-dimensional processes which may be viewed as restrictive. However, from other studies with a different focus it appears that small variations in the dimension are likely to result in qualitatively similar findings. That is, for processes with dimension two, for example, we expect to also find size and power distortions for increasing lag length. Of course, in such processes there are fewer possibilities to under-estimate the cointegrating rank if the process is stationary, say.

In this study we have exclusively focused on processes without deterministic trend terms. Given the importance of processes with deterministic linear trends in applied work, an extension of the present results to this case is desirable. We have not considered it here because it appears to be nontrivial at least as far as the asymptotic theory is concerned. Similar remarks are true for other deviations from the simple standard case considered here. For instance, investigating processes with structural shifts or heavy tailed, ARCH type residuals may be of interest from a practical point of view.

Appendix: Proofs

A.1 Preliminaries and Intermediate Results

Following Saikkonen (1992) and Saikkonen and Lütkepohl (1996) we shall first reparameterize equation (3.6) as

$$\Delta y_t = \sum_{j=1}^{K} \underline{\Gamma}_j u_{t-1} + \underline{\Gamma}_{K+1,1} u_{1,t-K-1} + \underline{\Pi}_2 y_{2,t-1} + e_t, \quad t = K+2,\dots,T, \qquad (A.1)$$

where $\underline{\Pi}_2 = 0$ and $\underline{\Gamma}_j = [\underline{\Gamma}_{j1} : \underline{\Gamma}_{j2}]$ with $\underline{\Gamma}_{11} = \Phi + \Gamma_{11}$, $\underline{\Gamma}_{j1} = \Gamma_{j1} - \Gamma_{j-1,1}$, $j = 2$, ..., K, $\underline{\Gamma}_{K+1,1} = -\Gamma_{K1} = 0$ and $\underline{\Gamma}_{j2} = \Gamma_{j1}A + \Gamma_{j2}$, $j = 1, \dots, K$. Define

$$q_t' = [u_{t-1}', \dots, u_{t-K}', u_{1,t-K-1}'], \quad p_t' = [q_t' : y_{2,t-1}']$$

and

$$\Xi = [\underline{\Gamma}_1 : \cdots : \underline{\Gamma}_K : \underline{\Gamma}_{K+1,1}], \quad \Lambda = [\Xi : \underline{\Pi}_2].$$

With these definitions we can write (A.1) as

$$\Delta y_t = \Lambda p_t + e_t, \quad t = K+2,\dots,T. \qquad (A.2)$$

Let $\tilde{\Lambda} = [\tilde{\Xi} : \tilde{\underline{\Pi}}_2]$ be the least squares estimator of Λ obtained from (A.2). Then it follows from the definitions that:

$$(\tilde{\Lambda} - \Lambda)D_T^{-1} = \sum_{t=K+2}^{T} e_t p_t' D_T \left[D_T \sum_{t=K+2}^{T} p_t p_t' D_T \right]^{-1}, \qquad (A.3)$$

where $D_T = \mathrm{diag}[N^{-1/2} I_{nK+n_1} : N^{-1} I_{n_2}]$. As in Saikkonen (1992) we have to study the asymptotic properties of the right hand side of (A.3). For this purpose it is convenient to introduce the matrix norm $\|C\|_1 = \sup\{\|Cx\| : \|x\| \le 1\}$ where the symbol $\|\cdot\|$ signifies the Euclidean norm. The useful inequality

$$\|C_1 C_2\| \le \|C_1\| \|C_2\|_1 \qquad (A.4)$$

is known to hold for any conformable matrices (see, e.g., Lütkepohl, 1996, ch. 8) and will be frequently used without explicit reference. Next define

$$\hat{R} = D_T \sum_{t=K+2}^{T} p_t p_t' D_T \quad \text{and} \quad R = \mathrm{diag}\left[\Gamma_{qq} : N^{-1} \sum_{t=K+2}^{T} y_{2,t-1} y_{2,t-1}' \right],$$

where $\Gamma_{qq} = E(q_t q_t')$. For the inverses of these matrices we have

$$\left\|\hat{R}^{-1} - R^{-1}\right\|_1 = O_p(K/N^{\frac{1}{2}}).   \tag{A.5}$$

This result follows directly from Lemmas A2–A4 of Saikkonen (1991) by observing that the proofs of these lemmas are based on moment calculations which require only Assumption 1. This fact will also be used in subsequent derivations without mentioning the difference in assumptions. We partition

$$\hat{R}^{-1} = [\hat{R}^{ij}]_{i,j=1,2}$$

conformably with the partition of R and prove the following auxiliary result.

Lemma A.1. Suppose that y_t is generated by (3.3) and (3.4) and that condition (3.5) holds. Then, as $T \to \infty$, uniformly in $K \le K_T = o(T^{1/3})$,

(a) $\|\hat{R}^{11}\|_1 = O_p(1)$;

(b) $\|\hat{R}^{11} - \Gamma_q^{-1}\|_1 = O_p(K_T/N^{1/2})$;

(c) $\|\hat{R}^{22} - (N^{-2}\sum_{t=K+2}^T y_{2,t-1}y'_{2,t-1})^{-1}\|_1 = O_p(K_T/N)$;

(d) $\|\hat{R}^{12}\|_1 = O_p((K_T/N)^{1/2})$.

Proof. We shall first give a proof for any chosen $K \le K_T$. From the inversion formula of a partitioned matrix one obtains:

$$(\hat{R}^{11})^{-1} - N^{-1}\sum_{t=K+2}^T q_t q'_t$$

$$= N^{-\frac{3}{2}}\sum_{t=K+2}^T q_t y'_{2,t-1}\left(N^{-2}\sum_{t=K+2}^T y_{2,t-1}y'_{2,t-1}\right)^{-1} N^{-\frac{3}{2}}\sum_{t=K+2}^T y_{2,t-1}q'_t.$$

The inverse on the r.h.s. is of order $O_p(1)$ by well-known properties of integrated processes whereas

$$\left\|N^{-\frac{3}{2}}\sum_{t=K+2}^T y_{2,t-1}q'_t\right\| = O_p((K_T/N)^{\frac{1}{2}})   \tag{A.6}$$

by arguments used to prove Lemma A2 of Saikkonen (1991) and by the assumption $K \le K_T$. Hence, since $\|\cdot\|_1 \le \|\cdot\|$, we have

$$\left\|(\hat{R}^{11})^{-1} - N^{-1}\sum_{t=K+2}^T q_t q'_t\right\|_1 = O_p(K_T/N).   \tag{A.7}$$

From Lemmas A3 and A4 of Saikkonen (1991) we find that the $\|\cdot\|_1$ norm of the inverse of the latter matrix on the l.h.s. is of order $O_p(1)$ and this holds even uniformly in $K \le K_T$. Thus, from Lemma A2 of Saikkonen and Lütkepohl (1996) it follows that (A.7) also holds for the corresponding inverses and, furthermore, that $\|\hat{R}^{11}\|_1 = O_p(1)$ for any $K \le K_T$. The same arguments and Lemma A2 of Saikkonen (1991) yield the second assertion and, after changing the roles of q_t and $y_{2,t-1}$, also the third one, for any $K \le K_T$. Finally, since

$$\hat{R}^{12} = -\left(N^{-1}\sum_{t=K+2}^{T}q_t q_t'\right)^{-1}\left(N^{-\frac{3}{2}}\sum_{t=K+2}^{T}q_t y_{2,t-1}'\right)\hat{R}^{22},$$

one can similarly show that the fourth result of the lemma holds for any $K \le K_T$.

To complete the proof, we have to establish uniformity in $K \le K_T$. This, however, only requires straightforward modifications to the above arguments. First note that, since $K_T = o(T^{1/3})$, it is easy to show that changing the range of summation from $t = K+2, \ldots, T$ to $t = K_T + 2, \ldots, T$ does not change the above conclusions and this holds uniformly in $K \le K_T$. This means that we have to establish the desired uniformity with respect to the dimension of q_t. This, however, follows because the above proof applies with $K = K_T$ and because the norm of a matrix does not decrease when its dimension is increased. Thus, the l.h.s. of (A.6) for example, is dominated by the corresponding quantity with $K = K_T$ plus a term which is of order $O_p((K/N)^{1/2})$ uniformly in $K \le K_T$. Hence, Lemma A.1 is established. ∎

In the following it is convenient to define

$$e_{1t} = -\sum_{j=K+1}^{\infty}G_j v_{t-j},$$

so that $e_t = \varepsilon_t + e_{1t}$. For e_{1t} we have, uniformly in t,

$$E\|e_{1t}\|^2 \le c\left(\sum_{j=K+1}^{\infty}\|G_j\|\right)^2 = o(K^{-2}), \tag{A.8}$$

where the first relation is given in (A12) of Saikkonen (1992) and the second one is an immediate consequence of condition (3.5). Here as well as below the symbol c signifies a finite positive constant (not necessarily the same throughout). We shall next prove the following lemma.

Lemma A.2. Under the conditions of Lemma A.1,
(a) $N^{-1}\sum_{t=K+2}^{T}e_{1t}y_{2,t-1}' = o_p(K^{-1})$;
(b) $\|N^{-1}\sum_{t=K+2}^{T}e_{1t}q_t'\| = o_p(K^{-1/2})$.

Proof. Denote the typical components of the vectors y_{2t} and e_{1t} by y_{2it} and e_{1jt}, respectively, and notice that

$$E\left\|N^{-1}\sum_{t=K+2}^{T}e_{1t}y_{2,t-1}'\right\|^2 = N^{-2}\sum_{t=K+2}^{T}\sum_{s=K+2}^{T}E(y_{2,t-1}'y_{2,s-1}e_{1s}'e_{1t})$$

$$= N^{-2}\sum_{i=1}^{n_2}\sum_{j=1}^{n}\sum_{t=K+2}^{T}\sum_{s=K+2}^{T}E(y_{2i,t-1}y_{2i,s-1}e_{1js}e_{1jt}). \tag{A.9}$$

In what follows we shall make the initial value assumption $y_{20} = 0$ which is easily seen to have no effect on asymptotic results. With this assumption we have the well-known identity:

$$E(y_{2i,t-1}y_{2i,s-1}e_{1js}e_{1jt}) = E(y_{2i,t-1}y_{2i,s-1})E(e_{1js}e_{1jt}) + E(y_{2i,t-1}e_{1jt})E(y_{2i,s-1}e_{1js})$$
$$+ E(y_{2i,t-1}e_{1js})E(y_{2i,s-1}e_{1jt}) + \text{cum}(y_{2i,t-1}, y_{2i,s-1}, e_{1jt}, e_{1js})$$
$$(\text{A.10})$$

where $\text{cum}(\cdot, \cdot, \cdot, \cdot)$ denotes the fourth order cumulant of the indicated random variables (see Stuart and Ord, 1987, p. 439). Well-known properties of integrated processes imply that $|E(y_{2i,t-1}y_{2i,s-1})| \leq c \min\{(t-1, s-1)\}$ which in conjunction with (A.8) shows that the contribution of the first term on the r.h.s. of (A.10) to (A.9) is of order $o(K^{-2})$. Next note that, since the covariance function of the process v_t is absolutely summable, we have

$$\left\| E(e_{1s}y'_{2,t-1}) \right\| = \left\| E\left(\sum_{i=K+1}^{\infty} G_i v_{s-i} \sum_{j=1}^{t-1} v'_{2j} \right) \right\|$$
$$\leq \sum_{i=K+1}^{\infty} \|G_i\| \sum_{j=1}^{t-1} \left\| E(v_{s-i}v'_{2j}) \right\|$$
$$\leq c \sum_{i=K+1}^{\infty} \|G_i\|.$$

By (A.8) the last quantity is of order $o(K^{-1})$ and it follows that the contribution of the second and third terms on the r.h.s. of (A.10) to (A.9) is of order $o(K^{-2})$. Finally, since cumulants are linear in each of their arguments and the fourth order cumulant function of the process v_t is absolutely summable, one readily finds that, uniformly in t and s,

$$\left| \text{cum}(y_{2i,t-1}, y_{2i,s-1}, e_{1jt}, e_{1js}) \right| = o(K^{-2}).$$

Hence, the contribution of the fourth term on the r.h.s. of (A.10) to (A.9) is also of order $o(K^{-2})$. Altogether we have thus shown that (A.9) is of order $o(K^{-2})$ so that the first assertion of the lemma follows from Markov's inequality.

As for the second assertion, we can use the argument in (2.9) of Lewis and Reinsel (1985, p. 397) and conclude that

$$E\left\| N^{-1} \sum_{t=K+2}^{T} e_{1t}q'_t \right\| \leq cK^{\frac{1}{2}} \sum_{j=K+1}^{\infty} \|G_j\|.$$

The r.h.s. is of order $o(K^{-1/2})$ which yields the desired result. ∎

We also need some intermediate results for estimators using the restriction $\Pi_2 = 0$ in (A.1). Therefore we write (A.2) as

$$\Delta y_t = \Xi(K)q_t + \varepsilon_{Kt}, \quad t = K+2,\ldots,T, \tag{A.11}$$

where

$$\Xi(K) = E(\Delta y_t q_t') E(q_t q_t')^{-1} \overset{def}{=} \Gamma_{\Delta yq} \Gamma_{qq}^{-1},$$

and ε_{Kt} is defined to make the identity hold. In other words, ε_{Kt} is the one-step ahead prediction error of the best linear predictor of Δy_t based on $u_{t-1}, \ldots,$ $u_{t-K}, u_{1,t-K-1}$. By stationarity, $\Xi(K)$ is independent of t and, by the definitions, $E(q_t \varepsilon_{Kt}') = 0$. Let $\hat{\Xi}(K)$ be the least squares estimator of $\Xi(K)$ obtained from (A.11). Since this least squares regression is a reparameterized form of (5.2) we have $\hat{\varepsilon}_{Kt} = \Delta y_t - \hat{\Xi}(K) q_t$. Furthermore,

$$\hat{\Xi}(K) - \Xi(K) = \left[N^{-1} \sum_{t=K+2}^{T} \varepsilon_{Kt} q_t' \right] \left[N^{-1} \sum_{t=K+2}^{T} q_t q_t' \right]^{-1}. \tag{A.12}$$

Since $\underline{\Pi}_2 = 0$ we can augment (A.11) to

$$\Delta y_t = \Lambda(K) q_t + \varepsilon_{Kt}, \quad t = K+2, \ldots, T, \tag{A.13}$$

where $\Lambda(K) = [\Xi(K) : \underline{\Pi}_2]$. Viewing $\tilde{\Xi}$ as an estimator of $\Xi(K)$ we thus have

$$\tilde{\Xi} - \Xi(K) = \left[N^{-1} \sum_{t=K+2}^{T} \varepsilon_{Kt} q_t' \right] \hat{R}^{11} + \left[N^{-\frac{3}{2}} \sum_{t=K+2}^{T} \varepsilon_{Kt} y_{2,t-1}' \right] \hat{R}^{21}, \tag{A.14}$$

where $\hat{R}^{11}$ and $\hat{R}^{21}$ are as in Lemma A.1. In order to study the difference between $\tilde{\Xi}$ and $\hat{\Xi}(K)$ and further to prove Lemma 5.1 we need the following results.

Lemma A.3. Suppose that the assumptions of Lemma 5.1 hold. Then,

(a) $||N^{-1}\sum_{t=K+2}^{T}\varepsilon_{Kt} q_t'|| = O_p(K_T/N^{1/2})$ uniformly in $K \leq K_T = o_p(T^{1/3})$ and

(b) $N^{-1}\sum_{t=K+2}^{T}\varepsilon_{Kt} y_{2,t-1}' - N^{-1}\sum_{t=K+2}^{T}\varepsilon_t y_{2,t-1}' = O_p(1)\sum_{j=K+1}^{\infty} j^a ||G_j|| + o_p(K_T^{-1})$

where the terms $O_p(1)$ and $o_p(K_T^{-1})$ are uniform in $K \leq K_T$.

Proof. By the definitions, $\varepsilon_{Kt} = \Delta y_t - \Xi(K) q_t$ and hence:

$$\left\| N^{-1} \sum_{t=K+2}^{T} \varepsilon_{Kt} q_t' \right\|$$

$$= \left\| N^{-1} \sum_{t=K+2}^{T} \Delta y_t q_t' - \Xi(K) N^{-1} \sum_{t=K+2}^{T} q_t q_t' \right\|$$

$$\leq \left\| N^{-1} \sum_{t=K+2}^{T} \Delta y_t q_t' - \Xi(K) \Gamma_{qq} \right\| + \left\| \Xi(K) \left(N^{-1} \sum_{t=K+2}^{T} q_t q_t' - \Gamma_{qq} \right) \right\|$$

$$\leq \left\| N^{-1} \sum_{t=K+2}^{T} \Delta y_t q_t' - \Gamma_{\Delta yq} \right\| + \left\| \Xi(K) \right\| \left\| N^{-1} \sum_{t=K+2}^{T} q_t q_t' - \Gamma_{qq} \right\|_1.$$

The first norm in the last expression is of order $O_p((K_T/T)^{1/2})$ for all $K \leq K_T$, because each element of the involved matrix has mean square of order $O(N^{-1})$ uniformly in the row and column index (see the proof of Lemma A2 of Saikkonen, 1991). Further, arguments used in the proof of Lemma A.1(b) show that that the $||\cdot||_1$ norm in the last expression is of order $O_p(K_T/N^{1/2})$ for all $K \le K_T$. Thus to prove the first result, it suffices to show that $||\Xi(K)|| = O(1)$ uniformly in $K \le K_T$. To see this, notice that $||\Xi(K)|| \le ||\Gamma_{\Delta yq}|| \, ||\Gamma_{qq}^{-1}||_1$ where the latter norm on the r.h.s. is of order $O(1)$ uniformly in $K \le K_T$ (see, e.g., the proof of Lemma A3 of Saikkonen, 1991). The former norm also has the same property because $\Delta y_{1t} = A u_{2t} + \Delta u_{1t}$ and $\Delta y_{2t} = u_{2t}$ and the covariance function of u_t is absolutely summable.

To prove the second assertion, observe that:

$$\varepsilon_{Kt} - \varepsilon_t = e_{1t} - (\Xi(K) - \Xi)q_t. \tag{A.15}$$

Thus, we can prove the result in two parts and first consider

$$-N^{-1} \sum_{t=K+2}^{T} e_{1t} y_{2,t-1}' = N^{-1} \sum_{t=K+2}^{T} \sum_{j=K+1}^{K_T+1} G_j v_{t-j} y_{2,t-1}'$$

$$+ N^{-1} \sum_{t=K+2}^{T} \sum_{j=K_T+2}^{\infty} G_j v_{t-j} y_{2,t-1}'.$$

Using (A.8) it is straightforward to check that changing the range of summation from $t = K + 2, \ldots, T$ to $t = K_T, \ldots, T$ has an effect which is at most of order $o_p(K_T^{-1})$. Thus, from Lemma A.2(a) it follows that the latter quantity on the r.h.s. is of order $o_p(K_T^{-1})$ uniformly in $K \le K_T$ and for the first one we can consider

$$\left\| N^{-1} \sum_{t=K_T+2}^{T} \sum_{j=K+1}^{K_T+1} G_j v_{t-j} y_{2,t-1}' \right\|$$

$$\le \sum_{j=K+1}^{K_T+1} j^a \|G_j\| \left\| j^{-a} N^{-1} \sum_{t=K_T+2}^{T} v_{t-j} y_{2,t-1}' \right\|$$

$$\le \max_{1 \le j \le K_T+1} \left\| j^{-a} N^{-1} \sum_{t=K_T+2}^{T} v_{t-j} y_{2,t-1}' \right\| \sum_{i=K+2}^{\infty} i^a \|G_i\|.$$

We have to show that the first factor in the last expression is of order $O_p(1)$. For $M > 0$ consider

$$P \left\{ \max_{1 \le j \le K_T+1} \left\| j^{-a} N^{-1} \sum_{t=K_T+2}^{T} v_{t-j} y_{2,t-1}' \right\| > M \right\}$$

$$\le \sum_{j=1}^{K_T+1} P \left\{ \left\| N^{-1} \sum_{t=K_T+2}^{T} v_{t-j} y_{2,t-1}' \right\| > j^a M \right\}$$

$$\le M^{-2} \sum_{j=1}^{K_T+1} j^{-2a} E \left\| N^{-1} \sum_{t=K_T+2}^{T} v_{t-j} y_{2,t-1}' \right\|^2,$$

where the last relation follows from Markov's inequality and the expectation therein is of order $O(1)$ uniformly in j (see the proof of Lemma A2 of Saikkonen, 1991). Thus, the last expression above can be bounded by cM^{-2} and, since this holds for any $0 < M < \infty$, the desired result follows.

To complete the proof of (b) in Lemma A.3 we still have to consider the second part related to the latter quantity on the r.h.s. of (A.15). This means that we have to find an appropriate bound for

$$\left\| (\Xi(K) - \Xi) N^{-1} \sum_{t=K+2}^{T} q_t y_{2,t-1}' \right\| \leq \left\| (\Xi(K) - \Xi) \right\| \left\| N^{-1} \sum_{t=K+2}^{T} q_t y_{2,t-1}' \right\|. \tag{A.16}$$

Consider the first norm on the r.h.s. and, analogously to the definition of Ξ, write $\Xi(K) = [\underline{\Gamma}_1(K) : \dots : \underline{\Gamma}_K(K) : \underline{\Gamma}_{K+1,1}(K)]$. Then,

$$\left\| \Xi(K) - \Xi \right\| \leq \sum_{j=1}^{K} \left\| \underline{\Gamma}_j(K) - \underline{\Gamma}_j \right\| + \left\| \underline{\Gamma}_{K+1,1}(K) - \underline{\Gamma}_{K+1,1} \right\|$$

$$\leq c \sum_{j=K+1}^{\infty} \left\| G_j \right\|. \tag{A.17}$$

Here the first inequality follows because the Euclidean norm is dominated by the L_1-norm. To justify the second inequality, notice that, since $\Delta y_{1t} = A u_{2t} + \Delta u_{1t}$ and $\Delta y_{2t} = u_{2t}$, the coefficient matrices involved in $\Xi(K)$ and Ξ are simple transformations of analogous coefficient matrices obtained from the infinite order autoregressive representation of u_t. Thus, since u_t is a linear transformation of v_t, it follows that we need to justify the last inequality for corresponding coefficient matrices obtained from G_j, the coefficient matrices of the infinite order autoregressive representation of v_t. After noticing this, the required result follows from Theorem 6.6.12 of Hannan and Deistler (1988, see also p. 271 after the theorem).

Thus, (A.17) and condition (3.5) imply that an appropriate upper bound for the r.h.s. of (A.16) is obtained by showing that

$$K^{-a} \left\| N^{-1} \sum_{t=K+2}^{T} q_t y_{2,t-1}' \right\| = O_p(1) \tag{A.18}$$

uniformly in $K \leq K_T$. In the same way as in the proof of the first part of the lemma it is again straightforward to check that K in the summation can be replaced by K_T and that, for any $M > 0$,

$$P\left\{ \max_{1 \leq K \leq K_T} K^{-a} \left\| N^{-1} \sum_{t=K_T+2}^{T} q_t y_{2,t-1}' \right\| > M \right\}$$

$$\leq M^{-2} \sum_{K=1}^{K_T} K^{-2a} E \left\| N^{-1} \sum_{t=K_T+2}^{T} q_t y_{2,t-1}' \right\|^2$$

where the expectation is of order $O(K)$ (see the proof of Lemma A2 of Saikkonen, 1991). Thus, we can conclude that the last expression is bounded by cM^{-2}. This implies (A.16) and completes the proof of Lemma A.3. ■

Lemma A.3 is used to prove the following result.

Lemma A.4. Suppose the assumptions of Lemma 5.1 hold. Then, uniformly in $K \leq K_T$,

(a) $\tilde{\underline{\Pi}}_2 = O_p(N^{-1})$;

(b) $\|\tilde{\Xi} - \hat{\Xi}(K)\| = o_p(K_T/N)$;

(c) $\|\hat{\Xi}(K) - \Xi(K)\| = O_p(K_T/N^{1/2})$.

Proof. Viewing $\tilde{\underline{\Pi}}_2$ as an estimator of $\underline{\Pi}_2$ in (A.13) yields:

$$N\tilde{\underline{\Pi}}_2 = N^{-\frac{1}{2}} \sum_{t=K+2}^{T} \varepsilon_{Kt} q_t' \hat{R}^{12} + N^{-1} \sum_{t=K+2}^{T} \varepsilon_{Kt} y_{2,t-1}' \hat{R}^{22}. \tag{A.19}$$

Here the first term on the r.h.s. is of order $O_p(K_T)O_p((K_T/N)^{1/2}) = o_p(1)$ uniformly in $K \leq K_T$ by Lemmas A.1(d) and A.3(a). That the second one is of order $O_p(1)$ uniformly in $K \leq K_T$ can be seen from Lemmas A.1(c) and A.3(b) and the fact that changing the range of summation from $t = K + 2, ..., T$ to $t = K_T + 2, ..., T$ does not change the conclusion.

To prove (b), notice that from (A.12) and (A.14) it follows that:

$$\left\| \tilde{\Xi} - \hat{\Xi}(K) \right\| \leq \left\| N^{-1} \sum_{t=K+2}^{T} \varepsilon_{Kt} q_t' \right\| \left\| \left(N^{-1} \sum_{t=K+2}^{T} q_t q_t' \right)^{-1} - \hat{R}^{11} \right\|_1$$

$$+ \left\| N^{-\frac{3}{2}} \sum_{t=K+2}^{T} \varepsilon_{Kt} y_{2,t-1}' \right\| \left\| \hat{R}^{21} \right\|_1$$

$$= O_p(K_T / N^{\frac{1}{2}})O_p(K_T / N) + O_p(N^{-\frac{1}{2}})O_p((K_T / N)^{\frac{1}{2}})$$

$$= o_p(K_T / N)$$

uniformly in $K \leq K_T$. Here the first equality can be justified by using (A.7) and Lemmas A.1(d) and A.3. Finally, (c) is an immediate consequence of (A.12), Lemma A.4(a) and the fact mentioned after (A.7). ■

Now we are able to prove Lemma 5.1.

A.2 Proof of Lemma 5.1

First note that

$$\tilde{\varepsilon} = \hat{\varepsilon}_{Kt} + (\hat{\Xi}(K) - \tilde{\Xi})q_t - \tilde{\underline{\Pi}}_2 y_{2,t-1}.$$

Thus, since $\hat{\varepsilon}_{Kt}$ and q_t are orthogonal,

$$\tilde{\Sigma}_K - \hat{\Sigma}_K = (\hat{\Xi}(K) - \tilde{\Xi})N^{-1}\sum_{t=K+2}^{T} q_t q_t'(\hat{\Xi}(K) - \tilde{\Xi})' + \underline{\tilde{\Pi}}_2 N^{-1}\sum_{t=K+2}^{T} y_{2,t-1}y_{2,t-1}'\underline{\tilde{\Pi}}_2'$$

$$-(\hat{\Xi}(K) - \tilde{\Xi})N^{-1}\sum_{t=K+2}^{T} q_t y_{2,t-1}'\underline{\tilde{\Pi}}_2' + \underline{\tilde{\Pi}}_2 N^{-1}\sum_{t=K+2}^{T} y_{2,t-1}q_t'(\hat{\Xi}(K) - \tilde{\Xi})'$$

$$-N^{-1}\sum_{t=K+2}^{T} \hat{\varepsilon}_{Kt}y_{2,t-1}'\underline{\tilde{\Pi}}_2' - \underline{\tilde{\Pi}}_2 N^{-1}\sum_{t=K+2}^{T} y_{2,t-1}\hat{\varepsilon}_{Kt}'.$$

It is not difficult to see that $\|\Gamma_{qq}\|_1 = O(1)$ uniformly in $K \leq K_T$, so that, using arguments similar to those in the proof of Lemma A.3(a), it can be shown that the $\|\cdot\|_1$-norm of the matrix in the middle of the first term on the r.h.s. is of order $O_p(1)$ uniformly in $K \leq K_T$. After dividing by N, a similar result clearly holds for the matrix in the middle of the second term on the r.h.s.. Using these facts, (A.6) and Lemma A.4 it can be seen that the first four terms on the r.h.s. are at most of order $o_p(K_T/T)$ uniformly in $K \leq K_T$. To show that this is also the case for the last two terms, notice that

$$N^{-1}\sum_{t=K+2}^{T} \hat{\varepsilon}_{Kt}y_{2,t-1}'\underline{\tilde{\Pi}}_2' = N^{-1}\sum_{t=K+2}^{T} \varepsilon_{Kt}y_{2,t-1}'\underline{\tilde{\Pi}}_2'$$

$$-(\hat{\Xi}(K) - \Xi(K))N^{-1}\sum_{t=K+2}^{T} q_t y_{2,t-1}'\underline{\tilde{\Pi}}_2'.$$

The desired result readily follows from this, Lemma A.3(b), Lemma A.4 and (A.6). ∎

A.3 Proof of Theorem 5.1

For the first assertion we have to show that $P\{\tilde{K} > K\}$ tends to unity for every fixed K. Observe that $\tilde{K} > K$ is implied by

$$\log\left|\tilde{\Sigma}_K\right| - \log\left|\tilde{\Sigma}_{K+k}\right| - kC_T/T > 0,$$

for some positive integer k. Denote $E(\varepsilon_{Kt}\varepsilon_{Kt}')$ by Σ_K. Using the result of Lemma 5.1 and arguments similar to those in its proof one can readily check that the l.h.s. of the above inequality converges in probability to $\log|\Sigma_K| - \log|\Sigma_{K+k}|$. When (3.4) is not a finite order autoregression this difference is strictly positive for some $k > 0$ and the required result follows.

To prove the second assertion, we first note that the above proof implies that we must have $\tilde{K} \geq K_0$ in probability. Thus, it suffices to show that here strict inequality is not possible. First observe that now $T^{1/2}\sum_{j=K+1}^{\infty}\|G_j\| \to 0$ as $K \to \infty$ and $T \to \infty$. Thus, we have $(\tilde{\Lambda} - \Lambda)D_T^{-1} = O_p(K^{1/2})$ for any $K_0 \leq K \leq K_T$ (see Saikkonen, 1992, p. 21). Standard arguments used to derive the limiting distribution of LR tests in VAR models readily show that $T(\log|\tilde{\Sigma}_K|$

$-\log|\tilde{\Sigma}_{K_0}|) = O_p(K)$. The desired result follows from this fact and the assumption $C_T \to \infty$.

A.4 Proof of Theorem 5.2

We shall first prove an auxiliary result about the estimators $\tilde{\underline{\Pi}}_2, \tilde{\Phi}$ and $\tilde{\Sigma}$ based on the estimated VAR order $\tilde{K}$. Notice that here $\tilde{\Phi} = \tilde{\Pi}_1$ is obtained from $\tilde{\Pi} = [\tilde{\Pi}_1 : \tilde{\Pi}_2]$. Since the theoretical counterpart of $\tilde{\Phi}$ depends on the VAR order (see (3.7)) it is convenient to consider the limiting version

$$\Phi_\infty = -\sum_{j=0}^\infty G_j J.$$

Now we can prove the following result.

Lemma A.5. Suppose the assumptions of Theorem 5.2 hold and that the estimators $\tilde{\underline{\Pi}}_2, \tilde{\Phi}$ and $\tilde{\Sigma}$ are based on the lag order $\tilde{K}$ selected by minimizing (5.1). Then,

(a) $N\tilde{\underline{\Pi}}_2 = N^{-1}\sum_{t=K_T+2}^T \varepsilon_t y_{2,t-1}' (N^{-2}\sum_{t=K_T+2}^T y_{2,t-1} y_{2,t-1}')^{-1} + o_p(1);$

(b) $\tilde{\Phi} = \Phi_\infty + o_p(1);$

(c) $\tilde{\Sigma} = \Sigma + o_p(1).$

Proof. To prove (a), note first that we again have (A.19) but with K on the r.h.s. replaced by $\tilde{K}$. Since we noticed below (A.19) that the first term on the r.h.s. is of order $o_p(1)$ uniformly in $K \le K_T$ the same order result is also obtained when K is replaced by $\tilde{K}$. From this fact and Lemma A.1(c) we find that:

$$N\tilde{\underline{\Pi}}_2 = N^{-1}\sum_{t=\tilde{K}+2}^T \varepsilon_{\tilde{K}t} y_{2,t-1}' \left[N^{-2}\sum_{t=\tilde{K}+2}^T y_{2,t-1} y_{2,t-1}'\right]^{-1} + o_p(1).$$

By Lemma A.3(b) and Theorem 5.1 we here have:

$$N^{-1}\sum_{t=\tilde{K}+2}^T \varepsilon_{\tilde{K}t} y_{2,t-1}' = N^{-1}\sum_{t=\tilde{K}+2}^T \varepsilon_t y_{2,t-1}' + O_p(1)\sum_{j=\tilde{K}+1}^\infty j^a \|G_j\| + o_p(K_T^{-1})$$

$$= N^{-1}\sum_{t=\tilde{K}+2}^T \varepsilon_t y_{2,t-1}' + o_p(1).$$

Thus, we have the equation stated in (a) except that the summation is started at $\tilde{K} + 2$ instead of $K_T + 2$. However, the stated result follows because, in the same way as in previous similar cases, it can be shown that changing the range of summation from $K + 2, ..., T$ to $K_T + 2, ..., T$ with a nonstochastic choice of K has an asymptotically negligible effect uniformly in $K \le K_T$.

To prove (b) first observe that:

$$\tilde{\Phi} - \Phi_\infty = \tilde{\Phi} - \Phi + \sum_{j=\tilde{K}+1}^{\infty} G_j J = \tilde{\Phi} - \Phi + o_p(1),$$

where the latter equality follows from Theorem 5.1. Here Φ depends on $\tilde{K}$ and, by the definitions,

$$\tilde{\Phi} - \Phi = \sum_{j=1}^{\tilde{K}+1} (\underline{\tilde{\Gamma}}_{j1} - \Gamma_{j1}) = (\tilde{\Xi} - \Xi) J_{\tilde{K}},$$

where $J_K = [-J' : \ldots : -J' : I_{n_1}]'$ is a $((Kn + n_1) \times n_1)$ matrix and $\|J_K\|_1 = (K+1)^{1/2}$. To prove the assertion, write:

$$\left\| \tilde{\Phi} - \Phi \right\| = \left\| (\tilde{\Xi} - \Xi) J_{\tilde{K}} \right\|$$
$$\leq \left\| (\tilde{\Xi} - \hat{\Xi}(\tilde{K})) J_{\tilde{K}} \right\| + \left\| (\hat{\Xi}(\tilde{K}) - \Xi(\tilde{K})) J_{\tilde{K}} \right\| + \left\| (\Xi(\tilde{K}) - \Xi) J_{\tilde{K}} \right\|$$
$$\leq o_p(K_T / N) O_p(K_T^{\frac{1}{2}}) + O_p(K_T / N^{\frac{1}{2}}) O_p(K_T^{\frac{1}{2}}) + c\tilde{K}^{\frac{1}{2}} \sum_{j=\tilde{K}+1}^{\infty} \left\| G_j \right\|$$
$$= o_p(1).$$

Here the third relation is based on Lemma A.4 and (A.17) and the fourth one on Theorem 5.1 and the assumption $K_T = o(T^{1/3})$.

As for (c), conclude first from Lemma 5.1 that it suffices to show that $\hat{\Sigma}_{\tilde{K}} = \Sigma + o_p(1)$, where $\hat{\Sigma}_{\tilde{K}}$ is obtained from the residuals $\hat{\varepsilon}_{\tilde{K}_t} = \varepsilon_{\tilde{K}_t} - (\hat{\Xi}(\tilde{K}) - \Xi(\tilde{K})) q_t$. Using Lemmas A.3(a) and A.4(b) in conjunction with (A.4) and the fact that the $\|\cdot\|_1$-norm of the matrix of second sample moments of q_t is of order $O_p(1)$ (cf. the proof of Lemma 5.1) it is straightforward to conclude from this fact that:

$$\hat{\Sigma}_{\tilde{K}} = N^{-1} \sum_{t=\tilde{K}+1}^{T} \varepsilon_{\tilde{K}t} \varepsilon'_{\tilde{K}t} + o_p(1).$$

From this and (A.15) it follows that:

$$\hat{\Sigma}_{\tilde{K}} - N^{-1} \sum_{t=\tilde{K}+1}^{T} \varepsilon_t \varepsilon'_t$$
$$= (\Xi(\tilde{K}) - \Xi) N^{-1} \sum_{t=\tilde{K}+1}^{T} q_t q'_t (\Xi(\tilde{K}) - \Xi)'$$
$$- (\Xi(\tilde{K}) - \Xi) N^{-1} \sum_{t=\tilde{K}+1}^{T} q_t \varepsilon'_t - N^{-1} \sum_{t=\tilde{K}+1}^{T} \varepsilon_t q'_t (\Xi(\tilde{K}) - \Xi)'$$
$$- N^{-1} \sum_{t=\tilde{K}+1}^{T} e_{1t} q'_t (\Xi(\tilde{K}) - \Xi)' - (\Xi(\tilde{K}) - \Xi) N^{-1} \sum_{t=\tilde{K}+1}^{T} q_t e'_{1t}$$
$$+ N^{-1} \sum_{t=\tilde{K}+1}^{T} \varepsilon_t e'_{1t} + N^{-1} \sum_{t=\tilde{K}+1}^{T} e_{1t} \varepsilon'_t + N^{-1} \sum_{t=\tilde{K}+1}^{T} e_{1t} e'_{1t} + o_p(1). \qquad (A.20)$$

From Theorem 5.1, (A.4), (A.17) and the above mentioned fact about the matrix of second sample moments of q_t it follows that the first term on the r.h.s. is of order $o_p(1)$. Since the second sample moments between the components of ε_t and q_t are readily seen to be of order $O_p(N^{-1})$ uniformly in the dimension of q_t (when the dimension is supposed to be nonstochastic) it similarly follows that the second and third terms on the r.h.s. of (A.20) are of order $o_p(1)$.

The remaining terms, which involve e_{1t}, are somewhat more complicated to deal with. Consider the last one of these and, for simplicity, denote its Euclidean norm by $Z_T(K)$ when $\tilde{K}$ is replaced by K. Let ϵ be arbitrary and K_0 an integer to be determined below. Then note that:

$$P\left\{\sup_{K\geq K_0} Z_T(K) > \epsilon\right\} \leq \sum_{K=K_0}^{\infty} P\{Z_T(K) > \epsilon\}$$

$$\leq \sum_{K=K_0}^{\infty} P\left\{N^{-1}\sum_{t=K+1}^{T}\|e_{1t}\|^2 > \epsilon\right\}$$

$$\leq \epsilon^{-1}c\sum_{K=K_0}^{\infty} K^{-2}. \tag{A.21}$$

Here the second inequality follows from the definition of $Z_T(K)$ and the third one from Markov's inequality and (A.8). For any $\epsilon > 0$ the last quantity can be made arbitrarily small by taking K_0 large enough. Next note that:

$$P\{Z_T(\tilde{K}) > \epsilon\} = P\{Z_T(\tilde{K}) > \epsilon; \tilde{K} \geq K_0\} + P\{Z_T(\tilde{K}) > \epsilon; \tilde{K} < K_0\}$$
$$\leq P\left\{\sup_{K\geq K_0} Z_T(K) > \epsilon\right\} + P\{\tilde{K} < K_0\}.$$

From (A.21) and Theorem 5.1 it can be seen that the last expression can be made arbitrarily small by taking K_0 large enough. Hence, $Z_T(\tilde{K}) = o_p(1)$ or, in other words, the term preceding $o_p(1)$ on the r.h.s. of (A.20) is of order $o_p(1)$. Combining this result with those obtained earlier in the proof and using (A.4) and the Cauchy–Schwarz inequality it is straightforward to show that the remaining terms on the r.h.s. of (A.20) are of order $o_p(1)$. Thus the last assertion follows because $\varepsilon_t\varepsilon_t'$ obeys a (weak) law of large numbers. ∎

Now we can prove Theorem 5.2. No detailed proof will be given because a proof can be obtained by following the proof of Theorem 3.1 of SL with appropriate modifications. Since SL assumed a deterministic order selection rule they were able to employ improved versions of Lemma A.5(b) and (c), where orders of consistency were also given. However, since these orders of consistency were actually not needed in the proof of SL, the results of Lemma A.5(b) and (c) are sufficient in this respect.

As in SL we first note that $\tilde{\lambda}_1 \geq \cdots \geq \tilde{\lambda}_n$ are identical to the eigenvalues of the matrix $\underline{M}_T\underline{\tilde{\Pi}}'\tilde{\Sigma}^{-1}\underline{\tilde{\Pi}}$, where $\underline{M}_T = \underline{A}M_T\underline{A}'$ and $\underline{\tilde{\Pi}} = \tilde{\underline{\Pi}}\underline{A}^{-1}$ with $\underline{A} = [\Theta : J_\perp]'$.

Notice that $\underline{\tilde{\Pi}} = [\tilde{\Phi} : \underline{\tilde{\Pi}}_2]$ and let $\mathrm{M}_T = [\mathrm{M}_{ij,T}]_{i,j=1,2}$ be a conformable partition of M_T. The next step in the proof of SL was to obtain some results, (A.13)–(A.15) in their paper, about the asymptotic behavior of the matrices $\mathrm{M}_{ij,T}$. The proofs of these results were based on asymptotic properties of second sample moments of $y_{2,t-1}$ and q_t with the dimension of q_t depending on a deterministically chosen order $K = o(T^{1/3})$. Since the results of Lemma A.1 and arguments used in their proofs hold uniformly in $K \le K_T$ it is straightforward to check that (A.13)–(A.15) of SL also hold in the present context, provided the order K is replaced by the maximum order K_T. After this the previous proof can be repeated in an obvious way to show that the $n - r_0$ smallest eigenvalues $\tilde{\lambda}_{r_0+1} \ge \cdots \ge \tilde{\lambda}_n$ are asymptotically equivalent to the solutions of the generalized eigenvalue problem:

$$N^2 \left| \underline{\tilde{\Pi}}_2' \tilde{\Sigma}^{-1} \underline{\tilde{\Pi}}_2 - \underline{\tilde{\Pi}}_2' \tilde{\Sigma}^{-1} \tilde{\Phi} (\tilde{\Phi}' \tilde{\Sigma}^{-1} \tilde{\Phi})^{-1} \tilde{\Phi}' \tilde{\Sigma}^{-1} \underline{\tilde{\Pi}}_2 - \lambda \sum_{t=\tilde{K}+2}^{T} y_{2,t-1} y_{2,t-1}' \right| = 0.$$

From Lemma A.5 and the arguments used in its proof it can be seen that in this eigenvalue problem the data dependent order $\tilde{K}$ can be replaced by the maximum order without changing asymptotic results. This means that the eigenvalues $\tilde{\lambda}_{r_0+1} \ge \cdots \ge \tilde{\lambda}_n$ are asymptotically equivalent to those in SL so that the desired result follows.

A.5 Models with an Intercept

When an intercept is included in the least squares regression (4.1) the estimator $\tilde{\Lambda}$ obtained from the least squares regression of (A.2) is defined by using mean corrected observations. This means that we still have (A.3) but with p_t measured as a deviation from its sample mean $\bar{p} = [\bar{q}' : \bar{y}_2']'$ with obvious notation. As pointed out in Saikkonen (1992, p. 22) we have $\|\bar{q}\| = O_p((K/N)^{1/2})$ and $\bar{y}_2 = O_p(N^{1/2})$ implying $\|D_T \bar{p}\| = O_p(N^{-1/2})$. (Note that in Saikkonen (1992, p. 22) this order is erroneously $O_p(K^{1/2}/N)$ but fortunately this has no effect on the subsequent conclusions of that paper.) Using these properties of sample means it is not difficult to check that the results of Lemmas A.1–A.5 hold even when q_t and $y_{2,t-1}$ are replaced by their mean corrected versions. In the same way one can also readily show that the mean correction has no effect on the other conclusions made above. Details are straightforward but somewhat tedious and will be omitted.

References

Agiagloglou, C. and P. Newbold (1996). "The balance between size and power in Dickey–Fuller tests with data-dependent rules for the choice of truncation lag." *Economics Letters*, 52: 229–34.

Helmut Lütkepohl and Pentti Saikkonen

Helmut Lütkepohl and Pentti Saikkonen

Cheung, Y.-W. and K. S. Lai (1993). "Finite-sample sizes of Johansen's likelihood ratio tests for cointegration." *Oxford Bulletin of Economics and Statistics*, 55: 313–28.

Engle, R. F. and C. W. J. Granger (1987). "Co-integration and error correction: representation, estimation and testing." *Econometrica*, 55: 251–76.

Granger, C. W. J. (1981). "Some properties of time series data and their use in econometric model specification." *Journal of Econometrics*, 16: 121–30.

Granger, C. W. J. (1986). "Developments in the study of cointegrated economic variables." *Oxford Bulletin of Economics and Statistics*, 48: 213–28.

Hall, A. (1994). "Testing for a unit root in time series with pretest data-based model selection." *Journal of Business and Economic Statistics*, 12: 461–70.

Hannan, E. J. and M. Deistler (1988). *The Statistical Theory of Linear Systems*. New York: Wiley.

Haug, A. A. (1996). "Tests for cointegration: a Monte Carlo comparison." *Journal of Econometrics*, 71: 89–115.

Horvath, M. T. K. and M. W. Watson (1995). "Testing for cointegration when some of the cointegrating vectors are prespecified." *Econometric Theory*, 11: 984–1014.

Johansen, S. (1988). "Statistical analysis of cointegration vectors." *Journal of Economic Dynamics and Control*, 12: 231–254.

Johansen, S. (1991). "Estimation and hypothesis testing of cointegration vectors in Gaussian vector autoregressive models." *Econometrica*, 59: 1551–81.

Johansen, S. (1995). *Likelihood-Based Inference in Cointegrated Vector Autoregressive Models*. Oxford: Oxford University Press.

Johansen, S. and K. Juselius (1990). "Maximum likelihood estimation and inference on cointegration—with applications to the demand for money." *Oxford Bulletin of Economics and Statistics*, 52: 169–210.

Lewis, R. and G. C. Reinsel (1985). "Prediction of multivariate time series by autoregressive model fitting." *Journal of Multivariate Analysis*, 16: 393–411.

Lütkepohl, H. (1991). *Introduction to Multiple Time Series Analysis*. Berlin: Springer-Verlag.

Lütkepohl, H. (1996). *Handbook of Matrices*. Chichester: John Wiley and Sons.

Lütkepohl, H. and D. S. Poskitt (1996). "Testing for causation using infinite order vector autoregressive processes." *Econometric Theory*, 12: 61–87.

Lütkepohl, H. and P. Saikkonen (1997). "Impulse response analysis in infinite order cointegrated vector autoregressive processes." *Journal of Econometrics*, 81: 127–57.

Ng, S. and P. Perron (1995). "Unit root tests in ARMA models with data-dependent methods for the selection of the truncation lag." *Journal of the American Statistical Association* 90: 268–81.

Phillips, P. C. B. (1991). "Optimal inference in cointegrated systems." *Econometrica*, 59: 283–306.

Reimers, H.-E. (1992). "Comparisons of tests for multivariate cointegration." *Statistical Papers*, 33: 335–59.

Reinsel, G. C. and S. K. Ahn (1992). "Vector autoregressive models with unit roots and reduced rank structure: estimation, likelihood ratio test, and forecasting." *Journal of Time Series Analysis*, 13: 353–75.

Said, S. E. and D. A. Dickey (1984). "Testing for unit roots in autoregressive-moving average models of unknown order." *Biometrika*, 71: 599–607.

Saikkonen, P. (1991). "Asymptotically efficient estimation of cointegration vectors." *Econometric Theory*, 7: 1–21.

Saikkonen, P. (1992). "Estimation and testing of cointegrated systems by an auto-regressive approximation." *Econometric Theory*, 8: 1–27.

Saikkonen, P. and H. Lütkepohl (1995). "Asymptotic inference on nonlinear functions of the coefficients of infinite order cointegrated VAR processes." Discussion Paper, Humboldt-Universität, Berlin, Institut für Statistik und Ökonometrie.

Saikkonen, P. and H. Lütkepohl (1996). "Infinite order cointegrated vector autoregress-ive processes: estimation and inference." *Econometric Theory*, 12: 814–44.

Saikkonen, P. and R. Luukkonen (1997). "Testing cointegration in infinite order vector autoregressive processes." *Journal of Econometrics*, 81: 93–126.

Schwert, G. W. (1989). "Tests for unit roots: a Monte Carlo investigation." *Journal of Business and Economic Statistics* 7: 147–59.

Stuart, A. and J. K. Ord (1987). *Kendall's Advanced Theory of Statistics*, 5th edn., vol. 1. London: Charles Griffin.

Yap, S. F. and G. C. Reinsel (1995). "Estimation and testing for unit roots in a partially nonstationary vector autoregressive moving average model." *Journal of the American Statistical Association*, 90: 253–67.

8
Granger's Representation Theorem and Multicointegration

TOM ENGSTED AND SØREN JOHANSEN

1 Introduction

Since Engle and Granger's (1987) seminal paper the concept of cointegration has developed progressively in several ways, and many extensions of the basic concept have been made. One such extension is the definition of multicointegration which refers to the case where the cumulation of equilibrium errors cointegrates with the original $I(1)$ variables of the system. Such situations arise naturally in economic models involving stock–flow relationships. One example, analyzed in detail by Granger and Lee (1989), is the case where the two $I(1)$ flow series production, X_t, and sales, Y_t, cointegrate such that inventory invest-ment $Z_t = X_t - Y_t$ is $I(0)$. It follows that $\sum_{i=1}^{t} Z_i$ is the level of inventories (stock) which might cointegrate with X_t and Y_t such that $U_t = \sum_{i=1}^{t} Z_i - aY_t - bX_t$ is $I(0)$. Thus, there are essentially two levels of cointegration between just two $I(1)$ time series. Other examples involve consumption, income, savings, and wealth, or new housing units started, new housing units completed, un-completed starts, and housing units under construction, see Lee (1992).

Granger (1986) anticipates the notion of multicointegration, and the concept is formally developed in Granger and Lee (1989, 1990). In particular, they prove a representation theorem stating that multicointegrated time series are generated by an error-correction model which contains both Z_{t-1} and U_{t-1} as error-correction terms. In addition, they show that multicointegration can be derived from a standard linear quadratic adjustment cost framework often used in economics.

The papers by Granger and Lee constitute an important starting point for the analysis of multicointegrated time series, but they are somewhat limited in scope since they analyze only bivariate systems. Furthermore, in the estima-tion procedure they assume that the cointegration vector at the first level is known and, hence, does not have to be estimated. In estimating the cointeg-rating vector at the second level they propose to use the simple OLS estimator which in general is not optimal and does not allow hypothesis testing using standard asymptotic theory. An asymptotically efficient two step estimation procedure for this situation can be found in Johansen (1995), whereas maximum likelihood inference in the unrestricted multicointegrated $I(2)$ model is given in Johansen (1997).

The purpose of the present paper is to provide a more detailed analysis of multicointegration in multivariate systems of $I(1)$ time series. It is shown that although the interest lies in the analysis of the $I(1)$ series one cannot achieve multicointegration in the cointegrated error correction model for $I(1)$ variables. If, however, we assume that the cumulated variables satisfy an error correction model for $I(2)$ variables then we have the possibility of modeling multicointegration for $I(1)$ variables.

Engle and Yoo (1991) also suggest relating multicointegration to $I(2)$ cointegration, and apply the Smith–McMillan decomposition to derive the VAR representation from the MA representation. Their results are discussed by Haldrup and Salmon (1998) for multivariate processes. Equivalently one can say that the process satisfies an integral control mechanism, see Hendry and Von Ungern Sternberg (1981).

The contents of the present paper are as follows. First we present a theorem about the inversion of matrix valued functions which is the essence of the Granger representation theorem. We then discuss multicointegration in the usual error correction model for $I(1)$ variables, and show that this phenomenon cannot occur. If, however, we assume that the cumulated process satisfies an $I(2)$ model, then the results about this model can be phrased in terms of multicointegration. Finally we show how the general formulation of Granger's theorem solves the problem of deriving the $I(2)$ model from the moving average representation. This generalizes the results of Granger and Lee (1990). Throughout we assume that the equations generating the process have no deterministic terms. The representation results given are easily generalized, but the statistical analysis becomes more complicated, see Johansen (1995, 1997) and Paruolo (1996).

2 A General Formulation of Granger's Representation Theorem

In this section we consider $n \times n$ matrix valued functions $A(z)$ with entries that are power series in a complex argument z. Let $|A(z)|$ denote the determinant and $adj\, A(z)$ the adjoint matrix.

Assumption 1. *The power series*

$$A(z) = \sum_{i=0}^{\infty} A_i z^i$$

is convergent for $|z| < 1 + \delta$, and satisfies the condition that if $|A(z)| = 0$, *then either $|z| > 1 + \gamma$ or $z = 1$. Here $0 < \gamma < \delta$. We assume further that $A(z) = I$ for $z = 0$.*

We are concerned with the power series for the function $A^{-1}(z)$. This function will have a power series expansion in a neighborhood of the origin, since $A(0) = I$ implies that $|A(z)| \neq 0$ for z sufficiently small, and hence $A^{-1}(z)$ exists.

We present a theorem that summarizes the Granger representation theorems for the $I(0)$, $I(1)$ and $I(2)$ variables given in Johansen (1992). We give the results a purely analytic formulation without involving any probability theory, since the basic structure is then more transparent. The result allows direct identification of the relevant coefficients of the inverse function in terms of the coefficients of the matrix function, and gives conditions for the presence of poles of the order 0, 1, and 2 respectively. The result will be applied below to derive the autoregressive representation from the moving average representation and vice versa, and the explicit formulae allow one to discuss the coefficients in the moving average representation in terms of the estimated coefficients from the autoregressive model.

We expand the function $A(z)$ around $z = 1$ and define the coefficients $\dot{A}(1)$ and $\ddot{A}(1)$ by the expansion

$$A(z) = A(1) + (z-1)\dot{A}(1) + \tfrac{1}{2}(z-1)^2 \ddot{A}(1) + \cdots,$$

which is convergent for $|z - 1| < \delta$. Thus

$$\dot{A}(1) = \left. \frac{dA(z)}{dz} \right|_{z=1}, \quad \ddot{A}(1) = \left. \frac{d^2 A(z)}{d^2 z} \right|_{z=1}.$$

For any $n \times m$ matrix a of full rank $m < n$, we denote by $a_\perp$ an $n \times (n-m)$ matrix of rank $n - m$ such that $a'a_\perp = 0$. We define $\bar{a} = a(a'a)^{-1}$, such that $a'\bar{a} = I$, and $\bar{a}a'$ is the projection of R^n onto the space spanned by the columns of a. For notational convenience we let $a_\perp = I$ if $a = 0$, and $m = 0$. Note that if we can write $a' = (a_1, a_2)$, where a_1 $(m \times m)$ has full rank, then we can choose

$$a_\perp = \begin{pmatrix} -a_1^{-1}a_2 \\ I_{n-m} \end{pmatrix}.$$

Note also that the choice of orthogonal complement is not unique. If $a_\perp^0$ and $a_\perp^1$ are any two choices, then $a_\perp^0 = a_\perp^1 \xi$ for some ξ $(n-m) \times (n-m)$ of full rank.

Theorem 2.1. *Let $A(z)$ be a matrix power series which satisfies Assumption 1. Then the following results hold for the function $A^{-1}(z)$.*

(a) *If $z = 1$ is not a root, then $A^{-1}(z)$ is a power series with exponentially decreasing coefficients.*

(b) *If $z = 1$ is a root then $A(1)$ is of reduced rank $m < n$, and $A(1) = \xi\eta'$, where ξ and η are of dimension $n \times m$ and rank m. If further*

$$\left|\xi'_\perp \dot{A}(1)\eta_\perp\right| \neq 0, \tag{2.1}$$

then

$$A^{-1}(z) = C\frac{1}{1-z} + C^*(z),$$

where $C^*(z)$ is a power series with exponentially decreasing coefficients, and where

$$C = -\eta_\perp \left(\xi'_\perp \dot{A}(1)\eta_\perp\right)^{-1}\xi'.$$

(c) *If $z = 1$ is a root such that $A(1) = \xi\eta'$ and if*

$$\xi'_\perp \dot{A}(1)\eta_\perp = \phi\zeta',$$

is of reduced rank, where ϕ and ζ are $(n-m) \times k$ matrices of rank $k < n-m$, and if

$$\left|\phi'_\perp\xi'_\perp(\tfrac{1}{2}\ddot{A}(1) - \dot{A}(1)\bar\eta\bar\xi'\dot{A}(1))\eta_\perp\zeta_\perp\right| \neq 0, \tag{2.2}$$

then

$$A^{-1}(z) = C_2\frac{1}{(1-z)^2} + C_1\frac{1}{1-z} + C^{**}(z),$$

where $C^{**}(z)$ is a power series with exponentially decreasing coefficients. Expressions for the coefficients C_1 and C_2 can be found in Johansen (1992, theorem 3). Here we give the expression

$$C_2 = \eta_\perp\zeta_\perp\left(\phi'_\perp\xi'_\perp(\tfrac{1}{2}\ddot{A}(1) - \dot{A}(1)\bar\eta\bar\xi'\dot{A}(1))\eta_\perp\zeta_\perp\right)^{-1}\phi'_\perp\xi'_\perp.$$

The proof can be found in the above mentioned reference for the case when $A(z)$ is a polynomial. The proof for the general case where infinitely many terms are allowed is the same. Note that the conditions (2.1), (2.2), and the expressions for the matrices C, C_1, and C_2 are invariant to the choice of orthogonal complement, such that it does not matter which orthogonal complement is chosen. Obviously the parameters ϕ and ζ will depend on the choice of orthogonal complement chosen for ξ and η.

Note that it is not enough to assume that the roots are outside the unit circle or equal to 1, since we could have infinitely many roots converging to the unit circle, which would ruin the proof. Hence we assume that the roots are bounded away from the unit disk or equal to 1. If $z = 1$ is a root then $A^{-1}(z)$ has a pole at the point $z = 1$, since

$$A^{-1}(z) = \frac{adjA(z)}{|A(z)|},$$

and $adjA(z)$ is a matrix valued power series with exponentially decreasing coefficients. The $I(1)$ condition (2.1) is necessary and sufficient for the pole to be of order 1. The function $C(1/(1-z))$ has a pole of order 1 at $z=1$ and the theorem says that the difference is a convergent power series. Thus the pole can be removed by subtracting the function $C(1/(1-z))$. The $I(2)$ condition (2.2) is necessary and sufficient for the pole to be of order 2, in which case it can be removed by subtracting the function $C_2(1/(1-z)^2) + C_1(1/(1-z))$, which also has a pole of order 2.

In order to apply this result in the autoregressive model,

$$X_t = \sum_{i=1}^{k} \Pi_i X_{t-i} + \varepsilon_t,$$

define $A(z)$ to be the matrix polynomial

$$A(z) = I - \sum_{i=1}^{k} \Pi_i z^i.$$

Then $A^{-1}(z)$ gives the solution to the equations, that is, the coefficients in the expansion for $A^{-1}(z)$ determine X_t as a function of the errors ε_t. The translation of the result is via the lag operator, such that for a function $C(z) = \sum_{i=0}^{\infty} C_i z^i$ with exponentially decreasing coefficients and a sequence of i.i.d. variables ε_t, we define the stationary process:

$$C(L)\varepsilon_t = \sum_{i=0}^{\infty} C_i \varepsilon_{t-i}.$$

For the expression $(1/(1-z))$, we use the interpretation

$$(1-L)^{-1}\varepsilon_t = \Delta^{-1}\varepsilon_t = \sum_{i=1}^{t} \varepsilon_i,$$

and $(1/(1-z)^2)$ is translated into

$$(1-L)^{-2}\varepsilon_t = \Delta^{-2}\varepsilon_t = \sum_{j=1}^{t}\sum_{i=1}^{j} \varepsilon_i.$$

The result of Theorem 2.1 can be used to check whether a given example of an autoregressive process is $I(0)$, $I(1)$, or $I(2)$. It is the fundamental tool in building $I(1)$ and $I(2)$ models for autoregressive processes as we shall show below.

3 Multicointegration in the $I(1)$ Model

In the following we apply these results to discuss the problem of multi-cointegration as defined by Granger and Lee (1989, 1990).

Definition 3.1. *The n-dimensional $I(1)$ process X_t is said to be multicointegrated with coefficient τ if $\tau' X_t$ is stationary and if the process $\sum_{i=1}^{t} \tau' X_i$ cointegrates with X_t, such that there exist coefficients ρ and ψ, that is, $\rho' \sum_{i=1}^{t} \tau' X_i + \psi' X_t$ is stationary.*

We want to prove that multicointegration cannot take place in the error correction model for $I(1)$ variables

$$\Delta X_t = \alpha \beta' X_{t-1} + \sum_{i=1}^{k-1} \Gamma_i \Delta X_{t-i} + \varepsilon_t, \quad t = 1, \ldots, T, \tag{3.1}$$

where α and β are $n \times r$, where $r < n$.

Theorem 3.2. *Multicointegration cannot appear in the $I(1)$ model (3.1) if the process X_t is $I(1)$, that is, if*

$$\left| \alpha'_{\perp} \left(I - \sum_{i=1}^{k-1} \Gamma_i \right) \beta_{\perp} \right| \neq 0. \tag{3.2}$$

Proof. We apply Theorem 2.1 to the polynomial

$$A(z) = (1 - z)I - \alpha \beta' z - \sum_{i=1}^{k-1} \Gamma_i (1 - z) z^i.$$

Here $A(1) = -\alpha \beta'$ and $\dot{A}(1) = -\alpha \beta' - I + \sum_{i=1}^{k-1} \Gamma_i$, such that the $I(1)$ condition (2.1) becomes the condition (3.2). The inverse polynomial has the expression as:

$$A^{-1}(z) = C \frac{1}{1-z} + C^*(z)$$
$$= C \frac{1}{1-z} + C^* + (1-z)C_1^*(z),$$

such that the process has the representation:

$$X_t = C \sum_{i=1}^{t} \varepsilon_i + C^* \varepsilon_t + \Delta Y_t + A, \tag{3.3}$$

where A depends on initial conditions, $\beta' A = 0$, and $Y_t = C_1^*(L)\varepsilon_t$ is a stationary process, see Johansen (1995). The matrix C is given by:

$$C = \beta_{\perp} \left[\alpha'_{\perp} \left(I - \sum_{i=1}^{k-1} \Gamma_i \right) \beta_{\perp} \right]^{-1} \alpha'_{\perp}.$$

The cumulated equilibrium error has the form:

$$\sum_{i=1}^{t} \beta' X_i = \beta' C * \sum_{i=1}^{t} \varepsilon_t + \beta Y_t - \beta' Y_0.$$

The common trends in the expression for X_t are of the form $\alpha'_{\perp}\sum_{i=1}^{t}\varepsilon_i$, and the common trends in the cumulated equilibrium error are of the form $\beta' C^*\sum_{i=1}^{t}\varepsilon_i$. In order to see if these cointegrate we have to find the matrix $\beta' C^*$. From the relation $A(z)A^{-1}(z) = I$ we find:

$$\left[(1-z)I - \alpha\beta' z - \sum_{i=1}^{k-1}\Gamma_i(1-z)z^i\right]\left[C\frac{1}{1-z} + C^* + (1-z)C_1^*(z)\right] = I.$$

or

$$\left[I - \sum_{i=1}^{k-1}\Gamma_i z^i\right]C + A(z)(C_1^* + (1-z)C_1^*(z)) = I.$$

For $z = 1$ we find:

$$\left[I - \sum_{i=1}^{k-1}\Gamma_i\right]C - \alpha\beta' C^* = I,$$

which when multiplied by $\bar{\alpha}'$ gives

$$\beta' C^* = \bar{\alpha}'\Gamma\beta_{\perp}(\alpha'_{\perp}\Gamma\beta_{\perp})^{-1}\alpha'_{\perp} - \bar{\alpha}',$$

where $\Gamma = I - \sum_{i=1}^{k-1}\Gamma_i$. This shows that the non-stationarity of the cumulated equilibrium errors is given in part by the $n - r$ common trends $\alpha'_{\perp}\sum_{i=1}^{t}\varepsilon_i$ of the process X_t, and in part by r random walks $\alpha'\sum_{i=1}^{t}\varepsilon_i$ which do not appear in X_t. Thus any linear combination of X_t and $\sum_{i=1}^{t}\beta' X_i$ will necessarily contain the trends $\alpha'\sum_{i=1}^{t}\varepsilon_i$ and hence be non-stationary. ∎

This shows that multicointegration cannot appear in the $I(1)$ model. Another way of formulating this result is that no process $\mu' X_t$, where X_t is generated by the $I(1)$ model, will be $I(-1)$. In order to see this assume that there is a stationary process Z_t, say, and a coefficient vector $\mu \in R^n$ such that $\mu' X_t = \Delta Z_t$. From (3.3) we find that we must have $\mu' C = \mu' C^* = 0$. Hence $\mu = \beta\kappa$ for some vector κ and $\mu' C^*\alpha = \kappa'\beta' C^*\alpha = -\kappa' = 0$ shows the impossibility. We therefore next discuss the $I(2)$ model for the cumulated variables.

4 Multicointegration in the $I(2)$ Model

Next we want to prove a more constructive result where we take as a starting point that the cumulated processes are generated by an $I(2)$ model, see Engle and Yoo (1991). Thus we define

$$S_t = \sum_{i=1}^{t} X_i,$$

and assume that this new process is given by an autoregressive model, restricted such that it generates $I(2)$ variables. This model can be parameterized in many ways. A parameterization that allows freely varying parameters is given by

$$\Delta^2 S_t = \alpha(\rho'\tau'S_{t-1} + \psi'\Delta S_{t-1}) + \Omega\alpha_\perp(\alpha'_\perp\Omega\alpha_\perp)^{-1}\kappa'\tau'\Delta S_{t-1} + \varepsilon_t. \qquad (4.1)$$

The parameters in this model are $(\alpha, \rho, \tau, \psi, \kappa, \Omega)$ and it is assumed that all parameters vary freely. This gives the possibility of deriving the maximum likelihood estimators and finding their asymptotic distributions, see Johansen (1997). We can add a lag polynomial applied to $\Delta^2 S_t$, to account for more short-term dynamics.

The characteristic polynomial is given by

$$A(z) = (1-z)^2 I - \alpha(\rho'\tau'z + \psi'(1-z)z) - \Omega\alpha_\perp(\alpha'_\perp\Omega\alpha_\perp)^{-1}\kappa'\tau'(1-z)z,$$

such that

$$A(1) = -\alpha\rho'\tau', \quad \dot{A}(1) = -\alpha\rho'\tau' + \alpha\psi' + \Omega\alpha_\perp(\alpha'_\perp\Omega\alpha_\perp)^{-1}\kappa'\tau'.$$

With $\beta = \tau\rho$ we find that $A(1) = -\alpha\beta'$ is of reduced rank and that

$$\alpha'_\perp \dot{A}(1)\beta_\perp = \kappa'\tau'\beta_\perp = \kappa'(\bar{\rho}_\perp\rho'_\perp + \bar{\rho}\rho')\tau'\beta_\perp = (\kappa'\bar{\rho}_\perp)(\rho'_\perp\tau'\beta_\perp),$$

since $\rho'\tau'\beta_\perp = \beta'\beta_\perp = 0$. This matrix is of reduced rank, and we can define $\phi = \kappa'\bar{\rho}_\perp$ and $\zeta = \beta'_\perp\tau\rho_\perp$. If further condition (2.2) is satisfied, the process S_t is $I(2)$, which implies that $X_t = \Delta S_t$ is $I(1)$. It is a consequence of the results in Johansen (1992) that $\tau'\Delta S_t = \tau'X_t$ is stationary, and furthermore that $\rho'\tau'S_t + \psi'\Delta S_t = \rho'\sum_{i=1}^{t}\tau'X_i + \psi'X_t$ is stationary. Thus we find that expressed in terms of the process X_t we have multicointegration and the error correction terms are exactly the integral correction term $\rho'\sum_{i=1}^{t}\tau'X_i + \psi'X_t$ and the usual error correction term $\tau'X_t$.

Thus this model is a general version of the error correction model derived by Granger and Lee (1990). The result shows that the general model for the $I(2)$ variable S_t can be formulated as an error correction model for $X_t = \Delta S_t$ which has both integral correction terms and equilibrium correction terms exactly as the model in Granger and Lee (1990). Model (4.1) can be written in this way as:

$$\Delta X_t = \alpha(\rho'\sum_{i=1}^{t-1}\tau'X_i + \psi'X_{t-1}) + \Omega\alpha_\perp(\alpha'_\perp\Omega\alpha_\perp)^{-1}\kappa'\tau'X_{t-1} + \varepsilon_t.$$

Note that when the cumulated X_t satisfies an autoregressive error correction model then X_t itself does not, since the equations we find for X_t by differencing will have $\Delta\varepsilon_t$ as an error term.

5 Multicointegration and Moving Average Models

The formulation of the result of Granger and Lee (1990) starts with the MA representation of the process and derives an (infinite) AR model for the process involving an integral correction term and an error correction term. We shall here show how Theorem 2.1 gives a necessary and sufficient condition for this construction to go through.

We consider the situation where we model the process in the usual form by its moving average form

$$\Delta X_t = C(L)\varepsilon_t = C_0\varepsilon_t + C_1\Delta\varepsilon_t + C^*(L)\Delta^2\varepsilon_t = C_0\varepsilon_t + C_1\Delta\varepsilon_t + \Delta^2 Y_t.$$

If we assume that C_0 is of reduced rank, such that $\tau'C_0 = 0$ for some $\tau \neq 0$, then we find

$$X_t = X_0 + C_0\sum_{i=1}^{t}\varepsilon_i + C_1(\varepsilon_t - \varepsilon_0) + \Delta Y_t - \Delta Y_0,$$
$$\tau'\Delta X_t = \tau'C_1\Delta\varepsilon_t + \tau'\Delta^2 Y_t,$$
$$\tau'X_t = \tau'X_0 + \tau'C_1(\varepsilon_t - \varepsilon_0) + \tau'(\Delta Y_t - \Delta Y_0),$$
$$\sum_{i=1}^{t}\tau'X_i = \tau'C_1\left(\sum_{i=1}^{t}\varepsilon_i - t\varepsilon_0\right) + \tau'(Y_t - Y_0 - t\Delta Y_0) + t\tau'X_0.$$

In order to find examples which exhibit multicointegration we only have to construct the matrices C_0 and C_1 such that there are coefficients ρ and ψ with the property that:

$$\psi'C_0 - \rho'\tau'C_1 = 0,$$

since

$$\psi'X_t - \rho'\tau'\sum_{i=1}^{t}X_i$$

does not contain any random walk. Thus, by choosing C_0 and C_1 appropriately it is easy to find examples of multicointegration. We shall now show how Theorem 2.1 generalizes the result of Granger and Lee.

Theorem 5.1. *Let the n-dimensional process X_t satisfy the equation*

$$\Delta X_t = C(L)\varepsilon_t,$$

where $C(0) = I$, and we assume that the roots of $|C(z)| = 0$ are either bounded away from the unit disk or equal to 1.

(a) If $z = 1$ is not a root, then ΔX_t satisfies an (infinite order) autoregressive equation

$$C^{-1}(L)\Delta X_t = \varepsilon_t.$$

The process X_t is $I(1)$ and does not cointegrate.

(b) *If $z = 1$ is a root, then $C(1) = \xi\eta'$ is of reduced rank $m < n$ and if further $\xi'_\perp \dot{C}(1)\eta_\perp$ has full rank then X_t satisfies an (infinite order) $I(1)$ model:*

$$\alpha\beta' X_t + A^*(L)\Delta X_t = \varepsilon_t,$$

with $\alpha\beta' = -\eta_\perp(\xi'_\perp \dot{C}(1)\eta_\perp)^{-1}\xi'_\perp$. Here $A^*(z) = C^{-1}(z) - \alpha\beta'(1/(1-z))$ has exponentially decreasing coefficients.

(c) *If $z = 1$ is a root, such that $C(1) = \xi\eta'$ is of reduced rank $m < n$ and if further $\xi'_\perp \dot{C}(1)\eta_\perp = \phi\zeta'$ is of reduced rank $k < n - m$ and condition (2.2) holds then X_t satisfies an (infinite order) autoregressive model with integral and error correction terms.*

Proof. (a) If the roots of $|C(z)| = 0$ are all bounded away from the unit disk, then the power series of $C^{-1}(z) = \sum_{i=0}^{\infty} A_i z^i$ is convergent for $|z| < 1 + \delta$, where $\delta > 0$. This means that the coefficients in $C^{-1}(z)$ are exponentially decreasing such that the stationary process $\sum_{i=0}^{\infty} A_i \Delta X_{t-i}$ is well defined and equal to ε_t. Expanding the function $C(z)$ around $z = 1$ we find

$$C(z) = C(1) + (1-z)C^*(z),$$

such that when summing the original equation from $s = 1$ to $s = t$ we find that

$$X_t = X_0 + C(1)\sum_{i=1}^{t} \varepsilon_i + Y_t - Y_0,$$

where $Y_t = C^*(L)\varepsilon_t$ is stationary. Thus X_t is an $I(1)$ process and since $C(1)$ has full rank it does not cointegrate.

(b) Now assume that $z = 1$ is a root such that $C(1) = \xi\eta'$ is of reduced rank, but $\xi'_\perp \dot{C}(1)\eta_\perp$ has full rank. We then find from Theorem 2.1, that

$$(1-z)C^{-1}(z) = A + (1-z)A^*(z), \tag{5.1}$$

with $A = -\eta_\perp(\xi'_\perp \dot{C}(1)\eta_\perp)^{-1}\xi'_\perp$. Inserting this expression into (5.1) we find

$$AX_t + A^*(L)\Delta X_t = C^{-1}(L)\Delta X_t = \varepsilon_t.$$

This is the required result if we define $\beta = \xi_\perp$ and $\alpha = -\eta_\perp(\xi'_\perp \dot{C}(1)\eta_\perp)^{-1}$.

(c) Finally assume that $C(1) = \xi\eta'$ and that $\xi'_\perp \dot{C}(1)\eta_\perp = \phi\zeta'$ is of reduced rank. In this case we have from Theorem 2.1

$$(1-z)^2 C^{-1}(z) = A_2 + (1-z)A_1 + (1-z)^2 A^{**}(z).$$

Insert this into the equation for $S_t = \sum_{i=1}^{t} X_i$

$$\Delta^2 S_t = C(L)\varepsilon_t,$$

and we find

$$A_2 S_t + A_1 \Delta S_t + A^{**}(z)\Delta^2 S_t = C^{-1}(L)\Delta^2 S_t = \varepsilon_t.$$

Expressing this in terms of X we find

$$A_2 \sum_{i=1}^{t} X_i + A_1 X_t + A^{**}(z)\Delta X_t = \varepsilon_t.$$

This shows the occurrence of integral correction terms and error correction terms in the same model. This model can be expressed in terms of freely varying parameters as (4.1) by using the explicit form for the matrices A_2 and A_1 given in Johansen (1992). ∎

6 An Example

Consider the example given by Granger and Lee (1990):

$$\Delta X_t = \begin{pmatrix} a + \Delta(1-a) & -a^2(1-\Delta) \\ 1 - \Delta & -a + \Delta(1+a) \end{pmatrix} \varepsilon_t.$$

In this case the polynomial is:

$$C(z) = \begin{pmatrix} a + (1-z)(1-a) & -a^2 z \\ z & -a + (1-z)(1+a) \end{pmatrix},$$

with

$$C(1) = \begin{pmatrix} a & -a^2 \\ 1 & -a \end{pmatrix} = \begin{pmatrix} a \\ 1 \end{pmatrix} \begin{pmatrix} 1 & -a \end{pmatrix},$$

$$\dot{C}(1) = \begin{pmatrix} -1+a & -a^2 \\ 1 & -1-a \end{pmatrix}.$$

In this case we find:

$$\begin{pmatrix} 1 \\ -a \end{pmatrix}' \begin{pmatrix} -1+a & -a^2 \\ 1 & -1-a \end{pmatrix} \begin{pmatrix} a \\ 1 \end{pmatrix} = 0.$$

Condition (2.2) is satisfied, since $\ddot{C}(1) = 0$ and we can take $\phi = \zeta = 0$. In this case the condition reduces to:

$$\xi'_\perp \dot{C}(1)\overline{\eta\xi}'\dot{C}(1)\eta_\perp = 1 \neq 0.$$

Thus the cumulated X_t satisfies an $I(2)$ model which gives multicointegration.

References

Engle, R. F. and Granger, C. W. J. (1987). "Co-integration and error correction: representation, estimation, and testing." *Econometrica*, 55: 251–76.
Engle, R. F. and Yoo, S. B. (1991). "Cointegrated economic time series: an overview

with new results." In R. F. Engle and C. W. J. Granger (eds.), *Long-run Economic Relations: Readings in Cointegration*, pp. 237–266. Oxford: Oxford University Press.

Granger, C. W. J. (1986). "Developments in the study of cointegrated economic variables." *Oxford Bulletin of Economics and Statistics*, 48: 213–28.

Granger, C. W. J. and Lee, T.-H. (1989). "Investigation of production sales and inventory relationships, using multicointegration and non-symmetric error correction models." *Journal of Applied Econometrics*, 4 (Suppl.): 145–59.

Granger, C. W. J. and Lee, T.-H. (1990). "Multicointegration." In G. F. Rhodes, Jr. and T. B. Fomby (eds.), *Advances in Econometrics: Cointegration, Spurious Regressions and Unit Roots*, pp. 71–84. Greenwich, CT: JAI Press.

Haldrup, N. and Salmon, M. (1998). "Representations of I(2) cointegrated systems using the Smith–McMillan form." *Journal of Econometrics* 84: 303–25.

Hendry, D. F. and von Ungern Sternberg, T. (1981). "Liquidity and inflation effects on consumer's expenditure." In A. S. Deaton (ed.), *Essays in the Theory and Measurement of Consumer's Behaviour*, pp. 237–261. Cambridge: Cambridge University Press.

Johansen, S. (1992). "A representation of vector autoregressive processes integrated of order 2." *Econometric Theory*, 8: 188–202.

Johansen, S. (1995). "A statistical analysis of cointegration for I(2) variables." *Econometric Theory*, 11: 25–59.

Johansen, S. (1996). *Likelihood-based Inference in Cointegrated Vector Autoregressive Models*, 2nd edn. Oxford: Oxford University Press.

Johansen, S. (1997). "Likelihood inference in the I(2) model." *Scandinavian Journal of Statistics*, 24: 433–62.

Lee, T.-H. (1992). "Stock–flow relationships in housing construction." *Oxford Bulletin of Economics and Statistics*, 54: 419–30.

Paruolo, P. (1996). "On the determination of integration indices in I(2) systems." *Journal of Econometrics*, 72: 313–56.

9
Dimensionality Effect in Cointegration Analysis

JESÚS GONZALO AND JEAN-YVES PITARAKIS

1 Introduction

During the past decade a considerable amount of research has focused on the issue of stochastic trends in economic variables and subsequently on whether such trends are common to some or all of the variables in question, a phenomenon known as cointegration (Granger, 1981; Engle and Granger, 1987). Despite an abundant literature dealing with the development of cointegration tests and their applications in economics (see Engle and Granger, 1991, for a comprehensive review), an important issue that has often been overlooked is the impact that the system dimension (number of variables) might have on the accuracy of inferences. The issue is not merely a degrees of freedom problem (see Abadir, Hadri and Tzavalis, 1997) and becomes relevant in a wide range of applied fields. Indeed, the analysis of cross country or sectoral comovements of economic variables in the new growth literature or the determination of the number of factors in asset pricing theories in finance, for instance, are some among numerous other examples that involve the handling of very large systems.

Currently a popular approach for conducting inferences about the presence of cointegration is the reduced rank vector autoregressive (VAR) framework proposed by Johansen (1988, 1991) and Ahn and Reinsel (1990) following earlier work by Anderson (1958) and leading to a likelihood ratio statistic (LR thereafter) of the cointegration hypothesis. Although commonly used in applied work, little is known about its properties in large dimensional systems since most of the published simulation studies rarely included higher than bivariate or trivariate systems.

We wish to thank seminar participants at CEMFI, CORE, Queens University, Université de Montréal, University of California San Diego, Universidad Carlos III de Madrid, Universidad Complutense de Madrid, the Tinbergen Institute and two anonymous referees for helpful suggestions and comments that led to a substantial revision of an earlier draft. Financial support from the Spanish Secretary of Education (PB 950298) and the European Union Human Capital and Mobility Program (ERBCHBICT941677) is gratefully acknowledged.

The main objective of our paper is to introduce a set of new tools for inferring the cointegrating rank and examine their relative robustness to the dimensionality problem together with that of the LR based testing strategy. The structure of the paper is as follows. Sections 2 and 3 introduce the new criteria and analyze their asymptotic and finite sample behavior as the system dimension increases. Section 4 focuses on an alternative to testing, namely a model selection approach for estimating the cointegrating rank, and Section 5 concludes.

2 Estimation of the Cointegrating Rank: Test-Based Approaches

2.1 Theoretical Framework and Alternative Test Criteria

From the Granger representation theorem (Engle and Granger, 1987) a p-dimensional vector of I(1) variables X_t with cointegrating rank r ($0 \leq r \leq p$) admits the following vector error correction model (VECM) representation

$$\Delta X_t = \Pi X_{t-1} + \sum_{j=1}^{k-1} H_j \Delta X_{t-j} + \epsilon_t, \tag{1}$$

where we assume that ϵ_t is $NID(0, \Omega)$ with $|\Omega| \neq 0$ and k finite. Under the hypothesis of cointegration, the long run impact matrix Π can be written as $\Pi = \alpha\beta'$ where α and β are $p \times r$ matrices with $r = rank(\Pi)$. Thus a test of the cointegration hypothesis is equivalent to a test of the rank of the Π matrix. When $r = 0$, the components of X_t are not cointegrated and the VECM takes the form of a VAR in first differences. Under $0 < r < p$ there exist r linear combinations of the I(1) variables that are stationary and when $r = p$ the vector X_t is in fact a stationary process. In a series of papers Johansen (1988, 1991) and Ahn and Reinsel (1990) have developed a full information maximum likelihood estimation of (1) subject to the constraint that $rank(\Pi) = r$, leading to a likelihood ratio (LR thereafter) test of the cointegration hypothesis. The LR statistic is given by $-T\sum_{i=r+1}^{p}\log(1 - \hat{\lambda}_i)$ where the $\hat{\lambda}_i$s are the ordered eigenvalues of the quantity $S_{11}^{-1}S_{10}S_{00}^{-1}S_{01}$ with $S_{ij} = (1/T)\sum_t R_{it}R'_{jt}$ and the R_{it}s denoting the respective residuals of the regression of ΔX_t and X_{t-1} on ΔX_{t-1}, ..., ΔX_{t-k+1}. Its asymptotic distribution obtained in Johansen (1988) was shown to be free of nuisance parameters, depending solely on the number of common stochastic trends $(p - r)$ driving the system. It is important to note that Johansen's framework is based on well known techniques in the multivariate analysis literature, namely the reduced rank regression and canonical correlation analysis (see Izenman, 1975, among others). The LR statistic is only one among many alternative test statistics proposed for inferring the rank of possibly rank deficient matrices (Hotelling, 1931; Pillai, 1954). Moreover simulation studies (see Olson, 1974) have shown that these test statistics behave very differently in a finite sample context despite the fact that they all share a common limiting distribution. Our initial objective here is to investigate their properties within the context of cointegration as well. Our interest is in finding a properly sized test statistic for conducting meaningful inferences in large dimensional systems. At this stage it is important to reiterate that the dimensionality problem does not arise solely because of the resulting degrees of freedom limitations. As shown in Abadir *et al.* (1997), when a VAR contains I(1) variables, increasing its dimension will proportionately raise the asymptotic bias of $\hat{\Pi}$ even when all regressors are independent of each other. In addition to the LR, the set of alternative test statistics considered in this paper are given by

(a) $PB = T\sum_{i=r+1}^{p}\hat{\lambda}_i$ (Pillai–Bartlett),

(b) $HL = T\sum_{i=r+1}^{p}(\hat{\lambda}_i/(1 - \hat{\lambda}_i))$ (Hotelling–Lawley).

Through a first order expansion of the functional forms it is straightforward to observe that the PB and HL statistics will have the same asymptotic distribution as that of the LR. Indeed, given that under $r = 0$ the $\hat{\lambda}_i$s are $O_p(1/T)$ we have $LR = PB + o_p(1)$ and $HL = LR + o_p(1)$, illustrating the fact that the asymptotic distribution of the *PB* statistic provides also an approximation to that of the *LR* or *HL*. Their finite sample distributions however will display important discrepancies both across each test statistic and compared with the asymptotic approximation. This can be noted by observing that the three criteria will satisfy the inequality $PB \leq LR \leq HL$, suggesting that in finite samples and when inferences are based on the asymptotic critical values the HL statistic will reject the null more frequently than the LR or PB and with the PB statistic rejecting it the least frequently. In order to isolate the impact of dimensionality this paper will mainly focus on models with $k = 1$. Although in applied work the lag issue raises serious modeling questions incorporating it here would prevent us from isolating the true impact of dimensionality on inferences.

2.2 Finite Sample Distributions and Dimensionality

In order to highlight the influence of the system dimension p on the distributions of the test statistics we initially focused on the empirical size of each test under the null of no cointegration. More specifically we generated p dimensional independent random walks and computed the rejection frequencies of the true null of no cointegration ($r_0 = 0$) using the common asymptotic critical values and a 5 percent nominal level. All our experiments have been performed using $N = 10{,}000$ replications and the asymptotic critical values were approximated using a sample of size $T = 10{,}000$. Results for these preliminary experiments are displayed in Table 1 for system dimensions ranging from $p = 2$ to $p = 10$.

Table 1. Empirical size under no cointegration (5% nominal level)

DGP: $\Delta x_{it} = \epsilon_{it}$, $\epsilon_{it} \equiv N(0, 1)$, $N = 10,000$ replications

p	LR	PB	HL	LCT	RALR	LR	PB	HL	LCT	RALR
	$T = 30$					$T = 90$				
2	7.00	2.90	12.96	4.86	5.24	5.12	4.00	7.15	4.69	4.60
3	9.42	1.13	24.69	4.63	4.88	6.21	3.18	9.45	4.58	4.77
4	13.04	0.34	44.00	4.22	3.94	6.64	2.58	12.82	4.54	4.62
5	20.75	0.07	72.06	4.44	3.59	8.10	1.71	21.2	4.27	4.27
6	31.66	0.00	91.62	5.04	2.68	10.48	1.12	31.44	4.26	3.90
7	47.44	0.00	99.02	5.78	1.98	12.12	0.72	43.76	4.12	3.78
8	67.42	0.00	100.00	7.90	2.00	14.00	0.20	57.78	3.62	2.82
9	85.00	0.00	100.00	10.46	1.32	19.96	0.12	76.30	4.04	2.72
10	96.69	0.00	100.00	19.41	0.96	25.03	0.05	88.11	3.87	2.23
	$T = 150$					$T = 400$				
2	5.02	4.18	5.78	4.78	4.74	5.10	5.20	6.37	5.10	5.45
3	5.90	4.29	7.91	5.10	4.76	5.13	4.47	5.80	4.70	4.80
4	6.46	3.38	9.98	4.76	4.96	5.17	4.27	5.97	4.67	4.80
5	7.11	3.12	13.13	4.84	4.90	5.93	4.53	8.20	5.37	5.37
6	7.84	2.44	18.50	4.68	4.50	5.87	3.70	8.30	4.40	4.40
7	8.18	1.44	23.52	4.10	3.90	6.70	3.77	9.83	4.97	4.87
8	9.70	1.12	31.40	4.08	3.58	6.50	2.87	11.13	4.63	4.44
9	11.60	0.92	42.26	4.28	3.58	8.27	3.37	15.27	5.47	5.27
10	14.69	0.55	55.75	4.25	3.17	8.70	3.07	19.03	5.30	4.90

A general picture that emerges from Table 1 is the strong negative impact of the system dimension on the size properties of the LR, PB and HL statistics. Although it is natural to expect a reduction in the accuracy of inferences as p increases, the magnitudes of the distortions are striking. The latter may increase substantially even when a system is augmented by a single additional variable. In addition the magnitudes presented in Table 1 also suggest that the inclusion of additional variables necessitates an extremely important incremental increase in the sample size so as to keep the distortions similar in the original and augmented models.

The distortions of the LR and HL statistics reach unacceptable levels as we move from a medium sized ($p = 5$) to larger systems. In the case of the LR statistic under $p = 8$ for instance the frequency of rejection of $r_0 = 0$ is 67.42 percent when $T = 30$, 14 percent when $T = 90$ and close to 10 percent for $T = 150$. In applied work such sample sizes are not uncommon especially when one is also interested in models with structural breaks or thresholds. The PB statistic on the other hand suffers from the opposite problem, being unable to move away from $r = 0$ unless a very large sample size becomes available. Clearly all three (LR, PB, HL) test criteria appear inappropriate for conducting inferences about the presence of cointegration in large dimensional systems, even when moderately large sample sizes are available: the LR and HL statistics will wrongly point towards too many stationary components and the PB towards too few. Although not reported here due to space considerations (available upon request) it is also important to point out that the results presented in this section and throughout the rest of the paper were highly robust to numerous alternative specifications that included deterministic components (i.e. constant and trend terms) in the fitted models.

In finite samples the poor approximation provided by the asymptotic distribution is not a problem novel to this nonstationary multivariate time series framework. Indeed it is also a well documented issue in the multivariate analysis and canonical correlation literature. Since Bartlett (1947) for instance, numerous authors introduced correction factors to the standard LR statistic with the motivation of having the first moment of the finite sample and asymptotic distributions match up to a certain order of magnitude (see Fujikoshi, 1977, for correction factors in the context of standard canonical correlation analysis and Taniguchi, 1991, for similar results in the stationary time series framework). Unfortunately such analytical corrections pose extremely challenging problems in multivariate systems with I(1) components and to our knowledge the issue has been tackled only partially in simple univariate AR(1) models (see Nielsen, 1997). However, the recent derivation of the multivariate joint moment generating function of S_{11} and S_{10} in Abadir and Larsson (1996) will almost surely open the path to further exact results in the nonstationary VAR framework for test statistics that are functions of these two moment matrices. Given the availability of powerful computer resources an alternative and perhaps more accurate strategy has been to use techniques such as response surface regressions for quantile estimation (see MacKinnon, 1994, 1996; MacKinnon, Haug, and Michelis, 1996, for an application to unit root distributions). Within our framework the specific behavior of the LR and PB test statistics may also allow us to design an alternative criterion with good size properties following the simulation path. Indeed a close analysis of the full densities of the LR and PB statistics across numerous sample sizes and system dimensions[1] prompts us to propose an alternative criterion based on the linear combination of LR and PB that minimizes the following distance:

$$\min_{\omega_1, \omega_2} \sum_{p=1}^{P} (q_p(\alpha) - \omega_1 LR(\alpha, T) - \omega_2 PB(\alpha, T))^2$$
$$s.t. \quad \omega_1 + \omega_2 = 1,$$

where $q_p(\alpha)$ denotes the α percent asymptotic critical value in the p-dimensional model and $LR(\alpha, T)$ and $PB(\alpha, T)$ the finite sample counterparts. In our estimations we used $p = 1, ..., 20$ for $T = 90$ and $T = 150$ respectively and an equal weighting $\omega_1 = \omega_2 = 0.5$ between LR and PB gave the best results with excellent diagnostics across all the experiments. This leads us to propose a linear combination test statistic (LCT thereafter) expressed as $0.5(LR + PB)$. Empirical size estimates corresponding to the LCT statistic under the null of no cointegration are also displayed in Table 1 together with the standard test criteria. Except for the extreme case where $p = 10$ and $T = 30$ the LCT statistic can be seen to track the asymptotic distribution very closely, with empirical size estimates extremely close to the nominal 5 percent level across all system dimensions. To gain further insight on its behavior Figures 1a and 1b also present the difference between the asymptotic and finite sample critical values across various values of the system dimension. The plot corresponding to the LCT criterion remains horizontal across all values of p clearly highlighting the absence of any distortion even within very large system dimensions.

Note that this result is robust to any specification of the covariance matrix of the errors in the VECM since the eigenvalues are invariant to any non-singular linear transformation of the variables. An important additional advantage of the LCT statistic comes from the fact that it shares the same asymptotic distribution as that of the LR or PB but this time without the distortions plaguing both statistics. As mentioned previously the main distortion characterizing the inferences based on the LR statistic arises from a drastic

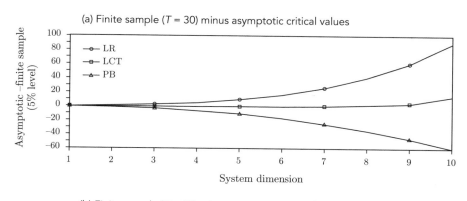

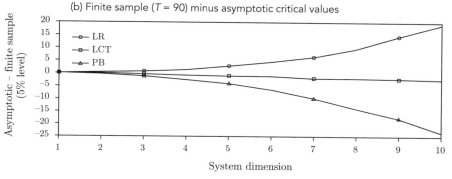

Figure 1

rightwards shift of the distribution as p increases for a given sample size. An intuitive explanation of this phenomenon can be inferred by analysing the $o_p(1)$ terms in the Taylor expansion of $LR = -T\sum_{i=r+1}^p \log(1 - \hat{\lambda}_i)$ where $\hat{\lambda}_i = O_p(1/T)$ for $i = r + 1, ..., p$. The latter consist of sums of powers of the estimated eigenvalues which are in turn premultiplied by a factor proportional to the sample size. In finite samples the $\hat{\lambda}_i$s are typically characterized by an important upward bias (the maximum eigenvalue in particular) the cumulated weight of which tends to increase the magnitude of the LR statistic relative to its asymptotic value. Similarly since the PB statistic is the first term in the expansion of LR, its lagging behavior (relative to its asymptotic distribution) can be explained by the fact that in small samples the normalizing factor T is not strong enough to make the statistic's finite sample distribution shift sufficiently rapidly towards its asymptotic counterpart. The LCT statistic offers a compromise between the LR and PB by reducing the weight of the $o_p(1)$ terms by half.

The size distortions characterizing the LR statistic have also been observed in previous studies focusing on possibly misspecified (due to residual auto-correlation for instance) small dimensional systems. A popular ad hoc correction taking the form $((T - p)/T)\ LR$ has been suggested in Reinsel and Ahn (1992) within the context of cointegration testing and was subsequently used in most empirical studies. In order to compare its size behavior with that of the LCT criterion Table 1 also presents corresponding size estimates for this corrected LR statistic (denoted RALR). Although the RALR statistic also appears to track the asymptotic distribution very closely (as judged by the empirical size estimates) even under limited sample sizes, its behavior seriously degenerates as the system dimension increases suggesting that inferences based on RALR might be unable to point to ranks other than zero. An empirical size of 0.96 percent or 2.23 percent under $T = 30$ and $T = 90$ when $p = 10$ for instance is an obvious indication of its limitation.

An extreme scenario that is worth mentioning, because it affects all the tests, is that of a model as in (1) at the border of the estimability region. More specifically the estimability condition in the context of model (1) under $k = 1$ requires $T \geq 2p + 1$ (see Brown, 1981) and if the system dimension p is such that $p \to T/2$, it is straightforward to show that $\hat{\lambda}_1 \to 1$ even when the true $\lambda_1 = 0$, a phenomenon that can be qualified as spurious cointegration.

3 Performance under the Presence of Cointegration

Our next concern is to evaluate the performance and overall behavior of the alternative test criteria when the systems are cointegrated. Given the highly distorted nature of the PB and HL statistics our analysis will mainly concentrate on the relative performance of the LR, LCT and RALR statistics. Our motivation here is to investigate whether distortions similar to the ones that were observed under $r_0 = 0$ will also be present when $r_0 > 0$ and whether the LCT statistic will maintain its attractive features under such scenarios. Since the sequential testing procedure (see Johansen, 1995, ch. 12) can be used to construct an estimate of the cointegrating rank we will also naturally investigate the ability of the various criteria to correctly detect the true rank and more importantly the influence of the system dimension when conducting such inferences.

So far we have seen that under the null of no cointegration the distorted behavior of the LR statistic manifests itself in the form of too many rejections of the true null $r_0 = 0$. Due to the sequential nature of the test however it is important to note that such distortions will not necessarily remain when testing ranks greater than zero. Specifically, if we let $LR(r)$ denote the LR statistic under r cointegrating relationships (i.e. $LR(r) = -T\sum_{i=r+1}^{p}\log(1 - \hat{\lambda}_i)$) and assuming that the sequential test is implemented starting from the hypothesis of no cointegration, we initially compare $LR(0)$ with its corresponding quantile c_p say and conclude $\hat{r} = 0$ if $LR(0) < c_p$. If $LR(0) \geq c_p$ we then proceed with $LR(1)$ and let $\hat{r} = 1$ if $LR(1) < c_{p-1}$ and so on. The fact that a large system dimension induces frequent rejections of the null of no cointegration due to the occurrence of $LR(0) > c_p$ beyond its theoretical level does not mean that the event $LR(1) > c_{p-1}$ will occur as frequently when $r_0 = 1$. An equivalent question to ask is whether in a $p - 1$ dimensional system with $r_0 = 0$ the discrepancies characterizing the distribution of $LR(0)$ will be similar to those occurring in the distribution of $LR(1)$ in a p dimensional system with $r_0 = 1$? Intuitively it is the bias in the first eigenvalue that might be causing an inflated value of the LR statistic. Before focusing more closely on this issue we will initially evaluate the influence of the system dimension on the ability of the sequential testing procedure to detect the true rank. In other words, given that a system is characterized by $r_0 > 0$ cointegrating relationship we ask how frequently will the three test statistics point to the true rank across different system dimensions. The DGP we have considered is given by $\Delta X_t = \Pi X_{t-1} + \epsilon_t$ with ϵ_t a $NID(0, I_p)$ random disturbance and $\Pi = diag(\rho - 1, 0, ..., 0)$. Thus the system is characterized by a single cointegrating relationship, the strength of which is determined by the magnitude of ρ. For this experiment we chose to set $\rho = 0.7$ which corresponds to a magnitude of the unique nonzero population eigenvalue of $\lambda_1 = (1 - \rho)/2 = 0.15$. Table 2 displays the relevant correct decision frequencies for values of p ranging from 2 to 10.

Given our previous findings on the behavior of LR under no cointegration we present the LR based frequencies using both asymptotic and finite sample critical values. The discrepancies between the two versions clearly support our analysis of the LR under the null of no cointegration. Although it is natural to expect a reduction in the accuracy of inferences as the system dimension increases, the magnitudes displayed in Table 2 are striking even when only a

Table 2. Correct decision frequencies $r_0 = 1$ (5% nominal level)

DGP: $x_{1t} = 0.7x_{1t-1} + \epsilon_{1t}$, $\Delta x_{it} = \epsilon_{it}$ $i = 2, ..., p$, $\epsilon_{it} \equiv N(0, 1)$, $N = 10{,}000$ replications

p	LR(ad)	LR(fsd)	LCT	RALR	LR(ad)	LR(fsd)	LCT	RALR
	$T = 30$				$T = 90$			
2	20.02	15.10	15.06	16.40	87.84	85.88	86.26	86.86
3	13.98	7.94	7.10	7.80	56.48	52.42	49.86	51.68
4	13.84	5.32	4.48	4.60	34.78	29.46	26.36	27.80
5	18.16	4.82	4.48	3.62	25.28	17.02	15.40	16.02
6	24.82	4.30	3.60	2.46	20.46	12.42	10.52	10.84
7	33.40	4.10	3.82	1.60	19.00	9.52	7.08	6.70
8	42.58	3.72	5.30	1.20	19.04	7.56	5.74	4.84
9	40.64	3.44	7.90	0.88	21.32	6.26	5.06	3.84
10	24.42	3.40	14.50	0.92	23.78	5.96	4.42	3.06
	$T = 150$				$T = 400$			
2	94.90	95.08	95.00	95.08	95.52	95.40	95.52	95.54
3	91.84	92.14	91.12	91.52	95.14	95.34	95.32	95.36
4	74.72	71.16	69.18	70.80	94.54	94.56	94.72	94.80
5	59.02	53.12	50.40	52.22	94.86	94.86	95.52	95.58
6	43.66	36.04	32.52	33.54	94.18	94.72	94.88	95.12
7	34.30	25.22	22.20	22.46	94.02	94.68	94.48	94.90
8	30.34	19.38	16.60	16.24	92.16	92.36	91.82	92.56
9	27.24	14.70	12.98	11.92	87.64	86.54	85.90	86.86
10	26.64	13.24	11.34	9.68	84.30	79.88	79.02	80.02

Note: LR(ad) and LR(fsd) refer to the correct decision frequencies based on the asymptotic and finite sample critical values respectively.

single additional variable is added to the system. Under $T = 90$ for instance the correct decision frequencies decrease by an amount close to 50 percent as we move from a bivariate to a trivariate system. A more extreme scenario is a reduction of the correct decision frequency by an amount close to 300 percent as we move from a bivariate to a ten dimensional system. Although these gaps tend to fade as we increase the sample size they remain highly significant. Overall these findings suggest that even the inclusion of a single additional variable might reduce the quality of inferences by an unexpectedly high proportion, an observation valid for all three test statistics. Comparing the magnitudes corresponding to LR(fsd), LCT and RALR it is also clear that for $T \geq 90$ the three statistics display a very similar ability to point to the true rank of $r_0 = 1$ across all system dimensions thus the advantageous size behavior of the LCT criterion observed in Table 1 is not coupled with any sort of distortion in its ability to point to the true rank *relative* to the other test statistics. It is also interesting to note the close agreement between the frequencies of the LCT statistic and those obtained using the "size corrected" LR statistic. This confirms our point about the ability of the LCT statistic to remain close to the asymptotic distribution across a wide range of sample size/system dimension pairs.

In order to gain further insight on the behavior of the LCT statistic when cointegration is present we next investigated the proximity of the finite sample distributions to their asymptotic counterparts under $r_0 = 1$ by computing the 5 percent critical values of the $LR(1)$ statistic in p-dimensional systems with $r_0 = 1$ and comparing them with their asymptotic counterparts from a $p - 1$ dimensional system with $r_0 = 0$. In a p-dimensional system with $r_0 = 1$ for instance it is clear that the *limiting distribution* of $LR(1) = -T\sum_{i=2}^{p}\log(1 - \hat{\lambda}_i)$ will be equivalent to that of the LR statistic in a $p - 1$ dimensional system with no cointegration. This will obviously be true asymptotically but important distortions might arise when dealing with small samples and/or large system dimensions. Using the same DGP as above Table 3 presents the relevant critical values for different sample sizes. For clarification purposes the first row in the LR column for instance refers to a DGP with $p = 2$ and $r_0 = 1$ while the column labeled $LR(p, r_0 = 0)$ represents the critical value computed using a DGP with $p = 1$ and $r_0 = 0$. The two should obviously coincide asymptotically.

Table 3. 5% critical values of LR, LCT, and RALR under $r_0 = 1$

DGP: $x_{1t} = 0.7x_{1t-1} + \epsilon_{1t}$, $\Delta x_{it} = \epsilon_{it}$ $i = 2, ..., p$, $\epsilon_{it} \equiv N(0, 1)$, $N = 10{,}000$ replications

$p - r_0$	LR	LR*	LCT	RALR	LR	LR*	LCT	RALR	Asymptotic
	$T = 30$				$T = 90$				
1	4.56	4.59	4.16	4.02	4.06	4.26	4.02	3.97	4.16
2	13.09	13.22	12.16	11.98	12.59	12.77	12.21	12.17	12.27
3	25.92	26.73	23.34	22.53	24.70	25.04	23.85	23.60	24.29
4	43.21	45.23	38.17	36.18	40.91	41.82	38.64	38.64	40.40
5	66.21	69.30	56.87	52.84	62.23	62.69	58.87	58.08	59.78
6	95.28	99.66	80.41	73.36	87.61	88.24	82.25	80.80	83.68
7	130.85	137.97	107.59	95.66	118.19	118.08	109.92	107.69	111.65
8	174.63	184.05	139.95	121.38	152.55	152.69	140.80	137.29	143.12
9	227.92	238.95	178.31	151.17	191.19	192.82	175.46	169.95	178.29
	$T = 150$				$T = 400$				
1	4.10	4.15	4.07	4.05	4.12	4.10	4.10	4.09	4.16
2	12.42	12.61	12.19	12.17	12.31	12.35	12.30	12.18	12.27
3	24.56	24.50	24.03	23.90	24.31	24.50	24.15	24.00	24.29
4	41.38	41.25	40.15	40.00	40.95	40.42	40.35	40.10	40.40
5	61.31	61.46	59.28	58.86	61.10	61.46	59.09	58.00	59.78
6	86.13	86.30	82.86	82.11	84.95	84.81	83.24	83.00	83.68
7	115.72	115.56	110.74	109.55	113.12	115.56	110.90	110.00	111.65
8	148.81	148.86	141.72	139.88	145.85	148.86	142.14	140.08	143.12
9	186.83	186.79	177.20	174.37	180.25	182.24	178.00	175.24	178.29

* $(p, r_0 = 0)$

It is again clear that the finite sample distribution of the LR statistic lies to the right of its asymptotic counterpart while that of the LCT tracks the latter very closely (although our judgement here is based solely on the 5 percent critical values similar discrepancies occur throughout the whole quantiles). It is however important to also note the discrepancies between the magnitudes appearing in the LR and $LR(p, r_0 = 0)$ columns respectively. Although both suggest that the finite sample distributions of the LR statistic lie to the right of their asymptotic counterpart it is also clear that for the same value of $p - r$ the critical values corresponding to $LR(p, r_0 = 0)$ are much larger. This suggests that the inflated empirical sizes we have observed under the null of no cointegration (i.e. Table 1) will be less pronounced when considering testing sequences involving ranks greater than zero. This is indeed what we observed when we evaluated the probability of pointing to ranks greater than one (i.e. $P[LR(0) > c_p$ and $LR(1) > c_{p-1}])$ for a DGP with $r_0 = 1$. It is important to note however that in this case the choice of the "strength" of the cointegrating relationship will play an important role in the sense that the discrepancies between the LR and $LR(p, r_0 = 0)$ columns appearing in Table 3 will not be robust to the chosen magnitude for ρ. Typically when we repeated the same experiment with smaller values of ρ (i.e. stronger cointegration) the discrepancies between LR and $LR(p, r_0 = 0)$ also appeared much stronger. Regarding the LCT statistic under the presence of cointegration it is again clear from Table 3 that its behavior under the presence of cointegration (judged by the closeness of its finite sample distributions to their asymptotic counterpart) does not present any significant difference to that observed under $r_0 = 0$ in the previous section.

4 Estimation of the Cointegrating Rank: Model Selection Procedure

In the previous section we saw that most standard tools for inferring the cointegrating rank were often ineffective when the ratio of the system dimension to the sample size was too large. Although the new criterion we introduced was able to significantly reduce the degree of size distortions plaguing the standard test statistics, by construction and regardless of the quality of the statistic being used the sequential testing strategy cannot lead to consistent estimates of the cointegrating rank because of the constraint imposed by the size of the test. This problem could become particularly intensified in large dimensional systems where the testing sequences are long. When consistency is a desired feature an alternative way of approaching the problem is to view the estimation of the cointegrating rank as a model selection problem where one chooses a model among a portfolio (assumed to contain the true model) of $p + 1$ competing models. The idea of using a model selection procedure for estimating the rank of a matrix was also recently investigated in Donald and Cragg (1995) within the context of a stationary multivariate normal framework. A general class of model selection criteria is given by $IC(\ell) = -2\log L_\ell + c_T m_\ell$ where m_ℓ denotes the number of free parameters to be estimated under the hypothesis that there are ℓ cointegrating relationships ($m_\ell = 2p\ell - \ell^2$), L_ℓ is the likelihood function and c_T is a deterministic penalty term. Many well known information theoretic criteria are encompassed in the above specification. Indeed, when $c_T = 2$, $IC(\ell)$ corresponds to the Akaike criterion (Akaike, 1969, 1976), $c_T = \log(T)$ corresponds to Schwarz's BIC criterion (Schwarz, 1978) and when $c_T = 2c \log(\log(T))$ with $c > 1$ we have the Hannan and Quinn (1979) criterion. According to the model selection procedure, r is estimated by $\hat{r}$ where $\hat{r}$ is chosen such that $IC(\hat{r}) = \arg \min \{IC(\ell), \ell = 0, ..., p\}$. More commonly, the general expression for the various criteria is given by

$$IC(\ell) = \log\left|\hat{\Omega}(\ell)\right| + \frac{c_T}{T} m_\ell, \tag{2}$$

where c_T and m_ℓ are defined as before and $\hat{\Omega}(\ell)$ corresponds to the estimated error covariance matrix from model (1) under the hypothesis that Rank(Π) $= \ell$. For computational convenience we can focus on a transformed objective function that involves directly the eigenvalues of $S_{00}^{-1}S_{01}S_{11}^{-1}S_{10}$ since those are readily available. Noting that the eigenvalues of $S_{00}^{-1}S_{01}S_{11}^{-1}S_{10}$ are the same as the eigenvalues of $I_p - S_{00}^{-1}\hat{\Omega}$, where $\hat{\Omega}$ is the covariance matrix of the residuals in the unrestricted VECM, it is straightforward to show that one can instead focus on the minimization of

$$\tilde{IC}(\ell) = IC(\ell) - IC(p) = -T \sum_{i=\ell+1}^{p} \log(1 - \hat{\lambda}_i) - c_T(p - \ell)^2 \tag{3}$$

where $\tilde{IC}(p) = 0$, thus rendering the approach trivial to implement once estimates of the eigenvalues have been obtained. Typically, as p the system dimension increases the LR portion of the criterion will increase and this latter increase will be balanced by the decrease due to the presence of the penalty term. The following proposition establishes the asymptotic properties of the resulting estimates.

Proposition 4.1. *Letting r_0 denote the true rank of Π in (1) and $\hat{r} = \arg \min_{0 \le \ell \le p}\{\tilde{IC}(\ell)\}$, then $\hat{r} \xrightarrow{p} r_0$ iff (i) $\lim_{T\to\infty} c_T = \infty$ and (ii) $\lim_{T\to\infty}(c_T/T) = 0$.*

Proof. See Appendix.

Thus provided that the chosen penalty in (2) or (3) satisfies both of the above requirements weak consistency of the rank estimate will follow. It is true, however, that the above two conditions allow for an extremely wide spectrum of possibilities beyond the conventional AIC, BIC or HQ type of penalties, thus leaving the choice of an appropriate penalty to become an empirical and model specific problem. The inconsistency of rank estimates resulting from constant penalty criteria (violation of condition (i) in proposition 4.1) is due to the fact that the probability of selecting some rank ℓ greater that r_0 does not vanish asymptotically. This is a well known problem in the model selection literature and its impact has often been downweighted for criteria such as the AIC by arguing that although positive, the limiting probability is usually very small. Within our framework, however, this nonzero limiting probability of overranking is much less innocuous and constant penalty criteria may lead to highly distorted results. This is due to the fact that in our setting the nonzero limiting probability of overranking is an increasing function of the system dimension with immediate consequences for the use of constant penalty based criteria in large dimensional systems. To illustrate this feature let us consider a p dimensional system having $r_0 = 0$. From (3) the probability that the model selection criterion will point to a rank greater than 0, say equal to 1 can be written as $P[\widetilde{IC}(1) < \widetilde{IC}(0)] = P[-T\log(1 - \hat{\lambda}_1) > c(2p-1)]$ where c represents a constant penalty term. In this setting the quantity $-T\log(1 - \hat{\lambda}_1)$ turns out to coincide with the well known likelihood ratio statistic (also called λ^{max}) for testing $r = 0$ against $r = 1$ proposed in Johansen (1991) and the full numerical distribution of which has been recently calculated in MacKinnon $et\ al.$ (1996). Using the companion program the authors provide it is therefore possible to evaluate very accurately the above limiting probability of overranking across various values of p. Using values of $p = 3, 5, 7$, and 10 respectively the computation of the above probability for the AIC criterion (i.e. $c = 2$) led to values of 48.52 percent, 69.86 percent, 84.10 percent and 95.04 percent clearly suggesting that the AIC or any other constant penalty criterion will persistently overrank, especially as the system dimension increases. This is in sharp contrast with the lag length estimation framework in which the AIC can be shown to point to the true lag as p increases (see Gonzalo and Pitarakis, 1997).

We now turn to the study of the performance of the criteria leading to consistent rank estimates, namely the BIC and HQ. For the sake of comparability we conducted the same experiments as the ones used in the evaluation of the testing procedure. Thus our initial goal is to examine the "size" behavior of the various model selection criteria as the system dimension increases. Results for this experiment are presented in Table 4a using samples of size $T = 30$, 90, 150 and 400.

The figures represent the number of times the criterion selected the true rank $r_0 = 0$. Given its strong penalty the BIC clearly converges to the true rank very rapidly, selecting it close to 100 percent most of the times for $T \geq 90$ and any value of p. Note that this characteristic of the BIC may be solely due to the strength of its penalty and not to its genuine ability to detect the true rank. The HQ criterion requires samples greater than $T = 90$ in order to achieve a correct decision frequency greater than 90 percent regardless of the

Table 4a. Model selection criteria—correct decision frequencies $r_0 = 0$
DGP: $\Delta x_{it} = \epsilon_{it}$, $\epsilon_{it} \equiv N(0, 1)$, $i = 1, ..., p$, $N = 10{,}000$ replications

p	AIC	BIC	HQ	AIC	BIC	HQ
	$T = 30$			$T = 90$		
2	59.32	89.32	72.38	61.88	97.96	87.90
3	39.96	89.06	61.90	47.48	98.98	85.80
4	24.14	87.08	49.24	34.08	99.56	85.40
5	12.82	84.62	38.14	23.02	99.54	82.40
6	4.48	80.28	24.22	14.88	99.78	81.64
7	1.38	73.86	13.86	9.06	99.88	80.64
8	0.24	63.36	6.08	4.46	99.90	79.66
9	0.00	49.68	1.94	2.14	99.90	76.06
10	0.00	33.40	0.34	0.86	99.96	74.74
	$T = 150$			$T = 400$		
2	63.34	98.82	89.86	63.64	99.64	93.64
3	49.52	99.66	90.14	50.14	99.98	95.08
4	34.84	99.88	90.32	36.98	100.00	95.98
5	24.18	99.98	90.36	27.44	100.00	96.88
6	17.62	99.96	91.66	19.52	100.00	97.50
7	11.22	99.98	91.34	13.32	100.00	98.04
8	6.42	100.00	91.54	8.90	100.00	98.44
9	3.72	100.00	91.42	5.44	100.00	98.50
10	1.92	100.00	92.04	3.30	100.00	98.72

magnitude of the system dimension. Although its penalty term is such that the resulting estimates of the cointegrating rank are consistent the quantity $2 \log(\log(T))$ converges to infinity very slowly explaining why the criterion has a rather strong tendency to overrank under smaller sample sizes. For $T \geq 150$ however its ability to point to the true rank improves drastically. At this stage it is also worth pointing out that the frequencies corresponding to the AIC criterion fully support our previous discussion about its behavior as p increases. Although not presented here, under $T = 400$ it pointed to $r = r_0 + 1 = 1$, 50 percent, 70 percent and 95 percent of the times under $p = 3, 5$, and 10 respectively, thus confirming the accuracy of our previous computations.

Bearing in mind their "size" behavior we now turn to the performance of the model selection criteria under cointegrated systems using models identical to the ones considered when evaluating the features of the test statistics (Table 4b).

The first point worth mentioning is the clear unreliability of the BIC criterion which has very little ability to point to the true rank $r_0 = 1$ even for moderately large sample sizes. For $T = 90$ or $T = 150$ for instance and when $p \geq 5$ its frequency of correct decision lies below 10 percent which is inferior to both the HQ and the LCT or RALR statistics. These frequencies confirm

Table 4b. Model selection criteria—correct decision frequencies $r_0 = 1$
DGP: $x_{1t} = 0.7x_{1t-1} + \epsilon_{1t}$, $\Delta x_{it} = \epsilon_{it}$, $i = 2, ..., p$, $\epsilon_{it} \equiv N(0, 1)$,
$N = 10,000$ replications

p	AIC	BIC	HQ	AIC	BIC	HQ
	$T = 30$			$T = 90$		
2	60.90	26.43	50.17	80.27	77.80	88.03
3	44.17	15.40	37.70	62.50	30.97	73.57
4	40.27	13.00	37.13	47.57	9.40	56.93
5	33.60	15.63	41.83	37.20	3.30	43.00
6	24.40	17.70	42.10	28.23	1.20	33.60
7	13.23	23.03	37.60	23.40	0.57	28.73
8	4.40	30.90	27.97	16.77	0.13	26.27
9	1.13	39.17	17.60	12.10	0.23	26.70
10	0.07	46.90	6.80	7.43	0.03	27.00
	$T = 150$			$T = 400$		
2	81.57	96.47	91.23	80.37	97.87	93.03
3	62.93	76.07	90.47	63.33	99.80	94.23
4	48.97	30.40	86.83	49.17	99.93	95.00
5	37.83	9.00	75.90	37.50	99.33	96.40
6	28.70	1.83	58.80	27.53	88.70	96.03
7	20.03	0.33	44.80	19.50	53.47	97.70
8	14.03	0.17	32.00	14.93	21.33	98.17
9	9.33	0.00	27.47	9.13	6.73	98.00
10	6.43	0.03	21.90	5.87	1.60	96.40

that in large dimensional systems the BIC will be unable to move away from $r = 0$ most of the time even if a sufficiently large sample size is available. Turning to the performance of the HQ criterion under values of T for which it displayed good size behavior (i.e. $T \geq 150$) its ability to point to the true rank is impressive when compared with either the standard test based inferences or the other model selection criteria. More importantly the HQ criterion turns out to be the only criterion able to achieve reasonable results even under a large dimensional system. Under $p = 5$ for instance it showed a tendency to outperform the test criteria by magnitudes as high as 25 percent. Similarly under $p = 10$ its performance was at least twice as good as the test based inferences across a wide range of system dimensions.

5 Conclusion

In this paper we studied various approaches for inferring the cointegrating rank by focusing on their robustness to the system dimensionality. We showed that standard (uncorrected) tools such as the LR statistic will lead to highly distorted inferences as the dimension of the system under study increases. We introduced a new test criterion (LCT) with the same limiting distribution as the LR, similar power properties and more importantly with no size distortions across a wide range of system dimensions. This of course is not meant to suggest that large dimensional systems can be dealt with as accurately as bivariate or trivariate systems since the improvements characterizing the LCT statistic do not make it more powerful (in absolute terms) for detecting the presence of cointegration in large systems.

As an alternative to testing we also examined the asymptotic and finite sample properties of a model selection based approach applied to the estimation of the cointegrating rank. Although commonly used information theoretic criteria such as the AIC or BIC were shown to perform poorly within our framework (with their performance deteriorating as the system dimension was allowed to increase), for moderately large sample sizes we found that the HQ criterion displayed excellent properties, particularly in large dimensional systems under which it consistently outperformed the test statistics. It is perhaps true that our results are based on a simple VAR model with no short run dynamics or any form of artificially induced misspecification but in this latter case it is well known for instance that the asymptotic critical values of the LR statistic become invalid and this would naturally have prevented us from isolating and evaluating the relative robustness of the various techniques to the dimensionality problem. More specifically any distortions characterizing the LR statistic under nonstandard conditions (such as MA or AR errors for instance) will also arise for the LCT or the model selection criteria an issue we leave for further research.

Appendix

Proof of Proposition 4.1. The proof follows by showing that under the chosen penalties the probabilities of "over" and "under" ranking vanish asymptotically.

- Case $\ell > r_0$: From (3) we have $P[IC(\ell) < IC(r_0)] = P[-T\sum_{i=r_0+1}^{\ell}\log(1 - \hat{\lambda}_i) > c_T(2p\ell - \ell^2 - 2pr_0 + r_0^2)]$. Since $-T\sum_{i=r_0+1}^{\ell}\log(1 - \hat{\lambda}_i)$ is $O_p(1)$ and the right hand side diverges towards infinity by condition (i) it follows that $\lim_{T\to\infty}P[IC(\ell) < IC(r_0)] = 0$ implying that overranking does not occur asymptotically.
- Case $\ell < r_0$: We have $P[IC(\ell) < IC(r_0)] = P[-\sum_{i=\ell+1}^{r_0}\log(1 - \hat{\lambda}_i) < (c_T/T)(2pr_0 - r_0^2 + \ell^2 - 2p\ell)]$. Since $\mathrm{plim}(-\sum_{i=\ell+1}^{r_0}\log(1 - \hat{\lambda}_i)) > 0$, from condition (ii) the right hand side converges to zero thus leading to $\lim_{T\to\infty}P[IC(\ell) < IC(r_0)] = 0$ and implying that underranking does not occur asymptotically. Taken together these two results imply that $\hat{r} \xrightarrow{p} r_0$ as $T \to \infty$.

In order to show that the requirements (i) and (ii) are necessary let us suppose that c_T is bounded by some constant δ. Condition (ii) still holds and $\lim_{T\to\infty} P[IC(\ell) < IC(r_0)] = 0 \; \forall \ell < r_0$. For $\ell > r_0$ we have $P[IC(\ell) < IC(r_0)]$ $= P[-T\sum_{i=r_0+1}^{\ell} \log(1 - \hat{\lambda}_i) > c_T(2p\ell - \ell^2 - 2pr_0 + r_0^2)]$ which will be nonzero since the right hand side does not tend to infinity when c_T is bounded. There is therefore a positive probability of overranking. In order to show that (ii) is necessary suppose that it fails, $(c_T/T) \to c > 0$. Clearly (i) is satisfied and for $\ell > r_0$ we have $\lim_{T\to\infty} P[IC(\ell) < IC(r_0)] = 0$. When $\ell < r_0$, $\lim_{T\to\infty} P[IC(\ell) < IC(r_0)] = P[-\sum_{i=\ell+1}^{r_0} \log(1 - \hat{\lambda}_i) < c(2pr_0 - r_0^2 + \ell^2 - 2p\ell)]$ and since $c > 0$ the result follows. ∎

Note

1. Full density plots for all test criteria and $T \in [30, 5000]$ are available upon request from the authors.

References

Abadir, K. and R. Larsson (1996) "The Joint Moment Generating Function of Quadratic Forms in Multivariate Autoregressive Series," *Econometric Theory*, 12: 682–704.

Abadir, K., K. Hadri, and E. Tzavalis (1997) "The Influence of VAR Dimensions on Estimator Biases," University of Exeter, Department of Economics, Discussion Paper.

Ahn, S. K. and G. C. Reinsel (1990) "Estimation for Partially Nonstationary Multivariate Autoregressive Models," *Journal of the American Statistical Association*, 85: 813–23.

Akaike, H. (1969) "Fitting Autoregressive Models for Prediction," *Annals of the Institute of Statistical Mathematics*, 21: 243–7.

Akaike, H. (1976) "Canonical Correlation Analysis of Time Series and the Use of an Information Criterion," in R. K. Mehra and D. G. Lainiotis (eds.), *System Identification: Advances and Case Studies*, New York: Academic Press, pp. 27–96.

Anderson, T. W. (1958) *An Introduction to Multivariate Statistical Analysis*. New York: John Wiley.

Bartlett, M. S. (1947) "Multivariate Analysis," *Journal of the Royal Statistical Society (Supplement)*, 9: 176–97.

Brown, B. W. (1981) "Sample Size Requirements in Full Information Maximum Likelihood Estimation," *International Economic Review*, 22: 443–459.

Donald, S. G. and J. Cragg (1997) "Inferring the Rank of a Matrix," *Journal of Econometrics*, 76: 223–50.

Engle, R. F. and C. W. J. Granger (1987) "Cointegration and Error Correction: Representation, Estimation and Testing," *Econometrica*, 55: 251–76.

Engle, R. F. and C. W. J. Granger (1991) *Long Run Economic Relationships*. Oxford: Oxford University Press.

Fujikoshi, Y. (1977) "Asymptotic Expansions for the Distributions of Some Multivariate Tests," in P. R. Krishnaiah (ed.), *Multivariate* Analysis, vol. 4. Amsterdam: North-Holland Publishing Company, pp. 55–71.

Gonzalo, J. and J. Y. Pitarakis (1997) "Lag Length Estimation in Large Dimensional Systems," University of Reading, Department of Economics, Manuscript.

Granger, C. W. J. (1981) "Some Properties of Time Series Data and Their Use in Econometric Model Specification," *Journal of Econometrics*, 16: 121–30.

Hannan, E. J. and Quinn, B. G. (1979) "The Determination of the Order of an Autoregression," *Journal of the Royal Statistical Society*, 41: 190–5.

Hotelling, H. (1931) "The Generalization of Student's Ratio," *Annals of Mathematical Statistics*, 2: 360–78.

Izenman, A. J. (1975) "Reduced Rank Regression for the Multivariate Linear Model," *Journal of Multivariate Analysis*, 5: 248–64.

Johansen, S. (1988) "Statistical Analysis of Cointegration Vectors," *Journal of Economic Dynamics and Control*, 12: 231–54.

Johansen, S. (1991) "Estimation and Hypothesis Testing of Cointegration Vectors in Gaussian Vector Autoregressive Models," *Econometrica*, 59: 1551–80.

Johansen, S. (1995) *Likelihood-Based Inference in Cointegrated Vector Autoregressive Models*. Oxford: Oxford University Press.

MacKinnon, J. G. (1994) "Approximate Asymptotic Distribution Functions for Unit Root and Cointegration Tests," *Journal of Business and Economic Statistics*, 12: 167–76.

MacKinnon, J. G. (1996) "Numerical Distribution Functions for Unit Root and Cointegration Tests," Queen's University, Institute for Economic Research, Discussion Paper no. 918.

MacKinnon, J. G., Haug, A. and L. Michelis (1996) "Numerical Distribution Functions of Likelihood Ratio Tests for Cointegration," Queen's University, Institute for Economic Research, Discussion Paper.

Nielsen, B. (1997) "Bartlett Correction for the Unit Root Test in Autoregressive Models," *Biometrika*, 84: 500–4.

Olson, C. L. (1974) "Comparative Robustness of Six Tests in Multivariate Analysis of Variance," *Journal of the American Statistical Association*, 69: 894–908.

Pillai, K. C. S. (1954) "Some New Test Criteria in Multivariate Analysis," *Biometrika*, 33: 117–21.

Reinsel, G. C. and Ahn, S. K. (1992) "Vector Autoregressive Models with Unit Roots and Reduced Rank Structure: Estimation, Likelihood Ratio Test, and Forecasting," *Journal of Time Series Analysis*, 13: 353–75.

Schwartz, G. (1978) "Estimating the Dimension of a Model," *Annals of Statistics*, 6: 461–4.

Taniguchi, M. (1991) *Higher Order Asymptotic Theory for Time Series Analysis*, Lecture Notes in Statistics 68. Springer.

10
Testing DHSY as a Restricted Conditional Model of a Trivariate Seasonally Cointegrated System

LUIGI ERMINI

1 Introduction

The UK consumption function has been analyzed in numerous studies, of which the model developed two decades ago by Davidson, Hendry, Srba and Yeo (1978), henceforth DHSY, is one of the best known and most successful (for a recent survey of these studies, see Muellbauer, 1994). Two main features of DHSY were the explicit modeling of the seasonal patterns present in the data through fourth-differencing and the presence of an error-correction term, whose central role in the empirical success of DHSY would be better understood a decade later in light of the newly developed literature on cointegration (for example, Granger, 1986); particularly, in light of the Granger representation theorem which formalizes the link between cointegration and error-correction (Engle and Granger, 1987). The introduction of the error-correction term in DHSY was based on intuitive rather than formal arguments to explicitly model the presence of a self-regulating mechanism that would keep consumption and income aligned in the long run. The link between error correction and cointegration for seasonally unadjusted data was later investigated by Hylleberg, Engle, Granger and Yoo (1990), henceforth HEGY, who developed unit-root tests for seasonal frequencies.

Most of the studies on the UK consumption function, including DHSY, adopt a single-equation framework; in DHSY, for example, consumer expenditures are explained by their past values and by current and past values of disposable income and inflation. To take into explicit account possible short- and

An earlier version of this paper was presented at the Meiji Gakuin University (Tokyo) conference "Recent Developments in the Analysis of Economic Time Series" in December 1996, as well as at seminars held at the European University Institute in Florence, at Nuffield College of Oxford University, the Stockholm School of Economics, the University of Rome and the University of Bologna. I thank Søren Johansen, Grayham Mizon, Rob Engle and an anonymous referee for very helpful comments.

long-run feedbacks from consumer expenditures to disposable income and inflation, multi-equation studies of the same trivariate system consumption–income–inflation have also appeared; for example, Hendry, Muellbauer and Murphy (1990) analyze this system by means of Johansen's maximum likelihood procedure for multivariate cointegration analysis at frequency zero (see Johansen, 1995, for a comprehensive reference). This paper analyzes the same trivariate system, but adopts a procedure that extends Johansen's approach to the seasonal frequencies as well; this procedure, commonly referred to as seasonal cointegration analysis, is conducted by estimating a *seasonal error-correction model*, or SECM, and is based on work by Lee (1992) and by Johansen and Schaumburg (1997); the latter improves upon Lee's work by providing a more accurate treatment of cointegration at the frequency of one cycle per year.

The purpose of this paper is to investigate the relation between the single-equation DHSY model and the multivariate SECM developed here, and to test the restrictions implied by the former. Although recent re-evaluations of DHSY inspired by its poor performance during the last few years have suggested the inclusion of other variables such as wealth as a significant explanatory variable of UK consumption—mostly to capture the effects of last-decade financial deregulation in Great Britain (see Muellbauer, 1994, and Hendry, 1994, for a discussion)—this paper will limit the investigation to the three variables of the original DHSY model, i.e. consumption, income, and inflation. One reason for this is practical: the addition of wealth potentially introduces at the seasonal frequencies issues of multi-cointegration—as defined, for example, in Granger and Lee (1991)—whose properties and implications have not yet been explored for seasonally cointegrated systems. A second reason is methodological: before extending the DHSY model in the direction that improves its performance (for example, by adding wealth), it is useful to assess whether and why the model is dominated by the alternative SECM approach.

This paper shows that DHSY is a restricted version of the conditional model of consumption, conditional on disposable income and inflation, that corresponds to the trivariate SECM developed here, and derives the implied restrictions. Three of these restrictions—full cointegration, stationarity of inflation and the absence of inflation from the cointegrating relations—are tested and rejected. The paper also tests and rejects the long-run strong exogeneity of disposable income and inflation, and thus establishes that the DHSY single-equation approach is inefficient. These results indicate that DHSY, despite having performed well over the years as a model of the UK consumption function to the point of being hailed as one of the most successful econometric models of the 1980s, is unambiguously dominated by the trivariate SECM model obtained through careful analysis of the cointegrating relations at each seasonal frequency. As the SECM model combines a number of important new

ideas and appeared in the analysis of time series after DHSY was developed
(particularly cointegration theory), rather than diminishing its importance
among older studies of UK consumption DHSY rejection should be interpreted
as an indirect tribute to the advances made in econometric modeling in the
last fifteen years, particularly in relation to integrated processes.

Regarding the seasonal cointegration analysis of the trivariate system, the
paper finds no cointegration at both the zero and the annual frequency, and
one cointegrating relation at the bi-annual frequency. These results can be
given the following interesting economic interpretation: the lack of cointegration
at frequency zero is consistent with life-cycle models of consumer behavior
whereby consumption is linearly related in the long run to permanent income
and not to current income; on the other hand, the presence of cointegration
at the seasonal frequency of two cycles per year indicates that consumers seem
to consume more out of the seasonal component of current income than
warranted by income smoothing over the life cycle. The latter possibility
contradicts the life-cycle hypothesis and lends support to the possible existence
of such restrictions as liquidity constraint in the consumer decision process.
As the lack of cointegration at the zero frequency can also be consistent with
the hypothesis of liquidity constraint, overall these results may indicate liquidity-
constraint effects in UK consumption. This issue will be investigated further
in a separate work.

The SECM of consumption–income–inflation presented here should be
viewed as a preliminary version of a more general model (greater details on
the SECM model presented here are found in Ermini, 1997, 1998). Possible
directions for further improvement are: (i) a better understanding of the
interplay between deterministic terms, cointegrating ranks, and restrictions
of the trend and seasonal dummies to the cointegrating spaces; (ii) testing of
specific linear restrictions on the seasonal cointegrating vectors to investigate
issues of economic theory, particularly the possibility previously mentioned
of liquidity constraint in consumption decisions; (iii) the extension of the seasonal cointegration analysis to a four-variable system (for example, by adding
wealth), or bigger; (iv) a more accurate modeling of inflation, particularly in
relation to its apparent variance shift in the early 1980s. Further investigations
along these directions will plausibly lead to more accurate seasonally cointegrated models; nonetheless, the rejection of DHSY against the SECM presented
here would still hold when compared to better models.

The paper is organized as follows. Section 2 describes the general structure
of a seasonal error-correction model (SECM). Section 3 shows that DHSY is
a restricted version of the conditional model of consumption corresponding to
the SECM of the trivariate system consumption–income–inflation. Section 4
reports the results of the seasonal cointegration analysis. Section 5 reports the
results of the tests of the restrictions implied by DHSY. Section 6 provides
some concluding remarks.

2 The Seasonal Error-Correction Model (SECM)

The N-dimensional vector process X_t is assumed to be generated by the following autoregressive process:

$$A(B)X_t = \Phi D_t + \varepsilon_t, \tag{2.1}$$

where ε_t is an N-dimensional vector innovation process of covariance matrix Σ; and D_t is a vector of deterministic functions of time (typically, a constant, a time trend, seasonal dummies and possibly other dummies to identify structural breaks). The following assumptions are made: (i) the polynomial matrix $A(B) = I - \sum_{j=1}^{p} A_j B^j$ is assumed to have finite order p and to have all the roots on or outside the unit circle; (ii) with quarterly data the unit-circle roots are assumed to be located only at 1, −1, or $\pm i$—corresponding to the frequency 0, π (two cycles per year) and $\pi/2$ (one cycle per year), respectively; (iii) each component of the vector process X_t is assumed to be at most first-order integrated at these frequencies; (iv) the initial conditions $X_0, ..., X_{t-p}$ are fixed, and the parameters $(A_1, ..., A_p \Phi, \Sigma)$ are constant.

In the most general case, the process X_t features a mixture of stationary (or cointegrated) and first-order integrated components at each of the frequencies 0, $\pi/2$ and π; for this reason, it is generically referred to as a *seasonally cointegrated process*. For this class of processes, Lee (1992) and Johansen and Schaumburg (1997) extend Johansen's maximum likelihood procedure for cointegration analysis at frequency zero to the seasonal frequencies π and $\pi/2$. As Lee's extension at the frequency $\pi/2$ is erroneously developed as an eigenvalue problem, this paper will follow the more accurate approach of Johansen and Schaumburg (1997).

Letting $z_1 = 1$, $z_2 = -1$, $z_3 = i$ and $z_4 = -i$, Johansen and Schaumburg (1997) show, following HEGY, that the VAR model in levels (2.1) can be rewritten in fourth differences as:

$$D(B)\Delta_4 X_t = -\sum_{j=1}^{4} A(z_j)Z_{j,t-1} + \Phi D_t + \varepsilon_t, \tag{2.2}$$

where $D(B)$ is a polynomial matrix of order $q = p - 4$ whose coefficient matrices D_j are defined in terms of the A_js of (2.1); and where the terms $Z_{j,t}$ are defined as:

$$Z_{j,t} = \frac{p_j(B)}{p_j(z_j)z_j} X_t, \tag{2.3}$$

with

$$p_j(B) = \frac{1 - B^4}{1 - \overline{z_j}B}, \quad p_j(z_j) = \left.\frac{1 - z^4}{1 - \overline{z_j}z}\right|_{z=z_j} ;$$

the bar denotes complex conjugate. As $Z_{3,t}$ and $Z_{4,t}$ are complex conjugate, so are $A(i)$ and $A(-i)$, and we can rewrite (2.2) as:

$$D(B)\Delta_4 X_t = -\sum_{j=1}^{2} A(z_j)Z_{j,t-1} - A(i)Z_{3,t-1} - \overline{A}(i)\overline{Z}_{3,t-1} + \Phi D_t + \varepsilon_t. \tag{2.4}$$

Indicating with superscript R and I the real and imaginary part of a complex number respectively, from (2.3) we have:

$$
\begin{align}
Z_{1,t} &= \tfrac{1}{4}(1 + B + B^2 + B^3)X_t \tag{2.5}\\
Z_{2,t} &= -\tfrac{1}{4}(1 - B)(1 + B^2)X_t\\
Z_{3,t}^R &= -\tfrac{1}{2}(1 - B^2)BX_t\\
Z_{3,t}^I &= \tfrac{1}{2}(1 - B^2)X_t;
\end{align}
$$

note that the imaginary process $Z_{3,t}^I$ is equal to the real process $Z_{3,t}^R$ led forward once.

For later use (Section 4), it is useful to rewrite (2.4) in the more compact form:

$$D(B)\Delta_4 X_t = \sum_{j=1}^{4} \Pi_j Y_{j,t-1} + \Phi D_t + \varepsilon_t. \tag{2.6}$$

where $\Pi_1 = -A(1)$, $\Pi_2 = -A(-1)$, $\Pi_3 = -A^R(i)$, and $\Pi_4 = -A^I(i)$; and where

$$
\begin{align}
Y_{1,t} &= Z_{1,t} \tag{2.7}\\
Y_{2,t} &= Z_{2,t}\\
Y_{3,t} &= Z_{3,t}^R\\
Y_{4,t} &= Z_{3,t}^I.
\end{align}
$$

The nature of integratedness of the process (2.1) at the frequency 0, π and $\pi/2$ is determined by the rank of the matrices $A(1)$, $A(-1)$ and $A(i)$ respectively. When all the components of the system are integrated at a given frequency, the corresponding rank is equal to the system dimension; when all the components are stationary at that frequency, the rank is zero; when the system exhibits a mixture of integrated and stationary components at that frequency, the corresponding matrix $A(\cdot)$ is of reduced rank $0 < r_j < N$ and can be decomposed into the product of two $N \times r_j$ matrices, $-\alpha_j\beta_j'$. In this case, (2.4) can be rewritten in the following seasonal error-correction form, or SECM:

$$D(B)\Delta_4 X_t = \sum_{j=1}^{2} \alpha_j\beta_j' Z_{j,t-1} + \alpha_3\overline{\beta}_3' Z_{3,t-1} + \overline{\alpha}_3\beta_3' \overline{Z}_{3,t-1} + \Phi D_t + \varepsilon_t; \tag{2.8}$$

or equivalently, letting $\zeta_{j,t} = \beta_j' Z_{j,t}$ for $j = 1, 2$, $\zeta_{3,t} = \overline{\beta}_3' Z_{3,t}$, and $\overline{\zeta}_{3,t} = \beta_3' \overline{Z}_{3,t}$,

$$D(B)\Delta_4 X_t = \sum_{j=1}^{2} \alpha_j \zeta_{j,t-1} + \alpha_3 \zeta_{3,t-1} + \bar{\alpha}_3 \bar{\zeta}_{3,t-1} + \Phi D_t + \varepsilon_t. \tag{2.9}$$

For $j = 1,\ 2$ the vector process $\zeta_{j,t} = \beta'_j Z_{j,t}$ is stationary in that the linear combination $\beta'_j Z_{j,t}$ eliminates the unit-circle roots of $Z_{j,t}$ at frequency 0 and π respectively. With regards to the annual frequency $\pi/2$, however, stationarity is achieved by simultaneously eliminating both roots at $+i$ and $-i$, and thus it is the overall process $\alpha_3 \zeta_{3,t-1} + \bar{\alpha}_3 \bar{\zeta}_{3,t-1}$ that is stationary, and not the two individual (complex) processes $\zeta_{3,t}$ and $\bar{\zeta}_{3,t}$. For this reason, while the two stationary processes $\zeta_{1,t}$ and $\zeta_{2,t}$ can be given the usual error-correction interpretation, with associated coefficients of adjustment α_1 and α_2, the same error-correction interpretation does not hold for frequency $\pi/2$, as we cannot disentangle the definition of an error correction term at this frequency from its coefficient of adjustment. It follows that we cannot identify at this frequency the deviations from equilibrium that generate changes in the levels of the vector X_t, nor can we properly identify a cointegrating sub-space: the column vectors of the complex matrices β_3 and $\bar{\beta}_3$ do not provide a basis for such a sub-space, as opposed to the matrices β_1 and β_2 which provide a basis for the cointegrating sub-spaces at frequency 0 and π respectively. In brief, the complex nature of the roots $\pm i$ prevents the usual interpretation of cointegration at frequency $\pi/2$.

We can obtain a better understanding of the complex nature of cointegration at frequency $\pi/2$ by explicitly expressing the complex conjugate elements of (2.8) in terms of their real and imaginary parts. Letting $\alpha_3 = \alpha_3^R + i\alpha_3^I$ and $\beta_3 = \beta_3^R + i\beta_3^I$, with some algebra the error-correction model (2.8) can be re-written as:

$$D(B)\Delta_4 X_t = \sum_{j=1}^{2} \alpha_j \beta'_j Z_{j,t-1} + 2(\alpha_3^R \beta_3^{R'} + \alpha_3^I \beta_3^{I'}) Z_{3,t-1}^R$$

$$+ 2(\alpha_3^R \beta_3^{I'} - \alpha_3^I \beta_3^{R'}) Z_{3,t-1}^I + \Phi D_t + \varepsilon_t. \tag{2.10}$$

As the impossibility of defining an error-correction term for the annual frequency $\pi/2$—and thus the difficulty of interpreting cointegration at this frequency in terms that can be appealing to economists—derives directly from β_3 being a complex matrix, it is natural to ask whether a more realistic interpretation might be obtained at the cost of assuming β_3 to be a real matrix ($\beta_3^I = 0$); this case will be referred to as the *real cointegration hypothesis*. By defining the error-correction term $\zeta_{3,t} = \beta_3^{R'} Z_{3,t}$, under this assumption the model (2.10) can be rewritten in a form that is directly conducive to the standard error-correction interpretation; that is

$$D(B)\Delta_4 X_t = \sum_{j=1}^{2} \alpha_j \zeta_{j,t-1} + \alpha_3(F)\zeta_{3,t-1} + \Phi D_t + \varepsilon_t, \tag{2.11}$$

with

$$\alpha_3(F) = 2(\alpha_3^R + \alpha_3^I F).$$

Now an identical real-valued cointegrating matrix β_3^R simultaneously eliminates both roots $+i$ and $-i$ and the column vectors of β_3^R properly identify the
cointegrating sub-space at frequency $\pi/2$. Note that the coefficient of
adjustment of the error-corrector $\zeta_{3,t}$ in this case is of polynomial nature. The
real cointegration hypothesis is routinely adopted in the literature on seasonal
cointegration, although—as pointed out in Johansen and Schaumburg (1997)
—it can be tested as a linear restriction on the cointegrating matrices. For
later use, and recalling (2.5), it is useful to rewrite (2.11) in the more compact
form

$$D(B)\Delta_4 X_t = \sum_{j=1}^{4} \alpha_j \zeta_{j,t-1} + \Phi D_t + \varepsilon_t, \tag{2.12}$$

with $\zeta_{4,t} = \beta_3^{R'} Z_{3,t}^I$, $\alpha_3 = 2\alpha^R$ and $\alpha_4 = -2\alpha^I$.

Another special case occasionally assumed in the literature (for example,
Lee, 1992; Ermini and Chang, 1996; Lee and Siklos, 1997), occurs when the
matrix of adjustments α_3 is also assumed to be real ($\alpha_3^I = 0$). In this case, the
error-correction model (2.12) reduces to

$$D(B)\Delta_4 X_t = \sum_{j=1}^{3} \alpha_j \zeta_{j,t-1} + \Phi D_t + \varepsilon_t; \tag{2.13}$$

this case corresponds to assuming that the imaginary part of $A(i)$ in (2.4) is
zero.

3 DHSY as a Restricted Conditional Model of the SECM

In this section, the DHSY model of UK consumption is shown to be a restricted
version of the conditional model of consumption, conditional on income and
inflation, corresponding to the SECM (2.8) when

$$X_t = \begin{bmatrix} c_t \\ i_t \\ \Delta p_t \end{bmatrix}; \tag{3.1}$$

here c_t, i_t and p_t are the log of quarterly, seasonally unadjusted, constant-£
(1955) UK expenditures on non-durable goods, disposable income and consumer price index respectively; the sample is from 1955:2 to 1992:2. Notice
that, as the price index appears to be integrated of order two at frequency
zero,[1] it is first-differenced in (3.1) to comply with the requirement that each
component of the process X_t is at most first-order integrated. Figure 1 reports
the time plots of these three variables, and of their first and fourth differences;

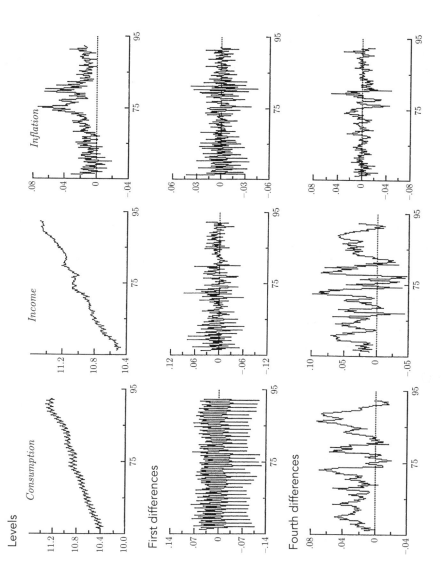

Figure 1. Timeplots of UK consumption, income, and inflation

the seasonal nature of these three variables is quite evident from these graphs. Univariate seasonal unit-root HEGY tests reveal that over the full sample all three variables exhibit unit-circle roots at the three frequencies 0, $\pi/2$ and π.[2]

The DHSY version considered here is (see DHSY, 1978; see also Hendry, Muellbauer and Murphy, 1990; Hendry, 1994):

$$\Delta_4 C_t = a_1 \Delta_4 i_t + a_2 \Delta \Delta_4 i_t + b_1 \Delta_4 p_t + b_2 \Delta \Delta_4 p_t + d(i_{t-4} - c_{t-4}) + \varepsilon_t; \qquad (3.2)$$

note the lack of a constant term and of seasonal dummies in the original DHSY estimation; a dummy variable for the introduction of the value-added tax system in the UK was included, but will not be considered in the present study.

DHSY is formally a conditional model of consumption, deseasonalized by fourth differencing and conditional on current deseasonalized values of disposable income ($\Delta_4 i_t$) and inflation ($\Delta_4 \Delta p_t$), with the additional property that consumption in any given quarter reacts to the deviation that occurred between income and consumption in the corresponding quarter of the previous year: if this deviation is positive (consumption too low with respect to income), next-year quarterly consumption in the corresponding quarter tends to increase on average; vice versa, if the deviation is negative.

DHSY exhibits two main features: (i) the explicit modeling of seasonality through fourth-differencing and (ii) the presence of the error-correction term $d(i_{t-4} - c_{t-4})$, whose central role in the empirical success of DHSY would be better understood a decade later in light of the newly developed theory of cointegration (for example, Granger, 1986); particularly in light of the Granger representation theorem (Engle and Granger, 1987) which formalized the link between cointegration and error-correction. The introduction of the error-correction term in DHSY was based on intuitive rather than formal arguments to explicitly model the presence of a self-regulating mechanism that would keep consumption and income aligned in the long run; error-correction mechanisms originated in the control theory literature (particularly, Phillips, 1954), but were seldom applied to economics until the DHSY study.

To show that DHSY is a restricted version of the seasonal error-correction model of the trivariate system (3.1), we first need to obtain the conditional model of consumption from the SECM (2.8) described in the previous paragraph. To this purpose, recall that if $D(c_t, i_t, \Delta p_t; \theta)$ is the probability density function underlying the data generating process (DGP) of the trivariate system (3.1), then an observationally equivalent representation of the same DGP is given by the product of conditional and marginal densities,

$$D(c_t, i_t, \Delta p_t; \theta) = D_C(c_t \mid i_t, \Delta p_t; \theta_1) \times D_M(i_t, \Delta p_t; \theta_2), \qquad (3.3)$$

where $D_C(c_t | i_t, \Delta p_t; \theta_1)$ is the density of consumption conditional on income and inflation, and $D_M(i_t, \Delta p_t; \theta_2)$ is the bivariate marginal density of income and inflation. For example, by letting

$$\mu = \begin{bmatrix} \mu_c \\ \mu_i \\ \mu_{\Delta p} \end{bmatrix} \quad \Sigma = \begin{bmatrix} \sigma_{cc} & \sigma_{ci} & \sigma_{c\Delta p} \\ \sigma_{ic} & \sigma_{ii} & \sigma_{i\Delta p} \\ \sigma_{\Delta pc} & \sigma_{\Delta pi} & \sigma_{\Delta p\Delta p} \end{bmatrix},$$

$$\Sigma_c = \begin{bmatrix} \sigma_{ic} & \sigma_{\Delta pc} \end{bmatrix} \quad \Sigma_{i\Delta p} = \begin{bmatrix} \sigma_{ii} & \sigma_{i\Delta p} \\ \sigma_{\Delta pi} & \sigma_{\Delta p\Delta p} \end{bmatrix} \quad \begin{bmatrix} \omega_i & \omega_{\Delta p} \end{bmatrix} = \Omega = \Sigma_c \Sigma_{i\Delta p}^{-1}, \tag{3.4}$$

the data generating process,

$$X_t = \mu + \varepsilon_t, \quad \varepsilon_t \sim NI(0, \Sigma), \tag{3.5}$$

can be decomposed into the conditional model,

$$c_t = (\mu_c - \omega_i \mu_i - \omega_{\Delta p} \mu_{\Delta p}) + \omega_i i_t + \omega_{\Delta p} \Delta p_t + \eta_t, \tag{3.6}$$

and the marginal model,

$$\begin{bmatrix} i_t \\ \Delta p_t \end{bmatrix} = \begin{bmatrix} \mu_i \\ \mu_{\Delta p} \end{bmatrix} + \begin{bmatrix} \varepsilon_{i,t} \\ \varepsilon_{\Delta p,t} \end{bmatrix}, \tag{3.7}$$

where

$$\eta_t = \varepsilon_{c,t} - \omega_i \varepsilon_{i,t} - \omega_{\Delta p} \varepsilon_{\Delta p,t} \sim NI(0, \Omega_c); \tag{3.8}$$

note that the modified innovation η_t has the property of being orthogonal to both $\varepsilon_{i,t}$ and $\varepsilon_{\Delta p,t}$. Note also that the conditional and marginal models (3.6)–(3.7) are obtained by pre-multiplying the model (3.5) by the triangular matrix

$$\Lambda = \begin{bmatrix} 1 & -\Omega \\ 0 & I_2 \end{bmatrix} = \begin{bmatrix} 1 & -\omega_i & -\omega_{\Delta p} \\ 0 & 1 & 0 \\ 0 & 0 & 1 \end{bmatrix}. \tag{3.9}$$

An identical procedure applies to the more general VAR model (2.1), as well as to any SECM parameterization. Referring to the SECM (2.8) or (2.9), and discarding the deterministic functions of time for simplicity, the conditional model of consumption can be shown to be:

$$\Delta_4 c_t = \omega_i \Delta_4 i_t + \omega_{\Delta p} \Delta_4 \Delta p_t$$
$$+ \sum_{k=1}^{q} G_{k,c} \Delta_4 X_{t-k} + \sum_{j=1}^{3} (\alpha_{j,c} - \omega_i \alpha_{j,i} - \omega_{\Delta p} \alpha_{j,\Delta p}) \zeta_{j,t-1}$$
$$+ (\bar{\alpha}_{3,c} - \omega_i \bar{\alpha}_{3,i} - \omega_{\Delta p} \bar{\alpha}_{3,\Delta p}) \bar{\zeta}_{3,t-1} + \eta_t, \tag{3.10}$$

where η_t is defined as in (3.8); where $G_{k,c}$ is the first row of the autoregressive matrix ΛD_k for $k = 1, \dots, q$; and where $\alpha_{j,c}$, $\alpha_{j,i}$ and $\alpha_{j,\Delta p}$ are the first, second, and third row of the $3 \times r_j$ matrix α_j of coefficients of adjustments, for $j = 1, 2, 3$ (and similarly for the complex conjugate $\bar{\alpha}_3$). The marginal model of income and inflation is:

$$\begin{bmatrix} i_t \\ \Delta p_t \end{bmatrix} = \sum_{k=1}^{q} \begin{bmatrix} D_{k,i} \\ D_{k,\Delta p} \end{bmatrix} \Delta_4 X_{t-k} + \sum_{j=1}^{3} \begin{bmatrix} \alpha_{j,i} \\ \alpha_{j,\Delta p} \end{bmatrix} \zeta_{j,t-1} + \begin{bmatrix} \bar{\alpha}_{3,i} \\ \bar{\alpha}_{3,\Delta p} \end{bmatrix} \bar{\zeta}_{3,t-1} + \begin{bmatrix} \varepsilon_{i,t} \\ \varepsilon_{\Delta p,t} \end{bmatrix}. \tag{3.11}$$

To derive the restrictions on the conditional model (3.10) implied by DHSY model, it is helpful to rewrite (3.2) as:

$$\Delta_4 c_t = (a_1 + a_2)\Delta_4 i_t + (b_1 + b_2)\Delta_4 \Delta p_t - a_2\Delta_4 i_{t-1} + b_1\Delta_4\Delta p_{t-1}$$
$$-d(c_{t-4} - i_{t-4}) + \varepsilon_t, \tag{3.12}$$

or equivalently as:

$$\Delta_4 c_t = (a_1 + a_2)\Delta_4 i_t + (b_1 + b_2)\Delta_4 \Delta p_t - a_2\Delta_4 i_{t-1} + 4b_1 Z^{\Delta p}_{1,t-1}$$
$$-dB^3(c_{t-1} - i_{t-1}) + \varepsilon_t; \tag{3.13}$$

in the latter expression we have used the fact that $\Delta_4 p_{t-1} = (1 + B + B_2 + B^3)\Delta p_{t-1}$, and thus from (2.5) $\Delta_4 p_{t-1} = 4Z^{\Delta p}_{1,t-1}$, the latter process being the inflation component of the vector process $Z_{1,t}$.

By comparing (3.14) with (3.11), we note that in DHSY the summation $\sum_{k=1}^q G_{k,c}\Delta_4 X_{t-k}$ reduces to the single term, $a_2\Delta_4 i_{t-1}$, and that all the error-correction terms reduce to the inflation component at frequency zero and to the term $dB^3(c_{t-4} - i_{t-4})$ which, as explained below, corresponds to the hypothesis of full cointegration. It is thus clear that the seasonal error-correction model offers a much richer parameterization of the DGP of the trivariate system consumption–income–inflation than DHSY. The issue then is whether the more parsimonious DHSY is a valid parameterization.

Four tests were conducted, one related to the efficiency of DHSY single-equation approach (weak exogeneity test) and three to the validity of the implied restrictions (stationary inflation, full cointegration, and absence of inflation from the cointegrating vectors). These tests are described next, and their results are discussed in Section 5.

(a) *Exogeneity of Income and Inflation*: DHSY is a single-equation model, and thus it is estimated independently from the joint estimation of the marginal model for income and inflation. As established in Engle, Hendry and Richard (1983), this single-equation approach leads to efficient estimation only under weak exogeneity of income and inflation for the parameters of interest of the conditional model. When the parameters of interest are the cointegrating vectors, Johansen (1992) shows that for the case of non-seasonal cointegration a necessary condition for the weak exogeneity of the conditioning variables is that the error-correction terms must not enter the marginal model. When weak exogeneity holds, the conditional model contains as much information about the parameters of interest as the full multivariate model, and thus no efficiency is lost in analyzing it in isolation as a single equation. The extension of Johansen condition to the seasonal case leads to the following restrictions:

$$\begin{bmatrix} \alpha_{1,i} \\ \alpha_{1,\Delta p} \end{bmatrix} = \begin{bmatrix} \alpha_{2,i} \\ \alpha_{2,\Delta p} \end{bmatrix} = \begin{bmatrix} \alpha^R_{3,i} \\ \alpha^R_{3,\Delta p} \end{bmatrix} = \begin{bmatrix} \alpha^I_{3,i} \\ \alpha^I_{3,\Delta p} \end{bmatrix} = 0. \tag{3.14}$$

It should be noted that these conditions impose a stronger form of exogeneity than weak exogeneity, as under these conditions the current levels of income and inflation affect the deviations $\zeta_{j,t}$ from the long-run equilibrium, but these deviations do not affect—in the Granger-causality sense—the current levels of income and inflation. For this reason, we suggest that conditions (3.14) be more appropriately referred to as conditions for *long-run strong exogeneity*: strong because they also imply Granger non-causality; long-run because they relate only to the deviations from the long-run equilibrium, i.e. the error-correction terms $\zeta_{j,t}$ (by contrast, short-run strong exogeneity would imply appropriate zero restrictions on the matrices D_k). Note also that, as a consequence of the strong exogeneity implied by conditions (3.14), testing these conditions simultaneously amounts to a test of efficiency (due to weak exogeneity) and specification (due to Granger non-causality).

(b) *Stationary Inflation*: the presence of the term $Z_{1,t-1}^{\Delta p}$ in (3.13) is equivalent to assuming the existence of the cointegrating vector $[0\ 0\ 1]'$ at frequency zero, with adjustment coefficient $4b_1$. Therefore, DHSY imposes the restriction that inflation is stationary at frequency zero, i.e. that the price index p_t is generated as $(1 - B_4)p_t = e_t$ and not as $(1 - B)(1 - B_4)p_t = e_t$, with $e_t \sim \mathrm{I}(0)$.

(c) *Full Cointegration*: full cointegration occurs when an identical cointegrating vector β_F simultaneously eliminates unit-circle roots at the three frequencies 0, π and $\pi/2$; that is, when the same cointegrating relation holds for each of these three frequencies. As in general the cointegrating matrix β_3 is complex but the matrices β_1 and β_2 are real, full cointegration requires the real cointegration hypothesis to hold; however, it does not require that *all* the unit-circle roots be simultaneously eliminated (for the latter condition to occur, the cointegrating ranks must be the same at all three frequencies, and so must be the associated cointegrating matrices, up to a non-singular transformation). By applying the condition $\beta_1 = \beta_2 = \beta_3^R = \beta_F$ to any of the cointegrating vectors of the SECM (2.10) or (2.11) under the real cointegration hypothesis, we obtain the term:

$$\alpha_1 \beta_F' Z_{1,t-1} + \alpha_2 \beta_F' Z_{2,t-1} + \alpha_3(F)\beta_F' Z_{3,t-1}^R, \tag{3.15}$$

which, recalling (2.5), can also be written as:

$$\alpha_F(B)\beta_F' X_{t-1}, \tag{3.16}$$

with $\alpha_F(B)$ a suitable polynomial in B. Thus in general under full cointegration the associated error-correction affects the system at several lags. By comparing (3.16) with DHSY, it is easily seen that the error-correction term $dB^3(c_{t-1} - i_{t-1})$ in (3.13) corresponds to the following special case of full cointegration:

$$\alpha_F(B) = \begin{bmatrix} -dB^3 & 0 & 0 \end{bmatrix}'$$
$$\beta_F = \begin{bmatrix} 1 & -1 & 0 \end{bmatrix}'. \tag{3.17}$$

It follows that DHSY implicitly assumes that (i) the real cointegration hypothesis holds, and that (ii) inflation is absent from the full cointegrating relation.

(d) *Additional Restrictions*: again comparing (3.14) with (3.11), the following additional restrictions are implied by DHSY: (i) lag values of $\Delta_4 X_t$ are only limited to the term $a_2\Delta_4 i_{t-1}$ (i.e. DHSY imposes the restriction $q = 1$); (ii) $\omega_i = a_1 + a_2$, and $\omega_{\Delta p} = b_1 + b_2$.

4 Seasonal Cointegrating Analysis of Consumption–Income–Inflation

4.1 Estimating the SECM

The maintained hypothesis in this paper is that the trivariate system (3.1) of consumption–income–inflation is generated by the autoregressive vector process (2.1), with the properties already listed in Section 2. We also assume the intercept and the seasonal dummies to be unrestricted, but the linear trend to be restricted to the cointegrating space at frequency zero. The latter assumption, which ensures that all the components of the system have at most a linear trend, is not as restrictive as it appears, given that the system is estimated in log values. As regards seasonal dummies, in the presence of unit roots unrestricted dummies generate cycles whose amplitude increases linearly with time (see, for example, Franses, 1996, for a discussion); as there is no a priori reason to believe that these increasing seasonal amplitudes are absent from the data, we prefer to leave the question to empirical testing, as explained below in Section 4.2. Besides, the critical values for the cointegrating rank test at the bi-annual frequency π are only available for unrestricted seasonal dummies.

The seasonal cointegration analysis will be thus applied to the SECM model

$$D(B)\Delta_4 X_t = \sum_{j=1}^{4} \Pi_j Y_{j,t-1} + m + d_1 + d_2 + d_3 + \varepsilon_t, \tag{4.1}$$

where m is a vector of unrestricted constants, and d_j are unrestricted centered seasonal dummies. To restrict the trend to the cointegrating space at frequency zero, in (4.1) $Y_{1,t}$ is redefined as $[Z_{1,t}\ t]'$ (see also Johansen, 1995). To test the hypothesis that the seasonal dummies also are restricted to their corresponding seasonal cointegrating spaces, the vectors $Y_{j,t}$ for $j = 2, 3, 4$ will be similarly redefined as (see Johansen and Schaumberg, 1997, for details):

$$Y_{2,t} = \begin{bmatrix} Z_{2,t} \\ (-1)^t \end{bmatrix}$$

$$Y_{3,t} = \begin{bmatrix} Z_{3,t}^R \\ \cos(t\pi/2) \end{bmatrix}$$

$$Y_{4,t} = \begin{bmatrix} Z_{3,t}^I \\ \sin(t\pi/2) \end{bmatrix}. \tag{4.2}$$

Table 1. Diagnostics for the SECM(3) with C + SD + T
(p-values in square brakets)

	$\Delta_4 c_t$	$\Delta_4 i_t$	$\Delta_4 \Delta p_t$
Standard error	0.0108	0.0171	0.0091
AR(1–5): $F(5, 108)$	1.91	2.27	1.38
	[0.099]	[0.053]	[0.236]
Normality: $\chi^2(2)$	5.63	9.93	15.47
	[0.060]	[0.007]	[0.000]
ARCH 4: $F(4, 105)$	1.13	1.27	0.87
	[0.348]	[0.285]	[0.482]
Xi^2: $F(42, 70)$	1.21	0.93	0.96
	[0.240]	[0.590]	[0.549]

Notes: (i) AR(1–5) is a likelihood ratio test for autocorrelated residuals; (ii) the test for normality is the test proposed by Doornik and Hansen (1994); (iii) ARCH is the likelihood ratio test for autocorrelated square residuals (Engle, 1982); (iv) Xi^2 is the White (1980) test of heteroskedasticity, based on the auxiliary regression of the squared residuals on the squares of the model regressors. These computations were done with the econometric package PC-Fiml; for further details, see Doornik and Hendry (1994).

As regards the choice of the lag length of the autoregressive polynomial $D(B)$ in (4.1), the value $p = 3$ was selected as the most parsimonious value among those that yielded congruent model residuals, i.e. homoskedastic residuals with no serial autocorrelation. The search was conducted over values of p between 6 and 1; for $p = 2$ and 1, the corresponding residuals exhibited serial autocorrelation. The model diagnostics associated with $p = 3$ are reported in Table 1; for further discussion on the selection procedure, see Ermini (1997). Notice from Table 1 that normality is rejected for both the income and the inflation residuals; although normality is restored when two outliers at 1979:III and 1979:IV are removed from the system (Ermini, 1997), the present study was conducted without outlier correction. Even if the rejection of normality invites some degree of caution in interpreting the results of seasonal cointegration, recall that the limit results of maximum likelihood inference hold as long as the residuals admit a central limit theorem in the sense of cumulative sums converging to Brownian motions.

It is worth noting that, although formal full-sample heteroskedasticity tests based on White (1980) are not rejected, a recursive estimation of the model revealed an apparent variance shift in the inflation residuals in mid-1973, i.e. in a period that coincides with the introduction of the value added tax (VAT) system in UK; although in the original DHSY model a dummy variable was added to account for this event, the introduction of an identical dummy variable in the SECM did not produce any noticeable effect on its stability.

4.2 Cointegration Rank Tests

Lee (1992) points out an important simplification in the conduct of the cointegration rank tests: as the regressors $Y_{j,t}$ are asymptotically uncorrelated in the sense that the probability limit of $T^{-1}\sum_{t=1}^{T} Y_{j,t} Y_{k,t}$ is zero, the maximum likelihood estimators of the cointegrating vectors and of the coefficients of adjustment at each frequency can be found by ignoring the constraint of reduced rank at the other frequencies, that is by concentrating out the associated regressors.

The cointegration rank tests at frequency zero and π are straightforward Johansen-type tests (see Lee, 1992) and thus do not require any detailed explanation. Table 2 reports the eigenvalues and the trace statistics for each rank at these two frequencies for the SECM (4.1) with $q = 3$, as well as the corresponding 5 percent level critical values, both asymptotic (Johansen, 1995) and for finite sample (Lee, 1992; Lee and Siklos, 1995); both sets of critical values are based on unrestricted seasonal dummies. From these results, we conclude that at the 5 percent level of significance there is no cointegrating relation at frequency zero and one relation at the bi-annual frequency π; the estimated cointegrating vector is

$$\hat{\beta}_2 = [1 \quad -4.3 \quad 20]'. \tag{4.3}$$

As anticipated in the introduction, the lack of cointegration at frequency zero is not surprising in light of life-cycle models, but a stable linear relation between consumption and current income at the semester seasonal may indicate a case of liquidity constraint in the consumer decision process, although the coefficients of the cointegrating vector (4.3) do not provide an immediate interpretation in this sense (see next paragraph for tests of linear restrictions).

Before proceeding to test for the cointegrating rank at the annual frequency $\pi/2$, we tested the hypothesis that the bi-annual seasonal dummy $(-1)^t$ is

Table 2. Seasonal cointegration analysis

Rank	Eigenvalues	Trace statistic	Asympt. crit. val.	Finite-sample crit. val.
(1) Frequency Zero (restricted trend)				
$r = 0$	0.1071	28.31	42.4	33.5
$r \leq 1$	0.0571	12.23	25.3	18.9
$r \leq 2$	0.0270	3.89	12.3	8.6
$r \leq 3$	0.0000	0.0000	—	—
(2) Frequency π (unrestricted seasonal dummy)				
$r = 0$	0.2007	49.21*	42.4	33.5
$r \leq 1$	0.0767	17.48	25.3	18.9
$r \leq 2$	0.0420	6.10	12.3	8.6

* denotes 5%-significance.

restricted to the cointegrating space at frequency π. This test is performed as a likelihood ratio test between the maximum likelihood obtained with unrestricted seasonal dummies, that is with the vectors $Y_{j,t}$ for $j = 2, 3, 4$ defined as in (2.7), against the maximum likelihood obtained by augmenting these vectors as in (4.2). It should be noticed that to perform this test we also restricted the annual seasonal dummies $\cos(t\pi/2)$ and $\sin(t\pi/2)$ to the seasonal cointegrating space at $\pi/2$. Following an argument similar to the one described in Johansen (1995) for the zero frequency, the test statistic for the restriction at the bi-annual frequency π can be shown to be:

$$-2\ln Q = -T \sum_{k=r_2+1}^{N} \left(\ln(1 - \lambda_{2,k}^r) - \ln(1 - \lambda_{2,k}) \right), \tag{4.4}$$

where $\lambda_{2,k}$ are the eigenvalues associated with vectors $Y_{j,t}$ defined as in (2.7), and $\lambda_{2,k}^r$ the restricted eigenvalues associated with vectors $Y_{j,t}$ defined as in (4.2). Johansen (1995) proves that for the zero frequency the asymptotic distribution of the statistic (4.4) is $\chi^2(N - r_1)$; although not proved here formally, the distribution $\chi^2(N - r_2)$ is presumed to hold for the frequency-π statistic as well. With a statistic $\chi^2(2) = 0.133$ (p-value $= 0.96$), one cannot reject the hypothesis that the seasonal dummy $(-1)^t$ is restricted to the cointegrating space at the bi-annual frequency π; the corresponding augmented cointegrating vector is estimated as:

$$\hat{\beta}_2 = [1 \quad -4.1 \quad 19.7 \quad 0.09]'; \tag{4.5}$$

note that the coefficients for consumption, income and inflation are quite similar to the unrestricted vector (4.3).

As regards the cointegration rank test at the frequency $\pi/2$, Johansen and Schaumburg (1997) show that the complex nature of cointegration at this frequency prevents the maximization of the loglikelihood function as an eigenvalue problem; as a useful alternative to keep the dimensionality of the maximization problem low, they propose the adoption of a switching algorithm. In the present study, however, given the low dimensionality of the system, we preferred to adopt a direct maximization of the loglikelihood function. It is useful to provide a few details on this procedure. Let R_{jt}, $j = 0$, $1, ..., 4$, be the OLS residuals of regressing $\Delta_4 X_t$ and $Y_{j,t-1}$, $j = 1, ..., 4$ on the lagged regressors $\Delta_4 X_{t-i}$, $i = 1, ..., q$, and on the unrestricted deterministic terms. Let $U_{0,t}$, $U_{3,t}^R$ and $U_{3,t}^I$ be the residuals of regressing $R_{0,t}$, $R_{3,t}$ and $R_{4,t}$ on $\{R_{1,t}, R_{2,t}\}$, respectively. Then, from (2.10) we have the equation:

$$U_{0,t} = 2(\alpha_3^R \beta_3^{R'} + \alpha_3^I \beta_3^{I'}) U_{3,t}^R + 2(\alpha_3^R \beta_3^{I'} - \alpha_3^I \beta_3^{R'}) U_{3,t}^I + u_t, \tag{4.6}$$

which can be rewritten more compactly as:

$$U_{0,t} = \tilde{\alpha}_3 \tilde{\beta}_3' \tilde{U}_{3,t} + u_t, \tag{4.7}$$

with

$$\tilde{\alpha}_3 = 2\begin{bmatrix} \alpha_3^R & -\alpha_3^I \end{bmatrix}, \quad \tilde{\beta}_3{}' = \begin{bmatrix} \beta_3^R & -\beta_3^I \\ \beta_3^I & \beta_3^R \end{bmatrix}, \quad \tilde{U}_{3,t} = \begin{bmatrix} U_{3,t}^R \\ U_{3,t}^I \end{bmatrix}; \tag{4.8}$$

notice that $\tilde{\alpha}_3$ and $\tilde{\beta}_3$ are $(2\ N)r_3$ and $(2\ N)(2\ r_3)$ matrices, respectively, r_3 being the cointegration rank at frequency $\pi/2$. Thus, upon defining the product moments $D_{00} = T^{-1}\sum_{t=1}^{T} U_{0,t}U_{0,t}'$, $D_{30} = T^{-1}\sum_{t=1}^{T}\tilde{U}_{3,t}U_{0,t}'$, and $D_{33} = T^{-1}\sum_{t=1}^{T}\tilde{U}_{3,t}\tilde{U}_{3,t}'$, the concentrated likelihood function can be written, apart from a constant factor, as:

$$L(\tilde{\beta}_3)^{-\frac{T}{2}} = |D_{00}|\frac{\left|\tilde{\beta}_3{}'(D_{33} - D_{30}D_{00}^{-1}D_{03})\tilde{\beta}_3\right|}{\left|\tilde{\beta}_3{}'D_{33}\tilde{\beta}_3\right|} \tag{4.9}$$

This function is maximized over the vector $[\beta_3^R\ \beta_3^I]'$, whose dimension is $2\,\mathrm{N}\,r_3$ (in our case, at most equal to 18).

Johansen and Schaumburg (1997) tabulate the asymptotic distribution of the likelihood ratio test statistic for the reduced rank hypothesis against the full rank alternative, for the following three cases: no deterministic terms in the model; both constant and seasonal dummies restricted (no trend); constant unrestricted and seasonal dummies restricted (no trend). As the critical values for the case when both the constant and the seasonal dummies are unrestricted are unavailable, for the present study we conducted the cointegration rank test at frequency $\pi/2$ by restricting the associated seasonal dummies to the seasonal cointegrating space; although this choice is somewhat arbitrary, some support for it may be lent by the previous result that the bi-annual seasonal dummy $(-1)^t$ is also restricted to the cointegrating space at frequency π. Thus table 3 of Johansen and Schaumburg (1997) offers the appropriate critical values for our study (recall also that the absence of cointegration at the zero frequency implies no restricted trend). The 5 percent level critical values from this table and the statistics of the cointegrating rank test at frequency $\pi/2$ are reported in Table 3.

Table 3. Seasonal cointegration analysis

Rank	Loglikelihood	LR test statistic	Asympt. crit. val.	Finite-sample crit. val.
(3) Frequency $\pi/2$ (restricted seasonal dummies)				
$r = 0$	1930.473	89.76	92.8	—
$r \leq 1$	1951.418	47.87	57.9	—
$r \leq 2$	1970.025	10.65	31.7	—
$r \leq 3$	1975.352	0.00	13.5	—

* denotes 5%-significance.

As the hypothesis $r = 0$ is not rejected at the 5 percent level of significance, we conclude that there is no cointegrating relation of the annual frequency $\pi/2$.

4.3 Testing Linear Restrictions on Cointegrating Vectors

Linear restrictions on the parameters of the cointegrating vectors for the two frequencies 0 and π can be tested by following the standard eigenvalue-based procedures for non-seasonal cointegration developed by Johansen and Juselius (1990, 1992) (see also Johansen, 1995, for a comprehensive treatment); linear restrictions on the parameters of the cointegrating vector at frequency $\pi/2$, instead, can be tested by directly calculating the likelihood ratio statistics from (4.9). Given the cointegration results of the previous section, linear restrictions were tested only on the cointegrating vector (4.5).

With a statistic $\chi^2(1) = 0.54$ (p-value $= 0.46$) we cannot reject the hypothesis that consumption and income enter the cointegrating vector at this frequency with coefficients 1 and -1, respectively; that is, the hypothesis $\beta_2 = [1 \ -1 \ * \ *]$. Under this hypothesis the restricted cointegrating vector becomes:

$$\hat{\beta}_2 = [1 \quad -1 \quad 4.7 \quad 0.036]' \tag{4.10}$$

However, with a statistic $\chi^2(2) = 32.79$ (p-value $= 0.00$) we do reject the hypothesis $\beta_2 = [1 \ -1 \ 0 \ 0]'$, i.e. the joint hypothesis that both inflation and the seasonal dummy $(-1)^t$ are absent from the cointegrating space at the bi-annual frequency. Furthermore, with a statistic $\chi^2(1) = 45.74$ (p-value $= 0.00$) we also reject the hypothesis $\beta_2 = [1 \ -1 \ * \ 0]'$, i.e. the hypothesis that only the seasonal dummy $(-1)^t$ is absent from the cointegrating space at the bi-annual frequency. The latter statistic was directly obtained as the ratio of the log-likelihood corresponding to the restriction $\beta_2 = [1 \ -1 \ * \ *]$ ($= 1966.74$) to the loglikelihood corresponding to the restriction $\beta_2 = [1 \ -1 \ *]$ in the SECM model with *no unrestricted* seasonal dummies ($= 1943.87$).

5 Testing DHSY Restrictions

As a result of the seasonal cointegration analysis of the previous section, we obtain a SECM characterized by the following features: unrestricted constant; no error-corrector terms at both the frequency zero and $\pi/2$; one-dimensional error-corrector term at frequency π, which includes the seasonal dummy $(-1)^t$. Upon endorsing the restriction that consumption and income appear in this cointegrating vector with coefficients 1 and -1, respectively, this error-corrector term is calculated on the basis of the estimate (4.10) of the cointegrating vector. These features are summarized in the seasonal model:

$$\Delta_4 X_t = \sum_{k=1}^{3} D_k \Delta_4 X_{t-k} + \alpha_2 \zeta_{2,t-1} + \mu + \varepsilon_t, \tag{5.1}$$

where μ is a vector of constant terms, and where

$$\zeta_{2,t} = Z_{2,t}^c - Z_{2,t}^i + 4.7 Z_{2,t}^{\Delta p} + 0.036(-1)^t. \tag{5.2}$$

It is worth noting that the error-corrector $\zeta_{2,t}$ has no unit-circle roots, is serially correlated, and exhibits a significant cluster of volatility (an ARCH test applied to the residuals of an AR(5) model for $\zeta_{2,t}$ yielded the statistic $F(4,126) = 2.88 \, [0.025]$; for more details, see Ermini, 1997). As already anticipated, the interpretation of these results in economic terms, and particularly of the time series properties of $\zeta_{2,t}$, are beyond the scope of this study.

The estimate of the SECM (5.1) is reported in Table 4, and the corresponding conditional model of consumption (see (3.10)) is reported in Table 5; for comparison, Table 6 reports DHSY model (3.2) (constant included) estimated with the same sample used for the SECM. All tables also report the relevant diagnostics.

A few comments on these results model are: (i) the original DHSY model (3.2) does not contain seasonal dummies, while our previous analysis reveals the presence of the seasonal dummy $(-1)^t$ restricted to the seasonal cointegrating space at frequency π; (ii) in the DHSY model the constant is insignificant when the error-corrector $i_{t-4} - c_{t-4}$ is included; (iii) the SECM model of Table 4 exhibits serial correlation of residuals, perhaps as a result of having eliminated from its final parameterization other possibly stationary error-correctors than $\zeta_{2,t}$ (in particular, note that the cointegration rank test at frequency $\pi/2$ is borderline); (iv) overall the SECM model appears to be stable, as White (1980) heteroskedasticity tests are not rejected; (v) by comparing

Table 4. Estimate of SECM (5.1) (s.e. in parentheses)

	$\Delta_4 c_t$	$\Delta_4 i_t$	$\Delta_4 \Delta p_t$		$\Delta_4 c_t$	$\Delta_4 i_t$	$\Delta_4 \Delta p_t$
$\Delta_4 c_{t-1}$	0.657	0.492	0.193	$\Delta_4 c_{t-2}$	0.334	0.513	−0.197
	(0.111)	(0.191)	(0.099)		(0.131)	(0.226)	(0.101)
$\Delta_4 c_{t-3}$	−0.042	−0.502	−0.037	$\Delta_4 i_{t-1}$	0.095	0.380	0.113
	(0.112)	(0.194)	(0.101)		(0.058)	(0.100)	(0.052)
$\Delta_4 i_{t-2}$	−0.167	0.049	0.031	$\Delta_4 i_{t-3}$	−0.048	−0.062	0.075
	(0.064)	(0.110)	(0.057)		(0.062)	(0.107)	(0.055)
$\Delta_4 \Delta p_{t-1}$	−0.005	0.056	0.053	$\Delta_4 \Delta p_{t-2}$	−0.063	−0.052	0.224
	(0.108)	(0.186)	(0.096)		(0.107)	(0.184)	(0.096)
$\Delta_4 \Delta p_{t-3}$	−0.034	0.309	−0.028	$\zeta_{2,t-1}$	0.196	0.335	−0.351
	(0.083)	(0.143)	(0.074)		(0.066)	(0.115)	(0.060)
Constant	0.004	0.005	−0.004	equat. s.e	0.0113	0.0195	0.0101
	(0.002)	(0.003)	(0.001)				
AR(1–5) $F(5, 126)$	2.286	4.260	5.255	Normal. $\chi^2(2)$	5.006	2.021	12.023
	[0.050]	[0.001]	[0.000]		[0.082]	[0.364]	[0.002]
ARCH 4 $F(4, 123)$	0.280	0.911	4.540	$Xi^2 \, F(20, 110)$	1.206	1.658	0.970
	[0.891]	[0.460]	[0.002]		[0.263]	[0.052]	[0.504]

Table 5. Conditional model of consumption, $\Delta_4 c_t$ (s.e. in parentheses)

Constant	0.0014	$\Delta_4 i_t$	0.248	$\Delta_4 p_t$	−0.365
	(0.001)		(0.043)		(0.082)
$\Delta_4 c_{t-1}$	0.606	$\Delta_4 c_{t-2}$	0.135	$\Delta_4 c_{t-3}$	0.069
	(0.093)		(0.107)		(0.092)
$\Delta_4 i_{t-1}$	0.042	$\Delta_4 i_{t-2}$	−0.170	$\Delta_4 i_{t-3}$	−0.006
	(0.051)		(0.051)		(0.050)
$\Delta_4 \Delta p_{t-1}$	0.0005	$\Delta_4 \Delta p_{t-2}$	0.031	$\Delta_4 \Delta p_{t-3}$	−0.121
	(0.086)		(0.087)		(0.067)
$\zeta_{2,t-1}$	−0.015	equat. s.e.	0.090	R^2	0.833
	(0.060)				
AR(1–5) $F(5, 124)$	2.581	Normal. $\chi^2(2)$	2.100	ARCH 4 $F(4, 121)$	1.009
	[0.030]		[0.350]		[0.406]
$Xi^2 F(24, 104)$	1.468				
	[0.096]				

Table 6. DHSY model of consumption, $\Delta_4 c_t$ (s.e. in parentheses)

Constant	0.0050	$\Delta_4 i_t$	0.566	$\Delta_4 p_t$	−0.122
	(0.004)		(0.041)		(0.025)
$\Delta \Delta_4 i_t$	−0.21	$\Delta \Delta_4 p_t$	−0.162	$i_{t-4} - c_{t-4}$	−0.070
	(0.052)		(0.087)		(0.024)
equat. s.e.	0.012	R^2	0.704		
AR(1–5) $F(5, 131)$	18.742	Normal. $\chi^2(2)$	0.368	ARCH 4 $F(4, 128)$	16.01
	[0.000]		[0.832]		[0.000]
$Xi^2 F(10, 125)$	1.813				
	[0.065]				

the R^2 and the equation standard error of the conditional model and of the DHSY model, the former appears to be a superior model; (vi) the residuals of both the single-equation models exhibit significant autocorrelation, but only DHSY residuals fail the ARCH test. The actual values of these residuals, together with their sample autocorrelations and spectra, are reported in Figure 2.

As regards testing the DHSY restrictions outlined in Section 3 by means of the SECM of Table 4, the following results were obtained.

(a) *Long-Run Strong Exogeneity of Income and Inflation*: as there is no error-correction at frequency zero and $\pi/2$, the restrictions (3.15) for the long-run strong exogeneity of income and inflation in the conditional model of consumption reduce to $\alpha_{2,i} = \alpha_{2,\Delta p} = 0$. The joint test of these two zero restrictions yielded a statistic $\chi^2(2) = 35.99$ (p-value $= 0.00$), and thus we reject the hypothesis that income and inflation are long-run strongly exogenous for consumption. It follows that the DHSY single-equation approach is inefficient, in that the marginal model of income and inflation contains useful information that is not taken into account in estimating the parameters of the consumption

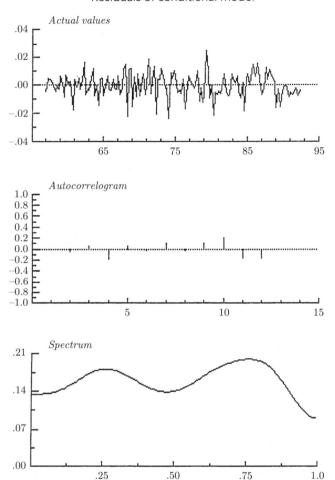

Figure 2. Sample properties of residuals

equation. It is fair to note that the original formulation of DHSY is of vintage 1978 and therefore its authors cannot be faulted for not taking into account concepts that were developed later (particularly, the notion of exogeneity as in Engle *et al.*, 1983); nonetheless, it is surprising that the issue of exogeneity of the explanatory variables in DHSY has not been addressed in more recent re-estimations of the model.

(b) *Stationary Inflation*: as explained in Section 3, DHSY imposes the restriction that inflation is stationary. Our findings, based on two related tests, contradict this assumption; more specifically: (i) as discussed in note 1, we

Residuals of DHSY model

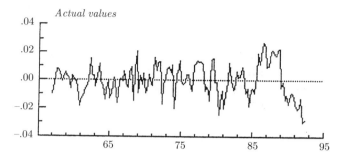

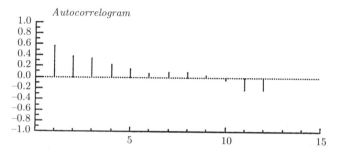

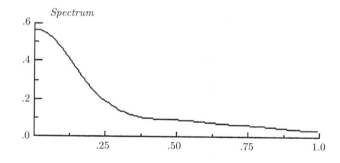

Figure 2. (*cont.*)

cannot reject the unit-root hypothesis for inflation based on a Dickey–Fuller test; (ii) as there is no cointegration at frequency zero, the system has no stationary components at the zero frequency. It might be argued that both the Dickey–Fuller and the Johansen tests have low power, or that the apparent shift in the inflation variance in mid-1973 (recall the comment in Section 4.1) is likely to bias these tests toward non-rejection. In any event, as mentioned in the introduction, a more accurate modeling of inflation might lead to improved SECM models, and thus to a better understanding of the long-run interactions between consumption, income, and inflation.

(c) *Full Cointegration*: as explained in Section 3, DHSY imposes on the trivariate system the full cointegrating vector $\beta_F = [1\ -1\ 0]'$ with coefficient of adjustment defined as in (3.18); this assumption, however, is contradicted by the lack of cointegration at both frequencies zero and $\pi/2$, as established in Section 4.2. Given the low power of seasonal cointegration analysis, one could conduct an alternative, more direct test of the full cointegration hypothesis as a likelihood ratio test between the unrestricted SECM (5.1) of Table 4 and the SECM restricted to full cointegration, i.e.

$$\Delta_4 X_t = \sum_{k=1}^{3} D_k \Delta_4 X_{t-k} + \alpha(c_{t-4} - i_{t-4}) + \mu + \varepsilon_t. \tag{5.3}$$

However, as (5.3) is not nested in (5.1), and as the non-standard distribution of the associated test statistic is unavailable, we chose to test the full-cointegration hypothesis by testing both (5.1) and (5.3) against the following encompassing SECM:

$$\Delta_4 X_t = \sum_{k=1}^{3} D_k \Delta_4 X_{t-k} + \alpha_2 \zeta_{2,t-1} + \alpha(c_{t-4} - i_{t-4}) + \mu + \varepsilon_t. \tag{5.4}$$

With a statistic $\chi^2(3) = 5.53$ (p-value $= 0.14$) we cannot reject the SECM (5.1) against the encompassing SECM (5.4); but with a statistic $\chi^2(3) = 35.27$ (p-value $= 0.00$) we strongly reject the restricted SECM (5.3) against the encompassing model. Thus, overall the full cointegration hypothesis is rejected. Recall that DHSY restriction is stronger than full-cointegration, as it also implies the absence of inflation from the full cointegrating vector. One interpretation of this rejection is that, by including the error-correction term $i_{t-4} - c_{t-4}$ into the DHSY model, its authors presumed more stationary components in the system than were apparently warranted by the data.

6 Conclusions

The arguments presented in the previous section provide enough evidence to conclude that DHSY, as a restricted version of the conditional model of consumption corresponding to the SECM developed in Section 4, is rejected against the latter, for the following main reasons: (i) inflation is not stationary; (ii) full cointegration is rejected; (iii) there exists a significant seasonal dummy, restricted to the seasonal cointegrating space at frequency π; (iv) inflation is present in the cointegrating relation. As the seasonally cointegrated model combines a number of important new ideas and appeared in the analysis of time series after DHSY was developed (particularly cointegration theory), rather than diminishing its importance among older studies of UK consumption, DHSY rejection should be interpreted as an indirect tribute to the advances made in econometric modeling in the last fifteen years, particularly in relation to integrated processes.

DHSY restrictions were tested on the basis of a satisfactory, albeit preliminary, model of the seasonal cointegration structure of the trivariate system consumption–income–inflation for the UK. Possible directions for further improvement are: (i) a better understanding of the interplay between deterministic terms, cointegrating ranks, and restrictions of the trend and seasonal dummies to the cointegrating spaces; (ii) testing of specific linear restrictions on the seasonal cointegrating vectors to investigate issues of economic theory, particularly the presence of liquidity constraint in consumption decisions; (iii) the extension of the seasonal cointegration analysis to a four-variable system (for example, by adding wealth), or bigger; (iv) a more accurate modeling of inflation, particularly in relation to its apparent variance shift in the early 1980s. Further investigations in these directions will quite possibly lead to more accurate seasonally cointegrated models; nonetheless, the rejection of DHSY against SECM as presented here would still hold when compared to better models.

Notes

1. A Dickey–Fuller (1981) test on $\Delta_4 p_t$ with constant does not reject the presence of a unit root at frequency zero with an adjusted t-statistic of -1.778 at lag 4 and of -2.272 at lag 5, against a 5 percent critical value of -2.882. A Dickey–Fuller test on the first-differences of $\Delta_4 p_t$ with constant rejects the unit root at frequency zero with an adjusted t-statistic of -7.571 at lag 3 and -4.9 at lag 4, against an identical critical value.
2. As in HEGY, several tests were performed, corresponding to the case of (i) no constant, no trend and no seasonal dummies; (ii) constant only; (iii) constant and trend only; (iv) constant, trend and seasonal dummies; (v) constant and seasonal dummies only. Our findings contrast with HEGY findings of unit-circle roots at 0 and π for both consumption and income but at $\pi/2$ for consumption only (HEGY does not study the price series); note however that HEGY investigates a shorter sample (55:2–84:4 as opposed to 55:2–92:2 here).

References

Davidson, J. H. E., D. F. Hendry, F. Srba, and S. Yeo (1978), "Econometric Modelling of the Aggregate Time-series Relationship between Consumers' Expenditures and Income in the United Kingdom," *Economic Journal*, 88: 661–92.

Dickey, D. A. and W. A. Fuller (1981), "Likelihood Ratio Statistics for Autoregressive Time Series with a Unit Root," *Econometrica*, 49: 1057–72.

Doornik, J. A. and H. Hansen (1994), "A Practical Test of Multivariate Normality," Nuffield College.

Doornik, J. A. and D. F. Hendry (1994), *PcFiml 8.0: Interactive Econometric Modelling of Dynamic Systems*. London: International Thomson Publishing.

Engle, R. F. (1982), "Autoregressive Conditional Heteroskedasticity, with Estimates of the Variance of United Kingdom Inflations," *Econometrica*, 50: 987–1007.

Engle, R. F., and C. W. J. Granger (1987), "Cointegration and Error-Correction: Representation, Estimation and Testing," *Econometrica*, 55: 251–76.

Engle, R. F., D. F. Hendry, and J. F. Richard (1983), "Exogeneity," *Econometrica*, 51: 277–304.

Ermini, L. (1997), "A Seasonal Cointegration Analysis of the UK Consumption Function," working paper.

Ermini, L. (1998), "Empirical Macroeconomic Modelling," manuscript.

Ermini, L. and D. Chang (1996), "Testing the Joint Hypothesis of Rationality and Neutrality under Seasonal Cointegration: The Case of Korea," *Journal of Econometrics*, 74: 363–86.

Franses, P. H. (1996), *Periodicity and Stochastic Trends in Economic Time Series*. Oxford: Oxford University Press.

Granger, C. W. J. (1986), "Developments in the Study of Cointegrated Economic Variables," *Oxford Bulletin of Economics and Statistics*, 48: 213–28.

Granger, C. W. J. and T.-H. Lee (1991), "Multicointegration," in R. F. Engle and C. W. J. Granger (eds.), *Long-Run Economic Relationships*. Oxford: Oxford University Press.

Hendry, D. F. (1994), "HUS Revisited," *Oxford Review of Economic Policy*, 10/2: 86–106.

Hendry, D. F., J. Muellbauer, and A. Murphy (1990), "The Econometrics of DHSY," in J. D. Hey and D. Winch (eds.), *A Century of Economics: 100 Years of the Royal Economic Society and the Economic Journal*. Oxford: Basil Blackwell, pp. 298–334.

Hylleberg, S., R. F. Engle, C. W. J. Granger, and B. S. Yoo (1990), "Seasonal Integration and Cointegration," *Journal of Econometrics*, 44: 215–38.

Johansen, S. (1992), "Testing Weak Exogeneity and the Order of Cointegration in UK Money Demand Data," *Journal of Policy Modelling*, 14: 313–35.

Johansen, S. (1995), *Likelihood-Based Inference on Cointegrated Vector Autoregressive Models*. Oxford: Oxford University Press.

Johansen, S. and K. Juselius (1990), "Maximum Likelihood Estimation and Inference on Cointegration—with Applications to the Demand for Money," *Oxford Bulletin of Economics and Statistics*, 52: 169–210.

Johansen, S. and K. Juselius (1992), "Testing Structural Hypotheses in a Multivariate Cointegration Analysis of the PPP and the UIP for UK," *Journal of Econometrics*, 53: 211–44.

Johansen, S. and E. Schaumburg (1997), "Likelihood Analysis of Seasonal Cointegration," manuscript.

Lee, H. S. (1992), "Maximum Likelihood Inference on Cointegration and Seasonal Cointegration," *Journal of Econometrics*, 54: 1–47.

Lee, H. S. and P. L. Siklos (1995), "A Note on the Critical Values for the Maximum Likelihood (Seasonal) Cointegration Tests," *Economic Letters*, 49/2: 137–45.

Lee, H. S. and P. L. Siklos (1997), "The Role of Seasonality in Economic Time Series: Reinterpreting Money–Output Causality in US Data," *International Journal of Forecasting*, 13/3: 381–91.

Muellbauer, J. (1994), "The Assessment: Consumer Expenditures," *Oxford Review of Economic Policy*, 10/2: 1–41.

Phillips, A. W. (1954), "Stabilisation Policy in a Closed Economy," *Economic Journal*, 64: 290–323.

White, H. (1980), "A Heteroskedastic-Consistent Covariance Matrix Estimator and a Direct Test for Heteroskedasticity," *Econometrica*, 48: 817–38.

11
A Unit Root Test in the Presence of Structural Changes in I(1) and I(0) Models

MICHIO HATANAKA AND KAZUO YAMADA

1 Introduction

In the unit root literature on structural changes of deterministic trends the changes are admitted *either* in I(0) models only, as in Zivot and Andrews (1992), *or* in both I(1) and I(0) models, as in Perron (1989). However, in Perron (1989) the break fractions (T_B/T) are specified outside the inference on the unit root, while the fractions are regarded as unknown parameters inside the inference in Zivot and Andrews (1992). Vogelsang and Perron (1994) compare the correctly and incorrectly specified break fractions that enter into both I(1) and I(0) models, and point out the inapplicability of Zivot and Andrews' procedure to such models. In the present paper we shall admit the structural changes in both I(1) and I(0) models, while incorporating the inference on the break fractions within the unit root test.

We have been motivated by analyses of Japanese macroeconomic data. Figure 1 shows logs of real GDP, seasonally adjusted, in Japan, the UK and the USA for the period since 1957.[1] A linear trend is fitted in each. It appears that simple linear trends with no breaks fit well to the UK and US data. As for Japan the differences between the data and the linear trend lack the regular oscillations to allow them to be described as business cycles. Indeed the common opinion among macroeconomists is that structural changes in growth rates possibly occurred in two steps, one about 1971–73, and the other about 1991. The first break is said to have occurred prior to the oil price crises, the validity of which is important for theoretical and empirical investigations on growth rates. A model of trends with breaks is fitted in Figure 1, and the

The authors are grateful to two anonymous referees of the Festschrift for their advice on revisions, and to Naoto Kunitomo (University of Tokyo), Kimio Morimune (Kyoto University) and Hidetaka Ohara (Meiji University), who have provided important suggestions in developing the present study. Sections 2 and 3 of the paper were presented at a conference of Institute of Statistical Mathematics (Tokyo) in November, 1996.

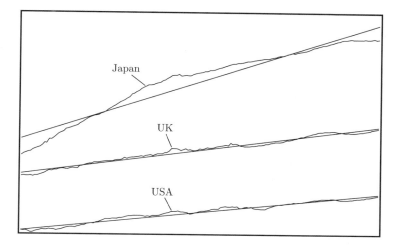

Figure 1. ln real GDP, 1957–1995

difference between the data and the trend involves more oscillations than in the earlier case where a simple linear trend is fitted.

In the unit root test on the Japanese GDP data it is necessary to allow the presence of structural changes in both I(1) and I(0) models. In selecting the break *point*, T_B, visual inspections introduce arbitrariness in the inference. The break *fraction*, T_B/T, should be treated as an unknown, nuisance parameter in the inference on the unit root. This is a problem that has not been dealt with in the literature.[2]

The following points will be made in the present paper.

(a) Alternative selection of a break fraction in the Dickey–Fuller OLS entails different constructions of independent variables. On the other hand, in most of the econometric literature on structural changes outside the unit root field, it is the regression coefficients rather than the independent variables that are affected when the break fraction is altered. The inference methods developed there may not work in the choice of a break fraction in the context of the unit root test. The inapplicability of Zivot and Andrews' method is an example of such failure.

(b) Assuming I(0) models, Bai and Perron (1998) made exceedingly comprehensive analyses of structural change in the sense of coefficient changes. The break fractions as well as the number of breaks are unknown parameters. Given the number of breaks, they estimate the break fractions by minimizing s^2. The present paper will show that this strategy *does* work in the unit root test. *If the number of breaks is given*, minimizing s^2 in the Dickey–Fuller OLS produces T-consistent estimators of break fractions, and as a result a usual consistent test is available for the unit root test, treating estimates of break *fractions* as though they were true values, and using the standard tables based

on functionals of the Wiener process. The estimates of break *points* should
have no biases.

(c) However this asymptotic test is not useful for the analyses of Japanese
GDP data. Models are constructed so that realizations of their observable
variables with $T = 150$ mimic the Japanese GDP data. The estimates of break
points have remarkable, negative biases, and the finite sample distributions
of test statistics seriously deviate from the limit distributions especially in their
tails. Our simulation studies indicate that the biases of break points estimates
being negative seem to be a finite sample property of s^2 in the OLS on the
Cochrane–Orcutt transformed variables, which is a common device in the regression with a stationary autoregressive disturbance. How to remove the biases
is an important task of future research.

(d) A logically rigorous procedure for the determination of the number of
break points does not appear to be straightforward in the framework of the
unit root test, but some practical methods can be proposed.

The plan of the paper is to present the above four points in order in Sections
2, 3, 4, and 5. Section 2 also explains our notation and models as well as a
summary of well known results.

2 Dickey–Fuller Tests with Breaks in Deterministic Trends

Other than in the last section of the paper, we shall assume that the number
of breaks is given. It is 2 in the following analysis, for the reason that it is
likely to be 2 in Japanese GDP data.

Let λ_1 and λ_2, $\lambda_1 < \lambda_2$, be real numbers in $(0, 1)$. The sample period, $1, \cdots,$
T, is divided into:

$$R_0 = \{t; 1 \leq t \leq [T\lambda_1]\}$$
$$R_1 = \{t; [T\lambda_1] < t \leq [T\lambda_2]\}$$
$$R_2 = \{t; [T\lambda_2] < t \leq T\},$$

where $[\ ]$ designates the integer part. $\lambda = [\lambda_1, \lambda_2]$ is called (the vector of) break
fractions. It is a parameter of our model. Even though it is a nuisance para-
meter in the unit root test, macroeconomists are interested in their estimates
just as much as in the integration order.

Let $T_i = [T\lambda_i]$, $i = 1, 2$. $T_* = [T_1, T_2]$ is called (the vector of) break points.
Let

$$dt(t, \lambda_1) = \begin{cases} 0 & \text{if } t \in R_0 \\ t - T_1 & \text{if } t \in R_1 \text{ or } R_2 \end{cases}$$

$$dt(t, \lambda_2) = \begin{cases} 0 & \text{if } t \in R_0 \text{ or } R_1 \\ t - T_2 & \text{if } t \in R_2. \end{cases}$$

Our model of the deterministic trend is

$$dt = \beta_1 + \beta_2 t + \gamma_1 dt(t, \lambda_1) + \gamma_2 dt(t, \lambda_2), \quad t = 1, \cdots, T, \tag{1}$$

i.e., a splined linear function of time.

Note that intercept shifts are not included in (1). The intercept is asymptotically unidentified in I(1) models, though identified in I(0) models. See Hatanaka (1996, pp. 75–6). The breaks on the intercept cannot be considered in the following asymptotic inference.

A scalar, time series $\{x_t\}$ is given by

$$x_t = d_t + u_t, \tag{2}$$

and $\{u_t\}$ is a possibly nonstationary autoregressive process,

$$(1 - a_1 L - \cdots - a_p L^p)u_t = \varepsilon_t, \tag{3}$$

where L is the lag operator and $\{\varepsilon_t\}$ is a white noise process with $E(\varepsilon_t) = 0$ and $E(\varepsilon_t^2) = \sigma_\varepsilon^2$. It is assumed in the proofs of the Mathematical Appendix that ε_t has a continuous distribution symmetric about zero, and $E(\varepsilon_t^4)$ exists. We shall not consider generalizations of (3) such as ARIMA models[3] and nonparametric model specifications. Moreover we shall assume that p in (3) is a priori known. Thereby we concentrate our attention on breaks in deterministic trends.

To construct the Dickey–Fuller equation the parameter $(a_1, \cdots, a_p)$ is reparameterized into $(\alpha, b_1, \cdots, b_{p-1})$ through

$$1 - a_1 L - \cdots - a_p L^p = (1 - L) - \alpha L - (1 - L)(b_1 L + \cdots + b_{p-1} L^{p-1}). \tag{4}$$

Indeed $\alpha = -(1 - a_1 - \cdots - a_p)$.

Concerning the characteristic equation that corresponds to $1 - a_1 L - \cdots - a_p L^p$, assume that it has stable (i.e. lying outside the unit circle) or real unit roots only, and also that it does not have double or more unit roots. It should be noted first that if the equation has one unit root, then $\alpha = 0$, and (3) is written as

$$(1 - b_1 L - \cdots - b_{p-1} L^{p-1})\Delta u_t = \varepsilon_t, \tag{5}$$

which defines a stationary $AR(p - 1)$ for $\{\Delta u_t\}$. Secondly, if all the roots are stable, (3) defines a stationary $AR(p)$ for $\{u_t\}$. It can be shown that $\alpha < 0$ in this case. The unit root test is to test for the presence against the absence of unit root in the characteristic equation.

From (2) and (3) it follows that

$$(1 - a_1 L - \cdots - a_p L^p)(x_t - d_t) = \varepsilon_t. \tag{6}$$

Other than in the last section of the paper our modeling of deterministic trend, (1), is given independently of integration orders of $\{u_t\}$; in particular I(1) and I(0) models share the same number and the same locations of break points.

Let

$$du(t, \lambda_1) = \Delta dt(t, \lambda_1) = \begin{cases} 0 & \text{if } t \in R_0 \\ 1 & \text{if } t \in R_1 \text{ or } R_2 \end{cases}$$

$$du(t, \lambda_2) = \Delta dt(t, \lambda_2) = \begin{cases} 0 & \text{if } t \in R_0 \text{ or } R_1 \\ 1 & \text{if } t \in R_2 \end{cases}$$

Ignoring some second order differences of d_t that appear when $p > 1$, it follows from (1), (4), and (6) that

$$\begin{aligned} \Delta x_t &\approx \mu_0 + \mu_1 du(t, \lambda_1) + \mu_2 du(t, \lambda_2) + \delta_0 t + \delta_1 dt(t, \lambda_1) + \delta_2 dt(t, \lambda_2) \\ &\quad + \alpha x_{t-1} + b_1 \Delta x_{t-1} + \cdots + b_{p-1} \Delta x_{t-p+1} + \varepsilon_t. \end{aligned} \tag{7}$$

The parameters in (7), μ_0, μ_1, μ_2, δ_0, δ_1, δ_2 and α can be expressed in terms of $\beta_1, \beta_2, \gamma_1, \gamma_2, a_1, \cdots, a_p$. Only two points in this relation deserve our attention. (a) If $(a_1, \cdots, a_p)$ is such that $\{u_t\}$ is I(1), then we have $\alpha = \delta_0 = \delta_1 = \delta_2 = 0$. (b) If $\gamma_i \neq 0$, then $\mu_i \neq 0$, $i = 1, 2$, regardless of the integration order of $\{u_t\}$ except in the case where $a_1 = \cdots = a_p = 0$.[4] (7) is called the Dickey–Fuller equation.

We wish to test the null hypothesis that $\{u_t\}$ is I(1), i.e., $\alpha = \delta_0 = \delta_1 = \delta_2 = 0$, against the alternative hypothesis that $\{u_t\}$ is I(0). All parameters other than α, δ_0, δ_1, and δ_2 are nuisance parameters. They include break fractions, $\lambda = [\lambda_1, \lambda_2]$.

If the break fractions *were* known, the hypothesis testing could be performed in the OLS along (7). Since the break fractions are in fact not known, we cannot even construct $du(t, \lambda_1)$, $du(t, \lambda_2)$, $dt(t, \lambda_1)$, $dt(t, \lambda_2)$, which are a part of independent variables in the OLS. In this respect *the present model differs from most of those in the econometric literature of structural changes*. In the latter the values of independent variables are not affected by structural changes. It is the regression coefficients that are affected by regime shifts.

The OLS with *hypothetically* given $\lambda = [\lambda_1, \lambda_2]$ turns out to be useful as a component in the inference procedure to be given below. The OLS uses

$$\begin{aligned} &\Delta x = [\Delta x_{p+1}, \cdots, \Delta x_t]', \quad \iota = [1, \cdots, 1]', \\ &t = [p+1, \cdots, T]', \quad x_{-1} = [x_p, \cdots, x_{T-1}]', \\ &du(\lambda_i) = [du(p+1, \lambda_i), \cdots, du(T, \lambda_i)]', \quad i = 1, 2 \\ &dt(\lambda_i) = [dt(p+1, \lambda_i), \cdots, dt(T, \lambda_i)]', \quad i = 1, 2 \\ &du(\lambda) = [du(\lambda_1), du(\lambda_2)], \quad ((T-p) \times 2) \\ &dt(\lambda) = [dt(\lambda_1), dt(\lambda_2)], \quad ((T-p) \times 2) \\ &\Delta x_{-j} = [\Delta x_{p+1-j}, \cdots, \Delta x_{T-j}]', \quad j = 1, \cdots, (p-1) \\ &X(\lambda) = [\iota, t, x_{-1}, du(\lambda), dt(\lambda), \Delta x_{-1}, \cdots, \Delta x_{-p+1}] \\ &X_1(\lambda) = [\iota, t, du(\lambda), dt(\lambda), \Delta x_{-1}, \cdots, \Delta x_{-p+1}] \\ &X_2(\lambda) = [\iota, du(\lambda), \Delta x_{-1}, \cdots, \Delta x_{-p+1}]. \end{aligned}$$

Let $P(\cdot)$ be the projection matrix of the matrix in ( ). Then

$$s^2(\lambda) = (T-p)^{-1}\Delta x'(I - P(X(\lambda)))\Delta x. \tag{8}$$

The t-statistic to test $\alpha = 0$ is

$$\hat{t}_\alpha(\lambda) = s^2(\lambda)^{-\frac{1}{2}}(x'_{-1}(I - P(X_1(\lambda)))x_{-1})^{-\frac{1}{2}}(x'_{-1}(I - P(X_1(\lambda)))\Delta x, \tag{9}$$

and the F-statistic to test $\alpha = \delta_0 = \delta_1 = \delta_2 = 0$ is given by

$$4F(\lambda) = (s^2(\lambda))^{-1}\Delta x'(P(X(\lambda)) - P(X_2(\lambda)))\Delta x. \tag{10}$$

The case where the true break fractions are a priori known has been treated in the literature such as Perron (1989), Hatanaka (1996), and Kunitomo (1996). Some of the results are summarily given here as they are used in the following explanations. The true values of parameters will be denoted by a $^-$ on top. The true break fractions are $\bar\lambda$. From (1) and (2):

$$x_t = \bar\beta_1 + \bar\beta_2 t + \bar\gamma_1 dt(t, \bar\lambda_1) + \bar\gamma_2 dt(t, \bar\lambda_2) + u_t.$$

Writing $u_{-1} = [u_p, \cdots, u_{T-1}]'$, $\Delta u = [\Delta u_{p+1}, \cdots, \Delta u_T]'$, $\gamma = [\gamma_1, \gamma_2]'$, the data generation equations of x_{-1} and Δx are given by:

$$x_{-1} = (\bar\beta_1 - \bar\beta_2)\iota + \bar\beta_2 t - du(\bar\lambda)\bar\gamma + dt(\bar\lambda)\bar\gamma + u_{-1} \tag{11}$$
$$\Delta x = \bar\beta_2 \iota + du(\bar\lambda)\bar\gamma + \Delta u. \tag{12}$$

Replace λ by $\bar\lambda$ in (8), (9), and (10) and substitute (11) and (12) in them. The asymptotic analysis of $s^2(\bar\lambda)$, $\hat{t}_\alpha(\bar\lambda)$, and $4F(\bar\lambda)$ produces the following results when $\{u_t\}$ is I(1). Initially

$$\text{plim } s_2(\bar\lambda) = \sigma_\varepsilon^2. \tag{13}$$

Then construct functions of $r \in [0, 1]$ as follows.

$$du(r, \lambda_i) = \begin{cases} 0 & \text{if } 0 \le r \le \lambda_i \\ 1 & \text{if } \lambda_i < r \le 1 \end{cases} \quad i = 1, 2$$

$$dt(r, \lambda_i) = \begin{cases} 0 & \text{if } 0 \le r \le \lambda_i \\ r - \lambda_i & \text{if } \lambda_i < r \le 1 \end{cases} \quad i = 1, 2$$

$$du(r, \lambda) = [du(r, \lambda_1), du(r, \lambda_2)], \quad dt(r, \lambda) = [dt(r, \lambda_1), dt(r, \lambda_2)],$$
$$a(r, \lambda) = [1, r, du(r, \lambda), dt(r, \lambda)]'.$$

Let $w(r)$ be the standard scalar Wiener process, and let $b_{wa}(r, \lambda)$ be the part of $w(r)$ orthogonal to $a(r, \lambda)$, i.e.,

$$b_{wa}(r, \lambda) = w(r) - \int_0^1 w(r)a(r, \lambda)' dr (\int_0^1 a(r, \lambda)a(r, \lambda)' dr)^{-1} a(r, \lambda). \tag{14}$$

A well known result is that

$$\hat{t}_\alpha(\overline{\lambda}) \xrightarrow{D} (\int_0^1 b_{wa}(r,\overline{\lambda})^2 dr)^{-\frac{1}{2}} \int_0^1 b_{wa}(r,\overline{\lambda})dw(r). \tag{15}$$

Moreover let

$$m(r,\lambda) = [r, dt(r,\lambda), w(r)]', \quad l(r,\lambda) = [1, du(r,\lambda)]', \tag{16}$$

and let $b_{ml}(r, \lambda)$ be the part of $m(r, \lambda)$ orthogonal to $l(r, \lambda)$,

$$b_{ml}(r,\lambda) = m(r,\lambda) - \int_0^1 m(r,\lambda)l(r,\lambda)'dr(\int_0^1 l(r,\lambda)l(r,\lambda)'dr)^{-1}l(r,\lambda).$$

Then

$$4F(\overline{\lambda}) \xrightarrow{D} (\int_0^1 dw(r)b_{ml}(r,\overline{\lambda})'(\int_0^1 b_{ml}(r,\overline{\lambda})b_{ml}(r,\overline{\lambda})'dr)^{-1} \int_0^1 b_{ml}(r,\overline{\lambda})dw(r). \tag{17}$$

Neither (15) nor (17) involves unknown parameters. In particular they are free from β_1, β_2, γ_1, γ_2.

Before turning to the case where λ is unknown, let us indicate a crucially important point in deriving (15) for the case where $\overline{\lambda}$ is known. (The analogous point is seen in deriving (17) as well.) When (9) is evaluated at $\lambda = \overline{\lambda}$ and the data generation equations (11) and (12) are substituted in it, it is seen that ι, t, $du(\overline{\lambda})$, and $dt(\overline{\lambda})$ in (11), and ι and $du(\overline{\lambda})$ in (12) are contained in $X_1(\overline{\lambda})$. Thus

$$x'_{-1}(I - P(X_1(\overline{\lambda})))x_{-1} = u'_{-1}(I - P(X_1(\overline{\lambda}_1)))u_{-1} \tag{18a}$$

and

$$x'_{-1}(I - P(X_1(\overline{\lambda})))\Delta x = u'_{-1}(I - P(X_1(\overline{\lambda}_1)))\Delta u. \tag{19a}$$

Since Δx_{-j}, $j = 1, \cdots, (p-1)$, is a linear combination of ι, $du(\overline{\lambda})$, Δu_{-j} (plus terms that can be ignored asymptotically), $P(X_1(\overline{\lambda}_1))$ can be replaced by $P(Y_1(\overline{\lambda}))$, where

$$Y_1(\overline{\lambda}) = [\iota, t, du(\overline{\lambda}), dt(\overline{\lambda}), \Delta u_{-1}, \cdots, \Delta u_{-p+1}].$$

The part of u_{-1} orthogonal to $Y_1(\overline{\lambda})$ leads us to b_{wa}. The present situation is identical to what we would have if $x_t \equiv u_t$ (d_t is absent) and ι, t, $du(\overline{\lambda})$, $dt(\overline{\lambda})$ are included in the Dickey–Fuller equation.

Zivot and Andrews (1992) consider λ not necessarily equal to $\overline{\lambda}$, but they assume that $\overline{\gamma} = 0$ in the I(1) model, which is the null model in the unit root test. The assumption eliminates $du(\overline{\lambda})$ and $dt(\overline{\lambda})$ from (11) and $du(\overline{\lambda})$ from (12). Since ι and t in (11) and ι in (12) are contained in $X_1(\lambda)$, $\lambda \neq \overline{\lambda}$,

$$x'_{-1}(I - P(X_1(\lambda)))x_{-1} = u'_{-1}(I - P(X_1(\lambda_1)))u_{-1} \tag{18b}$$

and

$$x'_{-1}(I - P(X_1(\lambda)))\Delta x = u'_{-1}(I - P(X_1(\lambda_1)))\Delta u. \tag{19b}$$

Since Δx_{-j}, $j = 1, \cdots, (p-1)$, is a linear combination of ι, Δu_{-j} (plus terms that can be ignored asymptotically), $P(X_1(\lambda))$ can be replaced by $P(Y_1(\lambda))$. It can be shown that plim $s^2(\lambda) = \sigma_\varepsilon^2$ for any λ in the present null model. Comparisons between (18a) and (18b) and between (19a) and (19b) lead us to

$$\hat{t}_\alpha(\lambda) \xrightarrow{D} (\int_0^1 b_{wa}(r,\lambda)^2 \, dr)^{-\frac{1}{2}} \int_0^1 b_{wa}(r,\lambda) dw(r)$$

for any λ. Zivot and Andrews (1992) propose $\inf_\lambda \hat{t}_\alpha(\lambda)$ as the unit root test statistic, and show

$$\inf_\lambda \hat{t}_\alpha(\lambda) \xrightarrow{D} \inf_\lambda (\int_0^1 b_{wa}(r,\lambda)^2 \, dr)^{-\frac{1}{2}} \int_0^1 b_{wa}(r,\lambda) dw(r) \tag{20}$$

in I(1) models.[5]

Let us then consider the case, $\lambda \neq \bar{\lambda}$, and $\bar{\gamma} \neq 0$ in both I(1) and I(0) models. It is only ι and t in (11) and ι in (12) that are contained in $X_1(\lambda)$, $\lambda \neq \bar{\lambda}$, and

$$x'_{-1}(I - P(X_1(\lambda)))x_{-1} = (-du(\bar{\lambda})\bar{\gamma} + dt(\bar{\lambda})\bar{\gamma} + u_{-1})'(I - P(X_1(\lambda)))$$
$$(-du(\bar{\lambda})\bar{\gamma} + dt(\bar{\lambda})\bar{\gamma} + u_{-1}) \tag{18c}$$

and

$$x'_{-1}(I - P(X_1(\lambda)))\Delta x = (-du(\bar{\lambda})\bar{\gamma} + dt(\bar{\lambda})\bar{\gamma} + u_{-1})'(I - P(X_1(\lambda)))$$
$$(du(\bar{\lambda})\bar{\gamma} + \Delta u). \tag{19c}$$

Deterministic terms, $du(\bar{\lambda})$ and $dt(\bar{\lambda})$, play major roles in the limit as $T \to \infty$, and (18c) and (19c) are entirely different from (18a) and (19a) respectively. The Wiener process does not appear in the limit.

What has caused this difference between the case, $\lambda \neq \bar{\lambda}$, and the case, $\lambda = \bar{\lambda}$, is that $du(\bar{\lambda})$ and $dt(\bar{\lambda})$ are involved in the data generations, while the independent variables in the Dickey–Fuller equation, $X_1(\lambda)$, involve $du(\lambda)$ and $dt(\lambda)$. Neither $du(\bar{\lambda})$ nor $dt(\bar{\lambda})$ vanishes when projected onto the orthogonal complement of the space spanned by $X_1(\lambda)$.

If we had used $\inf_\lambda \hat{t}_\alpha(\lambda)$, it would diverge to $-\infty$ as $T \to \infty$, and if the critical value were set according to (20), the test would reject the null hypothesis asymptotically a.s. in spite of the fact that the hypothesis is indeed correct. This has been pointed out in Vogelsang and Perron (1994).

3 Two-Step Procedure: Asymptotic Theory

We shall consider the model given by (1), (2), and (3). In particular $\gamma_1 \neq 0$ and $\gamma_2 \neq 0$. A two-step procedure is available for the unit root test. In its first step the break fractions are estimated by minimizing $s^2(\lambda)$ over λ, $0 < \lambda_1 < \lambda_2 < 1$, i.e.,

$$\hat{\lambda} = \arg\inf_{\lambda} s^2(\lambda), \quad \hat{\lambda} = [\hat{\lambda}_1, \hat{\lambda}_2], \quad \hat{\lambda}_1 < \hat{\lambda}_2. \tag{21}$$

In the second step the unit root test statistics, $\hat{t}_\alpha(\lambda)$ and $4F(\lambda)$, are calculated on the OLS along (7), in which λ is replaced by $\hat{\lambda}$. The critical values are obtained by applying the limit distributions (15) and (17) for $\hat{t}_\alpha(\overline{\lambda})$ and $4F(\overline{\lambda})$ respectively, replacing $\overline{\lambda}$ there by $\hat{\lambda}$.

Initially we prove the asymptotic validity of this two step procedure.

Proposition I. plim $\hat{\lambda} = \overline{\lambda}$ when $\overline{\gamma}_1 \neq 0$, $\overline{\gamma}_2 \neq 0$, and $\{u_t\}$ is I(1).

Proposition II. $\hat{\lambda} - \overline{\lambda}$ is $O_p(T^{-1})$, and $\hat{T}_1 - \overline{T}_1$ and $\hat{T}_2 - \overline{T}_2$ are asymptotically independent, when $\overline{\gamma}_1 \neq 0$, $\overline{\gamma}_2 \neq 0$, and $\{u_t\}$ is I(1).

These propositions can be proved by adapting the methods of proofs in Bai and Perron (1998), which has analyzed inf s^2 of the least squares with regime shifts and I(0) disturbances. However in their model regression coefficients are affected but independent variables are unaffected by a change in break fractions. Our proofs have to be constructed from the beginning. They are presented in the Mathematical Appendix.

Proposition III. When $\{u_t\}$ is I(1), and $\overline{\gamma}_1 \neq 0$, $\overline{\gamma}_2 \neq 0$,
$\hat{t}_\alpha(\hat{\lambda}) \xrightarrow{D}$ the right hand side of (15),
$4F(\hat{\lambda}) \xrightarrow{D}$ the right hand side of (17).

A proof is provided in the Mathematical Appendix. The right hand sides of (15) and (17) are useless for setting the critical values, but it is asymptotically valid to replace $\overline{\lambda}$ there by $\hat{\lambda}$.

Proposition IV. plim $\hat{\lambda} = \overline{\lambda}$ when $\overline{\gamma}_1 \neq 0$ and $\overline{\gamma}_2 \neq 0$, and $\{u_t\}$ is I(0).

Proposition V. When $\{u_t\}$ is I(0), $\hat{t}_\alpha(\hat{\lambda}) \to -\infty$, and $4F(\hat{\lambda}) \to +\infty$.

These propositions establish the consistency of the test based on the two-step procedure. Proofs of Proposition IV and V are omitted.

The following results are useful to compare the asymptotic theory and the finite sample performance to be given in the next section.

Proposition VI. When $\{u_t\}$ is I(0) and $\overline{\gamma}_1 \neq 0$, $\overline{\gamma}_2 \neq 0$, $\hat{\lambda} - \overline{\lambda}$ is $O_p(T^{-1})$, and $\hat{T}_1 - \overline{T}_1$ and $\hat{T}_2 - \overline{T}_2$ are asymptotically independent.

Proposition VII. Regardless of $\{u_t\}$ being I(1) or I(0), the limiting distributions of $\hat{T}_i - \overline{T}_i$, $i = 1, 2$, are each symmetric about zero, if ε_t has a continuous distribution symmetric about zero.

A proof of Proposition VII for the case where $\{u_t\}$ is I(1) is given as Corollary of Proposition II in the Mathematical Appendix. The proofs for the other part of Proposition VII and for Proposition VI are omitted.[6]

4 Two-Step Procedure: Finite Sample Simulation Studies

Finite sample distributions of the above test statistics, $\hat{t}_\alpha(\hat{\lambda})$ and $4F(\hat{\lambda})$ have been investigated in two groups of simulations.

(a) In the first group of simulations we postulate a model of deterministic trend which can produce data like the Japanese real GDP per capita.[7] $\bar{T}_1 = 60$ and $\bar{T}_2 = 135$, while $T = 150$. The parameter values in relation to (1) are $\bar{\beta}_1 = 1.72, \bar{\beta}_2 = 0.021, \bar{\gamma}_1 = -0.014, \bar{\gamma}_2 = -0.002$, which have been obtained by fitting (1) to the data.

In the null model $\{\Delta u_t\}$ is generated by $(1 - 0.5L)(1 - 0.2L)\Delta u_t = \varepsilon_t$,[8] and $p = 2$ is regarded as a priori known in calculating the test statistics. An important parameter value is $\sigma_\varepsilon^2 = 10^{-5}$, which has also been adopted to make realizations of the model mimic the data mentioned above.

Cumulative distributions of our two-step test statistics with 1,000 replications are given in Table 1 for this null model. In comparison Table 2 presents the limit distribution of $4F$ reproduced from Kunitomo and Sato (1995), which is based on either 5,000 or 8,000 replications of random numbers. Moreover Table 2' presents the limit distribution of $\hat{t}_\alpha$, the right hand side of (15), evaluated by 5,000 replications of pseudo-random numbers. The finite sample distribution of $4F$ has a larger mean and much larger dispersion than the limit

Table 1. Finite sample distributions of $\hat{t}_\alpha$ and $4F$ in I(1)
$\bar{T}_1 = 60, \bar{T}_2 = 135, \bar{\beta}_2 = 0.021, \bar{\gamma}_1 = -0.014, \bar{\gamma}_2 = -0.002, \sigma_\varepsilon^2 = 10^{-5}$

	0.05	0.1	0.2	0.3	0.4	0.5	0.6	0.7	0.8	0.9	0.95
$\hat{t}_\alpha$	−6.8	−6.3	−5.6	−4.9	−4.4	−4.0	−3.7	−3.4	−3.0	−2.4	−2.0
$4F$	11.3	13.5	16.5	18.8	21.3	23.9	27.5	32.4	39.0	46.5	52.2

Table 2. Limit distribution of $4F$ with known break points in I(1)
$\bar{\lambda}_1 = 60/150, \bar{\lambda}_2 = 135/150$

	0.05	0.1	0.5	0.9	0.95
$4F$	6.67	7.78	12.70	19.97	22.26

Table 2'. Limit distribution of $\hat{t}_\alpha$ with known break points in I(1)
$\bar{\lambda}_1 = 60/150, \bar{\lambda}_2 = 135/150$

	0.05	0.1	0.2	0.3	0.4	0.5	0.6	0.7	0.8	0.9	0.95
$\hat{t}_\alpha$	−4.46	−4.17	−3.82	−3.59	−3.39	−3.19	−2.99	−2.78	−2.53	−2.16	−1.84

Table 3. Distribution of $(\hat{T}_1, \hat{T}_2)$ in I(1)
$\bar{T}_1 = 60, \bar{T}_2 = 135, \bar{\beta}_2 = 0.021, \bar{\gamma}_1 = -0.014, \bar{\gamma}_2 = -0.002, \sigma_\varepsilon^2 = 10^{-5}$

$\hat{T}_1$	$\hat{T}_2$			
	110–118	119–129	130–140	
35–43	4	10	10	24
44–54	75	62	51	188
55–59	98	61	53	212
60	222	180	170	572
61–65	1	2	0	3
66–76	1	0	0	1
77–85	0	0	0	0
	401	315	284	1000

distribution. The asymptotic property in Proposition III does not hold even approximately with $T = 150, \bar{T}_1 = 60, \bar{T}_2 = 135$, and the parameter values given above.

The finite sample distribution of $(\hat{T}_1, \hat{T}_2)$ is given in Table 3 for the null I(1) model. In searching for $\inf_{T_1, T_2} s^2(T_1, T_2)$ we have confined T_1 into [35, 85] and T_2 into [110, 140] in order to save computation time. $\bar{T}_1$ is estimated fairly well with some negative bias. The probability of $\hat{T}_1 = \bar{T}_1$, i.e. no error of estimation of T_1, is 0.57, but the direction of bias is overwhelming. $\bar{T}_2$ is estimated very badly with enormous dispersion and negative bias.

In the alternative model $\{u_t\}$ is generated by I(0), $(1 - 0.7L)(1 - 0.5L)(1 - 0.2L)u_t = \varepsilon_t$, $\sigma_\varepsilon^2 = 10^{-5}$, and this is combined with the same deterministic trend as above. Biases of $\hat{T}_1$ and $\hat{T}_2$ are substantially smaller than in the case of I(1), but they are still negative. See Table 4.

(b) We would like to investigate which aspects of the above models have caused the extremely poor performance of our test. The biases in $(\hat{T}_1, \hat{T}_2)$ may

Table 4. Distribution of $(\hat{T}_1, \hat{T}_2)$ in I(0)
$\bar{T}_1 = 60, \bar{T}_2 = 135, \bar{\beta}_2 = 0.021, \bar{\gamma}_1 = -0.014, \bar{\gamma}_2 = -0.002, \sigma_\varepsilon^2 = 10^{-5}$

$\hat{T}_1$	$\hat{T}_2$			
	110–118	119–129	130–140	
35–43	0	0	0	0
44–54	13	18	31	61
55–59	84	89	134	307
60	146	198	287	631
61–65	0	0	1	1
66–76	0	0	0	0
77–85	0	0	0	0
	243	305	453	1000

well be due to the facts (i) that $\bar{T}_2 = 135$ is close to the end of the sample period, and (ii) that the coefficient on the third regime, $\bar{\gamma}_2 = -0.002$, is small (in absolute value) in relation to $\bar{\beta}_2 = 0.021$ and $\bar{\gamma}_1 = -0.014$ in (1). (iii) It might also be worth investigating to see whether both $\bar{\gamma}_1$ and $\bar{\gamma}_2$ being negative or $\bar{\beta}_2$ being positive has anything to do with the biases in $\hat{T}_* - \bar{T}_*$ being negative. (iv) Moreover it can be generally said that, the smaller σ_ε, the easier to estimate the parameters that generate the deterministic trend, $\{d_t\}$. It would be interesting to see the performance under more favorable conditions. Thus our second group of simulations experiment on (a) $\bar{\beta}_2 = \pm 0.028$, $\bar{\gamma}_1 = \pm 0.010$, and $\bar{\gamma}_2 = \pm 0.010$; (b) two alternative sets of $\bar{T}_*$, $[\bar{T}_1 = 50, \bar{T}_2 = 101]$, and $[\bar{T}_1 = 60, \bar{T}_2 = 135]$; and (c) two alternative values of σ_ε^2, 10^{-5}, which is the same as in the first group of experiments, and $10^{-6} \times 3$.

The results are as follows. In so far as $\sigma_\varepsilon^2 = 10^{-5}$ the finite sample distributions of $\hat{t}_\alpha$ and $4F$ do not differ much from those in the first group in all cases, even though considerable improvements are observed on $\hat{T}_2 - \bar{T}_2$ because $|\gamma_2|$ in the second group of simulations is larger than in the first group. Concerning $\hat{T}_* - \bar{T}_* = [\hat{T}_1 - \bar{T}_1, \hat{T}_2 - \bar{T}_2]$, neither the different locations of $[\bar{T}_1, \bar{T}_2]$ nor different signs of $\bar{\beta}_2, \bar{\gamma}_1$, and $\bar{\gamma}_2$ make much difference. Indeed negative biases on $\hat{T}_* - \bar{T}_*$ still remain in all cases.

When $\sigma_\varepsilon^2 = 10^{-6} \times 3$, the distributions of $(\hat{T}_* - \bar{T}_*)$ are excellent as seen in Table 5 for the null model, though negative biases are still appreciable. The finite sample null distribution of $4F$ is given in Table 6. Compare it with the

Table 5. Distribution of $(\hat{T}_1, \hat{T}_2)$ in I(1)

$\bar{T}_1 = 60, \bar{T}_2 = 135, \bar{\beta}_2 = 0.028, \bar{\gamma}_1 = -0.010, \bar{\gamma}_2 = -0.010, \sigma_\varepsilon^2 = 10^{-6} \times 3$

$\hat{T}_1$	$\hat{T}_2$					
	110–118	119–129	130–140	135	136–140	
35–43	0	0	0	5	0	5
44–54	0	9	5	53	0	67
55–59	0	6	12	76	0	94
60	7	49	61	716	0	833
61–65	0	0	0	1	0	1
66–76	0	0	0	0	0	0
77–85	0	0	0	0	0	0
	7	64	78	851	0	1000

Table 6. Finite sample distribution of $\hat{t}_\alpha$ and $4F$

$\bar{T}_1 = 60, \bar{T}_2 = 135, \bar{\beta}_2 = 0.028, \bar{\gamma}_1 = -0.010, \bar{\gamma}_2 = -0.010, \sigma_\varepsilon^2 = 10^{-6} \times 3$

	0.05	0.1	0.2	0.3	0.4	0.5	0.6	0.7	0.8	0.9	0.95
$\hat{t}_\alpha$	-6.5	-5.2	-3.9	-3.5	-3.2	-2.9	-2.6	-2.4	-2.0	-1.6	-1.2
$4F$	6.3	7.6	9.6	11.1	12.9	14.8	17.1	20.7	27.3	44.0	55.9

limit distribution in Table 2. The two distributions coincide well in their lower parts, say, up to the points where probabilities accumulate to 0.5. However the finite sample distribution greatly deviates from the limit distribution in their upper parts, which are the parts that are crucial for significant tests. Table 6 also gives the finite sample distribution of $\hat{t}_\alpha$. It is close to the limit distribution in Table 2' between cumulative probabilities, 0.2 and 0.5, but it deviates radically in the lower tail part, which is used for significance tests.

In the rest of the present section we shall digress from the unit root problem, and perform a few simulations to search for a source of the persistently negative biases in the estimates of break points. The model of deterministic trend is simplified to a single break, $d_t = \beta_0 + \beta_1 + \gamma dt(t, \lambda)$, with $T = 150, \bar{\lambda} = 60/150$, $\bar{\beta}_0 = 1.72, \bar{\beta}_1 = 0.028, \bar{\gamma} = -0.01$.

First, consider the case where $p = 0$ so that $\{u_t\}$ is a white noise, a very special case of $I(0)$. The break point is estimated by minimizing the s^2 in the regression of x_t on $[1, t, dt(t, \tau/150)]$ over various values of τ. No bias is found in the estimate of the break point.

Second, consider the case where $p = 1$ and $\{u_t\}$ is a stationary AR(1), $u_t = au_{t-1} + \varepsilon_t$. As was pointed out above in equation (7), no approximations are required to derive the Dickey–Fuller equation when $p = 1$. The break point is estimated by minimizing the s^2 in the regression of Δx_t on $[1, du(t, \tau/150)$, $dt(t, \tau/150), x_{t-1}]$ over different values of τ. The s^2 is identical to that of the OLS on the Cochrane–Orcutt transformation,

$$x_t = c_0 + c_1 du(t, \tau/150) + c_2 t + c_3 dt(t, \tau/150) + ax_{t-1} + \varepsilon_t,$$

where we have ignored the restrictions on c_0, c_1, c_2, and c_3 that follow from $c_0 = \beta_0(1 - a) - a\beta_1$, $c_1 = -a\gamma$, $c_2 = \beta_1(1 - a)$, $c_3 = \gamma(1 - a)$. The estimate of the break point does have a negative bias though not as conspicuous as in Table 4. Shifting $\bar{\lambda}$ to 75/150 does not eliminate the bias.

We are led to conjecture that the negative biases in the estimates of break points are due to some finite sample problem on the OLS applied to the dynamic model involving x_{t-1} among regressors. How to remove the biases is an important problem of future research.

5 Number of Break Points

So far we have assumed that an a priori known number of break points is common to both $I(1)$ and $I(0)$ models. That number is used to construct the statistic of our 2 step unit root test. The condition that the $\bar{\gamma}$s are not zero in (1) is used to prove the consistency of the test and to derive the limit distributions.

However the number of break points had better be treated as an unknown parameter. Suppose that a number, q, is to be selected from $\{q; q_{\min} \leq q \leq$

$q_{max}\}$, where q_{min} and q_{max} are known integers. (q_{min} may be zero.) Starting from $q = q_{min}$, q is increased sequentially as long as one rejects the null hypothesis that the true number is q against the hypothesis that the true number is $q + 1$ or larger. The methods used for this hypothesis testing depend upon the integration order of $\{u_t\}$. Therefore it is necessary to abandon the assumption that I(1) and I(0) models share the same number of break points. The selection of q in I(1) and I(0) models are explained below for the case where $q_{min} = 1$ and $q_{max} = 2$. Incidentally the sequential search should not start from q_{max}, because it is not easy to assess consequences of the true $\bar{q}$ being less than the q that is specified in a null hypothesis, which is tested against $q + 1$ or larger.

(a) Suppose that $\{u_t\}$ is I(1) and that the true number of break points is 1. Then:

$$\Delta x_t \approx \mu_0 + \mu_1 du(t, \lambda_1) + b_1 \Delta x_{t-1} + \cdots + b_{p-1} \Delta x_{t-p+1} + \varepsilon_t, \qquad (22)$$

and λ_1 is estimated by minimizing $s^2(\lambda_1)$ on the OLS along (22). Let $\hat{\lambda}_1$ be the estimate. The equation

$$\Delta x_t = \mu_0 + \mu_1 du(t, \hat{\lambda}_1) + \mu_2 du(t, \lambda_2) + b_1 \Delta x_{t-1} + \cdots + b_{p-1} \Delta x_{t-p+1} + \varepsilon_t \qquad (23)$$

contains a redundant term, $\mu_2 du(t, \lambda_2)$. The t-statistic to test $\mu_2 = 0$ in (23) is denoted by $\hat{t}_{\mu 2}(\lambda_2)$ for each λ_2 in (0, 1). Then

$$\sup_{\lambda_2} |\hat{t}_{\mu_2}(\lambda_2)| \qquad (24)$$

is distributed asymptotically as

$$\sup_{\lambda_2} |(\int b_{u_2}(r, \lambda_2, \bar{\lambda}_1)^2 dr)^{-\frac{1}{2}} \int b_{u_2}(r, \lambda_2, \bar{\lambda}_1) dw(r)|, \qquad (25)$$

where $b_{u_2}(r, \lambda_2, \bar{\lambda}_1)$ is the part of $du(r, \lambda_2)$ that is orthogonal to $[1, du(r, \bar{\lambda}_1)]$. The $\bar{\lambda}_1$ in (25) may be replaced by $\hat{\lambda}_1$.

If the true number of break points is 2, (24) diverges to $+\infty$.

(b) Suppose that $\{u_t\}$ is I(0) and the true number of break points is 1. Then

$$x_t \approx \mu_0 + \mu_1 du(t, \lambda_1) + \delta_0 t + \delta_1 dt(t, \lambda_1) + a_1 x_{t-1} + \cdots + a_p x_{t-p} + \varepsilon_t, \qquad (26)$$

and λ_1 is estimated by minimizing s^2 in (26). Adding redundant terms,

$$\mu_2 du(t, \lambda_2) + \delta_2 dt(t, \lambda_2),$$

to the right hand side of (26), where λ_2 is in (0, 1), let $F_{\mu\delta_2}(\lambda_2)$ be the F-statistic to test $\mu_2 = \delta_2 = 0$. Then

$$\sup_{\lambda_2} 2F_{\mu\delta_2}(\lambda_2) \qquad (27)$$

is distributed asymptotically as

$$\sup_{\lambda_2} \int dw(r) b_{ut_2}(r, \lambda_2, \overline{\lambda}_1) (\int b_{ut_2}(r, \lambda_2, \overline{\lambda}_1)' b_{ut_2}(r, \lambda_2, \overline{\lambda}_1) dr)^{-1}$$

$$\int b_{ut_2}(r, \lambda_2, \overline{\lambda}_1)' dw(r), \tag{28}$$

where $b_{ut_2}(r, \lambda_2, \overline{\lambda}_1)$ is the part of $[du(r, \lambda_2), dt(r, \lambda_2)]$ which is orthogonal to $[1, du(r, \overline{\lambda}_1), r, dt(r, \overline{\lambda}_1)]$. The $\overline{\lambda}_1$ may be replaced by $\hat{\lambda}_1$.

If the true number of break points is 2, (27) diverges to $+\infty$.

The distributions of (25) and (28) have been tabulated for various specifications of $\overline{\lambda}_1$, and both distributions are found to be very insensitive to $\overline{\lambda}_1$.

Each of the above two tests, (a) and (b), has been investigated on its finite sample performance. As for (a) the (finite sample) joint distribution of $\hat{\lambda}_1$ (obtained from (22)) and the statistic, (24), is tabulated, and the distributions of (24) conditional upon $\hat{\lambda}_1$ are derived from it. For a given value of the conditioning variable, $\hat{\lambda}_1$, the conditional distribution is compared with the (limit) distribution of (25) with $\overline{\lambda}_1$ replaced by that value of $\hat{\lambda}_1$. The two are fairly close though the finite sample distributions are a little more widely dispersed than the limit distributions. For example, the probabilities beyond 3.0 in the finite sample distributions are 0.06 ~ 0.08, while the probabilities are about 0.03 in the limit distributions. A similar investigation has been made on the test for the I(0) model, and a similar result has been obtained.

Let us return to the unit root test. It may be performed with estimates of break points, if the number, q_1, of break points in I(1) models does not exceed the number, q_0, in I(0) models, and if one can assume that I(1) and I(0) models share the same q_1 break points. Suppose that the above tests on the significance of the second break have led to the decision that $q_1 = 1$ and $q_0 = 2$. Since the null model is I(1), the Dickey–Fuller equation to consider is:

$$\Delta x_t \approx \mu_0 + \mu_1 du(t, \lambda_1) + \delta_0 t + \delta_1 dt(t, \lambda_1) + \alpha x_{t-1}$$
$$+ b_1 \Delta x_{t-1} + \cdots + b_{p-1} \Delta x_{t-p+1} + \varepsilon_t. \tag{7'}$$

Initially $\hat{\lambda}_1$ is determined by $\inf_{\lambda} s^2(\lambda)$. Secondly, substituting $\hat{\lambda}_1$ for λ_1 in (7'), the null hypothesis, $\delta_0 = \delta_1 = \alpha = 0$, is tested by the F-test. In proceeding along the reasoning in section III we ignore the errors involved in deciding that $q_1 = 1$ and $q_2 \geq q_1$. Here we have followed a fairly common practice of econometrics, i.e., when the total test consists of a pre-test and a subsequent test and the method of the subsequent test depends upon the result of the pre-test, one ignores the errors involved in the result of the pre-test. Admittedly this practice cannot be recommended, but it still provides a pragmatic solution for difficult problems.

The above methods have been applied to the Japanese data of logs of real GDP per capita. If $\{u_t\}$ is I(0), the significance of the second break is overwhelmingly high. If $\{u_t\}$ is I(1), the P-value of the test statistic is between 0.1 and 0.05 in terms of its limit distribution. In view of the finite sample distribu-

tions being a little wider than the limit distributions we had better imagine
P-values between 0.1 and 0.2. Thus (i) $q_1 = q_0 = 2$ and (ii) $q_1 = 1$, $q_0 = 2$ are
both plausible selections of the numbers of break points. The presence of a
unit root is rejected in terms of the limit distributions given in Proposition
III. But the simulation results in Section 4 cast doubt on any definitive
judgments on the unit root. In both cases of the above (i) and (ii) the estimate
of the first break point is 1973 II, which precedes the oil price crisis, but we
should keep in mind the negative bias revealed in Section 4.

Mathematical Appendix

Hereafter T will denote $T - p$. $s^2(\lambda)$ is given in (8), and $\hat{\lambda}$ in (21). In the data
generation (11) and (12) hold for x_{-1} and Δx respectively.

$$X(\lambda) = [\iota, t, x_{-1}, du(\lambda), dt(\lambda), \Delta x_{-1}, \cdots, \Delta x_{-p+1}].$$

Proof of Proposition I. $\{\Delta u_t\}$ is generated by a stationary $AR(p-1)$, (5).

$$T^{-1}\Delta x'(I - P(X(\hat{\lambda})))\Delta x = \inf_{\lambda} s^2(\lambda) \leq s^2(\bar{\lambda}), \tag{A1}$$

and it is known that

$$s^2(\bar{\lambda}) = T^{-1}\varepsilon'\varepsilon + o_p(1), \tag{A2}$$

where $\varepsilon = (\varepsilon_{p+1}, \cdots, \varepsilon_T)'$. Because of

$$\Delta x_{-j} \approx \bar{\beta}_2 \iota + du(\bar{\lambda})\bar{\gamma} + \Delta u_{-j}, \quad j = 1, \cdots, p-1,$$

we initially have

$$T^{-1}\Delta x' P(X(\hat{\lambda}))\Delta x = T^{-1}\Delta x' P(\tilde{X}(\hat{\lambda}))\Delta x + o_p(1),$$

where $\tilde{X}(\lambda) = [\iota,\ t,\ x_{-1},\ du(\lambda),\ dt(\lambda),\ (du(\bar{\lambda})\ \bar{\gamma} + \Delta u_{-1}),\ \cdots,\ (du(\bar{\lambda})\bar{\gamma} + \Delta u_{-p+1})]$.
Write $dj(\bar{\lambda} - \lambda) = du(\bar{\lambda}) - du(\lambda)$. Then we further have

$$T^{-1}\Delta x' P(X(\hat{\lambda}))\Delta x = T^{-1}\Delta x' P(Y(\hat{\lambda}))\Delta x + o_p(1),$$

where $Y(\lambda) = [\iota,\ t,\ x_{-1},\ du(\lambda),\ dt(\lambda),\ dj(\bar{\lambda} - \lambda)\bar{\gamma}\iota'_{p-1} + \Delta U_-]$,

$$\iota_{p-1}' = [1, \cdots, 1], (1 \times (p-1)); \Delta U_- = [\Delta u_{-1}, \cdots, \Delta u_{-p+1}], (T \times (p-1)).$$

With $dj(\bar{\lambda} - \lambda)$ (12) is rewritten as:[9]

$$\Delta x \approx \bar{\beta}_2 \iota + du(\lambda)\bar{\gamma} + dj(\bar{\lambda} - \lambda)\bar{\gamma} + \Delta u.$$

It can be seen that $\inf s^2(\lambda) = s^2(\hat{\lambda})$ is

$$T^{-1}(dj(\bar{\lambda} - \hat{\lambda})\bar{\gamma} + \Delta u)'(I - P(Y(\hat{\lambda})))(dj(\bar{\lambda} - \hat{\lambda})\bar{\gamma} + \Delta u) + o_p(1). \tag{A3}$$

Moreover partitioning $Y(\lambda)$ as $[Y_1(\lambda),\ Y_2(\lambda)]$

$$Y_1(\lambda) = [i, \boldsymbol{t}, x_{-1}, du(\lambda), dt(\lambda)]$$
$$Y_2(\lambda) = [dj(\bar{\lambda} - \lambda)\bar{\gamma}\iota_{p-1}{}' + \Delta U_{-}],$$

and writing $\xi = dj(\bar{\lambda} - \hat{\lambda})\bar{\gamma} + \Delta u$, (A3) is written as

$$
\begin{aligned}
&T^{-1}\xi'(I - P(Y_1(\hat{\lambda})))\xi \\
&\quad -T^{-1}\xi'(I - P(Y_1(\hat{\lambda})))Y_2(\hat{\lambda})(Y_2(\hat{\lambda})'(I - P(Y_1(\hat{\lambda})))Y_2(\hat{\lambda}))^{-1} \times \\
&\quad Y_2(\hat{\lambda})'(I - P(Y_1(\hat{\lambda})))\xi.
\end{aligned}
\tag{A3$'$}
$$

On the first term in (A3$'$) it can be shown that

$$T^{-1}\xi'(I - P(Y_1(\hat{\lambda})))\xi = d_T{}^2(\hat{\lambda}, \bar{\lambda}) + T^{-1}\Delta u'\Delta u + o_p(1) \tag{A4}$$

where

$$d_T{}^2(\lambda, \bar{\lambda}) = T^{-1}\bar{\gamma}'dj(\bar{\lambda} - \lambda)'(I - P(Y_1(\lambda)))dj(\bar{\lambda} - \lambda)\bar{\gamma}. \tag{A5}$$

The reasons are as follows. Let r_T be the largest eigenvalue of $E(\Delta u\Delta u')$. Since $\{\Delta u_t\}$ is a stationary AR, r_T is bounded above. (Indeed as $T \to \infty$ r_T converges to $2\pi\times$ (the maximum of the spectral density function).) (a) $T^{-1}\Delta u'dj(\bar{\lambda} - \hat{\lambda})\bar{\gamma}$ is $o_p(1)$. This is because $E(T^{-1/2}\Delta u'dj(\bar{\lambda} - \lambda)\bar{\gamma})^2 \leq ||\bar{\gamma}||^2 r_T$. $T^{-1/2}\Delta u'dj(\bar{\lambda} - \lambda)\bar{\gamma}$ is bounded in probability *uniformly* with respect to λ, and $T^{-1}\Delta u'dj(\bar{\lambda} - \hat{\lambda})\bar{\gamma}$ is $o_p(1)$. (b) $T^{-1}\Delta u'P(Y_1(\hat{\lambda}))dj(\bar{\lambda} - \hat{\lambda})\bar{\gamma} = T^{-1/2}\Delta u' \times P(Y_1(\hat{\lambda}))dj(\bar{\lambda} - \hat{\lambda})\bar{\gamma}T^{-1/2}$ is also $o_p(1)$. Note

$$P(Y_1(\lambda)) = Y_1(\lambda)D_T{}^{-1}(D_T{}^{-1}Y_1(\lambda)'Y_1(\lambda)D_T{}^{-1})^{-1}D_T{}^{-1}Y_1(\lambda)' \tag{A6}$$

where

$$D_T{}^{-1} = \mathrm{diag}[T^{-\frac{1}{2}}, T^{-\frac{3}{2}}, T^{-\frac{3}{2}}, T^{-\frac{1}{2}}I_2, T^{-\frac{3}{2}}I_2]. \tag{A6$'$}$$

It can be seen that $T^{-1/2}\Delta u'Y_1(\hat{\lambda})D_T^{-1}$ is $o_p(1)$, while $(D_T^{-1}Y_1(\hat{\lambda})'Y_1(\hat{\lambda})D_T^{-1})^{-1}$ and $D_T^{-1}Y_1(\hat{\lambda})'dj(\lambda - \bar{\lambda})\bar{\gamma}T^{-1/2}$ are $O_p(1)$. The reason why $T^{-1/2}\Delta u'Y_1(\hat{\lambda})D_T^{-1}$ is $o_p(1)$ is that $\Delta u'Y_1(\hat{\lambda})D_T^{-1}$ is bounded in probability uniformly with respect to λ, which in turn can be shown as in (a) above. (For $\lambda = \bar{\lambda}$ collinearity between $-du(\bar{\lambda})\bar{\gamma} + dt(\bar{\lambda})\bar{\gamma}$ in x_{-1} and $[du(\bar{\lambda}), dt(\bar{\lambda})]$ in $X(\bar{\lambda})$ necessitates construction of $Y_1(\bar{\lambda}) = [\iota, \boldsymbol{t}, u_{-1}, du(\bar{\lambda}), dt(\bar{\lambda})]$ and $D_T^{-1} = diag[T^{-1/2}, T^{-3/2}, T^{-1}, T^{-1/2}I_2, T^{-3/2}I_2]$, but the above conclusion can be extended to cover $\bar{\lambda}$.) (c) $T^{-1}\Delta u'P(Y_1(\hat{\lambda}))\Delta u$ is also $o_p(1)$ in so far as $E(\varepsilon_t^4)$ exists. This completes our proof of (A4).

As for the second term of (A3$'$) it is written as $-v'W^{-1}v$ with

$$
\begin{aligned}
W &= T^{-\frac{1}{2}}Y_2(\hat{\lambda})'(I - P(Y_1(\hat{\lambda})))Y_2(\hat{\lambda})T^{-\frac{1}{2}} \\
v &= T^{-\frac{1}{2}}Y_2(\hat{\lambda})'(I - P(Y_1(\hat{\lambda})))\xi T^{-\frac{1}{2}}.
\end{aligned}
$$

It can be shown in the same way as above that

$$W = d_T^{\,2}\iota_{p-1}\iota_{p-1}{}' + T^{-1}\Delta U'_{-}\Delta U_{-} + o_p(1)$$
$$v = d_T^{\,2}\iota_{p-1} + T^{-1}\Delta U'_{-}\Delta u + o_p(1),$$

where $d_T^2(\hat\lambda, \bar\lambda)$ has been abbreviated as d_T^2. With $\hat B = T^{-1}\Delta U'_{-}\,\Delta U_{-}$,

$$-v'W^{-1}v = -(d_T^{\,2}\iota_{p-1} + T^{-1}\Delta U'_{-}\Delta u)'(\hat B^{-1} - d_T^{\,2}(1 + d_T^{\,2}\iota_{p-1}{}'\hat B^{-1}\iota_{p-1})^{-1}$$
$$\hat B^{-1}\iota_{p-1}\iota_{p-1}{}'\hat B^{-1})(d_T^{\,2}\iota_{p-1} + T^{-1}\Delta U'_{-}\Delta u) + o_p(1). \tag{A7}$$

Combining (A4) and (A7), (A3) is seen to be equal to:

$$T^{-1}\Delta u'(I - \Delta U_{-}(\Delta U'_{-}\Delta U_{-})^{-1}\Delta U'_{-})\Delta u + d_T^{\,2}(1 + d_T^{\,2}\iota_{p-1}{}'B^{-1}\iota_{p-1})^{-1} \times$$
$$(1 - c'B^{-1}\iota_{p-1})^2 + o_p(1), \tag{A8}$$

where $B = \operatorname{plim} \hat B$ and $c = \operatorname{plim} \hat B(T^{-1}\Delta U'_{-}\,\Delta u)$. Because of (5) in the text,

$$T^{-1}\Delta u'(I - \Delta U_{-}(\Delta U'_{-}\Delta U_{-})^{-1}\Delta U'_{-})\Delta u = T^{-1}\varepsilon'\varepsilon + o_p(1),$$

and we have obtained from (A1), (A2), and (A8) that

$$T^{-1}\varepsilon'\varepsilon + d_T^{\,2}(1 + d_T^{\,2}\iota_{p-1}{}'B\iota_{p-1})^{-1}(1 - c'B^{-1}\iota_{p-1})^2 + o_p(1) \qquad = \inf_\lambda s^2(\lambda)$$
$$\le T^{-1}\varepsilon'\varepsilon + +o_p(1).$$

This implies that:

$$\operatorname{plim}\inf_\lambda s^2(\lambda) = \sigma_\varepsilon^2 \tag{A9}$$
$$\operatorname{plim} d_t^2(\hat\lambda, \bar\lambda) = 0, \tag{A10}$$

because $c'B^{-1}\iota_{p-1}$ is $(b_1 + \cdots + b_{p-1})$ in the notation of (5) and hence $(1 - c'B^{-1}\iota_{p-1})^2 > 0$.

What remains is to demonstrate that (A10) implies $\operatorname{plim}(\hat\lambda - \bar\lambda) = 0$. In relation to (A5) $P(Y_1(\lambda))$ there has been expressed on the right hand side of (A6). Noting (11) in the text for x_{-1}, of which ι and t are in $Y_1(\lambda)$ and $\|T^{-3/2}du(\bar\lambda)\bar\gamma\|$ and $\|T^{-3/2}u_{-1}\|$ go to zero as $T \to \infty$, construct

$$\tilde Y_1(\lambda) = [i, t, dt(\bar\lambda)\bar\gamma, du(\lambda), dt(\lambda)], \quad \lambda \ne \bar\lambda.$$

Then in relation to (A5)

$$d_T^{\,2}(\lambda, \bar\lambda) = d_T^{*2}(\lambda, \bar\lambda) + o_p(1),$$

where

$$d_T^{*2}(\lambda, \bar\lambda) = T^{-1}\bar\gamma'dj(\bar\lambda - \lambda)'(I - P(\tilde Y_1(\lambda)))dj(\bar\lambda - \lambda)\bar\gamma, \tag{A5'}$$

which is a nonstochastic function of λ. It is now sufficient to show that when

λ is looked upon as a function of $d_T^{*2}(\lambda, \bar{\lambda})$, $\lambda \to \bar{\lambda}$ as $d_T^{*2}(\lambda, \bar{\lambda}) \to 0$ in large T.

$(A5')$ is the squared norm of that part of $T^{-1/2}dj(\bar{\lambda} - \lambda)\bar{\gamma}$ that is orthogonal to the space spanned by columns of $\bar{Y}_1(\lambda)D_T^{-1}$, where D_T^{-1} is defined in (A6'). Since $T^{-1/2}dj(\bar{\lambda} - \lambda)\bar{\gamma}$ "stay away" from the space while $T \to \infty$, $d_T^{*2}(\lambda, \bar{\lambda}) \to 0$ if and only if $||T^{-1/2}dj(\bar{\lambda} - \lambda)\bar{\gamma}|| \to 0$. Under the assumption that $\bar{\gamma}_1 \neq 0$ and $\bar{\gamma}_2 \neq 0$ it is easy to show that $||T^{-1/2}dj(\bar{\lambda} - \lambda)\bar{\gamma}|| \to 0$ if and only if $(\bar{\lambda} - \lambda) \to 0$. If $\lambda_1 \neq \bar{\lambda}_1$ and $\lambda_2 \neq \bar{\lambda}_2$, $T^{-1}dj(\bar{\lambda} - \lambda)'dj(\bar{\lambda} - \lambda)$ is positive definite, and $||T^{-1/2}dj(\bar{\lambda} - \lambda)\bar{\gamma}|| > 0$. If one of λ_i is equal to $\bar{\lambda}_i$, this matrix has zero except at one diagonal element, which is positive, and $||T^{-1/2}dj(\bar{\lambda} - \lambda)\bar{\gamma}|| > 0$. It is only when $\lambda_1 = \bar{\lambda}_1$ and $\lambda_2 = \bar{\lambda}_2$ that $||T^{-1/2}dj(\bar{\lambda} - \lambda)\bar{\gamma}|| = 0$.   QED

Proof of Proposition II. Our reasoning can be presented more clearly in terms of break points, $T_* = [T_1, T_2]$, than in break fractions. What has been written earlier as $s^2(\lambda)$, $du(\lambda)$, and $dt(\lambda)$ will be denoted by $s^2(T_*)$, $du(T_*) = [du(T_1), du(T_2)]$, and $dt(T_*) = [dt(T_1), dt(T_2)]$. Let

$$X(T_*) = [\iota, t, x_{-1}, du(T_*), dt(T_*), \Delta x_{-1}, \cdots \Delta x_{-p+1}],$$
$$s^2(T_*) = T^{-1}\Delta x'(I - P(X(T_*)))\Delta x \qquad (A11)$$
$$\hat{T}_* = \arg\inf_{T_*} s^2(T_*).$$

The true value of T_* is $\bar{T}_* = [\bar{T}_1, \bar{T}_2]$.

The basic framework of our proof has been transferred from Bai and Perron (1998). We wish to show that $\hat{T}_* - \bar{T}_*$ is $O_p(1)$ as $T \to \infty$, i.e., that for an arbitrarily small η (> 0) there exists a constant c (> 0) such that:

$$P[||\hat{T}_* - \bar{T}_*|| > c] < \eta$$

for all sufficiently large T. The event that

$$\left\|\arg\inf_{T_*} s^2(T_*) - \bar{T}_*\right\| > c$$

is logically contained in the event that there exists c such that $|T_1 - \bar{T}_1| > c$ or $|T_2 - \bar{T}_2| > c$, and $s^2(T_*) \leq s^2(\bar{T}_*)$. Therefore we may show for all sufficiently large T that there exists c such that

$$P[|T_1 - \bar{T}_1| > c \text{ or } |T_2 - \bar{T}_2| > c, \text{ and } s^2(T_*) \leq s^2(\bar{T}_*)] < \eta. \qquad (A12)$$

Notice that we are examining T_* such that $||T_* - \bar{T}_*||$ does not expand to ∞ with T, even though $\bar{T}_i = [T\bar{\lambda}_i] \to \infty$ as $T \to \infty$.

The rest of the proof is basically different from Bai and Perron (1998) due to differences in the models. The third column of $X(T_*)$ is

$$x_{-1} = (\bar{\beta}_1 - \bar{\beta}_2)\iota + \bar{\beta}_2 t - du(\bar{T}_*)\bar{\gamma} + dt(\bar{T}_*)\bar{\gamma} + u_{-1}, \qquad (A13)$$

and different normalizers D_T^{-1} are necessitated for $T_* =$ and $\neq \bar{T}_*$ as mentioned in the above proof of Proposition I, in the parenthesis below (A6′). Here we can remove the problem. Noting:[10]

$$dt(\overline{T}_i) \approx dt(T_i) + (T_i - \overline{T}_i)du(\overline{T}_i), \quad i = 1, 2,$$

and also writing:

$$du(\overline{T}_i) = du(T_i) + dj(\overline{T}_i - T_i), \quad i = 1, 2,$$

$-du(\overline{T}_*)\overline{\gamma} + dt(\overline{T}_*)\,\overline{\gamma}$ in (A13) is approximately

$$-du(T_*)\overline{\gamma} + dt(T_*)\overline{\gamma} - dj(\overline{T}_1 - T_1)\overline{\gamma}_1 - dj(\overline{T}_2 - T_2)\overline{\gamma}_2$$
$$+(T_1 - \overline{T}_1)du(\overline{T}_1)\overline{\gamma}_1 + (T_2 - \overline{T}_2)du(\overline{T}_2)\overline{\gamma}_2.$$

The space spanned by columns of $X(T_*)$ is also approximately spanned by columns of

$$\tilde{X}(T_*) = [\iota, t, \xi, du(T_*), dt(T_*), \Delta u_{-1}, \cdots, \Delta u_{-p+1}],$$

where

$$\xi = -dj(\overline{T}_* - T_*)\overline{\gamma} + du(\overline{T}_*)[(T_1 - \overline{T}_1)\overline{\gamma}_1, (T_2 - \overline{T}_2)\overline{\gamma}_2]' + u_{-1}.$$

We have written $dj(\overline{T}_* - T_*) = [dj(\overline{T}_1 - T_1), dj(\overline{T}_2 - T_2)]$. When $T_* = \overline{T}_*$, $dj(\overline{T}_* - T_*)$ and $du(\overline{T}_*)$ vanish from ξ, leaving only u_{-1} in it. The same normalizer, T^{-1}, applies to ξ whether $T_* =$ or $\neq \overline{T}_*$, because $T^{-2}u'_{-1}u_{-1} = O_p(1)$, $T^{-2}du(\overline{T}_*)'du(\overline{T}_*) = O(T^{-1})$, and $T^{-2}dj(\overline{T}_* - T_*)'dj(\overline{T}_* - T_*) = O(T^{-2})$.

Construct $Y(T_*) = \tilde{X}(T_*)D_T^{-1}$ with $D_T^{-1} = diag[T^{-1/2}, T^{-3/2}, T^{-1}, T^{-1/2}I_2, T^{-3/2}I_2, T^{-1/2}I_{p-1}]$. $P(X(T_*))$ in (A11) is $P(Y(T_*))$. Since

$$\Delta x = \overline{\beta}_2 \iota + du(\overline{T}_*)\overline{\gamma} + \Delta u$$
$$= \overline{\beta}_2 \iota + du(T_*)\overline{\gamma} + dj(\overline{T}_* - T_*)\overline{\gamma} + \Delta u,$$
$$s^2(T_*) = T^{-1}(dj(\overline{T}_* - T_*)\overline{\gamma} + \Delta u)'(I - P(Y(T_*)))(dj(\overline{T}_* - T_*)\overline{\gamma} + \Delta u)$$
$$= T^{-1}\overline{\gamma}'dj(\overline{T}_* - T_*)'(I - P(Y(T_*)))dj(\overline{T}_* - T_*)\overline{\gamma}$$
$$+ 2T^{-1}\Delta u'(I - P(Y(T_*)))dj(\overline{T}_* - T_*)\overline{\gamma}$$
$$+ T^{-1}\Delta u'(I - P(Y(T_*)))\Delta u. \tag{A14}$$

On the other hand

$$s^2(T_*) = T^{-1}\Delta u'(I - P(Y(\overline{T}_*)))\Delta u. \tag{A15}$$

To prove (A12) we investigate (A14) minus (A15). We shall (a) confirm that the terms larger than $O_p(T^{-1})$ all vanish, (b) retain all terms that are $O_p(T^{-1})$, and drop all terms that are smaller than $O_p(T^{-1})$.

(i) Within the first term of (A14)

$$T^{-1}\overline{\gamma}'dj(\overline{T}_* - T_*)'Y(T_*)(Y(T_*)'Y(T_*))^{-1}Y(T_*)'dj(\overline{T}_* - T_*)\overline{\gamma} \tag{A16}$$

is $O_p(T^{-2})$. As for elements of $T^{-1/2}dj(\overline{T}_1 - T_1)'Y(T_*)$, for example,

$$T^{-\frac{1}{2}}dj(\overline{T}_* - T_*)'t T^{-\frac{3}{2}} = [\overline{\lambda}_1 T^{-1}(T_1 - \overline{T}_1), \overline{\lambda}_2 T^{-1}(T_2 - \overline{T}_2)]' + o(T^{-1})$$

$$T^{-\frac{1}{2}}dj(\overline{T}_* - T_*)'u_{-1}T^{-1} = [\overline{T}_1^{-\frac{1}{2}}u_{\overline{T}_1}\overline{\lambda}_1^{\frac{1}{2}}T^{-1}(T_1 - \overline{T}_1),$$

$$\overline{T}_2^{-\frac{1}{2}}u_{\overline{T}_2}\overline{\lambda}_2^{\frac{1}{2}}T^{-1}(T_2 - \overline{T}_2)]' + o_p(T^{-1}),$$

which are $O(T^{-1})$ and $O_p(T^{-1})$ respectively. Similarly for other elements, and thus $T^{-1/2}\overline{\gamma}'dj(\overline{T}_* - T_*)'Y(T_*)$ is $O_p(T^{-1})$. $(Y(T_*)'Y(T_*))^{-1}$ is $O_p(1)$. Thus (A16) is $O_p(T^{-2})$.

(ii) Within the second term of (A14)

$$2T^{-1}\Delta u'Y(T_*)(Y(T_*)'Y(T_*))^{-1}Y(T_*)'dj(\overline{T}_* - T_*)\overline{\gamma}$$

is $O_p(T^{-3/2})$. As for elements of $T^{-1/2}\Delta u'Y(T_*)$, for example,

$$T^{-\frac{1}{2}}\Delta u'\,t\,T^{-\frac{3}{2}} = O_p(T^{-\frac{1}{2}}), \quad T^{-\frac{1}{2}}\Delta u'u_{-1}T^{-1} = O_p(T^{-\frac{1}{2}}).$$

Similarly for other elements, and thus $T^{-1/2}\Delta u'Y(T_*)$ is $O_p(T^{-1/2})$, while $T^{-1/2}Y(T_*)'dj\,(\overline{T}_* - T_*)\overline{\gamma}$ is $O_p(T^{-1})$.

(iii) It can be shown that (the third term of (A14)) minus (A15), i.e.,

$$T^{-1}\Delta u'(P(Y(\overline{T}_*)) - P(Y(T_*)))\Delta u \tag{A17}$$

is $O_p(T^{-3/2})$. The reason is as follows. Abbreviating $Y(\overline{T}_*)$ and $Y(T_*)$ as $\overline{Y}$ and Y respectively,

$$T^{-1}\Delta u'\overline{Y}(\overline{Y}'\overline{Y})^{-1}\overline{Y}'\Delta u - T^{-1}\Delta u'Y(Y'Y)^{-1}Y'\Delta u$$
$$\approx 2T^{-1}\Delta u'(\overline{Y} - Y)(\overline{Y}'\overline{Y})^{-1}\overline{Y}'\Delta u$$
$$-T^{-1}\Delta u'\overline{Y}(\overline{Y}'\overline{Y})^{-1}(Y'Y - \overline{Y}'\overline{Y})(\overline{Y}'\overline{Y})^{-1}Y'\Delta u.$$

The first term is $O_p(T^{-3/2})$. As for the second term it can be shown that all elements of $Y'Y - \overline{Y}'\overline{Y}$ are $O_p(T^{-1})$. Thus the second term is $O_p(T^{-2})$, and (A17) is $O_p(T^{-3/2})$.

(iv) What remain in (A14) minus (A15) are $O_p(T^{-1})$. Thus, apart from the terms in $o_p(T^{-1})$, $s^2(T_*) - s^2(\overline{T}_*)$ is equal to:

$$T^{-1}\overline{\gamma}'dj(\overline{T}_* - T_*)'dj(\overline{T}_* - T_*)\overline{\gamma} + 2T^{-1}\Delta u'dj(\overline{T}_* - T_*)\overline{\gamma}$$
$$= T^{-1}\{\overline{\gamma}_1^2\left|T_1 - \overline{T}_1\right| + 2g_1(T_1 - \overline{T}_1) + \overline{\gamma}_2^2\left|T_2 - \overline{T}_2\right| + 2g_2(T_2 - \overline{T}_2)\} \tag{A18}$$

where

$$g_i(T_i - \overline{T}_i) = \begin{cases} 0 & \text{if } T_i - \overline{T}_i = 0 \\ (T_i - \overline{T}_i)^{\frac{1}{2}}\overline{\gamma}_i(\left|T_i - \overline{T}_i\right|^{-\frac{1}{2}}\sum_{s=1}^{T_i - \overline{T}_i}\Delta u_{\overline{T}_i + s}) & \text{if } T_i - \overline{T}_i > 0 \\ -\left|T_i - \overline{T}_i\right|^{\frac{1}{2}}\overline{\gamma}_i(\left|T_i - \overline{T}_i\right|^{-\frac{1}{2}}\sum_{s=T_i-\overline{T}_i}^{-1}\Delta u_{\overline{T}_i + s}) & \text{if } T_i - \overline{T}_i < 0 \end{cases}$$

$$i = 1, 2.$$

We have assumed that $dj(\bar{T}_1 - T_1)'dj(\bar{T}_2 - T_2) = 0$ because, $(\hat{\lambda}_1, \hat{\lambda}_2)$ being consistent, $P[|\hat{T}_i - \bar{T}_i| > T\delta]$, $i = 1, 2$, can be made as small as we wish for arbitrarily small δ. The probability that (A18) is negative (in spite of the fact that $\bar{\gamma}_i^2|T_i - \bar{T}_i|$ is necessarily positive) can be made as small as we wish by making either one of $|T_i - \bar{T}_i|$ sufficiently large. (A12) has been proved.

Finally the asymptotic independence between $\hat{T}_1 - \bar{T}_1$ and $\hat{T}_2 - \bar{T}_2$ can be derived from (A18). Observe that $\arg\inf s^2(T_*) = \arg\inf(s^2(T_*) - s^2(\bar{T}_*))$, and that the dominating part of $s^2(T_*) - s^2(\bar{T}_*)$ is (A18). $\hat{T}_1$ and $\hat{T}_2$ are to minimize the first and the second parts of (A18) respectively, and the two partial sums of Δu_t become independent as $T \to \infty$.   QED

Corollary of Proposition II. In relation to Proposition II $\hat{T}_i - \bar{T}_i$, $i = 1, 2$, are each distributed symmetrically about zero, if ε_t has a continuous distribution symmetric about zero.

Proof. In general the limit distribution of $\hat{T}_i - \bar{T}_i$ depends on the distribution function of ε_t, but the above symmetry can be derived without specifying a particular distribution function of ε_t. We shall consider $\{\varepsilon_t, t = \cdots, -2, -1, 0, 1, 2, \cdots\}$ and $\{\Delta u_t, t = \cdots, -2, -1, 0, 1, 2, \cdots\}$. In relation to (A18) construct for $\tau = \cdots, -2, -1, 0, 1, 2, \cdots$

$$f(\tau, \bar{\gamma}_i) = \begin{cases} \left|\bar{\gamma}_i^2\tau\right| + 2\bar{\gamma}_i\sum_{s=1}^{\tau}\Delta u_s & \text{for } \tau > 0 \\ 0 & \text{for } \tau = 0 \\ \left|\bar{\gamma}_i^2\tau\right| - 2\bar{\gamma}_i\sum_{s=\tau}^{-1}\Delta u_s & \text{for } \tau < 0. \end{cases}$$

$f(\tau, \bar{\gamma}_i) \to +\infty$ a.s. as $\tau \to \pm\infty$. $T_1 - \bar{T}_1$ and $T_2 - \bar{T}_2$ are asymptotically independent, and ε_t has a continuous distribution. As proved in Bai (1997, proof of proposition 2) on a similar situation, $\hat{T}_i - \bar{T}_i$ is asymptotically distributed as $\arg\inf_\tau f(\tau, \bar{\gamma}_i)$. We shall show that the probability that the arg inf is s is equal to the probability that it is $-s$.

In relation to (5), $\Delta u_t = b_1\Delta u_{t-1} + \cdots + b_{p-1}\Delta u_{t-p+1} + \varepsilon_t$ and $\Delta u_t = b_1\Delta u_{t+1} + \cdots + b_{p-1}\Delta u_{t+p-1} + \varepsilon_t$ generate the identical probability structure of $\{\Delta u_t\}$. In particular, for any integer k (> 0) $U_{2k+1} = [\Delta u_{-k}, \cdots, \Delta u_{-1}, \Delta u_0, \Delta u_1, \cdots, \Delta u_k]$ and $\tilde{U}_{2k+1} = [\Delta u_k, \cdots, \Delta u_1, \Delta u_0, \Delta u_{-1}, \cdots, \Delta u_{-k}]$ are identically distributed. Let $I_{*,2k+1}$ be a $(2k + 1) \times (2k + 1)$ matrix such that its (i, j) element is 1 if $i + j = 2k + 2$, and is zero otherwise. $\tilde{U}_{2k+1} = U_{2k+1}I_{*,2k+1}$.

The stochastic terms involved in $f(\tau, \bar{\gamma}_i)$ are:

$$V_{2k+1} = \left[-\sum_{s=-k}^{1}\Delta u_s, \cdots, -\Delta u_{-1}, 0, \Delta u_1, \cdots, \sum_{s=1}^{k}\Delta u_s\right]$$
$$= U_{2k+1}\,\text{diag}[-I_k, 0, I_k]\,\text{diag}[S, 0, S'],$$

where 0 in the *diag* is the scalar, zero, and S is the $k \times k$ lower triangular matrix of unities. We shall show that V_{2k+1} and $V_{2k+1}I_{*,2k+1}$ are identically distributed.

$$V_{2k+1}I_{*,2k+1} = \left[\sum_{s=1}^{k}\Delta u_s, \cdots, \Delta u_1, 0, -\Delta u_{-1}, \cdots, -\sum_{s=-k}^{1}\Delta u_s\right]$$
$$= \tilde{U}_{2k+1}\,\mathrm{diag}[I_k,0,-I_k]\,\mathrm{diag}[S,0,S'].$$

The distribution of the last expression is identical to that of

$$U_{2k+1}\,\mathrm{diag}[I_k,0,-I_k]\,\mathrm{diag}[S,0,S'],$$

and the latter distribution is identical to that of V_{2k+1}, because ε_t is distributed symmetrically about zero.

    Let $D_{2k+1} = [|k\overline{\gamma}_i^2|, \cdots, |\overline{\gamma}_i^2|, 0, |\overline{\gamma}_i^2|, \cdots, |k\overline{\gamma}_i^2|]$, and note that $D_{2k+1}I_{*,2k+1} = D_{2k+1}$. Let E_{2k+1} be a realization of V_{2k+1}. E_{2k+1} and $E_{2k+1}I_{*,2k+1}$ have the identical probability measure. Moreover, if the elements of $2\overline{\gamma}_i E_{2k+1} + D_{2k+1}$ attain their minimum in their sth element, $1 \le s \le 2k+1$, the elements of $(2\overline{\gamma}_i E_{2k+1} + D_{2k+1})I_{*,2k+1}$ attain their minimum in their $(2k+2-s)$th element. The probability that the elements of $2\overline{\gamma}_i V_{2k+1} + D_{2k+1}$ are minimum at the sth element is equal to the probability that they are minimum at the $(2k+2-s)$th element. The proof is completed by letting $k \to \infty$.[11]   QED

To prove Proposition III we shall prepare two lemmas. Let $X_1(\lambda) = [\iota, t, du(\lambda), dt(\lambda), \Delta x_{-1}, \cdots, \Delta x_{-p+1}]$, $D_T^{-1} = diag\,[T^{-1/2}, T^{-3/2}, T^{-1/2}I_2, T^{-3/2}I_2, T^{-1/2}I_{p-1}]$, $Y_1(\lambda) = X_1(\lambda)\,D_T^{-1}$, $dY_1 = Y_1(\hat\lambda) - Y_1(\overline\lambda), \overline{Y}_1 = Y_1(\overline\lambda)$. Note that $\overline{Y}_1'\overline{Y}_1$ is $O_p(1)$ and $\hat\lambda - \overline\lambda$ is $O_p(T^{-1})$.

Lemma 1. $dY_1'\overline{Y}_1$ is $O_p(T^{-1})$. Moreover:

$$Y_1(\hat\lambda)'Y_1(\hat\lambda) - Y_1(\overline\lambda)'Y_1(\overline\lambda) = dY_1'\overline{Y}_1 + \overline{Y}_1'dY_1 + W + O_p(T^{-2}),$$

where W is zero except at the 2×2 principal submatrix that corresponds to $du(\lambda)$ row-wise and column-wise. The submatrix is $O_p(T^{-1})$.

    The reason for W is that $T^{-1/2}(du(\hat\lambda_i) - du(\overline\lambda_i))'(du(\hat\lambda_i) - du(\overline\lambda_i))T^{-1/2}$, an element of $dY_1'dY_1$, is identical to $T^{-1/2}(du(\hat\lambda_i) - du(\overline\lambda_i))'du(\overline\lambda_i)T^{-1/2}$, an element of $dY_1'\overline{Y}_1$, apart from signs.

Lemma 2. Let a and b be each a column of a matrix A such that $A'A$ is nonsingular, and let dA and $dP(A)$ be differentials of A and $P(A)$ respectively. If

$$dP(A) = dA(A'A)^{-1}A' + A(A'A)^{-1}dA' - A(A'A)^{-1}(dA'A + A'dA)(A'A)^{-1}A',$$

then $b'dP(A)a = 0$. Moreover if a is not a column of A but b is the ith column, $b'dP(A)a = e_i'dA'(I - P(A))a$, where e_i is the ith unit vector.
    $T^{-1/2}du(\overline\lambda)$ is in $\overline{Y}_1$. Therefore

$$T^{-\frac{1}{2}}du(\overline\lambda)'(P(Y_1(\hat\lambda)) - P(Y_1(\overline\lambda)))du(\overline\lambda)T^{-\frac{1}{2}}$$
$$= -(\text{the } 2 \times 2 \text{ principal submatrix of } W) + O_p(T^{-2}). \tag{A19a}$$

Suppose that η_a is not in $\bar{Y}_1$. Then

$$
T^{-\frac{1}{2}}du(\bar{\lambda})'(P(Y_1(\hat{\lambda})) - P(Y_1(\bar{\lambda})))\eta_a
$$
$$
= -T^{-\frac{1}{2}}(du(\hat{\lambda}) - du(\bar{\lambda}))'(I - P(Y_1(\bar{\lambda})))\eta_a
$$
$$
-[(\text{the rows of } W \text{ that correspond to } T^{-\frac{1}{2}}du(\bar{\lambda}))(\bar{Y}_1'\bar{Y}_1)^{-1}\bar{Y}_1'
$$
$$
+O_p(T^{-2})]\eta_a. \tag{A19b}
$$

Proof of Proposition III. (a) On the t-statistic

$$
\hat{t}_\alpha(\hat{\lambda}) = s^2(\hat{\lambda})^{-\frac{1}{2}}(x_{-1}'(I - P(X_1(\hat{\lambda})))x_{-1})^{-\frac{1}{2}}x_{-1}'(I - P(X_1(\hat{\lambda})))\Delta x.
$$

It has been proved that plim $s^2(\hat{\lambda}) = \sigma_\varepsilon^2$ in (A9). From (11) of the text

$$
T^{-2}x_{-1}'(I - P(X_1(\hat{\lambda})))x_{-1}
$$
$$
= T^{-2}(dt(\bar{\lambda})\bar{\gamma} + u_{-1})'(I - P(X_1(\hat{\lambda})))(dt(\bar{\lambda})\bar{\gamma} + u_{-1}) + o_p(1)
$$
$$
= T^{-2}(\xi + u_{-1})'(I - P(X_1(\hat{\lambda})))(\xi + u_{-1}) + o_p(1),
$$

(where $\xi = du(\bar{\lambda})[(\hat{T}_1 - \bar{T}_1)\bar{\gamma}_1, (\hat{T}_2 - \bar{T}_2)\bar{\gamma}_2]'$, see the proof of Proposition II)

$$
= T^{-2}(\xi + u_{-1})'(I - P(Y_1(\bar{\lambda})))(\xi + u_{-1})
$$
$$
+T^{-2}(\xi + u_{-1})'(P(Y_1(\bar{\lambda})) - P(Y_1(\hat{\lambda})))(\xi + u_{-1}) + o_p(1)
$$
$$
= T^{-2}u_{-1}'(I - P(Y_1(\bar{\lambda})))u_{-1}
$$
$$
+T^{-2}(\xi + u_{-1})'(P(Y_1(\bar{\lambda})) - P(Y_1(\hat{\lambda})))(\xi + u_{-1}) + o_p(1).
$$

From (A19a) we get

$$
T^{-1}T^{-\frac{1}{2}}\xi'(P(Y_1(\bar{\lambda})) - P(Y_1(\hat{\lambda})))T^{-\frac{1}{2}}\xi = O_p(T^{-2}).
$$

From (A19b) we get

$$
T^{-\frac{3}{2}}u_{-1}'(P(Y_1(\bar{\lambda})) - P(Y_1(\hat{\lambda})))T^{-\frac{1}{2}}\xi = O_p(T^{-\frac{3}{2}}).
$$

Finally $T^{-2}u_{-1}'(P(Y_1(\bar{\lambda})) - P(Y_1(\hat{\lambda})))u_{-1} = O_p(T^{-1})$. Thus

$$
T^{-2}x_{-1}'(I - P(X_1(\hat{\lambda})))x_{-1} = T^{-2}u_{-1}'(I - P(Y_1(\bar{\lambda})))u_{-1} + o_p(1)
$$

$\xrightarrow{D} \sigma_\varepsilon^2 \int b_{wa}(r, \bar{\lambda})^2 dr$, where b_{wa} is defined in (14).
In an analogous way it can be shown that:

$$
T^{-1}x_{-1}'(I - P(X_1(\hat{\lambda})))\Delta x = T^{-1}u_{-1}'(I - P(Y_1(\bar{\lambda})))\Delta u + o_p(1)
$$

$\xrightarrow{D} \sigma_\varepsilon^2 \int b_{wa}(r, \bar{\lambda}) dw(r)$.
(b) On the F-statistic

$$
4F(\hat{\lambda}) = s^2(\hat{\lambda})^{-1}\Delta x'(P(X(\hat{\lambda})) - P(X_2(\hat{\lambda})))\Delta x,
$$

where $X(\hat{\lambda}) = [\iota, \boldsymbol{t}, x_{-1}, du(\hat{\lambda}), dt(\hat{\lambda}), \Delta x_{-1}, \cdots, \Delta x_{-p+1}]$ and $X_2(\hat{\lambda}) = [\iota, du(\hat{\lambda}), \Delta x_{-1}, \cdots, \Delta x_{-p+1}]$. Let

$$X_3(\hat{\lambda}) = [\boldsymbol{t}, x_{-1}, dt(\hat{\lambda})],$$

so that columns of $X(\hat{\lambda})$ consist of those in $X_2(\hat{\lambda})$ and $X_3(\hat{\lambda})$. Since ι and $du(\hat{\lambda})$ are in both $X(\hat{\lambda})$ and $X_2(\hat{\lambda})$,

$$
\begin{aligned}
\Delta x'&(P(X(\hat{\lambda})) - P(X_2(\hat{\lambda})))\Delta x \\
&= (dj(\overline{\lambda} - \hat{\lambda})'\overline{\gamma} + \Delta u)'(P(X(\hat{\lambda})) - P(X_2(\hat{\lambda})))(dj(\overline{\lambda} - \hat{\lambda})'\overline{\gamma} + \Delta u) \\
&= (dj(\overline{\lambda} - \hat{\lambda})'\overline{\gamma} + \Delta u)'(I - P(X_2(\hat{\lambda})))X_3(\hat{\lambda}) \times \\
&\quad (X_3(\hat{\lambda})'(I - P(X_2(\hat{\lambda})))X_3(\hat{\lambda}))^{-1} \times \\
&\quad X_3(\hat{\lambda})'(I - P(X_2(\hat{\lambda})))(dj(\overline{\lambda} - \hat{\lambda})'\overline{\gamma} + \Delta u). \tag{A20}
\end{aligned}
$$

Express $dt(\overline{\lambda})\overline{\gamma}$ in x_{-1} as a linear combination of $dt(\hat{\lambda})$ and $du(\overline{\lambda})$. Also express this $dt(\hat{\lambda})$ in x_{-1} and $dt(\hat{\lambda})$ in $X_3(\hat{\lambda})$ as a linear combination of $dt(\overline{\lambda})$ and $du(\overline{\lambda})$. Since $du(\hat{\lambda})$ are columns of $X_2(\hat{\lambda})$, it follows that

$$
\begin{aligned}
X_3(\hat{\lambda})'&(I - P(X_2(\hat{\lambda})))X_3(\hat{\lambda}) \\
&= B'[\boldsymbol{t}, u_{-1}dt(\overline{\lambda})]'(I - P(X_2(\hat{\lambda})))[\boldsymbol{t}, u_{-1}, dt(\overline{\lambda})]B,
\end{aligned}
$$

where

$$
B = \left[
\begin{array}{cc|c}
I_2 & & 0 \\
0 & \overline{\gamma}_1 & I_2 \\
0 & \overline{\gamma}_2 &
\end{array}
\right]
$$

Thus with $\tilde{X}_3(\overline{\lambda}) = [\boldsymbol{t}, u_{-1}, dt(\overline{\lambda})]$, (A20) is

$$
\begin{aligned}
(dj(\overline{\lambda} - \hat{\lambda})'\overline{\gamma} + \Delta u)'&(I - P(X_2(\hat{\lambda})))\tilde{X}_3(\overline{\lambda})(\tilde{X}_3(\overline{\lambda})'(I - P(X_2(\hat{\lambda})))\tilde{X}_3(\overline{\lambda}))^{-1} \\
&\tilde{X}_3(\overline{\lambda})'(I - P(X_2(\hat{\lambda})))(dj(\overline{\lambda} - \hat{\lambda})'\overline{\gamma} + \Delta u).
\end{aligned}
$$

The rest of the proof is analogous to the t-statistic. The term that is not $o_p(1)$ is

$$
\begin{aligned}
\Delta u'&(I - P(X_2(\overline{\lambda})))\tilde{X}_3(\overline{\lambda})(\tilde{X}_3(\overline{\lambda})'(I - P(X_2(\overline{\lambda})))\tilde{X}_3(\overline{\lambda}))^{-1} \\
&\tilde{X}_3(\overline{\lambda})'(I - P(X_2(\hat{\lambda})))\Delta u,
\end{aligned}
$$

which converges to $\sigma_\varepsilon^2 \times$ (the right hand side of (17)).   QED

Notes

1. In Figure 1 identical scales are adopted on the Y axis among different countries so that the slopes of linear trends may be compared.
2. The previous, empirical tests on the Japanese GDP data may be summarized as follows. Soejima (1995) chooses a plausible time interval within which a break point might be located, and performs a sequence of unit root tests of Perron (1989) while

sliding the break point over the interval. The result is that the Japanese GDP is I(0) unless the break point is after 1974 I. Ohara (1997) extends the method in Zivot and Andrews (1992) to multiple breaks. The result is that the Japanese GDP is I(0).

3. See Said and Dickey (1985).
4. Indeed $\mu_i = \gamma_i (\alpha + 1 - b_1 - \cdots - b_{p-1})$, $i = 1, 2$. Suppose that at least one of a_1, $\cdots$, a_p is not zero. The assumption made on the roots of the characteristic equation of (4) implies $\alpha + 1 - b_1 - \cdots - b_{p-1} \neq 0$. Then suppose that $a_1 = \cdots = a_p = 0$. It directly follows that $\alpha = -1$ and $b_1 = \cdots = b_{p-1} = 0$.
5. See Andrews (1993) for general discussions of this kind of statistic.
6. However see note 11.
7. The Japanese data in Figure 1 are not per capita. GDP per capita is used more frequently in macroeconomics.
8. $\{\varepsilon_t\}$ is a series of normal random numbers in all the simulations.
9. Another representation of Δx is

$$\Delta x = \overline{\mu}_0 \iota + du(\overline{\lambda})\overline{\mu} + \overline{b}_1 \Delta x_{-1} + \cdots + \overline{b}_{p-1}\Delta x_{-p+1} + \varepsilon$$

along equation (7). Use of this representation simplifies (A7) and (A8). But this kind of representation cannot be used for $\Delta x_{-1}, \cdots, \Delta x_{-p+1}$ in $X(\lambda)$, necessitating two representations to appear side by side. It might make it more difficult to follow through the proof.

10. Concerning $\approx$ the norm of the vector that represents the error of approximation is $\sum_{j=0}^{|T_i - \overline{T}_i|} j$, which is O(1), while $\| (T_i - \overline{T}_i) du(\overline{T}_i) \| = O(T)$.
11. When $\{u_t\}$ is I(0), $\hat{T}_i - \overline{T}_i$ is asymptotically arg inf$_\tau$ $g(\tau, \overline{\gamma}_i)$, where

$$g(\tau, \overline{\gamma}_i) = \begin{cases} \left| \overline{\gamma}_i^2 \tau \right| + 2\overline{\gamma}_i \sum_{s=1}^{\tau} \varepsilon_s & \text{for } \tau > 0 \\ 0 & \text{for } \tau = 0 \\ \left| \overline{\gamma}_i^2 \tau \right| - 2\overline{\gamma}_i \sum_{s=\tau}^{-1} \varepsilon_s & \text{for } \tau < 0. \end{cases}$$

References

Andrews, D. (1993), "Tests for Parameter Instability and Structural Change with Unknown Change Points," *Econometrica*, 61: 821–56.

Bai, J. (1997), "Estimation of a Change Point in Multiple Regression Models," *The Review of Economics and Statistics*, 79: 551–63.

Bai, J. and P. Perron (1998), "Estimating and Testing Linear Models with Multiple Structural Changes," *Econometrica*, 66: 47–78.

Hatanaka, M. (1996), *Time Series Based Econometrics*. Oxford: Oxford University Press.

Kunitomo, N. (1996), "Tests of Unit Roots and Cointegration Hypotheses in Econometric Models," *Japanese Economic Review*, 47: 79–109.

Kunitomo, N. and S. Sato (1995), "Tables of Limiting Distributions for Testing Unit Roots and Co-integration with Multiple Structural Breaks," mimeo.

Ohara, H. (1997), "Unit Root Test against a Trend Stationary Alternative with Multiple Trend Breaks," *Japanese Economic Review*. Forthcoming.

Perron, P. (1989), "The Great Crash, the Oil Price Shock, and the Unit Root Hypothesis," *Econometrica*, 57: 1361–1401.

Said, E. S. and D. A. Dickey (1985), "Hypothesis Testing in ARIMA(p, 1, q) Models," *Journal of the American Statistical Association*, 80: 369–74.

Soejima, Y. (1995), "Unit Root Test of the Japanese Macroeconomic Variables," *Monetary Economic Studies* (Bank of Japan), 13: 53–68.

Vogelsang, T. J. and P. Perron (1994), "Additional Tests for a Unit Root Allowing for a Break in the Trend Fraction at an Unknown Time," mimeo.

Zivot, E. and D. Andrews (1992), "Further Evidence on the Great Crash, the Oil-Price Shock, and Unit-Root Hypothesis," *Journal of Business and Economic Statistics*, 10: 251–70.

12
Investigating Inflation Transmission by Stages of Processing

TAE-HWY LEE AND STUART SCOTT

1 Introduction

At the time of the 1973–74 oil price shock, the featured index for the US Bureau of Labor Statistics Producer Price Index program was "All Commodities." For some time, this index was dominated by effects of oil prices as their effects spread to refined petroleum producers and other producers experiencing higher energy prices. Critics complained that the single summary index gave a very limited picture of what was happening in prices. In 1978, BLS shifted its publication emphasis to a stage of processing (SOP) system. As explained by Gaddie and Zoller (1988):

The basic idea of a stage of process system is that the economy can be subdivided into distinct economic segments which can be arranged sequentially so that the outputs of earlier segments become inputs to subsequent ones, up through final demand. . . . To the extent that such a sequential system of processing stages can be defined, it is possible to trace the transmission of price change through the economy and to develop information on both the timing and magnitude of price pass-throughs to final demand.

The initial SOP system (Popkin, 1974) is based on allocating products or commodities to three stages, Crude, Intermediate, and Finished, based on their degree of fabrication and end use. These will be denoted CSOP, since they are commodity-based. The Finished Goods index, representing goods nearest final consumption, is usually emphasized in press releases. Crude and Intermediate indexes are watched as possible indicators of future movements in Finished Goods.

A second SOP system (Gaddie and Zoller, 1988), denoted ISOP, with data available from June 1985, dovetails with an improved, industry-based sample

We wish to thank two referees, the editors, Jim Buszuwski, Brian Catron, Bill Cleveland, Jack Galvin, Irwin Gerduk, Pat Getz, Soon Paik, and Roslyn Swick for comments, discussions or for data, and Dimitri Paliouras for research assistance. The work was conducted while the first author visited the BLS under the ASA/NSF/BLS fellowship. The views expressed are those of authors and do not necessarily represent those of the BLS. All errors are our own.

design, introduced gradually over the 1978–85 period. In statistical terms, the redesign represents probability sampling of products made by individual industries under the SIC (Standard Industrial Classification) system. In conceptual terms, the ISOP represents an interindustry flow model for the economy. Using the Bureau of Economic Analysis (BEA) Input/Output tables, transaction flows between producing and consuming industries can be estimated. Four stages, Crude, Primary, Semifinished, and Finished Goods Producers, are derived as weighted averages of component SIC indexes.

Table 1 shows ISOP industry composition and transaction flow. Overall, the Crude stage represents about 10 percent of covered transactions, and the other stages roughly 30 percent each. The CSOP distribution for the three stages Crude, Intermediate, and Finished is roughly 10–50–40. Since these stages are formed by putting together commodities, wherever made, other statistics like those in Table 1 are not available for the CSOP. Following many analysts, we emphasize "core" SOPs, that is, indexes which exclude Food and Energy sectors, each representing about 15 percent of the total. These components are obviously important, but their volatility may mask other relationships in the data. The core PPI is almost entirely manufacturing; in moving from Crude to Finished the shares of Durable and Nondurable roughly reverse with Crude containing about 20 percent Durable and Finished about 80 percent Durable. The current ISOP industry coverage is quite limited. In recent years, many indexes in the service-producing industries have been added, but they are not yet in the existing ISOP.

As a starting point for partitioning industries into stages, we have an input/output table showing transaction flows between producing and consuming industries, a matrix like Table 1C, but with roughly 500 detailed industries. As indicated in the definition, the aim is to order these industries so that for a given row, representing a producing industry, most of the output is to subsequent industries, i.e., to industries to the right of the matrix diagonal. Companies, however, make such a variety of products, and their products are consumed by such a variety of industries, that no ordering produces a purely upper triangular matrix. Gaddie and Zoller's efforts to maximize "forward flow" and limit "internal flow" (consumption within the stage where produced) and "backward flow" (consumption by previous stages) are rather successful. The flow summary of Table 1D shows that the ISOP achieves a forward flow exceeding 80 percent, while backward flow and internal flow are 6 percent and 11 percent, respectively. A possible shortcoming, however, is that 30 percent of transactions skip one or more stages. For example, roughly 30–40 percent of output of each of the first three stages goes to Final Demand (products for personal consumption or capital investment). Thus, for instance, output from Primary differs considerably from input to Semifinished.

Success in analyzing price transmission among stages and to consumer prices has been limited. Mattey (1990), who makes an extra effort to extend the

Table 1. Composition of SOPs by industry sector (based on 1992 value of shipments)

A. Transactions (billions of dollars)

	Crude	Primary	Semifinished	Finished	Total
Food	39.4	134.9	200.3	198.7	573.3
Energy	138.7	389.8	0	0	528.5
Core	253.0	543.8	858.4	831.8	2487.0
Total	431.1	1068.5	1058.7	1030.5	3588.8

B. Industry sector distribution within core SOPs

Industry sector	Crude	Primary	Semifinished	Finished
Mining	6	1	0	0
Nondurable manufacturing	75	53	30	22
Durable manufacturing	19	46	70	78
Total	100	100	100	100

C. Transaction flows among ISOP

Producing stages	Consuming stages					
	Crude	Primary	Semifinished	Finished	Final demand	Total
Crude	22	23	9	17	29	100
Primary	8	14	21	20	37	100
Semifinished	6	6	11	34	43	100
Finished	2	2	1	5	90	100

We would like to thank Soon Paik at BLS for this table.

D. Transaction flow summary (%)

Backward	Internal	Forward (1)	Skip
6	11	53	30

ISOP data available at the time, has the only analytic study we have seen which explicitly compares CSOP and ISOP. Pointing out large flow differences between output from one stage and input to the next stage, due to skips and leakage, in the ISOP equations he uses the ISOP input indexes for input prices, an advantage with the ISOP, and finds forecast performance are similar for the two SOPs. Engle (1978), Silver and Wallace (1980), Granger, Robins, and Engle (1986), Blanchard (1987), Boughton and Branson (1991), Clark (1995), and many others have found evidence of price transmission among stages or evidence that changes in producer prices Granger-cause changes in consumer prices. Boughton and Branson find that producer prices and the CPI are not cointegrated, yet find a weak short-run relationship in which commodity prices help predict future CPI inflation. It is often found that the relationships between PPI and CPI are weak especially in terms of out-of-sample forecast performance.

The focus of the present paper is on inflation transmission among stages of producer prices and on transmission to consumer prices, and has been undertaken as part of a BLS effort to examine the usefulness of SOPs. The study employs multiple time series methods, and benefits from greater data availability for some of the indexes than the previous studies. Our results show that meaningful relationships exist between processing stages, and that consumer prices are strongly related to CSOP Finished Goods prices.

2 Modeling Inflation Transmission

In this section we describe how vector error correction models (VECM) can be employed to examine the sources of inflation and its transmission. We show how cointegration can be used in a VAR system to identify common stochastic trends subject to permanent changes in inflation rates and how we may investigate the system's responses to permanent shocks.

The data we will analyze are the CSOP which has been generated back to 1947 and the ISOP which starts in June 1985. Thus, our analyses are carried out for 11-year spans, June 1985 through May 1996. All PPI series are core indexes, excluding Food and Energy. CPI series is a core index excluding food, energy, and used cars. All series are monthly, seasonally adjusted, and transformed in logarithms.

In our empirical study the logarithms of all series are characterized as I(1) processes according to the augmented Dickey–Fuller and Phillips–Perron tests. The PPI inflation series in all stages are clearly mean-reverting in both ISOP and CSOP. CPI series display upward trends and their first difference shows rather smoother series than PPI series. In other studies where CPI series is used (e.g. Mehra, 1991), it is often found that the inflation series, the first differences of log prices, are I(1). However, it was not the case in our data.

Consider an SOP system with p stages, and let $X_t = (x_{1t} \ldots x_{pt})'$ be the PPI indexes. For example, in the ISOP output index system, $p = 4$ and the elements of X_t are PPI indexes for Crude, Primary, Semifinished, and Finished processors. Let X_t be I(1) and cointegrated with cointegrating rank r; that is, there exists a $p \times r$ matrix β of rank r ($< p$) such that $\beta' X_t$ is I(0). Then the system can be generated from the VECM

$$\Delta X_t = \mu + \Pi X_{t-1} + \Gamma_1 \Delta X_{t-1} + \cdots + \Gamma_k \Delta X_{t-k} + \epsilon_t, \tag{1}$$

where Π and Γs are $p \times p$, and ϵ_t is a $p \times 1$ vector white noise. The long-run impact matrix Π should then be of rank r and can be expressed as $\Pi = \alpha\beta'$ for suitable $p \times r$ matrices α and β.

We estimate the VECM given by (1) following Johansen (1995), and then transform it to a vector moving average model

$$\Delta X_t = \mu + C(B)\epsilon_t, \qquad (2)$$

where $C(B)$ is a $p \times p$ matrix polynomial in the backshift operator B. To identify the common factor h_t we rewrite (2) as

$$\Delta X_t = \mu + \Gamma(B)\eta_t, \qquad (3)$$

where $\Gamma(B) = C(B)\Gamma_0$ and $\eta_t = \Gamma_0^{-1}\epsilon_t$ for some nonsingular $p \times p$ matrix Γ_0. Partition the structural shocks $\eta_t = (\eta_t^{1\prime}\ \eta_t^{2\prime})'$ such that η_t^1 consists of η_{it} ($i = 1, ..., p - r$) and η_t^2 is $r \times 1$. We choose Γ_0 so that $\Gamma(1) = (A\ \mathbf{0})$ with $\mathbf{0}$ being a $p \times r$ null matrix. Then, using the expansion $\Gamma(B) = \Gamma(1) + \Delta\Gamma^*(B)$, (3) can be written:

$$X_t = X_0 + \mu t + A h_t + \tilde{X}_t, \qquad (4)$$

where X_0 is initial values at $t = 0$, μ is $p \times 1$, A is $p \times (p - r)$, $h_t = \sum_{n=0}^{\infty}\eta_{t-n}^1$ is $(p - r) \times 1$ I(1) common stochastic trends, and $\tilde{X}_t \equiv \Gamma^*(B)\eta_t$ consists of $p \times 1$ I(0) transitory components. Apart from the initial values and the deterministic trend, X_t can thus be decomposed into the permanent component $X_t^P = A h_t$ and the transitory component $X_t^T = \tilde{X}_t$. The elements of X_t can be explained in terms of a smaller number $(p - r)$ of I(1) variables comprising h_t, which are thus called common factors.

Let η_{it} ($i = 1, ..., p - r$) be the innovations to each stochastic trend h_{it}, i.e., $h_{it} = h_{i,t-1} + \eta_{it}$. η_t^1 may be called the permanent shocks because they construct X_t^P, while the remaining shocks η_t^2 may be called the transitory shock. The elements of A are the long-run multipliers of the permanent shock η_t^1, that is, $A = \lim_{n\to\infty}\partial X_t/\partial\eta_{t-n}^1$. The long-run multiplier of the transitory shock η_t^2 is zero because $\Gamma^*(B)$ is absolutely summable.

If X_t is cointegrated, i.e., $\beta'X_t$ is I(0), then $\beta'X_t^P = 0$ so $\beta'A = 0$ (because the process X_t^P is not cointegrated). Thus let $A = \beta_\perp\Theta$ where $\beta_\perp$ is a $p \times (p - r)$ matrix of full rank such that $\beta'\beta_\perp = 0$. $\hat{\beta}_\perp$ may be estimated following Johansen (1995, p. 95). Keeping in mind our prices application, we make several assumptions leading to the estimation of the long-run multipliers A and the short-run multipliers (impulse responses) of the permanent shocks η_t^1.

Assumption 1. Θ is a $(p - r) \times (p - r)$ lower triangular matrix of full rank. ∎

Assumption 2. The permanent shocks and the transitory shocks are uncorrelated, i.e., $\Sigma_\eta = E(\eta_t\eta_t')$ is block diagonal. ∎

Assumption 3. The permanent shocks η_t^1 are uncorrelated, i.e., $\Sigma_{\eta^1} = E(\eta_t^1\eta_t^{1\prime})$ is diagonal. ∎

Under Assumptions 1 and 2 we have

$$C(1)\Sigma_\epsilon C(1)' = \Gamma(1)\Sigma_\eta \Gamma(1)' = A\Sigma_{\eta^1} A' = \hat{\beta}_\perp \Theta \Sigma_{\eta^1} \Theta' \hat{\beta}'_\perp, \tag{5}$$

where Σ_ϵ is cov($\hat{\epsilon}$). Pre- and post-multiplying this by $\overline{\beta}_\perp = \hat{\beta}_\perp (\hat{\beta}'_\perp \hat{\beta}_\perp)^{-1}$ yields:

$$\Theta \Sigma_{\eta^1} \Theta' = \overline{\beta}'_\perp C(1)\Sigma_\epsilon C(1)' \overline{\beta}_\perp. \tag{6}$$

Under Assumption 3, Θ and Σ_{η^1} can be estimated from a Choleski decomposition of (6) either by normalizing the diagonal elements of Θ or by standardizing the permanent shocks with $\Sigma_{\eta^1} = I_{(p-r)}$.

When there is one common factor ($p - r = 1$), the permanent shock η_{1t} may be easily attached with some structural meaning. When there are more than one permanent shocks ($p - r > 1$), it may be hard to give η_{it} ($i = 1, ..., p - r$) structural interpretation unless some additional a priori structural information is provided on the long-run multiplier A or on $\beta_\perp$. Let $\beta_\perp = \tilde{A}Q$ and $\Pi = Q\Theta$ so that $A = \beta_\perp \Theta = \tilde{A}Q\Theta = \tilde{A}\Pi$. Then we can obtain:

$$\Pi\Sigma_{\eta^1}\Pi' = \overline{A}' C(1)\Sigma_\epsilon C(1)' \overline{A}, \tag{7}$$

where $\overline{A} = \tilde{A}(\tilde{A}'\tilde{A})^{-1}$. Having derived this expression, King *et al.* (1991, p. 831) impose structural information obtained from economic theory onto $\tilde{A}$ and assume Π is lower triangular, that requires Q be lower triangular (which we will also assume). To estimate Π and Σ_{η^1} from the Choleski decomposition of (7) the diagonal element of Π is normalized (i.e., $\pi_{ii} = 1$).

If an SOP system is effective, it will contain information on the size and direction of inflation transmission. Forward flow corresponds to supply shocks, and backward flow to demand shocks. Recall that in the ISOP only 6 percent of shipment flows are backward flow, so the stages do contain directionality in terms of supply and demand. We assume that permanent inflation shocks are supply-driven and demand-driven effects are transitory:

Assumption 4. Let $\tilde{A} = (I_p - c(\beta'c)^{-1}\beta')c_\perp$ where $c = (0\ I_r)'$ is $p \times r$ and $c_\perp = (I_{p-r}\ 0)'$ is $p \times (p - r)$. Q is a $(p - r) \times (p - r)$ lower triangular matrix of full rank. ■

For the expression of $\tilde{A}$, see Johansen (1995, p. 48). Under Assumptions 1 and 4, $\Pi = Q\Theta$ is lower triangular, which makes the first ($p - r$) rows of $\beta_\perp = \tilde{A}Q$ lower triangular. This means that only forward shock propagation has a long-run effect. The price indexes in the later stages include the permanent components of the previous stages (x^P_{i+1} contains x^P_i, $i = 1, 2, ..., p - 1$), but not vice versa. It should be noted that no such an assumption is imposed for the transitory components.

With the normalization $\beta = (-\phi\ I_r)'$ where ϕ is $r \times (p - r)$, $\tilde{A} = (I_{p-r}\ \phi')'$. Then the permanent component $X^P_t = Ah_t = \tilde{A}\Pi h_t$ is partitioned to $X^{1P}_t = \Pi h_t$ and $X^{2P}_t = \phi\Pi h_t$. In this representation of a cointegrated system, the first

$(p - r)$ elements (X_t^1) are considered as common factors because the remaining r elements (X_t^2) can be expressed as a linear combination of X_t^1; that is, $\Delta X_t^1 = u_t^1$ and $X_t^2 = \phi X_t^1 + u_t^2$ where $u_t = (u_t^{1\prime}\ u_t^{2\prime})'$ is a stationary stochastic process with full rank spectral density matrix. This triangular representation has been used by Phillips (1991) and Stock and Watson (1993).

Assumption 4 may be tested using $\hat{\beta}_\perp$ but it is not so simple and the test has not yet been available. Instead, we check the validity of Assumption 4 by testing for Granger-causality between x_i and x_j $(i, j = 1, ..., p, i \neq j)$. The p-values of the F-statistics to test the hypothesis that x_i does not Granger-cause x_j for ISOP and CSOP are shown below. The significant p-values, smaller than 0.050 (say), indicate the presence of Granger-causality and suggest the infla-tion transmission from x_i and x_j. The p-value matrices with insignificant p-values above the diagonal would be consistent with Assumption 4. For ISOP, the Granger causality tests generally support Assumption 4 except for one case where feedback exists from Primary (x_2) to Crude (x_1). For CSOP the test results are consistent with Assumption 4 for all cases (with one marginal excep-tion).

ISOP $x_j \backslash x_i$	x_1	x_2	x_3	x_4
x_1		.000	.983	.868
x_2	.000		.185	.975
x_3	.015	.010		.754
x_4	.769	.243	.002	

CSOP $x_j \backslash x_i$	x_1	x_2	x_3
x_1		.115	.079
x_2	.054		.154
x_3	.032	.002	

Because Assumption 4 is about permanent shocks, we also focus on causality in the *long* run. The full causal relationship can be decomposed by frequency based on the spectral decomposition of the series. Causality may be different in extent or direction at low frequencies than at other frequencies. Using the definition provided by Hosoya (1991), Granger and Lin (1995) show that Granger-causality at low frequencies in a cointegrated system depend on the error correction coefficients α. In Tables 2 and 3 discussed in the next section, the results of testing $H_0 : \alpha_i = 0$ $(i = 1, ..., p)$ are entirely consistent with the above Granger causality results.

The representation $A = \beta_\perp \Theta$ admits more general forms than those adopted in Assumption 4. Future work could adopt other forms fitting a particular ap-plication or use the general form for testing assumptions such as Assumption 4.

So far in this section we have discussed the long-run multipliers A. Under the assumptions, we can also determine short-run multipliers of the permanent shocks. The first $(p - r)$ columns of $\Gamma(B)$ show how the series ΔX_t respond to the permanent shocks η_t^1, and their accumulated sums show how the series X_t respond to the permanent shocks η_t^1. See King $et\ al.$ (1991) for estimation of the first $(p - r)$ columns of $\Gamma(B)$. Denoted by $_iR_j(n) = \partial x_{it}/\partial \eta_{j,t-n}$ is the response of x_{it} $(i = 1, ..., p)$ to each permanent shock $\eta_{j,t-n}$ that occurred n periods ago

$(j = 1, ..., p - r, n = 0, 1, ...)$. It may be noted that the ijth element of A is $\lim_{n\to\infty} {}_iR_j(n)$.

Since the VECM can be used for forecasting, we also compute the fraction of the h step ahead forecast error variance of $\Delta x_{i,t+h}$ $(i = 1, ..., p)$ attributed to each permanent shock η_{jt} $(j = 1, ..., p - r)$, which is given by:

$$\omega_{ij,h} = \sum_{n=0}^{h-1} (\gamma_{ij,n}^2 \Sigma_{\eta^1}^{jj}) / \mathrm{MSE}_i(h),$$

where $\gamma_{ij,n}$ is the ijth element of Γ_n with Γ_n being defined from $\Gamma(B) = \sum_{n=0}^\infty \Gamma_n B^n$, $\Sigma_{\eta^1}^{jj}$ is the jth diagonal element of Σ_{η^1}, and $MSE_i(h)$ is the ith diagonal element of the mean squared error matrix of the optimal h step ahead forecast of ΔX_t, $MSE(h) = \sum_{n=0}^{h-1} \Gamma_n \Sigma_\eta \Gamma_n' = \sum_{n=0}^{h-1} C_n \Sigma_\epsilon C_n'$. The estimated $\omega_{ij,h}$ provides information about the relative importance of permanent shocks in h step ahead forecasts of ΔX_t.

3 Inflation Transmission among SOPs

3.1 ISOP

We have analyzed and found positive results based on the reduced form model (2) and with respect to the shocks ε_t, allowing backward transmission, as found between the Primary and Crude stages. Here, however, we apply the structural model (3) with Assumptions 1–4, both for comparison with CSOP and for the appeal of the simplified generating mechanism with the common factor representation (4).

Table 2 reports the results of testing for cointegration (Panel A), testing for restrictions on α and β, testing for residual autocorrelations in each equation in the system (Panel B), the ML estimates of $\tilde{A}$, Π, and A (Panel C), and variance decompositions with simulated standard errors computed using 300 replications in parentheses (Panel D). The lag length $k = 5$ in the VECM is chosen using the Akaike and Schwarz information criteria (AIC and SIC) as well as the battery of residual diagnostics. The ISOP series $X_t = (x_{1t}\ x_{2t}\ x_{3t}\ x_{4t})'$ are cointegrated with three common stochastic trends.

In Panel B, following Johansen (1995), we test for weak exogeneity and for long-run exclusion. The tests for long-run exclusion are based on the hypothesis that a subset of the variables in X_t does not enter the cointegration space, which, if not rejected, implies that the variables in question can be omitted from the long-run relations between the ISOPs. The hypothesis is $H_0 : \beta_i = 0$ for each $i = 1, 2, 3, 4$. The results show that all of them are significant. Similar tests have been performed on the rows of α, corresponding to tests for weak exogeneity and also for Granger-causality in the long run. They can be formulated as $H_0 : \alpha_i = 0$ for each $i = 1, 2, 3, 4$, that the ith component in X_t is not

Table 2. ISOP

A. *Testing for cointegrating rank*
(with $k = 5$ lags)

H_0	trace	$\lambda_{\max}$
$r = 0$	64.65***	46.21***
$r = 1$	18.44	13.11
$r = 2$	5.33	4.28
$r = 3$	1.06	1.06

*** denotes significance at 1% level.

B. *Testing for $H_0 : \alpha_i = 0$ and $H_0 : \beta_i = 0$, and residual diagnostics (p-values)*

ith equation	$H_0 : \alpha_i = 0$	$H_0 : \beta_i = 0$	Ljung-Box tests for $\hat{\varepsilon}_i$
$i = 1$	.00013	.00000	.86
$i = 2$	.42919	.00000	.65
$i = 3$	.00006	.00379	.93
$i = 4$	.03046	.04109	.87

C. *Estimation of the long run multiplier*

$$\tilde{A} = \begin{bmatrix} 1 & 0 & 0 \\ 0 & 1 & 0 \\ 0 & 0 & 1 \\ 1.08 & -2.77 & 2.19 \end{bmatrix} \quad \Pi = \begin{pmatrix} 1 & 0 & 0 \\ .42 & 1 & 0 \\ -.002 & 1.76 & 1 \end{pmatrix} \quad A = \begin{bmatrix} 1 & 0 & 0 \\ .42 & 1 & 0 \\ -.002 & 1.76 & 1 \\ .08 & 1.10 & 2.19 \end{bmatrix}$$

D. *Fractions of forecast error variance, $\omega_{ij,h}$, for $\Delta x_{i,t+h}$ attributed to η_j*

h	η_1				η_2				η_3			
	$i=1$	$i=2$	$i=3$	$i=4$	$i=1$	$i=2$	$i=3$	$i=4$	$i=1$	$i=2$	$i=3$	$i=4$
1	.805	.487	.051	.000	.014	.265	.581	.161	.040	.017	.218	.749
	(.047)	(.085)	(.058)	(.022)	(.026)	(.079)	(.161)	(.171)	(.030)	(.042)	(.168)	(.172)
2	.818	.708	.453	.025	.043	.106	.258	.150	.040	.011	.093	.695
	(.060)	(.073)	(.105)	(.059)	(.028)	(.040)	(.082)	(.157)	(.032)	(.019)	(.078)	(.162)
12	.861	.770	.452	.300	.035	.069	.241	.155	.068	.058	.137	.454
	(.060)	(.064)	(.084)	(.083)	(.035)	(.028)	(.072)	(.094)	(.030)	(.024)	(.058)	(.113)
60	.848	.774	.451	.305	.038	.066	.241	.155	.082	.065	.140	.452
	(.058)	(.061)	(.084)	(.085)	(.035)	(.027)	(.073)	(.091)	(.034)	(.026)	(.057)	(.112)

Monte Carlo standard errors are in brackets.

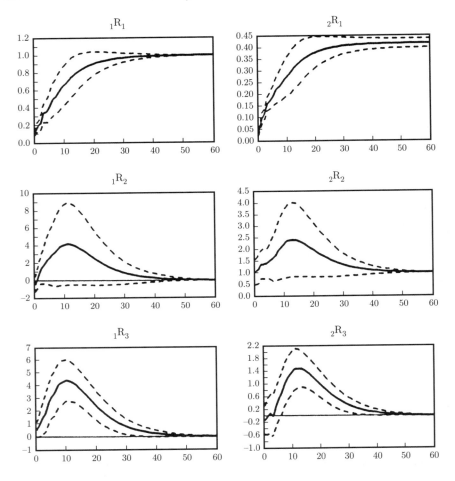

Figure 1. ISOP: Responses ($_iR_j$) of variable x_i to shock η_j

adjusting toward the estimated long-run relations. If not rejected it implies that the variable in question itself takes the role of a common trend in the system. No rejection of $H_0 : \alpha_2 = 0$ indicates that there is some backward inflation flow from Primary to Crude, consistent with the Granger-causality tests in the previous section.

From Panel D, it is observed that the first permanent shock η_1, the permanent shock to the Crude processor, explains a significant portion of the inflation fluctuations in all stages, the amount declining through the stages, but increasing in the long run (as the forecast horizon h increases) with faster speed in earlier stages. The second permanent shock η_2, which is another permanent shock to Primary processor, accounts for substantial variations in Primary and Semifinished processors. Its role declines for the longer forecast

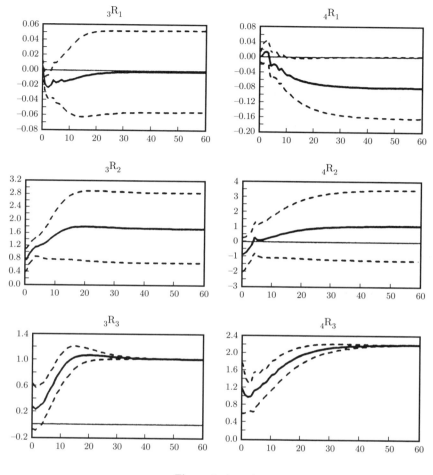

Figure 1. (*cont.*)

horizons. The third permanent shock η_3 that arrives at the third stage of processing to the Semifinished processor shows very significant inflation transmission from Semifinished to Finished stages.

Turning to Figure 1, which graphs the dynamic responses to the three shocks along with the two standard deviation confidence bands computed by Monte Carlo simulation using 300 replications (dashed lines), we see significant long-run effects of the first shock on Primary, the second shock on Semifinished, and the third shock on Finished. None of the other effects in the forward direction appear significant. In the backward direction, some of the short-run effects are substantial, implying that demand shocks matter in the short run. However, the long-run effects are zero by construction. ISOP captures the inflation transmissions throughout the economic segments fairly well with significant one-step forward-flow of the inflation transmissions. The multi-step forward transmissions of inflation are insignificant.

3.2 CSOP

Table 3 and Figure 2 present the results for CSOP. The lag length $k = 3$ is chosen using the multivariate portmanteau test although univariate Ljung–Box portmanteau tests are not significant for $k = 2$. See Johansen (1995, p. 22). For $k = 3$, the Johansen tests suggest $r = 1$. The error correction coefficients are all significant except α_1 (Panel B). Its insignificance indicates that Crude PPI does not adjust toward the estimated long-run relations and takes the role of a common trend in the system. The impulse responses in Figure 2 show a strong, fairly rapid response of Crude and Primary, but not Finished, to the first permanent shock. Finished responds rapidly to the second permanent shock. Similarly, the variance decomposition statistics (Panel D) show that the first permanent shock strongly influences the first two stages and the second permanent shock influences stages 2 and 3. The speed of response by each stage is different, faster in earlier stages to response to η_1. In general, the results for CSOP are similar to those for ISOP, showing significant forward inflation transmission through the three stages. The multi-step forward transmissions of inflation are insignificant.

4 Inflation Transmission to CPI

To examine how each PPI system is related to CPI, we add the CPI series to both ISOP and CSOP systems. The results are presented in Table 4, but not all those corresponding to Tables 2, 3 and Figures 1, 2 are reported to save space. Overall, the results give support to Popkin's original notions of stages. Later stages respond to earlier stages, and the CPI responds to PPI. The CPI responds to the shocks to the PPI systems, most strongly to the last permanent shock, more when CSOP is used than when ISOP is used. CSOP Finished relates more closely to the CPI than ISOP Finished. The latter pair has slightly inferior cointegration test statistics. In Panel A, it is shown that when CPI is added to the CSOP the rank of cointegration increases from $r = 1$ to $r = 2$, and thus adding CPI to CSOP does not increase the dimension of the common factors or the number of the permanent shocks. This is not the case for ISOP. Although Panel B shows that both ISOP and CSOP Granger-cause CPI, Panel C shows that only CSOP Granger-causes CPI in the long run. The CPI series adjusts to correct the deviations from the cointegrating relationship only with CSOP. The entire ISOP system relates less strongly to the CPI than the CSOP does.

A criterion for usefulness of time series models is forecast performance.

Table 3. CSOP

A. *Testing for cointegrating rank (with $k = 3$ lags)*

H_0	trace	$\lambda_{\max}$
$r = 0$	35.02**	19.60*
$r = 1$	15.42	11.13
$r = 2$	4.29	4.29

** and * denote significance at 5% and 10% level, respectively.

B. *Testing for $H_0 : \alpha_i = 0$ and $H_0 : \beta_i = 0$, and residual diagnostics (p-values)*

ith equation	$H_0 : \alpha_i = 0$	$H_0 : \beta_i = 0$	Ljung-Box tests for $\hat{\varepsilon}_i$
$i = 1$	.76284	.01102	1.00
$i = 2$	.04836	.00283	.96
$i = 3$	.00399	.00332	.72

C. *Estimation of the long run multiplier*

$$\tilde{A} = \begin{bmatrix} 1 & 0 \\ 0 & 1 \\ -.53 & 2.01 \end{bmatrix} \qquad \Pi = \begin{pmatrix} 1 & 0 \\ .24 & 1 \end{pmatrix} \qquad A = \begin{bmatrix} 1 & 0 \\ .24 & 1 \\ -.039 & 2.01 \end{bmatrix}$$

D. *Fractions of forecast error variance, $\omega_{ij,h}$, for $\Delta x_{i,t+h}$ attributed to η_j*

h	η_1			η_2		
	$i = 1$	$i = 2$	$i = 3$	$i = 1$	$i = 2$	$i = 3$
1	.923	.007	.000	.068	.682	.410
	(.038)	(.024)	(.016)	(.037)	(.051)	(.074)
2	.902	.002	.000	.059	.697	.386
	(.033)	(.028)	(.019)	(.027)	(.049)	(.071)
12	.893	.331	.102	.059	.488	.369
	(.031)	(.075)	(.042)	(.024)	(.071)	(.060)
60	.889	.429	.103	.062	.412	.369
	(.030)	(.076)	(.042)	(.023)	(.069)	(.060)

Monte Carlo standard errors are in brackets.

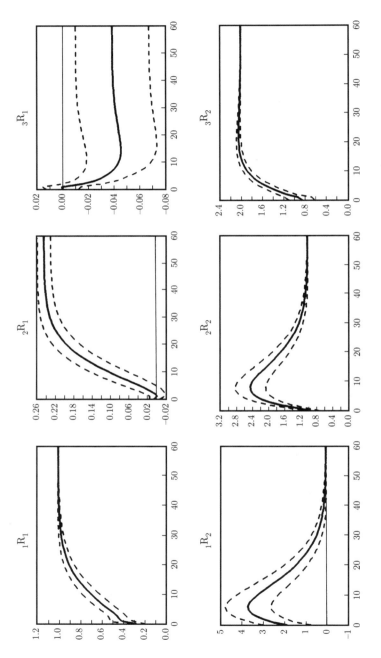

Figure 2. CSOP: Responses $({}_iR_j)$ of variable x_i to shock η_j

Table 4. Forecasting CPI using the SOP systems

A. Testing for cointegrating rank (Johansen trace test)

H_0	ISOP + CPI ($k = 5$)	CSOP + CPI ($k = 3$)
$r = 0$	79.03**	60.98***
$r = 1$	36.28	37.25**
$r = 2$	19.34	21.53**
$r = 3$	8.17	6.87
$r = 4$	3.80	N/A

B. In-sample Granger causality test for CPI

	$H_0 : \text{ISOP} \overset{G}{\nrightarrow} \text{CPI}$	$H_0 : \text{CSOP} \overset{G}{\nrightarrow} \text{CPI}$
p-values of F-test	0.013	0.039

$H_0 : \text{SOP} \overset{G}{\nrightarrow} \text{CPI}$ (SOP does not Granger-cause CPI)

C. In-sample long-run Granger causality test for CPI; $H_0 : \alpha_i = 0$ in the CPI equation

	ISOP + CPI	CSOP + CPI ($r = 3$)	CSOP + CPI ($r = 2$)	CSOP + CPI ($r = 3$)
p-value	.463	.011	.037	.014

$H_0 : \text{CPI is weakly exogenous for each SOP system augmented with CPI.}$

D. Out-of-sample forecast for CPI inflation

	MSE	RMSE	MAE
Model 1: Univariate AR(7) for CPI	.00000279	.00167	.00133
Model 2: ISOP + CPI with $r = 1$ and $k = 5$	.00000371	.00193	.00156
Model 3: CSOP + CPI with $r = 1$ and $k = 3$	.00000321	.00179	.00147
Model 4: CSOP + CPI with $r = 2$ and $k = 3$	.00000309	.00176	.00144

E. Comparing MSEs by Granger–Newbold test (p-values are reported)

A \ B	Model 1	Model 2	Model 3	Model 4
Model 1		.988	.879	.801
Model 2	.012**		.146	.091*
Model 3	.121	.854		.130
Model 4	.199	.909	.870	

$H_0 :$ Models A and B have the same MSEs.
$H_1 :$ MSE of Model A is larger than MSE of Model B.

Ashley, Granger, and Schmalensee (1980) argue that a sound and natural approach to Granger-causality must rely primarily on the out-of-sample forecasting performance of models relating the series of interest. Our evaluation of CPI forecasts using the SOPs in terms of out-of-sample forecasting performance proceeds as follows. The VECMs are estimated for ISOP plus CPI (with $p = 5$, $k = 5$ and $r = 1$) and CSOP plus CPI (with $p = 4$, $k = 3$ and $r = 1, 2$) using the observations until five years before May 1996, to have post-sample of 60 months. Based on the estimated models, one-step-ahead forecasts are generated for those post-samples, resulting in 60 pairs of forecast errors to evaluate. For each of the SOP augmented with CPI, we calculated the mean squared errors (MSE), root mean square errors (RMSE), and the mean absolute errors (MAE), which are reported in Panel D.

For the quadratic loss (MSE), we use the tests of Granger and Newbold (1977, GN henceforth), Meese and Rogoff (1988), Diebold and Mariano (1995), the sign test, and the Wilcoxon signed-rank test to investigate whether the loss-differences are significant. See Diebold and Mariano (1995) for an exposition of the tests in detail. In Panel E, the probability values (p-values) of the one-sided tests of GN are reported. To save space, we only report for GN tests, but all the other tests give similar results (available on request). Since the CPI has grown fairly slowly and steadily over most of the last decade, great differences cannot be expected. Still, Model 4 for CSOP has a smaller loss than ISOP (Model 2), achieving significance at the 10 percent level. The forecast evaluation seems to favor the CSOP over the ISOP system in terms of forecasting the CPI. However, both CSOP and ISOP have larger losses than the univariate AR(7) model for CPI (Model 1). Model 2 with ISOP plus CPI is significantly inferior to the univariate model (Model 1) almost at the 1 percent level.

These forecast results are somewhat disappointing, but have been seen before. For example, Clark (1995) shows producer price inflation Granger-causes consumer price inflation in-sample but fails to improve out-of-sample forecasts of consumer price inflation. It is widely recognized that price variability or volatility decreases through the stages of production and in consumer prices. Producers and retailers often attempt to avoid inflicting their customers with too many price fluctuations. The rather steady, low rate of inflation in the CPI in the study period may explain the lack of forecasting power. Still, overall, our results show inflation transmission from the earlier, more volatile stages to the later, more stable stages.

5 Conclusions

Using vector error correction models, the sources of inflation and its transmission in terms of direction, speed, and magnitude are examined for stages of processing. Both ISOP and CSOP give strong evidence of forward inflation transmission among stages; connections to the CPI are stronger with CSOP. By a small amount, CSOP outperforms ISOP in forecasting the CPI.

The ISOP system has conceptual and analytic advantages, e.g., it can be studied with other industry-based variables, such as wages. In addition to the "output" price indexes discussed in this article, this system includes "input" indexes to stages beyond Crude and an index to Final Demand. This last index, like CSOP Finished, relates closely to the CPI.

References

Ashley, R., C. W. J. Granger, and R. Schmalensee (1980), "Advertising and Aggregate Consumption: An Analysis of Causality," *Econometrica*, 48: 1149–67.

Blanchard, O. J. (1987), "Aggregate and Individual Price Adjustment," *Brookings Papers on Economic Activity*, 57–121.

Boughton, J. M. and W. Branson (1991), "Commodity Prices as a Leading Indicator of Inflation," in Lahiri and G. Moore (eds.), *Leading Economic Indicators*, ch. 17.

Clark, T. E. (1995), "Do Producer Prices Lead Consumer Prices?" *Economic Review*, Federal Reserve Bank of Kansas City, Third Quarter 1995, 25–39.

Diebold, F. X. and R. S. Mariano (1995), "Comparing Predictive Accuracy," *Journal of Business and Economic Statistics*, 13: 253–63.

Engle, R. F. (1978), "Testing Price Equations for Stability across Spectral Frequency Bands," *Econometrica*, 46: 869–881.

Gaddie, R. and M. Zoller (1988), "New Stages of Process Price System Developed for the Producer Price Index," *Monthly Labor Review*, April: 3–16.

Granger, C. W. J. and J.-L. Lin (1995), "Causality in the Long Run," *Econometric Theory*, 11: 530–6.

Granger, C. W. J. and P. Newbold (1977), *Forecasting Economic Time Series*. San Diego: Academic Press.

Granger, C. W. J., R. P. Robins, and R. F. Engle (1986), "Wholesale and Retail Prices: Bivariate Time-Series Modeling with Forecastable Error Variances," in David A. Belsley and Edwin Kuh (eds.), *Model Reliability*. Cambridge, MA: MIT Press, pp. 1–17.

Hosoya, Y. (1991), "The Decomposition and Measurement of the Interdependence between Second-Order Stationary Processes," *Probability Theory and Related Fields*, 88: 429–44.

Johansen, S. (1995), *Likelihood-Based Inference in Cointegrated Vector Autoregressive Models*. Oxford: Oxford University Press.

King, R. G., C. I. Plosser, J. H. Stock, and M. W. Watson (1991), "Stochastic Trends and Economic Fluctuations," *American Economic Review*, 81: 819–40.

Mattey, J. P. (1990), "Prices by Industry-Based Stages of Process," Working Paper No. 111, Economic Activity Section, Division of Research and Statistics, Board of Governors of the Federal Reserve System.

Meese, R. A. and K. Rogoff (1988), "Was It Real? The Exchange Rate–Interest Differential Relation Over the Modern Floating Rate Period," *Journal of Finance*, 43: 933–48.

Mehra, Y. P. (1991), "Wage Growth and the Inflation Process: An Empirical Note," *American Economic Review*, 81: 931–7.

Phillips, P. C. B. (1991), "Optimal Inference in Cointegrated Systems," *Econometrica*, 59: 283–306.

Popkin, J. (1974), "Consumer and Wholesale Prices in a Model of Price Behavior by Stage of Processing," *Review of Economics and Statistics*, 56: 486–501.

Silver, J. L. and T. D. Wallace (1980), "The Lag Relationship between Wholesale and Consumer Prices," *Journal of Econometrics*, 12: 375–387.

Stock, J. H. and M. W. Watson (1993), "A Simple Estimator of Cointegrating Vectors in Higher Order Integrated Systems," *Econometrica*, 61: 783–820.

13

Price Convergence
in the Medium and Long Run:
An I(2) Analysis of Six Price Indices

KATARINA JUSELIUS

1 Introduction

There has recently been an increased interest in the econometric relationship between so called commodity price indices and general price indices, like the CPI and the WPI (see Baillie, 1989; Kugler, 1991; Trivedi, 1995; Granger and Jeon, 1996; Gallo, Marcellino, and Trivedi, 1997). The economic background for this interest is the assumption that commodity prices should react faster to inflationary signals, for instance originating from changes in money stock, and hence could act as forward indicators of general price inflation.

Econometrically, these studies differ a lot. Baillie (1989), Kugler (1991) and Granger and Jeon (1996) essentially investigate bivariate relationships. Trivedi (1995) and Gallo *et al.* (1997) investigate multivariate relationships between four commodity price indices and two general price indices as indicators of US inflation. Some of the studies investigate relationships between inflation rates, others relationships between levels, and as in Granger and Jeon (1996) a relationship between a commodity price index in levels and a general price index in differences. The order of integration of the individual time series are discussed and tested using univariate test procedures. In general, the conclusion is that price levels are $I(1)$ or, possibly, $I(2)$. None of the papers test the order of integration (and cointegration) based on a multivariate analysis of all price variables allowing for $I(2)$ features.

This paper illustrates the scope of Clive Granger's original observation in Granger (1981, 1986) and Engle and Granger (1987) that series could individually be integrated, but jointly cointegrated. The implication of $I(2)$ series was first appreciated in Granger and Lee (1989) and formalized in Engle and Yoo (1991) and Johansen (1995).

This paper has benefited from very useful comments from two unknown referees, Søren Johansen, Niels Haldrup and Massimiliano Marcellino. Financial support from the Danish Social Sciences Research Council is gratefully acknowledged.

The purpose of this paper is twofold. First, to investigate the multivariate relationships between levels, differences, and acceleration rates of the six price indices analyzed in Trivedi (1995) and Gallo *et al.* (1997) based on the polynomially cointegrated VAR model. Since the previously analyzed models are sub-models of this general model one should be able to evaluate some of the puzzling and (sometimes) inconsistent empirical results reported in the above studies. Second, to demonstrate the potential usefulness of the $I(2)$ model for analyzing price movements in the short, medium, and long run. The methodological approach is similar to Juselius (1994, 1995, 1998a) but they use the method to address different problems.

Because the $I(2)$ model has a complicated structure, empirical results are not easily accessible to the nonexpert reader. Therefore, I first give a detailed interpretation of the different components of the $I(2)$ model in terms of long-run and medium-run steady-state relationships, driving forces and short-run adjustment behavior. I then argue, using the empirical results as illustrations, that an analysis based on sub-sets of the six price indices can lead to inconsistent results and misleading conclusions. For instance, I show that a minimum of three price indices are needed to produce cointegration and that bivariate analyses will, therefore, fail to find evidence on price convergence. I also show that long-run price homogeneity (between levels of prices) only exceptionally implies medium-run price homogeneity (between inflation rates). Hence, differencing the data to avoid the $I(2)$ analysis, i.e. analyzing the inflation rates instead of the prices, is likely to distort the analysis and produce puzzling and implausible results.

The organization of the paper is as follows: in Section 2 the $I(2)$ model is introduced as a parameter restriction on the general VAR model. The different levels of integration and their relationship are discussed and interpreted in terms of adjustment to dynamic steady-state relations and driving trends of first and second order. The concept of long-run and medium-run price homogeneity is formally defined and discussed using the $I(2)$ model structure. In Section 3 the empirical model is introduced and empirically checked for misspecification. The orders of integration and cointegration are tested within the multivariate model. As a sensitivity analysis I investigate in Section 4 how the choice of cointegration rank affects the classification of single price indices as $I(1)$ or $I(2)$, as excludable or non-excludable from the long-run relations, and as adjusting or non-adjusting to the long-run relations. In Section 5 the vector x_t is decomposed into the so called $(\beta, \beta_\perp)$ and $(\alpha, \alpha_\perp)$ directions and interpreted accordingly. Price homogeneity in the long and medium run is also analyzed in this section. Section 6 investigates cointegration relationships between commodity and general price indices and a fully specified overidentified model is estimated. Section 7 summarizes the basic findings.

2 The Statistical Model and Its Interpretation

The $I(2)$ model is introduced in Section 2.1 as a parameter restriction on the unrestricted VAR model and its corresponding moving average representation is presented. In Section 2.2 two different ways to classify the components of the model are discussed which relate to the two-step and FIML estimation procedure. The interpretation of the components takes advantage of the dual decomposition into long-run cointegration relations and driving common trends. The long-run relations are classified as

(a) cointegrating relations from $I(2)$ to $I(1)$ i.e. $CI(2, 1)$ relations,
(b) cointegrating relations from $I(2)$ to $I(0)$ i.e. $CI(2, 2)$ relations, and finally
(c) polynomially cointegrating relations combining $CI(2, 1)$ relations with relations between differences.

The driving trends are classified as common driving trends of first and second order. In Section 2.3 this decomposition is used to discuss long-run and medium-run price homogeneity and, hence, price convergence in the long and medium run.

2.1 The I(2) Model

The VAR model for x_t, $(p \times 1)$, with a constant term, μ, $(p \times 1)$, and centered seasonal dummies, S_t, $(p \times 3)$, is given by:

$$\Delta^2 x_t = \Gamma_1 \Delta^2 x_{t-1} + \Gamma \Delta x_{t-1} + \Pi x_{t-2} + \Phi S_t + \mu + \varepsilon_t,$$
$$\varepsilon_t \sim N_p(0, \Sigma), \quad t = 1, ..., T. \tag{2.1}$$

The parameters $\{\Gamma_1, \Gamma, \Pi, \Phi, \mu, \Sigma\}$ are all unrestricted.

The hypothesis that x_t is $I(2)$ is formulated in Johansen (1992) as two reduced rank hypotheses: $\Pi = \alpha \beta'$ and $\alpha'_\perp \Gamma \beta_\perp = \zeta \eta'$, where α, β are $p \times r$ and ζ, η are $(p - r) \times s_1$ matrices. We need further to decompose $\alpha_\perp = \{\alpha_{\perp 1}, \alpha_{\perp 2}\}$ and $\beta_\perp = \{\beta_{\perp 1}, \beta_{\perp 2}\}$, where $\alpha_{\perp 1} = \alpha_\perp (\alpha'_\perp \alpha_\perp)^{-1} \zeta$, $\alpha_{\perp 2} = \alpha_\perp \zeta_\perp$, $\beta_{\perp 1} = \beta_\perp (\beta'_\perp \beta_\perp)^{-1} \eta$, $\beta_{\perp 2} = \beta_\perp \eta_\perp$, and $\zeta_\perp$, $\eta_\perp$ are the orthogonal complements of ζ and η, respectively.

The moving average representation is given by:

$$x_t = C_2 \sum_{s=1}^{t} \sum_{i=1}^{s} \varepsilon_i + C_2 \Phi \tfrac{1}{2} \mu t^2 + C_2 \Phi \sum_{s=1}^{t} \sum_{i=1}^{s} S_i + C_1 \sum_{s=1}^{t} \varepsilon_s + C_1 \Phi \sum_{s=1}^{t} S_s$$
$$+ (C_1 + \tfrac{1}{2} C_2) \mu t + Y_t + A + Bt, \quad t = 1, ..., T \tag{2.2}$$

where Y_t defines the stationary part of the process, A and B are a function of the initial values x_0, x_{-1}, ..., x_{-k+1}, and the coefficient matrices satisfy:

$$C_2 = \beta_{\perp 2}(\alpha'_{\perp 2} \Psi \beta_{\perp 2})^{-1} \alpha'_{\perp 2}, \quad \beta' C_1 = -\bar{\alpha}' \Gamma C_2, \quad \beta'_{\perp 1} C_1 = -\bar{\alpha}'_{\perp 1}(I - \Psi C_2)$$

where $\Psi = \Gamma\bar{\beta}\bar{\alpha}'\Gamma + I - \Gamma_1$ and the shorthand notation $\bar{\alpha} = \alpha(\alpha'\alpha)^{-1}$ is used (see Johansen, 1992, 1995).

From (2.2) it appears that an unrestricted constant in the model allows for linear and quadratic trends in the DGP. Johansen (1992) suggested the decomposition of the constant term μ into the α, $\alpha_{\perp 1}$, $\alpha_{\perp 2}$ projections:

$$\mu = \alpha'\mu_0 + \alpha'_{\perp 1}\mu_1 + \alpha'_{\perp 2}\mu_2,$$

where

$\mu_0 = (\alpha'\alpha)^{-1}\alpha'\mu$ is related to the intercept of the stationary cointegration relations,

$\mu_1 = (\alpha'_{\perp 1}\alpha_{\perp 1})^{-1}\alpha'_{\perp 1}\mu$ is related to the slope coefficient of linear trends in the variables, and

$\mu_2 = (\alpha'_{\perp 2}\alpha_{\perp 2})^{-1}\alpha'_{\perp 2}\mu$ determines the slope coefficient of quadratic trends in the variables.

In the subsequent empirical analysis I will restrict $\alpha'_{\perp 2}\mu_2 = 0$, i.e. I will allow linear but no quadratic trends in the price levels. The motivation is that price inflation in general should be modeled as a nonzero mean process, but that linear trends in inflation are only reasonable as local phenomena and, therefore, should be modeled stochastically, not deterministically.

In the subsequent empirical analysis I sometimes need to distinguish between individual vectors and elements of a vector. The following notation will be used.

For a matrix β, $\beta_{.i}$ denotes the ith column, $\beta_{.ij}$ the jth element of the ith column. The r stationary relations $\beta = \{\beta_0, \beta_1\}$, such that $\beta_{.i}$, $i = 1, ..., r$, indicate CI vectors in the $I(1)$ space, $\beta_{0.i}$, $i = 1, ..., r_0$, indicate directly stationary CI vectors, and $\beta_{1.i}$, $i = 1, ..., r_1$, indicate polynomially stationary CI vectors. The $p - r$ nonstationary relations $\beta_{\perp} = \{\beta_{\perp 1}, \beta_{\perp 2}\}$, such that $\beta_{\perp 1.i}$, $i = 1, ..., s_1$, indicate $CI(2, 1)$ vectors that cannot be made stationary by polynomial cointegration, and $\beta_{\perp 2.i}$, $i = 1, ..., s_2$, indicate the $I(2)$ vectors that do not cointegrate at all.

A similar notation is used for α.

2.2 Interpretation and Estimation

The $I(2)$ model has a rich but complicated structure. It is no easy task to give the intuition for the many relationships and the different levels of integration and cointegration such that they become more easy to interpret. To facilitate the interpretation of the subsequent empirical results within the $I(2)$ model, Table 1 decomposes the vector process x_t into the $I(0)$, $I(1)$ and $I(2)$ directions. The first part of the table (column 2) describes the classification of the process into r stationary polynomially cointegrating relations, $\beta'x_t + \omega'\Delta x_t$, and $p - r$ nonstationary relations, $\beta'_{\perp}x$. The nonstationary relations $\beta'_{\perp}x_t$ can further be

Table 1. Decomposing the price vector using the $I(2)$ model

$x_t = [\beta, \beta_{\perp 1}, \beta_{\perp 2}]' x_t$	$x_t = [\beta_0, \beta_1, \beta_{\perp 1}, \beta_{\perp 2}]' x_t$
$r = 3$	$r_0 = 1$ $\quad \beta_{0.1}' x_t \sim I(0)$
$\quad [\beta_{.1}' x_t \sim I(1),\ \omega_{.1}' \Delta x_t \sim I(1)]$	
$\quad [\beta_{.2}' x_t \sim I(1),\ \omega_{.2}' \Delta x_t \sim I(1)]$	$r_1 = 2 \quad [\beta_{1.1}' x_t \sim I(1),\ \kappa_{1.1}' \Delta x_t \sim I(1)]$
$\quad [\beta_{.3}' x_t \sim I(1),\ \omega_{.3}' \Delta x_t \sim I(1)]$	$\qquad\ \ \ [\beta_{1.2}' x_t \sim I(1),\ \kappa_{1.2}' \Delta x_t \sim I(1)]$
$s_1 = 1 \quad \beta_{\perp 1}' x_t \sim I(1)$	
$s_2 = 2 \quad \beta_{\perp 2.1}' x_t \sim I(2)$	
$\qquad\ \ \ \beta_{\perp 2.2}' x_t \sim I(2)$	

Note: Components between [ ] are cointegrating CI(1, 1).

divided into the s_1 first order nonstationary relations, $\beta_{\perp 1}' x_t$, which are the $CI(2, 1)$ relations that cannot become stationary by polynomial cointegration, and the s_2 second order nonstationary relations, $\beta_{\perp 2}' x_t$, which are not cointegrating at all. The second part of the table (column 4) illustrates that for $r > s_2$ the r polynomially cointegrating relations can be further decomposed into $r_0 = r - s_2$ directly cointegrating relations, $\beta_0' x_t$, and $r_1 = r - r_0 = s_2$ polynomially cointegrating relations, $\beta_1' x_t + \kappa' \Delta x_t$.

For given values of $\{\beta_0, \beta_1, \beta_{\perp 1}, \beta_{\perp 2}\}$ one can derive $\{\alpha_0, \alpha_1, \alpha_{\perp 1}, \alpha_{\perp 2}\}$. There is an interesting duality between $\{\alpha_0, \alpha_1, \beta_{\perp 1}, \beta_{\perp 2}\}$ and $\{\beta_0, \beta_1, \alpha_{\perp 1}, \alpha_{\perp 2}\}$ in the sense that α_0 and α_1 determine the loadings (i.e. speed of adjustment) to the r_0 directly, $\beta_0' x_t$, and r_1 polynomially cointegrated relations, $\beta_1' x_t$, and $\beta_{\perp 1}$ and $\beta_{\perp 2}$ determine the loadings to the first, $\alpha_{\perp 1}' \sum_{s=1}^{t} \varepsilon_s$, and second order stochastic trends, $\alpha_{\perp 2}' \sum_{s=1}^{t} \sum_{i=1}^{s} \varepsilon_i$.

It appears from Table 1 that both $\beta' x_t$ and $\beta_{\perp 1}' x_t$ are $CI(2, 1)$ but that they differ in the following sense: the former can become stationary by polynomial cointegration, whereas the latter can only become stationary by differencing. The two-step estimation procedure in Johansen (1995) is based on the polynomial cointegration property of $\beta' x_t$, whereas the FIML procedure in Johansen (1997) is based on the $CI(2, 1)$ property of $\beta' x_t$ and $\beta_{\perp 1}' x_t$.

The first step of the two-step procedure is based on the $I(1)$ model and an estimate of β (and α) is obtained by solving the usual $I(1)$ eigenvalue problem, ignoring the reduced rank restriction on Γ. In the second step the estimate of $\beta_{\perp 1}$ is obtained by solving a second reduced rank problem based on the estimates $\{\hat\beta, \hat\alpha\}$. This is essentially done by deriving an equation which only involves differences by multiplying (2.1) for $\Pi = \hat\alpha\hat\beta'$ by $\hat\alpha_\perp'$. These equations can be used to find the $CI(2, 1)$ directions $\beta_{\perp 1}' x_t$ by applying cointegration techniques. Johansen (1995) showed that the two-stage procedure gives asymptotically efficient ML estimates.

The FIML estimates of $\{\beta, \beta_{\perp 1}\}$ are obtained using an iterative procedure that at each step delivers the solution of just one reduced rank problem. In this case the eigenvectors are the estimates of the $CI(2, 1)$ relations among the

$I(2)$ variables x_t, i.e. they give a decomposition of the vector x_t into the $p - s_2$ directions $(\beta, \beta_{\perp 1})$ in which the process is $I(1)$ and the s_2 directions $\beta_{\perp 2}$ in which it is $I(2)$.

Independently of the estimation procedure the crucial estimates are $\{\hat{\beta}, \hat{\beta}_{\perp 1}\}$, because for given values of these it is possible to derive the corresponding estimates of $\{\alpha, \alpha_{\perp 1}, \alpha_{\perp 2}, \beta_{\perp 2}\}$ and, if $r > s_2$, the further decomposition of $\beta = \{\beta_0, \beta_1\}$ and $\alpha = \{\alpha_0, \alpha_1\}$.

2.3 Long-Run and Medium-Run Price Homogeneity

As discussed above, the $I(2)$ model can distinguish between the $CI(2, 1)$ relations between levels $\{\beta' x_t, \beta'_{\perp 1} x_t\}$, the $CI(1, 1)$ relations between levels and differences $\{\beta' x_{t-1} + \omega' \Delta x_t\}$, and finally the $CI(1, 1)$ relations between differences $\{\beta'_{\perp 1} \Delta x_t\}$. When discussing the economic interpretation of these components there is a need to modify the generic concept of "long-run" steady-state relations accordingly. I will here use the concept of:

- a static long-run steady-state relation for $\beta'_0 x_t$,
- a dynamic long-run steady-state relation for $\{\beta'_1 x_t + \kappa' \Delta x_t\}$, and
- a medium-run steady-state relation for $\beta'_{\perp 1} \Delta x_t$.

In the subsequent empirical analysis the notion of price homogeneity plays an important role for the analysis of price convergence in the long run and the medium run. Both in the $I(1)$ and the $I(2)$ model long-run price homogeneity can be defined as zero sum restrictions on β. In the $I(2)$ model there is the additional possibility of medium-run price homogeneity defined as homogeneity between the inflation rates. To illustrate the interpretational difficulties in the latter case I follow the ideas in Johansen (1995) and rewrite the levels and difference components of model (2.1) as:

$$\Gamma \Delta x_{t-1} + \Pi x_{t-2} = (\Gamma \bar{\beta})\beta' \Delta x_{t-1} + (\alpha \bar{\alpha}' \Gamma \bar{\beta}_{\perp 1} + \alpha_{\perp 1})\beta'_{\perp 1} \Delta x_{t-1}$$
$$+ (\alpha \bar{\alpha}' \Gamma \bar{\beta}_{\perp 2})\beta'_{\perp 2} \Delta x_{t-1} + \alpha_0 \beta'_0 x_{t-2} + \alpha_1 \beta'_1 x_{t-2}. \tag{2.3}$$

The Γ matrix has been decomposed into three parts describing different effects from the lagged inflation rates and the Π matrix has been decomposed into two parts describing the effects from the stationary, $\beta'_0 x_{t-1}$, and the nonstationary, $\beta'_1 x_{t-1}$, cointegration relations. Note that the matrices in parentheses can be interpreted as adjustment coefficients. It is useful to study the order of integration of each component:

$$\beta'_{\perp 1} \Delta x_{t-1} \sim I(0), \quad \beta' \Delta x_{t-1} \sim I(0), \quad \beta'_0 x_{t-2} \sim I(0),$$
$$\beta'_{\perp 2} \Delta x_{t-1} \sim I(1), \quad \beta'_1 x_{t-2} \sim I(1).$$

Because there are only two $I(1)$ components they have to be polynomially cointegrating, i.e. combine to $\alpha_1(\beta'_1 x_{t-2} + \kappa' \Delta x_{t-1})$, where $\alpha_1 \kappa' = (\alpha \bar{\alpha}' \Gamma \bar{\beta}_{\perp 2})\beta'_{\perp 2}$. I will now examine the conditions for medium-run price homogeneity under the assumption of long-run price homogeneity in β. If $R'\beta_i = 0$, $i = 1, 2, ...,$ r, where $R' = [1, 1, ..., 1]$, then the first r.h.s component of (2.3), $(\Gamma\bar{\beta})\beta'\Delta x_{t-1}$, gives a homogeneous effect from lagged inflation rates. The interpretation is that prices are adjusting both to the equilibrium error between the prices, $\beta'x_{t-2}$, and to the change in the disequilibrium error, $\beta'\Delta x_{t-1}$.

Because $\beta'x_t$ is $I(1)$, a homogeneous adjustment of inflation rates is not sufficient for convergence to a stationary steady-state and a non-homogeneous adjustment has to take place. The latter is described by the third component, $(\alpha\bar{\alpha}'\Gamma\bar{\beta}_{\perp 2})\beta'_{\perp 2}\Delta x_{t-1}$. If $R'\beta = 0$, then in most cases $R'\beta_{\perp 2} \neq 0$ and the inflationary effect from the third component is non-homogeneous.

When $R'\beta_{\perp 1} = 0$, there is overall long-run homogeneity between prices and the second r.h.s. component corresponds to a homogeneous effect from lagged inflation rates. If $R'\beta_{\perp 1} \neq 0$, there exists inflation convergence in a nonhomogeneous direction, in the sense of $\beta'_{\perp 1}\Delta x_{t-1}$ being a stationary cointegration relation between inflation rates. This case corresponds to a non-homogeneous effect from lagged inflation rates.

To conclude, the condition for overall long-run price homogeneity is $R'\beta = 0$ and $R'\beta_{\perp 1} = 0$. I will use the notion of a weak form for long-run price homogeneity when $R'\beta = 0$ and $R'\beta_{\perp 1} \neq 0$. Note, however, that medium-run price homogeneity is, in general, not possible, even if overall long-run price homogeneity holds. This is because $\beta'_1 x_{t-1} \sim I(1)$ needs a non-homogeneous reaction in the inflation rates to achieve convergence to long-run steady state.

3 The Empirical Model

This section defines the variables of the VAR model and reports some multivariate and univariate residual misspecification tests. The cointegration rank, r, and $I(2)$ trends, s_2, is investigated based on the roots of the characteristic polynomial and the trace tests of the two-step procedure.

3.1 Checking the VAR Model

Model (2.1) with three lags and $\alpha'_{12}\mu = 0$ is the baseline model. Hence, no quadratic trends are allowed in the data. The vector $x'_t = [p1, p2, p3, p4, p5, p6]$ is based on quarterly observations for $t = 1970{:}4{-}1993{:}4$ where:

$p1$ = CPI, the US consumer price index
$p2$ = WBI, the World Bank commodity index
$p3$ = CRBI, the Commodity Research Bureau index
$p4$ = GSCI, the Goldman–Sachs index
$p5$ = ECI, the Economist commodity index
$p6$ = WPI, the US wholesale price commodity index.

Table 2. Misspecification tests and characteristic roots

Multivariate tests						
Residual autocorr. LM_1	$\chi^2(36) = 2.5$	p-val. 0.21				
LM_4	$\chi^2(36) = 43.2$	p-val. 0.19				
Normality: LM	$\chi^2(12) = 16.3$	p-val. 0.18				

Univariate tests	Δcpi	$\Delta crbi$	$\Delta gsci$	Δwbi	Δeci	Δwpi
ARCH(3)	2.0	5.6	12.8	7.2	4.4	1.8
Jarq.–Bera(2)	4.7	4.0	7.3	6.6	0.5	0.2
R^2	0.80	0.45	0.35	0.42	0.43	0.70
Eigenvalues of the Π-matrix	0.37	0.29	0.21	0.14	0.06	0.03
The trace test	118.9	76.5	44.7	23.0	8.4	2.8
The asymp. 90% quant.	89.4	64.7	43.8	26.7	13.3	2.7
6 largest roots of the process						
Unrestricted model	0.98	0.98	0.87	0.84	0.84	0.78
$r = 4$	1.00	1.00	0.91	0.91	0.79	0.79
$r = 3$	1.00	1.00	1.00	0.90	0.90	0.80
$r = 2$	1.00	1.00	1.00	1.00	0.87	0.87

The price indices $p1$ and $p6$ measure general price movements, whereas $p2$–$p5$ are so called commodity price indices. All variables are in logarithmic values. The definition of the special commodity price indices are given in Appendix A and the graphs of the levels and differences of all six variables are shown in Appendix B.

All estimates are based on the Johansen (1995) two-step procedure and have been calculated using a computer routine developed by C. Jørgensen within the package CATS for RATS (Hansen and Juselius, 1995).

The multivariate tests for residual normality, heteroskedasticity, and first and fourth order residual independence reported in Table 2 do not suggest misspecification. Since a single significant outcome can easily "drown" in the multivariate test, the univariate ARCH and Jarque–Bera normality tests are also included. The univariate tests give some indication of ARCH effects and non-normality for $p3$ and $p4$. Inspection of the residuals showed that these effects were mainly related to the turmoil of the breakdown of the previous Bretton Woods system in 1973 and the first oil crisis at the end and beginning of 1974.

As a sensitivity analysis I have re-estimated the model accounting for these effects. All basic results remained unchanged but the model without dummies produced more clearcut results. Since these shocks were "true" price shocks I have preferred to treat them as "normal" shocks, albeit quite large and all subsequent results are based on the no-dummy model. There were no signs of parameter non-constancy in the model based on the recursive tests procedures reported in Hansen and Johansen (1993).

All subsequent empirical results will be based on the VAR model, which means that current correlations are left unmodeled. To give the reader an impression of the magnitude of these correlations the estimated residual correlation matrix is given below:

$$
\hat{\Sigma} = \begin{bmatrix}
1.0 & & & & & \\
0.3 & 1.0 & & & & \\
0.2 & 0.7 & 1.0 & & & \\
0.4 & 0.4 & 0.7 & 1.0 & & \\
0.1 & 0.8 & 0.7 & 0.4 & 1.0 & \\
0.6 & 0.4 & 0.6 & 0.7 & 0.4 & 1.0
\end{bmatrix}.
$$

3.2 Determining the Two Rank Indices

In the $I(2)$ model the choice of cointegration rank r and the number of $I(2)$ components s_2 can be based on the trace tests. In the two-step procedure $r = \bar{r}$ is first determined and $s_1 = \bar{s}_1$ is found by solving another eigenvalue problem. Paruolo (1996) showed that the joint hypothesis (r, s_1) can be tested by combining the two test procedures. He also simulated the asymptotic distributions for the $I(2)$ model with different restrictions on the constant term.

There has recently been an increased interest in the small sample properties of the cointegration tests. For instance, Johansen (1999) derives Bartlett corrections that significantly improve the size of the tests on cointegration relations, but also demonstrates the low power of these tests. Jørgensen (1998) reports similar results based on a broad simulation study. She demonstrates the low power of the trace tests in $I(2)$ or near $I(2)$ models for samples sizes and adjustment coefficients similar to the present study.

Since the null of a unit root is not necessarily reasonable from an economic point of view, the low power is a serious problem. This is a strong argument for basing the choice of r and s_1 on economic theory as well as the statistical information in the data (Juselius, 1998, 1999). Economic theory often suggests a prior hypothesis for the number of independent trends, i.e. for $p - r$. For instance, based on the assumption of completely flexible prices, no market regulations or trade barriers, economic theory would suggest just one common stochastic price trend.

This assumption is clearly unrealistic for the price behavior in the investigated period. Therefore, the choice of r and s_1 will be empirically based in this study. I will, however, use all available information, economic as well as statistical, instead of relying exclusively on the trace tests. In particular, I will exploit the information provided by the roots of the characteristic polynomial of the VAR model when there are $I(2)$ or near $I(2)$ components in the data as described below.

The number of unit roots in the characteristic polynomial is $s_1 + 2s_2$, where

s_1 and s_2 are the number of $I(1)$ and $I(2)$ components respectively. The intuition is that the additional s_2 unit roots belong to Δx_t, and, hence, to the Γ matrix in (2.1). Therefore, the roots of the characteristic polynomial contain information on unit roots associated with both Γ and Π, whereas the standard $I(1)$ trace test only contain information on unit roots in the Π matrix. If there are no $I(2)$ components the number of unit roots (or near unit roots) should be $p - r$, otherwise $p - r + s_2$. In Table 2 I report the characteristic roots of the unrestricted VAR for $r = 2, 3, 4$. It appears that there remain two large roots in the model whatever value of r is chosen. This is strong evidence of two stochastic $I(2)$ trends.

The test statistics reported in Table 3 are based on the joint determination of (r, s_1) as described in Paruolo (1996) for the model with $\alpha'_{\perp 2}\mu = 0$. The 95 percent quantiles are given in italics. The test procedure starts with the most restricted model $(r = 0, s_1 = 0, s_2 = 6)$ in the upper left hand corner, continues to the end of the first row, and proceeds similarly row-wise from left to right until the first acceptance. This procedure delivers a correct size asymptotically, but does not solve the problem of low power. Because economic theory suggests few rather than many common trends, a reversed order of testing might be preferable from an economic point of view.

It appears that $(r = 2, s_1 = 2, s_2 = 2)$ is first accepted, but also that $(r = 3, s_1 = 1, s_2 = 2)$ is equally acceptable. In terms of economic interpretation the two cases are quite different. In the first case $r_0 = r - s_2 = 2 - 2 = 0$ implies no stationary cointegration relation between price indices that satisfies long-run price homogeneity, whereas in the second case there exists one stationary homogeneous steady-state relation. Because of the low power and the lack of a strong economic prior the choice between the two cases is not straight-forward. Nevertheless, the presence of three rather than four common trends seem more likely in a reasonably deregulated economy like the USA. Moreover,

Table 3. Testing the joint hypothesis $Q(s_1, r)$

$p-r$	r	$Q(s_1, r)$					
6	0	350.1	279.3	220.7	179.0	148.8	125.9
		240.4	*203.1*	*174.8*	*148.5*	*126.7*	*109.2*
5	1		240.4	180.5	139.8	109.7	82.6
			171.9	*142.5*	*117.6*	*98.0*	*81.9*
4	2			153.7	105.8	**66.7**	**51.2**
				116.3	*91.4*	*73.0*	*58.0*
3	3				96.7	**50.5**	**33.2**
					70.9	*51.4*	*38.8*
2	4					64.5	18.5
						36.1	*22.6*
1	5						13.9
							12.9
s_2		6	5	4	3	2	1

the case ($r = 3$, $s_1 = 1$, $s_2 = 2$) allows for a much richer description of inter-relations and dynamic interactions between the price indices and is, therefore, the preferred choice.

Because the choice of $r = 2$ or 3 leads to quite different decompositions of the data and the evidence from the test procedure was partly inconclusive, I report sensitivity analyses of the two choices of r in the next section.

4 Sensitivity Analyses

To investigate the consequences of choosing $r = 2$ or 3 three different types of sensitivity tests are performed. In the $I(1)$ model the tests are called tests of stationarity, long-run exclusion, and weak exogeneity (Hansen and Juselius, 1995). In the $I(2)$ model both their formulation and interpretation change. The first two hypotheses now involve restrictions on $\beta_{\perp 1}$ besides β, and the weak exogeneity hypothesis involves additional restrictions on $\alpha_{\perp 1}$ and $\beta_{\perp 1}$ (Paruolo and Rahbek, 1998).

For reasons related to the estimation procedure discussed in Section 2.2, it is difficult within the two-stage procedure to derive LR tests for hypotheses involving restrictions on $\beta_{\perp 1}$ and $\alpha_{\perp 1}$. The FIML procedure of Johansen (1997) provides a more unified framework for inference in the $I(2)$ model. Because of its novelty, well-tested computer programs are not yet available. Therefore, I apply the three test procedures exclusively to β and α and discuss how the interpretation has to be modified accordingly.

Section 4.1 investigates whether any of the price indices is empirically an $I(1)$ variable by testing whether any single price index corresponds to a unit vector in the cointegration space β. Section 4.2 investigates whether any of the price indices can be excluded from the β space, implying no long-run relationship with the remaining variables. Section 4.3 investigates absence of long-run levels feedback on any of the price indices.

4.1 Are Any of the Prices I(1)?

Univariate test procedures are usually adopted when testing for the order of integration of each of the variables. Here I will investigate the order of integration using the more complete information of the multivariate model.

The test whether a variable is at most $I(1)$ can be formulated as $\{\beta, \beta_{\perp 1}\}$ $= \{b, \psi_1\}$, where b is a unit vector and ψ_1 is a $p \times (r + s_1 - 1)$ vector of unrestricted coefficients. Accepting H_0 implies that the variable in question is $I(1)$, or alternatively $I(0)$ if b is in $sp(\beta_0)$. Since tests involving restrictions on $\beta_{\perp 1}$ cannot be performed within the two-stage procedure I test instead $\beta = (b, \psi)$ where ψ is a $p \times (r - 1)$ vector of unrestricted coefficients. If the $I(1)$ hypothesis is accepted in $sp(\beta)$ it would equally be accepted in $sp(\beta, \beta_{\perp 1})$,

Table 4. Stochastic properties of the data

r	ν	$\chi^2(\nu)$	$p1$	$p2$	$p3$	$p4$	$p5$	$p6$
Tests of I(1):ness								
2	4	9.49	21.70	11.01	17.09	16.05	16.80	18.70
3	3	*7.81*	*14.50*	*8.22*	*9.89*	**7.08**	*11.53*	*12.39*
Tests of long-run exclusion								
2	2	5.99	8.33	**4.56**	8.59	16.10	**5.89**	13.66
3	3	*7.81*	*15.05*	*11.10*	*9.10*	*20.68*	*8.61*	*20.14*
Tests of zero rows in α								
2	2	5.99	**1.69**	6.39	**0.50**	**3.25**	**5.89**	7.44
3	3	*7.81*	**1.86**	*9.54*	**0.72**	**7.28**	**6.88**	*12.28*

but if the hypothesis is rejected in $sp(\beta)$ it might nevertheless be accepted in $sp(\beta, \beta_{\perp 1})$.

The test statistics are reported in Table 4. To improve readability, insignificant values have been indicated in bold face and the preferred case $r = 3$ in italics. The smaller the value of r, the more "conservative" the test, the larger r the more "permissive" the test. For $r = 3$ the hypothesis is rejected for all variables, possibly with the exception of $p4$ for which there is weak evidence of acceptance. For $r = 2$ there is strong rejection of the unit vector hypothesis.

I conclude that all price indices are best approximated as $I(2)$ variables.

4.2 Long-Run Exclusion

Here I ask whether some of the price indices can be excluded from the long-run analysis. For instance, if any of the $I(2)$ price indices is long-run unrelated with the remaining indices, then one of the two $I(2)$ trends would be exclusively related to that price index. For instance if p_1 can be long-run excluded, then:

$$\beta' = \begin{bmatrix} 0,0,0 \\ *,*,* \\ *,*,* \\ *,*,* \\ *,*,* \\ *,*,* \end{bmatrix}, \quad \beta'_{\perp 1} = \begin{bmatrix} 0 \\ * \\ * \\ * \\ * \\ * \end{bmatrix} \Rightarrow \beta'_{\perp 2} = \begin{bmatrix} *,0 \\ 0,* \\ 0,* \\ 0,* \\ 0,* \\ 0,* \end{bmatrix}.$$

In this case the exclusion of p_1 would reduce the number of stochastic $I(2)$ trends and hence simplify the analysis considerably. At the same time the tests can be used as a check on the empirical adequacy of previously selected sets of price indices.

The hypothesis of long-run exclusion can be expressed as a zero row in $\{\beta, \beta_{\perp 1}\}$ or, equivalently, a unit vector in $\beta_{\perp 2}$. This hypothesis involves restrictions on both β and $\beta_{\perp 1}$, alternatively $\beta_{\perp 2}$ and cannot be tested with the two-step procedure. The modified hypothesis $\beta = H\phi$, alternatively $H'_\perp \beta = 0$, where $H_\perp$ is a unit vector leaves β_{11} unrestricted. If long-run exclusion is rejected in β it would also be rejected in $\{\beta, \beta_{11}\}$, but if long-run exclusion is accepted in β, it might, however, be rejected when tested on β_{11}.

The LR test statistic is approximately distributed as $\chi^2(r)$. For $r = 3$ all test statistics are significant on the 5 percent level, and none of the variables can be excluded from $sp(\beta)$. For $r = 2$ there is weak evidence of long-run exclusion of $p2$ (WBI) and $p5$ (ECI).

We conclude that there is no convincing evidence that any of the price indices are unrelated with the other indices in the long run. Hence, reducing the set of variables under study is likely to leave out important information on price convergence in the long run.

4.3 Hypotheses on the Adjustment Coefficients

The hypothesis of zero restrictions on a row of α is usually interpreted in terms of weak exogeneity of the corresponding variable w.r.t. the long-run parameters of interest β. As discussed in Paruolo and Rahbek (1999) this is no longer the case in the $I(2)$ model. The test of weak exogeneity involves complicated restrictions on the parameters $\{\alpha_{11}, \beta_{11}\}$. Since I do not intend to make inference in a partially specified model, weak exogeneity *per se* is not important. It is, however, of interest to test hypotheses on the strength of adjustment of each price index to the long-run relations, $\beta' x_t$. This can be investigated within the two-step procedure.

The test is of the form $R'\alpha = 0$, where R is a unit vector. The LR test statistics, approximately distributed as $\chi^2(r)$, are reported in the lower part of Table 4. Independently of the choice of r there is clear evidence of no adjustment for $p1$ and $p3$ and of weak adjustment for $p4$ and $p5$. Because the single hypotheses tests are not independent I also test the joint hypothesis of no adjustment for different sets of prices indices. Since no more than r of the variables can be jointly non-adjusting, a maximum of three indices are jointly tested. The hypothesis of no adjustment for $p1$ and $p3$ based on $r = 3$ was strongly accepted with a test statistic of 2.82, approximately distributed as $\chi^2(6)$. Adding any of the other price indices significantly increased the test statistic.

Altogether I conclude that $p1$ (CPI) and $p3$ (CRBI) are not adjusting to the long-run relations.

5 The Components of the I(2) Model

Based on the rank tests in Section 3 and the sensitivity analyses in Section 4, I continue the analyses with the preferred case ($r = 3$, $s_1 = 2$) and the estimates

Table 5. Decomposing the process into the $I(0)$, $I(1)$, and $I(2)$ directions

	$\hat{\beta}_0$	$\hat{\beta}_{1.1}$	$\hat{\kappa}_1$	$\hat{\beta}_{1.2}$	$\hat{\kappa}_2$	$\hat{\beta}_{\perp 1.1}$	$\hat{\beta}_{\perp 2.1}$	$\hat{\beta}_{\perp 2.2}$
$p1$ (CPI)	−0.81	0.03	−5.10	−0.55	1.84	−3.10	−0.14	−3.87
$p2$ (WBI)	−0.51	−0.16	1.90	0.05	−1.94	1.41	1.29	4.08
$p3$ (CRBI)	0.19	1.00	0.36	−0.17	−1.11	0.35	0.98	2.34
$p4$ (GSCI)	−0.04	−0.55	2.80	−0.24	−1.85	−4.27	0.91	3.89
$p5$ (ECI)	0.10	−0.56	−4.13	−0.13	0.71	3.16	0.65	−1.50
$p6$ (WPI)	1.00	0.26	−2.69	1.00	0.56	−2.35	0.33	−1.18
Σcoef.	0.07	0.01	−6.86	−0.04	−1.79	4.80		

	$\alpha_{0.1}$	$\alpha_{1.0}$	$\alpha_{1.1}$	$\hat{\alpha}_{\perp 1.1}$	$\hat{\alpha}_{\perp 2.1}$	$\hat{\alpha}_{\perp 2.2}$
$p1$ (CPI)	−0.011	−0.004	−0.013	−0.02	−0.02	**0.12**
$p2$ (WBI)	**0.441**	0.213	−0.107	**−0.06**	0.02	0.00
$p3$ (CRBI)	−0.071	0.046	0.111	**−0.07**	**−0.11**	−0.03
$p4$ (GSCI)	−0.262	**0.491**	**0.235**	−0.03	**0.05**	0.01
$p5$ (ECI)	0.083	**0.306**	0.052	**0.11**	**−0.07**	−0.01
$p6$ (WPI)	**−0.052**	0.022	**−0.090**	−0.04	**−0.07**	−0.04

reported in Table 5 are for this case. In Section 5.1 I interpret the estimates of β and α, and in Section 5.2 of $\beta_\perp$ and $\alpha_\perp$. Finally, in Section 5.3 I investigate long-run price homogeneity in β, and medium-run homogeneity in Γ.

5.1 Interpreting β and α

The stationary component $\beta_0' x_t$ seems to describe a homogeneous steady-state relation between $p1$ and $p6$ with some additional effects from $p2$ and $p3$. The two polynomially cointegrating relations $\beta_{1.i}' x_{t-1} + \kappa_i' \Delta x_t$, $i = 1, 2$ are not uniquely determined in terms of stationarity in the sense that the transformation $\alpha_1 M M^{-1\prime}(\beta_1', \kappa')$ where M is a non-singular 2×2 matrix, leaves the likelihood function unchanged. However, choosing M such that $\beta_{1.11} = 0$, $\beta_{1.22} = 0$ and a normalization at $\beta_{1.13}$ and $\beta_{1.26}$ hardly changes the estimates at all. Therefore, the above estimates can be given an economic interpretation under this identifying assumption.

The first dynamic steady-state relation can now be described as a relation between all price levels excluding $p1$ (CPI) and all six price differences, whereas the second is between all price levels excluding $p2$ (WBI) and all six price differences. The sum of the estimated coefficients suggests long-run price homogeneity for $\beta' x_t$, but probably not for $\beta_\perp' x_t$. Consistent with the results of Section 2.3 the κ coefficients do not sum to zero.

All three cointegration relations are significant in some of the price equations, which provides additional support for the choice of $r = 3$. The strength of the adjustment of each variable on itself in each equation can be inferred from the product coefficients $\alpha_{k.ij}\beta_{k.ij}$, $k = 0$, $i = 1, ..., 6$, $j = 1$ and $k = 1$, $i =$

1, ..., 6, $j = 1$, 2 reported below. Significant adjustment coefficients are given in bold face. For the directly cointegrating relation the result is:

$$\alpha_{0.i1}\beta_{0.i1} = [0.008, -\mathbf{0.225}, -0.0133, 0.0105, 0.008, -\mathbf{0.052}].$$

The results indicate that only $p2$ and $p6$ adjust significantly to this relation. For the polynomially cointegrating relations the $\alpha_{1.k}$ coefficients relate both to the levels $(\beta_{1.k})$ and the differences $(\omega_{1.k})$ of the process. Since the adjustment to the levels seems more important we focus on the former effect. For the first and second relation the result is:

$$\alpha_{1.i1}\beta_{1.i1} = [-0.000, -0.034, 0.046, -\mathbf{0.270}, -\mathbf{0.171}, 0.005],$$
$$\alpha_{1.i2}\beta_{1.i2} = [0.007, -0.005, -0.019, -\mathbf{0.056}, -0.006, -\mathbf{0.090}].$$

which suggests that $p4$ and $p5$ adjust significantly to the first relation, whereas $p6$ and $p4$ adjust to the second relation. Consistent with the results of Section 4.3, there is no sign of significant adjustment to any of the three relations in $p1$ (CPI) and $p3$ (CRBI), suggesting that shocks to these two price indices act as the main driving forces within this data set.

5.2 Interpreting $\alpha_\perp$ and $\beta_\perp$

The individual vectors $\{\alpha_{\perp 1.i}, \alpha_{\perp 2.j}\}$ and $\{\beta_{\perp 1.i}, \beta_{\perp 2.j}\}$, $i = 1, ..., s_1$, $j = 1, ..., s_2$, are often difficult to interpret unless identifying restrictions are imposed. In the present case $\alpha_{\perp 2}$ and $\beta_{\perp 2}$ are of dimension $p \times 2$, but since the unrestricted estimates were both interesting and perfectly interpretable I saw no need to rotate the vector space. From (2.2) it appears that $\alpha_{\perp 2}$ determines the second order stochastic trends, $\alpha'_{\perp 2}\sum_{s=1}^{t}\sum_{i=1}^{s}\varepsilon_i$, and $\beta_{\perp 2}$ the loadings of the trends in each variable, with the qualification that the weight matrix $(\alpha'_{\perp 2}\Psi\beta_{\perp 2})^{-1}$ can be referred to either the common trends or the loadings. The estimates in Table 5 are based on $\tilde{\beta}_{\perp 2} = \beta_{\perp 2}(\alpha'_{\perp 2}\Psi\beta_{\perp 2})^{-1}$ and $\alpha_{\perp 2} = \alpha_{\perp 2}$.

The estimates of the two $I(2)$ trends, $\hat{\alpha}'_{\perp 2.j}\sum\sum\hat{\varepsilon}_i$, $j = 1$, 2, where $\hat{\varepsilon}_i$ is the vector of estimated residuals from (2.1), suggest that the first $I(2)$ trend derives from the twice cumulated disturbances of $p3$, $p4$, $p5$, and $p6$, i.e. primarily of the commodity prices, whereas the second $I(2)$ trend is almost completely determined by the twice cumulated disturbances of $p1$. The corresponding estimate of $\beta_{\perp 2}$ indicates that all price indices are influenced by the second $I(2)$ trend (the CPI trend), and that all price indices, except the CPI are influenced by the first $I(2)$ trend. This is strong evidence of the dominant role of the CPI index. Moreover, judging from the magnitude of the estimated coefficients, $\beta_{\perp 2}$ does not seem to have any zero row, implying that all price indices are $I(2)$, consistent with the test results in Section 4.2.

The estimate of $\alpha'_{\perp 1}\sum_{s=1}^{t}\varepsilon_s$ determines the "autonomous" stochastic $I(1)$ trend and suggests that it is essentially a weighted average of the cumulated disturbances of the commodity indices. The estimate of $\beta_{\perp 1}$ determines the

$CI(2,1)$ relation that cannot be made stationary by cointegration between prices and inflation rates, only by cointegration between inflation, i.e $\beta'_{\perp 1}\Delta x_t \sim I(0)$. The estimate suggests the existence of a non-homogeneous medium-run steady-state relation between commodity price inflation and general price inflation. Econometrically, it is an interesting result because it demonstrates the danger of differencing the price variables to get rid of the $I(2)$ problem. One will usually fail to find a homogeneous relation between inflation rates, though such a relation is strongly present between the price levels.

A tentative economic interpretation of $\beta'_{\perp 1}\Delta x_t \sim I(0)$ is that in the medium run a change in a commodity price, say, results in other prices changing, but not necessarily such that a sustainable long-run relationship is achieved. One could, for instance, think of $\beta'_{\perp 1}x_t$ as a "rational expectations" medium-run steady-state relation, as opposed to a "neoclassical" long-run steady-state relation $\beta'x_t$. The former can be interpreted as a steady-state relation for a fixed institutional setup, and the latter as a long-run sustainable steady-state relation consistent with structural changes in institutions.

5.3 Long-Run Price Homogeneity

It appears from Table 5.1 that $\sum_j \beta_{ij} \approx 0$, $i = 1, 2, 3$, suggesting long-run price homogeneity in the r cointegrating relations $\beta'x_t$. The test of the hypothesis $R'\beta = 0$, was 1.86. It is approximately distributed as $\chi^2(3)$ and long-run homogeneity between the price indices in $sp(\beta)$ is strongly supported by the data. Hence, the weak form of long-run price homogeneity seems satisfied.

The hypothesis of overall long-run homogeneity involves restrictions on $\beta_{\perp 1}$ as well, i.e. $(\beta, \beta_{\perp 1}) = H\psi$ where ψ is $(p-1) \times (r + s_1)$. This hypothesis cannot be formally tested within the two-step procedure. But, as already discussed, the requirement $\sum_j \beta_{\perp 1.j} = 0$ does not seem to be satisfied and I conclude that weak, but not overall, long-run price homogeneity is present in the data.

As discussed in Section 2.4. empirical support for long-run price homogeneity in levels by no means implies medium-run price homogeneity in differences. Only in the direction of a homogeneous static long-run relation is medium-run price homogeneity likely to be found. Since it is of considerable economic interest to understand price movements both in the long and the medium run, I will further examine this question in Section 6.2.

6 Which Price Indices Are Related in the Long Run?

To investigate the relationship between individual price indices I have proceeded in the following way. I first ask whether the two general price indices cointegrate, and if not, which other variable(s) have to be added. I then investigate cointegration properties between combinations of the special indices.

Finally, I report the estimates and the joint test for three (overidentified) relations; one between the CPI, WPI, and WBI, another between the CRBI, WBI, and WPI, and finally one between the four commodity indices.

6.1 Partial Cointegration Tests

All hypotheses reported in Table 6 test whether a single restricted relation is in $sp(\beta)$ and are of the form $\beta = \{H\phi, \psi\}$, where H is a $p \times m$ design matrix imposing $p - m$ restrictions on one of the relations, ϕ is a $m \times 1$ vector of free parameters, and ψ is a $(p-1) \times r$ matrix of unrestricted coefficient. For derivation of the test procedures, see Johansen and Juselius (1992). I have grouped the hypotheses such that $\mathcal{H}_1$–$\mathcal{H}_5$ test hypotheses about the general price indices CPI and WPI relative to the commodity price indices, $\mathcal{H}_6$–$\mathcal{H}_{13}$ test hypotheses about the special commodity indices, and $\mathcal{H}_{14}$–$\mathcal{H}_{20}$ test hypotheses about the special commodity indices relative to one of the general price indices.

In the first group I find that CPI and WPI do not cointegrate by themselves, but that a combination with either WBI or CRBI is strongly cointegrating. In the second group I find that none of the special commodity prices indices cointegrate bivariately, but that the combination of WBI, CRBI, and ECI is

Table 6. Cointegration properties

	p1	p2	p3	p4	p5	p6	$\chi^2(\nu)$	p.val.
General versus commodity price indices								
$\mathcal{H}_1$	1	0	0	0	0	-1	15.16(3)	0.00
$\mathcal{H}_2$	-0.68	-0.32	0	0	0	1	1.34(2)	0.51
$\mathcal{H}_3$	-0.62	0	-0.38	0	0	1	1.32(2)	0.52
$\mathcal{H}_4$	-0.73	0	0	-0.27	0	1	4.97(2)	0.08
$\mathcal{H}_5$	1	0	0	0	-0.88	-0.12	9.77(2)	0.01
Commodity price indices								
$\mathcal{H}_6$	0	1	-1	0	0	0	6.24(3)	0.10
$\mathcal{H}_7$	0	1	0	-1	0	0	6.00(3)	0.11
$\mathcal{H}_8$	0	1	0	0	-1	0	14.52(3)	0.00
$\mathcal{H}_9$	0	0	1	-1	0	0	12.04(3)	0.01
$\mathcal{H}_{10}$	0	0	0	1	-1	0	14.51(3)	0.00
$\mathcal{H}_{11}$	0	1	-0.65	-0.35	0	0	3.62(2)	0.16
$\mathcal{H}_{12}$	0	-0.78	1	0	-0.22	0	1.71(2)	0.43
$\mathcal{H}_{13}$	0	0	1	-0.61	-0.39	0	5.66(2)	0.06
Commodity versus general price indices								
$\mathcal{H}_{14}$	0	-0.68	1	0	0	-0.32	0.03(2)	0.98
$\mathcal{H}_{15}$	0	0	1	-0.67	0	-0.33	11.01(2)	0.00
$\mathcal{H}_{16}$	0	0	-0.05	0	-0.95	1	12.08(2)	0.00
$\mathcal{H}_{17}$	0	0	0	-0.28	-0.72	1	10.83(2)	0.00
$\mathcal{H}_{18}$	0	1	0	-0.89	0	-0.11	5.83(2)	0.05
$\mathcal{H}_{19}$	0	-0.19	0	0	-0.81	1	12.03(2)	0.00
$\mathcal{H}_{20}$	-0.33	-0.77	1	0	0	0	0.01(2)	0.99

strongly cointegrating. The result that there is no bivariate cointegration is consistent with the results in Table 5, where the two $I(2)$ trends seemed to influence all price variables. In the third group I find that WBI and CRBI are strongly cointegrating with either CPI or WPI.

6.2 A Complete Specification

The joint hypothesis $\{\mathcal{H}_2, \mathcal{H}_{12}, \mathcal{H}_{14}\}$ was first tested but was strongly rejected based on a test statistic of 23.4 distributed as $\chi^2(6)$. For the derivation of the test procedure see Johansen and Juselius (1994). The main reason for rejection was that $\{\mathcal{H}_2, \mathcal{H}_{12}, \mathcal{H}_{14}\}$ long-run excludes $p4$, i.e. the GSCI index. Adding $p4$ to $\mathcal{H}_{14}$ resulted in a test statistics of 1.73, distributed as $\chi^2(5)$, and, hence, the modified joint hypothesis is clearly acceptable. The estimates are reported in Table 7 together with the adjustment coefficients. Adjustment coefficients being significant with a p-value > 0.05 are indicated in bold face and with a p-value of approximately 0.10 in italics.

The first relation is very similar to the directly stationary cointegrating relation $\beta_0'x$ in Table 5 and $p6$ (WPI) is significantly adjusting to it as well as $p2$ (WBI), albeit less significantly. The next relation is between $p3$ (CRBI), $p2$ (WBI) and $p6$ (WPI), and there is significant adjustment in $p6$ (WPI), and $p4$ (GSCI), and a less significant adjustment in $p5$ (ECI). The last relation ties all the special commodity price indices together, and shows significant adjustment in $p4$ (GSCI) and $p5$ (ECI), and weak adjustment in $p2$ (WBI).

Note, however, that the three $\beta'x$ relations are strictly speaking $I(1)$ (though the first one is probably $I(0)$). A test of joint restrictions on the levels and the differences is not yet available. Instead, I report the estimates of the levels matrix $\Pi = \alpha'\beta$ and the differences matrix Γ in Table 8. The estimates of Π are based on α and β in Table 7 and Γ is estimated under the reduced rank restriction $\alpha_\perp'\Gamma\beta_\perp = \zeta\eta'$.

The Γ matrix shows that $p1$ (CPI) does not seem to react on any relation between the lagged differences, hence confirming the role of CPI as the main driving force in this system, whereas $p3$ (CRBI) seems to react quite strongly to changes in the CPI and the WPI. Medium-run price homogeneity seems

Table 7. A complete specification of the cointegration relations

	$\hat{\beta}_1$	$\hat{\beta}_2$	$\hat{\beta}_3$	$\hat{\alpha}_1$	$\hat{\alpha}_2$	$\hat{\alpha}_3$
$p1$	−0.71	0	0	−0.02	0.01	−0.01
$p2$	−0.29	−0.67	−0.39	*0.30*	0.02	*0.32*
$p3$	0	1.00	1.00	−0.08	−0.13	0.14
$p4$	0	0	−0.33	−0.19	**−0.60**	**1.02**
$p5$	0	0	−0.28	0.09	*−0.25*	**0.57**
$p6$	1.0	−0.33	0	**−0.12**	**0.05**	−0.03

Table 8. The estimates of Γ and Π

Var.	$\Delta p1$	$\Delta p2$	$\Delta p3$	$\Delta p4$	$\Delta p5$	$\Delta p6$	sum
The Γ matrix							
$\Delta p1$	−0.01	−0.07	0.08	−0.04	0.05	−0.13	−0.12
$\Delta p2$	**1.28**	**−0.99**	0.07	−0.54	**0.93**	**0.70**	1.45
$\Delta p3$	**−2.94**	−0.42	−0.54	−0.62	0.62	**3.72**	−0.18
$\Delta p4$	0.05	**−0.96**	**0.83**	**−2.12**	**1.07**	**4.78**	4.01
$\Delta p5$	**2.15**	−0.30	0.09	−0.56	0.16	**1.49**	3.03
$\Delta p6$	**0.84**	−0.19	0.17	−0.14	0.20	**−0.89**	0.01

	$p1$	$p2$	$p3$	$p4$	$p5$	$p6$	sum
The Π matrix							
$p1$	0.02	0.00	−0.00	0.00	0.00	−0.02	0.0
$p2$	*−0.22*	**−0.22**	**0.33**	*−0.10*	*−0.09*	*0.30*	0.0
$p3$	0.05	0.06	0.01	−0.05	−0.04	−0.03	0.0
$p4$	0.14	0.06	**0.42**	**−0.33**	**−0.29**	0.00	0.0
$p5$	−0.07	−0.08	**0.32**	**−0.18**	**−0.16**	0.17	0.0
$p6$	**0.08**	0.01	0.03	0.01	0.01	**−0.14**	0.0

only to be present for $p3$ and $p6$ (and $p1$). Because $p3$ does not adjust to any of the long-run relations $\beta' x_t$ and $p6$ primarily adjusts to the static steady-state relation $\beta_0' x_t$ this is consistent with the results of Section 2.3. Altogether, the price adjustment seems to take place primarily in $p2$, $p4$, and $p5$, while $p1$ seems to be pushing all the other indices.

An interesting result is that the major part of the medium-run effects seems to derive from changes in the CPI and the WPI. There are essentially no effects from changes in the commodity indices on the general price indices.

7 Summary of Results

Based on the cointegrated VAR model I found convincing evidence for all six prices being $I(2)$, which motivated the decomposition of the vector process x_t into the $I(0)$, $I(1)$, and $I(2)$ directions. These were interpreted in terms of pushing and pulling forces. I demonstrated that the statistical concept of directly cointegrating, polynomially cointegrating and difference cointegrating relations can be given a natural economic interpretation as static long-run, dynamic long-run, and medium-run steady-state relations. Using the rich structure of the $I(2)$ model I was able to formally address the question of long-run price homogeneity (between price levels) and medium-run price homogeneity (between inflation rates). I showed that even under assumption of long-run price homogeneity, medium-run price homogeneity can only exceptionally be present. Hence, analyzing price homogeneity based on inflation rates instead of price levels is likely to give misleading results.

Several empirical results emerged from this study.

First, the usefulness of calculating the roots of the characteristic polynomial for the choice of cointegration rank indices was pointed out. In particular, when there are $I(2)$ or near $I(2)$ components in the data this turned out to be a valuable diagnostic tool. As a further help in choosing the cointegration indices (r, s_1) the paper demonstrated the use of sensitivity analyses as a complement to the formal tests.

Second, long-run price homogeneity was found to be present in $\beta' x_t$, but probably not in $\beta'_{\perp 1} x_t$. Consistent with the theoretical model medium-run price homogeneity between the differences was present in one of the long-run relations, the directly $CI(2, 2)$ cointegrating relation, but not in the others. Among the six price variables medium-run price homogeneity seemed to be present for the CPI, WPI, and CRBI, i.e. in those of the price indices that primarily act as driving forces in this system.

Third, the question whether commodity price indices can be used as forward indicators of the permanent part of price inflation measured by the CPI or the WPI index did not receive much empirical support. I found no significant effects on the CPI from the cointegrating relations, neither in levels nor in differences. The finding that the CPI was the driving force within the present system was a very strong result that carried through in all different tests.

Fourth, I found three common stochastic trends among the six price indices, of which two were of second order and one of first order. One of the second order trends seemed to derive exclusively from permanent shocks to the CPI index, whereas the other derived from shocks to the commodity indices. All six price indices were affected by the two $I(2)$ trends and a minimum of three price indices were, therefore, needed for cointegration. This result explains previous findings of no cointegration in bivariate cointegration analyses and points to the importance choosing a sufficiently large set of price indices for this kind of analysis.

As a complement I performed a similar analysis (not reported in the paper) exclusively based on the four commodity price indices. The results were on the whole inconclusive and disappointing: only weak evidence of $I(2)$ effects, no evidence of long-run price proportionality, only weakly significant adjustment to the cointegrating relations, etc., strengthening the conclusion that the complex relationships between price indices would be difficult to trace within a smaller set of variables.

Appendix A

*The composition of the four commodity price indices
(from Gallo et al., 1997)*

Commodity index	CRBI	GSCI	WBI	ECI
Energy	14.3	51.3	—	—
Livestock	14.3	13.6	—	47.4
Crops	42.8	25.4	53.2	—
Misc.[a]	9.5	—	19.7	19.3
Base metals[b]	4.8	6.6	27.1	33.3
Precious metals	14.3	3.2	—	—

a For the CRBI this component includes orange juice and lumber; for the WBI it includes agricultural nonfood items—cotton, jute, tobacco, and rubber.

b The CRBI includes only copper; the GSCI includes aluminum, copper, zinc, nickel, lead, and tin; the WBI further includes phosphate rock and iron ore.

Appendix B

The graphs of the data in levels and differences

LPCI

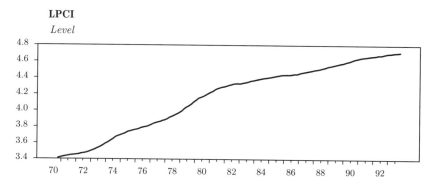

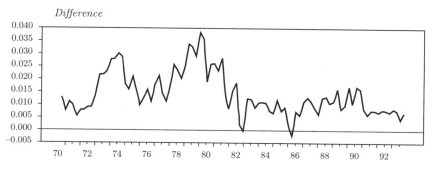

Katarina Juselius

LWBI

Level

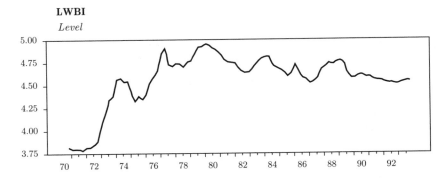

Difference

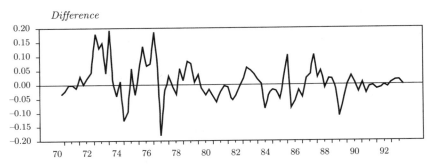

LCRBI

Level

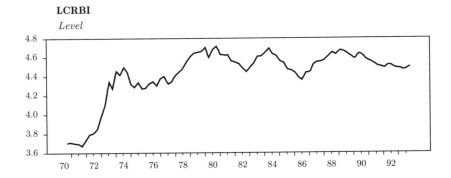

Difference

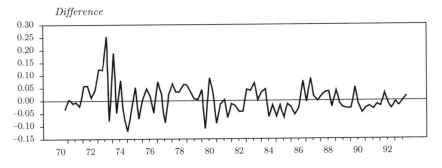

LGSCI

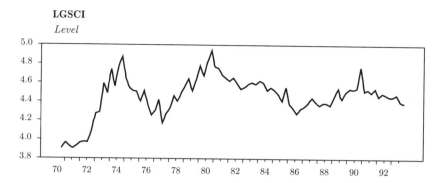

Level

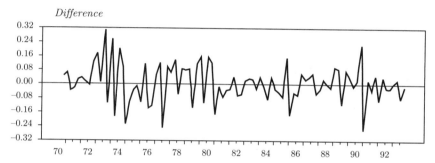

Difference

LECI

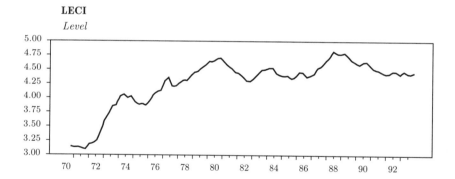

Level

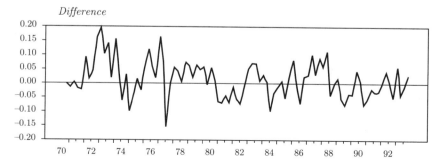

Difference

LWPI

Level

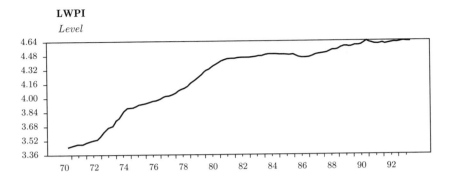

Difference

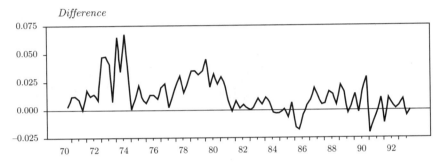

References

Baillie, R. T. (1989), "Commodity Prices and Aggregate Inflation: Would a Commodity Price Rule Be Worthwhile?" *Carnegie–Rochester Conference Series on Public Policy*, 31: 185–240.

Engle, R. F. and C. W. J. Granger (1987), "Co-integration and Error Correction: Representation, Estimation, and Testing," *Econometrica*, 55: 251–76.

Engle, R. F. and B. S. Yoo (1991), "Cointegrated Economic Time Series: An Overview with New Results," in R. F. Engle and C. W. J. Granger (eds.), *Long-Run Economic Relationships*. Oxford: Oxford University Press, pp. 237–66.

Gallo, G. M., M. Marcellino, and P. K. Trivedi (1997), "Forward Indicators of Inflation: The Message in Commodity Prices," unpublished report, European University Institute, Italy.

Granger, C. W. J. (1981), "Some Properties of Time Series Data and Their Use in Econometric Model Specification," *Journal of Econometrics*, 16: 121–30.

Granger, C. W. J. (1986), "Developments in the Study of Cointegrated Economic Variables," *Oxford Bulletin of Economics and Statistics*, 48/3: 213–28.

Granger, C. W. J. and Y. Jeon (1996), "Does the Commodity Price Index Lead Inflation?," unpublished report, Economics Department, University of California, San Diego.

Granger, C. W. J. and T.-H. Lee (1989), "Multicointegration," in G. F. Rhodes and

T. B. Fomby (eds.), *Advances in Econometrics: Co-Integration, Spurious Regressions and Unit Roots*, 8. Greenwich, CT: JAI Press, pp. 71–84.

Hansen, H. and S. Johansen (1993), "Recursive Estimation in Cointegrated VAR-Models," preprint 1, Institute of Mathematical Statistics, University of Copenhagen.

Hansen, H. and K. Juselius (1995), "CATS in RATS, Manual to Cointegration Analysis of Time Series, Estima," Evanston, IL.

Johansen, S. (1992), "A Representation of Vector Autoregressive Processes Integrated of Order 2," *Econometric Theory*, 8: 188–202.

Johansen, S. (1995), "A Statistical Analysis of Cointegration for I(2) Variables," *Econometric Theory*, 11: 25–59.

Johansen, S. (1997), "A Likelihood Analysis of the I(2) Model," *Scandinavian Journal of Statistics*, 24: 433–62.

Johansen, S. (1999), "A Bartlett Correction Factor for Test on the Cointegrating Relations," forthcoming in *Econometric Theory*.

Johansen, S. and K. Juselius (1992), "Testing Structural Hypotheses in a Multivariate Cointegration Analysis of the PPP and the UIP for UK," *Journal of Econometrics*, 53: 211–24.

Johansen, S. and K. Juselius (1994), "Identification of the Long-Run and the Short-Run Structure: An Application to the ISLM Model," *Journal of Econometrics*, 63: 7–36.

Jørgensen, C. (1998), "A Simulation Study of Tests in the Cointegrated VAR Model," unpublished report, Institute of Economics, University of Copenhagen.

Juselius, K. (1994), "On the Duality Between Long-Run Relations and Common Trends in the I(1) and the I(2) Case: An Application to Aggregate Money Holdings," *Econometric Reviews*, 13: 151–78.

Juselius, K. (1995), "Do Purchasing Power Parity and Uncovered Interest Parity Hold in the Long Run? An Example of Likelihood Inference in a Multivariate Time Series Model," *Journal of Econometrics*, 69: 211–40.

Juselius, K. (1998), "A Structured VAR in Denmark under Changing Monetary Regimes," *Journal of Business and Economics Statistics*, 16: 400–12.

Juselius, K. (1999), "Models and Relations in Economics and Econometrics," *Journal of Economic Methodology*, 6(2): 259–90.

Kugler, P. (1991), "Common Trends, Commodity Prices and Consumer Prices," *Economic Letters*, 37: 345–9.

Paruolo, P. (1996), "On the Determination of Integration Indices in *I*(2) Systems," *Journal of Econometrics*, 72: 313–56.

Paruolo, P. and A. Rahbek (1999), "Weak Exogeneity in I(2) VAR Systems," *Journal of Econometrics*, forthcoming.

Trivedi, P. K. (1995), "Commodity Price Indexes: Their Interrelationships and Usefulness as Forward Indicators of Future Inflation," unpublished report, Department of Economics, Indiana University, Bloomington.

14
M-Testing Using Finite and Infinite Dimensional Parameter Estimators

HALBERT WHITE AND YONGMIAO HONG

1 Introduction, Motivation, and Heuristics

A prominent theme recurring throughout Clive Granger's extensive body of work is his concern with the adequacy of econometric models. Granger (1990) gives this concern the status of an axiom in his general introduction to his volume *Modelling Economic Series*. In fact, it is his first axiom:

Axiom A. Any model will only be an approximation to the generating mechanism, with there being a preference for the best available approximation.

Granger's second axiom is:

Axiom B. The basic objective of a modeling exercise is to affect the beliefs— and hence the behavior—of other research workers.

Taken together, Axioms A and B require us not merely to report the results of our econometric modeling, but to evaluate the models as well, providing "comparisons with other models, the results of specification tests, out-of-sample evaluation, and so forth" (Granger, 1990, p. 3).

Indeed, one of the most useful approaches to specification testing involves the direct comparison of the results of two different models of the same phenomenon. This approach to specification testing, pioneered by Durbin (1954), Wu (1973), and Hausman (1978), has undergone substantial evolution and extension. Specification tests have progressed from purely parametric contexts, as in Durbin (1954), Wu (1973), Hausman (1978), Newey (1985), and Tauchen (1985), to contexts involving both nonparametric and parametric approaches, as in Whang and Andrews (1993) and Hong and White (1991, 1995). Our purpose here is to extend and unify these approaches in a way that permits

This is a revised version of our UCSD Department of Economics Discussion Paper 1993–1. We wish to thank Randy Eubank, Clive Granger, Kurt Honik, Sing-Chee Lee, Whitney Newey, Yosef Rinott, Max Stinchcombe, Jeff Wooldridge, and two anonymous referees for useful comments. All remaining errors are ours. White's participation was supported by NSF grants SES–8921382 and SES–9209023.

hypothesis testing about parametric, semi-parametric, and nonparametric models in a manner not previously possible, providing new tools to aid in achieving the objective of Granger's Axiom B.

To illustrate the issues involved, consider the consistent test for the correctness of a parametric regression model $f(X_t, \alpha)$ for the conditional expectation $\theta_o(X_t) = E(Y_t|X_t)$ given by Hong and White (1991, 1995), where Y_t is the dependent variable, X_t is the vector of explanatory variables and α is a finite dimensional parameter vector. The test is based on the sample covariance:

$$\hat{m}_n = n^{-1}\sum_{t=1}^{n}(\hat{\theta}_n(X_t) - f(X_t, \hat{\alpha}_n))(Y_t - f(X_t, \hat{\alpha}_n)). \qquad (1.1)$$

Here $\hat{\alpha}_n$ is an appropriate estimator, such as the nonlinear least squares estimator, and $\hat{\theta}_n$ is a nonparametric series estimator for θ_o. The statistic $\hat{m}_n$ estimates the covariance

$$m_o = E[(\theta_0(X_t) - f(X_t, \alpha^*))(Y_t - f(X_t, \alpha^*))],$$

where $\alpha^* = p \lim \hat{\alpha}_n$. Under the null hypothesis of correct specification (and only then) we have $m_o = 0$, as correct specification implies $\theta_o(X_t) = f(X_t, \alpha_o)$ a.s. for some $\alpha^* = \alpha_o$. Thus, a test based on $\hat{m}_n$ has asymptotic power one whenever $f(X_t, \alpha)$ is misspecified.

Although Hong and White (1995, theorem A.3) give a version of their statistic that does not suffer from the effects of neglecting heteroskedasticity of unknown form, this immunity is achieved essentially by use of a heteroskedasticity-consistent covariance matrix estimator. An attractive alternative is to correct for heteroskedasticity of unknown form directly, using a consistent nonparametric estimator for the conditional variance, as this may deliver better power. Letting $\pi_o(X_t) = (var(Y_t|X_t))^{1/2}$ and $\theta_o = \mu_o/\pi_o$, where $\mu_o(X_t) = E(Y_t|X_t)$, we now estimate θ_o nonparametrically by $\hat{\theta}_n$ and π_o nonparametrically, say by $\hat{\pi}_n$ (e.g., as in Robinson, 1987). The statistic of interest is now:

$$\hat{m}_n = n^{-1}\sum_{t=1}^{n}(\hat{\theta}_n(X_t) - f(X_t, \hat{\alpha}_n)/\hat{\pi}_n(X_t))(Y_t - f(X_t, \hat{\alpha}_n))/\hat{\pi}_n(X_t). \qquad (1.2)$$

This estimates

$$m_o = E[(\mu_o(X_t) - f(X_t, \alpha^*))^2 / \pi_o^2(X_t)],$$

which is again zero only under correct specification. We see that $\hat{m}_n$ is a particular value of

$$m_n(\alpha, \theta, \pi) = n^{-1}\sum_{t=1}^{n}m(Z_t, \alpha, \theta, \pi),$$

where $Z_t = (X'_t, Y_t)'$ and $m(Z_t, \alpha, \theta, \pi) = (\theta(X_t) - f(X_t, \alpha)/\pi(X_t))(Y_t - f(X_t, \alpha))/\pi(X_t)$.

We distinguish between the two infinite dimensional parameters θ and π, as it turns out that the effects of replacing them with $\hat{\theta}_n$ and $\hat{\pi}_n$ are quite different: $\hat{\theta}_n$ plays a key role in determining the asymptotic distribution of a suitably scaled version of $\hat{m}_n$, while $\hat{\pi}_n$ plays essentially no role in determining this distribution.

Although we are motivated by consideration of (1.1) and (1.2), it is conceptually simpler and notationally much simpler to work first with the general statistic $m_n(\hat{\alpha}_n, \hat{\theta}_n, \hat{\pi}_n)$ and then specialize. A not inconsiderable additional benefit to this is that many other interesting specification testing procedures fall into the same framework, saving a great deal of effort that might otherwise be required in treating them. We discuss several new applications in considerable detail, including a new test for regression error normality in a nonparametric regression and a new test for omitted variables in nonparametric regression, as well as two new consistent regression specification tests based on (1.1) and (1.2).

To make clear the contribution of our approach and its relation to prior work, we recall that Newey (1985) and Tauchen (1985) treated the case of "m-testing" based on the statistic:

$$m_n(\hat{\alpha}_n),$$

while White (1987, 1994) treated the case:

$$m_n(\hat{\alpha}_n, \hat{\pi}_n),$$

where $\hat{\alpha}_n$ is a parametric estimator that affects the asymptotic distribution of the test statistic, and $\hat{\pi}_n$ is a finite dimensional parametric estimator not affecting the asymptotic distribution. Whang and Andrews (1993) achieved a substantial advance by letting $\hat{\pi}_n$ be a nonparametric estimator not affecting the asymptotic distribution. This framework can be used to test parametric and semiparametric models (see Whang and Andrews, 1993).

To handle the specific examples above, we introduce the nonparametric estimator $\hat{\theta}_n$, leading to:

$$m_n(\hat{\alpha}_n, \hat{\theta}_n, \hat{\pi}_n).$$

This m-statistic cannot be handled within any previously studied framework (e.g., Whang and Andrews, 1993), because $\hat{\theta}_n$ plays a key role in determining its asymptotic distribution. Our goal, therefore, is to develop an appropriate theory to permit us to test hypotheses based on such statistics. A major consequence of introducing $\hat{\theta}_n$ is that the distribution and power theory for the tests of interest can differ substantially from that previously developed. Indeed, the joint presence of $\hat{\alpha}_n$, $\hat{\pi}_n$ and $\hat{\theta}_n$ introduces the potential for a variety of interesting possibilities. Our framework can be used to test hypotheses about parametric, semiparametric and nonparametric models.

Although the notation in the sections that follow is unavoidably complicated by the need to keep separate track of α, θ, and π, the basic underlying idea for developing our distribution theory is straightforward: essentially, we just take a Taylor series expansion appropriate to the situation at hand.

To see what is involved, we first replace $\hat{\pi}_n$ with its limit, say π_o: at each step we will impose conditions ensuring that this has no effect on the asymptotic distribution of interest. Now take a first order Taylor expansion around α_o and θ_o:

$$m_n(\hat{\alpha}_n, \hat{\theta}_n, \pi_o) = m_n(\alpha_o, \theta_o, \pi_o) + \nabla'_\alpha m_n^o(\hat{\alpha}_n - \alpha_o) + \nabla'_\theta m_n^o(\hat{\theta}_n - \theta_o) + r_n.$$

In the second term, $\nabla'_\alpha m_n^o$ denotes the Jacobian of m_n with respect to α evaluated at $(\alpha_o, \theta_o, \pi_o)$. The third term is a flagrant abuse of notation, but it greatly helps us to see what is going on. If θ were finite dimensional, then the Jacobian $\nabla'_\theta m_n^o$ of m_n with respect to θ at $(\alpha_o, \theta_o, \pi_o)$ could multiply $(\hat{\theta}_n - \theta_o)$ as we have written. Because θ is infinite dimensional, what we have written is invalid; however, by using the Frechet differential, we get a term that behaves essentially just as $\nabla'_\theta m_n^o(\hat{\theta}_n - \theta_o)$ does. Later, the Frechet notation δm_n^o appears in its place. For now, we stick with our abuse. The final term (r_n) is a remainder.

To obtain the desired null distributions, we need to find the orders of the different terms under the null, rescale by the rate for the slowest converging (i.e., dominant) term(s), and apply appropriate central limit results. Clearly, different cases may arise in which the orders of the various terms bear different relationships to each other.

A particularly interesting possibility is that r_n dominates, i.e., the first three terms in the first order expansion vanish under the null hypothesis at a rate faster than r_n vanishes. In particular, this occurs for our motivating case $m(Z_t, \alpha_o, \theta_o) = (\theta_o(X_t) - f(X_t, \alpha_o))(Y_t - f(X_t, \alpha_o))$ because $\theta_o(X_t) = f(X_t, \alpha_o)$ a.s., causing the first term to vanish for all n. The terms involving $\nabla'_\alpha m_n^o$ and $\nabla'_\theta m_n^o$ essentially vanish in probability at rates fast enough to overwhelm the more slowly converging $(\hat{\alpha}_n - \alpha_o)$ and $(\hat{\theta}_n - \theta_o)$. We refer to cases in which this does *not* happen as "first order," because the analysis can be based on the first order Taylor expansion. Cases in which we *do* have this sort of degeneracy will be called "second order," because it turns out that a second order Taylor expansion works.

The second order cases involve an approximation that acts like

$$m_n(\hat{\alpha}_n, \hat{\theta}_n, \pi_o) = \tfrac{1}{2}(\hat{\theta}_n - \theta_o)'\nabla^2_\theta m_n^o(\hat{\theta}_n - \theta_o) + r_n.$$

Again we abuse notation. The term on the right involving $\nabla^2_\theta m_n^o$ is really a second order Frechet derivative later denoted $\delta^2 m_n^o$. All but the dominant term have been placed in the remainder r_n. Analysis of the dominant term turns out to be straightforward using the distribution theory for U- or V-statistics. As might be expected, the dominant term has non-zero expectation and so must be recentered properly; estimation of the requisite recentering is usually straightforward. Interestingly, the rate of convergence of the leading term is typically quite rapid. In the past, this has often been viewed as a form of degeneracy, with a variety of special measures introduced to avoid it. (See Section 2.3 below and Hong and White, 1995, for a discussion.) We view this "degeneracy" as a potential advantage to be exploited: the rapid convergence rate leads to re-scalings that deliver statistics with better power under both local and global alternatives.

The preceding discussion suggests that for the first order case we will obtain conditions ensuring that $n^{1/2}\hat{m}_n$ converges in distribution to a normal random vector with mean zero under the null, as is usual; from this we can construct asymptotic χ^2 statistics in the usual way (i.e., by forming an appropriate quadratic form in $\hat{m}_n$). For the second order case, we find that, after recentering by R_n (say) and scaling by a_n (say), where a_n grows faster than $n^{1/2}$, $a_n(\hat{m}_n - R_n)$ converges to a normal random vector with mean zero under the null. Again, we can construct asymptotic χ^2 statistics.

With this heuristic picture of what we are going to do and why, we can now turn to a rigorous development of our theory, treating first and second order cases separately.

2 The Basic Framework

2.1 Fundamentals of M-Testing

To begin, we describe the data generating process (DGP) and the estimators of interest.

Assumption A.1. $(\Omega, \mathcal{F}, P)$ is a complete probability space on which is defined the stochastic process $\{Z_{nt} : \Omega \to \mathbb{R}^\nu\}$, $t = 1, ..., n$, $n = 1, 2, ..., \nu \in \mathbb{N}$, where P is such that for each n $\{Z_{nt}\}$ is independently but not necessarily identically distributed (i.n.i.d.).

Assumption A.2. For pseudo-metric spaces (Θ, ρ_Θ) and (Π, ρ_Π) suppose $\hat{\theta}_n : \Omega \to \Theta$ and $\hat{\pi}_n : \Omega \to \Pi$, $n = 1, 2, ...$, are measurable such that $\rho_\Theta(\hat{\theta}_n, \theta_o) \to^p 0$ for $\theta_o \in \Theta$ and $\rho_\Pi(\hat{\pi}_n, \pi_o) \to^p 0$ for $\pi_o \in \Pi$. Furthermore, $\hat{\alpha}_n : \Omega \to \mathbb{A} \subset \mathbb{R}^p$, $p \in \mathbb{N}$, is measurable with $\hat{\alpha}_n - \alpha_n^o \to^p 0$ for some nonstochastic sequence $\{\alpha_n^o \in \mathbb{A}\}$.

For notational simplicity, below we let the dependence of Z_{nt} on n be implicit. Put $\Gamma = \mathbb{A} \times \Theta \times \Pi$. We consider a measurable "moment" function $m_{nt} : \mathbb{R}^\nu \times \Gamma \to \mathbb{R}^q$, $q \in \mathbb{N}$, that satisfies

$$E[m_{nt}(Z_t, \alpha_o, \theta_o, \pi_o)] = 0 \text{ for some } \alpha_o \in \mathbb{A} \text{ and all } t = 1, ..., n, \quad n \geq 1,$$

when the model is correctly specified. Under model misspecification, such a moment condition does not hold generally, giving the test its power. The specific form taken by m_{nt} will be dictated by the null hypothesis of interest and the alternatives against which power is desired. Sections 3 and 4 provide a variety of examples illustrating choice of m_{nt}.

Throughout, we put $m_t(\gamma) = m_{nt}(Z_t, \gamma)$ and $\bar{m}_n(\gamma) = n^{-1}\sum_{t=1}^{n}Em_t(\gamma)$. Given the i.n.i.d. assumption and that $\hat{\theta}_n$ may affect the convergence rate of our statistics, we define the null hypothesis based on $\{m_t\}$ to be:

$$H_o : a_n\bar{m}_n(\alpha_o,\theta_o,\pi) \to 0 \text{ for some } (\alpha_o,\theta_o) \in \mathbb{A} \times \Theta \text{ and all } \pi \in \Pi_o \subseteq \Pi,$$

for a nonstochastic sequence $\{a_n : a_n \to \infty, a_n/n \to 0\}$. Local alternatives are:

$$H_{an} : a_n\bar{m}_n(\alpha_n^o,\theta_o,\pi) = O(1) \text{ for some } (\alpha_n^o,\theta_o) \in \mathbb{A} \times \Theta \text{ and all } \pi \in \Pi_o \subseteq \Pi.$$

We specify the global alternative as:

$$H_A : \left\|\bar{m}_n(\gamma)\right\| \geq c > 0 \text{ for all } \gamma \in \Gamma \text{ and all } n \text{ sufficiently large.}$$

Note that H_{an} can be generated by the functional form of $\{m_t\}$ and/or sequence $\{\alpha_n^o\}$. The factor a_n is determined by $\{m_t\}$ and $\hat{\theta}_n$. In first order m-testing, $a_n = n^{1/2}$; for second order, $a_n = n^{1/2+\epsilon}$ for some $\epsilon > 0$. These hypotheses may or may not coincide with the null hypothesis originally of interest (say H_o^*) and its alternatives. In first order m-testing, there is often a discrepancy between H_o and H_o^*. In second order, however, H_o generally coincides with H_o^*, thus delivering consistent tests. These issues are addressed further in the applications of Sections 3 and 4.

Stochastic equicontinuity plays a key role in ensuring that $\hat{\pi}_n$ has no asymptotic effect.

Definition 2.1. [Stochastic Equicontinuity]: *Let $(\Omega, \mathcal{F}, P)$ be a probability space and (Π, ρ_Π) be a pseudo-metric space. The stochastic process $\{Q_n : \Omega \times \Pi \to \mathbb{R}^q\}$, $n = 1, 2, ...$, $q \in \mathbb{N}$, is stochastically ρ_Π-equicontinuous at $\pi_o \in \Pi$ if for each $\epsilon > 0$ there exists $\delta > 0$ such that*

$$\lim_{n\to\infty} P^*[\sup_{\pi\in\mathbb{B}(\pi_o,\delta)} \left\|Q_n(\cdot,\pi) - Q_n(\cdot,\pi_o)\right\| > \epsilon] < \epsilon,$$

where P^* is outer probability and $\mathbb{B}(\pi_o, \delta) = \{\pi \in \Pi : \rho_\Pi(\pi, \pi_o) \leq \delta\}$.

Primitive conditions can be found in Andrews (1994); Theorem 3.6 below also provides an alternative method to ensure stochastic equicontinuity.

Assumption A.3. (a) Given $(\alpha_n^o, \theta_o) \in \mathbb{A} \times \Theta$ and a nonstochastic sequence $\{a_n : a_n \to \infty, a_n/n \to 0\}$, $a_n(m_n(\alpha_n^o, \theta_o, \cdot) - \bar{m}_n(\alpha_n^o, \theta_o, \cdot))$ is stochastically ρ_Π-equicontinuous at $\pi_o \in \Pi$; and (b) $a_n\bar{m}_n(\alpha_n^o, \theta_o, \hat{\pi}_n) = a_n\bar{m}_n(\gamma_n^o) + o_P(1)$, where $\gamma_n^o = (\alpha_n^o, \theta_o, \pi_o)$.

We also make use of the concept of uniform equicontinuity (cf. Billingsley, 1986).

Definition 2.2. [Uniform Equicontinuity]: *Let (Γ, ρ_Γ) be a product pseudo-metric space. For each n, let $Q_n : \Gamma \to \mathbb{R}^q \times \mathbb{R}^k$, $q, k \in \mathbb{N}$, be a given mapping.*

Then $\{Q_n\}$ is uniformly equicontinuous on Γ with respect to ρ_Γ if for each $\epsilon > 0$ there exists $\delta > 0$ such that

$$\limsup_n \sup_{(\gamma_1, \gamma_2) \in \mathbb{B}_n(\delta)} \left\| Q_n(\gamma_1) - Q_n(\gamma_2) \right\| < \epsilon,$$

where $\mathbb{B}_n(\delta) = \{(\gamma_1, \gamma_2) \in \Gamma \times \Gamma : \rho_\Gamma(\gamma_1, \gamma_2) \le \delta\}$.

Assumption A.4. For each n denote $\hat{\gamma}_n = (\hat{\alpha}_n, \hat{\theta}_n, \hat{\pi}_n)$. Let ρ_Γ be a product pseudo-metric on Γ such that $\rho_\Gamma(\hat{\gamma}_n, \gamma_n^o) \to^p 0$. (a) For each $\gamma \in \Gamma, \bar{m}_n(\gamma)$ is $O(1)$ and is uniformly equicontinuous on Γ with respect to ρ_Γ; (b) $\{m_t(\gamma)\}$ obeys a weak uniform law of large numbers (ULLN) on Γ, i.e., $\sup_{\gamma \in \Gamma} \|m_n(\gamma) - \bar{m}_n(\gamma)\| \to^p 0$.

Weak ULLNs are given by Andrews (1991a), Newey (1991), and White and Wooldridge (1991).

2.2 First Order M-Testing

We now treat the case in which the first order terms of a Taylor expansion determine the behavior of our test statistics. The next two assumptions permit a first order expansion.

Assumption B.1. (a) For each $(\theta, \pi) \in \Theta \times \Pi$, $m_t(\cdot, \theta, \pi)$ is continuously differentiable *a.s.* on $\mathbb{A}$ and $\bar{m}_n(\cdot, \theta, \pi)$ is continuously differentiable on $\mathbb{A}$; (b) for each $\gamma \in \Gamma$, $\nabla_\alpha \bar{m}_n(\gamma) = n^{-1}\sum_{t=1}^n E\nabla_\alpha m_t(\gamma)$ is $O(1)$ and is uniformly equicontinuous on Γ with respect to a product pseudo-metric ρ_Γ such that $\rho_\Gamma(\hat{\gamma}_n, \gamma_n^o) \to^p 0$; and (c) $\{\nabla_\alpha m_t(\gamma)\}$ obeys a weak ULLN on Γ.

Assumption B.2. (a) For each $\pi \in \Pi$, $m_t(\alpha_n^o, \cdot, \pi)$ is Frechet differentiable with respect to ρ_Θ *a.s.* on a neighborhood Θ_o of θ_o such that $E(\delta m_t(\theta - \theta_o; \gamma_n^o)) < \infty$ for all $\theta \in \Theta_o$; (b) there exist some $\lambda > 0$ and $D_{nt} : \mathbb{R}^\nu \to \mathbb{R}^+$, $n^{-1}\sum_{t=1}^n ED_{nt}(Z_t) = O(1)$, such that

$$\left\| m_t(\alpha_n^o, \theta, \pi) - m_t(\alpha_n^o, \theta_o, \pi) - \delta m_t(\theta - \theta_o; \alpha_n^o, \theta_o, \pi) \right\| \le D_{nt}(Z_t)\rho_\Theta(\theta, \theta_o)^{1+\lambda} \ a.s.$$

for all $\theta \in \Theta_o$ and all $\pi \in \Pi$; (c) $\rho_\Theta(\hat{\theta}_n, \theta_o) = o_P(n^{-1/2(1+\lambda)})$.

The product pseudo-metric ρ_Γ in Assumption B.1 may differ from that of Assumption A.4. In Assumption B.2, $\delta m_t(\theta - \theta_o; \alpha_n^o, \theta_o, \pi)$ is the Frechet differential of $m_t(\alpha_n^o, \cdot, \pi)$ with respect to ρ_Θ at θ_o with increment $\theta - \theta_o$, corresponding to $\nabla'_\theta m_n^o(\hat{\theta}_n - \theta_o)$ in Section 1. The inequality in Assumption B.2(b) controls the Taylor series remainder. For $\{m_t\}$ linear in θ, set $\lambda = \infty$.

Assumption B.3. For each n denote $\delta m_n^o(\theta - \theta_o; \pi) = n^{-1}\sum_{t=1}^n \delta m_t(\theta - \theta_o; \alpha_n^o, \theta_o, \pi)$ and $\delta\bar{m}_n^o(\theta - \theta_o; \pi) = E\delta m_n^o(\theta - \theta_o; \pi)$. (a) $n^{1/2}\sup_{\pi \in \Pi} \|\delta m_n^o(\hat{\theta}_n - \theta_o; \pi) - \delta\bar{m}_n^o(\hat{\theta}_n - \theta_o; \pi)\| \to^p 0$; (b) $n^{1/2}(\delta\bar{m}_n^o(\hat{\theta}_n - \theta_o; \hat{\pi}_n) - \delta\bar{m}_n^o(\hat{\theta}_n - \theta_o; \pi_o)) \to^p 0$; (c) $n^{1/2} \|\delta\bar{m}_n^o(\hat{\theta}_n - \theta_o; \pi_o) - V_n\| \to^p 0$, where $V_n = n^{-1}\sum_{t=1}^n v_{nt}(Z_t, \gamma_n^o)$ and $v_{nt} : \mathbb{R}^\nu \times \Gamma \to \mathbb{R}^q$ is measurable with $n^{1/2}EV_n \to 0$.

For each $\pi \in \Pi$, $\delta m_n^o(\hat{\theta}_n - \theta_o; \pi)$ is asymptotically a second order V-statistic, so Assumption B.3(a) is a uniform V-statistic projection. Assumption B.3(b) ensures that replacing $\hat{\pi}_n$ with π_o does not affect the limiting distribution of $\delta \bar{m}_n^o(\hat{\theta}_n - \theta_o; \hat{\pi}_n)$. Ensuring Assumption B.3(c) typically involves an "undersmoothing" procedure to make the bias of $\hat{\theta}_n$ vanish faster than its variance.

Assumption B.4. $n^{1/2}(\hat{\alpha}_n - \alpha_n^o) = n^{1/2}S_n + o_P(1)$, where $S_n = n^{-1}\sum_{t=1}^n s_{nt}(Z_t, \alpha_n^o)$, $s_{nt} : \mathbb{R}^\nu \times \mathbb{A} \to \mathbb{R}^p$ is measurable, and $n^{1/2}ES_n \to 0$.

This includes most parametric and semiparametric estimators that are $n^{1/2}$-consistent and asymptotically normal. In parametric maximum likelihood estimation, for example, s_{nt} is the score function premultiplied by the inverse of the information matrix.

Assumption B.5. $J_n^{o-1/2}n^{1/2}W_n \to^d N(0, I_q)$, where $W_n = m_n(\gamma_n^o) - \bar{m}_n(\gamma_n^o) + \nabla'_\alpha \bar{m}_n(\gamma_n^o)S_n + V_n$ and J_n^o is a $q \times q$ nonstochastic $O(1)$ uniformly positive definite matrix.

This ensures that $n^{1/2}W_n$ is nondegenerate. It occurs when $\delta \bar{m}_n^o(\hat{\theta} - \theta_o; \pi_o) = O_P(n^{-1/2})$, so that this functional of $\hat{\theta}_n$ achieves the parametric rate. Here, $n^{1/2}V_n$, $n^{1/2}(m_n(\gamma_n^o) - \bar{m}_n(\gamma_n^o))$ and $n^{1/2}\nabla'_\alpha \bar{m}_n(\gamma_n^o)S_n$ jointly determine the limiting distribution of $n^{1/2}\hat{m}_n$. This possibility arises when $\delta \bar{m}_n^o(\hat{\theta}_n - \theta_o; \pi_o)$ can be approximated asymptotically as a weighted integral of $\hat{\theta}_n - \theta_o$, providing additional smoothing. See Andrews (1991b, section 4), Goldstein and Messer (1992), Härdle and Stoker (1989), Lavergne and Vuong (1996), Newey (1994), Powell, Stock and Stoker (1989), Robinson (1988), and Stoker (1989).

Assumption B.6. For each n there exists a measurable $\hat{J}_n : \Omega \to \mathbb{R}^q \times \mathbb{R}^q$ such that $\hat{J}_n - J_n \to^p 0$, where J_n is a $q \times q$ nonstochastic $O(1)$ uniformly positive definite matrix with $J_n = J_n^o$ under H_{an}, where J_n^o is as in B.5.

We now state the first main result, a substantive extension of Whang and Andrews (1993).

Theorem 2.3. Define $M_n = n\hat{m}_n'\hat{J}_n^-\hat{m}_n$, where $\hat{m}_n = m_n(\hat{\gamma}_n)$. (i) Suppose Assumptions A.1–A.3 (with $a_n = n^{1/2}$) and Assumptions B.1–B.6 hold. Then under H_{an} with $a_n = n^{1/2}$,

$$M_n \to^d \chi_q^2(\zeta_n^o),$$

where $\chi_q^2(\zeta_n^o)$ is a chi-square distribution with q degrees of freedom and noncentrality $\zeta_n^o = n\bar{m}_n'(\gamma_n^o)J_n^{o-1}\bar{m}_n(\gamma_n^o)$; (ii) Suppose Assumptions A.1, A.2, A.4 and B.6 hold. Then under H_A and for any nonstochastic sequence $\{C_n = o(n)\}$,

$$P[M_n > C_n] \to 1.$$

When the limiting random variable depends on n as in (i) above, the convergence in distribution is as defined by White (1994, definition 8.3). Theorem

2.3 implies that M_n is able to detect the class of local alternatives converging to the null at the parametric rate $n^{-1/2}$. Compared to Whang and Andrews (1993), who consider only the infinite dimensional parameter estimators that do not affect the limit distribution of the m-test statistic, we permit use of infinite dimensional parameter estimators that may or may not affect the limit distribution of interest. This extends the scope of m-testing to test parametric, semiparametric, and nonparametric models against various alternatives, as illustrated by the examples in Sections 3 and 4 below.

2.3 Second Order M-Testing

We now consider the case in which second order terms dominate in our Taylor approximation. To characterize the relevant cases, we use the following definition.

Definition 2.4. [Degenerate Moment Function]: *Let Assumptions A.1, B.1(a) and B.2(a) hold. Then $\{m_t\}$ is a_n-degenerate at $\gamma_n^o = (\alpha_n^o, \theta_o, \pi_o) \in \Gamma$ if there exists a nonstochastic sequence $\{a_n : a_n/n^{1/2} \to \infty, a_n/n \to 0\}$ such that (a) $a_n(m_n(\gamma_n^o) - \bar{m}_n(\gamma_n^o)) \to^p 0$; (b) $(a_n/n^{1/2})\nabla_\alpha \bar{m}_n(\gamma_n^o) \to 0$; and (c) $a_n \delta \bar{m}_n^o(\theta - \theta_o; \pi_o) \to 0$ for all $\theta \in \Theta_o \subseteq \Theta$, where Θ_o contains a neighborhood of θ_o.*

Under H_o, $m_t(\gamma_o) = 0$ a.s., $\nabla_\alpha \bar{m}_n(\gamma_o) = 0$ and $\delta \bar{m}_n^o(\theta - \theta_o; \pi_o) = 0$ for all $\theta \in \Theta_o$ and all t, n. Assumption B.5 thus fails. Consequently, Theorem 2.3 does not apply to DMFs.

The examples at the outset of Section 1 are DMFs. Hong and White (1995) give numerous other examples relevant for testing specification hypotheses about models of conditional densities or expectations. In the past, the standard response to degeneracy has been to remove it, e.g., by sample splitting (Yatchew, 1992; Whang and Andrews, 1993, section 5), use of nonparametric estimators not nesting the parametric model (Wooldridge, 1992), or special weightings (Fan and Gencay, 1993; Lee, 1988; Robinson, 1991). These approaches base the limiting distribution of the test statistics essentially on modified first order terms. As it turns out, these approaches do not fully exploit the possible efficiency gains provided by the degeneracy. In addition, each has features one may consider drawbacks: sample-splitting uses relatively inefficient nonparametric estimators; non-nested approaches require slow convergence of the nonparametric estimator to the true function; and weighting may introduce unnecessary noise or make the asymptotic covariance matrix depend on a nuisance parameter, the choice of which may affect size and power in finite samples. Further, these procedures may work only in certain cases. For example, non-nested testing and deterministic weighting may not apply when θ_o is constant under the null, as in testing homoskedasticity.

We therefore part with tradition and avoid these drawbacks by basing tests on the dominant second order terms. As our statistics are quadratic forms,

CLTs for generalized quadratic forms (e.g., de Jong, 1987) or degenerate U-statistics (e.g., Hall, 1984) apply. In addition to being straightforward, a main advantage of our approach is that it improves asymptotic power under both local and global alternatives, as will be seen below.

We now introduce two conditions that permit a two-term Taylor expansion.

Assumption C.1. (a) For each $(\theta, \pi) \in \Theta \times \Pi$, $m_t(\cdot, \theta, \pi)$ is twice continuously differentiable *a.s.* on $\mathbb{A}$, with $\|\nabla'_\alpha m_t(\cdot)\|$ and $\|\nabla^2_\alpha m_t(\cdot)\|$ dominated by $D_{nt} : \mathbb{R}^\nu \to \mathbb{R}^+$, $n^{-1}\sum_{t=1}^n E D_{nt}(Z_t) = O(1)$; (b) with $\{a_n\}$ as in Assumption A.3, $a_n n^{-1/2}(\nabla'_\alpha m_n(\alpha^o_n, \hat\theta_n, \hat\pi_n) - \nabla'_\alpha \bar m_n(\alpha^o_n, \hat\theta_n, \hat\pi_n)) \to^p 0$; and (c) $a_n n^{-1/2}(\nabla'_\alpha \bar m_n(\alpha^o_n, \hat\theta_n, \hat\pi_n) - \nabla'_\alpha \bar m_n(\gamma^o_n)) \to^p 0$.

This ensures that the first two terms in the Taylor expansion of $a_n \hat m_n$ around α^o_n do not affect its limit distribution.

Assumption C.2. (a) For each $\pi \in \Pi$, $m_t(\alpha^o_n, \cdot, \pi)$ is twice Frechet differentiable with respect to ρ_Θ *a.s.* on a neighborhood Θ_o of θ_o and there exist some $\lambda > 0$ and $D_{nt} : \mathbb{R}^\nu \to \mathbb{R}^+$, $n^{-1}\sum_{t=1}^n E D_{nt}(Z_t) = O(1)$, such that for all $\theta \in \Theta_o$ and $\pi \in \Pi$,

$$\left\| m_t(\alpha^o_n, \theta, \pi) - m_t(\alpha^o_n, \theta_o, \pi) - \delta m_t(\theta - \theta_o; \alpha^o_n, \theta_o, \pi) - \delta^2 m_t(\theta - \theta_o; \alpha^o_n, \theta_o, \pi) \right\|$$
$$\leq D_{nt}(Z_{nt})\rho_\Theta(\theta, \theta_o)^{2+\lambda} \; a.s.;$$

(b) with $\{a_n\}$ as in Assumption A.3 and λ as in (a), $\rho_\Theta(\hat\theta_n, \theta_o) = o_P(a_n^{-1/(2+\lambda)})$.

Here, $\delta^2 m_t(\theta - \theta_o; \alpha^o_n, \theta_o, \pi)$ corresponds to $\frac{1}{2}(\theta - \theta_o)' \nabla^2_\theta m_n(\theta - \theta_o)$ in Section 1. The inequality imposes a rate condition on the remainder term of the Taylor expansion.

Assumption C.3. For $(\theta, \pi) \in \Theta_o \times \Pi$ denote $\delta^2 m^o_n(\theta - \theta_o; \pi) = n^{-1}\sum_{t=1}^n \delta^2 m_t(\theta - \theta_o; \alpha^o_n, \theta_o, \pi)$ and $\delta^2 \bar m^o_n(\theta - \theta_o; \pi) = E \delta^2 m^o_n(\theta - \theta_o; \pi)$. Let $\{a_n\}$ be as in Assumption A.3. (a) $a_n \sup_{\pi \in \Pi} \|\delta^2 m^o_n(\hat\theta_n - \theta_o; \pi) - \delta^2 \bar m^o_n(\hat\theta_n - \theta_o; \pi)\| \to^p 0$; (b) $\delta m^o_n(\hat\theta_n - \theta_o; \pi) - \delta \bar m^o_n(\theta - \theta_o; \pi) + \delta^2 \bar m^o_n(\hat\theta_n - \theta_o; \pi) = W_n(\pi) + o_P(a_n^{-1})$ uniformly in $\pi \in \Pi$, where $W_n(\pi) = n^{-2}\sum_{t=1}^n \sum_{s=1}^n W_{nts}(Z_t, Z_s; \pi)$ and $W_{nts} : \mathbb{R}^\nu \times \mathbb{R}^\nu \times \Pi \to \mathbb{R}^q$ is measurable; (c) $a_n(W_n(\hat\pi_n) - E W_n(\hat\pi_n)) = a_n(W_n(\pi_o) - E W_n(\pi_o)) + o_P(1)$; (d) $a_n E W_n(\hat\pi_n) = a_n E W_n(\pi_o) + o_P(1)$ and $a_n \delta \bar m^o_n(\hat\theta_n - \theta_o; \hat\pi_n) = a_n \delta \bar m^o_n(\hat\theta_n - \theta_o; \pi_o) + o_P(1)$.

For each $\pi \in \Pi$, $\delta^2 m^o_n(\hat\theta_n - \theta_o; \pi)$ is asymptotically a third order V-statistic, so Assumption C.3(a) is a uniform V-statistic projection. Assumption C.3(b) says that $\delta m^o_n(\hat\theta_n - \theta_o; \pi) - \delta \bar m^o_n(\hat\theta_n - \theta_o; \pi) + \delta^2 \bar m^o_n(\hat\theta_n - \theta_o; \pi)$ is asymptotically a generalized quadratic form $W_n(\pi)$ (see de Jong, 1987). When $W_{nts}(Z_t, Z_s; \pi) = W_n(Z_t, Z_s; \pi)$, $W_n(\pi)$ is a second order V-statistic. In first order m-testing, the term $\delta m^o_n(\hat\theta_n - \theta_o; \pi) - \delta \bar m^o_n(\hat\theta_n - \theta_o; \pi)$ vanishes (cf. Assumption B.3(a)), but here it matters. Generically, it is of the same order as the second term in Assumption C.3(b). In specific cases, the limiting distribution of the m-test statistic may be determined by: (i) the first term only (when $\{m_t\}$ is linear in θ, as in (1.1) and (1.2)); (ii) the second term only; or (iii) both jointly (e.g., Hong and White, 1993, 1995). Assumption C.3(b) provides a useful decomposition of DMFs; there may exist alternative decompositions, leading to different tests. For example, Hong and White (1991) show that different decompositions for (1.1) lead to a nested test (Hong and White, 1991) and a non-nested test (Wooldridge, 1992). Assumption C.3(c) ensures that replacing $\hat{\pi}_n$ with π_o does not matter asymptotically. While $a_n EW_n(\pi_o)$ dominates $a_n(W_n(\pi_o) - EW_n(\pi_o))$, it can be subtracted from $a_n \hat{m}_n$ so that $a_n(W_n(\pi_o) - EW_n(\pi_o))$ becomes dominant, a "recentering" procedure. This can have an appealing interpretation. For example, with $\hat{\theta}_n$ a nonparametric series estimator, Hong and White (1995) interpret recentering as subtracting the degrees of freedom from a χ^2 random variable.

Assumption C.4. $n^{1/2}(\hat{\alpha}_n - \alpha_n^o) = O_P(1)$.

We need not know the structure of $\hat{\alpha}_n$, as it will not affect the limit distribution of the test.

Assumption C.5. For $\{a_n\}$ as in Assumption A.3, $J_n^{o-1/2} a_n(W_n(\pi_o) - EW_n(\pi_o))$ $\to^d N(0, 1)$ as $a_n \to \infty$, where J_n^o is a $q \times q$ nonstochastic $O(1)$ uniformly positive definite matrix.

Given the i.n.i.d. assumption, we generally have $var(W_{nts}(Z_t, Z_s)|Z_t) = var(W_{nts}(Z_t, Z_s)|Z_s) = 0$ for $t \neq s$. Thus, $W_n(\pi_o) - EW_n(\pi_o)$ is a degenerate U-statistic. Here, CLTs for non-degenerate U-statistics (e.g., Power $et\ al.$, 1989; Lavergne and Vuong, 1996) do not apply. Instead, we must use CLTs for degenerate generalized quadratic forms (or degenerate U-statistics). For CLTs for quadratic forms, see (e.g.) de Jong (1987), Hall (1984), Mikosch (1991), Rotar (1973), and Whittle (1964).

Assumption C.6. (a) $\hat{J}_n : \Omega \to \mathbb{R}^q \times \mathbb{R}^q$ is measurable such that $\hat{J}_n - J_n \to^p 0$, where J_n is a $q \times q$ nonstochastic $O(1)$ uniformly positive definite matrix with $J_n = J_n^o$ under H_{an}, where J_n^o is as in C.5; (b) $\hat{R}_n : \Omega \to \mathbb{R}^q$ is measurable such that $a_n(\hat{R}_n - R_n) \to^p 0$, where $\{a_n\}$ is as in A.3 and R_n is a $q \times 1$ nonstochastic vector with $R_n = EW_n(\pi_o)$ under H_{an} and $||R_n|| = o(||\bar{m}_n(\gamma_n^o)||)$ under H_A.

Our second main result can now be given.

Theorem 2.5. Suppose $\{m_t\}$ satisfies Definition 2.4 with $\{a_n\}$ as in A.3. Define $M_n = a_n^2(\hat{m}_n - \hat{R}_n)'\hat{J}_n(\hat{m}_n - \hat{R}_n)$, where $\hat{m}_n = m_n(\hat{\gamma}_n)$. (i) Suppose Assumptions A.1–A.3 and C.1–C.6 hold. Then under H_{an},

$$M_n \to^d \chi_q^2(\zeta_n^o),$$

where $\zeta_n^o = a_n^2 \bar{m}_n'(\gamma_n^o) J_n^{o-1} \bar{m}_n(\gamma_n^o)$. (ii) Suppose Assumptions A.1, A.2, A.4 and C.6 hold. Then under H_A and for any nonstochastic sequence $\{C_n = o(a_n^2)\}$,

$P[M_n > C_n] \to 1.$

To interpret H_{an} for the DMFs, we consider the case in which H_{an} is generated by the sequence $\{\alpha_n^o\}$, where $\alpha_n^o \to \alpha_o$, and α_o is as in H_o. Recall that for DMFs, $\bar{m}_n(\gamma_o) = 0$ and $\nabla_\alpha \bar{m}_n(\gamma_o) = 0$, so a two-term Taylor expansion gives:

$$a_n \bar{m}_n(\gamma_n^o) = \tfrac{1}{2} a_n (\alpha_n^o - \alpha_o)' \nabla_\alpha^2 \bar{m}_n(\gamma_o)(\alpha_n^o - \alpha_o) + o(a_n \left\| \alpha_n^o - \alpha_o \right\|^2).$$

It follows that M_n has nontrivial power against $H_{an}^* : \alpha_n^o - \alpha_o = c a_n^{-1/2}$ for some $c \neq 0$. Obviously, this local alternative converges to H_o faster than $n^{-1/4}$ because $a_n/n^{1/2} \to \infty$. We thus achieve an efficiency improvement in terms of local power, compared to the various previous approaches that avoid rather than exploit the degeneracy. For these approaches, typical local alternatives are $n^{-1/4}$ (see Hong and White, 1993, for an example).

Theorem 2.5(i) shows that M_n cannot detect local alternatives H_{an}^* of $O(n^{-1/2})$, because $a_n/n \to 0$. In other words, the second order tests are less efficient than those that are able to detect local alternatives vanishing at the parametric rate $n^{-1/2}$. However, this conclusion is specific to the local power criterion. Using other appropriate efficiency criteria, the conclusion can be different for second order m-tests. Specifically, we can apply Bahadur's (1960) asymptotic slope criterion, suitable for comparing two large sample tests under fixed alternatives. The basic idea is to hold power fixed and compare the resulting test sizes. Bahadur's relative efficiency is the limit of the ratio of the sample sizes required by two tests to achieve the same asymptotic significance level (p-value) under a fixed alternative. This criterion has been used by (e.g.) Geweke (1981a, b) among others.

For parametric testing, the asymptotic slope is the rate at which minus twice the logarithm of the asymptotic significance level of the test statistic tends to infinity as n increases. Because the rate of divergence of second order m-tests is different from that of the parametric tests, we cannot use Bahadur's approach directly. Instead, we extend it appropriately. Given $M_n \to^d \chi_q^2$ under H_o, the asymptotic significance level of M_n is $1 - F_q(M_n)$, where F_q is the cdf of χ_q^2. We now define

$$K_n = -2\ln(1 - F_q(M_n)).$$

Because $\ln(1 - F_q(\zeta)) = -\tfrac{1}{2}\zeta^2(1 + o(1))$ as $\zeta \to +\infty$ (cf. Bahadur, 1960, section 5), it follows from Theorem 2.5(ii) that

$$K_n / a_n^2 = \bar{m}_n'(\gamma_n^o) J_n^{-1} \bar{m}_n(\gamma_n^o) + o_P(1).$$

Following Bahadur, we call $\bar{m}_n'(\gamma_n^o) J_n^{-1} \bar{m}_n(\gamma_n^o)$ the "asymptotic slope" of the sequence of tests based on $\{M_n\}$ under H_A. Obviously, a larger asymptotic slope or a faster rate a_n implies a faster rate at which the asymptotic significance level decreases to zero as $n \to \infty$. For parametric tests and first order m-tests,

$a_n = n^{1/2}$. For second order m-tests, however, $a_n/n^{1/2} \to \infty$. For example, Hong and White (1995) have $a_n = n^{1/2+\epsilon}$ for $\epsilon > 0$. Therefore, second order m-tests are more efficient than parametric tests or first order m-tests under fixed alternatives in the sense that Bahadur's relative efficiency is infinite. This conclusion is in sharp contrast to that reached under H_{an}.

3 Application to Nonparametric Series Estimation

3.1a First Order M-Testing: Results with Fixed Regressors

We first apply Theorem 2.3 to robust nonparametric series regressions. For simplicity and convenience, we assume the following DGP.

Assumption D.1. (a) For each n, $Y_t = \mu_o(X_t) + \sigma_o(X_t)\epsilon_t$, $t = 1, ..., n$, where $\mu_o \in \mathcal{C}^r(\mathbb{X})$ and $\mathbb{X} \subset \mathbb{R}^d$ contains the support of X_t, r, $d \in \mathbb{N}$. Suppose $\{X_t\}$ are nonrandom and $\{\epsilon_t\}$ are independently and identically distributed (i.i.d.) with $E(\epsilon_t) = 0$ and $E(\epsilon_t^2) = 1$; (b) $\sigma_o : \mathbb{X} \to \mathbb{R}^+$ is constant.

Here $\{X_t\}$ (hence $\{Y_t\}$) may implicitly depend on n. The analysis extends to random regressors (see Andrews, 1991b, or Gallant and Souza, 1991). Homoskedasticity (Assumption D.1(b)) can be relaxed; we do so in Section 3.2.

A nonparametric series estimator for μ_o is $\hat{\mu}_n = \arg\min_{\mu \in \Theta_n} Q_n(Z^n, \mu)$, where $Q_n : \Omega \times \Theta_n \to \mathbb{R}$, $Z^n = (Z_1, ..., Z_n)$, $Z_t = (Y_t, X_t')'$, and

$$\Theta_n = \{\theta : \mathbb{X} \to \mathbb{R} \mid \theta(x) = \sum_{j=1}^{p_n} \beta_j \psi_j(x), \quad \beta_j \in \mathbb{R}\}, \tag{3.1}$$

for given $\{\psi_j : \mathbb{X} \to \mathbb{R}\}$ and $p_n \in \mathbb{N}$. We take $Q_n(Z^n, \mu) = n^{-1}\sum_{t=1}^{n} \phi(Y_t - \mu(X_t))$, with $\phi : \mathbb{R} \to \mathbb{R}$. If ϕ is convex with derivative φ, then $\hat{\mu}_n(\cdot) = \psi_{np}' \hat{\beta}_n$ solves

$$n^{-1}\sum_{t=1}^{n} \psi_{np}(X_t)\varphi(Y_t - \hat{\mu}_n(X_t)) = 0, \tag{3.2}$$

where $\psi_{np_n}(X_t) = \{\psi_1(X_t), ..., \psi_{pn}(X_t)\}'$ and $\hat{\beta}_n$ are $p_n \times 1$ vectors.

Andrews (1991b) treats least squares. We complement Andrews by giving new results for robust estimators. We follow Yohai and Maronna (1979), Mammen (1989) by restricting φ.

Assumption D.2. $\varphi : \mathbb{R} \to \mathbb{R}$ is a monotonic bounded function with three bounded derivatives such that $E\varphi(\epsilon_t) = 0$ and $E\varphi'(\epsilon_t) > 0$.

Monotonicity ensures a unique solution for $\hat{\beta}_n$. Boundedness ensures robustness to outliers; it rules out least squares. Differentiability is for convenience.

Denote $D^\lambda\theta = (\partial^{\lambda_1}/\partial x_1^{\lambda_1}) \cdots (\partial^{\lambda_d}/\partial x_d^{\lambda_d})\theta$, where $\theta \in \mathcal{C}^r(\mathbb{X})$ and $\lambda = (\lambda_1, ..., \lambda_d)'$ is a $d \times 1$ vector of nonnegative integers. The order of $D^\lambda\theta$ is $|\lambda| = \sum_{i=1}^{d}\lambda_i \leq r$. When $|\lambda| = 0$, put $D^0\theta = \theta$. We use certain Sobolev spaces.

Definition 3.1. [Sobolev Space]: *Let $\theta \in \mathcal{C}^r(\mathbb{X})$, $r \in \mathbb{N}$. For $0 \leq s \leq r$, define*

$\rho_{s,\infty}(\theta_1, \theta_2) = ||\theta_1 - \theta_2||_{s,\infty}$, where $||\theta||_{s,\infty} = \max_{|\lambda| \le s} \sup_{x \in \mathbb{X}} |D^\lambda \theta(x)|$. When $s = 0$, write $\rho_\infty = \rho_{0,\infty}$. Define the Sobolev spaces

$$\mathcal{W}^s_{\infty,r}(\mathbb{X}) = \left\{ \theta \in \mathcal{C}^r(\mathbb{X}) : ||\theta||_{s,\infty} < \infty \right\}, \quad 0 \le s \le r, \quad \mathcal{W}_{\infty,r}(\mathbb{X}) = \mathcal{W}^0_{\infty,r}(\mathbb{X}).$$

Assumption D.3. Let $\lambda_{\min}(A)$ denote the minimum eigenvalue of square matrix A and $\Psi_n = \{\psi'_{np_n}(X_1), ..., \psi'_{np_n}(X_n)\}'$. Suppose (a) $\lambda_{\min}(\Psi'_n \Psi_n) \to \infty$; (b) putting $\xi_{np_n} = \sup_{1 \le t \le n} \{\psi'_{np_n}(X_t)(\Psi'_n \Psi_n)^- \psi_{np_n}(X_t)\}$, then $\max(n^{1/3}[\ln(n)]^{2/3}, p_n \xi_{np_n}) \to 0$; (c) $\max_{0 \le j \le pn} ||\psi_j||_{s,\infty} \le B_s(p_n)$, $0 \le s \le r$, where $B_s : \mathbb{N} \to \mathbb{R}^+$ is non-decreasing.

Assumption D.3(a) is key for consistency of $\hat{\mu}_n$ for μ_o. Assumption D.3(b) is a strengthened Lindeberg condition, implying $p^2/n \to 0$. We allow $B_0(p_n)$ to increase with p_n. For such series as B-splines, Gallant's (1981) Fourier Flexible Form (FFF) and the trigonometric series, $B_0(\cdot)$ is bounded if $\mathbb{X}$ is. For $1 \le s \le r$, $B_s(p_n)$ grows with p_n generally.

Assumption D.4. There exists a sequence of $p_n \times 1$ nonstochastic vectors $\{\beta_n^o\}$ such that $\mu_n^o(\cdot) = \psi'_{np_n}(\cdot)\beta_n^o \in \mathcal{W}^s_{\infty,r}(\mathbb{X})$ and (a) $\rho_\infty(\mu_n^o, \mu_o) = o(n^{-1/2})$; or (b) $\rho_{s,\infty}(\mu_n^o, \mu_o) = o(n^{-1/2(1+\lambda)})$, $0 \le s \le r$, for λ as in Assumption B.2(a).

Given $\{\psi_j\}$, Assumption D.4 is ensured by imposing smoothness on μ_o with appropriate choice of p_n. For example, if $\{\psi_j\}$ is the Fourier series, $\mu_o \in \mathcal{C}^r(\mathbb{X})$, $\mathbb{X} = (0, 2\pi)^d$, then there exists $\mu_n^o(\cdot) = \psi'_{np_n}(\cdot)\beta_n^o \in \mathcal{W}^s_{\infty,r}(\mathbb{X})$, $0 \le s < r$, such that $\rho_{s,\infty}(\mu_n^o, \mu_o) = o(p_n^{-(r-s)/d+\epsilon})$ for any $\epsilon > 0$ (e.g. Edmunds and Moscatelli, 1977). Hence, Assumption D.4(a) holds if $p_n = n^{d/2r+\epsilon}$ and Assumption D.4(b) holds if $p_n = n^{d/2(r-s)(1+\lambda)+\epsilon}$.

We now establish consistency and asymptotic normality for $\hat{\mu}_n$.

Proposition 3.2. [Consistency]: *Suppose Assumptions D.1–D.2, D.3(a) and D.4(a) hold, and $p_n \to \infty$, $p_n \xi_{np_n} \to 0$. Let $\hat{\mu}_n$ be as in (3.2). Then $n^{-1}\sum_{t=1}^n (\hat{\mu}_n(X_t) - \mu_o(X_t))^2 = O_P(p_n/n)$ and $||\hat{\beta}_n - \beta_n^o|| = O_P(p_n^{1/2}/\lambda_{\min}^{1/2}(\Psi'_n \Psi_n))$.*

Proposition 3.3. [Normality]: *Suppose Assumptions D.1–D.3(a, b) and D.4(a) hold. Let G_{np_n} be a sequence of $p_n \times q$ nonstochastic matrices such that $I_n^o = G'_{np_n}(\Psi'_n \Psi_n)^- G_{np_n} E\varphi^2(\epsilon_t)/E^2\varphi'(\epsilon_t)$ is a $q \times q$ uniformly nonsingular matrix. Let $v_{nt}(Z_t) = G'_{np_n}(\Psi'_n \Psi_n)^- \psi_{np_n}(X_t)\varphi(\epsilon_t)/E\varphi'(\epsilon_t)$. Then $I_n^{o-1/2}G'_{np_n}(\hat{\beta}_n - \beta_n^o) = I_n^{o-1/2}\sum_{t=1}^n v_{nt} + o_P(1)$, and*

$$I_n^{o-1/2}G'_{np_n}(\hat{\beta}_n - \beta_n^o) \to^d N(0, I_q).$$

This complements Andrews (1991b, theorem 1(a)). We will approximate $\delta\bar{m}_n^o(\hat{\theta}_n - \theta_o; \pi_o)$ as $G_{np}^{o\prime}(\hat{\beta}_n - \beta_n^o)$ for some $G_{np_n}^o$. For this, the following is appropriate.

Assumption D.5. (a) For each $\pi \in \Pi$ and $\theta \in \Theta_o$, $\delta\bar{m}_n^o(\theta - \theta_o; \pi) = n^{-1}\sum_{t=1}^n g_{nt}(X_t, \pi)(\theta(X_t) - \theta_o(X_t))$, where $g_{nt} : \mathbb{X} \times \Pi \to \mathbb{R}^q$ and $n^{-1}\sum_{t=1}^n g_{nt}(X_t, \pi_o)g_{nt}(X_t, \pi_o)'$

is a $q \times q$ $O(1)$ uniformly positive definite matrix; (b) there exist some $\eta > 0$ and $D_{nt} : \mathbb{X} \to \mathbb{R}^+$, $n^{-1}\sum_{t=1}^n D_{nt}(X_t) = O(1)$, such that for all $x \in \mathbb{X}$ and $\pi_1, \pi_2 \in \Pi$, $\|g_{nt}(x, \pi_1) - g_{nt}(x, \pi_2)\| \le D_{nt}(x)^{1/2}\rho_\Pi(\pi_1, \pi_2)^\eta$; and (c) $\rho_\Pi(\hat{\pi}_n, \pi_o) = o_P(p_n^{-1/2\eta})$.

Assumption D.5(a) is a "smoothness" (Goldstein and Messer, 1992, definition 3.2) or "full mean" (Newey, 1994, assumption 3.5) condition. Assumptions D.5(b, c) ensure Assumption B.3(b).

The main result of this section follows.

Theorem 3.4. *Suppose Assumptions A.2 (for α, π), A.3, B.1, B.3(a), B.4, B.5 with $v_{nt}(Z_t) = G_{np_n}^{o\prime}(\Psi_n'\Psi_n/n)^{-}\psi_{np_n}(X_t)\varphi(\epsilon_t)/E\varphi'(\epsilon_t)$, B.6, D.1–D.3(a, b), D.4– D.5 hold. Define $M_n = n\hat{m}_n'\hat{J}_n^{-}\hat{m}_n$, where $\hat{m}_n = m_n(\hat{\alpha}_n, \hat{\theta}_n, \hat{\pi}_n)$ and $\hat{\theta}_n = \hat{\mu}_n$ as in (3.2). Suppose either (a) $\{m_t\}$ is linear in θ; or (b) Assumption B.2(a, b) with $(\Theta, \rho_\Theta) = (\mathcal{W}_{\infty,\mathbb{R}}^s(\mathbb{X}), \rho_{s,\infty})$, and Assumption D.3(c) hold, and $n^{1/2(1+\lambda)}p_n B_s(p_n)/\lambda_{\min}^{1/2}(\Psi_n'\Psi_n) \to 0$, where λ is as in Assumption B.2(a). Then (i) under H_o,*

$$M_n \to^d N(0,1);$$

(ii) under H_A and for any nonstochastic sequence $\{C_n = o(n)\}$,

$$P[M_n > C_n] \to 1.$$

Hence, asymptotic $n^{1/2}$-normality is attainable, with $\hat{\theta}_n$ a series m-estimator. We omit treatment of local alternatives for the sake of brevity.

3.1b First Order M-Testing: Application to Testing Normality

We now apply Theorem 3.4 to construct a new test for normality of the regression error of a nonparametric regression. For this purpose, we use the following moment vector:

$$m_t(\alpha, \theta, \pi) = \{(Y_t - \mu(X_t))^3, (Y_t - \mu(X_t))^4 - 3\sigma^4\}',$$

where $(\alpha, \theta) = (\sigma^2, \mu)$, and $\alpha_o = \sigma_o^2$ is the unconditional variance of the regression error.

Here we recognize quantities with expectations proportional to the standard measures of skewness and excess kurtosis. White (1982) shows that the vanishing of these two moments is necessary and sufficient for validity of the information matrix equality when estimating the mean and variance of a normal random variable using maximum likelihood. Thus, testing for skewness and excess kurtosis gives an information matrix test for normality. Alternatively, Bera and Jarque (1982) obtain a normality test based on these moments by nesting the normal within the Pearson family. This example clearly demonstrates a typical feature of first order m-testing: the hypothesis H_o^* originally of interest (normality) does not exactly coincide with the null hypothesis H_o

tested (absence of skewness and excess kurtosis), as there are non-normal distributions with no skewness and excess kurtosis. It is for this reason that first order m-testing often fails to deliver consistent tests against H_o^*.

We have the following new result.

Theorem 3.5. [Testing for Normality]: *Suppose for each n, (a) $Y_t = \mu_o(X_t) + \epsilon_t$, where $X_t = (2t-1)/2n$, $t = 1, ..., n$, and ϵ_t is i.i.d. with $E(\epsilon_t) = 0$, $E(\epsilon_t^2) = \sigma_o^2$; (b) $\mu_o \in C^r(0,1)$ for some $r > 2$; (c) $\psi_j(x) = \sqrt{2}\cos (j-1)\pi x$, $j = 1, 2, ...$; (d) φ satisfies Assumption D.2; and (e) $p_n^4/n \to 0$, $p_n^{2r-\delta}/n \to \infty$ for any arbitrarily small $\delta > 0$.*

Put $\hat\sigma_n^2 = n^{-1}\sum_{t=1}^n \epsilon_t^2$ and $\hat\eta_t = \varphi(\hat\epsilon_t)/(n^{-1}\sum_{t=1}^n \varphi'(\hat\epsilon_t))$, where $\hat\epsilon_t = Y_t - \hat\mu_n(X_t)$, with $\hat\mu_n$ as in (3.2). Define $M_n = n\hat m_n'\hat J_n^{-1}\hat m_n$, $\hat m_n = n^{-1}\sum_{t=1}^n(\hat\epsilon_t^3, \hat\epsilon_t^4 - 3\hat\sigma_n^4)'$, and

$$\hat J_n = \begin{bmatrix} \hat J_{11} & \hat J_{12} \\ \hat J_{12} & \hat J_{22} \end{bmatrix},$$

where $\hat J_{11} = 15\hat\sigma_n^6 - 6\hat\sigma_n^2 n^{-1}\sum_{t=1}^n\hat\epsilon_t^3\hat\eta_t + 9\hat\sigma_n^4 n^{-1}\sum_{t=1}^n\eta_t^2$, $\hat J_{12} = -3\hat\sigma_n^2 n^{-1}\sum_{t=1}^n\hat\epsilon_t^4\hat\eta_t + 18\hat\sigma_n^4 n^{-1}\sum_{t=1}^n\hat\epsilon_t^2\hat\eta_t$, and $\hat J_{22} = 24\hat\sigma_n^8$. Then (i) under H_o,

$$M_n \to^d \chi_2^2;$$

(ii) under H_A, if $E(\epsilon_t^6) < \infty$, then for any nonstochastic sequence $\{C_n = o(n)\}$,

$$P[M_n > C_n] \to 1.$$

Compared to Bera and Jarque's (1982) test, our test is insensitive to model misspecification for μ, because we use a nonparametric model rather a parametric model. A similar result holds for more general regression designs; we omit this for brevity.

3.2 Second Order M-Testing

Next, we apply Theorem 2.5 to give a new consistent specification test for parametric models in the presence of heteroskedasticity of unknown form, as motivated us at the outset. The following parametric specification applies.

Assumption E.1. Let $\{X_t\}$ be a nonstochastic sequence with $v_n \Rightarrow v$, $v_n(\mathbb{B}) = n^{-1}\sum_{t=1}^n 1[X_t \in \mathbb{B}]$, $\mathbb{B} \subseteq \mathbb{R}^d$. For each $x \in \mathbb{X}$, $f(x, \cdot) : \mathbb{A} \to \mathbb{R}$ is twice continuously differentiable on $\mathbb{A}$, with $|f(x, \cdot)|$, $||\nabla_\alpha f(x, \cdot)||^2$ and $||\nabla_\alpha^2 f(x, \cdot)||$ dominated by functions integrable with respect to v.

The null hypothesis originally of interest (correct model specification) is

$$H_o^* : v[f(X, \alpha_o) = \mu_o(X)] = 1 \text{ for some } \alpha_o \in \mathbb{A},$$

for μ_o as in Assumption D.1, and the global alternative is

$$H_A^* : v[f(X, \alpha_o) \neq \mu_o(X)] > 0 \text{ for all } \alpha \in \mathbb{A}.$$

Using a nonparametric series estimator for μ_o, Hong and White (1995, theorem A.3) propose a consistent test for H_o^* based on (1.1) achieving robustness to heteroskedasticity through use of a heteroskedasticity consistent covariance matrix estimator. This limitation can be avoided by using

$$m_t(\alpha, \theta, \pi) = (\theta(X_t) - f(X_t, \alpha) / \sigma(X_t))(Y_t - f(X_t, \alpha)) / \sigma(X_t), \qquad (3.3)$$

where $(\theta, \pi) = (\mu/\sigma, \sigma)$. Observe that at $(\theta_o, \pi_o) = (\mu_o/\sigma_o, \sigma_o)$, $m_n(\alpha, \theta_o, \pi_o) = 0$ if and only if $\alpha = \alpha_o$ under H_o^*. Hence, tests based on (3.3) are consistent against H_o^*. Because (3.3) is degenerate at γ_o, Theorem 2.5 applies.

Using Θ_n as in (3.1), we form an adaptive nonparametric least squares estimator for θ_o as:

$$\hat{\theta}_n = \arg\min_{\theta \in \Theta_n} n^{-1} \sum_{t=1}^n (Y_t / \hat{\sigma}_n(X_t) - \theta(X_t))^2, \qquad (3.4)$$

where $\hat{\sigma}_n$ is a nonparametric estimator for σ_o. To verify that using $\hat{\sigma}_n$ in place of σ_o has no asymptotic effect, we use the following uniform convergence result, extending a method of Hall (1988, 1989) from a finite dimensional space to an infinite dimensional space. This can also be used to verify stochastic equi-continuity.

Theorem 3.6. *Let $(\Omega, \mathcal{F}, P)$ be a complete probability space and $\Pi = \{\pi : \mathbb{X} \subset \mathbb{R}^d \to [c, c^{-1}] \mid |\pi(x_1) - \pi(x_2)| \leq \Delta ||x_1 - x_2|| \text{ for any } x_1, x_2 \in \mathbb{X}\}$, where $0 < \Delta < \infty$ and $\mathbb{X}$ is bounded, $d \in \mathbb{N}$. For each n suppose Π_n is a compact subset of Π, and $Q_n : \Omega \times \Pi_n \to \mathbb{R}$ is a stochastic mapping such that $EQ_n(\pi) = 0$ for each $\pi \in \Pi_n$.*

Suppose (a) for each pair $\epsilon, \lambda > 0$, $\sup_{\pi \in \Pi_n} P[|Q_n(\pi)| > \epsilon] \leq C_1 n^{-\lambda}$; and (b) for each $\lambda > 0$, there exists $\lambda_1 = \lambda_1(\lambda) > 0$ such that $E \sup_{(\pi_1, \pi_2) \in \mathbb{B}_n(\delta_n)} |Q_n(\pi_1) - Q_n(\pi_2)| \leq C n^{-\lambda}$, where $\mathbb{B}_n(\delta_n) = \{(\pi_1, \pi_2) \in \Pi_n \times \Pi_n : \rho_\infty(\pi_1, \pi_2) < \delta_n = n^{-\lambda_1}\}$, then for each pair $\epsilon, \lambda > 0$,

$$P[\sup_{\pi \in \Pi_n} |Q_n(\pi)| > \epsilon] \leq C_2 n^{-\lambda}.$$

Assumption D.1. (b′) $\sigma_o \in \Sigma = \{\sigma : \mathbb{X} \to [c, c^{-1}] \mid |\sigma(x_1) - \sigma_2(x_2)| \leq \Delta ||x_1 - x_2||$ for any $x_1, x_2 \in \mathbb{X}\}$, where $0 < \Delta < \infty$ and $\mathbb{X} \subset \mathbb{R}^d$ is bounded; (c) all moments of ϵ_t are finite.

Assumption E.2. $\hat{\sigma}_n : \Omega \to \Sigma$ is measurable such that $\rho_\infty(\hat{\sigma}_n, \sigma_o) = o_P(\min[p_n^{-1/2}, (p_n/n)^{1/2+\delta}])$ for any arbitrarily small $\delta > 0$.

Assumption E.3. For ξ_{np_n} as in D.3, $\xi_{np_n} \to 0$.

Assumption E.4. There exists a nonstochastic sequence $\{\beta_n^o\}$ such that $\theta_n^o(\cdot) = \psi'_{np_n}(\cdot)\beta_n^o \in \mathcal{W}_{\infty, r}(\mathbb{X})$ and $\rho_\infty(\theta_n^o, \theta_o) = o(p_n^{1/2}/n^{1/2})$.

We now state a CLT for the quadratic form of $\{\psi_{np_n}(X_t)\epsilon_t\}$ in the presence of σ.

Theorem 3.7. *Suppose Assumptions D.1(a, b', c), D.3(a) and E.2–E.3 hold. Let $p_n \to \infty$ as $n \to \infty$. Define $W_n(\sigma) = \sum_{t=1}^n \sum_{s=1}^n W_{nts}(\sigma)$, where*

$$W_{nts}(\sigma) = (\sigma_o(X_t)/\sigma(X_t))\epsilon_t \psi'_{np_n}(X_t)(\Psi'_n \Psi_n)^{-1} \psi_{np_n}(X_s)\epsilon_s(\sigma_o(X_s)/\sigma(X_s)).$$

Then

$$(W_n(\hat\sigma_n) - p_n)/(2p_n)^{1/2} \to^d N(0,1).$$

This is obtained by first showing $p_n^{-1/2}(W_n(\hat\sigma_n) - W_n(\sigma_o)) \to^p 0$ using Theorem 3.6 and then showing $(W_n(\sigma_o) - p_n)/(2p_n)^{1/2} \to^d N(0,1)$ using de Jong's (1987) CLT for quadratic forms.

A new heteroskedasticity-insensitive test complementing Hong and White (1995) follows.

Theorem 3.8. *Suppose Assumptions C.4, D.1(a, b', c), D.3(a) and E.1–E.4 hold. Define $M_n = (n\hat m_n - p_n)/(2p_n)^{1/2}$, where $\hat m_n = n^{-1}\sum_{t=1}^n (\hat\theta_n(X_t) - f(X_t, \hat\alpha_n)/\hat\sigma_n(X_t))(Y_t - f(X_t, \hat\alpha_n))/\hat\sigma_n(X_t)$, with $\hat\theta_n$ as in (3.4). Let $p_n \to \infty$ as $n \to \infty$. Then (i) under H_o^*,*

$$M_n \to^d N(0,1);$$

(ii) under H_A^* and for any nonstochastic sequence $\{C_n = o(n/p_n^{1/2})\}$,

$$P[M_n > C_n] \to 1.$$

4 Application to Nonparametric Kernel Estimation

4.1a First Order M-Testing for the i.i.d. Case

Assumption F.1. (a) For each n the random sample $\{Z_1, ..., Z_n\}$ is i.i.d., where $Z_t = (X'_t, Y_t)' \in \mathbb{R}^{d+1}$, $d \in \mathbb{N}$, and $E|Y_t| < \infty$; (b) the support $\mathbb{X} \subset \mathbb{R}^d$ of X is compact and the distribution of X is absolutely continuous on $\mathbb{X}$ with respect to Lebesgue measure, with density p_o bounded above and away from zero on $\mathbb{X}$. Furthermore, the sample $\{X_1, ..., X_n\}$ does not include the boundary points of $\mathbb{X}$; and (c) for some $\delta > 0$, $E|Y_t|^{2+\delta} < \infty$ and $\sup_{x \in \mathbb{X}} E[|Y|^{2+\delta} \mid X = x] < \infty$.

Boundedness of p_o away from below can be relaxed using moving trimming (e.g. Härdle and Stoker, 1989, or Robinson, 1988). To avoid boundary effects, we assume $\{X_1, ..., X_n\}$ does not include boundary points of $\mathbb{X}$. Part (c) gives moment conditions for uniform convergence of kernel estimators (e.g. Mack and Silverman, 1982; Newey, 1994).

We use the Nadaraya–Watson kernel estimator for $\mu_o(x) = E(Y|X = x)$:

$$\hat\mu_n(x) = \begin{cases} (n\hat p_n(x))^{-1}\sum_{t=1}^n Y_t K_n(x - X_t) & \text{if } \hat p_n(x) \neq 0 \\ 0 & \text{otherwise,} \end{cases} \tag{4.1}$$

where $\hat{p}_n(x) = n^{-1}\sum_{t=1}^n K_n(x - X_t)$, $K_n(x - X_t) = b_n^{-d}K[(x - X_t)/b_n]$, and b_n is a bandwidth. We now impose regularity conditions on K, μ_o and p_o.

Assumption F.2. $K : \mathbb{T} \to \mathbb{R}$ is a symmetric bounded kernel of finite order k with compact support $\mathbb{T} = [-\tau, \tau]^d$, $0 < \tau < \infty$, such that K is differentiable of order $s \geq 0$, with Lipschitz sth derivative, $\int_{\mathbb{T}} K(u)\,du = 1$, $\int_{\mathbb{T}} u_1^{i_1} u_2^{i_2} \cdots u_d^{i_d} K(u)\,du = 0$ for $|i| = \sum_{j=1}^d i_j < k$, and $\int_{\mathbb{T}} u_1^{i_1} u_2^{i_2} \cdots u_d^{i_d} K(u)\,du \neq 0$ for $|i| = k$.

Assumption F.3. There exist extensions of p_o and $p_o\mu_o$ such that these extensions are in $\mathcal{W}_{\infty,r}^r(\mathbb{R}^d)$ for some integer $r > 0$.

We use a uniform convergence result due to Newey (1994).

Lemma 4.1. [Newey, 1994, theorem B.1]: *Suppose Assumptions F.1–F.3 hold with $r \geq s + k$. Let $b_n \to 0$, $n^{\delta/(2+\delta)} b_n^d/\ln(n) \to \infty$, where δ is as in Assumption F.1. Then (i) $\rho_{s,\infty}(\hat{\mu}_n, \mu_o) = O_P([nb_n^{d+2s}/\ln(n)]^{-1/2} + b_n^k)$; and (ii) $\rho_{s,\infty}(\hat{p}_n, p_o) = O_P([nb_n^{d+2s}/\ln(n)]^{-1/2} + b_n^k)$.*

This delivers explicit rates for b_n satisfying certain conditions of Theorem 2.3. We now impose conditions on $m_t(\alpha, \theta, \pi) = m(Z_t, \alpha, \mu, \pi)$.

Assumption F.4. (a) Let $\theta_o \in \Theta_o \subset \Theta$. For each $\theta \in \Theta_o$ and each $\pi \in \Pi$, $\delta\bar{m}_n^o(\theta - \theta_o; \pi) = E[g(X, \pi)(\theta(X) - \theta_o(X))]$, where $g : \mathbb{X} \times \Pi \to \mathbb{R}^q$ is such that for each $\pi \in \Pi$, $g(\cdot, \pi) \in \mathcal{C}^k(\mathbb{X})$, $E[g(X, \pi_o)g(X, \pi_o)']$ is a $q \times q$ finite positive semi-definite matrix and $\sup_{x \in \mathbb{X}}\|D^k g(x, \pi_o)\| \leq \Delta < \infty$; (b) there exist some $\eta > 0$ and $D : \mathbb{R}^d \to \mathbb{R}^+$, $ED(X) < \infty$, such that for all $x \in \mathbb{X}$ and $\pi_1, \pi_2 \in \Pi$, $\|g(x, \pi_2) - g(x, \pi_1)\| \leq D(x)^{1/2}\rho_{\Pi}(\pi_1, \pi_2)^{\eta}$; and (c) $\rho_{\Pi}(\hat{\pi}_n, \pi_o) = o_P((nb_n^d)^{-1/2\eta})$.

Assumption F.4(a) is a "smoothness" or "full mean" assumption. Assumptions F.4(b, c) ensure that replacing $\hat{\pi}_n$ with π_o does not affect the limiting distribution of $\delta\bar{m}_n^o(\theta - \theta_o; \hat{\pi}_n)$. We use the following key result.

Proposition 4.2. *Suppose Assumptions F.1(a, b) and F.2–F.4(a) hold and $V_o = E[g(X, \pi_o)g(X, \pi_o)'\epsilon^2]$ is finite and nonsingular, where $\epsilon = Y - \mu_o(X)$. Let $n^{\delta/(2+\delta)} b_n^d/\ln(n) \to \infty$, $nb_n^{2d}/\ln(n) \to \infty$, $nb_n^{2k} \to 0$, and $2k > d$. Then $n^{1/2}\delta\bar{m}_n^o(\hat{\theta}_n - \theta_o; \pi_o) = n^{-1/2}\sum_{t=1}^n g(X_t, \pi_o)\epsilon_t + o_P(1)$, and*

$$n^{1/2}\delta\bar{m}_n^o(\hat{\theta}_n - \theta_o; \pi_o) \to^d N(0, V_o).$$

This is necessary but not sufficient for Assumption B.5; the following suffices.

Assumption F.5. For $W(Z_t, \gamma_o) = m(Z_t, \gamma_o) + \nabla'_\alpha \bar{m}(\gamma_o)s(Z_t, \alpha_o) + g(X_t, \pi_o)\epsilon_t$, $J_o = E(W(Z, \gamma_o)W(Z, \gamma_o)')$ is a $q \times q$ finite positive definite matrix.

Theorem 4.3. *Suppose Assumptions A.2 (for α, π), A.3, B.1, B.3(a), B.4, B.6 with $J_n^o = J_o$, F.1(a, b) and F.2–F.5 hold. Define $M_n = n\hat{m}_n'\hat{J}_n\hat{m}_n$, where $\hat{m}_n = m_n(\hat{\alpha}_n, \hat{\theta}_n, \hat{\pi}_n)$ and $\hat{\theta}_n = \hat{\mu}_n$ is as in (4.1). Let $nb_n^d \to \infty$, $nb_n^{2k} \to 0$, $2k > d$. Suppose either (a) $\{m_t\}$ is linear in θ or (b) Assumptions B.2(a, b) with $(\Theta, \rho_\Theta) = (\mathcal{W}_{r,\infty}^s(\mathbb{X}), \rho_\infty)$, and F.1(c) hold, $n^{\delta/(2+\delta)} b_n^d/\ln(n) \to \infty$, $n^\lambda b_n^{(d+2s)(1+\lambda)}/$*

$\ln^{(1+\lambda)}(n) \to \infty$, $nb_n^{2k(1+\lambda)} \to 0$, *where δ is as in Assumption F.1 and λ as in Assumption B.2. Then (i) under H_o*

$$M_n \to^d \chi_q^2;$$

(ii) under H_A and for any nonstochastic sequence $\{C_n = o(n)\}$,

$$P[M_n > C_n] \to 1.$$

Asymptotic $n^{1/2}$-normality is thus achieved, despite the presence of $\hat{\theta}_n$.

4.1b First Order M-Testing: Application to Testing Omitted Variables

Although nonparametric regressions do not require specification of functional form, they do require a priori knowledge of relevant explanatory variables. One may be interested in testing the relevance of additional variables. We now give a new test for omitted variables insensitive to model misspecification.

Put $Z_t = (Y_t, X_t')' = (Y_t, (X_{1t}', X_{2t}'))'$, where X_{1t} is a $d_1 \times 1$ random vector with density p_1^o and X_{2t} is a $d_2 \times 1$ random vector, $d_1 + d_2 = d$. Suppose one is interested in testing the relevance of X_{2t} in explaining Y_t. Then the hypotheses originally of interest are

$$H_o^* : P[E(Y_t|X_{1t}) = E(Y_t|X_t)] = 1 \ \text{vs.} \ H_A^* : P[E(Y_t|X_{1t}) = E(Y_t|X_t)] < 1.$$

Put $\mu_1^o(X_{1t}) = E(Y_t|X_{1t})$ and consider the moment function

$$m(Z_t, \alpha, \theta, \pi) = \psi(X_{2t})(Y_t - \mu_1(X_{1t})),$$

where $\theta = \mu_1$, ψ is a given weighting function, and α and π are null. Now H_o^* implies $Em(Z_t, \alpha, \theta_o, \pi) = 0$ for $\theta_o = \mu_1^o$. We note that Robinson (1989, 5.52(e)) suggests a similar approach to testing H_o^* with the choice of $\psi(X_{2t}) = X_{2t}$, but does not construct a test statistic.

To construct our statistic, we use a kernel estimator for μ_1^o:

$$\hat{\mu}_{1n}(x_1) = \begin{cases} (n\hat{p}_{1n}(x_1))^{-1} \sum_{t=1}^n Y_t K_n(x_1 - X_{1t}) & \text{if } \hat{p}_{1n}(x_1) \neq 0 \\ 0 & \text{otherwise,} \end{cases} \quad (4.2)$$

where $\hat{p}_{1n}(x_1) = n^{-1} \sum_{t=1}^n K_n(x_1 - X_{1t})$, $K_n(x_1 - X_{1t}) = b_n^{-1} K((x_1 - X_{1t})/b_n)$, with $K : \mathbb{R}^{d_1} \to \mathbb{R}$ a kernel and b_n a bandwidth.

We also use the following kernel estimator for $g(X_{1t}) = E(\psi(X_{2t})|X_{1t})$:

$$\hat{g}_n(x_1) = \begin{cases} (n\hat{p}_{1n}(x_1))^{-1} \sum_{t=1}^n \psi(X_{2t}) K_n(x_1 - X_{1t}) & \text{if } \hat{p}_{1n}(x_1) \neq 0 \\ 0 & \text{otherwise.} \end{cases}$$

Theorem 4.4. [Testing for Omitted Variables]: *Suppose (a) Assumption F.1 with $\delta = 2$ holds; (b) $\psi : \mathbb{R}^{d_2} \to \mathbb{R}$ is measurable such that $E\psi^4(X_{2t}) < \infty$ and $\sup_{x_1 \in \mathbb{X}_1} E(\psi^4(X_{2t})|X_{1t} = x_1) < \infty$, where $\mathbb{X}_1$ is the compact support of X_1; (c)*

Assumption F.2 with $s = 0$ holds; (d) p_1^o and $p_1^o\mu_1^o$ satisfy Assumption F.3; (e)
$g(X_{1t}) = E(\psi(X_{2t})|X_{1t}) \in C^k(\mathbb{X}_1)$ with $\sup_{x_1 \in \mathbb{X}_1} ||D^k g(x_1)|| < \infty$; (f) $nb_n^{2d_1}/\ln^2(n)$
$\to \infty$, $b_n \to 0$.

Define $M_n = n\hat{m}_n' \hat{J}_n^{-1} \hat{m}_n$, where $\hat{m}_n = n^{-1}\sum_{t=1}^n \psi(X_{2t})(Y_t - \hat{\mu}_{1n}(X_{1t}))$, $\hat{J}_n =$
$n^{-1}\sum_{t=1}^n (\psi(X_{2t}) - \hat{g}_n(X_{1t}))^2 (Y_t - \hat{\mu}_{1n}(X_t))^2$. Then (i) under H_o: $E[\psi(X_{2t})(E(Y_t|X_t)$
$- E(Y_t|X_{1t}))] = 0$,

$$M_n \to^d \chi_1^2;$$

(ii) suppose H_A: $E[\psi(X_{2t})(Y_t - \mu_1^o(X_{1t}))] \neq 0$ holds. Then for any nonstochastic
sequence $\{C_n = o(n)\}$,

$$P[|M_n| > C_n] \to 1.$$

This test is not necessarily consistent against H_A^* as H_o^* implies H_o but the
converse may fail. Power depends on choice of ψ. For consistency we must
choose ψ so that H_o^* coincides with H_o. Such choices exist; see Bierens (1990)
and Stinchcombe and White (1998).

Lavergne and Vuong (1996) propose a method to determine relevant
regressors using kernel estimators, but this does not apply here, due to the
degeneracy of their statistic. Our approach complements theirs. One could
also use Theorem 2.5 to construct a consistent test for H_o^*; we leave this for
further work.

4.2 Second Order M-Testing

In Section 3.2 we gave a new heteroskedasticity-insensitive consistent specification test for the parametric model $f(X_t, \alpha)$ using an estimate of conditional
variance. We now give a heteroskedasticity-insensitive consistent specification
test using kernel regression and a new heteroskedasticity-consistent covariance
matrix estimator.

We use a weighted version of (1.1), i.e. $m_t(\alpha, \theta, \pi) = p(X_t)(\mu(X_t) -$
$f(X_t, \alpha))(Y_t - f(X_t, \alpha))$. Put $\theta = (\theta_1, \theta_2) = (r, p) = (p\mu, p)$ and let π be null.
Then

$$m_t(\alpha, \theta, \pi) = (r(X_t) - p(X_t)f(X_t, \alpha))(Y_t - f(X_t, \alpha)). \tag{4.3}$$

As (4.3) is degenerate at $(\alpha_o, \theta_o) = (\alpha_o, (p_o\mu_o, p_o))$, where $\alpha_o \in \mathbb{A}$ is such that
H_o^*: $P[f(X_t, \alpha_o) = \mu_o(X_t)] = 1$ holds, Theorem 2.5 applies. A consistent test
against H_A^*: $P[f(X_t, \alpha) \neq \mu_o(X_t)] > 1$ for all $\alpha \in \mathbb{A}$ can be based on

$$\hat{m}_n = n^{-1}\sum_{t=1}^n (\hat{r}_n(X_t) - \hat{p}_n(X_t)f(X_t, \hat{\alpha}_n))(Y_t - f(X_t, \hat{\alpha}_n)), \tag{4.4}$$

where $\hat{r}_n = \hat{p}_n\hat{\mu}_n$, and $\hat{\mu}_n$ and $\hat{p}_n$ are as in (4.1). We make following additional
assumptions.

Assumption F.6. For each $\alpha \in \mathbb{A}$, $f(\cdot, \alpha) : \mathbb{X} \to \mathbb{R}$ is measurable; (b) $f(X, \cdot)$ is twice continuously differentiable *a.s.* on $\mathbb{A}$, with $|f(X, \cdot)|$, $||\nabla_\alpha f(X, \cdot)||^2$ and $||\nabla_\alpha^2 f(X, \cdot)||$ dominated by $D : \mathbb{X} \to R^+$, $ED^2(X) < \infty$.

Assumption F.7. $\sigma_o^2(X) = var(Y|X)$ is continuous on $\mathbb{X}$.

The next result is the key to obtaining the distribution of our statistic.

Theorem 4.5. *Suppose Assumptions F.1 (with $\delta = 2$), F.2–F.3 and F.7 hold. Let $W_n = n^{-2}\sum_{t=1}^n \sum_{s=1}^n W_{nts}$, $W_{nts} = \epsilon_t \epsilon_s K_n(X_t - X_s)$, $\epsilon_t = Y_t - \mu_o(X_t)$. Define $J_o = 2C(K)E(\sigma_o^4(X)p_o(X))$, $C(K) = \int_T K^2(u)\, du$. Let $nb_n^d \to \infty$, $b_n \to 0$. Then*

$$J_o^{-1/2} nb_n^{d/2}(W_n - EW_n) \to^d N(0,1).$$

This is obtained by applying de Jong's (1987) CLT for generalized quadratic forms. Next, we propose a heteroskedasticity-consistent U-statistic estimator for J_o.

Proposition 4.6. *Suppose Assumptions F.1 (with $\delta = 2$), F.2–F.3 and F.7 hold. Define $\hat{J}_n = 4C(K)b_n^d n^{-2}\sum_{t=1}^n \sum_{s=1}^n \hat{\epsilon}_{nt}^2 \hat{\epsilon}_{ns}^2 K_n(X_t - X_s)$, where $\hat{\epsilon}_{nt} = Y_t - \hat{\mu}_n(X_t)$ and $\hat{\mu}_n$ is as in (4.1). Let $nb_n^{3d} \to \infty$, $b_n \to 0$ and $2k > d$. Then $\hat{J}_n - J_o \to^p 0$.*

Now the new heteroskedasticity-insensitive consistent test can be given.

Theorem 4.7. *Suppose Assumptions C.4, F.1 (with $\delta = 2$), F.2 (with $s = 0$), F.3 and F.6–F.7 hold. Define $M_n = \hat{J}_n^{-1/2} nb_n^{d/2}(\hat{m}_n - \hat{R}_n)$, where $\hat{J}_n$ is as in Proposition 4.6, $\hat{m}_n$ is as in (4.4) and $\hat{R}_n = (nb_n^d)^{-1}K(0)\hat{\sigma}_n^2$, with $\hat{\sigma}_n^2 = n^{-1}\sum_{t=1}^n \hat{\epsilon}_{nt}^2$, $\hat{\epsilon}_{nt} = Y_t - \hat{\mu}_n(X_t)$ and $\hat{\mu}_n$ as in (4.1). Let $nb_n^{3d} \to \infty$, $nb_n^{2k+d} \to 0$, $2k > d$. Then (i) under H_o^*,*

$$M_n \to^d N(0,1);$$

(ii) under H_A^* and any nonstochastic sequence $\{C_n = o(nb_n^{d/2})\}$,

$$P[M_n > C_n] \to 1.$$

The growth rate of M_n under H_A is $nb_n^{d/2}$, faster than $n^{1/2}$ because $nb_n^d \to \infty$; however, M_n can only detect local alternatives of $O(n^{-1/2}b_n^{-d/4})$, slightly slower than $O(n^{-1/2})$.

Mathematical Appendix

Proof of Theorem 2.3. (i) Given Assumption B.2 and by Hölder's inequality, we have

$$\left\| m_n(\alpha_n^o, \hat{\theta}_n, \hat{\pi}_n) - m_n(\alpha_n^o, \theta_o, \hat{\pi}_n) - \delta m_n^o(\hat{\theta}_n - \theta_o; \hat{\pi}_n) \right\|$$
$$\leq D_n \rho_\Theta(\hat{\theta}_n, \theta_o)^{1+\lambda} = o_P(n^{-1/2}), \tag{A1}$$

where $D_n = n^{-1}\sum_t D_{nt}(Z_t) = O_P(1)$ by Markov's inequality. By the mean value theorem,

$$\hat{m}_n = m_n(\alpha_n^o, \hat{\theta}_n, \hat{\pi}_n) + \nabla_\alpha' m_n(\tilde{\alpha}_n, \hat{\theta}_n, \hat{\pi}_n)(\hat{\alpha}_n - \alpha_n^o)$$

given Assumption B.1(a), where a different $\tilde{\alpha}_n$ ($||\tilde{\alpha}_n - \alpha_n^o|| \leq ||\hat{\alpha}_n - \alpha_n^o||$) appears in each row of $\nabla_\alpha m_n(\cdot, \hat{\theta}_n, \hat{\pi}_n)$. Substituting $m_n(\alpha_n^o, \hat{\theta}_n, \hat{\pi}_n)$ into (A1) and rearranging, we obtain

$$\hat{m}_n = m_n(\alpha_n^o, \theta_o, \hat{\pi}_n) + \nabla_\alpha' m_n(\tilde{\alpha}_n, \hat{\theta}_n, \hat{\pi}_n)(\hat{\alpha}_n - \alpha_n^o) + \delta m_n^o(\hat{\theta}_n - \theta_o; \hat{\pi}_n)$$
$$+ o_P(n^{-1/2}). \tag{A2}$$

For the first term in (A2), we have

$$\begin{aligned} m_n(\alpha_n^o, \theta_o, \hat{\pi}_n) &= \bar{m}_n(\alpha_n^o, \theta_o, \hat{\pi}_n) + (m_n(\alpha_n^o, \theta_o, \hat{\pi}_n) - \bar{m}_n(\alpha_n^o, \theta_o, \hat{\pi}_n)) \\ &= \bar{m}_n(\gamma_n^o) + (m_n(\gamma_n^o) - \bar{m}_n(\gamma_n^o)) + o_P(n^{-1/2}), \end{aligned} \tag{A3}$$

given Assumption A.3 and $a_n = n^{1/2}$. For the second term in (A2), we have

$$\begin{aligned} \left\| \nabla_\alpha m_n(\tilde{\alpha}_n, \hat{\theta}_n, \hat{\pi}_n) - \nabla_\alpha \bar{m}_n(\gamma_n^o) \right\| &\leq \left\| \nabla_\alpha m_n(\tilde{\alpha}_n, \hat{\theta}_n, \hat{\pi}_n) - \nabla_\alpha \bar{m}_n(\tilde{\alpha}_n, \hat{\theta}_n, \hat{\pi}_n) \right\| \\ &\quad + \left\| \nabla_\alpha \bar{m}_n(\tilde{\alpha}_n, \hat{\theta}_n, \hat{\pi}_n) - \nabla_\alpha \bar{m}_n(\gamma_n^o) \right\| \\ &= o_P(1), \end{aligned} \tag{A3}$$

by the triangle inequality and Assumption B.1. Hence, we obtain

$$\nabla_\alpha' m_n(\tilde{\alpha}_n, \hat{\theta}_n, \hat{\pi}_n)(\hat{\alpha}_n - \alpha_n^o) = \nabla_\alpha' \bar{m}_n(\gamma_n^o) S_n + o_P(n^{-1/2}), \tag{A4}$$

given Assumptions B.4 and B.5, which implies $\hat{\alpha}_n - \alpha_n^o = O_P(n^{-1/2})$. For the last term in (A2), we have

$$\begin{aligned} \delta m_n^o(\hat{\theta}_n - \theta_o; \hat{\pi}_n) &= \delta \bar{m}_n^o(\hat{\theta}_n - \theta_o; \pi_o) + (\delta m_n^o(\hat{\theta}_n - \theta_o; \hat{\pi}_o) - \delta \bar{m}_n^o(\hat{\theta}_n - \theta_o; \hat{\pi}_n)) \\ &\quad + (\delta \bar{m}_n^o(\hat{\theta}_n - \theta_o; \hat{\pi}_n) - \delta \bar{m}_n^o(\hat{\theta}_n - \theta_o; \pi_o)) \\ &= \delta \bar{m}_n^o(\hat{\theta}_n - \theta_o; \pi_o) + o_P(n^{-1/2}) \\ &= V_n + o_P(n^{-1/2}), \end{aligned} \tag{A5}$$

given Assumption B.3. Substituting (A3)–(A5) into (A2), we obtain $\hat{m}_n = \bar{m}_n(\gamma_n^o) + W_n + o_P(n^{-1/2})$. It follows that $J_n^{o-1/2} n^{1/2} \hat{m}_n \to^d N(J_n^{o-1/2} n^{1/2} \bar{m}_n(\gamma_n^o), I_q)$ by Assumption B.5. By Slutsky's Theorem, we have $n^{1/2} \hat{J}_n^{-1/2} \hat{m}_n \to^d N(J_n^{o-1/2} n^{1/2} \bar{m}_n(\gamma_n^o), I_q)$ given $\hat{J}_n^- - J_n^{o-1} = o_P(1)$ from Assumption B.6. Hence, $M_n \to^d \chi_q^2(\zeta_n^o)$.

(ii) Given Assumptions A.2, A.4 and B.6, we have $\hat{m}_n - \bar{m}_n(\gamma_n^o) \to^p 0$ and $\hat{J}_n^- - J_n^{-1} \to^p 0$. Hence, $M_n/n = \bar{m}_n'(\gamma_n^o) J_n^{-1} \bar{m}_n(\gamma_n^o) + o_P(1)$ by continuity, where $\bar{m}_n'(\gamma_n^o) J_n^{-1} \bar{m}_n(\gamma_n^o) \geq c > 0$ for all n sufficiently large under H_A. The desired result follows immediately. ■

Proof of Theorem 2.5. (i) Given Assumption C.2 and Hölder's inequality, we have

$$m_n(\alpha_n^o, \hat{\theta}_n, \hat{\pi}_n) - m_n(\alpha_n^o, \theta_o, \hat{\pi}_n) - \delta\hat{m}_n^o(\hat{\theta}_n - \theta_o; \hat{\pi}_n)$$
$$-\delta^2\hat{m}_n^o(\hat{\theta}_n - \theta_o; \hat{\pi}_n) = o_P(a_n^{-1}). \tag{A6}$$

Under Assumption C.1(a), a second order Taylor expansion of $\hat{m}_n$ about α_n^o yields

$$\hat{m}_n = m_n(\alpha_n^o, \hat{\theta}_n, \hat{\pi}_n) + \nabla_\alpha' m_n(\alpha_n^o, \hat{\theta}_n, \hat{\pi}_n)(\hat{\alpha}_n - \alpha_n^o)$$
$$+ \tfrac{1}{2}(\hat{\alpha}_n - \alpha_n^o)'\nabla_\alpha^2 m_n(\tilde{\alpha}_n, \hat{\theta}_n, \hat{\pi}_n)(\hat{\alpha}_n - \alpha_n^o),$$

where a different $\tilde{\alpha}_n$ ($\|\tilde{\alpha}_n - \alpha_n^o\| \le \|\hat{\alpha}_n - \alpha_n^o\|$) appears in each row of $\nabla_\alpha^2 m_n(\cdot, \hat{\theta}_n, \hat{\pi}_n)$. Substituting $m_n(\alpha_n^o, \hat{\theta}_n, \hat{\pi}_n)$ into (A6) and rearranging, we obtain

$$\hat{m}_n = m_n(\alpha_n^o, \theta_o, \hat{\pi}_n) + \nabla_\alpha' m_n(\alpha_n^o, \hat{\theta}_n, \hat{\pi}_n)(\hat{\alpha}_n - \alpha_n^o)$$
$$+ \tfrac{1}{2}(\hat{\alpha}_n - \alpha_n^o)'\nabla_\alpha^2 m_n(\tilde{\alpha}_n, \hat{\theta}_n, \hat{\pi}_n)(\hat{\alpha}_n - \alpha_n^o)$$
$$+ [\delta\hat{m}_n^o(\hat{\theta}_n - \theta_o; \hat{\pi}_n) + \delta^2\hat{m}_n^o(\hat{\theta}_n - \theta_o; \hat{\pi}_n)] + o_P(a_n^{-1}) \tag{A7}$$

Given Assumption C.1 and Definition 2.4(b), we have

$$\nabla_\alpha m_n(\alpha_n^o, \hat{\theta}_n, \hat{\pi}_n) = \nabla_\alpha \overline{m}_n(\gamma_n^o) + (\nabla_\alpha m_n(\alpha_n^o, \hat{\theta}_n, \hat{\pi}_n) - \nabla_\alpha \overline{m}_n(\gamma_n^o))$$
$$= o_P(n^{1/2}/a_n), \tag{A8}$$

and

$$\left\|\nabla_\alpha^2 m_n(\tilde{\alpha}_n, \hat{\theta}_n, \hat{\pi}_n)\right\| \le n^{-1}\sum_t D_{nt}(Z_t) = O_P(1), \tag{A9}$$

by Markov's inequality. On the other hand,

$$\delta\hat{m}_n^o(\hat{\theta}_n - \theta_o; \hat{\pi}_n) = (\delta\hat{m}_n^o(\hat{\theta}_n - \theta_o; \hat{\pi}_n) - \delta\overline{m}_n^o(\hat{\theta}_n - \theta_o; \hat{\pi}_n))$$
$$+ (\delta\overline{m}_n^o(\hat{\theta}_n - \theta_o; \hat{\pi}_n) - \delta\overline{m}_n^o(\hat{\theta}_n - \theta_o; \pi_o)) + \delta\overline{m}_n^o(\hat{\theta}_n - \theta_o; \pi_o)$$
$$= (\delta\hat{m}_n^o(\hat{\theta}_n - \theta_o; \hat{\pi}_n) - \delta\overline{m}_n^o(\hat{\theta}_n - \theta_o; \hat{\pi}_n)) + o_P(a_n^{-1}),$$

given Assumption C.3(d) and Definition 2.4(c), and

$$\delta^2\hat{m}_n^o(\hat{\theta}_n - \theta_o; \hat{\pi}_n) = \delta^2\overline{m}_n^o(\hat{\theta}_n - \theta_o; \hat{\pi}_n) + (\delta^2\hat{m}_n^o(\hat{\theta}_n - \theta_o; \hat{\pi}_n) - \delta^2\overline{m}_n^o(\hat{\theta}_n - \theta_o; \hat{\pi}_n))$$
$$= \delta^2\overline{m}_n^o(\hat{\theta}_n - \theta_o; \hat{\pi}_n) + o_P(a_n^{-1}),$$

given Assumption C.3(a). It follows that:

$$\delta\hat{m}_n^o(\hat{\theta}_n - \theta_o; \hat{\pi}_n) + \delta^2\hat{m}_n^o(\hat{\theta}_n - \theta_o; \hat{\pi}_n)$$
$$= \delta\hat{m}_n^o(\hat{\theta}_n - \theta_o; \hat{\pi}_n) - \delta\overline{m}_n^o(\hat{\theta}_n - \theta_o; \hat{\pi}_n) + \delta^2\overline{m}_n^o(\hat{\theta}_n - \theta_o; \hat{\pi}_n) + o_P(a_n^{-1})$$
$$= W_n(\hat{\pi}_n) + o_P(a_n^{-1})$$
$$= EW_n(\pi_o) + (EW_n(\hat{\pi}_n) - EW_n(\pi_o)) + (W_n(\hat{\pi}_n) - EW_n(\hat{\pi}_n)) + o_P(a_n^{-1})$$
$$= EW_n(\pi_o) + (W_n(\pi_o) - EW_n(\pi_o)) + o_P(a_n^{-1}), \tag{A10}$$

given Assumptions C.3(b, c, d). Substituting (A8–A10) into (A7) and using Assumptions A.3 and C.4, $a_n/n \to 0$, and Definition 2.4(a), we obtain:

$$\hat{m}_n = \bar{m}_n(\gamma_n^o) + (m_n(\gamma_n^o) - \bar{m}_n(\gamma_n^o)) + EW_n(\pi_o) + (W_n(\pi_o) - EW_n(\pi_o))$$
$$+ o_P(a_n^{-1})$$
$$= \bar{m}_n(\gamma_n) + EW_n(\pi_o) + (W_n(\pi_o) - EW_n(\pi_o)) + o_P(a_n^{-1}).$$

Consequently, given Assumption C.5, we have $J_n^{o-1/2} a_n(\hat{m}_n - EW_n(\pi_o)) \to^d N(J_n^{o-1/2} a_n \bar{m}_n(\gamma_n^o), I_q)$. It follows by Slutsky's Theorem that $\hat{J}_n^{-1/2} a_n(\hat{m}_n - \hat{R}_n) \to^d N(J_n^{o-1/2} a_n \bar{m}_n(\gamma_n^o), I_q)$ given $\hat{J}_n - J_n^{o-1} \to^P 0$ and $a_n(\hat{R}_n - EW_n(\pi_o)) \to^P 0$ by Assumption C.6. Therefore, $M_n \to^d \chi_q^2(\zeta_n^o)$.

(ii) The proof of consistency is similar to that of Theorem 2.3(ii). ∎

Proof of Proposition 3.2. Put $\hat{\mu}_{nt} = \hat{\mu}_n(X_t)$, $\mu_{nt}^o = \mu_n^o(X_t)$, and $\mu_t^o = \mu_o(X_t)$. We first apply Yohai and Maronna (YM) (1979, theorem 2.2) to show $n^{-1}\sum_t(\hat{\mu}_{nt} - \mu_{nt}^o)^2 = O_P(p_n/n)$. YM assume a linear model of the form (see YM, eq. (1.1))

$$Y_{nt}^o = \psi_{np_n}'(X_t)\beta_n^o + \epsilon_t = \mu_n^o(X_t) + \epsilon_t, \quad t = 1,2,\ldots,n, \quad n = 1,2,\ldots,$$

where $\psi_{np_n}(X_t)$ is a given $p_n \times 1$ vector, and ϵ_t is i.i.d. This is a moving DGP assumption. With this in mind, we must control the bias $\mu_n^o - \mu_o$ properly to apply YM's results to $\hat{\mu}_n$.

Put $\zeta_{nt} = (\Psi_n'\Psi_n)^{-1/2}\psi_{np_n}(X_t)$, $\tilde{\beta}_n = (\Psi_n'\Psi_n)^{1/2}\hat{\beta}_n$, $\beta_n^+ = (\Psi_n'\Psi_n)^{1/2}\beta_n^o$. Then $Y_{nt}^o = \zeta_{nt}'\beta_n^+ + \epsilon_t$. Following the proof of YM, we see that to apply YM's Theorem 2.2 to $\tilde{\beta}_n$, it suffices that

$$\left\| b_n' \sum_t \zeta_{nt}\varphi(Y_{nt}^o - \zeta_{nt}'\tilde{\beta}_n) \right\| \to 0 \quad a.s. \tag{A11}$$

for any $b_n \in \mathbb{R}^{p_n}$ with $\|b_n\| = O(1)$. By applying the mean value theorem to the first order condition (3.2) term by term, we obtain:

$$0 = \sum_t \zeta_{nt}\varphi(Y_t - \zeta_{nt}'\tilde{\beta}_n) = \sum_t \zeta_{nt}\varphi(Y_{nt}^o - \zeta_{nt}'\tilde{\beta}_n) + \sum_t \zeta_{nt}\varphi'(\bar{Y}_{nt})(\mu_{nt}^o - \mu_t^o),$$

where $\bar{Y}_{nt}$ lies between Y_{nt} and Y_{nt}^o. Hence, it suffices for (A11) to hold if $\|b_n'\sum_t\zeta_{nt}\varphi'(\bar{Y}_{nt})(\mu_{nt}^o - \mu_t^o)\| \to 0$ a.s. Given Assumptions D.2 and D.4(a), the identity $\sum_t\zeta_{nt}\zeta_{nt}' = I_{pn}$ and the Cauchy–Schwarz inequality, we have

$$\left\| b_n'\sum_t \zeta_{nt}\varphi'(\bar{Y}_t)(\mu_{nt}^o - \mu_t^o)\right\| \le c^{-1}\{b_n'(\sum_t \zeta_{nt}\zeta_{nt}')b_n\}^{1/2}\{\sum_t(\mu_{nt}^o - \mu_t^o)^2\}^{1/2}$$
$$\le c^{-1}n^{1/2}\|b_n\|^2 \rho_\infty(\mu_n^o, \mu_o) \to 0.$$

Hence, asymptotically, $\tilde{\beta}_n$ can be viewed as a solution to (A11), which is equivalent to Eq. (2.7) of YM. The results of YM then apply to (A11). Given Assumptions D.1–D.2, D.3(a), D.4(a) and $p_n\zeta_{np_n} \to 0$, the conditions of YM (1979, theorem 2.2) are satisfied. Hence, $p_n^{-1/2}\|\tilde{\beta}_n - \beta_n^+\| = O_P(1)$, i.e., $(\hat{\beta}_n - \beta_n^o)'(\Psi_n'\Psi_n)(\hat{\beta}_n - \beta_n^o) = O_P(p_n)$. It follows that

$$\sum_t (\hat{\mu}_{nt} - \mu_t^o)^2 \le 2\sum_t (\hat{\mu}_{nt} - \mu_{nt}^o)^2 + 2\sum_t (\mu_{nt}^o - \mu_t^o)^2$$
$$\le 2(\hat{\beta}_n - \beta_n^o)'(\Psi_n'\Psi_n)(\hat{\beta}_n - \beta_n^o) + O_P(n\rho_\infty^2(\mu_n^o, \mu_o))$$
$$= O_P(p_n),$$

given Assumption D.4(a). Because $(\hat{\beta}_n - \beta_n^o)'(\Psi_n'\Psi_n)(\hat{\beta}_n - \beta_n^o) \ge \lambda_{\min}(\Psi_n'\Psi_n)\|\hat{\beta}_n - \beta_n^o\|^2$, we also have $\|\hat{\beta}_n - \beta_n^o\|^2 = O_P(p_n^{1/2}/\lambda_{\min}^{1/2}(\Psi_n'\Psi_n))$. ∎

Proof of Proposition 3.3. We apply Mammen (1989, theorem 4). Like YM, Mammen also considers a linear model of the form of (A11). Following the proofs of both his Theorems 1 and 4, we see that Mammen's results can be applied to (A11), which holds given Assumptions D.2 and D.4(a), as has been shown in the proof of Proposition 3.2.

Let b_n be any sequence of $p_n \times q$ nonstochastic matrices such that $b_n'b_n$ is a $q \times q$ uniformly nonsingular matrix with $\|b_n'b_n\|$ bounded. We first show

$$\tilde{I}_n^{-1/2}b_n'(\tilde{\beta}_n - \beta_n^+) \to^d N(0, I_q), \tag{A12}$$

where $\tilde{\beta}_n = (\Psi_n'\Psi_n)^{1/2}\hat{\beta}_n$, $\beta_n^+ = (\Psi_n'\Psi_n)^{1/2}\beta_n^o$, and $\tilde{I}_n = b_n'b_n\sigma^2(\varphi)$, with $\sigma^2(\varphi) = E\varphi^2(\epsilon_t)/E^2\varphi'(\epsilon_t)$. Since Mammen only considers the univariate case ($q = 1$), we use the Cramer–Wold device (e.g. White, 1984, p. 108) to prove (A12).

Let $h \in \mathbb{R}^q$ be an arbitrary constant with $h'h = 1$. Define $c_n = b_n h$, a $p_n \times 1$ vector (thus c_n is equivalent to α_n in Mammen, 1989). Given Assumptions D.1–D.3(a, b), Condition (2.1) of Mammen (1989) is satisfied. Note that we impose $p_n\zeta_{np_n} \to 0$ to ensure that $b_n'(\tilde{\beta}_n - \beta_n^+)$ is centered at zero asymptotically. It remains to show that $\|c_n\|$ is bounded below and above. Since $b_n'b_n$ is a $q \times q$ symmetric bounded uniformly nonsingular matrix, $0 < c \le \lambda_{\min}(b_n'b_n) \le \lambda_{\max}(b_n'b_n) \le c^{-1} < \infty$. Hence, $\lambda_{\min}(b_n'b_n) \le c_n'c_n = h'b_n'b_n h \le \lambda_{\max}(b_n'b_n)$, i.e., $\|c_n\|$ is bounded below and above. Thus, (A12) now follows by Mammen (1989, theorem 4). Next we show

$$I_n^{o-1/2}G_{np_n}'(\hat{\beta}_n - \beta_n^o) \to^d N(0, I_q) \tag{A13}$$

for $I_n^o = G_{np_n}'(\Psi_n'\Psi_n)^- G_{np}\sigma^2(\varphi)$. Define the $p_n \times 1$ vector $b_n^o = a_n(\Psi_n'\Psi_n)^{-1/2}G_{np_n}$, where $a_n^{-1} = \|G_{np_n}'(\Psi_n'\Psi_n)^- G_{np_n}\|$. It follows immediately that $b_n^{o'}b_n^o$ is a $q \times q$ $O(1)$ symmetric uniformly nonsingular matrix and $\mathrm{tr}(b_n^{o'}b_n^o) = 1$. Hence, from (A12) we have $\tilde{I}_n^{o-1/2}a_n G_{np_n}'(\Psi_n'\Psi_n)^{-1/2}(\tilde{\beta}_n - \beta_n^+) \to^d N(0, I_q)$, where $\tilde{I}_n^o = b_n^{o'}b_n^o\sigma^2(\varphi) = a_n^2 I_n^o$. Because $\tilde{\beta}_n - \beta_n^+ = (\Psi_n'\Psi_n)^{1/2}(\hat{\beta}_n - \beta_n^o)$, this is equivalent to (A13). ∎

Proof of Theorem 3.4. Put $\hat{\mu}_{nt} = \hat{\mu}_n(X_t)$, $\mu_{nt}^o = \mu_n^o(X_t)$, and $\mu_t^o = \mu_o(X_t)$. (i) We verify the conditions of Theorem 2.3(i). Assumption A.1 is ensured by D.1; Assumptions A.2–A.3 and B.1 are either imposed directly or ensured (in Assumption A.2, we take $(\Theta, \rho_\Theta) = (\mathcal{W}_{\infty,r}^s, \rho_{s,\infty})$ and $\hat{\theta}_n = \hat{\mu}_n$ as in (3.2)). When $\{m_t\}$ is linear in θ, Assumption B.2 holds trivially with $\lambda = \infty$ for any pseudo-metric ρ_Θ; otherwise Assumptions B.2(a, b) are assumed, and Assumption B.2(c) holds because

$$\rho_{s,\infty}(\hat{\mu}_n, \mu_o) \le \rho_{s,\infty}(\hat{\mu}_n, \mu_n^o) + \rho_{s,\infty}(\mu_n^o, \mu_o)$$
$$\le p_n^{1/2} \sup_{1 \le j \le p_n} \|\psi_j\|_{\infty,s} \|\hat{\beta}_n - \beta_n^o\| + \rho_{s,\infty}(\mu_n^o, \mu_o)$$
$$\le p_n^{1/2} B_s(p_n) O_P(p_n^{1/2} / \lambda_{\min}^{1/2}(\Psi_n' \Psi_n)) + \rho_{s,\infty}(\mu_n^o; \mu_o)$$
$$= o(n^{-1/2(1+\lambda)}),$$

given Assumptions D.3(c), D.4(b), $n^{1/2(1+\lambda)} p_n B_s(p_n)/\lambda_{\min}(\Psi_n'\Psi_n) \to 0$ and Proposition 3.2.

Next, we verify Assumption B.3. B.3(a) is imposed directly; given D.5, we have

$$\delta \bar{m}_n^o(\hat{\theta}_n - \theta_o; \hat{\pi}_n) = n^{-1} \sum_t g_{nt}(X_t, \hat{\pi}_n)(\hat{\mu}_{nt} - \mu_t^o)$$
$$= n^{-1} \sum_t g_{nt}(X_t, \pi_o)(\hat{\mu}_{nt} - \mu_t^o) + r_n,$$

where $r_n = n^{-1}\sum_t(g_{nt}(X_t, \hat{\pi}_n) - g_{nt}(X_t, \pi_o))(\hat{\mu}_{nt} - \hat{\mu}_t^o) = o_P(n^{-1/2})$ by the Cauchy–Schwarz inequality, Proposition 3.2 and Assumptions D.5(b, c). Hence, B.3(b) holds. B.3(c) also holds because

$$n^{-1} \sum_t g_{nt}(X_t, \pi_o)(\hat{\mu}_{nt} - \mu_t^o)$$
$$= n^{-1} \sum_t g_{nt}(X_t, \pi_o)(\hat{\mu}_{nt} - \mu_{nt}^o)$$
$$+ n^{-1} \sum_t g_{nt}(X_t, \pi_o)(\mu_{nt}^o - \mu_t^o)$$
$$= [n^{-1} \sum_t g_{nt}(X_t, \pi_o)\psi_{np_n}'(X_t)](\hat{\beta}_n - \beta_n^o) + o_P(n^{-1/2})$$
$$= n^{-1} \sum_t v_{nt}(Z_t) + o_P(n^{-1/2}),$$

by Proposition 3.3 and using the fact that $\|n^{-1}\sum_t g_{nt}(X_t, \pi_o)(\mu_{nt}^o - \mu_t^o)\| = o_P(n^{-1/2})$ given Assumptions D.4(a) and D.5(a) by the Cauchy–Schwarz inequality. Finally, Assumptions B.4–B.6 are assumed directly. It follows from Theorem 2.3(i) that $M_n \to^d \chi_q^2$.

(ii) Consistency follows immediately from Theorem 2.3(ii). ∎

Proof of Theorem 3.5. We apply Theorem 3.4. (i) First we verify Assumptions D.1–D.5. Both D.1 and D.2 hold given (a) and (d). Given (a) and (c), we have $\sum_t \psi_i(X_t)\psi_j(X_t) = n\delta_{ij}$, where $\delta_{ii} = 1$ and $\delta_{ij} = 0$, $i \ne j$. Therefore, $\lambda_{\min}(\Psi_n'\Psi_n) = n$, so Assumption D.3(a) holds. Since $\max_j \sup_{x \in [0,1]} |\psi_j(x)| \le \sqrt{2}$, D.3(c) (for $s = 0$) holds with $B_0(p_n) = \sqrt{2}$ for all p_n. Because $\xi_{np_n} = \sup_t(\psi_{np_n}'(X_t)(\Psi_n'\Psi_n)^- \psi_{np_n}(X_t)) \le 2p_n/n$, Assumption D.3(b) holds given $p_n^4/n \to 0$.

Next, we verify Assumptions D.4–D.6. Given (b), there exists $\mu_n^o(\cdot) = \psi_{np_n}'(\cdot)\beta_n^o \in \mathcal{C}^r(0,1)$ such that $\rho_\infty(\mu_n^o, \mu_o) = o(p_n^{-r+\delta})$ for all $\delta > 0$ (e.g., Edmunds and Moscatelli, 1977). It follows that Assumption D.4 with $s = 0$ holds given (e). Also, with $B_0(p_n) = \sqrt{2}$ and $\lambda = 1$, the condition $n^{1/2(1+\lambda)} p_n B_0(p_n)/$

$\lambda_{\min}^{1/2}(\Psi_n'\Psi_n) = O(p_n/n^{1/4}) \to 0$ holds given (e). From (A14) below, we see that Assumption D.5(a) holds with $g_{nt}(X_t, \pi) = (-3\sigma_o^2, 0)'$; Assumptions D.5(b, c) are null because π does not appear.

We now verify the remaining conditions. We put $\mu_t = \mu(X_t)$, $\hat{\mu}_{nt} = \hat{\mu}_n(X_t)$, $\mu_{nt}^o = \mu_n^o(X_t)$. Assumption A.2 holds with $(\hat{\alpha}_n, \alpha_o) = (\hat{\sigma}_n^2, \sigma_o^2)$, $(\Theta, \rho_\Theta) = (\mathcal{C}^r(0, 1), \rho_\infty)$, and $\hat{\theta}_n = \hat{\mu}_n$ as in (3.2). Assumption A.3 is null since π does not appear. Assumption B.1 holds given $\{m_t\}$. Next we verify Assumptions B.2(a, b). For $\mu \in \Theta_o = \{\mu \in \mathcal{C}^r(0, 1) : \rho_\infty(\mu; \mu_o) \le \Delta\}$, we have $|(Y_t - \mu_t)^3 - \epsilon_t^3 + 3\epsilon_t^2(\mu_t - \mu_t^o)| \le (3|\epsilon_t| + \Delta)(\mu_t - \mu_t^o)^2$ and $|(Y_t - \mu_t)^4 - \epsilon_t^4 + 4\epsilon_t^3(\mu_t - \mu_t^o)| \le (8\epsilon_t^2 + 3\Delta^2)(\mu_t - \mu_t^o)^2$. It follows that

$$\left| m_t(\alpha_o, \theta, \pi) - (\epsilon_t^3, \epsilon_t^4 - 3\sigma_o^4)' + (3\epsilon_t^2, 4\epsilon_t^3)'(\mu_t - \mu_t^o) \right| \le D_{nt}(Z_t)\rho_\infty^2(\mu, \mu_o) \quad (A14)$$

for all $\mu \in \Theta_o$, where $D_{nt}(Z_t) = 8\epsilon_t^2 + 3|\epsilon_t| + 3\Delta^2 + \Delta$. Therefore, Assumptions B.2(a, b) with $\lambda = 1$ hold. From (A14) we have $\delta\hat{m}_n^o(\theta - \theta_o; \pi) = -n^{-1}\sum_{t=1}^n (3\epsilon_t^2, 4\epsilon_t^3)'(\mu_t - \mu_t^o)$, and $\delta\overline{m}_n^o(\theta - \theta_o; \pi) = (-3\sigma_o^2, 0)'n^{-1}\sum_t(\mu_t - \mu_t^o)$. Hence, Assumption B.3(a) holds because

$$\begin{aligned}
\delta\hat{m}_n^o(\hat{\theta}_n - \theta_o; \pi) - \delta\overline{m}_n^o(\hat{\theta}_n - \theta_o; \pi) &= -n^{-1}\sum_t (3(\epsilon_t^2 - \sigma_o^2), 4\epsilon_t^3)'(\hat{\mu}_{nt} - \mu_t^o) \\
&= -n^{-1}\sum_t (3(\epsilon_t^2 - \sigma_o^2), 4\epsilon_t^3)'(\hat{\mu}_{nt} - \mu_{nt}^o) \\
&\quad -n^{-1}\sum_t (3(\epsilon_t^2 - \sigma_o^2), 4\epsilon_t^3)'(\mu_{nt}^o - \mu_t^o) \\
&= o_P(n^{-1/2}), \quad (A15)
\end{aligned}$$

where for the first term $||n^{-1}\sum_t(3(\epsilon_t^2 - \sigma_o^2), 4\epsilon_t^3)'(\hat{\mu}_{nt} - \mu_{nt}^o)|| \le ||n^{-1}\sum_t(3(\epsilon_t^2 - \sigma_o^2), 4\epsilon_t^3)'\psi_{np_n}'(X_t)|| \, ||\hat{\beta}_n - \beta_n^o|| = O_P(p_n/n^{1/2})O_P(p_n^{1/2}/\lambda_{\min}^{1/2}(\Psi_n'\Psi_n)) = o_P(n^{-1/2})$ by Chebyshev's inequality and Proposition 3.2; and for the second term $n^{-1}\sum_t(3(\epsilon_t^2 - \sigma_o^2), 4\epsilon_t^3)(\mu_{nt}^o - \mu_t^o) = O_P(n^{-1/2}\rho_\infty(\mu_n^o; \mu_o)) = o_P(n^{-1/2})$ by Chebyshev's inequality. Similarly, we can show that $\hat{\sigma}_n^2 - \sigma_o^2 = n^{-1}\sum_{t=1}^n(\epsilon_t^2 - \sigma_o^2) + o_P(n^{-1/2})$, so Assumption B.4 with $s_{nt} = \epsilon_t^2 - \sigma_o^2$ holds. By definition, $G_{np_n}^o = n^{-1}\sum_t\psi_{np_n}(X_t)(-3\sigma_o^2, 0) = ((-\sqrt[3]{2}\sigma_o^2, 0, ..., 0), (0, 0, ..., 0))'$. It follows that $v_{nt}(Z_t) = G_{np_n}^{o'}(\Psi_n'\Psi_n/n)^-\psi_n(X_t)\varphi(\epsilon_t)/E\varphi'(\epsilon_t) = (-3\sigma_o^2\eta_t, 0)'$, where $\eta_t = \varphi(\epsilon_t)/E\varphi'(\epsilon_t)$. Therefore, we have $W_{nt} = (\epsilon_t^3 - 3\sigma_o^2\eta_t, (\epsilon_t^4 - 3\sigma_o^4) - 6\sigma_o^2(\epsilon_t^2 - \sigma_o^2))'$. By the Lindeberg–Levy CLT, $J_o^{-1/2}n^{1/2}W_n \to^d N(0, I_2)$, where

$$J_o = \begin{bmatrix} J_{11} & J_{12} \\ J_{12} & J_{22} \end{bmatrix},$$

with $J_{11} = 15\sigma_o^6 - 6\sigma_o^2 E(\epsilon_t^3\eta_t) + 9\sigma_o^4 E(\eta_t^2)$, $J_{22} = 24\sigma_o^8$ and $J_{12} = -3\sigma_o^2 E(\epsilon_t^4\eta_t) + 18\sigma_o^4 E(\epsilon_t^4\eta_t)$. Hence, Assumption B.5 holds. Assumption B.6 also holds given $\hat{J}_n$ by straightforward verification using appropriate weak ULLNs and $\rho_\infty(\hat{\mu}_n; \mu_o) \to^p 0$ by Proposition 3.2. The desired result then follows from Theorem 3.4(i).

(ii) Consistency follows immediately from Theorem 3.4(ii). ∎

Proof of Theorem 3.6. Given $\delta_n = n^{-\lambda_1}$, we choose a subset $\{\pi_n^1, ..., \pi_n^{\#G_n}\}$ from

Π_n such that for each $\pi \in \Pi_n$, there exists at least one π_n^j such that $\rho_\infty(\pi, \pi_n^j)$ $< \delta_n$, where $G_n = G_n(\delta_n)$ is a finite open covering of Π_n of cardinality of $\# G_n$. This cardinality is finite as Π (and hence Π_n) has finite metric entropy. For arbitrary $\epsilon > 0$,

$$
\begin{aligned}
&P[\sup_{\pi \in \Pi_n} |Q_n(\pi)| > \epsilon] \\
&\quad \le P[\max_{1 \le i \le \# G_n} \sup_{\pi \in \mathbb{B}_n(\pi_n^i, \delta_n)} |Q_n(\pi)| > \epsilon] \\
&\quad \le P[\max_{1 \le i \le \# G_n} |Q_n(\pi_n^i)| > \epsilon/2] \\
&\qquad + P[\max_{1 \le i \le \# G_n} \sup_{\pi \in \mathbb{B}_n(\pi_n^i, \delta_n)} |Q_n(\pi) - Q_n(\pi_n^i)| > \epsilon/2] \\
&\quad \le P[\max_{1 \le i \le \# G_n} |Q_n(\pi_n^i)| > \epsilon/2] \\
&\qquad + P[\sup_{\pi' \in \Pi_n} \sup_{\pi \in \mathbb{B}_n(\pi', \delta_n)} |Q_n(\pi) - Q_n(\pi')| > \epsilon/2],
\end{aligned}
$$

where $\mathbb{B}_n(\pi_n^i, \delta_n) = \{\pi \in \Pi_n : \rho_\infty(\pi, \pi_n^i) < \delta_n\}$. For the first term

$$
\begin{aligned}
P[\max_{1 \le i \le \# G_n} |Q_n(\pi_n^i)| > \epsilon/2] &\le \sum_{i=1}^{\# G_n} P[|Q_n(\pi_n^i)| > \epsilon/2] \\
&\le \# G_n \max_{1 \le i \le \# G_n} P[|Q_n(\pi_n^i)| > \epsilon/2] \\
&\le \# G_n \sup_{\pi \in \Pi_n} P[|Q_n(\pi)| > \epsilon/2] \\
&\le \# G_n C_1 n^{-\lambda}
\end{aligned}
$$

given (a). This holds in particular for $\lambda_2 = \lambda + d\lambda_1$. Next, for the second term

$$
P[\sup_{\pi' \in \Pi_n} \sup_{\pi \in \mathbb{B}_n(\pi', \delta_n)} |Q_n(\pi) - Q_n(\pi')|] > \epsilon/2 \le 2\epsilon^{-1} C n^{-\lambda}
$$

by Markov's inequality, given (b). Therefore,

$$
P[\sup_{\pi \in \Pi_n} |Q_n(\pi)| > \epsilon] \le \# G_n C_1 n^{-(\lambda + d\lambda_1)} + 2\epsilon^{-1} C n^{-\lambda}.
$$

Because $\Pi_n \subseteq \Pi$, $\# G_n \le \# G_n(\delta_n)$ for any $\delta_n > 0$, where $\# G(\delta_n)$ is the metric entropy of Π. Given Π and $\delta_n = n^{-\lambda_1}$, we have from Kolmogorov and Tihomirov (1961, section 2.3) that $\# G(\delta_n) = \Delta n^{d\lambda_1}$. (Kolmogorov and Tihomirov prove this only for $d = 1$, but the proof for $d > 1$ follows analogously.) Substituting this into the above expression, we obtain $P[\sup_{\pi \in \Pi_n} |Q_n(\pi)| > \epsilon] \le C_2 n^{-\lambda}$ for some C_2. This completes the proof. ∎

Proof of Theorem 3.7. Put $\zeta_{nt} = (\Psi_n' \Psi_n)^{-1/2} \psi_{np_n}(X_t)$, $\hat{\sigma}_{nt} = \hat{\sigma}_n(X_t)$, $\sigma_t = \sigma(X_t)$ and $\sigma_t^o = \sigma_o(X_t)$. Then $W_{nts} = \epsilon_t \zeta_{nt}' \zeta_{ns} \epsilon_s \sigma_t^o \sigma_s^o / \sigma_t \sigma_s$. The proof consists of showing: (i) $\sum_t (W_{nt}(\hat{\sigma}_n) - W_{nt}(\sigma_o)) = o_P(p_n^{1/2})$; (ii) $\sum\sum_{t \ne s} (W_{nt}(\hat{\sigma}_n) - W_{nt}(\sigma_o)) = o_P(p_n^{1/2})$; and (iii) $(\sum_t \sum_s W_{nts}(\sigma_o) - p_n)/(2p_n)^{1/2} \to^d N(0, 1)$.

We first consider (i). Given Assumption E.2 and the identity $\sum_t \zeta_{nt}' \zeta_{nt} = p_n$, we have $|\sum_t W_{ntt}(\hat{\sigma}_n) - W_{ntt}(\sigma_o)| \le C \rho_\infty(\hat{\sigma}_n, \sigma_o) \sum_t \epsilon_t^2 \zeta_{nt}' \zeta_{nt} = o_P(p_n^{1/2})$ by Markov's inequality.

Next, we apply Theorem 3.6 to show (ii). Choose $\Pi_n = \{\sigma \in \Sigma : \rho_\infty(\sigma, \sigma_o)$

$\leq n^{-\delta}\}$ for some $0 < \delta < 1$. Note that $\hat{\sigma}_n \in \Pi_n$ in probability. Let $Q_n(\sigma) = \sum\sum_{t\neq s}(W_{nt}(\hat{\sigma}_n) - W_{nt}(\sigma_o)) = \sum_{t=2}^n Q_{nt}$, where $Q_{nt} = 2\sum_{s=1}^{t-1}(W_{nts}(\sigma) - W_{nts}(\sigma_o))$.

To show (ii), it suffices to show $\sup_{\sigma\in\Pi_n}|Q_n(\sigma)| = o_p(p_n^{1/2})$. Given Assumptions D.1(a, b', c), $\sum_t \zeta'_{nt}\zeta_{nt} = p_n$ and $p_n/n \to 0$ (as implied by Assumption E.3), we have $E[\sup_{(\sigma_1,\sigma_2)\in\mathbb{B}_n(n^{-\lambda_1})}|Q_n(\sigma_1) - Q_n(\sigma_2)|] \leq c^{-1}n^{-\lambda_1}\sum\sum_{t\neq s}\zeta'_{nt}\zeta_{nt} \leq c^{-1}n^{-\lambda_1} + 1p_n \leq c^{-1}n^{-\lambda_1} + 2$. Hence, condition (b) of Theorem 3.6 holds by choosing $\lambda_1 \geq \lambda + 2$. Next, we verify condition (a). Since $E(Q_{nt}|\epsilon_1, \epsilon_2, ..., \epsilon_{t-1}) = 0$ given $\{X_t\}$ nonstochastic, $\{Q_{nt}, \mathcal{F}_{t-1}\}$ is a martingale difference sequence, where $\{\mathcal{F}_t\}$ is the sequence of σ-fields consisting of ϵ_s, $s \leq t$. By Hölder's inequality and Rosenthal's inequality (see Hall and Heyde, 1980, p. 23, or Hall, 1989, for its application), we have that for $k = 1, 2, ...,$

$$E\left(Q_n^{2k}(\sigma)\right) \leq \left\{\sum_{t=2}^n\left(EQ_{nt}^{2k}(\sigma)\right)^{1/k}\right\}^k.$$

Conditional on ϵ_t, $Q_{nt}(\sigma)$ is sum of independent random variables, and so given Assumption D.1(c) and $\sum_t \zeta_{nt}\zeta'_{nt} = I_n$, $EQ_{nt}^{2k}(\sigma) \leq c(k)^{-1}\rho_\infty^{2k}(\sigma, \sigma_o)\{\sum_{s=1}^{t-1}(\zeta'_{nt}\zeta_{ns})^2\}^k \leq c(k)^{-1}\rho_\infty^{2k}(\sigma, \sigma_o)(\zeta'_{nt}\zeta_{nt})^k$. It follows that $EQ_n^{2k}(\sigma) \leq c(k)^{-1}\rho_\infty^{2k}(\sigma, \sigma_o)\{\sum_{t=2}^n \zeta'_{nt}\zeta_{nt}\}^k \leq c(k)^{-1}\rho_\infty^{2k}(\sigma, \sigma_o)p_n^k$. Therefore, by Markov's inequality, we have for any $\eta > 0$ and for $k = 1, 2, ...,$

$$P\left[|Q_n(\sigma)| > \eta p_n^{1/2}\right] \leq EQ_n^{2k}(\sigma)/(p_n^k\eta^{2k}) = c(k)^{-1}\eta^{-2k}\rho_\infty^{2k}(\sigma,\sigma_o) \leq c(k)^{-1}\eta^{-2k}n^{-\delta k}$$

It follows from Theorem 3.6 that $\sup_{\sigma\in\Sigma_n}|Q_n(\sigma)| = o(p_n^{1/2})$ a.s. Thus, (ii) is proved. Finally, the proof of (iii) follows exactly that of Hong and White (1995, theorem A.1). ∎

Proof of Theorem 3.8. We use the following notations: $f_t^o = f(X_t, \alpha_o)$, $\nabla_\alpha f_t^o = \nabla_\alpha f(X_t, \alpha_o)$, $\mu_t^o = \mu_o(X_t)$, $\theta_t = \theta(X_t)$, $\theta_t^o = \theta_o(X_t)$, $\hat{\theta}_{nt} = \hat{\theta}_n(X_t)$, $\theta_{nt}^o = \theta_n^o(X_t)$, $\sigma_t = \sigma(X_t)$, $\sigma_t^o = \sigma_o(X_t)$, $\hat{\sigma}_{nt} = \hat{\sigma}_n(X_t)$. Under H_o^* we have $m_t(\gamma_o) = (\theta_t^o - f_t^o/\sigma_t^o)(Y_t - f_t^o)/\sigma_t^o = 0$, $\nabla_\alpha \bar{m}_n(\gamma_o) = -E[\nabla_\alpha f_t^o(Y_t - f_t^o)/(\sigma_t^o)^2 + (\theta_t^o - f_t^o/\sigma_t^o)/\sigma_t^o] = 0$ and $\delta\bar{m}_n^o(\theta - \theta_o; \pi_o) = E[(\theta_t - \theta_t^o)(Y_t - f_t^o)/\sigma_t^o] = 0$ for $\theta \in \mathcal{W}_{\infty,r}(\mathbb{X})$. It follows that (3.3) is a_n-degenerate at γ_o under H_o^* for any given sequence a_n. Hence, Theorem 2.5 is relevant. (i) We first consider asymptotic normality: Assumption A.1 is ensured by Assumptions D.1(a, b', c); Assumption A.2 holds with $(\Theta, \rho_\Theta) = (\mathcal{W}_{\infty,r}(\mathbb{X}), \rho_\infty)$ and $(\Pi, \rho_\Pi) = (\Sigma, \rho_\infty)$. Assumption A.3(a) with $a_n = n/p_n^{1/2}$ holds because

$$a_n(m_n(\alpha_o,\theta_o,\pi) - \bar{m}_n(\alpha_o,\theta_o,\pi)) = a_n n^{-1}\sum_{t=1}^n(\theta_t^o - f_t^o/\sigma_t^o)(Y_t - f_t^o)/\sigma_t^o$$
$$= a_n n^{-1}\sum_{t=1}^n \mu_t^o \epsilon_t(1/\sigma_t\sigma_t^o - \sigma_t^2)$$
$$= o_P(1)$$

given Assumptions D.1(a, b', c) and E.2 by applying Theorem 3.6 (following the analogous reasoning of (ii) in the proof of Theorem 3.7); Assumption A.3(b) also holds trivially since $\bar{m}_n^o(\alpha_o, \theta_o, \pi) = 0$ for all $\pi = \sigma \in \Sigma$. Assumption C.1(a) holds given D.1(a, b′, c) and E.1; Assumption C.1(b) holds since

$$
\begin{aligned}
\nabla_\alpha m_n(\alpha_o, \hat{\theta}_n, \hat{\pi}_n) - \nabla_\alpha \bar{m}_n(\alpha_o, \hat{\theta}_n, \hat{\pi}_n) &= n^{-1}\sum_{t=1}^{n}(\nabla_\alpha f_t^o / \hat{\sigma}_{nt})(Y_t - f_t^o)/\hat{\sigma}_{nt} \\
&= n^{-1}\sum_{t=1}^{n}\nabla_\alpha f_t^o \epsilon_t / \sigma_t^o \\
&\quad - n^{-1}\sum_{t=1}^{n}\nabla_\alpha f_t^o \sigma_t^o \epsilon_t(\hat{\sigma}_{nt}^{-2} - \sigma_t^{o-2}) \\
&= O_P(n^{-1/2}) \\
&= o_P(n^{1/2}/a_n).
\end{aligned}
$$

Above, the first term is $O_P(n^{-1/2})$ by Chebyshev's inequality and the second term is $o_P(n^{-1/2})$ given Assumption E.2 by Theorem 3.6 following the analogous reasoning of (ii) of the proof of Theorem 3.7. Assumption C.1(c) holds under H_o^* since

$$
\begin{aligned}
\nabla_\alpha' \bar{m}_n^o(\alpha_o, \hat{\theta}_n, \hat{\pi}_n) &- \nabla_\alpha' \bar{m}_n^o(\gamma_o) \\
&= -n^{-1}\sum_{t=1}^{n}\nabla_\alpha' f_t^o(\hat{\theta}_{nt} - f_t^o / \hat{\sigma}_{nt})/\hat{\sigma}_{nt} \\
&= n^{-1}\sum_t(\nabla_\alpha' f_t^o / \hat{\sigma}_{nt})(\hat{\theta}_{nt} - \theta_t^o) + n^{-1}\sum_{t=1}^{n}\nabla_\alpha' f_t^o \mu_t^o(1/\hat{\sigma}_{nt}\sigma_t^o - 1/\hat{\sigma}_{nt}^2) \\
&= n^{-1}\sum_t(\nabla_\alpha' f_t^o / \sigma_t^o)(\hat{\theta}_{nt} - \theta_t^o) + n^{-1}\sum_{t=1}^{n}\nabla_\alpha' f_t^o(1/\hat{\sigma}_{nt} - 1/\sigma_t^o)(\hat{\theta}_{nt} - \theta_t^o) \\
&\quad + n^{-1}\sum_t\nabla_\alpha' f_t^o \mu_t^o(1/\hat{\sigma}_{nt}\sigma_t^o - 1/\hat{\sigma}_{nt}^2) \\
&= o_P(p_n^{1/2}/n^{1/2}),
\end{aligned}
$$

where for the first term (a weighted average of $\hat{\theta}_n - \theta_o$) we have $n^{-1}\sum_t(\nabla_\alpha' f_t^o/\sigma_t^o)(\hat{\theta}_{nt} - \theta_t^o) = o_P(p_n^{1/2}/n^{1/2})$ by straightforward but tedious algebra, given Assumptions D.1(a), E.2 and E.4. Also, the last two terms are $o_P(p_n^{1/2}/n^{1/2})$ by the Cauchy–Schwarz inequality given Assumptions E.2 and E.4.

We now verify the remaining conditions. Since (3.3) is linear in θ, Assumption C.2 with $\lambda = \infty$ holds. C.3(a) also holds trivially since $\delta^2 m_{nt}(\theta - \theta_o; \alpha_o, \theta_o, \pi) = 0$; for Assumption C.3(b),

$$
\begin{aligned}
\delta \hat{m}_n^o(\hat{\theta}_n - \theta_o; \hat{\pi}_n) \\
&= n^{-1}\sum_t(\hat{\theta}_n - \theta_t^o)\epsilon_t\sigma_t^o / \hat{\sigma}_{nt} \\
&= n^{-1}\sum_t(\hat{\theta}_n - \theta_{nt}^o)\epsilon_t\sigma_t^o / \hat{\sigma}_{nt} + n^{-1}\sum_t(\theta_{nt}^o - \theta_t^o)\epsilon_t\sigma_t^o / \hat{\sigma}_{nt} \\
&= n^{-1}\sum_t\sum_s(\sigma_t^o / \hat{\sigma}_{nt})\epsilon_t\zeta_{nt}'\zeta_{ns}\epsilon_s(\sigma_s^o / \hat{\sigma}_{ns}) \\
&\quad + n^{-1}\sum_t\sum_s(\sigma_t^o / \hat{\sigma}_{nt})\epsilon_t\zeta_{nt}'\zeta_{ns}(\mu_t^o / \hat{\sigma}_{ns} - \theta_{nt}^o) \\
&\quad + n^{-1}\sum_t(\theta_t - \theta_t^o)\epsilon_t\sigma_t^o / \hat{\sigma}_{nt} \\
&= n^{-1}\sum_t\sum_s\epsilon_t\zeta_{nt}'\zeta_{ns}\epsilon_s + o_P(p_n^{1/2}/n),
\end{aligned}
$$

by Theorem 3.6, given Assumptions E.2 and E.4. Also, Assumption C.3(d) holds since $\delta \bar{m}_n^o(\hat{\theta}_n - \theta_o; \pi) = 0$ for all $\pi \in \Pi$; C.4 is given directly; and C.5 with $J_n^o = 2$ holds by Theorem 3.7. Finally, Assumption C.6 holds with $\hat{J}_n = 2$ and $\hat{R}_n = R_n^o = p_n/n$. The result now follows from Theorem 2.5(i).

(ii) Consistency follows immediately from Theorem 2.5(ii). ∎

Proof of Lemma 4.1. See Appendix B of Newey (1994). Note that the proof for $\rho_\infty(\hat{p}, p_o) = O_P([nb_n^d/\ln(n)]^{-1/2} + b_n^k)$ follows analogously to that of Newey with $y_{ni} = 1$. ∎

Proof of Proposition 4.2. Given Assumption F.4(a) and $\hat{\theta}_n = \hat{r}_n/\hat{p}_n$, we have

$$
\begin{aligned}
\delta \bar{m}_n^o(\hat{\theta}_n - \theta_o; \pi_o) &= E[g(X, \pi_o)(\hat{\theta}_n(X) - \theta_o(X))] \\
&= \int_{\mathbb{X}} g(x, \pi_o)[\hat{r}_n(x) - \theta_o(x)\hat{p}_n(x)]dx \\
&\quad + \int_{\mathbb{X}} g(x, \pi_o)[\hat{r}_n(x) - \theta_o(x)\hat{p}_n(x)][p_o(x)/\hat{p}_n(x) - 1]dx \quad \text{(A16)}
\end{aligned}
$$

For the first term, we can write

$$
\begin{aligned}
\int_{\mathbb{X}} & g(x, \pi_o)[\hat{r}_n(x) - \theta_o(x)\hat{p}_n(x)]dx \\
&= \int_{\mathbb{X}} g(x, \pi_o)[n^{-1}\sum_t (Y_t - \theta_o(X))K_n(X_t - x)]dx \\
&= n^{-1}\sum_t g(X_t, \pi_o)\epsilon_t + n^{-1}\sum_t \epsilon_t[\int_{\mathbb{X}} g(x, \pi_o)K_n(X_t - x)dx - g(X_t, \pi_o)] \\
&\quad + n^{-1}\sum_t \int_{\mathbb{X}} g(x, \pi)(\theta_o(X_t) - \theta_o(x))K_n(X_t - x)dx \\
&= n^{-1}\sum_t g(X_t, \pi_o)\epsilon_t + o_P(n^{-1/2}) + O_P(b_n^k) \\
&= n^{-1}\sum_t g(X_t, \pi_o)\epsilon_t + o_P(n^{-1/2}) \quad \text{(A17)}
\end{aligned}
$$

given $nb_n^{2k} \to 0$, where the second term is $o_P(n^{-1/2})$ by Chebyshev's inequality and the fact that $\int_{\mathbb{X}} g(x, \pi_o)K_n(X_t - x)dx - g(X_t, \pi_o) = o(1)$ uniformly in t given Assumptions F.1(b), F.2 and F.4(a). Also, the third term is $O(b_n^k)$ by Markov's inequality and the fact that $\int_{\mathbb{X}} g(x, \pi_o)(\theta_o(x') - \theta_o(x))K_n(x' - x)dx = O(b_n^k)$ uniformly in $x' \in \mathbb{X}$ given Assumptions F.1(b) and F.2–F.4(a).

Next, we consider the last term of (A16). By the Cauchy–Schwarz inequality, we obtain:

$$
\begin{aligned}
\left| \int_{\mathbb{X}} \right. & \left. g(x, \pi_o)[\hat{r}_n(x) - \theta_o(x)\hat{p}_n(x)][p_o(x)/\hat{p}_n(x) - 1]dx \right| \\
&\leq \sup_{x \in \mathbb{X}} |p_o(x)/\hat{p}_n(x) - 1|(\int_{\mathbb{X}} \|g(x, \pi_o)\|^2 dx)^{1/2}(\int_{\mathbb{X}} [\hat{r}_n(x) - \theta_o(x)\hat{p}_n(x)]^2 dx)^{1/2} \\
&= O_P(\ln^{1/2}(n)(nb_n^d)^{-1/2} + b_n^k))O_P((nb_n^d)^{-1/2} + b_n^k) \\
&= o_P(n^{-1/2}), \quad \text{(A18)}
\end{aligned}
$$

given $nb_n^{2d}/\ln(n) \to \infty$, $nb_n^{2k} \to 0$, and $2k > d$, where we have made use of the fact that $\sup_{x \in \mathbb{X}} |p_o(x)/\hat{p}_n(x) - 1| = O_P((nb_n^d/\ln(n))^{-1/2} + b_n^k)$ by Lemma 4.1, and $\int_{\mathbb{X}} [\hat{r}_n(x) - \theta_o(x)\hat{p}_n(x)]^2 dx = O_P((nb_n^d)^{-1} + b_n^{2k})$ by Markov's inequality given Assumptions F.1–F.3. Combining (A16)–(A18) yields $n^{1/2}\delta\bar{m}_n^o(\hat{\theta}_n - \theta_o; \gamma_o) = n^{-1/2}\sum_t g(X_t, \pi_o)\epsilon_t + o_P(1)$. Because $V_o = E[g(X, \pi_o)g(X, \pi_o)'\epsilon^2]$ is $O(1)$ and nonsingular, $n^{-1/2}\sum_t g(X_t, \pi_o)\epsilon_t \to^d N(0, V_o)$ by the Lindeberg–Levy CLT. ∎

Proof of Theorem 4.3. (i) We verify the conditions of Theorem 2.3(i). Assumption A.1 is ensured by F.1; Assumption A.2 holds with $(\Theta, \rho_\Theta) = (\mathcal{W}_{\infty,r}^s(\mathbb{X}), \rho_\infty)$ and $\hat{\theta}_n = \hat{\mu}_n$ as in (4.1); Assumptions A.3 and B.1 are imposed directly. When (a) $m(Z_t, \alpha, \theta, \pi)$ is linear in θ, Assumption B.2 with $\lambda = \infty$ holds for any norm ρ_Θ; or when (b) Assumptions B.2(a, b) hold, B.2(c) is ensured by Lemma 4.1 given $n^{\delta/(2+\delta)}b_n^d \ln n(n) \to \infty$, $n^\lambda b_n^{(d+2s)(1+\lambda)}/\ln^{1+\lambda}(n) \to \infty$ and $nb_n^{2k(1+\lambda)} \to 0$. Assumption B.3(a) is assumed directly; given F.4, Assumption B.3(b) holds because

$$\delta\bar{m}_n^o(\hat{\theta}_n - \theta_o; \pi_o) = E[g(X, \hat{\pi}_n)(\hat{\theta}_n(X) - \theta_o(X))]$$
$$= E[g(X, \pi_o)(\hat{\theta}_n(X) - \theta_o(X))]$$
$$+ E[(g(X, \hat{\pi}_n) - g(X, \pi_o))(\hat{\theta}_n(X) - \theta_o(X))]$$
$$= E[g(X, \pi_o)(\hat{\theta}_n(X) - \theta_o(X))] + o_P(n^{-1/2}),$$

where the second term is $o_P(n^{-1/2})$ by the Cauchy–Schwarz inequality, Assumptions F.4(b, c) and $E(\hat{\theta}_n(X) - \theta_o(X))^2 = O_P((nb_n^d)^{-1} + b_n^{2k})$. By Proposition 4.2, Assumption B.3(c) holds with $v_{nt}(Z_t) = g(X_t, \pi_o)\epsilon_t$. Assumption B.4 is given directly; Assumption B.5 holds by the Lindeberg–Levy CLT given F.5. Finally, Assumption B.6 is imposed directly. All conditions of Theorem 2.3(i) are satisfied, so the desired result follows.

(ii) Consistency follows immediately from Theorem 2.3(ii). ∎

Proof of Theorem 4.4. Put $\hat{\mu}_{1t} = \hat{\mu}_{1n}(X_{1t})$, $\mu_1^o(X_{1t}) = \mu_{1t}^o$, $\hat{p}_{1t} = \hat{p}_{1n}(X_{1t})$, $p_{1t}^o = p_1^o(X_{1t})$, and $\hat{r}_{1t} = \hat{\mu}_{1t}\hat{p}_{1t}$. (i) We apply Theorem 4.3(i.a) as $\{m_t\}$ is linear in $\theta = \mu_1$. Given that α and π do not appear, Assumption A.2 with $(\Theta, \rho_\Theta) = (\mathcal{W}_{\infty,r}(\mathbb{X}), \rho_2)$ holds, where $\rho_2(\theta_1, \theta_2) = (\int_{\mathbb{X}}(\theta_2(x) - \theta_1(x))^2 p_o(x) dx)^{1/2}$. Assumptions A.3 and B.1 are null since $\mathbb{A}$ and Π are null. The proofs of Assumptions B.3(a) and B.6 are deferred to the end.

Next, we verify Assumptions F.1–F.5. F.1 with $\delta = 2$ holds given (a); F.2 with $s = 0$ holds given (b); F.3 (for μ_1^o and p_1^o) holds given (d); F.4(a) holds with $g(X_{1t}, \pi) = g(X_{1t})$ since, with p_o the joint density of X_t,

$$\delta\bar{m}_n^o(\hat{\theta}_n - \theta_o; \pi_o) = E(\psi(X_{2t})(\hat{\mu}_{1t} - \mu_{1t}^o)) = E(g(X_{1t})(\hat{\mu}_{1t} - \mu_{1t}^o)),$$

where g satisfies conditions in Assumption F.4(a) given (e); Assumptions F.4(b, c) are null. Assumption F.5 holds with $W(Z_t, \pi_o) = (\psi(X_{2t}) - g(X_{1t}))\epsilon_{1t}$ given (a) and (b), where $\epsilon_{1t} = Y_t - \mu_{1t}^o$. Finally, $nb_n^{2d_1}/\ln^2(n) \to \infty$, $nb_n^{2k} \to 0$, $2k > d_1$ are imposed directly. All conditions of Theorem 4.3(i.a) are satisfied. Hence, $M_n \to^d \chi_1^2$, provided Assumptions B.3(a) and B.6 hold.

It remains to prove Assumptions B.3(a) and B.6. For B.3(a), note that

$$\delta m_n^o(\hat{\theta}_n - \theta_o; \pi_o) = n^{-1}\sum_t \psi(X_{2t})(\hat{\mu}_{1t} - \mu_{1t}^o)$$
$$= n^{-1}\sum_t \psi(X_{2t})(\hat{r}_{1t} - \mu_{1t}^o \hat{p}_{1t})p_{1t}^{o-1}$$
$$+n^{-1}\sum_t \psi(X_{2t})(\hat{r}_{1t} - \mu_{1t}^o \hat{p}_{1t})(\hat{p}_{1t}^{-1} - p_{1t}^{o-1})$$
$$= n^{-1}\sum_t \psi(X_{2t})(\hat{r}_{1t} - \mu_{1t}^o \hat{p}_{1t})p_{1t}^{o-1} + o_P(n^{-1/2}),$$

where the second term is $o_P(n^{-1/2})$ given the conditions on p_1^o, μ_1^o and ψ, by following reasoning analogous to (A18). Similarly, we can also obtain:

$$\delta \overline{m}_n^o(\hat{\theta}_n - \theta_o; \pi) = \int_{\mathbb{X}_1} g(x_1)(\hat{r}_{1n}(x_1) - \mu_1^o(x_1)\hat{p}_{1n}(x_1))dx_1 + o_P(n^{-1/2}).$$

Thus, to show $\delta m_n^o(\hat{\theta}_n - \theta_o; \pi) - \delta \overline{m}_n^o(\hat{\theta}_n - \theta_o; \pi) = o_P(n^{-1/2})$, it suffices to show

$$A_n = n^{-1}\sum_t \psi(X_{2t})(\hat{r}_{1t} - \mu_{1t}^o \hat{p}_{1t})p_{1t}^{o-1}$$
$$= \int_{\mathbb{X}} g(x_1)(\hat{r}_n(x_1) - \mu_1^o(x_1)\hat{p}_{1n}(x_1))dx_1 + o_P(n^{-1/2}). \tag{A19}$$

For this purpose, we write

$$A_n = n^{-2}\sum_t\sum_s \psi(X_{2t})(Y_s - \mu_{1t}^o)p_{1t}^{o-1}K_n(X_{1t} - X_{1s})$$
$$= n^{-2}\sum_t\sum_{t \neq s} \psi(X_{2t})(Y_s - \mu_{1t}^o)p_{1t}^{o-1}K_n(X_{1t} - X_{1s}) + h_n$$
$$= U_n + o_P(n^{-1/2}),$$

where $h_n = b_n^{-1}K(0)n^{-2}\sum_t\psi(X_{2t})\epsilon_{1t}p_{1t}^{o-1} = O_P(n^{-3/2}b_{1n}^{-1}) = o_P(n^{-1/2})$ by Chebyshev's inequality given conditions (a)–(d). We now consider U_n.

Define $U_{nts} = [\psi(X_{2t})(Y_s - \mu_{1t}^o)p_{1t}^{o-1} + \psi(X_{2s})(Y_t - \mu_{1s}^o)p_{1s}^{o-1}]K_n(X_{1t} - X_{1s})$. Then $U_n = n^{-2}\sum\sum_{s<t}U_{nts} = (1 - n^{-1})EU_n + n^{-2}\sum\sum_{s<t}\hat{U}_{nts}$, where $\hat{U}_{nts} = U_{nts} - EU_n$, $EU_n = EU_{nts}$. Given $nb_n^{2d_1}\ln^2(n) \to \infty$, we have $E\hat{U}_{nts}^2 = O(b_n^{-d_1}) = o(n)$. Hence, by the extended U-statistic projection theorem of Powell et al. (1989, lemma 3.1), we have $U_n = (1 - n^{-1})[EU_n + n^{-1}\sum_t E(\hat{U}_{nts}|Z_t)] + o_P(n^{-1/2})$, where

$$E(\hat{U}_{nts}|Z_t) = \int_{\mathbb{X}}\psi(x_2)(Y_t - \mu_1^o(x_1))p_1^{o-1}(x_1)K_n(X_{1t} - x_1)p_o(x_1)dx_1$$
$$+\psi(X_{2t})p_{1t}^{o-1}\int_{\mathbb{X}}(\mu_1^o(x_1) - \mu_1^o(X_{1t}))K_n(X_{1t} - x_1)p_o(x)dx - EU_n$$
$$= \int_{\mathbb{X}_1} g(x_1)(Y_t - \mu_1^o(x_1))p_1^{o-1}(x_1)K_n(X_{1t} - x_1)p_1^o(x_1)dx_1 - EU_n$$
$$+O(b_n^k),$$

given the conditions on μ_1^o and K. It follows that

$$U_n = EU_n + n^{-1}\sum_t\int_{\mathbb{X}_1} g(x_1)(Y_t - \mu_1^o(x_1))K_n(X_{1t} - x_1)dx_1 + o_P(n^{-1/2}),$$

given $nb_n^{2k} \to 0$. Therefore, (A19) holds. Thus, Assumption B.3(a) holds. Finally, by Lemma 4.1, we have $\rho_\infty(\hat{\mu}_{1n}, \mu_1^o) \to^p 0$ and $\rho_\infty(\hat{g}_n, g) \to^p 0$ given conditions (a)–(f). Hence, it is straightforward to show $\hat{J}_n \to^p J_o = E((\psi(X_{2t}) - g(X_{1t}))^2 \epsilon_{1t}^2)$, so Assumption B.6 holds.

(ii) Consistency follows immediately from Theorem 4.3(ii). ∎

Proof of Proposition 4.5. Because $E(W_{nts}|X_t) = E(W_{nts}|X_s) = 0$, $t \neq s$, given Assumption F.1(a), we have $EW_n = (nb_n^d)^{-1}K(0)\sigma_o^2$, where $\sigma_o^2 = E(\epsilon_t^2)$. Hence, $W_n - EW_n = n^{-2}\sum\sum_{s<t}2W_{nts} + (nb_n^d)^{-1}K(0)n^{-1}\sum_t(\epsilon_t^2 - \sigma_o^2) = n^{-2}\sum\sum_{s<t}2W_{nts} + O_P(n^{-3/2}b_n^{-d})$ by Chebyshev's inequality given Assumptions F.2(a, c) with $\delta = 2$. Put $a_n = nb_n^{d/2}$. Then $a_n(W_n - EW_n) = n^{-1}b_n^{d/2}\sum\sum_{s<t}2W_{nts} + o_P(1)$ given $nb_n^d \to \infty$. Therefore, to show $a_n(W_n - EW_n) \to^d N(0,1)$, it suffices to show $U_n \to^d N(0,1)$, where $U_n = \sum\sum_{s<t}U_{nts}$, $U_{nts} = 2n^{-1}b_n^{d/2}W_{nts}$. Because $E(U_{nts}|Z_t) = E(U_{nts}|Z_s) = 0$ for $t \neq s$, U_n is a degenerate second order U-statistic. de Jong's (1987) CLT for generalized forms then applies. By de Jong (1987, proposition 3.2), it suffices for $J_n^{-1/2}U_n \to^d N(0,1)$ that $G_{ni}/J_n^2 = o(1)$ for $i = 1, 2, 4$, where G_{ni} and J_n are defined as follows. Put $K_n^{ts} = K_n(X_t - X_s)$. Then, by change of variable, it is straightforward to compute that:

$$J_n = \text{var}(U_n) = \sum\sum_{s<t}EU_{nts}^2$$
$$= (1 - n^{-1})2b_n^d E(\epsilon_1^2\epsilon_2^2(K_n^{12})^2)$$
$$= 2C(K)E(\sigma_o^4(X)p_o(X))(1 + o(1))$$
$$= J_o(K)(1 + o(1));$$

$$G_{n1} = \sum\sum_{s<t}EU_{nts}^4 \leq 8n^{-2}b_n^{2d}E(\epsilon_1^4\epsilon_2^4(K_n^{12})^4)$$
$$\leq \Delta^2 n^{-2}b_n^{2d}E(K_n^{12})^4$$
$$= \Delta^2 n^{-2}b_n^{-d}(\int_T K^4(v)dv)E(p_o(X))(1 + o(1));$$

$$G_{n2} = \sum\sum\sum_{s<t<j}E[U_{nts}^2U_{ntj}^2]$$
$$\leq 16n^{-1}b_n^{2d}E[\epsilon_1^2\epsilon_2^2(K_n^{12})^2\epsilon_1^2\epsilon_3^2(K_n^{13})^2]$$
$$\leq \Delta^2 n^{-1}b_n^{2d}E[(K_n^{12})^2(K_n^{13})^2]$$
$$= \Delta^2 n^{-1}C^2(K)E(p_o^2(X))(1 + o(1));$$

$$G_{n4} = \sum\sum\sum\sum_{i<j<s<t}[E(U_{nij}U_{nis}U_{ntj}U_{nts})$$
$$+ E(U_{nij}U_{nit}U_{nsj}U_{nst}) + E(U_{nis}U_{nit}U_{njs}U_{njt})]$$
$$\leq b_n^{2d}E(\epsilon_1^2\epsilon_2^2\epsilon_3^2\epsilon_4^2 K_n^{12}K_n^{13}K_n^{42}K_n^{43})$$
$$\leq \Delta^2 b_n^{2d}E(K_n^{12}K_n^{13}K_n^{42}K_n^{43})$$
$$= \Delta^2 b_n^d(\int_T K(v)K(v+w)K(w)dvdw)E(p_o^3(X))(1 + o(1)).$$

It follows that $G_{ni}/J_n^2 = o(1)$ for $i = 1, 2, 4$ given $nb_n^d \to \infty$, $b_n \to 0$. Hence, $J_o(K)^{-1/2}U_n \to^d N(0,1)$, and therefore $J_o(K)^{-1/2}nb_n^{d/2}(W_n - EW_n) \to^d N(0,1)$. ∎

Proof of Proposition 4.6. Put $\hat{v}_{nt} = \mu_o(X_t) - \hat{\mu}_n(X_t)$ and $\hat{S}_n = 2n^{-2}\sum\sum_{s<t}\hat{\epsilon}_{nt}^2\hat{\epsilon}_{ns}^2 K_n^{ts}$,

where $K_n^{ts} = K_n(X_t - X_s)$. Then $\hat{J}_n = 2C(K)\hat{S}_n$. Straightforward but tedious algebra delivers that:

$$
\begin{aligned}
\hat{S}_n &= 2n^{-2}\sum\sum_{s<t}\epsilon_t^2\epsilon_t^2 K_n^{ts} \\
&\quad + n^{-2}\sum\sum_{s<t}(8\epsilon_t^2\epsilon_s\hat{v}_{ns} + 4\epsilon_t^2\hat{v}_{ns}^2 + 8\epsilon_t\epsilon_s\hat{v}_{nt}\hat{v}_{ns} + 8\epsilon_t\hat{v}_{nt}\hat{v}_{ns}^2 + 2\hat{v}_{nt}^2\hat{v}_{ns}^2)K_n^{ts}, \\
&= \tilde{S}_n + 8A_{1n} + 4A_{2n} + 8A_{3n} + 8A_{4n} + 2A_{5n}, \text{ say} \\
&= \tilde{S}_n + o_P(1),
\end{aligned}
$$

where $A_{jn} = o_P(1)$, $j = 1, ..., 5$, by straightforward but tedious algebra. For example, $A_{2n} \le \Delta b_n^{-d}(n^{-1}\sum_t\epsilon_t^2)(n^{-1}\sum_s\hat{v}_{ns}^2) = O_P(n^{-1}b_n^{-2d} + b_n^{2k-d}) = o_P(1)$ given boundedness of K, $nb_n^{3d} \to \infty$, $b_n \to 0$ and $2k > d$, where we have also made use of $n^{-1}\sum_s\hat{v}_{ns}^2 = O_P(n^{-1}b_n^{-d} + b_n^{2k})$.

Next, we show $\tilde{S}_n = E(\sigma_o^4(X)p_o(X)) + o_P(1)$. Since $E[\epsilon_1^2\epsilon_2^2(K_n^{12})^2] = O(b_n^{-d}) = o(n)$ given $nb_n^d \to \infty$, it follows by Powell $et\ al.$ (1989, lemma 3.1) that:

$$
\tilde{S}_n = S_n^o + 2n^{-1}\sum_{t=1}^n[\epsilon_t^2\int_{\mathbb{X}}\sigma_o^2(x)K_n(X_t - x)p_o(x)dx - S_n^o] + o_P(n^{-1/2}),
$$

where $S_n^o = b_n^d E[\epsilon_1^2\epsilon_2^2 K_n^{12}]$. Furthermore, by Chebyshev's inequality, $\sum_{t=1}^n[\epsilon_t^2\int_{\mathbb{X}}\sigma_o^2(x)K_n(X_t - x)p_o(x)dx - S_n^o] = O_P(n^{-1/2})$ given Assumptions F.1 (with $\delta = 2$) and F.2. It follows that $\tilde{S}_n = S_n^o + O_P(n^{-1/2})$; on the other hand, $S_n^o = E(\sigma_o^4(X_t)p_o(X_t)) + o(1)$ by continuity of σ_o^2 and p_o. Since $\hat{J}_n = 2C(K)\hat{S}_n$, we have $\hat{J}_n = J_o + o_P(1)$. ∎

Proof of Theorem 4.7. We first verify that (4.3) is degenerate under H_o^*: noting $f(X_t, \alpha_o) = \mu_o(X_t)$ and $\epsilon_t = Y_t - f(X_t, \alpha_o)$, we have $m_t(\alpha_o, \theta_o, \pi) = (r_o(X_t) - p_o(X)f(X_t, \alpha_o))\epsilon_t = 0$ a.s., $\nabla'_\alpha \bar{m}_n(\alpha_o, \theta_o, \pi) = E[-\nabla'_\alpha f(X_t, \alpha_o)(r_o(X_t) - p_o(X_t)f(X_t, \alpha_o) + \epsilon_t)] = 0$, and $\delta \bar{m}_n^o(\theta - \theta_o; \pi) = E\{[(r(X_t) - r_o(X_t)) - (p(X_t) - p_o(X_t))f(X_t, \alpha_o)]\epsilon_t\} = 0$ for all $\theta = (r, p) \in \Theta = \mathcal{W}_{\infty,r}^r(\mathbb{X}) \times \mathcal{W}_{\infty,r}^r(\mathbb{X})$. It follows by Definition 2.4 that (4.3) is a_n-degenerate at γ_o under H_o^* for any given sequence a_n. Theorem 2.5 is applicable. (i) We first show asymptotic normality: Assumption A.1 is ensured by F.1; Assumption A.2 holds with $(\Theta, \rho_\Theta) = (\mathcal{W}_{\infty,r}^r(\mathbb{X}) \times \mathcal{W}_{\infty,r}^r(\mathbb{X}), \rho)$, where $\rho(\theta, \theta') = \rho_\infty(\mu, \mu') + \rho_\infty(p, p')$. Assumption A.3 is null because π does not appear. Given Assumption F.6, (4.3) is twice differentiable a.s. on $\mathbb{A}$, with $\|\nabla_\alpha^2 m_t(\alpha, \theta, \pi)\| = \|[r(X_t) + p(X_t)Y_t - 2p(X_t)f(X_t, \alpha)] - 2p(X_t)\nabla_\alpha f(X_t, \alpha)\nabla'_\alpha f(X_t, \alpha)\|$ dominated by some integrable function. Hence, Assumption C.1(a) holds; C.1(b, c) are null since Π is null. Next, because

$$
\begin{aligned}
m_t(\alpha_o, \theta, \pi) &= m_t(\alpha_o, \theta_o, \pi) + \delta m_t(\theta - \theta_o; \alpha_o, \theta_o, \pi) \\
&= m_t(\alpha_o, \theta_o, \pi) + [(r(X_t) - r_o(X_t)) - (p(X_t) - p_o(X_t))f(X_t, \alpha_o)]\epsilon_t,
\end{aligned}
$$

Assumption C.2(a) with $\lambda = \infty$ holds; and C.2(b) holds trivially. C.3(a) is null because $\delta^2 m_t(\alpha, \theta, \pi) = 0$. In addition, since $\delta \bar{m}_n^o(\theta - \theta_o; \pi) = 0$ for all $\theta \in \Theta$ under H_o^*, we have

$$\delta \hat{m}_n^o(\hat{\theta}_n - \theta_o; \pi) - \delta \overline{m}_n^o(\hat{\theta}_n - \theta_o; \pi) + \delta^2 \overline{m}_n^o(\theta - \theta_o; \pi)$$
$$= n^{-1} \sum_t [(\hat{r}_n(X_t) - r_o(X_t)) - (\hat{p}_n(X_t) - p_o(X_t))f(X_t, \alpha_o)]\epsilon_t.$$

Put $\hat{\mu}_{nt} = \hat{\mu}_n(X_t)$, $\mu_t^o = \mu_o(X_t)$ and $K_n^{ts} = K_n(X_t - X_s)$. Substituting expressions for $\hat{r}_n$ and $\hat{p}_n$, we obtain

$$\delta \hat{m}_n^o(\hat{\theta}_n - \theta_o; \pi) = n^{-2} \sum_t \sum_s \epsilon_t (Y_s - \mu_t^o) K_n^{ts}$$
$$= n^{-2} \sum_t \sum_s \epsilon_t \epsilon_s K_n^{ts} + n^{-2} \sum_t \sum_s \epsilon_t (\mu_s^o - \mu_t^o) K_n^{ts}$$
$$= W_n + O_P(n^{-1}b_n^{1-d/2} + n^{-1/2}b_n^k)$$
$$= n^{-2} \sum_t \sum_s W_{nts} + o_P(n^{-1}b_n^{-d/2}),$$

given $nb_n^{2k+d} \to 0$, where $W_{nts} = \epsilon_t \epsilon_s K_n^{ts}$, and we have made use of

$$n^{-2} \sum_t \sum_s \epsilon_t (\mu_s^o - \mu_t^o) K_n^{ts} = O_P(n^{-1}b_n^{1-d/2} + n^{-1/2}b_n^k), \tag{A20}$$

as is shown at the end of this proof. Therefore, Assumption C.3(b) holds for $a_n = nb_n^{d/2}$; C.3(c, d) are null since Π is null. C.4 is given directly. C.5 holds with $J_n^o = J_o = 2C(K)E(\sigma_o^4(X_t)p_o(X_t))$ by Theorem 4.5. Finally, C.6(a) is ensured by Proposition 4.6; and Assumption C.6(b) with $R_n = n^{-1}b_n^{-d}K(0)\sigma_o^2$ holds because $\hat{R}_n = n^{-1}b_n^{-d}K(0)\hat{\sigma}_n^2$, and

$$\hat{\sigma}_n^2 - \sigma_o^2 = n^{-1}\sum_t (\epsilon_t^2 - \sigma_o^2) + 2n^{-1}\sum_t \epsilon_t(\hat{\mu}_{nt} - \mu_t^o) + n^{-1}\sum_t(\hat{\mu}_{nt} - \mu_t^o)^2$$
$$= O_P(n^{-1/2}) + O_P(n^{-1/2}b_n^{-d/2} + b_n^k) + O_P(n^{-1}b_n^{-d} + b_n^{2k})$$
$$= o_P(b_n^{d/2}),$$

given $nb_n^{3d} \to \infty$, $nb_n^{2k+d} \to 0$ and $2k > d$. Therefore, $M_n \to^d N(0, 1)$ by Theorem 2.5(i).

It remains to show (A20). Define $U_{nts} = (\epsilon_t(\mu_s^o - \mu_t^o) + \epsilon_s(\mu_t^o - \mu_s^o))K_n^{ts}$, and put $\hat{U}_{nts} = (U_{nts} - U_{nt} - U_{ns})$, $U_{nt} = E(U_{nts}|Z_s)$. Then we can write

$$U_n = n^{-2}\sum_t \sum_s \epsilon_t(\mu_s^o - \mu_t^o)K_n^{ts}$$
$$= n^{-2}\sum \sum_{t<s}(\epsilon_t(\mu_s^o - \mu_t^o) + \epsilon_s(\mu_t^o - \mu_s^o))K_n^{ts}$$
$$= n^{-2}\sum \sum_{t<s}\hat{U}_{nts} + 2(1 - n^{-1})n^{-1}\sum_t U_{nt}.$$

Because $E(\hat{U}_{nts}|Z_t) = E(\hat{U}_{nts}|Z_s) = 0$ and $E\hat{U}_{nts}^2 \le 2EU_{nts}^2 = O(b_n^{2-d})$, we have $var(\sum\sum_{s<t}\hat{U}_{nts}) = \sum\sum_{s<t}E\hat{U}_{nts}^2 = O(n^2b_n^{2-d})$. It follows by Chebyshev's inequality that $n^{-2}\sum\sum_{t<s}\hat{U}_{nts} = O_P(n^{-1}b_n^{1-d/2})$. Next, noting that $U_{nt} = \epsilon_t\int_{\mathbb{X}}(\mu_o(x) - \mu_o(X_t))K_n(X_t - x)p_o(x)dx$ and $E(U_{nt}^2) = O(b_n^{2k})$ given Assumptions F.1–F.3, we have $n^{-1}\sum_t U_{nt} = O_P(n^{-1/2}b_n^k)$ by Chebyshev inequality. It follows that $U_n = O_P(n^{-1}b_n^{1-d/2} + n^{-1/2}b_n^k)$. This completes the proof for asymptotic normality.

(ii) Consistency follows immediately from Theorem 2.5(ii). ∎

References

Andrews, D. W. K. (1991a), "An Empirical Process Central Limit Theorem for Dependent Nonidentically Distributed Random Variables," *Journal of Multivariate Analysis*, 38: 187–203.

Andrews, D. W. K. (1991b), "Asymptotic Normality of Series Estimators for Nonparametric and Semiparametric Regression Models," *Econometrica*, 59: 307–45.

Andrews, D. W. K. (1994), "Asymptotics for Semiparametric Econometrics Models via Stochastic Continuity," *Econometrica*, 62: 43–72.

Bahadur, R. R. (1960), "Stochastic Comparison of Tests," *Annals of Mathematical Statistics*, 31: 276–95.

Bera, A. K. and C. M. Jarque (1982), "Model Misspecification Tests: A Simultaneous Approach," *Journal of Econometrics*, 20: 59–82.

Bierens, H. J. (1990), "A Consistent Conditional Moment Test for Functional Forms," *Econometrica*, 58: 1443–58.

Billingsley, P. (1986), *Probability and Measure*, 2nd ed. New York: John Wiley.

De Jong, P. (1987), "A Central Limit Theorem for Generalized Quadratic Forms," *Probability Theory and Related Fields*, 75: 261–77.

Durbin, J. (1954), "Errors in Variables," *Review of the International Statistical Institute*, 22: 23–32.

Edmunds, D. E. and V. B. Moscatelli (1977), "Fourier Approximation and Embeddings of Sobolev Space," *Dissertationes Mathematicae*, Warsaw: Polish Scientific Publishers.

Fan, Y. and R. Gencay (1993), "Hypothesis Testing Based on Modified Nonparametric Estimation of an Affine Measure between Two Distributions," *Journal of Nonparametric Statistics*, 2: 389–403.

Gallant, A. R. (1981), "Unbiased Determination of Production Technologies," *Journal of Econometrics*, 30: 149–69.

Gallant, A. R. and G. Souza (1991), "On the Asymptotic Normality of Fourier Flexible Form Estimates," *Journal of Econometrics*, 50: 329–53.

Granger, C. W. J. (1990), "General Introduction," in C. W. J. Granger (ed.), *Modelling Economic Time Series*. Oxford: Oxford University Press, pp. 1–23.

Geweke, J. (1981a), "The Approximate Slopes of Econometric Tests," *Econometrica*, 49: 1427–42.

Geweke, J. (1981b), "A Comparison of Tests of Independence of Two Covariance Stationary Time Series," *Journal of the American Statistical Association*, 76: 363–73.

Goldstein, L. G. and K. Messer (1992), "Optimal Plug-in Estimators for Nonparametric Functional Estimation," *Annals of Statistics*, 30: 1306–28.

Hall, P. (1984), "Central Limit Theorem for Integrated Square Error of Multivariate Nonparametric Density Estimators," *Journal of Multivariate Analysis*, 14: 1–16.

Hall, P. (1988), "Estimating the Direction in Which a Data Set is Most Interesting," *Probability Theory and Related Fields*, 80: 51–77.

Hall, P. (1989), "On Polynomial-Based Projection Indices for Exploratory Projection Pursuit," *Annals of Statistics*, 17: 589–605.

Hall, P. and C. Heyde (1980), *Martingale Limit Theory and Its Application*. New York: Academic Press.

Härdle, W. and T. M. Stoker (1989), "Investigating Smooth Multiple Regression by the Method of Average Derivatives," *Journal of the American Statistical Association*, 84: 986–95.

Hausman, J. A. (1978), "Specification Tests in Econometrics," *Econometrica*, 46: 1251–72.

Hong, Y. and H. White (1991), "Consistent Specification Testing via Nonparametric Series Regression," University of California, San Diego, Department of Economics Discussion Paper.

Hong, Y. and H. White (1993), "Consistent Nonparametric Entropy-Based Testing," University of California, San Diego, Department of Economics Discussion Paper.

Hong, Y. and H. White (1995), "Consistent Specification Testing via Nonparametric Series Regression," *Econometrica*, 63, 1133–1159.

Kolmogorov, A. N. and V. M. Tihomirov (1961), "ϵ-Entropy and ϵ-Capacity of Sets in Functional Spaces," *American Mathematical Society Translations*, 2/17: 277–364.

Lavergne, P. and Q. Vuong (1996), "Nonparametric Selection of Regressors: The Nonnested Case," *Econometrica*, 64: 207–19.

Lee, B. J. (1988), "A Nonparametric Model Specification Test Using a Kernel Regression Method," University of Wisconsin, Department of Economics Doctoral Dissertation.

Mack, Y. P. and B. W. Silverman (1982), "Weak and Strong Uniform Consistency of Kernel Regression Estimates," *Zeitschrift für Wahrscheinlichkeitstheorie und Verwandte Gebiete*, 61: 405–15.

Mammen, E. (1989), "Asymptotics with Increasing Dimension for Robust Regression with Application to the Bootstrap," *Annals of Statistics*, 17: 382–400.

Mikosch, T. (1991), "Functional Limit Theorems for Random Quadratic Forms," *Stochastic Processes and Their Applications*, 37: 81–98.

Newey, W. K. (1985), "Maximum Likelihood Specification Testing and Conditional Moment Tests," *Econometrica*, 53: 1047–70.

Newey, W. K. (1991), "Uniform Convergence in Probability and Stochastic Equicontinuity," *Econometrica*, 59: 1161–67.

Newey, W. K. (1994), "Kernel Estimation of Partial Means and a General Variance Estimator," *Econometric Theory*, 10: 233–53.

Powell, J., J. Stock, and T. Stoker (1989), "Semiparametric Estimation of Index Coefficients," *Econometrica*, 57: 1403–30.

Robinson, P. M. (1987), "Asymptotically Efficient Estimation in the Presence of Heteroskedasticity of Unknown Form," *Econometrica*, 55: 875–91.

Robinson, P. M. (1988), "Root-N-Consistent Semiparametric Regression," *Econometrica*, 56: 931–54.

Robinson, P. M. (1989), "Hypothesis Testing in Nonparametric and Semiparametric Models for Econometric Time Series," *Review of Economic Studies*, 56: 511–34.

Robinson, P. M. (1991), "Consistent Nonparametric Entropy-Based Testing," *Review of Economic Studies*, 58: 437–453.

Rotar, I. V. (1973), "Some Limit Theorems for Polynomials of Second Degree," *Theory of Probability and Its Applications*, 18: 499–507.

Stinchcombe, M. and H. White (1998), "Consistent Specification Testing With Nuisance Parameters Present only under the Alternative," *Econometric Theory*, 14: 295–325.

Stoker, T. M. (1989), "Tests of Additive Derivative Constraints," *Review of Economic Studies*, 56: 535–52.

Tauchen, G. (1985), "Diagnostic Testing and Evaluation of Maximum Likelihood Models," *Journal of Econometrics*, 30: 415–443.

Whang, Y.-J. and D. W. K. Andrews (1993), "Tests of Specification for Parametric and Semiparametric Models," *Journal of Econometrics*, 57: 277–318.

White, H. (1982), "Maximum Likelihood Estimation of Misspecified Models," *Econometrica*, 50: 1–25.

White, H. (1984), *Asymptotic Theory for Econometricians*. San Diego: Academic Press.

White, H. (1987), "Specification Testing in Dynamic Models," in T. F. Bewley (ed.), *Advances in Econometrics, Fifth World Congress*, vol. 1. New York: Cambridge University Press, pp. 1–58.

White, H. (1994), *Estimation, Inference and Specification Analysis*. New York: Cambridge University Press.

White, H. and J. Wooldridge (1991), "Some Results on Sieve Estimation with Dependent Observations," in W. Barnett, J. Powell, and G. Tauchen (eds.), *Nonparametric and Semiparametric Methods in Econometrics and Statistics: Proceedings of the Fifth International Symposium in Economic Theory and Econometrics*. New York: Cambridge University Press, pp. 459–93.

Whittle, P. (1964), "On the Convergence to Normality of Quadratic Forms in Independent Variables," *Theory of Probability and Its Applications*, 9: 113–18.

Wooldridge, J. (1992), "A Test for Functional Form Against Nonparametric Alternatives," *Econometric Theory*, 8: 452–75.

Wu, D.-M. (1973), "Alternative Tests of Independence between Stochastic Regressors and Disturbances," *Econometrica*, 41: 733–50.

Yatchew, A. J. (1992), "Nonparametric Regression Tests Based on an Infinite Dimensional Least Squares Procedure," *Econometric Theory*, 8: 435–51.

Yohai, V. J. and R. A. Maronna (1979), "Asymptotic Behavior of *M*-Estimators for the Linear Model," *Annals of Statistics*, 7, 258–68.

15
Asymptotic Properties of Some Specification Tests in Linear Models with Integrated Processes

JEFFREY M. WOOLDRIDGE

1 Introduction

Much work has been done recently on analyzing ordinary least squares estimators in linear time series models when one or more of the regressors are integrated processes (that is, contain a unit root). A fairly complete asymptotic theory exists due to the work of Phillips (1986, 1987, 1988, 1991), Park and Phillips (1988, 1989), Stock (1987), Sims, Stock, and Watson (1990), Phillips and Hansen (1990), Saikkonen (1991), Stock and Watson (1993), Kitamura and Phillips (1995, 1997), and others. What has not been systematically treated is specification testing in linear models when some explanatory variables are integrated. This has not stopped researchers from applying such tests in regressions with integrated processes. For example, the book by Banerjee, Dolado, Galbraith, and Hendry (1993) contains several instances where diagnostic tests are reported after running regressions with integrated processes.

The kinds of tests I have in mind are standard tests for serial correlation, tests against non-nested alternatives, and tests for endogeneity of some of the explanatory variables. When the explanatory variables are stationary and weakly dependent, a general asymptotic theory is available. See, for example, Engle (1984), Godfrey (1988), and MacKinnon (1992). In Wooldridge (1991a) I covered a class of tests and showed that simple, regression-based statistics have asymptotic chi-square distributions under general assumptions. I also offered methods for adjusting the statistics to make them robust to violations of certain auxiliary assumptions.

The purpose of this paper is to analyze a class of specification tests in linear models when some of the regressors are integrated of order one. The kinds of specification tests allowed are not completely general: I focus on regression-based, variable addition tests where the auxiliary regressors are themselves

I would like to thank two anonymous reviewers for helpful suggestions on an earlier draft.

fitted values or residuals from a first stage estimation. While somewhat special, the setup does allow treatment of the kinds of tests mentioned above. The main result is that, under the assumption that the misspecification indicators are cointegrated with the explanatory variables in the model under H_0, standard tests—and robust versions of them—have limiting chi-square distributions.

The rest of the paper is organized as follows. Section 2 discusses some features of the null model and briefly summarizes the relevant asymptotic theory. Section 3 introduces the general specification testing setup and the key assumptions; it concludes with a general limiting distribution result. Section 4 considers various forms of the tests based on different sets of auxiliary assumptions imposed under H_0.

The emphasis in this paper is on models with $I(0)$ and $I(1)$ regressors without drift. Nevertheless, in Section 5 I show how the analysis extends to the case where some explanatory variables are either trend-stationary or $I(1)$ with drift. Section 6 contains some concluding remarks and suggests topics for future research.

2 Preliminaries

2.1 Conventions and Definitions

In the following I will use some terms that are fairly standard in the time series econometrics literature, so I just summarize the most important ones used here. First, I will use the phrases *stationary* and *integrated of order zero* $(I(0))$, interchangeably. There is some conflict in the literature on what $I(0)$ actually implies about the nature of dependence in a time series, but for current purposes the key assumption is: if a series is $I(0)$ with zero mean then it satisfies the central limit theorem (CLT). Further, if $\{(\mathbf{r}_t, u_t) : t = 1, 2, ..., \}$ is an $I(0)$ sequence where $\mathbf{r}_t$ is $1 \times Q$ with $E(\mathbf{r}_t' u_t) = \mathbf{0}$ then $\{\mathbf{r}_t' u_t\}$ is assumed to follow the CLT. Conditions under which the CLT holds for stationary, weakly dependent processes and functions of such processes are widely available; see, for example, Anderson (1971), Hall and Heyde (1980), Domowitz and White (1982), and Wooldridge and White (1988).

I will also assume that various functions of an $I(0)$ process satisfy the weak law of large numbers (WLLN). For example, $T^{-1}\sum_{t=1}^{T} u_t^2 \mathbf{r}_t' \mathbf{r}_t$ converges in probability to its expectation.

A process $\{x_t\}$ is *trend-stationary* if it can be written as:

$$x_t = \mu_0 + \mu_1 t + v_t, \qquad (2.1)$$

where $\{v_t\}$ is a zero-mean $I(0)$ process such that:

$$\omega_v^2 = \sigma_v^2 + 2\sum_{j=1}^{\infty} E(v_t v_{t-j}) > 0, \qquad (2.2)$$

where $\sigma_v^2 = E(v_t^2) > 0$. The inequality in (2.2) is needed for $\{v_t\}$ to satisfy the

CLT; it rules out degenerate situations. One could allow for additional poly-nomials in t in this definition, but in this paper I only cover the linear trend case.

A process $\{x_t\}$ is *integrated of order one*, or I(1), if it can be written as:

$$x_t = \mu + x_{t-1} + v_t \tag{2.3}$$

where $\{v_t\}$ is a zero-mean I(0) process satisfying (2.2). $\{x_t\}$ is said to be an I(1) process *without drift* if $\mu = 0$; otherwise it contains drift.

The notion of two or more I(1) series being *cointegrated* (CI) has become a central focus in time series econometrics. In the simplest case, two I(1) series without drift $\{x_{t1}\}$ and $\{x_{t2}\}$ are cointegrated if there exists some constant c_1 (necessarily different from zero) such that $\{x_{t1} - c_1 x_{t2}\}$ is I(0). If $\{\mathbf{x}_t\}$ is a $1 \times K$ vector process of I(1) variables without drift, then *no* cointegrating (CI) rela-tionships exist among the elements of $\mathbf{x}_t$ if $\{\mathbf{x}_t \mathbf{c}_1\}$ is I(1) for all $K \times 1$ vectors $\mathbf{c}_1 \neq \mathbf{0}$. See Engle and Granger (1987) and Watson (1994) for discussions of the interpretation and uses of cointegration in econometrics. For the purposes of this paper, I need a slightly more general notion of cointegration. This is given by the following definition.

Definition 1. (Cointegration in the Generalized Sense): Let $\{\mathbf{x}_t : t = 1, 2, ..., \}$ be a $1 \times K$ vector process that can contain I(0) as well as I(1) processes without drift. Partition $\mathbf{x}_t$ as $\mathbf{x}_t = (\mathbf{x}_{t1}, \mathbf{x}_{t2})$, where $\mathbf{x}_{t1}$ is $1 \times K_1$ and $\mathbf{x}_{t2}$ is $1 \times K_2$. Then $\mathbf{x}_{t1}$ is *cointegrated in the generalized sense* (hereafter, CIGS) with $\mathbf{x}_{t2}$ if there exists at least one $K_2 \times K_1$ matrix $\mathbf{A}_1$ such that

$$\mathbf{x}_{t1} - \mathbf{x}_{t2}\mathbf{A}_1 \sim I(0). \tag{2.4}$$

There are several points worth making about this definition. First, if $\{\mathbf{x}_{t1}\}$ is I(0) then this definition holds trivially because one can just take $\mathbf{A}_1 = \mathbf{0}$. Second, there is no presumption that $\mathbf{A}_1$ is unique; we simply require that there is one matrix such that (2.4) holds. Third, this definition is asymmetric in $\mathbf{x}_{t1}$ and $\mathbf{x}_{t2}$; it is not necessarily true that if $\mathbf{x}_{t1}$ is CIGS with $\mathbf{x}_{t2}$ then $\mathbf{x}_{t2}$ is CIGS with $\mathbf{x}_{t1}$.

If $\{\mathbf{x}_t\}$ contains either trend-stationary or I(1) variables with drift, then the same definition holds if a pair $(\mathbf{b}_1, \mathbf{A}_1)$ can be found such that

$$\mathbf{x}_{t1} - \mathbf{b}_1 t - \mathbf{x}_{t2}\mathbf{A}_1 \sim I(0), \tag{2.5}$$

where $\mathbf{b}_1$ is a $1 \times K_1$ vector.

2.2 The Model

I begin with a single equation linear model for time series data:

$$y_t = \alpha + \mathbf{x}_t \boldsymbol{\beta} + u_t, \quad t = 1, 2, ..., \tag{2.6}$$

where $\mathbf{x}_t$ is a $1 \times K$ vector that can contain both I(0) and I(1) variables without drift, α is a scalar, $\boldsymbol{\beta} \equiv (\beta_1, \beta_2, ..., \beta_K)'$ is a $K \times 1$ vector, and u_t is the un-observable error. In Section 5 I allow $\mathbf{x}_t$ to contain I(1) elements with drift as well as trend-stationary variables, but for now I rule that out. The dependent variable y_t can be either I(0) or I(1).

I assume that (2.6) is estimated by ordinary least squares (OLS); let $\hat{\alpha}$ and $\hat{\boldsymbol{\beta}}$ denote the OLS estimators from the regression y_t on 1, $\mathbf{x}_t$, $t = 1, 2, ..., $ T. As shown in Wooldridge (1991b) and Hamilton (1994, proposition 19.3), the following assumption is essential for the OLS estimators to be consistent for α and $\boldsymbol{\beta}$.

Assumption 1. $\{u_t\}$ is a zero-mean I(0) process and u_t is uncorrelated with *every* I(0) linear combination of $\mathbf{x}_t$, $t = 1, 2, ...$ ∎

As discussed in Wooldridge (1991b) and Hamilton (1994), Assumption 1 serves to identify the vector $\boldsymbol{\beta}$ along with the intercept α. When $\mathbf{x}_t$ is I(0), Assumption 1 reduces to the usual assumption for OLS to be consistent: $E(u_t) = 0$ and $E(\mathbf{x}_t'u_t) = \mathbf{0}$. When $\mathbf{x}_t$ is I(1) and there are no CI relationships among the $\mathbf{x}_t$, then Assumption 1 only requires $\{u_t\}$ to be a zero-mean I(0) process: because there are no I(0) linear combinations of $\mathbf{x}_t$ there is nothing one must assume about the relationship between $\mathbf{x}_t$ and u_t in order for OLS to consistently estimate $\boldsymbol{\beta}$, and the zero mean assumption identifies α. When $\{\mathbf{x}_t\}$ is an I(1) vector process with no CI relationships among its elements, (2.6) is the model studied extensively by Phillips and Durlauf (1986), Park and Phillips (1988, 1989), and Phillips and Hansen (1990). Kitamura and Phillips (1995, 1997) have recently studied such models under weaker assumptions.

Assumption 1 is reasonable in many other cases where $\mathbf{x}_t$ contains both I(0) and I(1) variables. For example, in the partitioned model:

$$y_t = \alpha + \mathbf{x}_{t1}\boldsymbol{\beta}_1 + \mathbf{x}_{t2}\boldsymbol{\beta}_2 + u_t, \qquad (2.7)$$

where $\{\mathbf{x}_{t1}\}$ is I(1) with no CI relationships among its elements, and $\{\mathbf{x}_{t2}\}$ is I(0), Assumption 1 is satisfied when $E(u_t) = 0$ and $E(\mathbf{x}_{t2}'u_t) = \mathbf{0}$, but where the relationship between $\mathbf{x}_{t1}$ and u_t is unrestricted.

In the AR(P) model,

$$y_t = \alpha + \beta_1 y_{t-1} + ... + \beta_P y_{t-P} + u_t, \qquad (2.8)$$
$$E(u_t | y_{t-1}, y_{t-2}, ...) = 0, \qquad (2.9)$$

it follows from (2.9) that u_t is uncorrelated with all I(0) linear combinations of $(y_{t-1}, y_{t-2}, ...)$, even if $\{y_t\}$ is an integrated process (in which case the β_j sum to unity). In the distributed lag model,

$$y_t = \alpha + \beta_0 z_t + \beta_1 z_{t-1} + ... + \beta_G z_{t-G} + u_t, \qquad (2.10)$$
$$E(u_t | z_t, z_{t-1}, ...) = 0, \qquad (2.11)$$

u_t is again uncorrelated with all I(0) linear combinations of $(z_t, z_{t-1}, ...)$, even if $\{z_t\}$ is an integrated process. This is true even if $\{u_t\}$ is not a martingale difference sequence with respect to the information sets $\{z_t, y_{t-1}, z_{t-1}, ...\}$. Assumption 1 also holds for error correction models. For example, if

$$\Delta y_t = \alpha + \beta_1 \Delta y_{t-1} + \beta_2 \Delta z_{t-1} + \beta_3 (y_{t-1} - \delta_1 z_{t-1}) + u_t, \tag{2.12}$$
$$E(u_t | y_{t-1}, z_{t-1}, y_{t-2}, z_{t-2}, ...) = 0, \tag{2.13}$$

where $\{y_t\}$ and $\{z_t\}$ are I(1) without drift and $\{y_t - \delta_1 z_t\}$ is I(0), then (2.13) implies that u_t is uncorrelated with all I(0) linear combinations of $\{y_{t-1}, z_{t-1}, y_{t-2}, z_{t-2}, ...\}$; in particular, u_t is uncorrelated with $\Delta y_{t-1}, \Delta z_{t-1}$, and the error correction term, $(y_{t-1} - \delta_1 z_{t-1})$.

While Assumption 1 is satisfied for many models, it is not for free. It can fail if some I(0) elements of $\mathbf{x}_t$ are correlated with u_t—such as in (2.7) when $E(\mathbf{x}'_{t2} u_t) \neq \mathbf{0}$—or when some I(0) linear combination of I(1) elements of $\mathbf{x}_t$ is correlated with u_t. For example, if x_{t1} and x_{t2} are each I(1), but $x_{t1} - x_{t2}$ is I(0) and correlated with u_t, then Assumption 1 fails. I will not cover estimation techniques, such as instrumental variables, that can be used when Assumption 1 fails. I do cover a test for endogeneity of elements of $\mathbf{x}_t$ as one of the specification testing examples.

2.3 Some Asymptotic Distribution Results

In order to derive the limiting distribution of the specification test statistics, I draw on some convergence results for unit root processes from the literature. The following definition is fundamental.

Definition 2. (Functional Central Limit Theorem): Let $\{\mathbf{w}_t : t = 1, 2, ...\}$ be an $M \times 1$ I(0) process such that

(a) $E(\mathbf{w}'_t \mathbf{w}_t) < \infty$

(b) $E(\mathbf{w}_t) = \mathbf{0}$

(c) $\mathbf{\Omega} \equiv \lim_{T \to \infty} \text{Var}(T^{-1/2} \sum_{t=1}^{T} \mathbf{w}_t)$ exists.

Then $\{\mathbf{w}_t\}$ is said to satisfy the *functional central limit theorem* (FCLT) if the stochastic process $\{B_T : T = 1, 2, ...\}$, defined by

$$B_T(r) \equiv T^{-1/2} \sum_{t=1}^{[Tr]} \mathbf{w}_t, \quad 0 \leq r \leq 1,$$

converges in distribution to $\mathcal{BM}(\mathbf{\Omega})$, an M-dimensional Brownian motion with covariance matrix $\mathbf{\Omega}$. Here, [Tr] denotes the integer part of Tr. ∎

The use of the FCLT to obtain limiting distribution results for OLS estimators was pioneered by Phillips (1986, 1987) in univariate contexts. The multivariate FCLT was first used in econometric applications by Phillips and Durlauf (1986). The FCLT is known to hold under conditions analogous to the CLT; for recent, fairly general, results see Phillips and Durlauf (1986), Phillips (1988), and Wooldridge and White (1988). For background material on the kind of convergence referred to in Definition 1 the reader is referred to Billingsley (1968).

The following lemma is very useful for analyzing least squares estimators with I(1) processes. Parts (i) to (iv) were proven by Park and Phillips (1988) and follow directly from the FCLT. Conditions under which (v) holds are given in Hansen (1992).

Lemma 1. Let $\{\mathbf{w}_t \equiv (\mathbf{u}_t', \mathbf{v}_t')'\}$ be an $M \times 1$ zero-mean I(0) process, where $\mathbf{u}_t$ is $M_1 \times 1$ and $\mathbf{v}_t$ is $M_2 \times 1$. Define

$$\mathbf{\Sigma} = E(\mathbf{w}_t \mathbf{w}_t'), \quad \mathbf{\Lambda} = \sum_{s=1}^{\infty} E(\mathbf{w}_t \mathbf{w}_{t-s}'),$$

and

$$\mathbf{\Omega} = \mathbf{\Sigma} + \mathbf{\Lambda} + \mathbf{\Lambda}' \equiv \lim_{T \to \infty} \operatorname{var}\left(T^{-1/2} \sum_{t=1}^{T} \mathbf{w}_t\right) \equiv \begin{pmatrix} \mathbf{\Omega}_{11} & \mathbf{\Omega}_{21}' \\ \mathbf{\Omega}_{21} & \mathbf{\Omega}_{22} \end{pmatrix}.$$

Note that

$$\mathbf{\Sigma}_{21} = E(\mathbf{v}_t \mathbf{u}_t'), \quad \mathbf{\Lambda}_{21} = \sum_{s=1}^{\infty} E(\mathbf{v}_t \mathbf{u}_{t-s}'),$$

and

$$\mathbf{\Delta}_{21} = \mathbf{\Sigma}_{21} + \mathbf{\Lambda}_{21}.$$

Assume that $\mathbf{\Omega}_{11}$ and $\mathbf{\Omega}_{22}$ are positive definite. Define $\mathbf{x}_t = \mathbf{x}_{t-1} + \mathbf{v}_t$, where $\mathbf{x}_0$ is any random vector. Let $\mathcal{B}$ denote a Brownian motion with covariance matrix $\mathbf{\Omega}$, and partition $\mathcal{B}$ as $\mathcal{B} \equiv (\mathcal{B}_1', \mathcal{B}_2')'$. Then, under additional regularity conditions, the following hold jointly as well as separately:

(i) $T^{-3/2}\sum_{t=1}^{T}\mathbf{x}_t \xrightarrow{d} \int_0^1 \mathcal{B}_2(r)\,dr$

(ii) $T^{-5/2}\sum_{t=1}^{T}t\mathbf{x}_t \xrightarrow{d} \int_0^1 r\mathcal{B}_2(r)\,dr$

(iii) $T^{-2}\sum_{t=1}^{T}\mathbf{x}_t\mathbf{x}_t' \xrightarrow{d} \int_0^1 \mathcal{B}_2(r)\mathcal{B}_2(r)'\,dr$

(iv) $T^{-3/2}\sum_{t=1}^{T}t\mathbf{u}_t \xrightarrow{d} \int_0^1 r\,d\mathcal{B}_1(r)$

(v) $T^{-1}\sum_{t=1}^{T}\mathbf{x}_t\mathbf{u}_t' \xrightarrow{d} \int_0^1 \mathcal{B}_2(r)\,d\mathcal{B}_1(r)' + \mathbf{\Delta}_{21}.$ ∎

Variations on this lemma have been used extensively to study the limiting distribution of the OLS estimator in models with integrated processes; see, for example, Park and Phillips (1988, 1989), Phillips (1988), Wooldridge (1991b, 1994), and Watson (1994). It underlies the asymptotic derivations for the specification tests in this paper.

3 A General Framework for Specification Testing

I now turn to a general framework for variable additions tests in model (2.6) under Assumption 1. The implicit null hypothesis defined below determines the alternatives against which the tests have power. Below I give several examples to illustrate how one uses the framework to analyze popular specification tests.

The initial variable addition tests I study involve regressing the OLS residuals $\hat{u}_t$, estimated under the null, onto all of the explanatory variables $(1, \mathbf{x}_t)$ and an additional variable or vector of variables. These "auxiliary regressors," which I also refer to as "misspecification indicators," can be chosen in a variety of ways depending on the kind of misspecification one is interested in. A general class of tests can be studied as follows. Let $\hat{\mathbf{a}}_t = \mathbf{q}_t\hat{\boldsymbol{\Psi}}$ denote the $1 \times Q$ vector of misspecification indicators, where the $1 \times G$ vector $\mathbf{q}_t$ can contain both I(0) and I(1) variables without drift satisfying arbitrary cointegrating relationships, and the $G \times Q$ matrix $\hat{\boldsymbol{\Psi}}$ is a matrix of estimators. I explicitly allow the misspecification indicators to be estimated in a preliminary stage to allow for a broader class of specification tests. However, I assume that the $\hat{\mathbf{a}}_t$ have a specific representation in terms of I(1) and I(0) processes.

Assumption 2. For $t = 1, 2, ..., \mathrm{T}$, $\hat{\mathbf{a}}_t = \mathbf{q}_{t1}\hat{\boldsymbol{\Psi}}_1 + \mathbf{q}_{t2}\hat{\boldsymbol{\Psi}}_2$, where $\mathbf{q}_{t1}$ is a $1 \times G_1$ vector of I(1) variables containing no CI relationships among its elements, $\mathbf{q}_{t2}$ is a $1 \times G_2$ vector of I(0) variables, $T(\hat{\boldsymbol{\Psi}}_1 - \boldsymbol{\Psi}_1) = O_p(1)$ where $\boldsymbol{\Psi}_1$ is a $G_1 \times Q$ nonrandom matrix, and $\sqrt{T}(\hat{\boldsymbol{\Psi}}_2 - \boldsymbol{\Psi}_2) = O_p(1)$ where $\boldsymbol{\Psi}_2$ is a $G_2 \times Q$ nonrandom matrix. ∎

Assumption 2 holds trivially in the case where $\hat{\mathbf{a}}_t = \mathbf{a}_t \equiv \mathbf{q}_{t1}\boldsymbol{\Psi}_1 + \mathbf{q}_{t2}\boldsymbol{\Psi}_2$ and $\{\mathbf{q}_{t1}\}$ and $\{\mathbf{q}_{t2}\}$ are as in Assumption 2. In other words, the misspecification indicator is a fixed linear combination of I(1) and I(0) processes. Moreover, Assumption 2 holds whenever the $\hat{\mathbf{a}}_t$ are fitted values or residuals from an OLS regression involving I(1) and I(0) processes (as the dependent or independent variables). This is because fitted values and residuals are invariant to nonsingular transformations: if $\hat{\mathbf{a}}_t = \mathbf{q}_t\hat{\boldsymbol{\Psi}}$ are fitted values or residuals (or both), where $\{\mathbf{q}_t\}$ is a $1 \times G$ vector process containing I(1) and I(0) variables, we can always express $\hat{\mathbf{a}}_t$ as in Assumption 2. From a practical perspective it is important that we do not actually have to find a suitable partition of $\mathbf{q}_t$ into $\mathbf{q}_{t1}$ and $\mathbf{q}_{t2}$; we just need to know one exists.

To show that Assumption 2 allows for several situations of interest, I now introduce three examples. The statistic that is available under "ideal" assumptions, which are discussed in Section 4, is obtained as TR_u^2 from the regression

$$\hat{u}_t \text{ on } 1, \mathbf{x}_t, \hat{\mathbf{a}}_t, \quad t = 1, 2, ..., T, \tag{3.1}$$

where $\hat{u}_t$ are the OLS residuals and R_u^2 is the usual R-squared from (3.1). By appropriately choosing $\hat{\mathbf{a}}_t$ we can treat many tests in the literature. A standard omitted variables test is obtained by choosing $\mathbf{a}_t = \mathbf{q}_t$, where $\mathbf{q}_t$ is the set of variables hypothesized not to appear in the model under H_0. For example, in the AR(P) model, $\mathbf{q}_t$ can contain Q additional lags of y_t; in the distributed lag model, $\mathbf{q}_t$ can contain additional lags of z_t. Some other important examples follow.

Example 1. (Testing for Serial Correlation): The test for AR(P) serial correlation tests $E(u_t u_{t-j}) = 0$, $j = 1, 2, ..., P$. This is obtained by setting $\hat{\mathbf{a}}_t = (\hat{u}_{t-1}, \hat{u}_{t-2}, ..., \hat{u}_{t-P})$ (and probably using $(T - P)R_u^2$ in place of TR_u^2). Engle (1984) and Godfrey (1988) cover the I(0) case. The setting here allows explicitly for random, I(1) as well as I(0) explanatory variables. ∎

Example 2. (Testing Against a Nonnested Alternative): Consider testing the model

$$y_t = \alpha + \mathbf{x}_t \boldsymbol{\beta} + u_t \tag{3.2}$$

against the alternative

$$y_t = \gamma + \mathbf{z}_t \boldsymbol{\delta} + v_t. \tag{3.3}$$

The elements in $\mathbf{x}_t$ and $\mathbf{z}_t$ can contain lags of y_t or lags of other explanatory variables. In the case where all variables—including $\mathbf{z}_t$—are I(0), what is usually intended is a test of $H_0 : E(y_t|\mathbf{x}_t, \mathbf{z}_t) = E(y_t|\mathbf{x}_t) = \alpha + \mathbf{x}_t\beta$ against $H_1 : E(y_t|\mathbf{x}_t, \mathbf{z}_t) = E(y_t|\mathbf{z}_t) = \gamma + \mathbf{z}_t\delta$. This is often reasonable in the more general case where both $\mathbf{x}_t$ and $\mathbf{z}_t$ contain I(1) elements. But popular tests against nonnested hypotheses take the null to be weaker than that. For linear models the Davidson–MacKinnon (1981) test looks for correlation between the OLS residuals $\{\hat{u}_t\}$ from (3.2) and the fitted values $\{\hat{\gamma} + \mathbf{z}_t\hat{\boldsymbol{\delta}}\}$ from the alternative model (3.3). In other words, the misspecification indicator is $\hat{a}_t = \hat{\gamma} + \mathbf{z}_t\hat{\boldsymbol{\delta}}$. ∎

Example 3. (Testing for Endogeneity): Consider the model (2.6) with x_{t1}—which can be either I(0) or I(1)—a potentially "endogenous" variable:

$$y_t = \alpha + \beta_1 x_{t1} + ... + \beta_K x_{tK} + u_t \tag{3.4}$$
$$x_{t1} = \gamma + \delta_2 x_{t2} + ... + \delta_K x_{tK} + \mathbf{z}_t \boldsymbol{\gamma}_2 + v_t. \tag{3.5}$$

Endogeneity here is defined as correlation between v_t and u_t. The maintained assumptions are that u_t and v_t are I(0) with zero means and each is uncorrelated with all I(0) linear combinations of $(x_{t2}, ..., x_{tK}, \mathbf{z}_t)$, where $\mathbf{z}_t$ is a set of either I(0) or I(1) additional "instruments." (This is the appropriate sense in which $x_{t2}, ..., x_{tK}, \mathbf{z}_t$ are "exogenous" when some of these may be I(1).) Unlike in the case where all variables are I(0), correlation between u_t and v_t need not affect the ability of OLS to consistently estimate the coefficients in (3.4)—for example, if the x_{tj} are all I(1) and there are no CI relationships among them—but sometimes it will. Validity of the test requires that $\boldsymbol{\gamma}_2 \neq \mathbf{0}$, that is, there are some additional variables in (3.5) not in (3.4). The misspecification indicator is $\hat{a}_t = \hat{v}_t$, the OLS residual from the first stage regression of x_{t1} onto $(1, x_{t2}, ..., x_{tK}, \mathbf{z}_t)$. This is analogous to Hausman (1978). ∎

The next assumption restricts the behavior of the misspecification indicator relative to $\mathbf{x}_t$. This is the crucial assumption for the test statistics to have limiting chi-square distributions. As I will show, it holds in many cases. In stating the assumption, recall that $\boldsymbol{\Psi} \equiv \text{plim } \hat{\boldsymbol{\Psi}}$ and $\mathbf{a}_t \equiv \mathbf{q}_t\boldsymbol{\Psi}$.

Assumption 3. $\{\mathbf{a}_t\}$ is cointegrated with $\{\mathbf{x}_t\}$ in the generalized sense. ∎

By the definition of CIGS, Assumption 3 holds automatically when $\{\mathbf{a}_t\}$ is I(0). This is the case in Example 1 under the assumption that $\{u_t\}$ is I(0), since $\mathbf{a}_t = (u_{t-1}, u_{t-2}, ..., u_{t-P})$. It is also true in Example 3 under the assumption that $\{v_t\}$ is I(0). In Example 2, $\{a_t \equiv \gamma + \mathbf{z}_t\boldsymbol{\delta}\}$ is not I(0) if $\{y_t\}$ is I(1). (Here $(\gamma, \boldsymbol{\delta})$ are the plims of the OLS estimators $\hat{\gamma}$, $\hat{\boldsymbol{\delta}}$ under H_0.) If $\{y_t\}$ is I(1) then $\{\mathbf{x}_t\boldsymbol{\beta}\}$ must be I(1), since Assumption 1 is maintained (that is, $\{u_t\}$ is I(0)). Any sensible competing model (3.3) should have at least some elements of $\mathbf{z}_t$ which are I(1). Assuming that y_t is CIGS with $\mathbf{z}_t$ whether or not H_0 holds, $\{\mathbf{z}_t\boldsymbol{\delta}\}$ is I(1). It is natural to assume that $\mathbf{z}_t\boldsymbol{\delta}$ *is* CIGS with $\mathbf{x}_t$, in which case Assumption 3 holds. This must be the case if x_t and z_t are each scalars and each is cointegrated with y_t. For example, if the competing models are $H_0 : E(y_t|y_{t-1}, z_{t-1}) = \alpha + \beta y_{t-1}$ and $H_1 : E(y_t|y_{t-1}, z_{t-1}) = \gamma + \delta z_{t-1}$, then Assumption 3 holds when y_t and z_t are cointegrated, which is necessary for H_1 to be a competitor to H_0.

Assumption 3 also holds when testing for additional lags of either y_t in (2.8) or z_t in (2.10), even when $\{y_t\}$ and $\{z_t\}$ are I(1), assuming that at least some lags appear in the null model. For example, y_{t-2} is always CIGS with y_{t-1} whether $\{y_t\}$ is I(0) or I(1).

So far, we have relied on intuition and examples in stating the null hypothesis for the specification tests. What the regression (3.1) tests is the asymptotic orthogonality condition

$$\operatorname*{plim}_{T \to \infty} T^{-1} \sum_{t=1}^{T} \hat{\mathbf{a}}_t' \hat{u}_t = \mathbf{0}.$$

When $\{\mathbf{a}_t\}$ is I(0), it is useful to think of this as the sample analog of $E(\mathbf{a}_t' u_t) = \mathbf{0}$. Under the more general Assumption 3, it is more informative to express the null in a different fashion. Define $\mathbf{r}_t \equiv \mathbf{a}_t - \boldsymbol{\theta}_0 - \mathbf{x}_t\boldsymbol{\Theta}$ as the population residuals in the CIGS relationship between $\mathbf{a}_t$ and $\mathbf{x}_t$, so that $\{\mathbf{r}_t\}$ is I(0) under Assumption 3. These population residuals are always well-defined even though the cointegrating parameters might not be unique, as discussed in Wooldridge (1991b). As with variable addition tests when all variables are stationary, the effective null hypothesis is

$$H_0 : E(\mathbf{r}_t' u_t) = \mathbf{0}. \tag{3.6}$$

The covariance in (3.6) is well-defined under Assumption 3 because $\mathbf{r}_t$ is I(0), whereas $E(\mathbf{a}_t' u_t)$ might not even be well-defined when $\{\mathbf{a}_t\}$ contains I(1) elements. In fact, for deriving the asymptotic distribution of the statistics, it is useful to look at the sample analog of (3.6). Let $\hat{\mathbf{r}}_t$ be the $1 \times Q$ residuals for observation t from the multivariate OLS regression:

$$\hat{\mathbf{a}}_t \text{ on } 1, \mathbf{x}_t, \ t = 1, 2, ..., T. \tag{3.7}$$

Then a test of (3.6) is based on the limiting distribution of

$$T^{-1/2}\sum_{t=1}^{T}\hat{\mathbf{r}}_t'\hat{u}_t. \tag{3.8}$$

Because $\sum_{t=1}^{T}\hat{\mathbf{r}}_t'\hat{u}_t = \sum_{t=1}^{T}\hat{\mathbf{a}}_t'\hat{u}_t$, (3.8) is the same sample orthogonality condition. However, the following theorem shows that (3.8) has a standard asymptotic normal distribution.

Theorem 1. Under Assumptions 1, 2, and 3, the null hypothesis (3.6), and standard regularity conditions, the following asymptotic equivalence holds:

$$T^{-1/2}\sum_{t=1}^{T}\hat{\mathbf{a}}_t'\hat{u}_t = T^{-1/2}\sum_{t=1}^{T}\hat{\mathbf{r}}_t'\hat{u}_t = T^{-1/2}\sum_{t=1}^{T}\mathbf{r}_t'u_t + o_p(1). \tag{3.9}$$

Proof. I prove this for the case where $\alpha = 0$ (and is not estimated) and where any I(0) elements in $\mathbf{x}_t$ and $\mathbf{q}_t$ have zero mean; the general case is quite similar but notationally more cumbersome. First, note that $\hat{\mathbf{r}}_t = \hat{\mathbf{a}}_t - \mathbf{x}_t\hat{\boldsymbol{\Theta}}$, where $\hat{\boldsymbol{\Theta}}$ is the $K \times Q$ matrix of OLS coefficients from the regression $\hat{\mathbf{a}}_t$ on $\mathbf{x}_t$. Therefore,

$$\sum_{t=1}^{T}\hat{\mathbf{r}}_t'\hat{u}_t = \sum_{t=1}^{T}(\hat{\mathbf{a}}_t - \mathbf{x}_t\hat{\boldsymbol{\Theta}})'\hat{u}_t = \sum_{t=1}^{T}(\hat{\mathbf{a}}_t - \mathbf{x}_t\boldsymbol{\Theta})'\hat{u}_t$$

because $\sum_{t=1}^{T}\mathbf{x}_t'\hat{u}_t \equiv \mathbf{0}$. Now, under Assumption 2, we can write $\hat{\mathbf{a}}_t = \mathbf{q}_{t1}\hat{\boldsymbol{\Psi}}_1 + \mathbf{q}_{t2}\hat{\boldsymbol{\Psi}}_2$, where $\mathbf{q}_{t1}$, $\mathbf{q}_{t2}$, $\hat{\boldsymbol{\Psi}}_1$, and $\hat{\boldsymbol{\Psi}}_2$ satisfy the conditions in Assumption 2. Similarly, one can write $\hat{u}_t = y_t - \mathbf{x}_{t1}\hat{\boldsymbol{\beta}}_1 - \mathbf{x}_{t2}\hat{\boldsymbol{\beta}}_2$, where $\mathbf{x}_{t1}$ is a $1 \times K_1$ vector of I(1) variables containing no CI relationships among its elements, $\mathbf{x}_{t2}$ is a $1 \times K_2$ vector of I(0) variables, $T(\hat{\boldsymbol{\beta}}_1 - \boldsymbol{\beta}_1) = O_p(1)$, and $\sqrt{T}(\hat{\boldsymbol{\beta}}_2 - \boldsymbol{\beta}_2) = O_p(1)$. Now

$$T^{-1/2}\sum_{t=1}^{T}(\hat{\mathbf{a}}_t - \mathbf{x}_t\boldsymbol{\Theta})'\hat{u}_t = T^{-1/2}\sum_{t=1}^{T}(\mathbf{a}_t - \mathbf{x}_t\boldsymbol{\Theta})'u_t$$

$$-(\hat{\boldsymbol{\Psi}} - \boldsymbol{\Psi})'T^{-1/2}\sum_{t=1}^{T}\mathbf{q}_t'u_t \tag{3.10}$$

$$-(\hat{\boldsymbol{\Psi}} - \boldsymbol{\Psi})'T^{-1/2}\sum_{t=1}^{T}\mathbf{q}_t'\mathbf{x}_t(\hat{\boldsymbol{\beta}} - \boldsymbol{\beta}).$$

Along with the convergence rates of the parameters, the results of Lemma 1—in particular $T^{-1}\sum_{t=1}^{T}\mathbf{q}_{t1}'u_t = O_p(1)$, $T^{-1/2}\sum_{t=1}^{T}\mathbf{q}_{t2}'u_t = O_p(1)$, $T^{-2}\sum_{t=1}^{T}\mathbf{q}_{t1}'\mathbf{x}_{t1} = O_p(1)$, $T^{-1}\sum_{t=1}^{T}\mathbf{q}_{t1}'\mathbf{x}_{t2} = O_p(1)$, $T^{-1}\sum_{t=1}^{T}\mathbf{q}_{t2}'\mathbf{x}_{t1} = O_p(1)$, and $T^{-1}\sum_{t=1}^{T}\mathbf{q}_{t2}'\mathbf{x}_{t2} = O_p(1)$—it follows that the last two terms in (3.10) are $o_p(1)$. But then

$$T^{-1/2}\sum_{t=1}^{T}\hat{\mathbf{r}}_t'\hat{u}_t = T^{-1/2}\sum_{t=1}^{T}(\mathbf{a}_t - \mathbf{x}_t\boldsymbol{\Theta})'u_t + o_p(1),$$

which is just (3.9). ∎

Given Theorem 1, the rest of the analysis is fairly straightforward. Because $\{\mathbf{r}_t' u_t : t = 1, 2, ...\}$ is a stationary, mean-zero, weakly dependent process, it satisfies the CLT under very general weak dependence conditions. Thus, $T^{-1/2}\sum_{t=1}^{T}\mathbf{r}_t' u_t$ has an asymptotic normal distribution, and (3.9) shows that the same limiting distribution results when all of the unknown parameters $\boldsymbol{\Psi}$, $\boldsymbol{\Theta}$, and $\boldsymbol{\beta}$ are replaced with their estimators $\hat{\boldsymbol{\Psi}}$, $\hat{\boldsymbol{\Theta}}$, and $\hat{\boldsymbol{\beta}}$. This is a very convenient simplification because one does not need to know the limiting distributions of $\hat{\boldsymbol{\Psi}}$, $\hat{\boldsymbol{\Theta}}$, and $\hat{\boldsymbol{\beta}}$ (scaled by the proper function of the sample size) in order to obtain the limiting distribution of the test statistic.

Next, let

$$\mathbf{V} \equiv \operatorname*{var}_{T \to \infty}\left(T^{-1/2}\sum_{t=1}^{T}\mathbf{r}_t' u_t\right)$$

be the *long-run variance* of $\{\mathbf{r}_t' u_t\}$, so that $T^{-1/2}\sum_{t=1}^{T}\hat{\mathbf{r}}_t' \hat{u}_t \overset{a}{\sim} \text{Normal}(\mathbf{0}, \mathbf{V})$ under Assumptions 1, 2, 3 and the null hypothesis (3.6). Assuming that $\text{rank}(\mathbf{V}) = Q$—so that Q nonredundant restrictions are being tested—and letting $\hat{\mathbf{V}}$ be a consistent estimator of $\mathbf{V}$,

$$\left(T^{-1/2}\sum_{t=1}^{T}\hat{\mathbf{r}}_t' \hat{u}_t\right)' \hat{\mathbf{V}}^{-1}\left(T^{-1/2}\sum_{t=1}^{T}\hat{\mathbf{r}}_t' \hat{u}_t\right) \overset{d}{\to} \chi_Q^2. \tag{3.11}$$

The left hand side of (3.11) is the general form of the test statistic, and it has a limiting chi-square distribution under the previous assumptions. In the next section, I discuss simplifications that are available under different assumptions; this corresponds to different choices for the estimator $\hat{\mathbf{V}}$ of $\mathbf{V}$.

Recognizing that the null hypothesis is (3.6) allows us to characterize the alternatives against which the statistic in (3.11) has power. If we maintain Assumptions 1, 2, and 3 under the alternative—in particular, $\mathbf{a}_t$ is CIGS with $\mathbf{x}_t$ under the alternative—then the statistic will have asymptotic unit power whenever $E(\mathbf{r}_t' u_t) \neq \mathbf{0}$. This alternative needs to be studied on a case-by-case basis. For example, when testing for omission of y_{t-2} in a AR(1) model when $\{y_t\}$ contains a unit root, we are really testing whether Δy_{t-1} is correlated with the innovations in the AR(1) model.

In the non-nested testing example above, where $H_0 : E(y_t|y_{t-1}, z_{t-1}) = \alpha + \beta y_{t-1}$, $H_1 : E(y_t|y_{t-1}, z_{t-1}) = \gamma + \delta z_{t-1}$, and y_t and z_t are I(1) and cointegrated, we are testing whether $y_{t-1} - \eta z_{t-1}$ is correlated with $y_t - \alpha - \beta y_{t-1}$, where α and β are generally the plims of the OLS estimators and η is the cointegrating parameter. It is possible that $\{y_t\}$ follows an AR(1) model (with a unit root) but that H_1 holds. Then, we are not testing whether z_{t-1} is uncorrelated with the innovations in the AR(1) model—as this correlation need not even be well-defined—but whether an I(0) linear combination of y_{t-1} and z_{t-1} is correlated with the AR(1) innovations.

The two previous examples suggest that when a regression model contains I(1) explanatory variables, one needs to carefully study the kinds of alternatives against which a specification test has power.

4 Forms of the Test under Various Assumptions

4.1 The "Ideal" Assumptions

Regression (3.1) is familiar from the specification testing literature, and leads to computationally simple tests. However, it is valid only when some additional assumptions hold under the null hypothesis. In this section I cover those assumptions and show what they entail in each example. The first assumption rules out serial correlation in the vector process $\{\mathbf{r}'_t u_t\}$ under H_0.

Assumption 4. $\{\mathbf{r}'_t u_t : t = 1, 2, ...\}$ is serially uncorrelated. ∎

Assumption 4 is not the same as simply assuming $\{u_t : t = 1, 2, ...\}$ is serially uncorrelated. The latter assumption is sufficient only when the explanatory variable can be treated as nonrandom (or strictly exogenous). In models with explicitly random regressors—as with most time series models—Assumption 4 is the appropriate no serial correlation assumption for specification testing. Assumption 4 always holds if

$$E(u_t \,|\, \mathbf{x}_t, \mathbf{a}_t, u_{t-1}, \mathbf{x}_{t-1}, \mathbf{a}_{t-1}, u_{t-2}, ...) = 0, \tag{4.1}$$

under H_0. This is often the case, especially when one is testing for dynamic misspecification, where the null is correct dynamic specification. In Example 1, Assumption 4 holds when the null hypothesis is

$$E(u_t \,|\, \mathbf{x}_t, u_{t-1}, \mathbf{x}_{t-1}, u_{t-2}, ...) = 0, \tag{4.2}$$

Usually, this is the intended null when testing $\{u_t\}$ for serial correlation because one is really testing for dynamic misspecification in the regression function, whether one begins with (2.8), (2.10), (2.12), or some other model. For practical purposes Assumption 4 is *always* satisfied when testing explicitly for dynamic misspecification.

The other "ideal" assumption is a form of homoskedasticity in the errors. Again, this is needed only under H_0.

Assumption 5. For $\sigma_u^2 = E(u_t^2)$, $E(u_t^2 \mathbf{r}'_t \mathbf{r}_t) = \sigma_u^2 E(\mathbf{r}'_t \mathbf{r}_t)$. ∎

It is *not* enough to simply assume that $E(u_t^2)$ is constant across t, which is always the case here because of the I(0) assumption. Assumption 5 is best interpreted as a *conditional* homoskedasticity assumption. It is easy to show, using the law of iterated expectations, that Assumption 5 holds if

$$E(u_t^2 \,|\, \mathbf{r}_t) = E(u_t^2). \tag{4.3}$$

Because $\mathbf{r}_t$ is a function of $(\mathbf{x}_t, \mathbf{a}_t)$, sufficient for (4.3) is $E(u_t^2 | \mathbf{x}_t, \mathbf{a}_t) = E(u_t^2)$. In any case, Assumption 5 is a natural starting point, although it can never be guaranteed a priori. When testing for dynamic misspecification, $\mathbf{r}_t$ contains lags of y_t or u_t, and so Assumption 5 rules out dynamic forms of heteroskedasticity such as ARCH (Engle, 1982).

When one imposes Assumptions 4 and 5, the regression (3.1) produces a valid test statistic.

Theorem 2. Under Assumptions 1 to 5, and the null hypothesis (3.6), TR_u^2 from regression (3.1) is distributed asymptotically as χ_Q^2.

Proof. Under Assumptions 4 and 5, the form of $\mathbf{V}$ simplifies to $\mathbf{V} = \sigma_u^2 E(\mathbf{r}_t'\mathbf{r}_t)$. The natural estimator of $\mathbf{V}$ is

$$\hat{\sigma}_u^2 \left(T^{-1} \sum_{t=1}^{T} \hat{\mathbf{r}}_t'\hat{\mathbf{r}}_t \right), \tag{4.4}$$

where $\hat{\sigma}_u^2 = T^{-1}\sum_{t=1}^{T}\hat{u}_t^2$. After tedious but standard algebra, and using the convergence results in Lemma 1, (4.4) can be shown to converge in probability to $\sigma_u^2 E(\mathbf{r}_t'\mathbf{r}_t)$. Plugging (4.4) in for $\hat{\mathbf{V}}$ in (3.11), and doing a little algebra, reduces (3.11) to TR_u^2 from the regression

$$\hat{u}_t \text{ on } \hat{\mathbf{r}}_t, \ t = 1, 2, ..., T. \tag{4.5}$$

Because $\{\hat{u}_t\}$ and $\{(1, \mathbf{x}_t)\}$ are orthogonal in sample, TR_u^2 from (4.5) is identical to TR_u^2 from (3.1). ∎

This regression-based statistic can be applied to any of Examples 1, 2, and 3, provided that the no serial correlation and homoskedasticity assumptions hold under H_0. As mentioned above, Assumption 4 can be assumed when testing the null of no serial correlation in $\{u_t\}$. The homoskedasticity assumption is often maintained as a simplification, although it is never guaranteed to hold. Under homoskedasticity, the regression-based test for AR(P) serial correlation is the usual one (for example, Engle, 1984; Godfrey, 1988; Wooldridge, 1991a): $(T - P)R_u^2$ from the regression

$$\hat{u}_t \text{ on } 1, \ \mathbf{x}_t, \ \hat{u}_{t-1}, ..., \hat{u}_{t-P}. \tag{4.6}$$

Theorem 2 shows that this statistic is valid under an appropriate homoskedasticity assumption, even when some elements of $\mathbf{x}_t$ are I(1).

In Examples 2 and 3, Assumptions 4 and 5 are both auxiliary assumptions, but they are often maintained. This leads to especially simple tests by choosing $\hat{a}_t = \hat{\gamma} + \mathbf{z}_t\hat{\boldsymbol{\delta}}$ for Example 2 and $\hat{a}_t = \hat{v}_t$ for Example 3.

Example 3 is easily extended to more than one potential endogenous variable. Write:

$$y_t = \alpha + \mathbf{x}_{t1}\boldsymbol{\beta}_1 + \mathbf{x}_{t2}\boldsymbol{\beta}_2 + u_t,$$

where $\mathbf{x}_{t1}$ denotes a $1 \times K_1$ vector of potentially endogenous variables, which can contain both I(0) and I(1) variables with arbitrary cointegration relationships among its elements. Write a "reduced-form" for $\mathbf{x}_{t1}$ as

$$\mathbf{x}_{t1} = \gamma_1 + \mathbf{x}_{t2}\Gamma_2 + \mathbf{z}_t\Gamma_3 + \mathbf{v}_t, \tag{4.7}$$

where Γ_2 is $K_2 \times K_1$ and Γ_3 is $L \times K_1$. Here, $\mathbf{x}_{t2}$ and $\mathbf{z}_t$ can contain I(0) and I(1) elements satisfying arbitrary CI relationships. I assume that u_t and the reduced-form errors $\mathbf{v}_t$ are zero-mean I(0) processes uncorrelated with all I(0) linear combinations of $(\mathbf{x}_{t2}, \mathbf{z}_t)$. To test the null of exogeneity of $\mathbf{x}_{t1}$, we estimate each of the K_1 equations in (4.7) by OLS (or perform a single multivariate regression) and form the $1 \times K_2$ OLS residuals $\hat{\mathbf{v}}_t$. Then take $\hat{\mathbf{a}}_t = \hat{\mathbf{v}}_t$ in (3.1); under H_0, $TR_u^2 \overset{\mathrm{a}}{\sim} \chi_{K_2}^2$.

4.2 Heteroskedasticity-Robust Tests

Even though Assumption 4 is natural to maintain for many specification tests, we might want a test robust to violations of Assumption 5. Calculation of a heteroskedasticity-robust test is easy and follows Wooldridge (1991a) for the weakly dependent case. To obtain the statistic, we observe that, under Assumptions 1 to 4, (3.6), and regularity conditions, a consistent estimator of $\mathbf{V} = E(u_t^2 \mathbf{r}_t' \mathbf{r}_t)$ is

$$T^{-1}\sum_{t=1}^{T} \hat{u}_t^2 \hat{\mathbf{r}}_t' \hat{\mathbf{r}}_t. \tag{4.8}$$

The algebra is a bit tedious and not particularly insightful. When (4.8) is plugged into (3.11), the statistic becomes

$$\left(\sum_{t=1}^{T} \hat{\mathbf{r}}_t' \hat{u}_t\right)' \left(\sum_{t=1}^{T} \hat{u}_t^2 \hat{\mathbf{r}}_t' \hat{\mathbf{r}}_t\right)^{-1} \left(\sum_{t=1}^{T} \hat{\mathbf{r}}_t' \hat{u}_t\right). \tag{4.9}$$

This is most easily computed as $T - \mathrm{SSR}$ from the regression

$$1 \text{ on } \hat{u}_t \hat{\mathbf{r}}_t, \quad t = 1, 2, ..., T, \tag{4.10}$$

where SSR is just the usual sum of squared residuals and $\hat{u}_t \hat{\mathbf{r}}_t = (\hat{u}_t \hat{r}_{t1}, \hat{u}_t \hat{r}_{t2}, ..., \hat{u}_t \hat{r}_{tQ})$ is a $1 \times Q$ vector.

This essentially proves the following theorem.

Theorem 3. Under Assumptions 1 to 4 and the null hypothesis (3.6), $T - \mathrm{SSR}$ from (4.10) is distributed asymptotically as χ_Q^2. ∎

To obtain this statistic, note that the $\hat{\mathbf{r}}_t$ from the auxiliary regression (3.7) must be obtained explicitly, and then used to compute the products $\hat{u}_t \hat{r}_{th}$, $h = 1, ..., Q$. The statistic is then obtained by regressing unity on all of these products.

Any of the statistics in Examples 1, 2, and 3 can be made heteroskedasticity-robust using this method. For Example 1, regression (3.7) becomes

$$(\hat{u}_{t-1}, \hat{u}_{t-2}, ..., \hat{u}_{t-P}) \text{ on } 1, \mathbf{x}_t, \quad t = P+1, ..., T.$$

The residuals $\hat{r}_{t1}$, ..., $\hat{r}_{tP}$ are then used in (4.10) (where the regression would be 1 on $\hat{u}_t\hat{r}_{t1}$, ..., $\hat{u}_t\hat{r}_{tP}$, and the statistic would be $(T - P) -$ SSR). In Example 3 with $\mathbf{x}_{t1}$ a vector, regression (3.7) becomes

$$\hat{\mathbf{v}}_t \text{ on } 1, \mathbf{x}_t, \tag{4.11}$$

and the $1 \times K_1$ residuals $\hat{\mathbf{r}}_t$ are used along with $\hat{u}_t$ in (4.10).

4.3 Serial Correlation-Robust Tests

Sometimes one wants a test robust to failure of Assumption 4 as well as to failure of Assumption 5. Remember that in testing for dynamic misspecification, one should probably always maintain Assumption 4 under H_0. But, for examples like Example 2 and Example 3, one might not be interested in the dynamics at all. Equations (3.2) and (3.3) might be two different static relationships, and one does not wish to take a stand on serial correlation in $\{u_t\}$ under H_0. Similarly, (3.4) might be a static model with an endogenous variable; $\{u_t\}$ may or may not be serially uncorrelated. In the distributed lag equation (2.10), (2.11) is not enough to ensure Assumption 4 when testing for additional lags of z_t. Relaxing Assumptions 4 and 5 requires a more general form for $\hat{\mathbf{V}}$.

One possibility is to construct the statistic (3.11) with $\hat{\mathbf{V}}$ a serial correlation and heteroskedasticity-robust variance matrix estimator. Following Newey and West (1987), one fairly simple estimator is given by

$$\hat{\mathbf{V}} = T^{-1}\sum_{t=1}^{T}\hat{u}_t^2\hat{\mathbf{r}}_t'\hat{\mathbf{r}}_t + \sum_{j=1}^{L}\left(1 - \frac{j}{L+1}\right)\left(T^{-1}\sum_{t=j+1}^{T}\hat{u}_t\hat{u}_{t-j}\{\hat{\mathbf{r}}_t'\hat{\mathbf{r}}_{t-j} + \hat{\mathbf{r}}_{t-j}'\hat{\mathbf{r}}_t\}\right), \tag{4.12}$$

where L is a lag length that must be chosen by the researcher, and the weights $1 - j/(L + 1)$ ensure that the estimator is a least positive semi-definite. The second term in (4.12) is a weighted sum of estimated autocovariances of $\{\hat{\mathbf{r}}_t'\hat{u}_t\}$. Adapting the approach of Newey and West (1987), $\hat{\mathbf{V}}$ can be shown to be consistent for $\mathbf{V}$ as $T \to \infty$, provided the growth of L is controlled. I do not investigate the exact conditions needed here since they are of limited practical value anyway. This estimator of $\mathbf{V}$ can be used in (3.11) to obtain a statistic that requires neither Assumption 4 nor Assumption 5. For other approaches to estimating $\mathbf{V}$ see Andrews (1991) and Andrews and Monohan (1992).

An alternative approach is to prewhiten the series $\hat{\mathbf{g}}_t \equiv \hat{u}_t\hat{\mathbf{r}}_t$ before using it in a specification test. For a selected lag length L, run a vector autoregression (VAR) of $\hat{\mathbf{g}}_t$ on $(\hat{\mathbf{g}}_{t-1}, \hat{\mathbf{g}}_{t-2}, ..., \hat{\mathbf{g}}_{t-L})$, and let $\{\hat{\mathbf{e}}_t\}$ be the $1 \times Q$ residuals from this VAR. Then, assuming L has been chosen to properly account for the serial correlation in $\{u_t r_t\}$ under H_0, a valid statistic is:

$$\left(\sum_{t=L+1}^{T} \hat{\mathbf{e}}_t\right)\left(\sum_{t=L+1}^{T} \hat{\mathbf{e}}_t'\hat{\mathbf{e}}_t\right)^{-1}\left(\sum_{t=L+1}^{T} \hat{\mathbf{e}}_t'\right),$$

which is just $(T-L)$ – SSR from the auxiliary regression

$$1 \text{ on } \hat{\mathbf{e}}_t, \quad t = L+1,\dots,T. \tag{4.13}$$

Under H_0, and without either Assumption 4 or 5, $(T-L)$ – SSR is asymptotically χ_Q^2. Berk (1974) shows how fairly general serial correlation is allowed provided L increases as some fractional power of T. See Wooldridge (1991a) for additional discussion of this statistic in the context of essentially stationary, weakly dependent data.

5 Models with Time Trends and Processes with Drift

So far I have assumed that the explanatory variables $\mathbf{x}_t$ are either I(0) or I(1) without drift. It turns out that the same tests are valid with slight modification if some regressors are trend-stationary or I(1) with drift. The model is now

$$y_t = \alpha_0 + \alpha_1 t + \mathbf{x}_t \boldsymbol{\beta} + u_t, \tag{5.1}$$

where $\mathbf{x}_t$ can contain trend-stationary variables and I(1) processes with drift, in addition to I(0) processes and I(1) processes without drift. Assumptions 1, 2, and 3 are still appropriate for this model. The only change is implicit in stating Assumption 3: $\mathbf{a}_t - \boldsymbol{\theta}_0 - \boldsymbol{\theta}_1 t - \mathbf{x}_t \boldsymbol{\Theta} \sim \text{I}(0)$ for some $1 \times Q$ vectors $\boldsymbol{\theta}_0$ and $\boldsymbol{\theta}_1$ and some $K \times Q$ matrix $\boldsymbol{\Theta}$. In other words, $\mathbf{a}_t$ is CIGS with $\mathbf{x}_t$, allowing for drift. The form of the statistic valid under the ideal assumptions is TR_u^2 from the regression:

$$\hat{u}_t \text{ on } 1, t, \mathbf{x}_t, \hat{\mathbf{a}}_t. \tag{5.2}$$

For the robust forms of the test, $\hat{\mathbf{r}}_t$ is obtained from auxiliary regression:

$$\hat{\mathbf{a}}_t \text{ on } 1, t, \mathbf{x}_t. \tag{5.3}$$

With these modifications, the computation of the statistics is the same as before.

In some cases one might wish to exclude "t" from (5.1). However, unless a special kind of cointegration occurs among the elements of $\mathbf{x}_t$ and between $\mathbf{a}_t$ and $\mathbf{x}_t$, the test procedures that use the chi-squared distribution are not generally valid without t in the regressions. It is safest to include a linear time trend in a model whenever one or more of the variables has some sort of linear trend, including an I(1) process with drift.

6 Conclusion

I have treated specification tests in linear models when the misspecification indicators are linear in observed variables. Among other things, the results justify the use of some standard diagnostics quite broadly in linear models with integrated processes.

When the indicators must be estimated I have essentially assumed that they are obtained either as OLS fitted values or residuals. While this covers several cases of interest, there is much else that can be done. An important extension is to test for nonlinear misspecification. My conjecture is that the same conclusions hold provided that the nonlinear functions comprising the misspecification indicator are I(0) when evaluated at the unknown coefficients. The details appear nontrivial to work out, as mean value expansions in I(1) variables are involved. Recent work of Phillips and Park (1998) should help in this regard. A natural application of results with nonlinear misspecification indicators would be to testing for the presence of nonlinear error correction terms—once cointegration between two or more series has been established—as in Escribano (1987).

I have also assumed that the elements of $\mathbf{x}_t$ are either I(0), trend-stationary, or I(1), and similarly for $\mathbf{a}_t$. An open question is what happens when some elements of $\{\mathbf{x}_t\}$ are strongly dependent processes (such as long-memory or fractionally integrated processes) but are not I(1); see, for example, Robinson (1991).

Another limitation of the tests is that I have assumed neither the null nor alternative models contain structural breaks, as in Perron (1989). In some cases the limiting distributions can be expected to be nonstandard, but in others—such as testing for serial correlation in the presence of structural breaks—the statistics may have standard limiting distributions. This, however, remains to be seen.

Finally, it is also of some interest to test hypotheses about the conditional variance of the errors $\{u_t\}$. Assuming that $\{u_t^2\}$ is I(0) under the null of homoskedasticity—which is certainly reasonable—it seems likely that the usual tests for ARCH (Engle, 1982) and other forms of dynamic heteroskedasticity will be valid. But verifying this requires using the functional CLT to obtain the appropriate asymptotic representations. Apparently, this has yet to be done.

References

Anderson, T. W. (1971), *The Statistical Analysis of Time Series*. New York: Wiley.
Andrews, D. W. K. (1991), "Heteroskedasticity and Autocorrelation Consistent Covariance Matrix Estimation," *Econometrica*, 59: 817–58.

Andrews, D. W. K. and J. C. Monohan (1992), "An Improved Heteroskedasticity and Autocorrelation Consistent Covariance Matrix Estimator," *Econometrica*, 60: 953–66.

Banerjee, A., J. Dolado, J. W. Galbraith, and D. F. Hendry (1993), *Co-integration, Error-Correction, and the Econometric Analysis of Non-stationary Data*. Oxford: Oxford University Press.

Berk, K. N. (1974), "Consistent Autoregressive Spectral Estimates," *Annals of Statistics* 2: 489–502.

Billingsley, P. (1968), *Convergence of Probability Measures*. New York: Wiley.

Davidson, R. and J. G. MacKinnon (1981), "Several Tests for Model Specification in the Presence of Alternative Hypotheses," *Econometrica*, 49: 781–93.

Domowitz, I. and H. White (1982), "Maximum Likelihood Estimation of Misspecified Models," *Journal of Econometrics*, 20: 35–58.

Engle, R. F. (1982), "Autoregression Conditional Heteroskedasticity with Estimates of United Kingdom Inflation," *Econometrica*, 50: 987–1008.

Engle, R. F. (1984), "Wald, Likelihood Ratio, and Lagrange Multiplier Tests in Econometrics," in Z. Griliches and M. D. Intriligator (eds.), *Handbook of Econometrics*, vol. 2. Amsterdam: North Holland, pp. 775–826.

Engle, R. F. and C. W. J. Granger (1987), "Cointegration and Error Correction: Representation, Estimation and Testing," *Econometrica*, 55: 251–76.

Escribano, A. (1987), "Error-Correction Systems: Nonlinear Adjustments to Linear Long-Run Relationships," CORE Discussion Paper No. 8730.

Fuller, W. (1976), *Introduction to Statistic Time Series*. New York: Wiley.

Godfrey, L. G. (1988), *Misspecification Tests in Econometrics: The LM Principle and Other Approaches*. New York: Cambridge University Press.

Hall, P. and C. C. Heyde (1980), *Martingale Limit Theory and Its Application*. New York: Academic Press.

Hamilton, J. (1994), *Time Series Analysis*. New York: Princeton University Press.

Hansen, B. E. (1992), "Convergence to Stochastic Integrals for Dependent Heterogeneous Processes," *Econometric Theory*, 8: 489–500.

Hausman, J. (1978), "Specification Tests in Econometrics," *Econometrica*, 46: 1251–71.

Kitamura, Y. and P. C. B. Phillips (1995), "Efficient IV Estimation in Non-stationary Regression: An Overview and Simulation Results," *Econometric Theory*, 11: 1095–1130.

Kitamura, Y. and P. C. B. Phillips (1997), "Fully Modified IV, GIVE, and GMM Estimation with Possibly Non-stationary Regressors and Instruments," *Journal of Econometrics*, 80: 85–123.

MacKinnon, J. G. (1992), "Model Specification Tests and Artificial Regressions," *Journal of Economic Literature*, 30, 102–46.

Newey, W. K. and K. D. West (1987), "A Simple, Positive Semi-Definite, Heteroskedasticity and Autocorrelation Consistent Covariance Matrix," *Econometrica*, 55: 703–8.

Park, J. Y. and P. C. B. Phillips (1988), "Statistical Inference in Regressions with Integrated Processes: Part 1," *Econometric Theory*, 4: 468–97.

Park, J. Y. and P. C. B. Phillips (1989), "Statistical Inference in Regressions with Integrated Processes: Part 2," *Econometric Theory*, 5: 95–131.

Perron, P. (1989), "The Great Crash, the Oil Price Shock, and the Unit Root Hypothesis," *Econometrica* 57: 1361–1401.

Phillips, P. C. B. (1986), "Understanding Spurious Regressions in Econometrics," *Journal of Econometrics*, 33: 311–40.

Phillips, P. C. B. (1987), "Time Series Regression with a Unit Root," *Econometrica*, 55: 277–301.

Phillips, P. C. B. (1988), "Multiple Regression with Integrated Time Series," *Contemporary Mathematics*, 80: 79–105.

Phillips, P. C. B. (1991), "Optimal Inference in Cointegrated Systems," *Econometrica*, 59: 283–306.

Phillips, P. C. B. and S. N. Durlauf (1986), "Multiple Time Series Regression with Integrated Processes," *Review of Economic Studies*, 53: 473–96.

Phillips, P. C. B. and B. E. Hansen (1990), "Statistical Inference in Instrumental Variables Regression with I(1) Processes," *Review of Economic Studies*, 57: 99–125.

Phillips, P. C. B. and J. Park (1998), "Nonlinear Regression with Integrated Time Series," mimeo, Cowles Foundation for Research in Economics.

Robinson, P. M. (1991), "Testing for Strong Serial Correlation and Dynamic Conditional Heteroskedasticity in Multiple Regression," *Journal of Econometrics*, 47: 67–84.

Saikkonen, P. (1991), "Asymptotically Efficient Estimation of Cointegration Regressions," *Econometric Theory*, 7: 1–21.

Sims, C. A., J. H. Stock, and M. W. Watson (1990), "Inference in Linear Time Series Models with Some Unit Roots," *Econometrica*, 58: 113–44.

Stock, J. H. (1987), "Asymptotic Properties of Least Squares Estimators of Cointegrating Vectors," *Econometrica*, 55: 1035–56.

Stock, J. H. and M. W. Watson (1993), "A Simple MLE of Cointegrating Vectors in Higher Order Integrated Systems," *Econometrica*, 61: 783–820.

Watson, M. W. (1994), "Vector Autoregressions and Cointegration," in R. F. Engle and D. McFadden (eds.), *Handbook of Econometrics*, vol. 4. Amsterdam: North-Holland, pp. 2843–915.

Wooldridge, J. M. (1991a), "On the Application of Robust, Regression-Based Diagnostics to Models of Conditional Means and Conditional Variances," *Journal of Econometrics*, 47: 5–46.

Wooldridge, J. M. (1991b), "Notes on Regression with Difference-Stationary Data," mimeo, Michigan State University Department of Economics.

Wooldridge, J. M. (1994), "Estimation and Inference for Dependent Processes," in R. F. Engle and D. L. McFadden (eds.), *Handbook of Econometrics*, vol. 4. Amsterdam: North-Holland, pp. 2639–738.

Wooldridge, J. M. and H. White (1988), "Some Invariance Principles and Central Limit Theorems for Dependent Heterogeneous Processes," *Econometric Theory*, 4: 210–30.

16
Residual Variance Estimates and Order Determination in Panels of Intercorrelated Autoregressive Time Series

VIDAR HJELLVIK AND DAG TJØSTHEIM

1 Introduction

A quite general linear dynamic model for a panel of time series observations $\{X_{(i)t}, i = 1, ..., n; t = 1, ..., T\}$ is given by

$$X_{(i)t} = \sum_{j=1}^{p} a_j X_{(i)t-j} + \eta_t + \lambda_i + \beta^\tau W_{(i)t} + \epsilon_{(i)t} \tag{1.1}$$

(see e.g. Hsiao, 1986, p. 71). Here t denotes time and i the individual series of the panel. Moreover, $\{W_{(i)t}\}$ is a (possibly) vector series of explanatory variables, η_t represents effects over time influencing all of the series, and similarly λ_i stands for individual effects not taken care of by the explanatory variables. Finally, $\{\epsilon_{(i)t}\}$ are the error terms assumed to be independent identically distributed (iid) in all of the following.

There is a large recent literature on estimation for panel time series described by a fixed parametric model such as (1.1), or rather for the subclass defined by $\eta_t \equiv 0$ (see e.g. Hsiao, 1986, Mátyás and Sevestre, 1992, Baltagi, 1995, and the special issue of *Journal of Econometrics*, vol. 68, 1995 and the references therein), but as remarked by Clive Granger (1996), little work has been done on specification and evaluation of models. In the present paper we make an attempt in the direction of model specification by looking at autoregressive order determination for a panel of time series. We are not aware of previous work on this problem, but we maintain that it is both of practical and theoretical interest. We look at the situation where the number of series n in the

This work has received support from the Norwegian Supercomputer Committee through a grant of computing time. We are grateful to N. C. Stenseth, T. Saitoh and O. N. Bjørnstad for supporting the vole data. This data set and the ensuing discussion with Stenseth and Bjørnstad have served as an inspiration and motivation for this paper.

panel is large whereas the number of observations T of each series is small (of order $2p$), and at the case where n is small and T large. In short, we always require nT to be large.

For some reason there seems to be a tradition for removing η_t, thus ignoring the common effects over time and hence effectively the contribution of this term to the intercorrelation across the panel. We claim that the neglect of intercorrelation implied by omitting η_t can in many instances not be justified, and it may have some severe consequences for the estimation of the AR-parameters of the model. This was demonstrated in Hjellvik and Tjøstheim (1999), to which we refer for more details.

In this paper we have gone to the opposite extreme by omitting λ_i (and $\beta^\tau W_{(i)t}$) from (1.1), i.e. we look at order determination in the model

$$X_{(i)t} = \sum_{j=1}^{p} a_j X_{(i)t-j} + \eta_t + e_{(i)t}. \tag{1.2}$$

We have done this simplification for several reasons: the order determination problem is difficult in the panel case, and it is important to understand the simpler situation (1.2) before embarking on models such as (1.1). One could argue that one might as well concentrate on the simplified situation where η_t is replaced by λ_i in (1.2), which would be relevant for some econometric settings. However, this would lead to a model where the individual time series are independent and in a sense the transition from the univariate to the panel case would be more straightforward and thus perhaps not of the same interest from a times series theory point of view. Moreover, (1.2) represents a direct continuation of the setup in Hjellvik and Tjøstheim (1999), and it is essential for biological time series panels of the type presented in Section 6 (cf. Figure 2), where intercorrelation cannot be ignored.

Our ultimate goal is to be able to cover the situation in (1.1). This general case as well as some other extensions and problems are briefly discussed in Section 7. Indeed, the extension from the univariate to the present setting is far from trivial. To illustrate, let us review very rapidly the univariate case, where one has to select the order p of the AR-process

$$X_t = \sum_{j=1}^{p} a_j X_{t-j} + e_t.$$

The available criteria (e.g. FPE, AIC, BIC, see Brockwell and Davis, 1996, ch. 5.5) are all based on a bias corrected estimate of the residual variance σ_e^2, which is also the one-step mean square prediction error, and on a penalty term depending on the number of estimated parameters. A fairly complete asymptotic theory as $T \to \infty$ exists, and it does not matter much which type of AR estimates $\hat{a}_j$ are used.

In the panel case one has to consider asymptotics as a function of both n

and T, and the way the AR coefficients are estimated becomes essential. Our estimates will be based on a conditional likelihood argument to be presented in Section 2. Constructing an estimate of the residual variance there are now two alternatives, $\sigma_e^2 = \sigma_\eta^2 + \sigma_\epsilon^2$ and σ_ϵ^2. It is not obvious which one should be used, and it is not clear how a bias corrected estimate can be obtained. We treat these problems in Sections 3 and 4. Finally, one has to be careful when implementing the estimated residual variance in the order determination criterion. Using a direct analogy of the univariate case will fail if T is small or moderate as will be seen in Section 5. Throughout we will present simulated examples as well as a real data application in Section 6 to a panel of biological catch data.

2 A Conditional Maximum Likelihood Approach

We start by writing (1.2) in vector notation,

$$X_{(i)t} = a^\tau x_{(i)t-1} + e_{(i)t}, \quad e_{(i)t} = \eta_t + \epsilon_{(i)t}, \tag{2.1}$$

where $a^\tau = [a_1, ..., a_p]$ and $x_{(i)t}^\tau = [X_{(i)t}, ..., X_{(i)t-p+1}]$, and we assume that $X_{(i)t}$ is observed for $1 \le i \le n$ and $1 \le t \le T$. The residuals $\{\epsilon_{(i)t}\}$ are supposed to be iid with a density f_ϵ, and the roots of the characteristic polynomial $z^p - \sum_{j=1}^p a_j z^{p-j}$ are all required to be inside the unit circle to guarantee stability. At the moment we make no assumptions about the sequence $\{\eta_t\}$ other than it being independent of $\{\epsilon_{(i)t}\}$. A deterministic sequence $\{\eta_t\}$ would also be allowed. Additional restrictions on $\{\eta_t\}$ will be introduced as needed.

With the lack of assumptions on $\{\eta_t\}$ unconditional likelihood methods cannot be employed. Even if $\{\eta_t\}$ were to consist of iid random variables, ordinary maximum likelihood arguments cannot in general be used, since if T is small, the intercorrelation introduced by $\{\eta_t\}$ would not be consistently estimated. Conditional on η_t, however, $X_{(i)t}$ and $X_{(j)t}$ are independent for $i \neq j$, $i, j = 1, ..., n$. Moreover, denoting by $\mathcal{F}_t^\eta$ the σ-algebra generated by $\{\eta_s, s \le t\}$, by X_t the vector given by $[X_{(1)t}, ..., X_{(n)t}]$, and by using a standard Markov argument, the likelihood conditional on $\mathcal{F}_T^\eta$ and the starting values $X_1, ..., X_p$ is given by

$$L(X_{p+1}, ..., X_T \,|\, X_1, ..., X_p, \mathcal{F}_T^\eta) = \prod_{t=p+1}^T \prod_{i=1}^n f_\epsilon(X_{(i)t} - a^\tau x_{(i)t-1} - \eta_t).$$

If f_ϵ is assumed to be Gaussian with zero mean and variance σ_ϵ^2, then

$$L(X_{p+1}, ..., X_T \,|\, X_1, ..., X_p, \mathcal{F}_T^\eta)$$
$$= (2\pi\sigma_\epsilon^2)^{-n(T-p)/2} \exp\left\{-\frac{1}{2\sigma_\epsilon^2} \prod_{i=1}^n \prod_{t=p+1}^T (X_{(i)t} - a^\tau x_{(i)t-1} - \eta_t)^2\right\}.$$

We can now obtain a consistent estimate of a by letting either n or T, but not necessarily both, tend to infinity. In fact, considering $\{\eta_1, ..., \eta_T\}$ to be nuisance parameters, and maximizing L with respect to a yields the estimator

$$\tilde{a}^\tau = [\tilde{a}_1, ..., \tilde{a}_p] = \frac{1}{n(T-p)} \sum_{i=1}^{n} \sum_{t=p}^{T-1} (X_{(i)t+1} - X_{.t+1})(x_{(i)t} - x_{.t})^\tau$$

$$\times \left\{ \frac{1}{n(T-p)} \sum_{i=1}^{n} \sum_{t=p}^{T-1} (x_{(i)t} - x_{.t})(x_{(i)t} - x_{.t})^\tau \right\}^{-1}, \qquad (2.2)$$

with $x_{.t} = \frac{1}{n}\sum_{i=1}^{n} x_{(i)t}$ and $X_{.t+1} = \frac{1}{n}\sum_{i=1}^{n} X_{(i)t+1}$. Alternatively, if one wants to avoid the Gaussian assumption, this can be looked at as a conditional least squares estimate. Much of the analysis goes through if $\{\epsilon_{(i)t}\}$ is an array of iid random variables satisfying some weak moment conditions.

The estimate $\tilde{a}$ was analyzed in Hjellvik and Tjøstheim (1999), where it was found that under weak restrictions as $nT \to \infty$, $\tilde{a}$ is consistent and asymptotically normal. In case $\{X_{(i)t}\}$ is stationary and $\{\eta_t\}$ consists of iid random variables, the covariance matrix is given by

$$\text{cov}(\tilde{a}) \sim \frac{\sigma_e^2 \Gamma_x^{-1}}{(n-1)(T-p)}$$

where $\Gamma_x = \text{E}(x_{(i)t}\, x_{(i)t}^\tau)$. For the more general case we refer to Hjellvik and Tjøstheim (1999).

For a small T it should be noted that an essential improvement can be obtained by replacing $\tilde{a}$ by Burg-type alternatives (cf. Hjellvik and Tjøstheim, 1999). However, these are more difficult to work with theoretically and will not be used here. Moreover, it may be mentioned that in the case of a large T and a weak intercorrelation, a likelihood estimate conditioned only on $X_1, ..., X_p$ will perform a little better than $\tilde{a}$.

Returning to the Gaussian log likelihood and minimizing with respect to η_t, we have

$$\tilde{\eta}_t = X_{.t} - \tilde{a}^\tau x_{.t-1}$$

and using standard arguments the conditional likelihood estimate of σ_ϵ^2 is obtained as

$$\tilde{\sigma}_\epsilon^2 = \frac{1}{n(T-p)} \sum_{i=1}^{n} \sum_{t=p+1}^{T} \{X_{(i)t} - \tilde{a}^\tau x_{(i)t-1} - (X_{.t} - \tilde{a}^\tau x_{.t-1})\}^2$$

$$= \frac{1}{n(T-p)} \sum_{i=1}^{n} \sum_{t=p+1}^{T} (\tilde{e}_{(i)t} - \tilde{e}_{.t})^2,$$

with

$$\tilde{e}_{(i)t} = X_{(i)t} - \tilde{a}^\tau x_{(i)t-1}.$$

It is not difficult to prove consistency as $nT \to \infty$, and a bias corrected estimate will be presented in Section 3.

As mentioned in the introduction, it is not obvious whether σ_ϵ^2 or $\sigma_e^2 = \sigma_\eta^2 + \sigma_\epsilon^2$ should be used as a basis for an order determination algorithm. In the latter case an estimate of σ_η^2 is required, and as a minimum one has to assume that $\{\eta_t\}$ is a stationary ergodic process independent of $\{\epsilon_{(i)t}\}$, and where second order moments exist. One may think that a natural estimator for σ_η^2 would be of type

$$\frac{1}{T-p} \sum_{t=p+1}^{T} (\tilde{\eta}_t - \tilde{\eta}_.)^2 = \frac{1}{T-p} \sum_{t=p+1}^{T} \{X_{\cdot t} - \tilde{a}^\tau x_{\cdot t-1} - (X_{\cdot\cdot,1} - \tilde{a}^\tau x_{\cdot\cdot,0})\}^2, \qquad (2.3)$$

where

$$\tilde{\eta}_. = \frac{1}{T-p} \sum_{t=p+1}^{T} \tilde{\eta}_t, \qquad X_{\cdot\cdot,1} = \frac{1}{n(T-p)} \sum_{i=1}^{n} \sum_{t=p}^{T-1} X_{(i)t+1},$$

$$\text{and } x_{\cdot\cdot,0} = \frac{1}{n(T-p)} \sum_{i=1}^{n} \sum_{t=p}^{T-1} x_{(i)t}.$$

However, this is not even a consistent estimator of σ_η^2 for a fixed n as $T \to \infty$. Indeed, since $\tilde{a} \to a$, as $nT \to \infty$, putting $\tilde{a} = a$ in (2.3):

$$\frac{1}{T-p} \sum_{t=p+1}^{T} \{X_{\cdot t} - a^\tau x_{\cdot t-1} - (X_{\cdot\cdot,1} - a^\tau x_{\cdot\cdot,0})\}^2 = \frac{1}{T-p} \sum_{t=p+1}^{T} \{\epsilon_{\cdot t} + \eta_t - (\epsilon_{\cdot\cdot} + \eta_.)\}$$

$$\to \frac{\sigma_\epsilon^2}{n} + \sigma_\eta^2,$$

in probability as $T \to \infty$. Adjusting for the first term, a consistent estimator for σ_η^2, as $T \to \infty$, is obtained by

$$\tilde{\sigma}_\eta^2 = \frac{1}{T-p} \sum_{t=p+1}^{T} \{X_{\cdot t} - \tilde{a}^\tau x_{\cdot t-1} - (X_{\cdot\cdot,1} - \tilde{a}^\tau x_{\cdot\cdot,0})\}^2 - \frac{1}{n} \tilde{\sigma}_\epsilon^2,$$

and correspondingly

$$\tilde{\sigma}_e^2 = \tilde{\sigma}_\eta^2 + \tilde{\sigma}_\epsilon^2.$$

Note that σ_η^2 (and hence σ_e^2) cannot be consistently estimated for a fixed T as $n \to \infty$, because only finitely many η_ts are available in this situation. Under the restricted assumption that the η_ts are iid random variables, $\sigma_e^2 = \sigma_\eta^2 + \sigma_\epsilon^2$ coincides with the one-step mean square prediction error. Further, under these circumstances it is not difficult to show (Hjellvik and Tjøstheim, 1999) that the intercorrelation between an arbitrary pair of time series $\{X_{(i)t}\}$ and $\{X_{(j)t}\}$ is given by

$$\text{Corr}(X_{(i)t}, X_{(j)t}) = \frac{\sigma_\eta^2}{\sigma_\epsilon^2 + \sigma_\eta^2} \doteq \rho \qquad (2.4)$$

which can be consistently estimated by $\tilde{\sigma}_\eta^2/\tilde{\sigma}_e^2$ as $T \to \infty$. Also note that $\sigma_\epsilon^2 = (1 - \rho)\,\sigma_e^2$.

In the case of a more general process $\{\eta_t\}$, neither σ_ϵ^2 nor σ_e^2 can be identified with the mean square prediction error, but it is perhaps worth remembering that

$$E\{X_{(i)t} - X_{\cdot t} - a^\tau(x_{(i)t-1} - x_{\cdot t-1})\}^2 = \frac{n}{n-1}\sigma_\epsilon^2$$

so that $\sigma_\epsilon^2 n/(n-1)$ can be interpreted as the one-step mean square forecast error for the mean-adjusted process $Y_{(i)t} = X_{(i)t} - X_{\cdot t}$. Also, $\tilde{\sigma}_\epsilon^2$ is more applicable than $\tilde{\sigma}_e^2$ in the sense that the former is consistent as $nT \to \infty$, whereas the latter requires $T \to \infty$. A comparison between the two in the case where $T \to \infty$, is presented in Section 4.

3 Bias Corrected Variance Estimates and a Standardization

In the univariate order determination it is vital that a bias corrected estimate of σ_e^2 is used. The aim of this section is to introduce bias corrected versions of $\tilde{\sigma}_\epsilon^2$ and $\tilde{\sigma}_\eta^2$. This requires considerably more work than in the time series case, and most of the computations are displayed in the Appendix.

However, before embarking on this, we look at another standardization problem, which is absent in the univariate case, but which is as important as bias correction in the panel situation. The univariate residual variance $\hat{\sigma}_{e,k}^2$ of an AR approximation of order k is estimated as

$$\hat{\sigma}_{e,k}^2 = \frac{1}{T-k}\sum_{t=k+1}^{T}(X_t - \tilde{a}^\tau(k)x_{t-1}^{(k)})^2 \tag{3.1}$$

where $\tilde{a}^\tau(k) = [\tilde{a}_{k,1}, ..., \tilde{a}_{k,k}]$ is a fitted vector of AR coefficients of order k and $x_{t-1}^{(k)} = [x_{t-1}, ..., x_{t-k}]^\tau$, and where k varies from 0 ($\tilde{a}(0) = x_{t-1}^{(0)} = 0$) to an upper pre-determined limit L. This means that the number of observations used to evaluate $\hat{\sigma}_{e,k}^2$ varies as k varies from 0 to L. This does not matter much when L is small compared to T (as it usually is for time series), but in the panel case where T may be moderate or even small, using an analogue of (3.1) does not work, and a standardization is required. The standardization essentially amounts to replacing the lower limit k by L, so that a fixed number of terms are used in the evaluation and comparisons of $\hat{\sigma}_{e,k}^2$, $k = 0, ..., L$. More precisely, first we estimate:

$$\tilde{a}^\tau(k) = [\tilde{a}_{k,1}, ..., \tilde{a}_{k,k}] = \frac{1}{n(T-L)}\sum_{t=L}^{T-1}\sum_{i=1}^{n}(X_{(i)t+1} - X_{\cdot t+1})(x_{(i)t}^{(k)} - x_{\cdot t}^{(k)})^\tau$$

$$\times\left\{\frac{1}{n(T-L)}\sum_{t=L}^{T-1}\sum_{i=1}^{n}(x_{(i)t}^{(k)} - x_{\cdot t}^{(k)})(x_{(i)t}^{(k)} - x_{\cdot t}^{(k)})^\tau\right\}^{-1}. \tag{3.2}$$

The corresponding kth order residuals are given by:

$$\tilde{e}_{(i)t,k} = X_{(i)t} - \sum_{j=1}^{k} \tilde{a}_{k,j} X_{(i)t-j}, \quad i = 1,...,n, \quad t = k+1,...,T. \tag{3.3}$$

In the definition of $\tilde{a}$ we have replaced p by L in the right hand side of (2.2). A standardized and bias corrected estimate of σ_ϵ^2 is given as:

$$\tilde{\sigma}_{\epsilon,k}^2 = \frac{1}{(n-1)(T-L)-k} \sum_{t=L+1}^{T} \sum_{i=1}^{n} (\tilde{e}_{(i)t,k} - \tilde{e}_{\cdot t,k})^2, \tag{3.4}$$

where $\tilde{e}_{\cdot t,k} = n^{-1} \sum_i \tilde{e}_{(i)t,k}$.

Comparing (3.1) and (3.4) it is seen that more data points are utilized in (3.1), but by letting t run from k to T in (3.4) there would be n new terms each time k is reduced by one unit, and if n is moderate or large the added variation produced by these new terms may dominate the ordering of the $\tilde{\sigma}_{\epsilon,k}^2$s in the order determination criterion, as will be seen in Section 5.

Concerning the bias correction we show in Appendix A for an AR(p) model with $p \leq k$ that $\tilde{\sigma}_{\epsilon,k}^2$ is an asymptotically unbiased estimator for σ_ϵ^2 as $nT \to \infty$, and in Appendix B we demonstrate that the standardized estimate

$$\tilde{\sigma}_{\eta,k}^2 = \frac{1}{T-L-1+k/(n-1)} \sum_{t=L+1}^{T} (\tilde{e}_{\cdot t,k} - \tilde{e}_{\cdot\cdot,k})^2 - \frac{1}{n} \tilde{\sigma}_{\epsilon,k}^2, \tag{3.5}$$

where $\tilde{e}_{\cdot\cdot,k} = (nT)^{-1} \sum_t \sum_i \tilde{e}_{(i)t,k}$, is asymptotically unbiased for σ_η^2 as $T \to \infty$. This will imply that

$$\tilde{\sigma}_{e,k}^2 = \tilde{\sigma}_{\epsilon,k}^2 + \tilde{\sigma}_{\eta,k}^2 \tag{3.6}$$

is asymptotically unbiased for σ_e^2 as $T \to \infty$. Finite sample properties are displayed in Table 1, which is based on 1,000 realizations of the AR(3) model

$$X_{(i)t} = 1.2X_{(i)t-1} - 0.2X_{(i)t-2} - 0.2X_{(i)t-3} + \eta_t + \epsilon_{(i)t}. \tag{3.7}$$

The tabulated results are computed from

$$\tilde{e}_{(i)t,3} = X_{(i)t} - \sum_{j=1}^{3} \tilde{a}_{3,j} X_{(i)t-j}, \quad i = 1,...,n, \quad t = L+1,...,T.$$

for $nT = 512$ and $nT = 128$ with various combinations of n and T and with L somewhat arbitrarily set to $\min(T/2, 10)$. Two cases are considered, $\sigma_\eta^2 = 0$, i.e. $\rho = 0$, and $\sigma_\eta^2 = \sigma_\epsilon^2 = 1$, i.e. $\rho = 0.5$. In the rightmost part of the table the inconsistency of σ_η^2 and σ_ϵ^2 for a small T is clearly indicated.

In an order determination context it is of interest to investigate how the residual variance estimates defined by (3.4) – (3.6) change for data generated from an AR(p) model as we increase the order $k \geq p$ in (3.3). That is, we want to investigate the effect of the correction terms k and $k/(n-1)$ in the de-

Table 1

			$\sigma_\epsilon^2 = 1$	$\sigma_\eta^2 = 0$	$\sigma_e^2 = 1$	$\sigma_\eta^2 = 1$	$\sigma_e^2 = 2$
n	T	L	$\tilde{\sigma}_{\epsilon,3}^2$	$\tilde{\sigma}_{\eta,3}^2$	$\tilde{\sigma}_{e,3}^2$	$\tilde{\sigma}_{\eta,3}^2$	$\tilde{\sigma}_{e,3}^2$
Empirical bias							
2	256	10	0.00067	−0.00052	0.00015	−0.00118	−0.00051
4	128	10	0.00067	0.00017	0.00084	−0.00427	−0.00359
8	64	10	−0.00191	−0.00012	−0.00203	0.00200	0.00008
16	32	10	−0.00500	0.00041	−0.00459	−0.00799	−0.01300
32	16	8	0.00737	−0.00017	0.00720	−0.02919	−0.02182
64	8	4	0.00239	−0.00018	0.00221	−0.04349	−0.04110
2	64	10	0.00220	−0.00213	0.00007	−0.00031	0.00189
4	32	10	0.00109	−0.00411	−0.00302	0.00308	0.00417
8	16	8	0.00131	0.00003	0.00134	−0.00205	−0.00074
16	8	4	−0.00464	−0.00292	−0.00755	−0.07098	−0.07562
Empirical variance							
2	256	10	0.00838	0.00470	0.00412	0.02078	0.02036
4	128	10	0.00566	0.00136	0.00409	0.02671	0.02852
8	64	10	0.00543	0.00065	0.00461	0.04829	0.05206
16	32	10	0.00606	0.00039	0.00587	0.10251	0.10450
32	16	8	0.00834	0.00026	0.00823	0.29400	0.30080
64	8	4	0.00828	0.00017	0.00814	0.61862	0.62761
2	64	10	0.03813	0.02240	0.01907	0.12242	0.11173
4	32	10	0.03220	0.00841	0.02361	0.16661	0.18339
8	16	8	0.03820	0.00538	0.03246	0.41774	0.44582
16	8	4	0.03610	0.00272	0.03418	0.67757	0.70619

The empirical bias and variance of $\tilde{\sigma}_{\epsilon,3}^2$, $\tilde{\sigma}_{\eta,3}^2$ and $\tilde{\sigma}_{e,3}^2$ computed from 1,000 realizations of model (3.7) with $\rho = 0$ (columns 1–3) and $\rho = 0.5$ (columns 1, 4 and 5).

nominators of (3.4) and (3.5), respectively. Using data generated from a white noise model, we define $\Delta_{\epsilon,k} = \tilde{\sigma}_{\epsilon,k}^2 - \tilde{\sigma}_{\epsilon,k-1}^2$, $k = 1, ..., L$, and the corresponding statistics $\Delta_{\eta,k}$ and $\Delta_{e,k}$ are defined in an analogous way. Table 2a indicates that there is very small systematic change in the estimates of $\tilde{\sigma}_{\epsilon,k}^2$, $\tilde{\sigma}_{\eta,k}^2$ and $\tilde{\sigma}_{e,k}^2$ as k changes, especially for $nT = 512$ and $\rho = 0$. To get an idea of the effect of dropping the correction terms k and $k/(n-1)$, the results achieved by setting $k = 0$ in the denominators of (3.4) and (3.5) are tabulated in Table 2b.

Simulation experiments with the AR(3) model defined in (3.7) gave for $k \geq 3$ similar results to those obtained for the white noise model.

4 The Choice between $\tilde{\sigma}_\epsilon^2$ and $\tilde{\sigma}_e^2$

For T small and $\eta_t \not\equiv$ constant it is clear that $\tilde{\sigma}_\epsilon^2$ should be preferred to $\tilde{\sigma}_e^2$ because the latter is inconsistent. For T large the situation is less clear. It

Table 2

(a)

n	T	L	$\sigma_\epsilon^2 = 1$ $\hat{\Delta}_\epsilon$	$\sigma_\eta^2 = 0$ $\hat{\Delta}_\eta$	$\sigma_e^2 = 1$ $\hat{\Delta}_e$	$\sigma_\eta^2 = 1$ $\hat{\Delta}_\eta$	$\sigma_e^2 = 2$ $\hat{\Delta}_e$
2	256	10	0.00011	−0.00002	0.00009	−0.00002	0.00009
4	128	10	0.00013	−0.00009	0.00004	0.00005	0.00019
8	64	10	0.00002	0.00000	0.00002	−0.00015	−0.00013
16	32	10	0.00002	−0.00001	0.00001	−0.00023	−0.00022
32	16	8	0.00007	−0.00001	0.00006	−0.00089	−0.00082
64	8	4	−0.00001	−0.00004	−0.00005	−0.00058	−0.00060
128	4	2	−0.00011	−0.00006	−0.00018	−0.00422	−0.00434
2	64	10	0.00192	−0.00060	0.00131	−0.00028	0.00164
4	32	10	0.00105	−0.00018	0.00088	0.00047	0.00153
8	16	8	0.00043	−0.00009	0.00034	0.00131	0.00173
16	8	4	0.00030	−0.00031	−0.00001	−0.00701	−0.00670
32	4	2	0.00025	−0.00058	−0.00034	−0.01466	−0.01442

(b)

n	T	L	$\hat{\Delta}_{\epsilon,0}$	$\hat{\Delta}_{\eta,0}$	$\hat{\Delta}_{e,0}$	$\hat{\Delta}_{\eta,0}$	$\hat{\Delta}_{e,0}$
2	256	10	−0.00398	0.00407	0.00009	0.00814	0.00416
4	128	10	−0.00270	0.00133	−0.00137	0.00433	0.00163
8	64	10	−0.00263	0.00068	−0.00195	0.00321	0.00058
16	32	10	−0.00302	0.00038	−0.00264	0.00327	0.00025
32	16	8	−0.00398	0.00026	−0.00371	0.00395	−0.00003
64	8	4	−0.00398	0.00011	−0.00387	0.00471	0.00073
128	4	2	−0.00405	0.00003	−0.00402	0.00410	0.00005
2	64	10	−0.01694	0.01837	0.00144	0.03779	0.02085
4	32	10	−0.01416	0.00772	−0.00643	0.02423	0.01007
8	16	8	−0.01746	0.00476	−0.01271	0.02646	0.00900
16	8	4	−0.01633	0.00209	−0.01424	0.01663	0.00030
32	4	2	−0.01592	0.00097	−0.01495	0.01822	0.00230

The table is based on 1,000 realizations of the white noise model $X_{(i)t} = \eta_t + \varepsilon_{(i)t}$ with $\rho = 0$ (columns 1–3) and $\rho = 0.5$ (columns 1, 4 and 5). (a) $\hat{\Delta}_\varepsilon = (L-1)^{-1}\sum_{k=1}^{L}\hat{\Delta}_{\epsilon,k}$ where $\hat{\Delta}_{\epsilon,k} = \text{ave}(\tilde{\sigma}_{\epsilon,k}^2) - \text{ave}(\tilde{\sigma}_{\epsilon,k-1}^2)$ and $\text{ave}(\tilde{\sigma}_{\epsilon,k}^2)$ is the average over the 1,000 realizations of $\tilde{\sigma}_{\epsilon,k}^2$. $\hat{\Delta}_\eta$ and $\hat{\Delta}_e$ are defined by replacing all occurrences of ϵ in the definition of $\hat{\Delta}_\epsilon$ by η and e, respectively. (b) $\hat{\Delta}_{\epsilon,0}$, $\hat{\Delta}_{\eta,0}$ and $\hat{\Delta}_{e,0}$ are defined as $\hat{\Delta}_\varepsilon$, $\hat{\Delta}_\eta$ and $\hat{\Delta}_e$ in Table 2a but with $k = 0$ in the denominators of (3.4) and (3.5).

resembles the choice between the AR estimates $\tilde{a}$ and $\hat{a}$ in Hjellvik and Tjøstheim (1999) where it was shown that $\tilde{a}$ is preferable to $\hat{a}$ unless ρ is less than the threshold $1/(n-1)$ as $T \to \infty$. The choice between $\tilde{\sigma}_\epsilon^2$ and $\tilde{\sigma}_e^2$ will also depend on the intercorrelation. Unfortunately, we have not been able to carry through the analysis in full generality. We have only been able to establish the existence of a threshold in the very special case where $p = k = L = 0$, and where $\{\epsilon_{(i)t}\}$ and $\{\eta_t\}$ are independent Gaussian variables. The simulations indicate the existence of such a threshold in the general case. In the special case of $p = k = L = 0$, we have $\sigma_\epsilon^{-2}\sum_t\sum_i(\epsilon_{(i)t} - \epsilon_{.t})^2 \sim \chi^2_{(n-1)T}$, and it follows that

$$\text{var}(\tilde{\sigma}_\epsilon^2) = \frac{2\sigma_\epsilon^4}{(n-1)T}. \tag{4.1}$$

For $\tilde{\sigma}_\eta^2$ we have that

$$\tilde{\sigma}_\eta^2 = \frac{1}{T-1}\sum_{t=1}^{T}(\eta_t - \eta_.)^2 + \frac{1}{T-1}\sum_{t=1}^{T}(\epsilon_{.t} - \epsilon_{..})^2$$
$$+\frac{2}{T-1}\sum_{t=1}^{T}(\eta_t - \eta_.)(\epsilon_{.t} - \epsilon_{..}) - \frac{1}{n}\tilde{\sigma}_\epsilon^2$$
$$\doteq \tilde{C}_1 + \tilde{C}_2 + \tilde{C}_3 + \tilde{C}_4. \tag{4.2}$$

Here $\sigma_\eta^{-2}\sum_t(\eta_t - \eta_.)^2 \sim \chi^2_{T-1}$ and $n\sigma_\epsilon^{-2}\sum_t(\epsilon_{.t} - \epsilon_{..})^2 \sim \chi^2_{T-1}$. This implies that $\text{E}(\tilde{\sigma}_\eta^2)$ $= \text{E}(\tilde{C}_1 + \tilde{C}_2 + \tilde{C}_3 + \tilde{C}_4) = \sigma_\eta^2 + \sigma_\epsilon^2/n + 0 - \sigma_\epsilon^2/n = \sigma_\eta^2$. Further, $\text{var}(\tilde{\sigma}_\eta^2) =$ $\sum_j\text{var}(\tilde{C}_j) + \sum_{j\neq k}\text{cov}(\tilde{C}_j, \tilde{C}_k)$ where $\text{var}(\tilde{C}_4) = 2\,\sigma_\epsilon^4/\{n^2(n-1)T\}$, and by chi-square arguments, $\text{var}(\tilde{C}_1) = 2\,\sigma_\eta^4/(T-1)$ and $\text{var}(\tilde{C}_2) = 2\sigma_\epsilon^4/\{n^2(T-1)\}$. For $\tilde{C}_3$ we have $\text{E}(\tilde{C}_3) = 0$ and straightforward computations yield $\text{var}(\tilde{C}_3) =$ $4\sigma_\eta^2\sigma_\epsilon^2/\{n(T-1)\}$. It can be shown that none of the covariance terms contribute. Thus we end up with

$$\text{var}(\tilde{\sigma}_\eta^2) = \sum_{j=1}^{4}\text{var}(\tilde{C}_j) = \frac{2\sigma_\eta^4}{T-1} + \frac{2\sigma_\epsilon^4}{n^2(T-1)} + \frac{4\sigma_\eta^2\sigma_\epsilon^2}{n(T-1)} + \frac{2\sigma_\epsilon^4}{n^2(n-1)T},$$

and as $n \to \infty$ for a fixed T, $\text{var}(\tilde{\sigma}_\eta^2) \sim \text{var}(\tilde{C}_1) = 2\sigma_\eta^4/(T-1)$, again showing the inconsistency of $\tilde{\sigma}_\eta^2$ as $n \to \infty$ if $\sigma_\eta^2 > 0$.

Since both $\tilde{\sigma}_\epsilon^2$ and $\tilde{\sigma}_\eta^2$ are unbiased, clearly so is $\tilde{\sigma}_e^2$. To find the variance of $\tilde{\sigma}_e^2$, note that we can write $\tilde{\sigma}_e^2$ as in (4.2) with C_4 replaced by $\tilde{\sigma}_\epsilon^2(n-1)/n$, and we get

$$\text{var}(\tilde{\sigma}_e^2) = \frac{2\sigma_\eta^4}{T-1} + \frac{2\sigma_\epsilon^4}{n^2(T-1)} + \frac{4\sigma_\eta^2\sigma_\epsilon^2}{n(T-1)} + \frac{2(n-1)\sigma_\epsilon^4}{n^2T}. \tag{4.3}$$

Thus, $\text{var}(\tilde{\sigma}_e^2) \to \text{var}(\tilde{\sigma}_\eta^2)$ as $n \to \infty$ for a fixed T, and $\tilde{\sigma}_e^2$ is not consistent. We are now ready to investigate the relative precision of $\tilde{\sigma}_\epsilon^2$ and $\tilde{\sigma}_e^2$ as $T \to \infty$. Using that $\sigma_\eta^2 = \sigma_\epsilon^2\rho/(1-\rho)$, we find from (4.1) and (4.3) that as $T \to \infty$

$$\frac{\text{var}(\tilde{\sigma}_\epsilon^2)}{\text{var}(\tilde{\sigma}_e^2)} \sim \frac{n}{n(n-1)C_\rho^2 + 2(n-1)C_\rho + (n-1)}, \tag{4.4}$$

where $C_\rho = \rho/(1-\rho)$. For $\rho = 0$ we see that $\text{var}(\tilde{\sigma}_\epsilon^2)/\text{var}(\tilde{\sigma}_e^2) \to n/(n-1)$ and $\tilde{\sigma}_e^2$ is clearly preferable, especially for n small. Setting the asymptotic variance ratio of (4.4) equal to 1, we get:

$$n(n-1)C_\rho^2 + 2(n-1)C_\rho - 1 = 0,$$

Table 3

n:	2	4	8	16	32	64	128	256
ρ_0	0.2679	0.1165	0.0548	0.0266	0.0131	0.0065	0.0032	0.0016
$T = 1000$	1.0241	0.9430	1.0049	1.0048				
$T = \ \ 100$	1.0559	1.0794	1.0157	0.9931				

The table shows the values of the cross-over point ρ_0 given by (4.5) for some values of n, and for $n \leq 16$ the ratio $\operatorname{var}(\tilde{\sigma}_\epsilon^2)/\operatorname{var}(\tilde{\sigma}_e^2)$ estimated from 1,000 realizations of the white noise model $X_{(i)t} = \eta_t + \epsilon_{(i)t}$ with $\rho = \rho_0$.

Table 4

n:	2	4	8	16
$T = 1000$	1.0367	0.9266	1.0151	0.9931
$T = \ \ 100$	0.9174	0.9452	1.0418	1.0277

The relation $\operatorname{var}(\tilde{\sigma}_{\epsilon,3}^2)/\operatorname{var}(\tilde{\sigma}_{e,3}^2)$ estimated from 1,000 realizations of model (3.7) with $\rho = \rho_0$ where ρ_0 is given by (4.5).

which has the solution:

$$C_\rho = \frac{-(n-1) + \sqrt{(n-1)(2n-1)}}{n(n-1)}.$$

This implies that for ρ equal to

$$\rho_0 = \frac{-(n-1) + \sqrt{(n-1)(2n-1)}}{(n-1)^2 + \sqrt{(n-1)(2n-1)}} \tag{4.5}$$

the asymptotic variances of $\tilde{\sigma}_\epsilon^2$ and $\tilde{\sigma}_e^2$ as $T \to \infty$ are equal, whereas for $\rho < \rho_0$, $\tilde{\sigma}_e^2$ is preferable. The values of ρ_0 are given in Table 3 for selected values of n together with some simulated values of $\operatorname{var}(\tilde{\sigma}_\epsilon^2)/\operatorname{var}(\tilde{\sigma}_e^2)$ for $T = 1,000$ and $T = 100$.

Using this threshold for the AR(3) process (3.7) also gave quite good results, as can be seen from Table 4. But in this case we have not been able to back it up with theoretical calculations.

5 Order Determination

The first order determination criterion in the time series case is the Final Prediction Error (FPE) criterion by Akaike (1969). If $\{\epsilon_{(i)t}\}$ and $\{\eta_t\}$ are iid such that σ_e^2 is the AR prediction error we can follow the same line of argument as in the traditional one-series case (cf. e.g. Brockwell and Davis, 1996, s. 5.5.1): Let $\{X_{(i)t}, \ i = 1, \ldots, n, \ t = 1, \ldots, T\}$ and $\{Y_{(i)t}, \ i = 1, \ldots, n, \ t = 1, \ldots, T\}$

be two independent realizations of an $AR(p)$ panel-process with coefficients $a_1, ..., a_p, p < T$, and let $\tilde{a}(p, Y)$, $k \geq p$ be the estimate obtained by replacing $\{X_{(i)t}\}$ by $\{Y_{(i)t}\}$ in (3.2). Then the mean square prediction error of the one-step predictor $\tilde{a}^\tau(p, Y)x_{(i)t}$ of $X_{(i)t+1}$ is

$$E\{X_{(i)t+1} - \tilde{a}^\tau(p,Y)x_{(i)t}\}^2 = E[X_{(i)t+1} - a^\tau(p)x_{(i)t} - \{\tilde{a}^\tau(p,Y) - a^\tau(p)\}x_{(i)t}]^2$$
$$= \sigma_e^2 + E[\{\tilde{a}(p,Y) - a(p)\}^\tau \Gamma_x \{\tilde{a}(p,Y) - a(p)\}], \qquad (5.1)$$

and where we write $a(p)$ for a. Assuming asymptotic normality for $\tilde{a}^\tau(p, Y)$ (cf. Hjellvik and Tjøstheim, 1999), we have that as $nT \to \infty$,

$$\tilde{a}(p,Y) \sim N\left(a, \frac{\sigma_e^2 \Gamma_x^{-1}}{(n-1)(T-L)}\right).$$

This implies that

$$\frac{(n-1)(T-L)}{\sigma_e^2}[\{\tilde{a}(p,Y) - a(p)\}^\tau \Gamma_x \{\tilde{a}(p,Y) - a(p)\}] \sim \chi_p^2$$

and

$$E[\{\tilde{a}(p,Y) - a(p)\}^\tau \Gamma_x \{\tilde{a}(p,Y) - a(p)\}] \sim \frac{p\sigma_e^2}{(n-1)(T-L)}.$$

Inserting in (5.1) we get

$$\text{FPE} = E[\{X_{(i)T+1} - \tilde{a}^\tau(p,Y)x_{(i)t}\}^2] \sim \sigma_e^2\left(1 + \frac{p}{(n-1)(T-L)}\right).$$

Using the asymptotically (as $T \to \infty$) unbiased estimator $\tilde{\sigma}_{e,k}^2$ of σ_e^2 defined in (3.6), the estimated mean square prediction error of $X_{(i)T+1}$ to be minimized is:

$$\text{FPE}_{\tilde{e},k} = \tilde{\sigma}_{e,k}^2\left(1 + \frac{k}{(n-1)(T-L)}\right), \quad k = 0,1,.... \qquad (5.2)$$

Unfortunately $\text{FPE}_{\tilde{e},k}$ depends on ρ through $\tilde{\sigma}_{e,k}^2$, which is not consistent for T fixed as $n \to \infty$ in the correlated case. However, it can be made totally independent of ρ by replacing $\tilde{\sigma}_{e,k}^2$ by $\tilde{\sigma}_{\epsilon,k}^2$ in (5.2). Then we obtain:

$$\text{FPE}_{\tilde{\epsilon},k} = \tilde{\sigma}_{\epsilon,k}^2\left(1 + \frac{k}{(n-1)(T-L)}\right). \qquad (5.3)$$

Note that $\text{FPE}_{\tilde{\epsilon},k}$ does not estimate the final prediction error FPE but rather $(1-\rho)\text{FPE}$ since $\sigma_\epsilon^2 = (1-\rho)\sigma_e^2$. However, in the order determination algorithm it is the relative—not absolute—magnitudes of FPE that are used, this justifying using $\text{FPE}_{\tilde{\epsilon},k}$ as an alternative to $\text{FPE}_{\tilde{e},k}$. The advantage of using the former is that if the correlation is increased, both $\tilde{a}(k)$ and $\tilde{\sigma}_{\epsilon,k}^2$ remain unchanged, and hence $\text{FPE}_{\tilde{\varepsilon},\text{k}}$ remains the same. In addition, both $\tilde{a}(k)$ and $\tilde{\sigma}_{\varepsilon,k}^2$ are consistent for T fixed as $n \to \infty$ for $k \geq p$. The drawback is that for n and ρ small, $\text{FPE}_{\tilde{\varepsilon},\text{k}}$ is unstable compared to $\text{FPE}_{\tilde{e},k}$ since $\text{var}(\tilde{\sigma}_{\varepsilon,k}^2)$ is larger than $\text{var}(\tilde{\sigma}_{e,k}^2)$ (cf. Section 4).

A closely related criterion is the AIC criterion. Since (Brockwell and Davis, 1996, ch. 5) the computation of the criterion again has the evaluation of the prediction error as its essential ingredient, it can be introduced and analyzed in the panel case in much the same manner as the FPE criterion. We have not actually carried out simulations with this criterion, but in view of its close analogy to the FPE-criterion for AR-models, it must be expected to give very similar results.

Both the AIC and FPE criteria overestimate the order of an AR(p) time series model asymptotically, and it seems safe to state the conjecture that this will be so in the panel case as well. To avoid this overestimation a stronger penalty term is needed as in the so-called BIC-criterion. We have used two ad hoc generalizations of that in the one-series case (cf. Schwarz, 1978), namely

$$\text{BIC}_{\tilde{e},\text{k}} = nT \log \tilde{\sigma}_{e,k}^2 + k \log(nT) \quad \text{and} \quad \text{BIC}_{\tilde{\varepsilon},\text{k}} = nT \log \tilde{\sigma}_{\varepsilon,k}^2 + k \log(nT).$$

These criteria generally give a lower order and they can be expected to outperform the FPE criteria for low order models. However, in practical terms the concept of "true order" is debatable, and perhaps efficiency of representation as discussed by Shibata (1980) is more relevant. For time series AIC (and FPE) are more efficient than BIC in an AR(∞) case. It would be of interest if similar results could be established in the panel case.

In Table 5, $\text{FPE}_{\tilde{e},k}$ is compared to $\text{FPE}_{\tilde{\varepsilon},\text{k}}$ for AR models of order $p = 0, 1,$ 5 and 9. To illustrate the use of BIC to reduce overestimation it has been included too. From the table we see for example that in the white noise case with $n = 2$ and $T = 256$, $\text{FPE}_{\tilde{\varepsilon},\text{k}}$ yields 721 correct identifications, independent of ρ, whereas $\text{FPE}_{\tilde{e},k}$ yields 838 and 730 correct identifications for $\rho = 0$ and $\rho = 0.5$, respectively. In general we see that for the FPE criteria, $\text{FPE}_{\tilde{e},k}$ is superior in the uncorrelated case and inferior in the correlated case, as expected. One exception is the case with $n = 2$ and $T = 64$ where $\text{FPE}_{\tilde{\varepsilon},k}$ is best also in the correlated case. This means that the cross-over point given by (4.5) should not be used uncritically to decide between $\text{FPE}_{\tilde{\varepsilon},\text{k}}$ and $\text{FPE}_{\tilde{e},k}$.

We also see that for $nT = 512$ the BIC criteria are superior to the FPE criteria except for the 9th order case. For $nT = 128$ the FPE criteria are superior both in the 5th and the 9th order cases. It remains to analyze these criteria asymptotically. We believe that this can be done using arguments similar to those in the one-series case (cf. Shibata, 1976, 1980).

In Section 3 we emphasized the importance of standardization using a fixed L in addition to bias correction. This can be illustrated quite dramatically for the order determination criteria (we look at FPE only). By using an analogue of (2.2) instead of $\tilde{a}(k)$ of (3.2) for estimating a, and replacing L by k in the

Table 5

n	T	L	$p = 0$			$p = 1$			$p = 5$			$p = 9$		
(a) FPE														
2	256	10	721	(838	730)	713	(847	707)	737	(851	717)	827	(871	805)
4	128	10	720	(781	613)	735	(794	595)	759	(816	608)	832	(856	733)
8	64	10	700	(749	481)	743	(763	481)	735	(749	508)	850	(847	636)
16	32	10	705	(732	402)	705	(722	360)	726	(724	372)	837	(846	538)
32	16	8	710	(700	369)	689	(699	238)	741	(748	308)			
64	8	4	746	(749	389)	751	(762	233)						
128	4	2	769	(762	455)	840	(835	348)						
2	64	10	715	(844	707)	540	(752	602)	305	(427	372)	163	(174	196)
4	32	10	698	(769	589)	616	(673	424)	390	(408	284)	243	(244	238)
8	16	8	704	(722	472)	559	(555	256)	365	(387	231)			
16	8	4	727	(741	446)	580	(574	222)						
32	4	2	771	(754	491)	719	(695	318)						
(b) BIC														
2	256	10	943	(985	973)	921	(985	981)	860	(946	914)	464	(524	518)
4	128	10	977	(987	970)	972	(987	957)	949	(964	886)	530	(519	459)
8	64	10	972	(981	919)	980	(981	891)	933	(944	746)	544	(533	413)
16	32	10	971	(980	851)	971	(974	687)	917	(922	536)	529	(533	361)
32	16	8	940	(939	643)	925	(925	406)	881	(881	372)			
64	8	4	945	(947	594)	949	(949	295)						
128	4	2	931	(929	598)	941	(944	379)						
2	64	10	879	(968	943)	620	(735	687)	168	(139	164)	28	(7	15)
4	32	10	914	(958	886)	669	(703	545)	188	(145	153)	25	(12	27)
8	16	8	879	(892	738)	604	(572	326)	219	(217	162)			
16	8	4	905	(914	679)	617	(594	251)						
32	4	2	919	(904	640)	684	(650	314)						

The table is based on 1,000 realizations of a white noise model and AR(p) models with $p = 1, 5,$ 9, $a_1 = a_p = 0.3$ and $a_2 = ... = a_{p-1} = 0$. (a) The number of cases in which the right order was chosen by FPE$_{\tilde{e},k}$. Corresponding numbers for FPE$_{\hat{e},k}$ are found in parentheses. The first of these numbers is for $\rho = 0$ and the other for $\rho = 0.5$. (b) Same as (a), but for BIC$_{\tilde{e},k}$ and BIC$_{\hat{e},k}$.

residual variance estimates (3.4)–(3.6) and in (5.2) and (5.3), more of the data would be exploited. This is usually done in the one-series case, and it is natural in order to exploit the available data. However, the resulting order determination algorithm yields very poor results, especially for n large. To illustrate, let $\tilde{\sigma}_{e,k}^{2\prime}$ be the adjusted version of $\tilde{\sigma}_{e,k}^2$ with L replaced by k, and FPE$'_{\tilde{e},k}$ the corresponding order determination criterion for $n \geq 2$. The associated, obviously defined statistics for $n = 1$ are $\hat{\sigma}_{e,k}^{2\prime}$ and FPE$'_{\hat{e},k}$. In Table 6, FPE$'_{\tilde{e},k}$ and FPE$'_{\hat{e},k}$ are compared to FPE$_{\tilde{e},k}$ and FPE$_{\hat{e},k}$, respectively. We see that FPE$'_{\tilde{e},k}$ is clearly inferior to FPE$_{\tilde{e},k}$, especially for n large. The explanation can be found in Figure 1 and in Table 7. In Figure 1, $\tilde{\sigma}_{e,k}^{2\prime}$ is compared to $\tilde{\sigma}_{e,k}^2$ for three realizations of an uncorrelated white noise model with $T = 16$. If we define

Table 6

n	T	L	$p = 0$		$p = 1$		$p = 5$		$p = 9$	
1	512	10	600	(703)	585	(692)	634	(746)	768	(830)
2	256	10	698	(838)	691	(847)	690	(851)	788	(871)
4	128	10	508	(781)	564	(794)	522	(816)	705	(856)
8	64	10	430	(749)	439	(763)	447	(749)	623	(847)
16	32	10	399	(732)	364	(722)	359	(724)	528	(846)
32	16	8	324	(700)	367	(699)	343	(748)		
64	8	4	348	(749)	353	(762)				
128	4	2	407	(762)	513	(835)				
1	128	10	616	(709)	596	(686)	472	(582)	390	(460)
2	64	10	733	(844)	667	(752)	349	(427)	154	(174)
4	32	10	615	(769)	534	(673)	272	(408)	191	(244)
8	16	8	536	(722)	438	(555)	176	(387)		
16	8	4	417	(741)	338	(574)				
32	4	2	458	(754)	414	(695)				

The table is based on the same realizations as Table 5. It shows the number of correct identifications achieved by $\mathrm{FPE}'_{\tilde{e},k}$ for $n \geq 2$ and $\mathrm{FPE}'_{\hat{e},k}$ for $n = 1$. The corresponding numbers for $\mathrm{FPE}_{\tilde{e},k}$ and $\mathrm{FPE}_{\hat{e},k}$ are given by the numbers in parentheses.

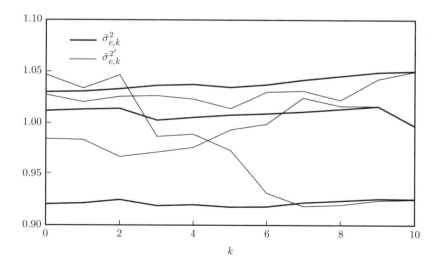

Figure 1

The figure shows for $k = 0, \ldots, 10$ $\tilde{\sigma}^2_{e,k}$ and $\tilde{\sigma}^{2\prime}_{e,k}$ for three independent realizations of the model $X_{(i)t} = \epsilon_{(i)t}$ with $n = 32$ and $T = 16$.

Table 7

n	T	L	$|\delta'|$	$|\delta|$	$|\delta'|/|\delta|$
1	512	10	0.00297	0.00196	1.51
2	256	10	0.00427	0.00267	1.60
4	128	10	0.00515	0.00218	2.36
8	64	10	0.00731	0.00233	3.14
16	32	10	0.01113	0.00280	3.98
32	16	8	0.01817	0.00388	4.68
64	8	4	0.02553	0.00385	6.63
128	4	2	0.03596	0.00409	8.79
1	128	10	0.01273	0.00837	1.52
2	64	10	0.02056	0.01356	1.56
4	32	10	0.02679	0.01257	2.13
8	16	8	0.04272	0.01684	2.54
16	8	4	0.05470	0.01566	3.49
32	4	2	0.07564	0.01583	4.78

The table is based on 1,000 realizations of the white noise model
$X_{(i)t} = \eta_t + \epsilon_{(i)t}$. For each realization δ_k and δ'_k is calculated, and
the table shows the average absolute values of δ_k and δ'_k.

$\delta'_k = \tilde{\sigma}^{2\prime}_{e,k} - \tilde{\sigma}^{2\prime}_{e,k-1}$ and $\delta_k = \tilde{\sigma}^2_{e,k} - \tilde{\sigma}^2_{e,k-1}$, we see that the absolute value of δ'_k tends
to be large compared to that of δ_k. In Table 7 the average absolute values of
δ'_k and δ_k, $k = 1, ..., 10$, computed from 1,000 realizations of the white noise
model are compared, and we see that even for $n = 1$ the difference is
substantial. The reason for the large variability of $\tilde{\sigma}^{2\prime}_{e,k}$ and hence of δ'_k is of
course that as we increase the order from k to $k + 1$, n sample points are taken
away, and this is a substantial part of the data if n is large and T small. Using
L instead of k means that exactly the same data points are used in the
evaluation of all $\tilde{\sigma}^2_{e,k}$, $k = 0, ..., L$, and the above mentioned variability as a
function of k is avoided, although for a *fixed* k the variance of $\tilde{\sigma}^2_{e,k}$ would in
general be higher than for $\tilde{\sigma}^{2\prime}_{e,k}$.

6 A Real Data Example

We end by taking a look at a real data example discussed in Bjørnstad,
Champley, Stenseth and Saitoh (1996) and in Stenseth, Bjørnstad and Saitoh
(1996). The data are presented in Figure 2 and consist of the logarithms of
the yearly catch of gray-sided voles over a period of $T = 31$ years at $n = 34$
different locations of the island of Hokkaido. In Table 8 the residual variance
estimates $\tilde{\sigma}^2_{\epsilon,k}$ and $\tilde{\sigma}^2_{\eta,k}$ are given for $k = 0, ..., 10$. Inserting these into (2.4) we
get an estimated correlation ranging from 0.305 for $k = 0$ to 0.335 for $k = 10$,
which means that common causes (σ^2_η) explain about 30 percent of the variation.

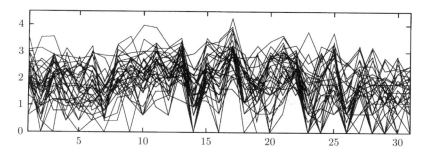

Figure 2

The figure shows $\log (X_{(i)t} + 1)$ where $\{X_{(i)t}, i = 1, ..., 34, t = 1, ..., 31\}$ is the number of gray-sided voles trapped each year from 1961 to 1992 at 34 different locations in Hokkaido, Japan.

Table 8

k	0	1	2	3	4	5	6	7	8	9	10
$\tilde{\sigma}^2_{\xi,3}$	0.610	0.570	0.560	0.550	0.533	0.534	0.534	0.534	0.527	0.525	0.518
$\tilde{\sigma}^2_{\eta,k}$	0.268	0.279	0.262	0.265	0.243	0.238	0.243	0.242	0.252	0.254	0.261

Estimates of residual variances for the voles data.

Alternatively, ρ can be estimated as in Section 5 of Hjellvik and Tjøstheim (1998). This gives an estimate of 0.31. These results imply that the order determination criteria based on $\tilde{\sigma}^2_{\epsilon,k}$ would be more appropriate than those based on $\tilde{\sigma}^2_{e,k}$.

It should be noted that there are indications of a weak nonlinearity in the data. Further, model (1.2) does not take into account a weak spatial dependence present in the correlation structure in the voles data. The correlation between two series within a group seems to depend on the distance between the corresponding locations. If $\hat{\rho}_{ij}$ is the estimated correlation between series i and series j, and δ_{ij} the distance between the corresponding locations, the correlation between $\hat{\rho}_{ij}$ and δ_{ij} estimated from all pairs $\{ij, i = 1, ..., 33, j = i + 1, ..., 34\}$ is –0.245. This is in contrast to model (1.2) where the pairwise correlation is the same between all possible pairs of series. Figure 3 shows a scatter plot of $\hat{\rho}_{ij}$ and δ_{ij}.

For $L = 10$ the order chosen by $\text{FPE}_{\tilde{\epsilon},k}$ and $\text{BIC}_{\tilde{\epsilon},k}$ is 10 and 4, respectively. From Figure 4 we see that the reduction in the estimated prediction error achieved by increasing the order from 4 to 10 is relatively small compared to the reduction achieved by going from $k = 0$ to $k = 4$. In fact we have that $\text{FPE}_{\tilde{\epsilon},4} - \text{FPE}_{\tilde{\epsilon},10} = 0.0113$ whereas $\text{FPE}_{\tilde{\epsilon},0} - \text{FPE}_{\tilde{\epsilon},4} = 0.0722$, so considering the approximation involved and the tendency of the FPE criterion to over-estimate, $k = 4$ seems to be a reasonable choice.

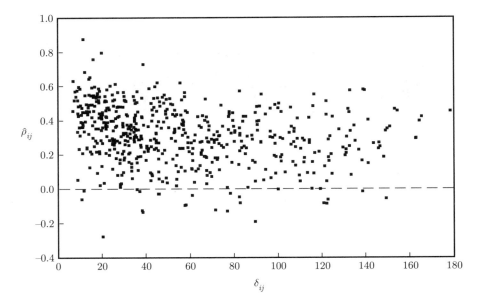

Figure 3

The figure shows the pairwise estimated correlation $\hat{\rho}_{ij}$ between the series in the voles data set as a function of the distance δ_{ij} between the series.

7 Discussion and Possible Extensions

There are a number of extensions and associated open problems which are worth mentioning. Looking at the model formulation itself, it is clear that a general model containing individual effects λ_i such as in (1.1) would be of more use to econometricians. By differencing such a model we obtain:

$$Z_{(i)t} = \sum_{j=1}^{p} a_j Z_{(i)t-j} + \eta_t + \eta_{t-1} + \epsilon_{(i)t} - \epsilon_{(i)t-1},$$

where we have omitted the explanatory variables $W_{(i)t}$, and where $Z_{(i)t} = X_{(i)t} - X_{(i)t-1}$. Averaging over i and then using instrumental variables, $a_1, ..., a_p$ and σ_ϵ^2 can be estimated. Work on this problem is in progress.

Another extension of model (2.1) is to allow for a time-varying $a = a_t$ or for individual effects $a = a_{(i)}$ in the AR parameters. In the first case, if we let $n \to \infty$,

$$\tilde{a}_t^\tau = \frac{1}{n}\sum_{i=1}^{n}(X_{(i)t+1} - X_{\cdot t+1})(x_{(i)t} - x_{\cdot t})^\tau \left\{ \frac{1}{n}\sum_{i=1}^{n}(x_{(i)t} - x_{\cdot t})(x_{(i)t} - x_{\cdot t})^\tau \right\}^{-1},$$

would be a consistent estimate of a_t. We can then estimate the residuals,

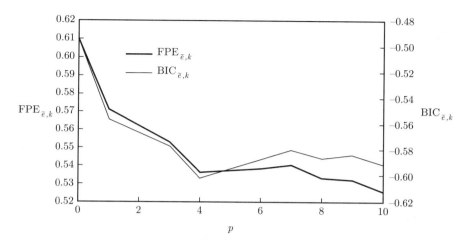

Figure 4

The figure shows $\text{FPE}_{\tilde{e},k}$ and $\text{BIC}_{\tilde{e},k}$ as a function of p for the voles data.

$$\tilde{e}_{(i)t} = X_{(i)t} - \tilde{a}_t^\tau x_{(i)t-1},$$

and we could try to proceed as before, but clearly the asymptotic theory in the Appendices would be more difficult.

In the case of dependence on i, with an obvious dot-notation for summation over t,

$$\tilde{a}_{(i)}^\tau = \frac{1}{T-p} \sum_{t=p}^{T-1} (X_{(i)t+1} - X_{(i)\cdot})(x_{(i)t} - x_{(i)\cdot})^\tau$$
$$\times \left\{ \frac{1}{T-p} \sum_{t=p}^{T-1} (x_{(i)t} - x_{(i)\cdot})(x_{(i)t} - x_{(i)\cdot})^\tau \right\}^{-1},$$

would be a consistent estimator of $a_{(i)}$ as $T \to \infty$, and residuals are formed as:

$$\tilde{e}_{(i)t} = X_{(i)t} - \tilde{a}_{(i)}^\tau x_{(i)t-1}.$$

Many economic time series are believed to be nonstationary, and an alternative extension to letting a be time dependent is to allow for unit roots in the characteristic polynomial. Unit root panels have been treated but not—to our knowledge—when they are intercorrelated. It is a challenging task.

Looking next at estimation, compared to Hjellvik and Tjøstheim (1998) we have simplified in that Burg estimators have not been used. For a panel with a small T and large n, such estimates have been shown to perform much better than the estimate $\tilde{a}$. This is due to edge effects being taken care of. The difference is especially startling for $T = 2$ or 3, but for such a small T, the appropriateness of doing an order determination analysis can be questioned of course.

A challenging design problem is the problem of choosing the upper limit L of allowable orders. In our simulation experiments we have chosen $L = \min(10,\ T/2)$ for a fixed number of observations $nT = 512$ and $nT = 128$. Clearly it is reasonable to let L increase with T, but even in the univariate case this is a question that has not received too much attention, but which is of considerable practical importance. An added difficulty in the panel case is the standardization in terms of L introduced in Section 3 and further discussed in Section 5.

Finally, the possibility of doing an asymptotic analysis of the FPE, AIC and BIC-type criteria themselves is an important problem. A good deal of work has been done in the univariate case (see e.g. Shibata, 1976, 1980), and it would be of large interest (and within reach, we believe) to extend this to the panel situation.

Appendix A

We want to show the asymptotic unbiasedness of $\tilde{\sigma}^2_{\epsilon,k}$, $k \geq p$, defined in (3.4). To ease notation we only treat the case $k = p$. An identical derivation holds for $k > p$. Let

$$Q = \sum_{t=L+1}^{T} \sum_{i=1}^{n} (\tilde{e}_{(i)t,p} - \tilde{e}_{\cdot t,p})^2 = \sum_{t=L+1}^{T} \sum_{i=1}^{n} (\tilde{\epsilon}_{(i)t,p} - \tilde{\epsilon}_{\cdot t,p})^2,$$

where

$$\tilde{e}_{(i)t,p} = X_{(i)t} - \tilde{a}^\tau x_{(i)t-1},$$

and $\tilde{a} = \{\tilde{a}_{p,1},\ ...,\ \tilde{a}_{p,p}\}^\tau$ is defined by (3.2). Then

$$Q = \sum_{t=L+1}^{T} \sum_{i=1}^{n} \{X_{(i)t} - \tilde{a}^\tau x_{(i)t-1} - (X_{\cdot t} - \tilde{a}^\tau x_{\cdot t-1})\}^2$$

$$= \sum_{t=L+1}^{T} \sum_{i=1}^{n} \{X_{(i)t} - X_{\cdot t} - a^\tau(x_{(i)t-1} - x_{\cdot t-1}) - (\tilde{a}^\tau - a^\tau)(x_{(i)t-1} - x_{\cdot t-1})\}^2$$

$$= \sum_{t=L+1}^{T} \sum_{i=1}^{n} \{e_{(i)t} - e_{\cdot t} - (\tilde{a}^\tau - a^\tau)(x_{(i)t-1} - x_{\cdot t-1})\}^2$$

$$= \sum_{t=L+1}^{T} \sum_{i=1}^{n} (e_{(i)t} - e_{\cdot t})^2 - 2 \sum_{t=L+1}^{T} \sum_{i=1}^{n} (e_{(i)t} - e_{\cdot t})(\tilde{a}^\tau - a^\tau)(x_{(i)t-1} - x_{\cdot t-1})$$

$$+ \sum_{t=L+1}^{T} \sum_{i=1}^{n} (\tilde{a}^\tau - a^\tau)(x_{(i)t-1} - x_{\cdot t-1})(x_{(i)t-1} - x_{\cdot t-1})^\tau (\tilde{a}^\tau - a^\tau)^\tau$$

$$\doteq Q_1 + Q_2 + Q_3.$$

For Q_1 we have that

$$\frac{1}{\sigma_\epsilon^2} \sum_{t=L+1}^{T} \sum_{i=1}^{n} (e_{(i)t} - e_{\cdot t})^2 = \frac{1}{\sigma_\epsilon^2} \sum_{t=L+1}^{T} \sum_{i=1}^{n} (\epsilon_{(i)t} - \epsilon_{\cdot t})^2,$$

and since $E(\epsilon_{(i)t} - \epsilon_{\cdot t})^2 = (1 - 1/n)\,\sigma_\epsilon^2$, we have

$$E(Q_1) = (n-1)(T-L)\sigma_\epsilon^2.$$

From Hjellvik and Tjøstheim (1999) we have that asymptotically

$$\tilde{a} - a \sim \sigma_e^{-2}\sigma_\epsilon^2\Gamma_x^{-1}\,\frac{1}{(n-1)(T-L)} \sum_{s=L+1}^{T} \sum_{j=1}^{n} (e_{(j)s} - e_{\cdot s})(x_{(j)s-1} - x_{\cdot s-1}), \qquad (A.1)$$

which implies that

$$Q_2 \sim \frac{-2}{(n-1)(T-L)} \sum_{t=L+1}^{T} \sum_{i=1}^{n} (\epsilon_{(i)t} - \epsilon_{\cdot t})$$

$$\times \sum_{s=L+1}^{T} \sum_{j=1}^{n} (e_{(j)s} - e_{\cdot s})(x_{(j)s-1} - x_{\cdot s-1})\sigma_e^{-2}\sigma_\epsilon^2\Gamma_x^{-1}(x_{(i)t-1} - x_{\cdot t-1}). \qquad (A.2)$$

It is not difficult to show, using the technique of Hjellvik and Tjøstheim (1999), that asymptotically Q_2 is χ^2-distributed and that the mean in the asymptotic distribution is obtained by taking expectations in the right hand side of (A.2). Taking expectations we only get contributions for $s = t$, so that asymptotically:

$$E(Q_2) \sim \frac{-2}{(n-1)(T-L)} \sum_{t=L+1}^{T} \sum_{i=1}^{n} \sum_{j=1}^{n} E(\epsilon_{(i)t} - \epsilon_{\cdot t})(\epsilon_{(j)t} - \epsilon_{\cdot t})$$

$$\times E(x_{(j)t-1} - x_{\cdot t-1})^\tau \sigma_e^{-2}\sigma_\epsilon^2\Gamma_x^{-1}(x_{(i)t-1} - x_{\cdot t-1}).$$

Using that in general for a $p \times p$ matrix A, $a^\tau A a = \mathrm{Tr}(a^\tau A a) = \mathrm{Tr}(aa^\tau A)$, we get

$$E(Q_2) \sim \frac{-2}{(n-1)(T-L)} \sum_{t=L+1}^{T} \sum_{i=1}^{n} \sum_{j=1}^{n} E(\epsilon_{(i)t} - \epsilon_{\cdot t})(\epsilon_{(j)t} - \epsilon_{\cdot t})$$

$$\times \mathrm{Tr}\{E(x_{(i)t-1} - x_{\cdot t-1})(x_{(j)t-1} - x_{\cdot t-1})^\tau \sigma_e^{-2}\sigma_\epsilon^2\Gamma_x^{-1}\}.$$

Further, we have

$$E\{(\epsilon_{(i)t} - \epsilon_{\cdot t})(\epsilon_{(j)t} - \epsilon_{\cdot t})\} = \begin{cases} (1-n^{-1})\sigma_\epsilon^2, & i = j \\ -n^{-1}\sigma_\epsilon^2, & i \neq j \end{cases},$$

$$E\{(x_{(i)t-1} - x_{\cdot t-1})(x_{(j)t-1} - x_{\cdot t-1})^\tau\} = \begin{cases} (1-n^{-1})\sigma_e^2\sigma_\epsilon^{-2}\Gamma_x, & i = j \\ -n^{-1}\sigma_e^2\sigma_\epsilon^{-2}\Gamma_x, & i \neq j \end{cases},$$

$$\mathrm{Tr}\{\sigma_e^{-2}\sigma_\epsilon^2\Gamma_x\sigma_e^{-2}\sigma_\epsilon^2\Gamma_x^{-1}\} = \mathrm{Tr}\{I_p\} = p,$$

where I_p is the p-dimensional identity matrix corresponding to the fact that $x_{(i)t}$ has dimension p. This gives

$$E(Q_2) \sim \frac{-2}{n-1}\{n(1-n^{-1})^2 + n(n-1)(-n^{-1})^2\}p\sigma_\epsilon^2 = -2p\sigma_\epsilon^2.$$

For Q_3 we get, using (A.1), that

$$Q_3 \sim \frac{1}{(n-1)^2(T-L)^2}$$
$$\times \sum_{t=L+1}^{T} \sum_{i=1}^{n} \sum_{s=L+1}^{T} \sum_{j=1}^{n} \sum_{u=L+1}^{T} \sum_{l=1}^{n} (\epsilon_{(j)s} - \epsilon_{\cdot s})(\epsilon_{(l)u} - \epsilon_{\cdot u})(x_{(j)s-1} - x_{\cdot s-1})^\tau$$
$$\times \sigma_e^{-2}\sigma_\epsilon^2\Gamma_x^{-1}(x_{(i)t-1} - x_{\cdot t-1})(x_{(i)t-1} - x_{\cdot t-1})^\tau \sigma_e^{-2}\sigma_\epsilon^2\Gamma_x^{-1}(x_{(l)u-1} - x_{\cdot u-1}).$$

Note that

$$\frac{1}{(n-1)(T-L)} E\left\{ \sum_{t=L+1}^{T} \sum_{i=1}^{n} (x_{(i)t-1} - x_{\cdot t-1})(x_{(i)t-1} - x_{\cdot t-1})^\tau \right\} = \sigma_e^2 \sigma_\epsilon^{-2}\Gamma_x$$

and that only $s = u$ contributes in the expression for Q_3. We therefore get that the mean in the asymptotic distribution for Q_3 is given by:

$$Q_3 \sim \frac{1}{(n-1)(T-L)} \sum_{s=L+1}^{T} \sum_{i=1}^{n} \sum_{j=1}^{n} (\epsilon_{(i)s} - \epsilon_{\cdot s})(\epsilon_{(j)s} - \epsilon_{\cdot s})$$
$$\times E(x_{(j)s-1} - x_{\cdot s-1})^\tau \sigma_e^{-2}\sigma_\epsilon^2\Gamma_x^{-1}(x_{(i)s-1} - x_{\cdot s-1}),$$

and since this is the same expression as was treated for $E(Q_2)$, we obtain:

$$E(Q_3) \sim p\sigma_\epsilon^2.$$

Collecting terms, we have

$$E(Q) = E(Q_1) + E(Q_2) + E(Q_3) \sim \sigma_\epsilon^2\{(n-1)(T-L) - p\},$$

and therefore

$$\tilde{\sigma}_{e,p}^2 = \frac{1}{(n-1)(T-L) - p} \sum_{t=L+1}^{T} \sum_{i=1}^{n} (\tilde{e}_{(i)t,p} - \tilde{e}_{\cdot t,p})^2$$

is an asymptotically unbiased estimator for σ_e^2.

Appendix B

We again restrict ourselves to the case of $k = p$, the derivation being identical but more notationally complex for $k > p$. To derive the asymptotic unbiased-ness of $\tilde{\sigma}_{\eta,k}^2$ defined in (3.5) with $k = p$ as $T \to \infty$, let

$$R = \frac{1}{T-L-1} \sum_{t=L+1}^{T} (\tilde{e}_{\cdot t,p} - \tilde{e}_{\cdot\cdot,p})^2,$$

where

$$\tilde{e}_{\cdot t,p} = X_{\cdot t} - \tilde{a}^\tau x_{\cdot t-1} \quad \text{and} \quad \tilde{e}_{\cdot\cdot,p} = X_{\cdot\cdot} - \tilde{a}^\tau x_{\cdot\cdot}.$$

Using that

$$X_{\cdot t} = a^\tau x_{\cdot t-1} + \epsilon_{\cdot t} + \eta_t \quad \text{and} \quad X_{\cdot\cdot} = a^\tau x_{\cdot\cdot} + \epsilon_{\cdot\cdot} + \eta_\cdot,$$

which implies that

$$X_{\cdot t} - X_{\cdot\cdot} = a^\tau (x_{\cdot t-1} - x_{\cdot\cdot}) + \epsilon_{\cdot t} - \epsilon_{\cdot\cdot} + \eta_t - \eta_\cdot,$$

we get

$$\begin{aligned}
R &= \frac{1}{T-L-1} \sum_{t=L+1}^{T} \{X_{\cdot t} - \tilde{a}^\tau x_{\cdot t-1} - (X_{\cdot\cdot} - \tilde{a}^\tau x_{\cdot\cdot})\}^2 \\
&= \frac{1}{T-L-1} \sum_{t=L+1}^{T} \{X_{\cdot t} - X_{\cdot\cdot} - a^\tau (x_{\cdot t-1} - x_{\cdot\cdot}) - (\tilde{a}-a)^\tau (x_{\cdot t-1} - x_{\cdot\cdot})\}^2 \\
&= \frac{1}{T-L-1} \sum_{t=L+1}^{T} \{\eta_t - \eta_\cdot + \epsilon_{\cdot t} - \epsilon_{\cdot\cdot} - (\tilde{a}-a)^\tau (x_{\cdot t-1} - x_{\cdot\cdot})\}^2 \\
&= \frac{1}{T-L-1} \sum_{t=L+1}^{T} (\eta_t - \eta_\cdot + \epsilon_{\cdot t} - \epsilon_{\cdot\cdot})^2 \\
&\quad - \frac{2}{T-L-1} \sum_{t=L+1}^{T} (\eta_t - \eta_\cdot + \epsilon_{\cdot t} - \epsilon_{\cdot\cdot})(\tilde{a}-a)^\tau (x_{\cdot t-1} - x_{\cdot\cdot}) \\
&\quad + \frac{1}{T-L-1} \sum_{t=L+1}^{T} (\tilde{a}-a)^\tau (x_{\cdot t-1} - x_{\cdot\cdot})(x_{\cdot t-1} - x_{\cdot\cdot})^\tau (\tilde{a}-a) \\
&\doteq R_1 - R_2 + R_3.
\end{aligned}$$

For R_1 we have:

$$\begin{aligned}
R_1 &= \frac{1}{T-L-1} \sum_{t=L+1}^{T} (\eta_t - \eta_\cdot)^2 + \frac{2}{T-L-1} \sum_{t=L+1}^{T} (\eta_t - \eta_\cdot)(\epsilon_{\cdot t} - \epsilon_{\cdot\cdot}) \\
&\quad + \frac{1}{T-L-1} \sum_{t=L+1}^{T} (\epsilon_{\cdot t} - \epsilon_{\cdot\cdot})^2 \doteq R_{11} - 2R_{12} + R_{13},
\end{aligned}$$

where $\mathrm{E}(R_{12}) = 0$, $\mathrm{E}(R_{11}) = \sigma_\eta^2$ and $\mathrm{E}(R_{13}) = n^{-1}\sigma_\epsilon^2$.

Since $x_{\cdot\cdot} \to \mathrm{E}(X_{(i)t}) = 0$, $\eta_\cdot \to \mathrm{E}(\eta_t) = 0$ and $\epsilon_{\cdot\cdot} \to \mathrm{E}(\epsilon_{(i)t}) = 0$ almost surely as $n \to \infty$, we have for R_2 that $\tilde{a} - a$ is given by (A.1) and

$$x_{\cdot t} - x_{\cdot\cdot} \sim x_{\cdot t}, \quad \eta_t - \eta_\cdot \sim \eta_t \quad \text{and} \quad \epsilon_{\cdot t} - \epsilon_{\cdot\cdot} \sim \epsilon_{\cdot t}.$$

Hence $(T - L - 1)R_2/2$ can be written as $\sum_t(R_{21t} + R_{22t})$ where

$$R_{21t} \sim \frac{\eta_t}{(n-1)(T-L)} \sum_{s=L+1}^{T} \sum_{j=1}^{n} (\epsilon_{(j)s} - \epsilon_{\cdot s})(x_{(j)s-1} - x_{\cdot s-1})^\tau \sigma_e^{-2}\sigma_\epsilon^2 \Gamma_x^{-1} x_{\cdot t-1},$$

and

$$R_{22t} \sim \frac{\epsilon_{\cdot t}}{(n-1)(T-L)} \sum_{s=L+1}^{T} \sum_{j=1}^{n} (\epsilon_{(j)s} - \epsilon_{\cdot s})(x_{(j)s-1} - x_{\cdot s-1})^\tau \sigma_e^{-2}\sigma_\epsilon^2 \Gamma_x^{-1} x_{\cdot t-1}.$$

For R_{21t} we have that:

for $t \geq s$, η_t is independent of $(\epsilon_{(j)s} - \epsilon_{\cdot s})(x_{(j)s-1} - x_{\cdot s-1})^\tau \sigma_e^{-2}\sigma_\epsilon^2 \Gamma_x^{-1} x_{\cdot t-1}$, and
for $t < s$, $(\epsilon_{(j)s} - \epsilon_{\cdot s})$ is independent of $\eta_t(x_{(j)s-1} - x_{\cdot s-1})^\tau \sigma_e^{-2}\sigma_\epsilon^2 \Gamma_x^{-1} x_{\cdot t-1}$.

Similarly we have for R_{22t} that:

for $t > s$, $\epsilon_{\cdot t}$ is independent of $(\epsilon_{(j)s} - \epsilon_{\cdot s})(x_{(j)s-1} - x_{\cdot s-1})^\tau \sigma_e^{-2}\sigma_\epsilon^2 \Gamma_x^{-1} x_{\cdot t-1}$,
for $t < s$, $(\epsilon_{(j)s} - \epsilon_{\cdot s})$ is independent of $\epsilon_{\cdot t}(x_{(j)s-1} - x_{\cdot s-1})^\tau \sigma_e^{-2}\sigma_\epsilon^2 \Gamma_x^{-1} x_{\cdot t-1}$ and
for $s = t$, $\epsilon_{\cdot t}(\epsilon_{(j)s} - \epsilon_{\cdot s})$ is independent of $(x_{(j)s-1} - x_{\cdot s-1})^\tau \sigma_e^{-2}\sigma_\epsilon^2 \Gamma_x^{-1} x_{\cdot t-1}$.

But $E\{\epsilon_{\cdot t}(\epsilon_{(j)s} - \epsilon_{\cdot s})\} = n^{-1}\sigma_\epsilon^2 - n^{-1}\sigma_\epsilon^2 = 0$, so asymptotically there are no contributions from the crossterm R_2.

From the above it follows that $(T - L - 1)R_3$ is given by:

$$(T - L - 1)R_3 \sim \sum_{t=L+1}^{T} \frac{1}{(n-1)^2(T-L)^2} \sum_{s=L+1}^{T} \sum_{j=1}^{n} \sum_{u=L+1}^{n} \sum_{k=1}^{n} (\epsilon_{(j)s} - \epsilon_{\cdot s})(\epsilon_{(k)u} - \epsilon_{\cdot u})$$
$$\times (x_{(j)s-1} - x_{\cdot s-1})^\tau \sigma_e^{-2}\sigma_\epsilon^2 \Gamma_x^{-1} x_{\cdot t-1} x_{\cdot t-1}^\tau \sigma_e^{-2}\sigma_\epsilon^2 \Gamma_x^{-1}(x_{(k)u-1} - x_{\cdot u-1}).$$

Here $E(x_{(i)t}x_{(i)t}^\tau) = \Gamma_x$ and $E(x_{(i)t}x_{(j)t}^\tau) = \rho\Gamma_x$, which implies that:

$$E(x_{\cdot t}x_{\cdot t}^\tau) = \frac{1}{n^2}E\left(\sum_{i=1}^{n}\sum_{j=1}^{n} x_{(i)t}x_{(j)t}^\tau\right) = \frac{1}{n}\Gamma_x + \frac{n(n-1)}{n^2}\rho\Gamma_x = \rho\Gamma_x + \frac{1}{n}(1-\rho)\Gamma_x.$$

Further, $\sigma_e^{-2}\sigma_\epsilon^2 = 1/(1 - \rho)$, so that:

$$\frac{1}{T-L}\sum_t x_{\cdot t-1}x_{\cdot t-1}^\tau \sigma_e^{-2}\sigma_\epsilon^2 \Gamma_x^{-1} \sim \left(\frac{\rho}{1-\rho} + \frac{1}{n}\right)I_p,$$

where I_p is the identity matrix of dimension p. As for Q_3 in Appendix A, only $s = u$ contributes for the other terms, and we obtain:

$$E\left\{\frac{1}{(n-1)(T-L)} \sum_{s=L+1}^{T} \sum_{i=1}^{n} \sum_{j=1}^{n} (\epsilon_{(i)s} - \epsilon_{\cdot s})(\epsilon_{(j)s} - \epsilon_{\cdot s})\right.$$
$$\left. \times (x_{(j)s-1} - x_{\cdot s-1})^\tau \sigma_e^{-2}\sigma_\epsilon^2 \Gamma_x^{-1}(x_{(i)s-1} - x_{\cdot s-1})\right\} \sim p\sigma_\epsilon^2 = \frac{p(1-\rho)}{\rho}\sigma_\eta^2.$$

Hence, we get for R_3

$$E\{(T - L - 1)R_3\} \sim \frac{1}{n-1}\left(\frac{\rho}{(1-\rho)} + \frac{1}{m}\right)\frac{p(1-\rho)}{\rho}\sigma_\eta^2 = \frac{p\sigma_\eta^2}{n-1} + \frac{p\sigma_\epsilon^2}{n(n-1)},$$

and for $R = R_1 - R_2 + R_3$

$$(T - L - 1)R \sim \left(T - L - 1 + \frac{p}{n-1}\right)\sigma_\eta^2 + \frac{(T-L-1)(n-1) + p}{n(n-1)}\sigma_\epsilon^2.$$

This implies that

$$E\left\{\frac{1}{T - L - 1 + p/(n+1)}\sum_{t=L+1}^{T}(\tilde{e}_{.t,p} - \tilde{e}_{..,p})^2\right\} \sim \sigma_\eta^2 + \frac{1}{n}\sigma_\epsilon^2,$$

and hence $\tilde{\sigma}_{\eta,p}^2$ defined in (3.5) with $k = p$ is an approximately unbiased estimator for σ_η^2 for T large.

References

Akaike, H. (1969). "Fitting autoregressive models for prediction." *Annals of the Institute of Statistical Mathematics*, 21: 243–7.

Baltagi, B. H. (1995). *Econometric Analysis of Panel Data*. New York: Wiley.

Bjørnstad, O. N., Champley, S., Stenseth, N. C., and Saitoh, T. (1996). "Cyclicity and stability of grey-sided voles, *Clethrionomys rufocanus*, of Hokkaido: spectral and principal components analyses." *Phil. Trans. R. Soc. Lond. B*, 351: 867–75.

Brockwell, P. J. and Davis, R. A. (1996). *Introduction to Time Series and Forecasting*. New York: Springer-Verlag Inc.

Granger, C. W. J. (1996). "Evaluation of panel models: some suggestions from time series." Preliminary draft.

Hjellvik, V. and Tjøstheim, D. (1999). "Modelling panels of intercorrelated autoregressive time series." To appear in *Biometrika*.

Hsiao, C. (1986). *Analysis of Panel Data*. Cambridge: Cambridge University Press.

Mátyas, L. and Sevestre, P. (1992). *The Econometrics of Panel Data*. Dordrecht: Kluwer Academic Publishers.

Schwarz, G. (1978). "Estimating the dimension of a model." *Ann. Statist.*, 6: 461–4.

Shibata, R. (1976). "Selection of the order of an autoregressive model by Akaike's information criterion." *Biometrika*, 63: 117–26.

Shibata, R. (1980). "Asymptotically efficient selection of the order of the model for estimation parameters of a linear process." *Ann. Statist.*, 8: 147–65.

Stenseth, N. C., Bjørnstad, O. N., and Saitoh, T. (1996). "A gradient from stable to cyclic populations of *Clethrionomys rufocanus* in Hokkaido, Japan." *Proc. R. Soc. Lond. B*, 263: 1117–26.

17
Partial Pooling: A Possible Answer to "To Pool or Not To Pool"

FARSHID VAHID

1 Introduction

In a panel discussion on future directions in econometrics,[1] Clive Granger expressed the opinion that statisticians and econometricians should pay more attention to methods of extracting information from large panels, given that such panels are becoming increasingly available. In this spirit, the present paper suggests a procedure for classifying linear conditional expectation functions in "medium-sized" panels, i.e. panels with a moderately large time dimension, and not too large a cross sectional dimension. We are motivated by regional and sectoral panel studies (such as the 50 states of the United States, the 18 OECD countries, 20 two digit manufacturing industries, etc.) where, for each region or sector, the parameters of the conditional expectation function of one (dependent) variable given some other (independent) variables are of interest, and regions or sectors are independent enough so that there are no feedbacks from one region or sector to the other, and hence a VAR analysis on the entire panel would not be appropriate.[2]

A central question in the study of panels with a relatively large time dimension is *when* and *how* the homogeneity assumption, which was particularly (or at least partially) made in earlier panel data studies because the time dimension was small, might be relaxed. This question has attracted some attention under the title of "To pool or not to pool" in the literature. The answer to *when*, seems, at least on the surface, easy: test the null hypothesis that coefficients are equal across the cross sectional units, and do not assume homogeneity if the null is rejected. There is a large body of applied work based on cross country or sectoral data which has tested and rejected the pooling restriction. For

Part of this research was performed while I was visiting the Department of Econometrics and Business Statistics at Monash University. I am indebted to David Dowe for introducing me to coding theory and the works of Professor C. Wallace. I gratefully acknowledge useful discussions with Heather Anderson, Brett Inder, Ann Maharaj and the participants of Monash brown bag workshop. This paper has benefited from many useful comments made by two anonymous referees and by Badi Baltagi, who also kindly provided me with the data used in Baltagi and Griffin (1997). Finally, I am solely responsible for all errors and omissions in this paper.

example, Burnside (1996) rejected the hypothesis that production function parameters across the US manufacturing sectors were equal, and Baltagi and Griffin (1997) rejected the hypothesis that gasoline demand elasticities across the OECD countries were equal. However in both cases, they noticed that the fully heterogeneous model, which assumed no cross equation restrictions, led to very imprecise parameter estimates, which in some cases had the wrong signs. In addition, Burnside observed that the general conclusion about the returns to scale of the US manufacturing sector would be quite different if one used the fully homogeneous, or the fully heterogeneous models. Baltagi and Griffin also noticed that the squared out of sample long-horizon forecast error of the pooled model was considerably smaller than that of the fully heterogeneous model.

This paper studies what can be done when the pooling hypothesis is rejected. We start with the observation that the alternative hypothesis to the pooling restriction is that at least one of the cross section units has different parameters from the rest. Therefore the rejection of the pooling hypothesis does not provide any evidence about the extent of heterogeneity across the cross sections, and in particular does not point to the alternative of a fully heterogeneous model. Of course, in the absence of any a priori reason to group a subset or subsets of cross sectional units, if there is a lot of structure in the time series data, in the sense that parameters can be precisely estimated from the individual time series models, then full heterogeneity will be a safe way to proceed.[3] However, our focus is the case where individual dynamic models do not lead to sharp inference about the parameters. The motivating application underlying this paper is that if an econometrician in country X is asked to predict the short- and long-run effects of a consumption tax on the demand for commodity Y, and if the time series data in that country do not lead to precise estimates of the price elasticity, should the econometrician stop looking at the historical evidence from other countries because the pooling restriction of equality of demand elasticities for *all* countries for which data are available is rejected? Our answer is no, and we suggest a systematic way in which cross sectional units can be partially pooled into homogeneous clusters.[4]

There are many ways that N cross sectional units can be partitioned into non-empty groups. Ideally one would like to find the partition that minimizes some loss function, subject to the constraint that the null hypothesis that the parameters of the cross sectional unit within each sub-group are equal, is not rejected. However, since a global search over all possible partitions might be infeasible, we suggest a hierarchical clustering procedure. It starts from the fully heterogeneous model, and pools the two cross sectional units that are "closest" to each other conditional on their distance being less than a threshold value c, and continues until there are no two groups within c of each other. The measure of inter-cluster distance that we use is the value of the χ^2 test statistic for the null that the parameters of the two clusters are equal. The threshold value that determines when two units can be pooled together is the 5 percent critical value of this null distribution.

It is conceivable that there are more than one non-nested partitions (i.e. partitions that one is not the same as the other with two or more of its sub-groups pooled together) of N cross sectional units for which the homogeneity of cross sectional units within each sub-group is not rejected. Hence it is important to have an appropriate loss function to be able to compare competing partitions and choose the "best" one. We combine features of measures of complexity introduced in coding and information theory in order to develop a loss functions that in addition to goodness of fit and parsimony, explicitly takes account of the (lack of) correspondence to theoretical priors and the (lack of) precision of parameter estimates, which are the two major concerns that have made the researchers wary of the fully heterogeneous models.

Even with the additional requirement that at each stage the closest clusters should be fused only if the resulting partition has a smaller loss than before, our hierarchical clustering algorithm is still a local search algorithm. Similar to other local optimization procedures, this algorithm is not guaranteed to lead to the globally optimal partially pooled model, and may lead to different local optima depending on the path of the search. If N is so large that considering all possible hierarchical paths is not feasible, we use an exchange method on the final outcome of the hierarchical algorithm to make sure that the loss cannot be lowered by moving a unit from one cluster to another.

This paper is structured as follows. Section 2 is the main section of the paper, which gives a more formal and detailed description of the points raised in the introduction. In this section the hierarchical clustering algorithm, the loss function and the exchange method that are the three ingredients of our partial pooling procedure are discussed. Section 3 applies this algorithm to the data used in Baltagi and Griffin (1997) to partially pool gasoline demand schedules of the OECD countries. Section 4 reviews the related literature and one possible alternative method of clustering regressions. We have, rather unconventionally, left the discussion of the related literature to the section after the empirical example, so that the type of empirical questions that have motivated this paper, will be clearer for the reader. The concluding Section 5 discusses some directions for future research on partial pooling of conditional models.

2 Partial Pooling of Dynamic Regressions

2.1 The Statement of the Problem

Suppose we have time series observations of length T, on K variables across N cross sectional units. Let z_{it} denote the period t observation on the K-vector of random variables in cross sectional unit i, and partition z_{it} into the scalar random variable y_{it} (the "dependent variable") and the $K-1$ vector of random variables x_{it} (the "independent variables"). The objective is to provide conditional models for y_{it} given (x_{it}, Φ_{it-1}) for all $i = 1, ..., N$, where Φ_{it-1} is the information set of the cross sectional unit i at time $t-1$, i.e. $\Phi_{it-1} = z_{it-1}$, $z_{it-2}, ...$.

It is important to be clear right at the outset that this paper studies the question of whether some parameters of the conditional expectation functions across cross sectional units are equal, and it assumes that these functions are linear. Throughout the paper, we assume that z_{it} is strictly stationary and ergodic, and that the distribution of y_{it} given (x_{it}, Φ_{it-1}) is normal. We also assume that conditioning on a finite number of lags of z_{it}, completely specifies the dynamics. This rules out moving average errors, and implies autoregressive distributed lag models for every cross section $i = 1, ..., N$:

$$y_{it} = \alpha_i + x'_{it}\beta_i + (z'_{it-1}, ..., z'_{it-p})\gamma_i + \varepsilon_{it}, \quad \varepsilon_{it} \sim \text{iid } N(0, \sigma_i^2), \forall t.$$

The classic "homogeneity assumption" in panel data analysis is the $\theta_i \equiv (\beta_i, \gamma_i, \sigma_i^2)$ of all N cross sectional units are equal, after one allows for cross section specific fixed or random effects α_i. This assumption is absolutely necessary and non-testable for the analysis of panel data with very small T. With panels of moderately large T, this assumption can be tested by the usual tests of parameter restrictions (see Baltagi, 1995, ch. 4). The null and the alternative of this test are:

$H_0 : \theta_1 = \theta_2 = ... = \theta_N$
$H_1 :$ at least one of the above does not hold.

This paper studies cases where the null is rejected. We only consider the fixed effects case, i.e. the case where α_i, $i = 1, ..., N$ are fixed cross section specific constants. The reason for this is that when the time dimension is moderately large, the fixed effect assumption is not too costly. With this assumption, the analysis can be performed on the mean subtracted data (i.e. $z_{it} - \bar{z}_{i.}$), and the constant terms can be ignored. For simplicity, we assume that there is no contemporaneous correlation between ε_{it} and ε_{jt} for $i \neq j$. This, of course, does not mean that the dependent variables in different cross sectional units are not subject to common shocks (for example world-wide shocks when the cross sectional units are countries, or industry-wide shocks when they are sectors of an industry); it only means that such shocks influence the dependent variables solely through the channel of the independent variables.

The rejection of homogeneity does not mean that all θ_i are necessarily different from each other. Our objective is to partition the N cross sectional units into m sub-groups of homogeneous units, so that $\theta_i = \theta_j$ if i and j belong to the same group, and $\theta_i \neq \theta_j$ if i and j belong to different groups. The number of possible ways that N units could be partitioned into m non-overlapping blocks is called the Sterling number of the second kind[5] which can be calculated from the recursion:

$$S(N,m) = S(N-1,m-1) + mS(N-1,m),$$
$$S(1,1) = 1,$$
$$S(N,N) = 1.$$

Hence, partitioning the 18 OECD countries into two non-overlapping blocks would require consideration of $131,071$ possible configurations, and this number would go up to 5.63×10^{14} for the 50 states of the United States. If we want all possible ways that N objects can be partitioned into non-overlapping blocks, we need to sum the Sterling numbers over m, which will give us the so called Bell number of order N, which can be computed through the following recursion:

$$B(N) = 1 + \sum_{m=1}^{N-1} \binom{N-1}{m} B(m),$$
$$B(1) = (1).$$

This leads to 6.82×10^{11} possibilities for the 18 OECD countries, or 1.86×10^{47} possibilities for the 50 states of the United States! Clearly, it is not feasible to search over all possible partitions and choose all partitions which have homogeneous blocks. Our solution is to use a hierarchical agglomerative clustering algorithm with some additional requirements for linking the clusters, rather than just minimizing a distance measure. These requirements, which are explained below, can potentially reduce the number of possible clusters to a manageable number.

2.2 The Clustering Algorithm

A clustering algorithm is based on a distance measure, and starts clustering the two objects which are "closest" to each other, and continues to do so until a desired number of clusters are formed, or another stopping criterion is reached. In our problem, the natural distance measure between clusters i and j, denoted by $d(C_i, C_j)$, would be the likelihood ratio test statistic (or the Chow, 1960, test statistic) that the parameters of the two clusters are equal. The natural stopping rule would be to stop when there are no two blocks whose distance is less than the critical value of that test.

An additional plausible requirement, which we call sub-group consistency, ensures that the formation of clusters is independent of irrelevant alternatives:

Definition 2.1. *A block of cross-sectional units for which the homogeneity restriction is not rejected is* sub-group consistent *if the homogeneity restriction is not rejected for any arbitrary subset of the cross sectional units in that block.*

This requirement ensures that the pooling of the cross sectional units i and j in one block is independent of whether k is in that block. We think this is important, because if two researchers work on the same data, but one of them does not include the cross section unit k in the analysis, the one with the smaller set of cross sectional units should not be surprised to see that the other one has pooled i and j together. This requirement leads us to consider hierarchical procedures which start with the fusion of two units, and only search for a possible third unit to be added to the group among those units that are close enough to both units in that block. In that sense, our procedure is a complete linkage clustering algorithm (Everitt, 1980).

This partial pooling procedure does not take into account the two main concerns that applied researchers have about heterogeneous models, namely that the parameters are imprecisely estimated and have the wrong signs. If partial pooling is based on the magnitude of the above test statistic only, the clustering algorithm may pool a group of cross sectional units that all happen to have imprecisely estimated parameters which have theoretically incorrect signs. Moreover, the between-variation of the right hand side variables of these cross sectional units may decrease standard errors of the estimated parameters of that block, and we may end up with a block with parameter estimates which seem to be precisely estimated, but have the wrong signs. In order to avoid this, we use an additional measure which leads the clustering algorithm to select, from all possible blocks that are close enough, one that leads to precisely estimated parameter estimates which accord with the researchers priors. In other words, we ask our clustering algorithm to move in a direction which reduces the "complexity" of the overall system. In the next sub-section we review how complexity is measured in stochastic systems, and we adopt a measure which explicitly accounts for priors about the parameters and their precision.

2.3 An ad hoc[6] Measure of Complexity

There is no agreement among different disciplines on what "complexity" means, if it can be measured, and how. The sense that we use the term here is closest to the statisticians' notion of "stochastic complexity" (see Rissanen, 1987), which quantifies how complicated a conditional model is, and how unstructured the dependent variable is given the model.[7] One might initially propose the traditional information criteria such as Akaike or the Schwarz criteria as suitable candidates for measuring complexity, at least for linear models. However, such measures do not use information about what the parameters are supposed to measure. For example, suppose two independent researchers are presenting the following two models (M1 and M2) as their estimated *demand* functions for the same commodity based on the same data,

$$\ln Q_t = 2.02 + 0.50 \ln RY_t - 0.01 \ln RP_t + \hat{u}_t$$
$$\quad\quad\;\; (.40) \quad (.25) \quad\quad\quad (.10)$$

$$\ln Q_t = 2.00 + 0.51 \ln RY_t + \hat{u}_t$$
$$\quad\quad\;\; (.40) \quad (.20)$$

where Q, RY and RP denote quantity demanded, real income and relative prices respectively. The information criteria unanimously prefer M2 over M1, the price elasticity is clearly not significantly different from zero, and the omission of relative prices does not change the estimate of income elasticity significantly. However, M2 creates substantial confusion if presented to a panel of economists as a *demand* function. The presenter of M2 is likely to be asked more questions and is likely to need more time to describe and justify her model than the presenter of M1. A good measure of complexity should be able to reflect the idea that in *the context of demand functions*, M2 is more complex (or confusing) than is M1. The analogy of complexity to the amount of description needed to present a model to a learned audience, motivates us to look at measures of complexity used in coding theory.

In coding theory, complexity is defined as the length of the shortest uniquely decipherable code that is needed to encode a data sequence. The two measures of complexity which have been developed on the basis of this principle are the minimum description length (MDL) proposed by Rissanen (1987) and the minimum message length (MML) developed by Wallace and Freeman (1987). For the application in this paper, the two measures are quite similar, and in what follows we provide a brief description of the MML measure.

For a discrete random variable Y which has n possible outcomes $(y_1, ..., y_n)$, the length of the most efficient code needed to code the value y_i is approximately[8] $-\log(\Pr(Y = y_i))$, where the base of logarithm is the number of distinct symbols in the coding alphabet.[9] Conditional on some explanatory variables X, and within the class of parametric conditional models indexed by the parameter vector θ, the length of the most efficient code for encoding a sequence of observed values of Y given an estimate for θ, (say $\hat{\theta}$), will therefore be $-\sum_{i=1}^{n}\log f(y_i|X, \hat{\theta})$. However, the parameters are unknown and are estimated from the sample, and they have to be coded as well. For simplicity assume that there is only one parameter. Assuming that the prior belief about θ is reflected by the density $h(\theta)$, the most efficient code for transmitting $\hat{\theta}$ to the precision δ (the smaller the δ the higher the precision), will be $-\log(h(\hat{\theta}) \delta)$. The precision level δ plays an important role, especially when the parameter space is not discrete, in which case, the coding of a parameter with infinite precision (i.e. $\delta = 0$) would require infinite code length. For a given precision δ, the average length of a code required for encoding the data given the model will be:

$$\frac{1}{\delta} \int_{\hat{\theta}-\delta/2}^{\hat{\theta}+\delta/2} -\sum_{i=1}^{n} \log f(y_i|X,\theta)d\theta.$$

One can derive the optimal precision analytically (i.e. concentrate δ out of the message length formula), and use this to find the minimum message length required for encoding the parameters and the data, given the parameters.

Following this logic, and after some simplifying approximations, for a multiple regression with k parameters, the MML criterion turns out to be:[10]

$$\text{MML} = -\sum_{i=1}^{n} \log f(y_i \mid X, \hat{\theta}) - \log(h(\hat{\theta})) + \frac{1}{2} \log \left| \mathcal{I}_n(\hat{\theta}) \right| + \frac{k}{2} + \frac{k}{2} \log \kappa_k,$$

where $\mathcal{I}_n(\hat{\theta})$ is the empirical Fisher-information matrix[11] and κ_k is a constant, decreasing function of k.

How appropriate is the MML criterion for leading our clustering algorithm? The answer is that although it is an improvement over the usual information criteria, it is not ideal. Its advantage over AIC is the incorporation of prior beliefs. MML uses the priors of the sender and receiver to minimize the code length. This is another way of saying that when the estimated parameters are highly unusual given the theoretical priors of a learned audience,[12] it takes a long discussion to justify the model. However, the MML criterion depends on the units of the regressors X, and it can be arbitrarily manipulated by changing the units of regressors. If the prior distribution is a proper prior, and the researcher is aware of the changes in the unit of measurement of X, then the prior will change accordingly and MML will stay the same. However, if we use MML to choose between competing models with qualitatively different regressors, it is easy to see that, given similar fits, the MML will choose the regressors with higher degree of collinearity. This is exactly the opposite to what we would like. This is not so much a flaw in the principle of MML, but rather a function of the assumptions made to derive the optimal precision at which the parameters are transmitted.

We remedy the above undesirable property of MML, by defining MML as the length of the shortest uniquely decodable code required to transmit the *standardized* coefficients $\psi = \Psi^{1/2}\theta$, ($\Psi = \text{diag}(E(\mathcal{I}_n^{-1}(\theta)/n))$), and the model given the parameters. The prior used for transmitting the parameters is also the prior over the standardized coefficients. When the priors have finite variance MML will be invariant to such change in variables, but when the priors are improper (diffuse priors, or priors on the signs of the parameters only, as often is the case in economics), this change will make a significant difference. The modified MML will have the form:

$$\begin{aligned}
\text{MML}^* &= -\sum_{i=1}^{n} \log f(y_i \mid X, \hat{\psi}) - \log(h(\hat{\psi})) + \frac{1}{2} \log \left| \mathcal{I}_n(\hat{\psi}) \right| + \frac{k}{2} + \frac{k}{2} \log \kappa_k \\
&= -\sum_{i=1}^{n} \log f(y_i \mid X, \hat{\theta}) - \log(h(\hat{\psi})) + \frac{1}{2} \sum_{j=1}^{k} \log \hat{\Psi}_{jj} + \frac{1}{2} \log \left| \mathcal{I}_n(\hat{\theta}) \right| \\
&\quad + \frac{k}{2}(1 + \log \kappa_k + \log n).
\end{aligned}$$

In this form, MML has an interesting interpretation. The third and the fourth terms can be written as:

$$\frac{1}{2}\sum_{j=1}^{k}\log\hat{\Psi}_{jj}+\frac{1}{2}\log\left|\mathcal{I}_{n}(\hat{\theta})\right|=\frac{1}{2}\sum_{j=1}^{k}\log\hat{\Psi}_{jj}-\frac{1}{2}\log\left|\mathcal{I}_{n}^{-1}(\hat{\theta})\right|$$

$$=\sum_{j=1}^{k}H(\hat{\theta}_{j})-H(\hat{\theta}_{1},\hat{\theta}_{2},...,\hat{\theta}_{k}),$$

where H is the entropy, assuming that $(\hat{\theta}_{1},\hat{\theta}_{2},...,\hat{\theta}_{k})$ are normally distributed. The difference between the sum of individual entropies and the joint entropy is a measure of dependence of random variables. This difference is always non-negative (Shannon, 1948), and it is equal to zero if and only if $\hat{\theta}_{1},\hat{\theta}_{2},...,\hat{\theta}_{k}$ are independent. Van Emden (1975) used this difference as a measure of complexity of a covariance structure (Van Emden, 1975, p. 61). In the regression context, it can be seen as a penalty for the redundancy of the regressors (i.e. multicollinearity), and it is minimized when regressors are uncorrelated with each other. This property is highly desirable for our purpose, and MML^{*} is therefore the model selection criterion that we choose to direct our clustering algorithm.

We end this section by comparing MML^{*} with another model selection criterion developed on the basis of Van Emden's measure of covariance complexity. Bozdogan (1990) has introduced the following measure of informational complexity:

$$ICOMP(IFIM)=-\sum_{i=1}^{n}\log f(y_{i}\big|X,\hat{\theta})+\frac{k}{2}\log(\mathrm{trace}(\mathcal{I}^{-1}(\hat{\theta}))/k)+\frac{1}{2}\log\left|\mathcal{I}(\hat{\theta})\right|,$$

which can be expressed alternatively as:

$$ICOMP(IFIM)=-\sum_{i=1}^{n}\log f(y_{i}\big|X,\hat{\theta})+\frac{k}{2}\log\frac{\overline{\lambda}_{a}}{\overline{\lambda}_{g}},$$

where $\overline{\lambda}_{a}$ and $\overline{\lambda}_{g}$ are the arithmetic average and the geometric average of the eigenvalues of $\mathcal{I}^{-1}(\hat{\theta})$. In this criterion, $\frac{k}{2}\log(\mathrm{trace}(\mathcal{I}^{-1}(\hat{\theta}))/k)$ replaces $\frac{1}{2}\sum_{j=1}^{k}\log\hat{\Psi}_{jj}$. Van Emden (1975) introduces this substitution in order to make his measure of covariance complexity invariant to orthonormal transformations of the parameter vector. This does not create a concern in our context, because our procedure is designed for applications in which parameters have specific interpretations. Although their units may be arbitrary, arbitrary orthonormal transformations of them are of no interest. Note that $ICOMP$ is not invariant to changes in units of only one or a subset of parameters, whereas MML^{*} is. Table 1 compares the penalty assigned by AIC, Schwarz, Hannan–Quinn, MML, MML^{*} and $ICOMP$ in three situations: (i) when all regressors are independent; (ii) same as (i) but a quarter of the regressors are multiplied by 100; and (iii) when regressors are highly correlated ($X_{j}=1.2X_{1}+0.5\varepsilon_{j}$, $j=2,...,k$, where $X_{1},\varepsilon_{2},...,\varepsilon_{k}$ are i.i.d.). In each case, the penalty is shown for 8, 16, 24 parameters and 50, 150 and 250 observations.

Table 1 shows the problem of *MML* with correlated regressors very clearly (*MML* actually favors overparameterized models in this case). One can also see the sensitivity of *ICOMP* to change in the units of a subset of regressors. Table 1 also shows that the penalty assigned by *MML** is roughly between

Table 1. Penalty assigned by different model selection criteria in a linear regression when regressors are independent and have equal variances

n	AIC	SC	HQ	ICOMP	MML	MML*
Independent regressors with equal variances, $k = 8$						
50	8	15.65	10.91	1.46	0.51	10.53
150	8	20.04	12.89	1.15	5.24	14.65
250	8	22.09	13.67	1.14	7.27	16.68
Independent regressors with equal variances, $k = 16$						
50	16	31.30	21.82	3.17	−1.30	20.84
150	16	40.09	25.79	1.80	8.47	28.32
250	16	44.17	27.34	1.64	12.66	32.25
Independent regressors with equal variances, $k = 24$						
50	24	46.94	32.74	6.07	−4.55	32.08
150	24	60.13	38.68	2.91	10.95	42.30
250	24	66.26	41.01	2.33	17.30	47.87
The case where regressors are independent but do not have equal variances						
Independent regressors with unequal variances, $k = 8$						
50	8	15.65	10.91	9.74	9.72	10.53
150	8	20.04	12.89	9.25	14.45	14.65
250	8	22.09	13.67	9.24	16.48	16.68
Independent regressors with unequal variances, $k = 16$						
50	16	31.30	21.82	19.37	17.12	20.84
150	16	40.09	25.79	18.02	26.89	28.32
250	16	44.17	27.34	17.84	31.08	32.25
Independent regressors with unequal variances, $k = 24$						
50	24	46.94	32.74	30.55	23.08	32.08
150	24	60.13	38.68	27.31	38.58	42.30
250	24	66.26	41.01	26.66	44.93	47.87
The case of correlated regressors						
Correlated regressors, $k = 8$						
50	8	15.65	10.91	2.92	−4.35	11.76
150	8	20.04	12.89	2.70	0.38	15.86
250	8	22.09	13.67	2.75	2.41	17.93
Correlated regressors, $k = 16$						
50	16	31.30	21.82	4.81	−11.70	22.04
150	16	40.09	25.79	3.58	−1.93	29.63
250	16	44.17	27.34	3.38	2.26	33.55
Correlated regressors, $k = 24$						
50	24	46.94	32.74	7.80	−20.49	33.40
150	24	60.13	38.68	4.56	−4.99	43.56
250	24	66.26	41.01	4.09	1.36	49.16

the Hannan–Quinn penalty, which is $k \ln \ln n$, and the Schwarz penalty, which is $\frac{k}{2} \ln n$. This suggests that MML^* is a consistent order selection criterion.

2.4 The Exchange Method and Other Modifications

Even though at each stage, from among all clusters that are within a critical distance of each other, our algorithm fuses two clusters which together form a subgroup consistent cluster and reduce the MML^* criterion the most, there is still no guarantee that it will lead to the globally optimal partition. Therefore, the algorithm should be amended with the usual enhancements to increase the chance of moving towards the global optimum. Depending on the size of the problem, these modifications might range from starting the clustering algorithm by fusing the second best options at the initial stage, to allowing for some possibility of non-optimal choice (like a mutation in a genetic algorithm) at each stage, and comparing the MML^* of the resulting final configurations.

One enhancement which is easy to implement, would be to add a so called exchange algorithm at the end, to check that the final configuration cannot be improved upon by moving one cross sectional unit from one partition to another, while preserving the sub-group consistency criterion. Suppose that the hierarchical algorithm partitions the n cross sectional units into $m(< n)$ groups and assigns cross sectional unit s to group j. An exchange method simply reevaluates MML^* using $\hat{\theta}_i (i = 1, ..., m; i \neq j)$ for the cross sectional unit s, and if the objective function is improved, s is moved from cluster j to cluster i. After all such exchanges have taken place, the parameters of the new partitions are re-estimated. Since re-estimation can only reduce the sum of squared errors of each cluster, the MML^* is guaranteed to improve at each round of exchange. The exchange method stops when no more MML^* improving exchanges are possible.

3 Empirical Example

Baltagi and Griffin (1983, 1997) consider the following model of gasoline demand for 18 OECD countries:

$$\ln\left(\frac{GAS}{CAR}\right)_{it} = \alpha_i + \beta_1^m \ln\left(\frac{GNP}{POP}\right)_{it} + \beta_2^m \ln\left(\frac{CAR}{POP}\right)_{it} + \beta_3^m \ln\left(\frac{P_{GAS}}{P_{GNP}}\right)_{it}$$

$$+ \beta_4^m \ln\left(\frac{GAS}{CAR}\right)_{it-1} + \beta_5^m \ln\left(\frac{GNP}{POP}\right)_{it-1} + \beta_6^m \ln\left(\frac{CAR}{POP}\right)_{it-1} + \varepsilon_{it},$$

where (GAS/CAR) is the gasoline consumption per auto, (GNP/POP) is the real income per capita, (CAR/POP) is cars per capita and (P_{GAS}/P_{GNP}) is the relative price of gasoline. The parameter α_i is the country specific fixed effect, and β_1^m to β_6^m are elasticities which are the same for all countries in group m.

Baltagi and Griffin consider only the two polar cases; the pooled case in which there is only one group which includes all countries, and the fully heterogeneous case in which each of the eighteen OECD countries is in a separate group. They estimate their model using data from 1960 to 1980, and use it to generate conditional forecasts for 1981 to 1990. They find that the pooled model leads to better forecasts than the individual country models, even though the pooling restriction is strongly rejected.

We ran their 1960 to 1980 data through the clustering algorithm explained in the previous section. The prior we used in the MML^* criterion was Baltagi and Griffin's (1997) prior that the long-run income and price elasticities should be positive and negative respectively. The algorithm produced the following final partition:

Group 1: USA, Japan, Denmark, Ireland, Italy, Netherlands.
Group 2: Belgium, Spain, Sweden, Switzerland, Turkey.
Group 3: Austria, Germany, Norway, UK.
Group 4: Canada, France.
Group 5: Greece.

The resulting parameter estimates are included in Table 2. Had subgroup consistency not been a requirement, combining the first and the third groups would have been an MML^* enhancing fusion, with no possible move after that. The closeness of the first and third groups is also apparent from the elasticity estimates in Table 2.

Using these elasticity estimates, we produced conditional forecasts for gasoline demand for the years 1981 to 1990. The resulting average of the root mean squared forecast errors for all OECD countries is included in Table 3.

Table 2. Parameter estimates for groups
(standard errors in parentheses)

	β_1	β_2	β_3	β_4	β_5	β_6
Group 1	0.289	−0.625	−0.119	0.789	−0.260	0.487
	(0.15)	(0.13)	(0.03)	(0.04)	(0.15)	(0.13)
Group 2	0.192	−1.12	−0.286	0.461	−0.050	0.812
	(0.20)	(0.08)	(0.03)	(0.07)	(0.20)	(0.08)
Group 3	0.248	−0.521	−0.186	0.634	−0.137	0.378
	(0.13)	(0.19)	(0.04)	(0.07)	(0.13)	(0.16)
Group 4	0.456	−1.13	−0.276	0.728	−0.249	0.855
	(0.17)	(0.14)	(0.04)	(0.07)	(0.17)	(0.13)
Group 5	0.571	−0.819	−0.402	−0.388	0.934	−0.155
	(0.57)	(0.25)	(0.14)	(0.20)	(0.71)	(0.32)

Table 3. Grouped vs. pooled average of root mean
squared forecast errors for all OECD countries

Year	Grouped	Pooled
1981	0.034	0.035
1982	0.045	0.046
1983	0.057	0.069
1984	0.063	0.075
1985	0.092	0.098
1986	0.098	0.107
1987	0.123	0.135
1988	0.140	0.155
1989	0.156	0.174
1990	0.177	0.189
10-year average	0.0985	0.108

Note: The figures reported in the third column are different from those reported in Baltagi and Griffin (1997).
They have made some adjustments to their forecasts
that are not fully explained in their paper, and hence
cannot be reproduced.

This table also includes the corresponding measure for the forecasts based on
the pooled (within) estimates of elasticities.

Table 3 shows that for this particular model, there is only a very slight improvement of the out-of-sample performance of the grouped model over the
pooled model. However, there is much more information in the grouping suggested by the data than in the two extreme cases of pooling all countries, or
not pooling at all.

4 Related Literature and an Alternative Procedure

There is an extensive literature on classification and discrimination in statistics. However, most of this literature is concerned with the assignment of a
new observation to one of k populations, given a training sample (see Anderson,
1984, ch. 6). There is also a literature in time series analysis on the classification
of ARMA processes (see Shumway, 1982, for a survey). However, the problem
of clustering time series into an unknown number of groups, according to estimated parameters has not been studied. Our problem is more difficult; we do
not know the number of possible classes, and we want to group cross sectional
units according to the closeness of coefficients estimated from individual unit
time series data. Our solution is basically a hierarchical clustering algorithm
(Everitt, 1980). Previous applications of clustering procedures in economics
include Hirschberg *et al.* (1991) who use them to develop a low dimensional
multivariate quality of life index, and Haruvy (1997) who uses them to explore
the levels of rationality of subjects in the analysis of experimental data.

An alternative to the clustering algorithm used in this paper could be a suitably modified variant of the classification and regression trees (CART) procedure (Breiman *et al.*, 1984). While this procedure is designed for uncovering threshold nonlinearities in the conditional expectation function of cross sectional data, its fundamentals can be used to design a procedure for clustering cross sectional units in a panel. However, it relies on a pre-specified set of threshold variables to group the data. These variables can be a subset of exogenous variables in the model, or they can be given from outside. Therefore, CART is useful only for problems in which there are good reasons to believe that coefficients might be closely related to some specific attributes of the cross sectional units. For example, the coefficients of money demand are often assumed to be similar for "high inflation" countries, and similar for "low inflation" countries (see for example Vogel, 1974, or Duck, 1993). Also, the regressions which study the convergence or non-convergence of per capita income in different countries are often grouped according to their initial level of income and development. Durlauf and Johnson (1995) use CART to cluster countries into homogeneous groups and then they study convergence.

It is interesting to see what cluster arrangement will arise out of an alternative procedure such as CART, and to determine how it will perform in the above forecasting exercise. To use CART, we have to start by specifying a set of threshold variables. Since we have no reason to prefer one of the exogenous variables in the data set over any of the others, we let all three exogenous variables (income per capita, cars per capita and relative gasoline price) be possible threshold variables. Given that we have time-series observations on all of these attributes, we have to decide which observation on these attributes should be chosen as the guide for the CART procedure. For lack of any specific reason to do otherwise, we use the average over the estimation period (21 years).

The CART procedure[13] at each level, uses one of the threshold variables to split the observations of a cluster into two groups. All possible binary splits according to all specified threshold variables, and all possible threshold values are examined. The split with the smallest sum of squared errors (SSE) is chosen and the algorithm is repeated. With cross sectional data sets, these splits have to stop when there are just enough observations in each group to estimate the coefficients. However, in our situation, the coefficients for each unit can be estimated from the time series dimension of that unit, and therefore each of the final nodes will contain only a single unit. Even though it is clear from the outset that the final split will lead to a fully heterogeneous model, it is the path to this final configuration, or the "tree," that matters, because in the next stage, this determines what can be "pruned." "Pruning," which is merging of the units that are the result of a former split, will allow a branch with a late split with a large effect on SSE to survive, while another branch, with successive splits that have less impact on SSE, may be pruned back. In the pruning stage, a penalty for the number of parameters is introduced, and the pruning stops when the increase in the SSE is no longer offset by the decrease in the penalty.

We have used the AIC criterion to guide us when to stop pruning. When there were only two or three countries remaining in each group, the threshold variable could not be identified (i.e. sorting of countries based on any of the three attributes resulted in the same order), but the initial splits were all based on either income per capita or relative price. The resulting final configuration was:

Group 1: Japan, France, Ireland, Italy, Netherlands, UK.
Group 2: Belgium, Norway.
Group 3: Austria, Denmark, Germany.
Group 4: USA, Canada, Sweden, Switzerland.
Group 5: Spain, Turkey.
Group 6: Greece.

If the penalty for overparameterization is increased, groups 1 and 2 are merged first, then they are joined by 3, then by 4, and so on until we get back to the fully homogeneous model. This algorithm also chooses Greece as a clear outlier. However, since CART does not use information on the signs of actual parameters as a guide, two of the above groups, (groups 3 and 5), produce estimates with the "wrong" signs. The average mean squared error of the conditional forecasts produced from this configuration is 0.117, which is larger than the averages of the fully homogeneous model and the partially pooled model reported in Table 3.

The purpose of the above comparison is not to show which algorithm is universally "better." After all, the aim of this paper is to argue that partial pooling should be taken seriously, and to suggest an algorithm which seems plausible for the specific applied problems which motivated this paper. The above comparison simply presents an alternative that might be useful under different circumstances. For example, if there were, in our data set, a measure which reflected the general attitude of the people of each country about energy conservation, then CART might have been a better algorithm than another which does not use this information. Different aspects of each algorithm can be mixed to produce better algorithms for other situations.

5 Summary and Suggestions for Further Research

This paper studies the use of clustering methods for the partial pooling of cross sectional units in a medium sized panel. Here, clustering is based on the closeness of conditional expectation functions, which are assumed to remain constant over time for each cross sectional unit. This assumption will not always be plausible. For instance, the production structure of rapidly industrializing countries will be similar to that of the non-industrial countries during the earlier years of the sample, and then similar to the industrial countries later on. Future work should allow for one or more group switches over time, for every cross sectional unit.

It is well known that the final outcome of any hierarchical clustering algorithm is sensitive to its initial conditions. In this paper we suggest a global objective function, the modified message length criterion, which allows us to choose the best of all different partitions that the clustering algorithm may lead to. We choose this particular objective function because it can easily accommodate prior beliefs, and because it penalizes imprecision in the parameter estimates as well as lack of parsimony. Little work has been done on the properties of this criterion (see Baxter and Dowe, 1996). Future research should compare the performance of this criterion against other model selection criteria.

Since our clustering algorithm uses beliefs about the coefficients to influence the formation of groups, it is natural to think about using a fully Bayesian approach.[14] However, given the enormous number of possible partitions, a fully Bayesian approach to this problem may become unwieldy. With uninformative prior on the possible partitions, and with prior only about the signs of coefficients, a fully Bayesian approach might not lead to a different result, given that there is at least one partition (i.e. the pooled regression) in which the estimated coefficients have the correct sign. Of course this is only a speculation, and the question deserves further research.

Our procedure is motivated by empirical studies in which researchers have no a priori reason to cluster the cross sectional units according to any specific variable. In some situations, there is a good reason to believe that one can group cross sectional units based on a single attribute. For example, countries are often grouped in high inflation and low inflation groups in money demand estimation, or grouped in low, medium and high income groups in growth analysis. It is easy to incorporate this into our algorithm, by fusing, among all units whose distance is less than the critical value, those units which are closer to each other in some specified attribute. The partial pooling procedure, can also be used to check if such a priori groupings are in fact suggested by the data. Alternatively, one can start from the grouping suggested by the algorithm in this paper, and investigate which particular attribute, or combination of attributes, can best determine which group a cross sectional unit belongs to.

In the empirical example of this paper, we clustered the OECD countries according to similarities in their short-run as well as their long-run elasticities. However, economic theory usually only provides good reasons to expect that long-run elasticities might be the same. Future research should investigate the partial pooling of the cross sectional units based on similarities in their long-run elasticities, while allowing the short-run elasticities to be different.

Such an analysis would no longer require the lag specification for all cross sectional units to be the same, and this would allow considerable flexibility in the specification of the dynamics.

Notes

1. "Interdisciplinary Workshop on Time-Series Analysis" organized by the Departments of Economics and Statistics at Texas A&M University, March 23–24, 1996.
2. The question of dimension reduction in linear and non-linear VARs have attracted considerable attention in the last ten years. See, inter alia, Engle and Granger (1987), Ahn and Reinsel (1988), Tiao and Tsay (1989), Vahid and Engle (1993, 1997) and Anderson and Vahid (1998).
3. For example, Ramanathan *et al.* (1997) estimate 24 fully heterogeneous models for conditional expectation of hourly electricity load given temperature, for the 24 hours of the day. In real time forecasting, their model has outperformed all competing linear and nonlinear pooled models.
4. An alternative solution, suggested by Maddala *et al.* (1997), is to assume that coefficients are random across the cross sectional units with a specific distribution. This will, in effect, lead to the shrinkage of the individual country estimates towards the pooled estimate.
5. See the Mathematics Forum web page at http://forum.swarthmore.edu.
6. ad hoc: for the particular end or purpose at hand and without reference to wider application or employment (*Webster's* dictionary).
7. Notice that this is quite different from the notion of complexity in deterministic nonlinear dynamic systems. There, complexity reflects an intricate structure, which can predict the dependent variable perfectly. Here complexity reflects a confused structure, which cannot predict the dependent variable well.
8. The approximation relates to cases where $-\log(p_i)$ is not an integer. However, Shannon (1948) proves the existence of a uniquely decipherable code whose average length is at most one unit larger than $\sum_{i=1}^{n} -p_i \log(p_i)$, which is the average length of the most efficient code if fractional coding were possible (a code theoretic definition for the entropy of Y). Hence $-\log(p_i)$ is taken as the approximate code length, even if it is non-integer.
9. For binary codes, all logarithms will be in base 2 and the code length will be in "bits." Here, in order to compare this measure with information criteria, we choose natural logarithms (the unit is "nits").
10. See Wallace and Freeman (1987) and Baxter and Dowe (1996) for details.
11. Specifically, by empirical Fisher-information matrix we mean $\mathcal{I}_n(\hat{\theta}) = -\sum_{i=1}^{n}(\partial^2 \log f(y_i|X, \hat{\theta})/\partial\theta\partial\theta')$.
12. By "theoretical priors" I mean restrictions implied by economic theory and generally expected by an audience of economists. These would generally involve simple sign restrictions.
13. For a concise and clear explanation of CART, refer to the Technical Appendix in Durlauf and Johnson (1995).
14. A referee has pointed out that a fully Bayesian approach has been used to study a similar sort of problem in biostatistics.

References

Ahn, S. K. and G. C. Reinsel (1988), "Nested Reduced Rank Autoregressive Models for Multiple Time Series," *Journal of the American Statistical Association*, 83: 849–56.

Anderson, H. M. and F. Vahid (1998), "Testing Multiple Equation Systems for Common Nonlinear Components," *Journal of Econometrics*, 84/1: 1–36.

Anderson, T. W. (1984), *An Introduction to Multivariate Statistical Analysis*, 2nd edn. Wiley.

Baltagi, B. H. (1995), *Econometric Analysis of Panel Data*. Wiley.

Baltagi, B. H. and J. M. Griffin (1983), "Gasoline Demand in the OECD: An Application of Pooling and Testing Procedures," *European Economic Review*, 22: 117–37.

Baltagi, B. H. and J. M. Griffin (1997), "Pooled Estimators vs. Their Heterogeneous Counterparts in the Context of Dynamic Demand for Gasoline," *Journal of Econometrics*, 77: 303–27.

Baxter, R. A. and D. L. Dowe (1996), "Model Selection in Linear Regression Using the MML Criterion," Technical Report 96/276, Department of Computer Science, Monash University.

Bearse, P. M., H. Bozdogan, and A. M. Schlottmann (1997), "Empirical Econometric Modelling of Food Consumption using a New Informational Complexity Approach," *Journal of Applied Econometrics*, 12: 563–92.

Bozdogan, H. (1990), "On the Information Based Measure of Covariance Complexity and Its Application to the Evaluation of Multivariate Linear Models," *Communications in Statistics, Theory and Methods*, 19: 221–78.

Breiman, L., J. L. Friedman, R. A. Olshen, and C. J. Stone (1984), *Classification and Regression Trees*. Wadsworth.

Burnside, C. (1996), "Production Function Regressions, Returns to Scale, and Externalities," *Journal of Monetary Economics*, 37: 177–201.

Chow, G. C. (1960), "Tests of Equality between Sets of Coefficients in Two Linear Regressions," *Econometrica*, 28: 591–605.

Duck, N. (1993), "Some International Evidence on the Quantity Theory of Money," *Journal of Money, Credit and Banking*, 25: 1–12.

Durlauf, S. N. and P. A. Johnson (1995), "Multiple Regimes and Cross-Country Growth Behaviour," *Journal of Applied Econometrics*, 10: 365–84.

Engle, R. F. and C. W. J. Granger (1987), "Cointegration and Error Correction: Representation, Estimation and Testing," *Econometrica*, 55: 251–76.

Everitt, B. (1980), *Cluster Analysis*, 2nd edn. Wiley.

Haruvy, E. (1997), "Testing Modes in the Population Distribution of Beliefs from Experimental Games," mimeo, Department of Economics, University of Texas at Austin.

Hirschberg, J. G., E. Maasoumi, and D. J. Slottje (1991), "Cluster Analysis for Measuring Welfare and Quality of Life across Countries," *Journal of Econometrics*, 50: 131–50.

Maddala, G. S., R. P. Trost, H. Li, and F. Joutz (1997), "Estimation of Short-Run and Long-Run Elasticities of Energy Demand From Panel Data Using Shrinkage Estimators," *Journal of Business and Economic Statistics*, 15: 90–100.

Ramanathan, R., R. F. Engle, C. W. J. Granger, F. Vahid, and C. Brace (1997), "Short-Run Forecasts of Electricity Loads and Peaks," *International Journal of Forecasting*, 13: 161–74.

Rissanen, J. (1987), "Stochastic Complexity," *Journal of the Royal Statistical Society, Series B*, 49: 223–39.

Shannon, C. E. (1948), "A Mathematical Theory of Communication," *Bell System Technical Journal*, 27: 379–423.

Shumway, R. H. (1982), "Discriminant Analysis for Time Series," in P. R. Krishnaiah and L. N. Kanal (eds.), *Handbook of Statistics*, vol. 2. North-Holland.

Tiao, G. C. and R. S. Tsay (1989), "Model Specification in Multivariate Time Series," *Journal of the Royal Statistical Society, Series B*, 51: 157–213.

Vahid, F. and R. F. Engle (1993), "Common Trends and Common Cycles," *Journal of Applied Econometrics*, 8: 341–60.

Vahid, F. and R. F. Engle (1997), "Codependent Cycles," *Journal of Econometrics*, 80: 199–221.

Van Emden, M. H. (1975), *An Analysis of Complexity*, 2nd printing, Mathematical Center Tracts: Amsterdam.

Vogel, R. (1974), "The Dynamics of Inflation in Latin America," *American Economic Review*, 64: 102–14.

Wallace, C. S. and P. R. Freeman (1987), "Estimation and Inference by Compact Coding," *Journal of the Royal Statistical Society, Series B*, 49: 240–65.

18
A Simultaneous Binary Choice/ Count Model with an Application to Credit Card Approvals

ANDREW A. WEISS

1 Introduction

In this paper I discuss one of the models that can be formed by combining an equation on count data and an equation on a binary choice variable: the model in which the count is an endogenous explanatory variable in the equation for the binary choice. An example of the model is where the binary choice involves the success or failure of a credit card application and the endogenous count variable is the number of major derogatory reports on the applicant's credit history. Such a model is estimated in Section 8 using data from Greene (1994).

The basic model for the count data is the poisson regression model. In particular, the rates in the poisson are assumed to depend on explanatory variables and a heterogeneous error term. The heterogeneity term allows for the overdispersion often found in real data (i.e., the variance exceeds the mean). It implies, for example, that the distribution of the count variable has a long tail and "excess zeros" relative to the poisson. More importantly for my purposes, the heterogeneity term facilitates the introduction of correlation across the count and binary choice equations—the heterogeneity term is assumed to be correlated with the error in the binary choice model.

A variant of the model is the zero-inflated (ZI) count variable model. This explicitly allows for excess zeros through a binary choice equation. If the ZI-binary choice gives a zero, the count variable is equal to zero. If the ZI-binary choice gives a one, then a poisson model applies. The ZI-binary choice model adds an additional error term potentially correlated with the error in the binary choice equation for the output variable.

The major issue in the specification of the model arises because the marginal distributions of the errors can have quite different forms. For example, a

I am grateful to Rob Engle and the referee for helpful comments, and to Bill Greene for making available the credit card data. Any errors are my own.

common assumption for the heterogeneity term in the poisson model is that it
follows a gamma distribution. This leads to a closed form solution, the negative
binomial (NB) model. The corresponding assumption for the output binary
choice equation is that the errors are normally distributed, leading to the probit
model. The problem is that estimation of the model requires the joint distribution of the errors. To form this, I use the device in Lee (1982)—a transformation
of the gamma is normal and this is assumed to be linearly related to the error
in the probit. An interesting special case is when the correlation between the
transformation of the gamma and the error in the probit is equal to one. Also,
this specification issue does not arise in the simultaneous probit model with a
normally distributed endogenous regressor (e.g., Rivers and Vuong, 1988).

The rest of the paper begins with a review of the poisson model in Section
2. In Section 3, I define and discuss in detail the specification of the binary
choice model with an endogenous NB count variable. In Section 4, I consider
the ZI model. I discuss maximum likelihood estimation of the model in Section
5, model specification and testing in Section 6, the results of a small Monte
Carlo experiment in Section 7, and the empirical example in Section 8. Some
concluding comments are given in Section 9.

2 Poisson and Negative Binomial Models

Let Y_i, $i = 1, ..., n$ be independent random variables giving the numbers of
occurrences of an event in a given period of time. If the distribution of Y_i
follows a poisson distribution with parameter λ_i, then

$$P(Y_i = y_i) \equiv Po(\lambda_i, y_i) = \frac{\lambda_i^{y_i} e^{-\lambda_i}}{y_i!} \quad y_i = 0, 1, ..., \tag{1}$$

where y_i is the realized value of Y_i. To include explanatory variables, λ_i is
modeled by $\lambda_i = \bar{\lambda}_i$ where $\log \bar{\lambda}_i = x_i'\beta_1$, log is the natural logarithm, and x_i is
a $(k \times 1)$ set of explanatory variables with first element unity.[1]

In this model, $E[Y_i|\lambda_i] = \text{var}[Y_i|\lambda_i]$. A common feature in data sets, however,
is that the variance exceeds the mean—there is overdispersion.[2] One way to
relax the mean/variance restriction in the poisson model is via the compound
poisson model. Let

$$\log \lambda_i = x_i'\beta_1 + \epsilon_{1i}, \tag{2}$$

where ϵ_{1i} is an i.i.d. error term representing unobserved heterogeneity. ϵ_{1i} is
assumed to be independent of x_i. The marginal distribution of Y_i is given by

$$P(Y_i = y_i) = \int P(Y_i = y_i | \epsilon_{1i}) g(\epsilon_{1i}) d\epsilon_{1i}$$
$$= \int Po(\lambda_i, y_i) g(\epsilon_{1i}) d\epsilon_{1i}, \tag{3}$$

where $g(.)$ is the probability density function of the ϵ_{1i}.[3] As noted by Cameron and Trivedi (1986), for example, there is some arbitrariness in the choice of g(.). A common assumption is that ϵ_{1i} is distributed as an exponential gamma, i.e., $e^{\epsilon 1i}$ is distributed as a gamma random variable, since this gives a closed form expression for $P(Y_i = y_i)$. With the normalization that $E[e^{\epsilon 1i}] = 1$, the p.d.f. of ϵ_{1i} is given by:

$$g(\epsilon_{1i}) \equiv g_{EG}(\epsilon_{1i}) = \frac{\theta^\theta}{\Gamma(\theta)} e^{-\theta e^{\epsilon_{1i}}} e^{\theta \epsilon_{1i}}, \tag{4}$$

where $\alpha = 1/\theta$ is the variance of the associated gamma and θ is the shape parameter. Substituting equation (4) into equation (3) and solving gives the negative binomial (NB) model:

$$P(Y_i = y_i) = \frac{\Gamma(y_i + \theta)}{\Gamma(\theta)y_i!} u_i^\theta (1 - u_i)^{y_i}, \tag{5}$$

where $u_i = \theta/(\theta + \bar{\lambda}_i)$. In this model, $E[Y_i] = \bar{\lambda}_i$ and $\text{var}[Y_i] = \bar{\lambda}_i + \alpha \bar{\lambda}_i^2$ $(\geq E[Y_i])$. Assuming that ϵ_{1i} is normal, or $e^{\epsilon 1i}$ lognormal, does not give a closed form expression. In this case, θ parameterizes the variance of the lognormal.

The difference between the gamma and lognormal is particularly important when the data is negative binomial with $\theta < 1$. The gamma density has an asymptote at zero for those values of θ, and the shape of the distribution is therefore quite different from that of the lognormal, which starts at the origin. While all values of θ give rise to excess zeros relative to the poisson, as a consequence of the Two Crossing result in Shaked (1980), values of θ less than one will give more draws of $e^{\epsilon 1i}$ and λ_i near zero, and hence high probabilities that $Y_i = 0$. An alternative model for excess zeros—the ZI model—is considered in Section 4 of the paper.

3 Endogenous Count Variable

In this section of the paper, I define and discuss the basic binary choice model with an endogenous NB count variable, derive the form of the likelihood function of the model, and consider some special cases of the model.

3.1 Model and Discussion

The binary choice model is based on a linear equation for an underlying latent variable z_i^*,

$$z_i^* = w_i'\beta_2 + \gamma Y_i + \epsilon_{2i}, \tag{6}$$

where ϵ_{2i} is i.i.d. with mean zero and variance one, w_i is a vector of exogenous

variables, and the first element of w_i is unity. The corresponding observed
variable is the indicator function $z_i = 1(z_i^* > 0)$, i.e.,

$$z_i = 1 \quad \text{if } z_i^* \geq 0$$
$$ = 0 \quad \text{otherwise.} \tag{7}$$

The count model is given by,

$$\log \lambda_i = x_i' \beta_1 + \epsilon_{1i}, \tag{8}$$
$$P(Y_i = y_i | \epsilon_{1i}) = Po(\lambda_i, y_i), \tag{9}$$

with $\epsilon_{1i} \sim g(\epsilon_{1i})$.

Endogeneity of Y_i in the z_i^* equation is implied by correlation between Y_i
and ϵ_{2i}, and it is natural to introduce this through the joint distribution of ϵ_{1i}
and ϵ_{2i}. The basic idea is to build up the joint distribution in such a way that
the marginal distributions for the count and binary choice can have standard
forms, that estimation is straightforward if it turns out that endogeneity is
not a relevant factor, and that there is consistency across models if the approach is to build the marginal models and then test for endogeneity.

I suppose that ϵ_{1i} and ϵ_{2i} satisfy the representation

$$\epsilon_{2i} = \rho_{12} h(\epsilon_{1i}) + \eta_i, \tag{10}$$

where $h(\cdot)$ is some function and, conditional on (ϵ_{1i}, Y_i), η_i is normally distributed with mean zero and variance $\sigma_\eta^2 = 1 - \rho_{12}^2$. The form of h depends on the
application at hand; but in this paper, I concentrate on the model with

$$h(\epsilon_{1i}) = \Phi^{-1}[G(\epsilon_{1i})], \tag{11}$$

where Φ is the c.d.f. of the standard normal and G is the c.d.f. of ϵ_{1i}. Lee (1982)
used the same device in the sample selection/regression model, and it implies
that $h(\epsilon_{1i})$ is standard normal.

In the rest of this subsection, I discuss some of the issues in the specification
of (10) and (11). In general, the comments also apply to the ZI model in the
next section. To begin, note that Y_i can be modeled ignoring the binary choice
equation and the expression in (11) does not restrict the distribution of the
heterogeneity. For example, ϵ_{1i} may be exponential gamma or normal. Next,
endogeneity is not a material issue if either $\gamma = 0$ or $\rho_{12} = 0$. If $\gamma = 0$, then
the modeling is simple if ϵ_{2i} is unconditionally normal—the binary choice model
can be estimated as a probit and an LM test for $\gamma = 0$ performed. If $\rho_{12} = 0$,
then it is convenient if the binary choice equation can be estimated as a probit,
i.e., if η_i is normal. I develop a test for endogeneity in Section 6.3 and, to see
the effects of allowing for endogeneity in the credit card example, I compare
the results in the model with $\rho_{12} \neq 0$ with those from the model with $\rho_{12} = 0$.

A simple alternative to (11) is

$$h(\epsilon_{1i}) = \epsilon_{1i} - E[\epsilon_{1i}]. \tag{12}$$

This leads to a normal distribution for ϵ_{2i} if ϵ_{1i} is normal, but the distribution of Y_i does not have a closed form. If ϵ_{1i} is exponential gamma then the unconditional distribution of ϵ_{2i} is given by[4]

$$f(\epsilon_{2i}) = \int \phi(\epsilon_{2i} - \rho_{12}h(\epsilon_{1i}))g_{EG}(\epsilon_{1i})d\epsilon_{1i}, \tag{13}$$

where ϕ is the p.d.f. of the standard normal. Depending on the value of θ in the gamma, this distribution is similar in shape to the normal, but skewed to the right.

Of course, more general choices for h can be considered. One extension is obtained by replacing the normal c.d.f. in (11) with that from a semi-nonparametric distribution. In Gallant and Nychka (1987) and Gabler, Laisney, and Lechner (1993), for example, the corresponding density has the form

$$s(x) = \sum_{i,j=0}^{D} \alpha_i \alpha_j x^{i+j} e^{-(x/\delta)^2}, \tag{14}$$

where the degree parameter D must be specified.[5] Alternatively, the five parameter generalized beta and three parameter generalized gamma distributions (e.g., McDonald and Xu, 1995) include the gamma and log normal as special cases. Taking logs gives the exponential gamma and normal. Under (14), equation (11) becomes

$$h(\epsilon) = S^{-1}[G(\epsilon)], \tag{15}$$

where $S(x)$ is the c.d.f. corresponding to $s(x)$; and it is relatively complicated to impose normalization restrictions on $S(x)$ so that ϵ_{2i} has mean zero and variance one (e.g., Gabler et al., 1993) and to calculate $S^{-1}(x)$. A more straightforward approach is to add a polynomial term to h directly, e.g.,

$$h^*(\epsilon_{1i}) = h(\epsilon_{1i})(\alpha_0 + \alpha_1\epsilon_{1i} + \ldots + \alpha_k\epsilon_{1i}^k). \tag{16}$$

I derive the LM test for the $H_0 : \alpha_1 = \ldots = \alpha_k$ in Section 6.6, but leave the topic of estimation with (16) to future work.

Recent variations on the NB model have used series expansions in the distribution for the heterogeneity and in the distribution for the counts themselves (e.g., Gurmu, 1997, and Cameron and Johansson, 1997, respectively). The former implies a more complicated form for G while it is not clear how to incorporate the latter in the current framework.

Note also that the model does not allow the special case of an endogenous poisson variable, since $\text{var}(\epsilon_{1i}) = 0$ implies that Y_i cannot be endogenous. One way to model this possibility is to write the poisson in terms of underlying waiting times and assume that these are correlated with ϵ_{2i}. Since I am interested in the case when the count variable is overdispersed, however, I do not pursue this approach in the current paper.[6]

The model is also different from certain other simultaneous probit models in the literature, e.g., Rivers and Vuong (1988). In that paper, the endogenous variable is represented by a linear model on a set of instruments and a normal error. Estimation can be based on substituting out the endogenous variable since the errors in the resulting equation are still normally distributed. Here, taking expectations shows that Y_i can be written as a nonlinear function of the variables in x_i, $Y_i = e^{x_i'\beta_i} + \omega_i$, for some ω_i. But the errors in the binary choice equation obtained by substituting for Y_i, i.e., $\epsilon_{2i} + \gamma\omega_i$, are not normally distributed. The equivalent of the two-stage conditional maximum likelihood estimator in Rivers and Vuong (1988) requires the distribution of $\epsilon_{2i} + \gamma\omega_i$, which in turn depends on the specification of the joint distribution of ϵ_{1i} and ϵ_{2i}. The same applies to the nonlinear least squares estimator based on $E[z_i]$, since $E[z_i] = P(z_i = 1) = P(\epsilon_{2i} + \gamma\omega_i > -w_i'\beta_2 - \gamma e^{x_i'\beta_i})$. Another alternative is semi-nonparametric estimation (e.g., Horowitz, 1992; Klein and Spady, 1994), but this is no simpler than the estimation suggested here. Also, it would not give an estimate of ρ_{12}.

Finally, note that h depends on unknown parameters in the distribution of ϵ_{1i}. This must be taken into account in the estimation of the model.

3.2 Joint Probabilities and Likelihood Function

The observed variables are z_i and Y_i; and

$$
\begin{aligned}
P(z_i = 1, Y_i = y_i) &= P(z_i = 1 | Y_i = y_i) P(Y_i = y_i) \\
&= \int P(z_i = 1 | Y_i = y_i, \epsilon_{1i}) P(Y_i = y_i | \epsilon_{1i}) g(\epsilon_{1i}) d\epsilon_{1i} \\
&= \int \Phi_i(\epsilon_{1i}) Po(\lambda_i, y_i) g(\epsilon_{1i}) d\epsilon_{1i},
\end{aligned}
\tag{17}
$$

where $Po(\lambda_i, y_i)$ was defined in equation (1) and $\Phi(\epsilon_{1i}) = \Phi((w_i'\beta_2 + \gamma y_i + \rho_{12} h(\epsilon_{1i}))/\sigma_\eta)$. The expression for $P(z_i = 0, Y_i = y_i)$ is given by (17), with Φ replaced by $1 - \Phi$.

The likelihood function is given by

$$
L(\psi) = \prod_{i=1}^{n} P(z_i = 1, Y_i = y_i)^{z_i} P(z_i = 0, Y_i = y_i)^{1-z_i},
\tag{18}
$$

where ψ is the vector of parameters, $\psi = (\beta_1', \beta_2', \gamma, \rho_{12}, \theta)'$. The likelihood function can also be written as:

$$
\begin{aligned}
L(\psi) &= \prod_{i=1}^{n} P(z_i = 1 | Y_i = y_i)^{z_i} P(Y_i = y_i)^{z_i} P(z_i = 0 | Y_i = y_i)^{1-z_i} P(Y_i = y_i)^{1-z_i} \\
&= \prod_{i=1}^{n} P(z_i = 1 | Y_i = y_i)^{z_i} P(z_i = 0 | Y_i = y_i)^{1-z_i} \times \prod_{i=1}^{n} P(Y_i = y_i) \\
&= L_2(\beta_2, \gamma, \rho_{12}, \beta_1, \theta) \times L_1(\beta_1, \theta).
\end{aligned}
\tag{19}
$$

Maximizing L_1 over β_1 and θ and then maximizing L_2 over β_2, γ, and ρ_{12} given the L_1-maximizing values of β_1 and θ gives a conditional maximum likelihood estimator (MLE).

Evaluating L_2 is no simpler than evaluating L, but some computational savings are obtained because L_2 is maximized over fewer parameters. The asymptotic covariance matrix of the conditional MLE takes into account the estimation of β_1 and θ (e.g., Murphy and Topel, 1985). Further details on the MLE are given in Section 5.

3.3 Special Cases

If $\rho_{12} = 0$, then, using equation (3),

$$P(z_i = 1, Y_i = y_i) = \Phi(w_i'\beta_2 + \gamma y_i) \int Po(\lambda_i, y_i) g(\epsilon_{1i}) d\epsilon_{1i}$$
$$= P(z_i = 1)P(Y_i = y_i). \tag{20}$$

If $\gamma = 0$ and $\rho_{12} \neq 0$, the system is a seemingly unrelated count/binary choice model. Depending on the specification of $h(\epsilon_{1i})$ and the distribution of ϵ_{1i}, the distribution of ϵ_{2i} may or may not be unconditionally normal. Unfortunately, however, it may be necessary to estimate the full model in order to determine $h(\epsilon_{1i})$, the distribution of ϵ_{1i}, and whether $\gamma = 0$.

Another special case is that with $\rho_{12} = 1$ (or –1). With the normalization that $\mathrm{var}(\epsilon_{2i}) = 1$, $\rho_{12} = 1$ implies that $\epsilon_{2i} = h(\epsilon_{1i})$ with probability one and that, conditionally on the heterogeneity term ϵ_{1i}, the binary choice is deterministic. If $\gamma < 0$, for example, a small value of Y_i implies that z_i^* is positive and $z_i = 1$. In the credit card example (where $\gamma < 0$) a small number of major derogatory reports would imply that the application is approved.[7]

The joint probabilities when $\rho_{12} = 1$ are obtained by arguing as in (17), giving,

$$P(z_i = 1, Y_i = y_i)\big|_{\rho_{12}=1} = \int 1(w_i'\beta_2 + \gamma y_i + h(\epsilon_{1i}) > 0)Po(\lambda_i, y_i)g(\epsilon_{1i})d\epsilon_{1i}. \tag{21}$$

The connect between (17) and (21) is as follows: $\Phi_i(\epsilon_{1i})$ in (17) converges pointwise to the indicator function in (21) as $\rho_{12} \to 1$ for almost all ϵ_{1i}. Hence, by the Lebesgue Dominated Convergence Theorem (LDCT), $P(z_i = 1, Y_i = y_i) \to P(z_i = 1, Y_i = y_i)|_{\rho_{12}=1}$ as $\rho_{12} \to 1$. In this way, the parameter space for the model can be extended to include $\rho_{12} = 1$ (and –1).[8] Similarly, the convergence implies that the likelihood function is continuous from the left at $\rho_{12} = 1$.

4 Zero-Inflated Models

In Section 4.1, I introduce the basic zero-inflated negative binomial (ZINB) model and in Section 4.2, I combine this with the probit model.

4.1 Zero-Inflated Negative Binomial Model

An alternative to the NB model is the ZINB model. Following Lambert (1992) and Greene (1994), for example, let the observed count variable be $Y_i^\#$ and write:

$$Y_i^\# = r_i Y_i, \tag{22}$$

where r_i is a binary choice variable and Y_i is negative binomial with heterogeneity term ϵ_{1i}. Hence $Y_i^\# = 0$ is observed if either $r_i = 0$ or $Y_i = 0$. Also define the latent variable r_i^* such that $r_i = 1(r_i^* > 0)$ and the model:

$$r_i^* = v_i'\beta_3 + \epsilon_{3i}, \tag{23}$$

where v_i is a vector of exogenous variables with first element unity and $\epsilon_{3i} \sim$ i.i.d. $N(0, 1)$. Then

$$
\begin{aligned}
P(Y_i^\# = y_i) &= P(r_i = 0) + P(r_i = 1, Y_i = 0) && \text{if } y_i = 0 \\
&= P(r_i = 1, Y_i = y_i) && \text{otherwise.}
\end{aligned} \tag{24}
$$

From (23), $P(r_i = 0) = 1 - \Phi(v_i'\beta_3)$. If ϵ_{1i} and ϵ_{3i} satisfy a model of the form of (10) and (11), i.e., $\epsilon_{3i} = \rho_{13}h(\epsilon_{1i}) + \xi_i$, where $\xi_i \sim N(0, \sigma_\xi^2)$ and $\sigma_\xi^2 = 1 - \rho_{13}^2$, then

$$P(r_i = 1, Y_i = y_i) = \int \Phi_i^\#(\epsilon_{1i}) Po(\lambda_i, y_i) g(\epsilon_{1i}) d\epsilon_{1i}, \tag{25}$$

where $\Phi_i^\#(\epsilon_{1i}) = \Phi((v_i'\beta_3 + \rho_{13}h(\epsilon_{1i}))/\sigma_\xi)$. The likelihood function is given by:

$$
\begin{aligned}
L^\#(\psi) &= \prod_{i=1}^n P(Y_i^\# = y_i) \\
&= \prod_{i=1}^n \{1(y_i = 0)P(r_i = 0) + P(r_i = 1, Y_i = y_i)\}.
\end{aligned} \tag{26}
$$

As Winkelmann (1998) notes, the correlation in this model, ρ_{13}, has typically been set to zero.

There is a complicated relationship between the NB and ZINB models. First, the ZINB model may make it possible to differentiate between heterogeneity and zero-inflation as the source of excess zeros (as Greene, 1994, notes). In any case, it is likely that the estimated value of θ will be smaller in the NB model than in the ZINB model since ϵ_{1i} in the ZINB model for Y_i does not need to be small in order to give a high probability that $Y_i^\# = 0$. Second, as $v_i'\beta_3 \to \infty$, $P(r_i = 0) \to 0$ and $\Phi_i^\#(\epsilon_{1i}) \to 1$, so that $P(r_i = 1, Y_i = y_i) \to P(Y_i = y_i)$. That is, the ZINB approaches the NB. But standard asymptotic theory assumes a compact parameter space and numerical problems will arise if the estimate of β_3 gets large. If the parameter space for β_3 is bounded, then the models are non-nested. This bounding is the approach taken in Greene (1994) and in Sections 6, 7, and 8 below. Alternatively, setting all but the intercept in β_3 to zero implies that $P(r_i = 0) = \Phi(\beta_{31}) = P_1$ (say), where β_{3i} is the ith element of β_3. If $\rho_{13} = 0$ and $P_1 = 0$, then ZINB $\equiv$ NB.

It is also interesting to note that if the counts are not observed when $r_i = 0$, rather than being equal to zero, then the model becomes a sample selection model with a count outcome variable. The likelihood function is given by:

$$L_S(\psi) = \prod_{i=1}^{n} P(r_i = 0)^{1-r_i} P(r_i = 1, Y_i = y_i)^{r_i}. \tag{27}$$

I do not consider this model further in this paper, although the analysis here clearly applies. See also Terza (1998).

4.2 Endogenous Zero-Inflated Count Variable

Corresponding to the endogenous count variable model in Section 3 is the binary choice model with an endogenous ZINB variable:

$$
\begin{aligned}
z_i^* &= w_i'\beta_2 + \gamma Y_i^{\#} + \epsilon_{2i} \\
z_i &= 1(z_i^* > 0) \\
Y_i^{\#} &= r_i Y_i \\
r_i^* &= v_i'\beta_3 + \epsilon_{3i} \\
r_i &= 1(r_i^* > 0) \\
P(Y_i = y_i | \epsilon_{1i}) &= Po(\lambda_i, y_i) \\
\log \lambda_i &= x_i'\beta_1 + \epsilon_{1i},
\end{aligned}
\tag{28}
$$

and $\epsilon_{1i} \sim g(\epsilon_{1i})$. The observed variables are $Y_i^{\#}$ and z_i. To complete the specification, I assume that $h(\epsilon_{1i})$, ϵ_{2i}, and ϵ_{3i} are trivariate normal with mean zero and covariance matrix,

$$
\begin{pmatrix}
1 & \rho_{12} & \rho_{13} \\
\rho_{12} & 1 & \rho_{23} \\
\rho_{13} & \rho_{23} & 1
\end{pmatrix}.
\tag{29}
$$

This implies that ϵ_{2i} can be written as:

$$\epsilon_{2i} = r_1 h(\epsilon_{1i}) + r_2 \epsilon_{3i} + \zeta_i, \tag{30}$$

where $\zeta_i \sim N(0, \sigma_\zeta^2)$ and

$$
\begin{aligned}
r_1 &= \frac{\rho_{12} - \rho_{23}\rho_{13}}{1 - \rho_{13}^2} \\
r_2 &= \frac{\rho_{23} - \rho_{12}\rho_{13}}{1 - \rho_{13}^2} \\
\sigma_\zeta^2 &= 1 - \frac{\rho_{12}^2 + \rho_{23}^2 - 2\rho_{12}\rho_{23}\rho_{13}}{1 - \rho_{13}^2}.
\end{aligned}
\tag{31}
$$

The likelihood function has the form

$$L(\psi) = \prod_{i=1}^{n} P(z_i = 1, Y_i^{\#} = y_i)^{z_i} P(z_i = 0, Y_i^{\#} = y_i)^{1-z_i}, \tag{32}$$

where, for example,

$$
\begin{aligned}
P(z_i &= 1, Y_i^{\#} = y_i) \\
&= P(z_i = 1 | Y_i^{\#} = y_i) P(Y_i^{\#} = y_i) \\
&= \int \int P(z_i = 1 | Y_i^{\#} = y_i, \epsilon_{1i}, \epsilon_{3i}) P(Y_i^{\#} = y_i | \epsilon_{1i}, \epsilon_{3i}) g(\epsilon_{1i}, \epsilon_{3i}) d\epsilon_{1i} d\epsilon_{3i} \\
&= \int \int \Phi_i(\epsilon_{1i}, \epsilon_{3i}) [1(\epsilon_{3i} < -v_i'\beta_3) 1(y_i = 0) \\
&\quad + 1(\epsilon_{3i} > -v_i'\beta_3) Po(\lambda_i, y_i)] g(\epsilon_{1i}, \epsilon_{3i}) d\epsilon_{1i} d\epsilon_{3i}. \tag{33}
\end{aligned}
$$

In (33), $\Phi_i(\epsilon_{1i}, \epsilon_{3i}) = \Phi((w_i'\beta_2 + \gamma y_i + r_1 h(\epsilon_{1i}) + r_2 \epsilon_{3i})/\sigma_\zeta)$ and

$$
\begin{aligned}
g(\epsilon_{1i}, \epsilon_{3i}) &= BN(h(\epsilon_{1i}), \epsilon_{3i}; \rho_{13}) \frac{g(\epsilon_{1i})}{\phi(h(\epsilon_{1i}))} \\
&= \frac{1}{\sqrt{2\pi}\sigma_\xi} \phi(\epsilon_{3i} | h(\epsilon_{1i})) g(\epsilon_{1i}), \tag{34}
\end{aligned}
$$

where $BN(.,.;\rho)$ is the bivariate normal p.d.f. with means zero, variances one, and correlation ρ, and $\sigma_\xi = \sqrt{(1 - \rho_{13}^2)}$.

Conditional MLE of $(\beta_2', \gamma, \rho_{12}, \rho_{23})'$ given estimates of $(\beta_1', \beta_3', \theta, \rho_{13})'$ is again potentially useful because of the large number of parameters in the model.

The special case corresponding to $\rho_{12} = 1$ in the endogenous NB model is $\sigma_\zeta^2 = 0$. I assume that $|\rho_{13}| < 1$, so that $\sigma_\zeta^2 = 0$ is equivalent to the covariance matrix of $(h(\epsilon_{1i}), \epsilon_{2i}, \epsilon_{3i})'$ having rank 2. An example would be when the three error terms are linear combinations of two independent error terms. To study the convergence of $P(z_i = 1, Y_i^{\#} = y_i)$ as $\sigma_\zeta^2 \to 0$, I define $\rho = (\rho_{12}, \rho_{13}, \rho_{23})'$ and assume that there exists a ρ^* such that $\rho \to \rho^*$ and at $\rho = \rho^*$, $\sigma_\zeta^2 = 0$. As $\rho \to \rho^*$, $\Phi_i(\epsilon_{1i}, \epsilon_{3i}) \to 1(\epsilon_{3i} \geq \epsilon_{3i}^*)$, where $\epsilon_{3i}^* = -(w_i'\beta_2 + (r_1^* + r_2^*\rho_{13})h(\epsilon_{1i}))/r_2^*$ and r_1^* and r_2^* are r_1 and r_2 evaluated at $\rho = \rho^*$. By the LDCT,

$$
\begin{aligned}
P(z_i &= 1, Y_i^{\#} = y_i) \\
&\to \int \int 1(\epsilon_{3i} \geq \epsilon_{3i}^*)[1(\epsilon_{3i} < -v_i'\beta_3)1(y_i = 0) \\
&\quad + 1(\epsilon_{3i} > -v_i'\beta_3) Po(\lambda_i, y_i)] g(\epsilon_{1i}, \epsilon_{3i}) d\epsilon_{1i} d\epsilon_{3i}, \tag{35}
\end{aligned}
$$

which is well-defined.

5 Maximum Likelihood Estimation

I sketch the properties of the MLE in Section 5.1, using the endogenous NB count variable model as the illustration. In Section 5.2 I discuss the numerical evaluation of the integrals appearing in the expressions for the probabilities; and in Section 5.3 I consider the behavior of derivatives of the probabilities, and therefore of the likelihood function, as $\rho_{12} \to 1$.

5.1 Sketch of Consistency and Asymptotic Normality

I illustrate the maximum likelihood estimation of the models using the endogenous NB count variable model in Section 3.1. Following Amemiya (1985), I define the maximum likelihood estimator, $\hat{\psi}$, as the solution to the equations:

$$\frac{\partial \log L(\psi)}{\partial \psi} = 0, \tag{36}$$

corresponding to a local maximum of log $L(\psi)$. To obtain the expression for the derivatives, write the log likelihood function as

$$\log L(\psi) = \sum_{i=1}^{n} \{z_i \log P_{i1y_i} + (1 - z_i) \log P_{i0y_i}\}$$
$$= \sum_{i=1}^{n} \sum_{\substack{j=0,1 \\ 0 \le k < \infty}} 1_{ijk} \log P_{ijk}, \tag{37}$$

where $1_{ijk} = 1$ if $z_i = j$ and $Y_i = k$ and zero otherwise and $P_{ijk} = P_{ijk}(\psi)$ is obtained from the right hand side of (17) evaluated at ψ and $y_i = k$. Hence, $P_{ijk}(\psi_0) = P(z_i = j, Y_i = k)$, which is denoted by P_{ijk}^0. Differentiating (37) gives:

$$\frac{\partial \log L(\psi)}{\partial \psi} = \sum_{i=1}^{n} \left[\frac{z_i}{P_{i1y_i}} \frac{\partial P_{i1y_i}}{\partial \psi} + \frac{1 - z_i}{P_{i0y_i}} \frac{\partial P_{i0y_i}}{\partial \psi} \right]$$
$$= \sum_{i=1}^{n} \sum_{\substack{j=0,1 \\ 0 \le k < \infty}} 1_{ijk} \frac{1}{P_{ijk}} \frac{\partial P_{ijk}}{\partial \psi}. \tag{38}$$

Expressions for the elements of $\partial P_{ijk}/\partial \psi$ are obtained from (17) and are given in Section 5.3. Since $E[1_{ijk}] = P_{ijk}^0$, taking expectations in the second expression in (38) implies that

$$E\left[\frac{\partial \log L(\psi)}{\partial \psi} \right]\bigg|_{\psi_0} = \sum_{i=1}^{n} \sum_{\substack{j=0,1 \\ 0 \le k < \infty}} \frac{\partial P_{ijk}}{\partial \psi}\bigg|_{\psi_0} = 0. \tag{39}$$

The second equality follows because $\sum_{k=0}^{\infty} P(Y_i = k) = 1$. From (39) and (42) below, $E[\log L(\psi)]$ attains a local maximum at ψ_0 and, from theorem 4.1.2 of Amemiya (1985), the equation $\partial \log L(\psi)/\partial \psi = 0$ has a strongly consistent root. Redefine $\hat{\psi}$ to be the consistent root.

Standard arguments also imply that $\hat{\psi}$ is asymptotically normal with asymptotic covariance matrix given by the inverse of the information matrix. That is,

$$n^{1/2}(\hat{\psi} - \psi_0) \xrightarrow{d} N(0, \mathbf{I}^{-1}), \tag{40}$$

where ψ_0 is the vector of true parameters and $\mathbf{I}$ is the information matrix. Since

$$\mathbf{I} = E\left[-n^{-1}\frac{\partial^2 \log L(\psi)}{\partial\psi\partial\psi'}\right]\bigg|_{\psi_0} = E\left[n^{-1}\frac{\partial \log L(\psi)}{\partial\psi}\frac{\partial \log L(\psi)}{\partial\psi'}\right]\bigg|_{\psi_0}, \tag{41}$$

it follows that

$$\mathbf{I} = n^{-1}\sum_{i=1}^{n}\sum_{\substack{j=0,1 \\ 0\le k<\infty}}\frac{1}{P_{ijk}^0}\frac{\partial P_{ijk}}{\partial\psi}\frac{\partial P_{ijk}}{\partial\psi'}\bigg|_{\psi_0}. \tag{42}$$

Equation (42) implies that the information matrix is positive semi-definite. It seems reasonable to assume that it is positive definite.

The MLE may be obtained using an iterative technique such as the Berndt, Hall, Hall, and Hausman (BHHH) algorithm (e.g., Berndt *et al.*, 1974) or the method of scoring (e.g., Amemiya, 1985, p. 138). The expression for $\mathbf{I}$ in (42) also shows that BHHH is much more convenient than scoring. In BHHH, $\mathbf{I}$ is estimated by the outer product of gradient (OPG) form,

$$\hat{\mathbf{I}}_{\text{OPG}} = n^{-1}\sum_{i=1}^{n}\left\{\frac{z_i}{P_{i1y_i}^2}\frac{\partial P_{i1y_i}}{\partial\psi}\frac{\partial P_{i1y_i}}{\partial\psi'} + \frac{1-z_i}{P_{i0y_i}^2}\frac{\partial P_{i0y_i}}{\partial\psi}\frac{\partial P_{i0y_i}}{\partial\psi'}\right\}\bigg|_{\hat{\psi}}, \tag{43}$$

whereas scoring would use an estimate of the right hand side of (42),

$$\hat{\mathbf{I}}_{\text{SC}} = n^{-1}\sum_{i=1}^{n}\sum_{\substack{j=0,1 \\ 0\le k<K}}\frac{1}{P_{ijk}}\frac{\partial P_{ijk}}{\partial\psi}\frac{\partial P_{ijk}}{\partial\psi'}\bigg|_{\hat{\psi}}, \tag{44}$$

for suitable K. K can be set to the maximum of the y_i, for example, corresponding to the value implicit in (43). $\hat{\mathbf{I}}_{SC}$ is computationally slower to evaluate because it involves probabilities and derivatives for each k, not just for $k = y_i$.

5.2 Evaluation of Integrals

In general, single integrals are evaluated numerically. I approximate $\int_{-\infty}^{\infty}$ by $\int_a^b$, where a and b are chosen so that the value of the integrand is small (e.g., $< 10^{-9}$) outside the interval $[a, b]$. I use the Legendre polynomials expanded from $[-1, 1]$ to $[a, b]$ and 60 terms in the summation approximation to the integral. I first evaluate the probability based on the interval $[a, b]$ defined such that $g(\epsilon_{1i}) < 10^{-9}$ outside $[a, b]$. If the probability is less than 0.2, I then refine the interval based on the value of the entire integrand. For larger probabilities, the percentage errors in the initial approximation, and hence the errors in the natural logs of the probabilities, are small. The bounds for the evaluation of the integrals in expressions for derivatives are the same as for the corresponding probability (unless $\rho_{12} \geq 0.98$, in which case I again refine the interval).

The exception to this is the evaluation of the double integral in (33), where I use Monte Carlo integration. Note that (33) can be written as:

$$
\begin{aligned}
P(z_i &= 1, Y_i^{\#} = y_i) \\
&= E[\Phi_i(\epsilon_{1i}, \epsilon_{3i})\{1(\epsilon_{3i} < -v_i'\beta_3)1(y_i = 0) + 1(\epsilon_{3i} > -v_i'\beta_3)Po(\lambda_i, y_i)\}] \\
&= E[s_i(\epsilon_{1i}, \epsilon_{3i})] \quad (\text{say}),
\end{aligned}
\tag{45}
$$

where the expectation is taken over the joint distribution $g(\epsilon_{1i}, \epsilon_{3i})$. Hence, $P(z_i = 1, Y_i^{\#} = y_i)$ can be estimated by:

$$
\hat{P}(z_i = 1, Y_i^{\#} = y_i) = M^{-1}\sum_{k=1}^{M} s_i(\epsilon_{1i}^{(k)}, \epsilon_{3i}^{(k)}),
\tag{46}
$$

where the $\epsilon_{1i}^{(k)}$, $\epsilon_{3i}^{(k)}$, $k = 1, ..., M$, are independent draws from $g(\epsilon_{1i}, \epsilon_{3i})$. I use $M = 5000$ and the same underlying draws throughout the maximization. Thus, the MLE is a maximum simulated likelihood estimate (MSLE); Lee (1992) gives the asymptotic properties of MSLEs. In particular, when $M = M(n) \to \infty$ as $n \to \infty$, the asymptotic distribution of the MSLE is the same as that of the MLE. I use the estimates of the asymptotic standard errors. It is also straightforward to calculate the variance of $\hat{P}(z_i = 1, Y_i^{\#} = y_i)$ and so measure the numerical accuracy (e.g., Geweke, 1989).[9]

Because of the integrals, obtaining the MLE is time consuming. This is particularly the case for the MSLE of the endogenous ZINB model and, as a result, I focus on the endogenous NB model in Sections 6, 7, and 8. I do not estimate the endogenous ZINB model in the Monte Carlo experiment nor do I calculate all of the statistics in the credit card example.

5.3 Special Cases

The case of ρ_{12} near to 1 again deserves a special mention. In particular, I argued in Section 3.3 that the likelihood function is continuous in ρ_{12} for ρ_{12} near to 1. Here, I demonstrate that the derivatives satisfy the same property. Differentiating (17) with respect to β_2 gives:

$$
\begin{aligned}
\frac{\partial P_{i1y_i}}{\partial \beta_2} &= \frac{w_i}{\sigma_\eta}\int \phi\left(\frac{w_i'\beta_2 + \gamma y_i + \rho_{12}h(\epsilon_{1i})}{\sigma_\eta}\right)Po(\lambda_i, y_i)g(\epsilon_{1i})d\epsilon_{1i} \\
&= \frac{w_i}{\rho_{12}}\int \phi(t)Po(\lambda_i^{(t)}, y_i)\phi\left(\frac{\sigma_\eta t - w_i'\beta_2 - \gamma y_i}{\rho_{12}}\right)dt
\end{aligned}
$$

$$\rightarrow w_i\phi(w_i'\beta_2 + \gamma y_i)Po(\lambda_i^{(0)}, y_i)$$

$$= \frac{\partial}{\partial\beta_2}\left(P(z_i = 1, Y_i = y_i)\big|_{\rho_{12}=1}\right), \tag{47}$$

as $\rho_{12} \rightarrow 1$, where $\lambda_i^{(t)} = \exp\{x_i\beta_1 + \epsilon_{1i}^{(t)}\}$, $\epsilon_{1i}^{(t)} = h^{-1}((\sigma_\eta t - w_i'\beta_2 - \gamma y_i)/\rho_{12})$, $\lambda_i^{(0)} = \exp\{x_i\beta_1 + \epsilon_{1i}^{(0)}\}$, and $\epsilon_{1i}^{(0)} = h^{-1}(-w_i'\beta_2 - \gamma y_i)$. The second equality follows from the change of variable $t = (w_i'\beta_2 + \gamma y_i + \rho_{12}h(\epsilon_{1i}))/\sigma_\eta$ and the convergence follows from the LDCT. Similar results apply for the derivatives with respect to γ, β_1, and θ, i.e., these derivatives are continuous in ρ_{12} for ρ_{12} near to 1. The second last line of (47) also shows that the derivatives are bounded.

Differentiating (17) with respect to ρ_{12} gives:

$$\frac{\partial P_{i1y_i}}{\partial\rho_{12}} = \int\phi\left(\frac{w_i'\beta_2 + \gamma y_i + \rho_{12}h(\epsilon_{1i})}{\sigma_\eta}\right)\times$$

$$\times\left[\frac{h(\epsilon_{1i})}{\sigma_\eta} + \frac{\rho_{12}(w_i'\beta_2 + \gamma y_i + \rho_{12}h(\epsilon_{1i}))}{\sigma_\eta^3}\right]Po(\lambda_i^{(t)}, y_i)g(\epsilon_{1i})d\epsilon_{1i}$$

$$= \int\phi(t)\left(\frac{t\sigma_\eta}{\rho_{12}^2} - \frac{w_i'\beta_2 + \gamma y_i}{\rho_{12}^2} + \frac{t}{\sigma_\eta}\right)Po(\lambda_i, y_i)\phi\left(\frac{\sigma_\eta t - w_i'\beta_2 - \gamma y_i}{\rho_{12}}\right)dt$$

$$\rightarrow \frac{(y_i - \lambda_i^{(0)})Po(\lambda_i^{(0)}, y_i)\phi(w_i'\beta_2 + \gamma y_i)^2}{g(\epsilon_{1i}^{(0)})}, \tag{48}$$

as $\rho_{12} \rightarrow 1$. The convergence follows from splitting the integral into three integrals and applying the LDCT. Details are given in the Appendix, as are the results for the endogenous ZINB model.

It is apparent from equations (47) and (48) that for ρ_{12} close to one, the coefficients on w_i, y_i, and $h(\epsilon_{1i})$ will be large and the numerical integration will be less accurate. For this reason, I refine the bounds on the integrals in the expressions for the derivatives when ρ_{12} greater than 0.98, as described above. The value 0.98 was chosen by inspecting the results.

6 Model Specification and Testing

6.1 Marginal Distribution of Y_i

In all the models, the marginal distribution of Y_i can be specified prior to considering the joint model. The different heterogeneity distributions are typically non-nested, suggesting that either model selection or non-nested hypothesis tests should be used.[10]

The Schwarz model selection criterion (Schwarz, 1978), for example, is given by $-2 \log L + k \log n$, where k is the number of parameters. Since (11) and (12) contain the same number of parameters, the choice reduces to comparing the values of the log-likelihood function.

To discuss non-nested hypothesis testing, I begin with the well-known Cox test. Let $f_{1i}(\psi_1)$ and $f_{2i}(\psi_2)$ be the contributions to the likelihoods of models 1 and 2 from observation i. That is, let $L_1(\psi_1) = \sum_{i=1}^{n} f_{1i}(\psi_1)$ and $L_2(\psi_2) = \sum_{i=1}^{n} f_{2i}(\psi_2)$, where ψ_i are the parameters in model i. For example, let f_{1i} be the contribution in the model with exponential gamma heterogeneity and f_{2i} be the contribution in the model with lognormal heterogeneity. Then the Cox test for testing model 1 against model 2 with model 1 as the null hypothesis is based on the distribution of $S_1 = \bar{d} - \hat{E}_1[\bar{d}]$, where $\bar{d} = n^{-1} \sum_{i=1}^{n} d_i(\hat{\psi}_1, \hat{\psi}_2)$, $d_i(\psi_1, \psi_2) = \log f_{1i}(\psi_1) - \log f_{2i}(\psi_2)$, $\hat{\psi}_i$ is the MLE of the parameters in model i, and $\hat{E}_1$ is an estimate of the expected value of $\bar{d}$ under the null. Calculating the expectation analytically is intractable in the models here, although it could be evaluated by simulation (e.g., Pesaran and Pesaran, 1993). A much simpler approach is that suggested by Vuong (1989). Under the null hypothesis that $E[d_i] = 0$, i.e., both models are wrong but equally close to the true data generation process, the statistic:

$$V = \frac{\sqrt{n}\,\bar{d}}{s_d} \xrightarrow{d} N(0,1), \tag{49}$$

where $s_d^2 = n^{-1} \sum_{i=1}^{n} (d_i - \bar{d})^2$. If $E[d_i] > 0$, i.e., model 1 is better, then $V \to \infty$ a.s.; and if $E[d_i] < 0$, i.e., model 2 is better, then $V \to -\infty$ a.s. I use the Vuong test rather than the Cox test with a simulated expectation because it is computationally much faster.

6.2 Comparing NB and ZINB Models

I apply the model selection and Vuong (1989) test.

6.3 Endogeneity of Y_i

Consider first the endogenous NB model. From equation (20), if $\rho_{12} = 0$ then the binary choice equation can be estimated by ordinary probit ML. It is therefore advisable to test for the endogeneity before undertaking ML estimation of the joint model. The null hypothesis is $H_0 : \rho_{12} = 0$ and the alternative is $\rho_{12} \neq 0$. The first test is based on Smith and Blundell (1986): substitute (10) into (6); replace the unobservable $h(\epsilon_{1i})$ by the corresponding generalized residual, $\hat{\epsilon}_{1i} = E[h(\epsilon_{1i}) | Y_i = y_i]|_{\hat{\psi}_1}$; and estimate the resulting equation by probit maximum likelihood. The test statistic is simply the t-ratio on the coefficient on the generalized residual. Under the null hypothesis, this is asymptotically distributed as a standard normal. The expression for the generalized residual is:

$$
\begin{aligned}
E[h(\epsilon_{1i})|Y_i = y_i] &= \int h(\epsilon_{1i}) f(\epsilon_{1i}|Y_i = y_i) d\epsilon_{1i} \\
&= \int h(\epsilon_{1i}) \frac{P(Y_i = y_i | \epsilon_{1i}) g(\epsilon_{1i})}{P(Y_i = y_i)} d\epsilon_{1i} \\
&= \frac{1}{P(Y_i = y_i)} \int h(\epsilon_{1i}) Po(\lambda_i, y_i) g(\epsilon_{1i}) d\epsilon_{1i}.
\end{aligned}
\tag{50}
$$

Next, consider the Lagrange multiplier (LM) test for H_0. The LM test statistic has the form

$$
\xi = n^{-1} \frac{\partial \log L(\psi)}{\partial \rho'_{12}} \hat{V}^{-1}_{\rho_{12}} \frac{\partial \log L(\psi)}{\partial \rho_{12}} \xrightarrow{d} \chi^2_1,
\tag{51}
$$

where $\hat{V}_{\rho_{12}}$ is an estimate of the block corresponding to ρ_{12} of

$$
E\left[-n^{-1} \frac{\partial^2 \log L(\psi_a)}{\partial \psi_a \partial \psi'_a}\right]\Bigg|_{\psi_{a0}} = E\left[n^{-1} \frac{\partial \log L(\psi_a)}{\partial \psi_a} \frac{\partial \log L(\psi_a)}{\partial \psi'_a}\right]\Bigg|_{\psi_{a0}},
\tag{52}
$$

$\psi_a = (\psi'_{-\rho_{12}}, \rho_{12})'$, $\psi_{a0} = (\psi'_{-\rho_{12}}, 0)'$, and $\psi_{-\rho_{12}}$ includes β_1, β_2, γ, and θ but not ρ_{12}.

More specifically, from (38),

$$
\frac{\partial \log L(\psi)}{\partial \rho_{12}} = \sum_{i=1}^n \left\{ \frac{z_i}{P_{i1y_i}} \frac{\partial P_{i1y_i}}{\partial \rho_{12}} + \frac{1 - z_i}{P_{i0y_i}} \frac{\partial P_{i0y_i}}{\partial \rho_{12}} \right\},
\tag{53}
$$

where $\partial P_{i0y_i}/\partial \rho_{12} = -\partial P_{i1y_i}/\partial \rho_{12}$. With $\rho_{12} = 0$,

$$
\frac{\partial P_{i1y_i}}{\partial \rho_{12}} = \phi(w'_i \beta_2 + \gamma y_i) \int h(\epsilon_{1i}) Po(\lambda_i, y_i) g(\epsilon_{1i}) d\epsilon_{1i}.
\tag{54}
$$

Hence, since $P_{i1y_i} = \Phi(w'_i \beta_2 + \gamma y_i) P(Y_i = y_i)$ under H_0,

$$
\begin{aligned}
\frac{\partial \log L(\psi)}{\partial \rho_{12}}\Bigg|_{\rho_{12}=0} &= \sum_{i=1}^n \frac{z_i - \Phi_{i0}}{\Phi_{i0}(1 - \Phi_{i0})} \frac{1}{P(Y_i = y_i)} \phi(w'_i \beta_2 + \gamma y_i) \int h(\epsilon_{1i}) Po(\lambda_i, y_i) g(\epsilon_{1i}) d\epsilon_{1i} \\
&= \sum_{i=1}^n \frac{z_i - \Phi_{i0}}{\Phi_{i0}(1 - \Phi_{i0})} \phi(w'_i \beta_2 + \gamma y_i) E[h(\epsilon_{1i})|Y_i = y_i] \\
&= \sum_{i=1}^n E[\epsilon_{2i}|\epsilon_{2i} > -w'_i \beta_2 - \gamma y_i] E[h(\epsilon_{1i})|Y_i = y_i],
\end{aligned}
\tag{55}
$$

where $\Phi_{i0} = \Phi(w'_i \beta_2 + \gamma y_i)$. This is just the first-order condition from the probit maximum likelihood of z_i on x_i, Y_i, and the generalized residual, evaluated with the coefficient on the generalized residual set to zero. Hence, the LM test is asymptotically equivalent under the null to the Smith–Blundell test. The latter is slightly easier to perform.

The endogeneity can also be tested by reversing the roles of ϵ_{1i} and ϵ_{2i}. That is, the generalized residuals for the binary choice model can be added to the count model. This test arises more naturally in the sample selection model and is not considered in this paper.

The corresponding tests for the endogenous ZINB model are obtained by substituting (30) into (6) and taking expectations conditional on $Y_i^\#$. There are two generalized residuals, expressions for which are given by (33) with $h(\epsilon_{1i})$ and ϵ_{3i} in place if $\Phi_i(\epsilon_{1i}, \epsilon_{3i})$.

6.4 Comparing Endogenous NB and Endogenous ZINB Models

I apply the model selection and Vuong (1989) test.

6.5 Testing $H_0 : \rho_{12} = 1$

The value of ρ_{12} under the null hypothesis lies on the boundary of the parameter space. Hence, of the classical Wald, Likelihood ratio (LR) and LM test, the LM test statistic is the most convenient—its asymptotic distribution is χ^2, whereas those of the Wald and LR test statistics involve mixtures of χ^2s (e.g., Moran, 1971; Chant, 1974). The LM test statistic has the form of (51), (52), and (53) with $\psi_{a1} = (\psi'_{-\rho_{12}}, 1)'$ replacing ψ_{a0} and the derivatives of P_{i1y_i} and P_{i0y_i} obtained from (47) and (48).

6.6 Testing (10) and (11)

I consider three tests for the specification of the joint distribution of ϵ_{1i} and ϵ_{2i}: an LM test for the inclusion of powers of $h(\epsilon_{1i})$ in (10), a RESET-type test for the normality of η_i, and an LM test for non-zero terms in the polynomial in (16). Note also that I concentrate on the endogenous NB model—the extra error term in the ZI models makes the tests more complicated.

For testing whether ϵ_{1i} and ϵ_{2i} satisfy the representation in (10), I consider the alternative,

$$\epsilon_{2i} = \rho_{12}h(\epsilon_{1i}) + \sum_{l=2}^{L} \rho_l(h(\epsilon_{1i})^l - E[h(\epsilon_{1i})^l]) + \eta_i. \tag{56}$$

A similar expression is derived in Pagan and Vella (1989, equation 32).[11] Let $\psi_3 = (\rho_2, ..., \rho_L)'$. Then the null hypothesis is given by $H_0 : \psi_3 = 0$; and the LM test statistic has the form

$$\xi_3 = n^{-1} \frac{\partial \log L(\psi)}{\partial \psi'_3} \hat{V}_{33}^{-1} \frac{\partial \log L(\psi)}{\partial \psi_3} \overset{d}{\to} \chi^2_{L-1}, \tag{57}$$

where $\hat{V}_{33}$ is an estimate of the block corresponding to ψ_3 of

$$V = E\left[-n^{-1}\frac{\partial^2 \log L(\psi_b)}{\partial \psi_b \partial \psi_b'}\right]\Bigg|_{\psi_{b0}} = E\left[n^{-1}\frac{\partial \log L(\psi_b)}{\partial \psi_b}\frac{\partial \log L(\psi_b)}{\partial \psi_b'}\right]\Bigg|_{\psi_{a0}}, \qquad (58)$$

$\psi_b = (\psi', \psi_3')'$, and $\psi_{b0} = (\psi_0', 0)'$. Expressions for the $\partial \log L(\psi)/\partial \rho_l$, $l = 2, \ldots,$ L are comparable to (53), with

$$\frac{\partial P_{i1y_i}}{\partial \rho_l} = \frac{1}{\sigma_\eta}\int (h(\epsilon_{1i})^l - E[h(\epsilon_{1i})^l])\phi_i(\epsilon_{1i})Po(\lambda_i, y_i)g(\epsilon_{1i})d\epsilon_{1i}, \qquad (59)$$

and $\phi_i(\epsilon_{1i}) = \phi((w_i'\beta_2 + \gamma y_i + \rho_{12}h(\epsilon_{1i}))/\sigma_\eta)$.

An important consideration is the estimation of V_{33}. As noted in Davidson and MacKinnon (1993, p. 477), for example, an LM test based on an OPG estimate of the covariance matrix can have actual size exceeding the nominal asymptotic size unless the sample size is very large. Monte Carlo evidence reported in the next section shows that this is the case here, and a scoring estimate should be used.

To test whether η_i is normally distributed, I follow Pagan and Vella (1989) and Ruud (1984) and consider the model with $P(\eta_i < x) = \Phi(x + \tau_1 x^2 + \tau_2 x^3)$. The null hypothesis is $H_0 : \tau_1 = \tau_2 = 0$; and under the null:

$$\frac{\partial P_{i1y_i}}{\partial \tau_j} = \int ((w_i'\beta_2 + \gamma y_i + \rho_{12}h(\epsilon_{1i}))/\sigma_\eta)^{1+j}\phi_i(\epsilon_{1i})Po(\lambda_i, y_i)g(\epsilon_{1i})d\epsilon_{1i}. \qquad (60)$$

The test has the same form as the LM test in (57). Also, equation (60) also appears in the derivative of $\log L$ with respect to τ_j, evaluated at $\tau_j = 0$, in the model:

$$z_i^* = w_i'\beta_2 + \gamma Y_i + \tau_1(w_i'\beta_2 + \gamma Y_i + rh(\epsilon_{1i}))^2 \\ + \tau_2(w_i'\beta_2 + \gamma Y_i + rh(\epsilon_{1i}))^3 + \epsilon_{2i}. \qquad (61)$$

Hence, as in the simple probit model (e.g., Pagan and Vella, 1989), a RESET-like test is obtained.

Finally, the null hypothesis in (16) is $H_0 : \alpha_1 = \ldots = \alpha_k = 0$; and under H_0,

$$\frac{\partial P_{i1y_i}}{\partial \alpha_k} = \frac{\rho_{12}}{\sigma_\eta}\int h(\epsilon_{1i})\epsilon_{1i}^k\phi_i(\epsilon_{1i})Po(\lambda_i, y_i)g(\epsilon_{1i})d\epsilon_{1i}. \qquad (62)$$

7 Monte Carlo Experiment

In this section, I briefly describe the results of a small Monte Carlo experiment exploring some of the properties of the procedures. As noted above, I focus on the endogenous NB model because of the time involved in estimating the endogenous ZINB model. I present results on the estimation of the endogenous NB model, the test for endogeneity based on adding the generalized residual to the probit equation, and the three specification tests in Section 6.6.

The model is loosely based on the distribution of the data in the credit card example. I use

$$\log \lambda_i = 0 + x_{1i} \times 0 + x_{2i} \times 1 + \epsilon_{1i}, \tag{63}$$
$$r_i^* = 0 + x_{1i} \times 1 + x_{2i} \times 0 + \epsilon_{3i}, \tag{64}$$
$$z_i^* = 1.25 + w_{1i} \times 0 + Y_i \times 1 + \epsilon_{2i}, \tag{65}$$
$$\epsilon_{2i} = r_i h(\epsilon_{1i}) + r_2 \epsilon_{3i} + \zeta_i, \tag{66}$$

$e^{\epsilon_{1i}} \sim Gamma(\theta, 1/\theta)$, $\zeta_i \sim N(0, \sigma_\zeta^2)$, and $\epsilon_{3i} \sim N(0, 1)$. I set $h(\epsilon_{1i}) = \Phi^{-1}[G(\epsilon_{1i})]$ as in (11), $\alpha = 1/\theta = 3.03$, $\rho_{23} = 0$, and $\rho_{13} = 0$. ρ_{12} is a choice variable in the experiment, and I allow $\rho_{12} = (0, 0.5, 0.8)$. The sample size is 1300.

There are six experiments in total, three with data generated from the endogenous NB model and three with data from the endogenous ZINB model. The number of replications is 100 and the ML estimation uses the BHHH algorithm.

I generate $w_{ji} \sim N(0, 1/9)$ and the x_{ji} using

$$x_{ji} \sim a_j + (b_j - a_j) * Beta(p_j, q_j), \quad j = 1, 2. \tag{67}$$

In the NB $(a_2, b_2, p_2, q_2) = (-8.0, 0.1, 9.9, 1.5)$, and in the ZINB $(a_1, b_1, p_1, q_1) = (-0.75, 3.0, 6.0, 8.0)$ and $(a_2, b_2, p_2, q_2) = (-7.0, -0.1, 10.0, 1.0)$. These choices are based on the distributions of $x_i \hat{\beta}_1$, $w_i' \hat{\beta}_2$, and $v_i' \hat{\beta}_3$ in the credit card example. The values of the x_i and w_i are fixed across replications within each experiment.

First, consider the results in the endogenous NB model. The rejection proportion under the null ($\rho_{12} = 0$) in the test for endogeneity using the nominal 5 percent critical values was 0.09, within two standard deviations of the nominal level. The rejection proportions for $\rho_{12} = 0.5$ and 0.8 were 0.79 and 1.00, respectively. Rejection proportions for the three specification tests in Section 6.6 using the nominal 5 percent critical values are given in Table 1. Those based on the OPG form are often too large, whereas those based on scoring are close to the nominal value. The MLEs of the parameters model were also well-behaved. For example, the averages across replications of the estimates of the three values of ρ_{12} were $(0.07, 0.51, 0.79)$. The corresponding standard errors were $(0.23, 0.16, 0.09)$, and the corresponding averages of the estimated standard errors, using the scoring estimate of the covariance matrix, were $(0.21, 0.14, 0.08)$. The estimates of the three parameters in the probit model (65) were biased when the endogeneity was ignored. For example, when $\rho_{12} = 0.5$ and 0.8, the average parameter values were $(1.16, -0.03, -0.69)$ and $(1.17, -0.01, -0.55)$, and the standard errors were $(0.05, 0.14, 0.05)$ and $(0.04, 0.13, 0.05)$. The rejection proportions in the Vuong test with the NB as the null model and the ZINB as the alternative averaged 20 percent and the Schwarz criterion picked the NB at least 98 times out of 100.

The corresponding results when the data were generated by the endogenous

Table 1. Rejection proportions, specification tests in Section 6.6
Endogenous NB model

	OPG			Scoring		
	$\rho = 0.0$	$\rho = 0.5$	$\rho = 0.8$	$\rho = 0.0$	$\rho = 0.5$	$\rho = 0.8$
Powers of $h(\varepsilon_1)$						
2–4	0.23	0.18	0.24	0.01	0.04	0.01
2	0.06	0.04	0.10	0.05	0.03	0.05
RESET						
2–3	0.36	0.22	0.29	0.03	0.03	0.04
2	0.10	0.06	0.17	0.03	0.02	0.03
3	0.24	0.16	0.12	0.02	0.00	0.02
Powers of ε_1						
1–2	0.09	0.05	0.14	0.07	0.02	0.03
1	0.06	0.03	0.10	0.03	0.02	0.05
2	0.04	0.02	0.06	0.03	0.02	0.04

Note: OPG means the outer product of gradient form of the test. Scoring means the form of the test based on the scoring-type estimate of the covariance matrix.

ZINB model were driven by the fact that there is not a large difference between these NB and ZINB models. The rejection proportions in the Vuong test averaged 33 percent and the Schwarz criterion again picked the NB in at least 98 replications. The estimates of the parameters in the NB were biased, the averages for the three parameters in (63) and α being around (–0.54, 0.33, 1.03, 4.12)—these were the values with $\rho_{12} = 0.5$. The averages were almost identical in the MLE of the endogenous NB model. The rejection proportions in the endogeneity test were almost the same as those in the endogenous NB model, and the rejection proportions in the specification tests were only slightly higher. The latter implies that the tests have little power against misspecifying the ZINB here by an NB.[12]

8 Example: Credit Card Applications

In this section, I illustrate the simultaneous equations model using a set of data describing the evaluations of credit card applications. The data were used in Greene (1994) to illustrate a sample selection model, although Greene also noted that "a simultaneous equations approach might be appropriate" (his footnote 32). The count variable in the number of major derogatory reports (MDRs), where a MDR is defined as a delinquency of sixty days or more on a credit account. The binary choice variable is the approval or not of the application for a major credit card. The sample covers 1319 individuals drawn from the population of applicants for the credit card. Of these, 1023 were given approval. The binary choice and count models are basically the same as those in Greene (1994)—I do not attempt to modify the data or specifications used in Greene (1994), other than adding MDR and MDR^2 terms to the probit equation.

The footnote in Greene (1994) gives background on the modeling situation—"Credit card vendors outsource the evaluation of card application to third parties who have automated the procedure of credit card scoring. Their exact procedures are closely guarded secrets . . . we have found that the number of MDRs is a highly significant covariate in any applicant acceptance equation." Hence, the correlation between the two equations can be thought of as arising from unobserved factors which influence both credit card use of individuals and decisions of agents of the credit card company on whether or not to accept applications. Alternatively, the specification allows for extra flexibility in the joint distribution of the endogenous variables; and once it is recognized that there are two behavioral variables, zero correlation is a strong assumption. Of course, the correlation could also be resulting from misspecification of the model (other than unobserved factors).

Table 2 gives the frequency distribution of MDRs and the independent variables are described in Table 3. The distribution of MDR appears to have both excess zeros and a long tail.

Tables 4 and 5 give a variety of models for the counts. In Table 4 the poisson model is clearly rejected in favor of the models with heterogeneity. The negative binomial is preferred over the model with normal heterogeneity (not

Table 2. Frequencies of MDRs

MDR	Full sample	Successful
0	1060	915
1	137	90
2	50	13
3	24	4
4	17	1
5	11	
6	5	
7	6	
8	0	
9	2	
10	4	
11	4	
12	1	
13	0	
14	1	

Notes: (*a*) MDR: number of major derogatory reports; (*b*) Full sample: 1,319 applications; Successful: 1,023 successful applications.

Table 3. Independent variables

Income	Income, in $10,000
Age	Age, in years
Curadd	Number of years residing at current address
Exp-inc	Average monthly expenditure divided by yearly income
Avgexp	Average monthly credit card expenditure
Ownrent	Binary variable indicating home ownership
Selfempl	Binary variable, one for self-employed
Depndt	Number of dependents
Inc-per	Income per dependent
Major	Binary variable, one if the individual holds a major credit card
Active	Number of active credit card accounts
Accounts	Number of open accounts

Table 4. Count models

Variable	Poisson	NB	ZINB	Endogenous NB	Endogenous ZINB
Constant	−0.370	−0.877	3.614	−0.434	3.388
	(0.174)	(0.384)	(1.453)	(0.363)	(1.137)
Income	−0.025	−0.006	−0.147	−0.026	−0.114
	(0.028)	(0.057)	(0.108)	(0.052)	(0.100)
Age	0.005	0.011	−0.057	0.007	−0.056
	(0.004)	(0.009)	(0.018)	(0.009)	(0.017)
Exp-inc	−17.98	−9.37	−8.31	−15.49	−9.16
	(2.20)	(1.73)	(1.79)	(1.62)	(1.86)
Avgexp	0.0014	0.0006	0.000	0.001	0.000
	(0.0006)	(0.0007)	(0.001)	(0.001)	(0.001)
Major	0.046	0.055	0.043	0.084	0.029
	(0.105)	(0.207)	(0.202)	(0.195)	(0.211)
α		4.811	2.983	3.578	3.090
		(0.52)	(0.005)	(0.412)	(0.909)
Log-L	−1367.48	−1028.25	−1016.38	−1485.73	−1478.39
V		−2.07	2.07	−0.75	0.75

Notes: (a) NB: negative binomial model; (b) ZINB: zero inflated negative binomial model; (c) Endogenous NB: endogenous negative binomial model; (d) Endogenous ZINB: endogenous zero inflated negative binomial model; (e) Standard errors based on BHHH/OPG estimate of information matrix in parentheses; (f) α: variance parameter in exponential gamma distribution; Log-L: value of log likelihood function; V: Vuong (1989) statistic, ZINB vs. NB and Endogenous ZINB vs. Endogenous NB, a positive value favours the model.

shown), which had log-likelihood value of −1051.9; and I concentrate on the models with gamma heterogeneity. The estimated value of α in the NB model implies a value of θ of 0.207, corresponding to a heterogeneity distribution with a long tail and an asymptote at zero. It is therefore not surprising that the gamma model is preferred to the normal heterogeneity model. The ZINB model has a lower log-likelihood value than the NB model and the Vuong test statistic of 2.07 favors the ZINB model. The Schwarz criterion, on the other

Table 5. Zero-inflating models

Variable	ZINB	Endogenous ZINB
Constant	−1.40	−1.33
	(0.319)	(0.406)
Income	0.072	0.059
	(0.088)	(0.088)
Age	0.048	0.049
	(0.013)	(0.012)
Ownrent	−0.263	−0.250
	(0.132)	(0.120)
Selfempl	0.020	0.009
	(0.182)	(0.185)
Depndt	0.050	0.043
	(0.086)	(0.089)
Inc-per	0.068	0.064
	(0.097)	(0.098)
ρ_{13}	−0.905	−0.897
	(0.095)	(0.088)
Log-L	−1016.38	−1478.39

Notes: (*a*) ZINB: zero inflated negative binomial model; (*b*) Endogenous ZINB: endogenous zero inflated negative binomial model; (*c*) Standard errors based on BHHH/OPG estimate of information matrix in parentheses; (*d*) Log-L: value of log likelihood function.

hand, favors the NB model 2106.8 to 2133.3. The large difference in these values comes about because many of the variables in the ZI equation have small *t*-ratios—see column one of Table 6. Asymptotically, a *t*-ratio of $\sqrt{(\log(1319))} = 2.68$ is required for a variable to decrease the Schwarz criterion. Including just the intercept and Age in the zero-inflating equation gave a log-likelihood value of −1022.47 and a value of Schwarz criterion of 2116.8. The latter still favors the NB model, but the *t*-ratio on Age was 2.67.

Another way to compare the models is through the estimated probabilities for MDR = 0, 1, ..., 14. For each observation, these probabilities were estimated; and averaging over the sample gives the values in Table 7, columns 1 and 2. The relative frequencies in the data are shown in column 5. Again, there is little to choose between the models. (Chi-squared statistics are shown; although, of course, the asymptotic distributions of the statistics are not χ^2s. I have also not aggregated over classes with small expected frequencies.)

Note also that ρ_{13} is strongly significant in the ZINB model. The negative value implies, for example, that a high probability for $Y_i = 0$ can be obtained with a low value of $v_i'\beta_3$ through either a small value of ϵ_{3i} or a large value of ϵ_{3i} and a small value of ϵ_{1i}, the latter giving $r_i = 1$ and a small value of λ_i.

The estimates of the parameters in the basic probit model are given in the

Table 6. Binary choice models

Variable	Probit	Endogenous NB	Endogenous ZINB
Constant	0.496	0.618	0.526
	(0.199)	(0.175)	(0.189)
Income	0.110	0.089	0.107
	(0.058)	(0.048)	(0.051)
Age	−0.007	−0.004	−0.004
	(0.005)	(0.005)	(0.006)
Curadd	0.0002	−0.000	−0.000
	(0.0008)	(0.001)	(0.001)
Ownrent	0.257	0.194	0.184
	(0.109)	(0.103)	(0.111)
Selfempl	−0.344	−0.264	−0.337
	(0.169)	(0.142)	(0.156)
Depndt	−0.134	−0.106	−0.115
	(0.073)	(0.064)	(0.070)
Inc-per	−0.010	0.010	0.064
	(0.080)	(0.063)	(0.098)
Major	0.265	0.235	0.251
	(0.109)	(0.104)	(0.110)
Active	−0.047	−0.032	−0.039
	(0.029)	(0.016)	(0.022)
Accounts	0.119	0.087	0.105
	(0.031)	(0.019)	(0.025)
MDR	−0.944	−1.60	−1.37
	(0.145)	(0.099)	(0.227)
MDR^2	0.046	0.095	0.080
	(0.047)	(0.021)	(0.066)
ρ_{12}		0.887	0.538
		(0.069)	(0.190)
ρ_{23}			−0.114
			(0.217)
Log-L	−486.36	−1485.73	−1478.39

Notes: (*a*) NB: negative binomial model; (*b*) ZINB: zero inflated negative binomial model; (*c*) Endogenous NB: endogenous negative binomial model; (*d*) Endogenous ZINB: endogenous zero inflated negative binomial model; (*e*) Standard errors based on BHHH/OPG estimate of information matrix in parentheses; (*f*) α: variance parameter in exponential gamma distribution; Log-L: value of log likelihood function.

first column of Table 6. Adding the generalized residuals based on the NB to the probit model gave a *t*-ratio of 8.8, strongly suggesting the endogeneity of MDR.

The estimates of the parameters in the endogenous NB and ZINB models are shown in the final two columns of Table 4, the final column of Table 5, and the final two columns of Table 6. In both models the values of the log likelihood function are higher than those for $\rho_{12} = 0$; and corresponding to

Table 7. Estimated probabilities for fitted models—all observations

MDR	NB	ZINB	Endogenous NB	Endogenous ZINB	Rel. freq.
0	.803	.802	.779	.776	.804
1	.104	.100	.118	.099	.104
2	.042	.044	.047	.043	.038
3	.021	.022	.023	.022	.018
4	.012	.012	.013	.012	.013
5	.007	.007	.008	.007	.008
6	.004	.004	.005	.004	.004
7	.003	.003	.003	.003	.005
8	.002	.002	.002	.002	.000
9	.001	.001	.001	.001	.002
10	.001	.001	.001	.001	.001
11	.001	.000	.001	.000	.003
12	.000	.000	.000	.000	.001
13	.000	.000	.000	.000	.000
14	.000	.000	.000	.000	.001
Chi-sq	24.8	31.5	38.8	50.7	

Notes: (*a*) NB: negative binomial model; (*b*) ZINB: zero inflated negative binomial model; (*c*) Endogenous NB: endogenous negative binomial model; (*d*) Endogenous ZINB: endogenous zero inflated negative binomial model.

this are the strongly significant estimates of ρ_{12} and ρ_{13} and the changes in the estimates of the coefficients on MDR and MDR^2.[13]

The implications of these estimates for estimated probabilities are shown in Tables 7 and 8. Table 8 gives the estimated probabilities for the data split into successful and non-successful applications and Table 7 gives the estimated probabilities for the data aggregated across these two categories. The column headed "rho = 0" in Table 8 gives the estimated probabilities in the Endogenous NB model with $\rho_{12} = 0$. Clearly, the endogenous NB and ZINB models fit the disaggregated data better than this model; although corresponding to the NB and ZINB models, there is little to choose between the Endogenous NB and ZINB model. The endogenous models fit the aggregated data worse than the marginal NB and ZINB models, but this is to be expected. The estimated value of σ_ζ^2 in the endogenous ZINB model is 0.017; and conditional MLE gave essentially the same results as the full MLE.

Next, I compare the binary choice/NB models with and without $\rho_{12} = 0$ through their estimates of the marginal effects of each of the regressors on the expected number of MDRs and the probability of approval, averaged over observations. In the model with $\rho_{12} = 0$, $E[Y_i] = e^{x_i'\beta_1}$, and the averaged marginal effect with respect to x_{im}, when x_{im} is continuous, is estimated by $n^{-1}\sum_{i=0}^{n}\hat{\beta}_{1m}e^{x_i'\beta_1}$. Standard errors are obtained using the delta method. The effects with respect to the elements of w_i are zero. In the model with $\rho_{12} \neq 0$,

$$E[Y_i] = \sum_{k=0}^{\infty} k \sum_{l=0}^{1} P(z_i = l, Y_i = k), \tag{68}$$

and the averaged marginal effect with respect to x_{im} is estimated by:

$$\frac{d}{dx_{im}} n^{-1} \sum_{i=1}^{n} \sum_{l=0}^{1} \sum_{k=0}^{K} kP(z_i = l, Y_i = k)\Big|_{\hat{\psi}}, \tag{69}$$

for some K. (I use $K = \max(Y_i) + 5$ and numerical derivatives.) Since the evaluation of both (69) and the corresponding equation for the probability of approval is slow, I did not estimate the associated standard errors. In the discussion below, I simply note if a confidence interval for the estimate from the model with $\rho_{12} = 0$ contains the estimate from the model with $\rho_{12} \neq 0$.

If x_{im} is a dummy variable, I evaluate the difference between the probability/expected value at $x_{im} = 0$ and $x_{im} = 1$. If x_{im} is a discrete variable, I evaluate the difference between the probability/expected value at the observed value and the observed value plus one.

The results are shown in Table 9 and show substantial differences in the effects of exp-inc. The derivative for exp-inc in the model with endogeneity lies outside a 95 percent confidence interval from the model with $\rho_{12} = 0$.

Next, consider the probability of approval. In the model with $\rho_{12} = 0$,

Table 8. Estimated probabilities for fitted models

MDR	Not successful				Successful			
	rho = 0	Endog. NB	Endog. ZINB	Rel. freq.	rho = 0	Endog. NB	Endog. ZINB	Rel. freq.
0	.177	.117	.107	.110	.625	.662	.669	.694
1	.024	.036	.036	.036	.080	.082	.063	.068
2	.010	.035	.030	.028	.032	.012	.013	.010
3	.005	.022	.020	.015	.016	.001	.002	.003
4	.003	.013	.012	.012	.009	.000	.000	.001
5	.002	.008	.007	.008	.005	.000	.000	.000
6	.001	.005	.004	.004	.003	.000	.000	.000
7	.001	.003	.003	.005	.002	.000	.000	.000
8	.001	.002	.002	.000	.001	.000	.000	.000
9	.000	.001	.001	.002	.001	.000	.000	.000
10	.000	.001	.001	.001	.001	.000	.000	.000
11	.000	.001	.000	.003	.001	.000	.000	.000
12	.000	.000	.000	.001	.000	.000	.000	.000
13	.000	.000	.000	.000	.000	.000	.000	.000
14	.000	.000	.000	.001	.000	.000	.000	.000

Notes: (*a*) NB: negative binomial model; (*b*) Endog. NB: endogenous negative binomial model; (*c*) Endog. ZINB: endogenous zero inflated negative binomial model.

Table 9. Derivatives of expected numbers of MDRs

Variable	Endogenous NB	NB	Standard error NB
Income	−0.012	−0.002	0.024
Age	0.003	0.005	0.004
Curadd	0	0	0
Exp-inc	−7.242	−4.041	0.818
Avgexp	0.001	0.000	0.000
Ownrent	0	0	0
Selfempl	0	0	0
Depndt	0	0	0
Inc-per	0	0	0
Major	0.039	0.023	0.086
Active	0	0	0
Accounts	0	0	0

$P(z_i = 1) = \Phi(w_i'\beta_2 + \gamma Y_i)$, and the averaged marginal effect with respect to w_{im}, the mth element of w_i, when w_{im} is continuous, is estimated by $n^{-1}\sum_{i=1}^{n}\hat{\beta}_{2m}\phi(w_i'\hat{\beta}_2 + \hat{\gamma}Y_i)$. Standard errors are again obtained by the delta method and now the effects with respect to the elements of x_i are zero. In the model with $\rho_{12} \neq 0$,

$$P(z_i = 1) = \sum_{k=0}^{\infty} P(z_i = 1, Y_i = k), \tag{70}$$

and the averaged marginal effect with respect to w_{im} is estimated by

$$n^{-1}\sum_{i=1}^{n}\sum_{k=0}^{K}\frac{d}{dw_{im}}P(z_i = 1, Y_i = k)\bigg|_{\hat{\psi}}. \tag{71}$$

Dummy and discrete variables are treated as above, and for the elements of x_i, replace w_{im} by x_{im}. In particular, the expressions are not necessarily zero. I also compute the marginal effects on the conditional probability of approval, $P(z_i = 1 | Y_i = y_i)$.

The results are shown in Table 10, and highlight the effects of the variables appearing only in the count equation (exp-inc and avgexp). The MDR difference in the conditional probability in the joint model lies outside a 95 percent confidence interval from the model with $\rho_{12} = 0$.

In summary, the NB and ZINB models give similar results by many of the measures used here. Exp-inc is the most important variable in the count models, while a number of variables play a role in the probit—income, selfempl, major, accounts, and MDR. The two models differ "significantly" in their conclusions about the effects of the number of MDRs on the probability of approval.

It is also apparent that there may still be problems with the specification

Table 10. Derivatives of P(Approval)

Variable	Endogenous NB	Probit	Standard Error Probit	P(Approval|MDR) Endogenous NB
Income	0.024	0.023	0.012	0.022
Age	−0.002	−0.001	0.001	−0.001
Curadd	0.000	0.000	0.000	0.000
Exp-inc	1.717	0	0	0.543
Avgexp	−0.001	0	0	−0.000
Ownrent	0.048	0.053	0.022	0.046
Selfempl	−0.072	−0.079	0.042	−0.069
Depndt	−0.028	−0.028	0.017	−0.027
Inc-per	0.001	0.000	0.016	0.002
Major	0.053	0.058	0.025	0.056
Active	−0.008	−0.010	0.006	−0.008
Accounts	0.021	0.024	0.006	0.020
MDR	—	−0.235	0.027	−0.141

Table 11. Specification test statistics

	OPG	Scoring
Powers of $h(\varepsilon_1)$ (eqn 56)		
2–4	58.4	115.2
2	26.0	85.1
3	10.2	53.9
4	6.8	62.3
RESET (eqn 61)		
2–3	15.6	84.8
2	3.5	8.1
3	10.3	45.8
Powers of ε_1 (eqn 16)		
1–2	48.3	132.5
1	14.4	26.9
2	4.3	0.1

Note: OPG means the outer product of gradient form of the test. Scoring means the form of the test based on the scoring-type estimate of the co-variance matrix.

of the model—the values of the statistics from the three specification tests are given in Table 11.[14] Note also the behavior of the estimates of the α and the coefficients on exp-inc in Table 4. The estimates are quite different in the NB and endogenous NB models but are similar in the ZINB and endogenous ZINB models. An informal Hausman test suggests misspecification of the NB model. On the other hand, the ZINB model is not clearly better than the NB model. Exploring a wider range of models and undertaking a more thorough Monte Carlo experiment may be necessary in order to explain this effect.

9 Concluding Comments

I have considered the estimation of a binary choice variable with an endogenous overdispersed count variable. The joint distribution of the variables is based on the assumption that a suitable transformation of the heterogeneity term in the count model is jointly normally distributed with the error in the binary choice equation. I have also considered two possible models for the count variable—an NB and a ZINB. I allowed correlation between the ZI-binary choice and poisson equations in the latter; and considered the special cases in which correlations between error terms are equal to zero and one.

I have also mentioned a number of extensions to the model—to the joint distribution of the random terms, to the distribution of the counts themselves, to the sample selection model, and to the framework involving waiting times rather than counts. All of these remain topics for future work.

Appendix

A.1 Derivation of Equation (48)

As in equation (48) in the text,

$$
\frac{\partial P_{i1y_i}}{\partial \rho_{12}} = \int \phi \left(\frac{w_i'\beta_2 + \gamma y_i + \rho_{12}h(\epsilon_{1i})}{\sigma_\eta} \right)
$$

$$
\times \left[\frac{h(\epsilon_{1i})}{\sigma_\eta} + \frac{\rho_{12}(w_i'\beta_2 + \gamma y_i + \rho_{12}h(\epsilon_{1i}))}{\sigma_\eta^3} \right] Po(\lambda_i, y_i) g(\epsilon_{1i}) d\epsilon_{1i}
$$

$$
= \int \phi(t) \left[\frac{t\sigma_\eta}{\rho_{12}^2} - \frac{w_i'\beta_2 + \gamma y_i}{\rho_{12}^2} + \frac{t}{\sigma_\eta} \right] Po(\lambda_i^{(t)}, y_i) \phi \left(\frac{\sigma_n t - w_i'\beta_2 - \gamma y_i}{\rho_{12}} \right) dt.
$$

Split this into three integrals. First:

$$
\int \phi(t) \left[\frac{t\sigma_\eta}{\rho_{12}^2} \right] Po(\lambda_i^{(t)}, y_i) \phi \left(\frac{\sigma_n t - w_i'\beta_2 - \gamma y_i}{\rho_{12}} \right) dt \to 0,
$$

as $\rho_{12} \to 1$ and $\sigma_\eta \to 0$, by the LDCT. Second:

$$
-\int \phi(t) \left[\frac{w_i'\beta_2 + \gamma y_i}{\rho_{12}^2} \right] Po(\lambda_i^{(t)}, y_i) \phi \left(\frac{\sigma_n t - w_i'\beta_2 - \gamma y_i}{\rho_{12}} \right) dt
$$

$$
\to -(w_i'\beta_2 + \gamma y_i) Po(\lambda_i^{(0)}, y_i) \phi(w_i'\beta_2 + \gamma y_i) \int \phi(t) \, dt
$$

$$
= -(w_i'\beta_2 + \gamma y_i) Po(\lambda_i^{(0)}, y_i) \phi(w_i'\beta_2 + \gamma y_i),
$$

as $\rho_{12} \to 1$ and $\sigma_\eta \to 0$, by the LDCT. Third:

$$\int \phi(t) \left[\frac{t}{\sigma_\eta} \right] Po(\lambda_i^{(t)}, y_i) \phi \left(\frac{\sigma_n t - w_i' \beta_2 - \gamma y_i}{\rho_{12}} \right) dt$$

$$\rightarrow (w_i' \beta_2 + \gamma y_i) Po(\lambda_i^{(0)}, y_i) \phi(w_i' \beta_2 + \gamma y_i)$$

$$+ \frac{(y_i - \lambda_i^{(0)}) Po(\lambda_i^{(0)}, y_i) \phi(w_i' \beta_2 + \gamma y_i)^2}{g(\epsilon_{1i}^{(0)})},$$

as $\rho_{12} \rightarrow 1$ and $\sigma_\eta \rightarrow 0$. To see this, expand $Po(\lambda_i^{(t)}, y_i)\phi((\sigma_n t - w_i' \beta_2 - \gamma y_i)/\rho_{12})$ in a mean value expansion about $\sigma_\eta = 0$:

$$Po(\lambda_i^{(t)}, y_i)\phi \left(\frac{\sigma_n t - w_i' \beta_2 - \gamma y_i}{\rho_{12}} \right)$$

$$= Po(\lambda_i^{(0)}, y_i)\phi(w_i' \beta_2 + \gamma y_i) + \left\{ -Po(\lambda_i^{(t)}, y_i)\phi \left(\frac{\sigma_n t - w_i' \beta_2 - \gamma y_i}{\rho_{12}} \right) \right.$$

$$\times \left[\frac{\sigma_n t - w_i' \beta_2 - \gamma y_i}{\rho_{12}} \right] \left[\frac{t}{\rho_{12}} - \frac{\sigma_n t - w_i' \beta_2 + \gamma y_i}{\rho_{12}^2} \frac{\partial \rho_{12}}{\partial \sigma_\eta} \right]$$

$$\left. + \phi \left(\frac{\sigma_n t - w_i' \beta_2 - \gamma y_i}{\rho_{12}} \right) Po(\lambda_i^{(t)}, y_i)(y_i - \lambda_i) \frac{1}{\lambda_i} \frac{\partial \lambda_i}{\partial \sigma_h} \right\} (\sigma_h - 0),$$

where the term in $\{\}$ is evaluated at a mean value and

$$\frac{\partial \lambda_i}{\partial \sigma_h} = \lambda_i \frac{\partial h^{-1} \left(\frac{\sigma_n t - w_i' \beta_2 - \gamma y_i}{\rho_{12}} \right)}{\partial \sigma_h}$$

$$= \lambda_i \frac{\phi \left(\frac{\sigma_n t - w_i' \beta_2 - \gamma y_i}{\rho_{12}} \right)}{g \left(h^{-1} \left(\frac{\sigma_n t - w_i' \beta_2 - \gamma y_i}{\rho_{12}} \right) \right)} \left[\frac{t}{\rho_{12}} - \frac{\sigma_n t - w_i' \beta_2 + \gamma y_i}{\rho_{12}^2} \frac{\partial \rho_{12}}{\partial \sigma_\eta} \right].$$

Substituting, applying the LDCT, and noting that $\partial \rho_{12}/\partial \sigma_\eta = 0$ at $\sigma_\eta = 0$ and that $\int t^2 \phi(t) dt = 1$, gives the result.

A.2 Derivatives of the ZINB Model as $\sigma_\zeta^2 \rightarrow 0$

From equation (33),

$$\frac{\partial P_{i1 y_i}}{\partial \beta_2} = \frac{w_i}{\sigma_\zeta} \int \int \phi_i(\epsilon_{1i}, \epsilon_{3i}) Z(\epsilon_{1i}, \epsilon_{3i}) \frac{1}{\sqrt{2\pi}} \phi(\epsilon_{3i} | h(\epsilon_{1i})) g(\epsilon_{1i}) d\epsilon_{1i} d\epsilon_{3i}$$

$$= \frac{w_i}{r_2} \int \int \phi_i(t) Z(\epsilon_{1i}, \tilde{t}) \frac{1}{\sqrt{2\pi}} \phi(\tilde{t}) g(\epsilon_{1i}) d\epsilon_{1i} dt$$

$$\rightarrow \frac{w_i}{r_2^*} \int Z(\epsilon_{1i}, \epsilon_{3i}^*) \frac{1}{\sqrt{2\pi}} \phi(\epsilon_{3i}^*) g(\epsilon_{1i}) d\epsilon_{1i},$$

as $\rho \to \rho^*$ by the LDCT, where $\phi_i(\epsilon_{1i}, \epsilon_{3i}) = \phi((w_i'\beta_2 + \gamma y_i + r_1 h(\epsilon_{1i}) + r_2 \epsilon_{3i})/\sigma_\zeta)$, ϵ_{3i}^* and r_2^* were defined above equation (35), $\tilde{t} = (\sigma_\zeta t - w_i'\beta_2 - \gamma y_i - r_1 h(\epsilon_{1i}))/r_2$, and

$$Z(\epsilon_{1i}, \epsilon_{3i}) = 1(y_i = 0)1(\epsilon_{3i} < -v_i'\beta_3) + 1(\epsilon_{3i} > -v_i'\beta_3)Po(\lambda_i, y_i).$$

Similar expressions are obtained for the derivations with respect to γ, β_1, ρ_{12}, ρ_{23}, and θ.

For β_3, begin with the change-of-variable $\epsilon_{3i} = \rho_{13} h(\epsilon_{1i}) + \sigma_\xi \eta$:

$$P_{1iy_i} = \int\int \Phi_i(\epsilon_{1i}, \rho_{13}h(\epsilon_{1i}) + \sigma_\xi \eta)[1(y_i = 0)1(\eta < \ddot{\eta})$$
$$+ 1(\eta > \ddot{\eta})Po(\lambda_i, y_i)]\phi(\eta)g(\epsilon_{1i})d\eta d\epsilon_{1i},$$

where $\ddot{\eta} = (-v_i'\beta_3 - \rho_{13}h(\epsilon_{1i}))/\sigma_\xi$. Hence:

$$\frac{\partial P_{1iy_i}}{\partial \beta_3} = -\frac{v_i}{\sigma_\xi}\int \Phi_i(\epsilon_{1i}, \rho_{13}h(\epsilon_{1i}) + \sigma_\xi\ddot{\eta})[1(y_i = 0) - Po(\lambda_i, y_i)]\phi(\ddot{\eta})g(\epsilon_{1i})d\epsilon_{1i}$$

$$\to -\frac{v_i}{\sigma_\xi}\int 1\left(\ddot{\eta} > \frac{-w_i'\beta_2 - \gamma y_i - (r_1^* + r_2^*\rho_{13})h(\epsilon_{1i})}{r_2^*\sigma_\xi}\right)$$
$$\times [1(y_i = 0) - Po(\lambda_i, y_i)]\phi(\ddot{\eta})g(\epsilon_{1i})d\epsilon_{1i},$$

as $\rho \to \rho^*$ by the LDCT, where the various terms are evaluated at ρ^*. A similar expression is obtained for the derivative with respect to ρ_{13}, also taking into account the facts that σ_ξ and $\Phi_i(.,.)$ are functions of ρ_{13}.

Notes

1. For convenience, I treat the explanatory variables as "fixed" and omit expectations over the distribution of the explanatory variables. In the asymptotic theory, the explanatory variables would be assumed to satisfy conditions such as those used in Gouriéroux, Monfort, and Trognon (1984), who reference Burguete, Gallant, and Souza (1982). I similarly assume that the relevant dominance conditions, etc., hold so that, for example, the various expectations exist.
2. See, for example, Cameron and Trivedi (1990) for a discussion of overdispersion.
3. The bounds on integrals are $-\infty$ to ∞ unless stated otherwise.
4. $f(\cdot)$ is used to denote a number of different densities, with the particular density given by the argument.
5. Gabler *et al.* (1993) treat the choice of D as a model selection problem.
6. Winkelmann (1995) and Lee (1996), for example, apply this approach.
7. Note that the correlation between ϵ_{1i} and ϵ_{2i} is still less than one when $\rho_{12} = 1$. The intercept in the binary choice equation may also change.
8. Otherwise, it is necessary to assume that $|\rho_{12}| \leq 1 - \delta$ for some $\delta > 0$ in order to make the parameter space compact—the usual assumption on the parameter space in the standard asymptotic theory.
9. For averages in (46) of around 0.3–0.4, the average variance across observations

was approximately 0.1. This implies the standard deviations of the averages of around 0.0045.

10. Both the lognormal and gamma are special cases of the generalized beta II distribution, e.g., MacDonald and Xu (1995); but I do not consider this wider family in this paper.

11. Pagan and Vella begin by assuming that the joint density of the two random variables they are concerned with has a particular form, and then impose the null of normality. I simply treat (56) as the alternative.

12. The difference between the NB and ZINB models will be greater in models in which the tail of the distribution of Y_i is driven by the dispersion of the independent variables rather than the heterogeneity (e.g., Weiss, 1998). As noted above, the model here was based on the example in the next section.

13. Strictly, the coefficients on MDR and MDR^2 imply that above some level, larger values of MDR increase the probability of the application being successful. The quadratic should be taken as an approximation.

14. Huge values of the test statistics sometimes occurred in the Monte Carlo experiment, but I have not yet investigated the cause of this in detail.

References

Amemiya, T. (1985), *Advanced Econometrics*. Cambridge, MA: Harvard University Press.

Berndt, E. R., B. H. Hall, R. E. Hall, and J. A. Hausman (1974), "Estimation and inference in non-linear structural models," *Annals of Economic and Social Measurement*, 3: 653–65.

Burguete, J., R. Gallant, and G. Souza (1982), "On unification of the asymptotic theory of nonlinear econometric models," *Econometric Reviews*, 1: 151–90.

Cameron, A. C. and P. Johansson (1997), "Count data regression using series expansions: with applications," *Journal of Applied Econometrics*, 12: 203–23.

Cameron, A. C. and P. K. Trivedi (1986), "Econometric models based on count data: comparison of some estimators and tests," *Journal of Applied Econometrics*, 1: 29–54.

Cameron, A. C. and P. K. Trivedi (1990), "Regression-based tests for overdispersion in the poisson model," *Journal of Econometrics*, 46: 347–64.

Chant, D. (1974), "On asymptotic tests of composite hypotheses in nonstandard conditions," *Biometrika*, 61: 291–8.

Davidson, R. and J. G. MacKinnon (1993), *Estimation and Inference in Econometrics*. Oxford: Oxford University Press.

Gabler, S., F. Laisney, and M. Lechner (1993), "Seminonparametric estimation of binary choice models with an application to labor-force participation," *Journal of Business and Economic Statistics*, 11: 61–80.

Gallant, A. R. and D. W. Nychka (1987), "Semi-nonparametric maximum likelihood estimation," *Econometrica*, 55: 363–90.

Geweke, J. (1989), "Bayesian inference in econometric models using Monte Carlo integration," *Econometrica*, 57: 1317–39.

Gouriéroux, C., A. Monfort, and A. Trognon (1984), "Pseudo maximum likelihood methods: theory," *Econometrica*, 52: 681–700.

Greene, W. H. (1994), "Accounting for excess zeros and sample selection in poisson and negative binomial regression models," Working paper EC-94-10, Department of Economics, New York University.

Gurmu, S. (1997), "Semi-parametric estimation of hurdle regression models with an application to Medicaid utilization," *Journal of Applied Econometrics*, 12: 225–43.

Horowitz, J. L. (1992), "A smoothed maximum score estimator for the binary response model," *Econometrica*, 60: 505–31.

Klein, R. W. and R. H. Spady (1993), "An efficient semiparametric estimator for binary response models," *Econometrica*, 61: 387–422.

Lambert, D. (1992), "Zero-inflated poisson regression, with an application to defects in manufacturing," *Technometrics*, 34: 1–14.

Lee, L.-F. (1982), "Some approaches to the correction of selectivity bias," *Review of Economic Studies*, 49: 355–72.

Lee, L.-F. (1992), "On efficiency of methods of simulated moments and maximum simulated likelihood estimation of discrete response models," *Econometric Theory*, 8: 518–52.

Lee, L.-F. (1996), "Specification and estimation of count data regression and sample selection models: a counting process and waiting time approach," Working paper, Department of Economics, The Hong Kong University of Science and Technology, Hong Kong.

McDonald, J. B. and Y. J. Xu (1995), "A generalization of the beta distribution with applications," *Journal of Econometrics*, 66: 133–52.

Moran, P. A. P. (1971), "Maximum likelihood estimators in non-standard conditions," *Proceedings of the Cambridge Philosophical Society*, 70: 414–50.

Murphy, K. and R. Topel (1985), "Estimation and inference in two-step econometric models," *Journal of Business and Economic Statistics*, 3: 370–9.

Pagan, A. and F. Vella (1989), "Diagnostic tests for models based on individual data: a survey," *Journal of Applied Econometrics*, 4: S29–S59.

Pesaran, M. H. and B. Pesaran (1993), "A simulation approach to the problem of computing Cox's statistic for nonnested models," *Journal of Econometrics*, 57: 337–92.

Rivers, D. and Q. H. Vuong (1988), "Limited information estimators and exogeneity tests for simultaneous probit models," *Journal of Econometrics*, 39: 347–66.

Rund, P. (1984), "Tests of specification in econometrics," *Econometric Reviews*, 3: 211–42.

Schwarz, G. (1978), "Estimating the dimension of a model," *Annals of Statistics*, 6: 461–4.

Shaked, M. (1980), "On mixtures of exponential families," *Journal of the Royal Statistical Society Series B*, 42: 192–198.

Smith, R. and R. Blundell (1986), "An exogeneity test for a simultaneous equation tobit model with an application to labor supply," *Econometrica*, 54: 679–85.

Terza, J. V. (1998), "Estimating count data models with endogenous switching: sample selection and endogenous treatment effects," *Journal of Econometrics*, 84: 129–54.

Vuong, Q. (1989), "Likelihood ratio tests for model selection and non-nested hypotheses," *Econometrica*, 57: 307–34.

Weiss, A. A. (1998), "On excess zeros in count data models," Working paper, School of Economics and Finance, Victoria University of Wellington.

Winkelmann, R. (1995), "Duration dependence and dispersion in count-data models," *Journal of Business and Economic Statistics*, 13: 467–74.

Winkelmann, R. (1998), "Count data models with selectivity," *Econometric Reviews*, 17: 339–59.

19
Statistical Properties of the Asymmetric Power ARCH Process

CHANGLI HE AND TIMO TERÄSVIRTA

1 Introduction

The temporal properties of power-transformed returns, r_t, from speculative assets have recently received considerable attention. Clive Granger, whose interest in commodity and stock markets can be traced back to Granger and Morgenstern (1963, 1970), has discussed them in a series of papers: see Ding, Granger and Engle (1993), henceforth DGE, Granger and Ding (1995a, b, 1996) and Ding and Granger (1996). In DGE the authors reminded the reader of the fact which Taylor (1986, pp. 52–6) first observed, namely, that $|r_t|$ is positively autocorrelated even at long lags. DGE found that $|r_t|^d$, $d > 0$, is even "long-memory" in that the autocorrelations remain not only positive but rather high at very long lags. Moreover, the authors observed that the property is strongest for $d = 1$ and near it. They noted that this may argue against ARCH specifications that are based on squared returns such as the classical GARCH model of Bollerslev (1986) and Taylor (1986, pp. 78–9). Consequently, DGE introduced a new GARCH model with a separate "heteroskedasticity parameter" δ. This model, the Asymmetric Power ARCH (A-PARCH) model, contained as special cases a host of previous GARCH models. DGE demonstrated its potential by fitting the model with normal errors to the long S&P 500 daily stock return series from January 3, 1928 to April 30, 1991, 17,054 observations in all.

In this paper we view the A-PARCH process from a different angle. If we transform the original process with a certain sign-preserving transformation and define a standard GARCH process for these observations then this GARCH

This work has received financial support from the Swedish Council for Research in the Humanities and Social Sciences and the Bank of Sweden Tercentenary Foundation. Earlier versions of the paper have been presented at the Fifth Workshop on Finance and Econometrics, Brussels, December 1997, and the Econometric Society European Meeting, Berlin, September 1998. Comments from participants at these occasions, Christian Hafner in particular, are gratefully acknowledged. We also wish to thank Robert Kunst and an anonymous referee for helpful comments and Rob Engle for very penetrating and useful remarks that have greatly improved the presentation. Any remaining errors and shortcomings are our own responsibility.

process is equivalent to the corresponding A-PARCH process. We can then discuss the effect of the transformation parameter which is related to the exponent in the A-PARCH process on the autocorrelation function of the squares of the transformed observations. We can also view the original A-PARCH process through this standard GARCH process. In particular, we are able to derive certain fractional moments for the A-PARCH process and consider the effect of the asymmetry parameter on the corresponding autocorrelation function. Furthermore, it is possible to obtain an existence condition for a fractional moment. This is helpful in practice because if the condition is satisfied then we know that all lower-order moments, integer ones included, exist as well. If it is not satisfied then no higher-order moment condition is satisfied either.

The paper is organized as follows. A transformation of observations implicit in the A-PARCH specification is the topic of Section 2. The fractional moments and the autocorrelation function of the A-PARCH process are also presented in this section. Section 3 considers the autocorrelation function of squares of the power-transformed series as a function of the power or heteroskedasticity parameter. Section 4 discusses possible advantages of the A-PARCH specification in the light of the empirical example in DGE. Section 5 concludes.

2 Moments and the Autocorrelation Function

Consider the general A-PARCH(p, q, δ) model

$$\varepsilon_t = z_t h_t \tag{1}$$

where $\{z_t\}$ is a sequence of independent identically distributed random variables with a symmetric density with zero mean and a finite 2δth unconditional absolute moment. Furthermore,

$$
\begin{aligned}
h_t^\delta &= \alpha_0 + \sum_{j=1}^{p} \alpha_j \left(\left| \varepsilon_{t-j} \right| - \phi_j \varepsilon_{t-j} \right)^\delta + \sum_{j=1}^{q} \beta_j h_{t-j}^\delta \\
&= \alpha_0 + \sum_{j=1}^{p} c_{\delta, t-j} h_{t-j}^\delta,
\end{aligned} \tag{2}
$$

where $c_{\delta,t-j} = \alpha_j (|z_{t-j}| - \phi_j z_{t-j})^\delta + \beta_j$, $|\phi_j| < 1$, $\alpha_0 > 0$, α_j, $\beta_j \geq 0$, $j = 1, ..., p$. Letting $\beta_j = 0$, $j = 1, ..., p$, in (2) yields the so-called β-ARCH model; see Guégan (1994, p. 169). Expression (2) for $\delta = 2$ and $\phi_j = 0$, $j = 1, ..., p$, appeared in He and Teräsvirta (1999a). We shall concentrate on the first-order case ($p = q = 1$). This implies that (2) becomes

$$h_t^\delta = \alpha_0 + c_{\delta,t-1} h_{t-1}^\delta, \tag{3}$$

where $c_{\delta t} = \alpha_1 (|z_t| - \phi z_t)^\delta + \beta_1$ and $\phi = \phi_1$, and $\{c_{\delta t}\}$ is a sequence of iid observations.

Now, consider (1) with (3), assume $\phi = 0$, and transform ε_t as follows:

$$\xi_t = \text{sgn}(\varepsilon_t)|\varepsilon_t|^{\delta/2} \tag{4}$$

and let

$$z_t^* = \text{sgn}(z_t)|z_t|^{\delta/2} .$$

Then $\xi_t = z_t^* h_t^{\delta/2}$ follows a standard GARCH(1, 1) process with conditional variance h_t^{δ}. Note, however, that if $z_t \sim N(0, 1)$, this is no longer true for z_t^*, but the density of z_t^* is still symmetric around zero. There does not exist a corresponding transformation for $\phi \neq 0$. Nonetheless, if we reparameterize the A-PARCH(1, 1) model by replacing the term $(|\varepsilon_{t-1}| - \phi\varepsilon_{t-1})$, $|\phi| < 1$, by $(\varepsilon_{t-1} - \phi|\varepsilon_{t-1}|)$ we may define

$$\xi_t^* = \text{sgn}(\varepsilon_t - \phi|\varepsilon_t|)|\varepsilon_t - \phi|\varepsilon_t|\|^{\delta/2} . \tag{5}$$

When $\{\varepsilon_t\}$ has the modified A-PARCH(1, 1) representation the sequence $\{\xi_t^*\}$ obeys a symmetric GARCH(1, 1) model. We can now apply either the general results in He and Teräsvirta (1999a), or those in He and Teräsvirta (1999b) to these transformed processes.

Setting $\gamma_\delta = \mathsf{E}c_{\delta t}$ and $\gamma_{2\delta} = \mathsf{E}c_{\delta t}^2$ thus yields

Theorem 1. *For the A-PARCH(1, 1, δ) model (1) with (3), a necessary and sufficient condition for the existence of the 2δth absolute moment $\mu_{2\delta} = \mathsf{E}|\varepsilon_t|^{2\delta}$ is*

$$\gamma_{2\delta} < 1. \tag{6}$$

If (6) holds, then

$$\mu_{2\delta} = \alpha_0^2 \nu_{2\delta}(1 + \gamma_\delta)/\{(1 - \gamma_\delta)(1 - \gamma_{2\delta})\}, \tag{7}$$

and the "moment coefficient"

$$\kappa_{2\delta} = \mu_{2\delta} / \mu_\delta^2 = \kappa_{2\delta}(z_t)(1 - \gamma_\delta^2)/(1 - \gamma_{2\delta}), \tag{8}$$

where $\nu_\psi = \mathsf{E}|z_t|^\psi$ and $\kappa_{2\delta}(z_t) = \nu_{2\delta}/\nu_\delta^2$. Furthermore, the autocorrelation function $\rho_n(\delta) = \rho(|\varepsilon_t|^\delta, |\varepsilon_{t-n}|^\delta)$, $n \geq 1$, of $\{|\varepsilon_t|^\delta\}$ has the form

$$\rho_n(\delta) = \frac{\nu_\delta \gamma_\delta^{n-1}\left[\overline{\gamma}_\delta(1 - \gamma_\delta^2) - \nu_\delta\gamma_\delta(1 - \gamma_{2\delta})\right]}{\nu_{2\delta}(1 - \gamma_\delta^2) - \nu_\delta^2(1 - \gamma_{2\delta})} \tag{9}$$

where $\overline{\gamma}_\delta = \mathsf{E}(|z_t|^\delta c_{\delta t})$.

In particular, when $\delta = 2$ (identity transformation), the kurtosis of $\{\varepsilon_t^2\}$ equals $\kappa_4 = \kappa_4(z_t)(1 - \gamma_2^2)/(1 - \gamma_4)$ and $\rho_n(2) = \kappa_4(z_t)\gamma_2^{n-1}(\overline{\gamma}_2 - \gamma_2\kappa_4^{-1})/(1 - \kappa_4^{-1})$, $n \geq 1$, where $\kappa_4(z_t)$ is the kurtosis of $\{z_t\}$; see He and Teräsvirta (1999b) for a discussion.

Theorem 1 completes results in DGE who also discussed γ_δ. Furthermore,

Ding and Granger (1996) derived the (conditional) autocorrelation function of $|\varepsilon_t|^{\delta}$ under the assumption $\nu_{\delta} = 1$. As DGE pointed out, many well-known GARCH models are special cases of the A-PARCH model. Theorem 1 applies to those as well, but they are considered in more detail in He and Teräsvirta (1999b).

The A-PARCH model was introduced to characterize processes $\{\varepsilon_t\}$ in which $\rho(|\varepsilon_t|, |\varepsilon_{t-n}|)$ decays slowly as a function of n. From (9) we have:

$$\rho_n(\delta) = \rho_1(\delta)\gamma_{\delta}^{n-1}, \quad n \geq 1. \tag{10}$$

The decay of the autocorrelation function is exponential, as Ding and Granger (1996) already noted, and γ_{δ} controls this decay. For a closer look at the first-order autocorrelation (9) note that, due to the symmetry of the density of z_t, we can express γ_{δ}, $\overline{\gamma}_{\delta}$ and $\gamma_{2\delta}$, respectively, as:

$$\gamma_{\delta} = (\alpha_1/2)\phi_{\delta}\nu_{\delta} + \beta_1, \tag{11}$$
$$\overline{\gamma}_{\delta} = (\alpha_1/2)\phi_{\delta}\nu_{2\delta} + \beta_1\nu_{\delta}, \tag{12}$$
$$\gamma_{2\delta} = (\alpha_1^2/2)\phi_{2\delta}\nu_{2\delta} + \alpha_1\beta_1\phi_{\delta}\nu_{\delta} + \beta_1^2, \tag{13}$$

where $\phi_{\delta} = (1+\phi)^{\delta} + (1-\phi)^{\delta}$ and $\phi_{2\delta} = (1+\phi)^{2\delta} + (1-\phi)^{2\delta}$. Using (11), expressions (12) and (13) may be rewritten as

$$\overline{\gamma}_{\delta} = \gamma_{\delta}\nu_{\delta} + (\alpha_1/2)\phi_{\delta}(\nu_{2\delta} - \nu_{\delta}^2), \tag{14}$$
$$\gamma_{2\delta} = \gamma_{\delta}^2 + (\alpha_1^2/2)\phi_{2\delta}\nu_{2\delta} - (\alpha_1^2/4)\phi_{\delta}^2\nu_{\delta}^2. \tag{15}$$

Inserting (14) and (15) into (9) yields:

$$\rho_1(\delta) = \frac{(\alpha_1/2)\nu_{\delta}\phi_{\delta}(\nu_{2\delta} - \nu_{\delta}^2)(1 - \gamma_{\delta}^2) + (\alpha_1^2/2)\nu_{\delta}^2\gamma_{\delta}(\phi_{2\delta}\nu_{2\delta} - (1/2)\phi_{\delta}^2\nu_{\delta}^2)}{(\nu_{2\delta} - \nu_{\delta}^2)(1 - \gamma_{\delta}^2) + (\alpha_1^2/2)\nu_{\delta}^2(\phi_{2\delta}\nu_{2\delta} - (1/2)\phi_{\delta}^2\nu_{\delta}^2)}. \tag{16}$$

From (16) it is seen that for given values of α_1, β_1 and ϕ, $\rho_1(\delta)$ is a function of δ expressed in terms of ϕ_{δ}, $\phi_{2\delta}$, ν_{δ} and $\nu_{2\delta}$. Assuming $\phi = 0$, $\rho_1(\delta)$ reduces to:

$$\rho_1(\delta) = \frac{\alpha_1\nu_{\delta}(1 - \gamma_{\delta}^2) + \alpha_1^2\gamma_{\delta}\nu_{\delta}^2}{(1 - \gamma_{\delta}^2) + \alpha_1^2\nu_{\delta}^2}. \tag{17}$$

On the other hand, setting $\beta_1 = 0$ in (16) yields the first-order autocorrelation of squares in the A-PARCH$(1, \delta)$ or β-ARCH$(1, \delta)$ model:

$$\rho_1(\delta) = \frac{(\alpha_1/2)\nu_{\delta}\phi_{\delta}(\nu_{2\delta} - \nu_{\delta}^2) + (\alpha_1^3/4)\nu_{\delta}^3\phi_{\delta}\nu_{2\delta}(\phi_{2\delta} - (1/2)\phi_{\delta}^2)}{(\nu_{2\delta} - \nu_{\delta}^2) + (\alpha_1^2/2)\nu_{\delta}^2\nu_{2\delta}(\phi_{2\delta} - (1/2)\phi_{\delta}^2)}$$
$$= (\alpha_1/2)\phi_{\delta}\nu_{\delta}. \tag{18}$$

Further giving up asymmetry by setting $\phi = 0$ in (18) leads to

$$\rho_1(\delta) = \gamma_{\delta} = \alpha_1\nu_{\delta}, \tag{19}$$

which is analogous to a familiar expression from an ARCH(1) model.

We may also note that the asymmetry parameter ϕ has a systematic effect on the autocorrelation function. Let $\rho_1^*(\delta)$ denote the first order autocorrelation $\rho_1(\delta)$ in (16) corresponding to $\phi \neq 0$ whereas $\rho_1^o(\delta) = \rho_1(\delta)$ in (17) where $\phi = 0$. We can then formulate:

Theorem 2. *Consider the A-PARCH model (1) with (3) and assume that $\rho_1^*(\delta)$ and $\rho_1^o(\delta)$ exist for some δ. Then*

$$\rho_1^*(\delta) > \rho_1^o(\delta), \quad \text{when } \delta \geq 1; \tag{20}$$

$$\rho_1^*(\delta) > \rho_1^o(\delta), \quad \text{when } 0{<}\delta < 1 \text{ and } \gamma_\delta \text{ is sufficiently large.} \tag{21}$$

Proof. See Appendix.

We only obtain this result for the autocorrelations of $|\varepsilon_t|^\delta$, but it may be indicative for other powers of $|\varepsilon_t|$ as well. The situation is illustrated in Figure 1. The solid curve is the theoretical autocorrelation as a function of δ obtained from (17) by assuming standard normal errors and setting $\alpha_1 = 0.091$ and $\beta_1 = 0.9$. The dashed–dotted curve is the counterpart of the solid one after introducing skewness by setting the asymmetry parameter $\phi = -0.3$. It is seen that the value of the theoretical autocorrelation function is higher when $\phi \neq 0$ than it is when the model is symmetric. Also note that the nonzero asymmetry parameter has the effect of shifting the autocorrelation-minimizing value

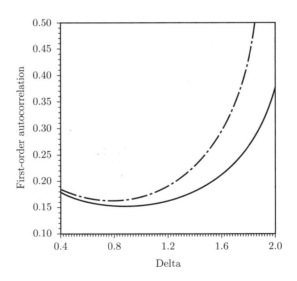

Figure 1

The figure shows the first-order theoretical autocorrelations from an A-PARCH(1, 1) model as a function of δ with $\alpha_1 = 0.091$, $\beta_1 = 0.9$, and $\phi = 0$ (solid convex curve) and $\phi = -0.3$ (dashed-dotted convex curve)

of δ to the left. We shall have a closer look at autocorrelations as a function of δ in the next section.

3 The Power Parameter

We shall now consider the sign-preserving power transformations (4) and (5). Suppose that $\{x_t\}$ follows an A-PARCH(1, 1, δ) process and that the 2δth moment exists. Then $\rho_n(\delta)$, $n = 1, 2, \ldots$, exist and the transformed sequence follows a standard GARCH(1, 1) process with a finite fourth moment. We consider the influence of δ on the higher-order dependence in the transformed sequence $\{\xi_t\}$ or $\{\xi_t^*\}$. If we do that by using $\rho_1(\delta)$, the first-order autocorrelation of $\{\xi_t^2\}$ or $\{\xi_t^{*2}\}$, as our measure of second-order dependence we may ask if there exists a $\delta > 0$ such that $\rho_1(\delta)$ attains a (global) maximum or minimum. Figure 1 already suggests an answer but we shall analyze the situation more formally. Let $I = (0, l)$, $l > 0$, be an open interval such that $\delta_0 \in I$ if and only if $\gamma_{2\delta_0} < 1$. Then there exists $I_\delta = [\delta_a, \delta_b]$, which is a closed interval, such that $I_\delta \subset I$. Obviously, for any $\delta \in I_\delta$ we have $\gamma_{2\delta} < 1$.

We obtain the following result:

Property 3.1. *Assume that ν_δ is a convex function of δ on I_δ with a finite second derivative for any $\delta \in I_\delta$. Then $\rho_1(\delta)$ given in (15) is a convex function of δ on I_δ. Furthermore, if $\partial\nu_\delta/\partial\delta|_{\delta=\delta_0} = 0$ and $\delta_0 \in I_\delta$, then $\partial\rho_1(\delta)/\partial\delta|_{\delta=\delta_0} = 0$.*

Proof. See Appendix.

Remark. The convexity assumption for ν_δ is not very restrictive. In fact, what we have assumed for z_t in Section 2 is sufficient for ν_δ to be a convex function of δ on I_δ. To see this, suppose that a random variable X has a continuous density $f(x)$ on $(-\infty, +\infty)$ such that $f(x)$ is nonnegative everywhere. Then $\nu_\delta'' = E(|X|^\delta \ln^2|X|) > 0$ on I_δ so that ν_δ is a convex function of δ on I_δ. Moreover, $\nu_\delta' = E(|X|^\delta \ln|X|)$ implies that there exists a unique δ_0 such that $\nu_{\delta_0}' = 0$.

Moreover the asymmetry terms ϕ_δ, $\phi_{2\delta}$ and ϕ_δ^2 in (16) are convex functions of δ on the interval $(0, 1)$ and they reach their minimum values on the interval $(0, 0.5]$. The minimizing value is a function of ϕ.

Remark 2. If $\phi = 0$, it follows from the convexity assumption of ν_δ that $\gamma_\delta = \alpha_1\nu_\delta + \beta_1$ is a convex function of δ on I_δ for given parameter values β_1 and α_1. Then $\rho_1(\delta)$ reaches its minimum value at $\delta_0 \in I_\delta$, in which γ_δ also has its minimum value as well as ν_δ does. This implies that $(\partial^2/\partial\delta^2)\rho_1(\delta)\gamma_\delta > 0$ at $\delta \in I_\delta$. We see that $\rho_2(\delta)$ is a convex function of δ on I_δ. In general, $\rho_n(\delta) = \rho_1(\delta)\gamma_\delta^{n-1}$ is a convex function of δ for any $n > 1$ when $\phi = 0$.

From (17) we see that $\rho_1(\delta)$ only depends on the δth absolute moment ν_δ if we do not allow asymmetry. If $\phi \neq 0$ then it follows from (16) that $\rho_1(\delta)$ also depends on $\nu_{2\delta}$, ϕ_δ and $\phi_{2\delta}$. This complicates the analysis. Nevertheless, assume as before that ν_δ with a second derivative for any $\delta \in I_\delta$ is a convex function of δ on I_δ. This implies that $\nu_{2\delta}$ is also a convex function of δ on I_δ. Moreover, $\phi_\delta'' = (1+\phi)^\delta \ln^2(1+\phi) + (1-\phi)^\delta \ln^2(1-\phi) \geq 0$ indicates that ϕ_δ is a convex function of δ on I_δ. Therefore, there exists a subset $I_{\delta_*} \subseteq I_\delta$ such that ν_δ', $\nu_{2\delta}'$, ϕ_δ', $\phi_{2\delta}' < 0$ for any $\delta \in I_{\delta_*}$. Then there exists an unique $\delta_0 \in I_\delta$ such that $u'v - uv' = 0$ at $\delta_0 \in I_\delta$, where $\rho_1(\delta) = u/v$ in (16). We thus have $\rho_1'(\delta_0) = 0$. Proving $\rho_1''(\delta_0) > 0$ seems complicated and we content ourselves with:

Conjecture 3.2. *Assume that ν_δ with a second derivative for any $\delta \in I_\delta$ is a convex function of δ on I_δ. Then, for $\phi \neq 0$, $\rho_1(\delta)$ is a convex function of δ on I_δ. Furthermore, if $\partial \nu_\delta / \partial \delta|_{\delta = \delta_0} = 0$ and $\delta_0 \in I_\delta$, then $\partial \rho_1(\delta)/\partial \delta|_{\delta = \delta_0} \neq 0$.*

Remark 3. When $\phi \neq 0$, $\rho_1(\delta)$ is still a convex function of δ on I_δ. However, the minimizing $\delta_0 \in I_\delta$ such that $\nu_{\delta_0}' = 0$ is not the same as the $\delta_* \in I_\delta$ for which $\rho_1'(\delta_*) = 0$. The inequality $\delta_* \neq \delta_0$ is due to the effects of the asymmetric terms ϕ_δ and $\phi_{2\delta}$ in (16).

As Remark 2 indicates, the minimizing value of $\rho(|\varepsilon_t|^\delta, |\varepsilon_{t-1}|^\delta)$ may also be shifted away from $\delta_{min} = 0.87$ where it is located under the assumption of normality by assuming another distribution for the error term. It can be shown that if the error term is t-distributed then $\delta_{min} < 0.87$. In fact, the minimizing value is an increasing function of degrees of freedom in the t-distribution. On the other hand, the t-distribution can be generalized further into a generalized t (GT) distribution with the density

$$f(x) = \frac{p}{2\sigma q^{1/p} B(1/p, q)\left(1 + \frac{|x|^p}{q\sigma^p}\right)^{q+1/p}}, \quad |x| < \infty, \quad \sigma, p, q > 0 \quad (22)$$

where B is the beta-function, see, for example, McDonald and Newey (1988). Bollerslev, Engle and Nelson (1994) employed the GT distribution as the error distribution when modeling US stock index returns. Suitable choices of the two shape parameters p and q shift the minimizing value to the right. For instance, $p = 1.5$ and $q = 200$ yield $\delta_{min} = 1.07$. For comparison, $p = 2$ for the t-distribution.

How can these results be interpreted? Parameter δ affects the second-order dependence of the observations transformed according to (4) or (5). This dependence can be minimized by an appropriate choice of δ. If the A-PARCH model is actually symmetric then the minimizing value of δ does not depend on the other parameters of the model. If δ has to do with explaining heteroskedasticity then one could perhaps expect an estimate close to the value minimizing the autocorrelation function of squares of the transformed observations. We shall consider this possibility in the light of an empirical example.

4 An Empirical Example

The above theory considers the role of δ and ϕ in the A-PARCH model under the *ceteris paribus* assumption that the other parameters remain constant. If a standard GARCH model is augmented by these parameters, the estimates of the other parameters almost certainly change. DGE applied the A-PARCH(1, 1, δ) to the long S&P 500 daily return series of 17,054 observations mentioned in the Introduction. Their estimation results are summarized in Table 1. Comparison of estimated likelihoods of the standard GARCH(1, 1), the absolute-value GARCH(1, 1) (AVGARCH(1, 1)) and the A-PARCH(1, 1, δ) models indicates that the last one fits the data significantly better than the other two. We focus on first-order autocorrelations. As discussed in Section 2, we can only obtain certain fractional moments analytically but would nonetheless like to compare the autocorrelations $\rho_1(|\varepsilon_t|^d, |\varepsilon_{t-1}|^d)$ for different values of d for the three models with what is obtained directly from the data. We have computed these autocorrelations by simulation from 1,000 series of 500,000 observations each for $d = 0.2, 0.4, ..., 2.6$. The results appear in Figure 2. Note that some of the estimated autocorrelations do not actually have a theoretic counterpart as the $2d$th moment condition is not satisfied for all values of d. For example, Table 1 shows that the estimated GARCH(1, 1) model does not possess a finite fourth moment. But then, the estimated autocorrelations always remain between zero and unity in absolute value by definition.

Figure 2 shows that the autocorrelations from the A-PARCH model are much closer to those estimated directly from the data than those from the other two models. The difference increases with d, but the $2d$th moment may

Table 1. GARCH specifications estimated for the S&P 500 daily stock return series, January 3, 1928 to April 30, 1991

Parameter estimate	GARCH $\delta = 2$	A-PARCH $\hat{\delta} = 1.43$	AVGARCH $\delta = 1$
$\hat{\alpha}_0$	8.0×10^{-7} (12.5)	1.4×10^{-6} (4.5)	9.6×10^{-6} (12.6)
$\hat{\alpha}_1$	0.091 (50.7)	0.083 (32.4)	0.104 (67)
$\hat{\beta}_1$	0.906 (43.4)	0.920 (474)	0.913 (517)
$\hat{\phi}$		−0.373 (−20.7)	
$\hat{\gamma}_{2\delta}$	1.0106	0.99526	0.99591

Note: $\hat{\gamma}_{2\delta}$ = left-hand side of the 2δ moment condition. A value less than unity indicates the existence of the 2δth moment of $\{|\varepsilon_t|\}$.

Source: DGE (value of the t-statistic in parentheses).

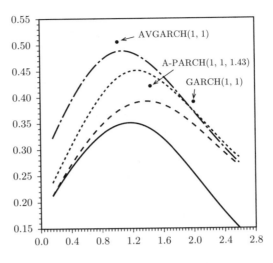

Figure 2

The figure shows the first-order autocorrelation for power-transformed observations
of the S&P 500 daily return series with 17,054 observations for powers from 0.2 to 2.6,
estimated directly from the data (solid curve), estimated by simulation from the
AVGARCH(1, 1) model (dashed-dotted curve), from the GARCH(1, 1) model (dashed
curve; short dashes) and from the A-PARCH(1, 1, 1.43) model (dashed curve; long
dashes), and autocorrelations for absolute values (AVGARCH) obtained by plug-in
from the AVGARCH model, and those for $\delta = 1.43$ obtained from the A-PARCH
model, and a (nonunique) asymptotic value for the autocorrelation of squares as the
fourth moment vanishes, estimated from the GARCH(1, 1) model (solid circles).

not exist for all d (it still does for $d = 1.43$). On the other hand, with the introduction of the two extra parameters not present in GARCH or AVGARCH
models the maximum of the autocorrelation function moves to the right,
further away from unity and the maximum of the autocorrelation estimated
directly from the data and not to the left. As $\widehat{\delta} = 1.43$ in the A-PARCH model,
the "heteroskedasticity parameter" δ may not have the property that it tends
to reduce autocorrelation in the squares of the transformed observations as
discussed in the previous section. It should be noted, however, that the estimated A-PARCH model also contains an asymmetry parameter whose contribution complicates the interpretation because the A-PARCH parameterization
does not accord with (5).

The contents of Table 2 also help interpret the contribution of the extra
parameters in the A-PARCH model. The table shows the autocorrelation
functions of absolute values of $|\varepsilon_t|^\delta$ for $\delta = 2, 1.43, 1$ at selected lags. The auto-
correlations are estimated directly from the data (D) or computed from the
estimated models (M) applying (16) and (17). As mentioned above, the fourth
moment does not exist for the standard GARCH model. We are thus not able
to compute any autocorrelations of squared observations from the model. Yet,
the left-hand side of the existence condition for the fourth moment is a mono-

Table 2. Autocorrelation functions of $\{|\varepsilon_t|^\delta\}$, $\delta = 2, 1.43, 1$, estimated from the linearly filtered S&P 500 daily stock return series, January 3, 1928 to April 30, 1991, and computed from estimated models

Model	D/M	Lag									
		1	2	3	4	5	10	20	30	40	50
GARCH	D	0.252	0.243	0.182	0.153	0.200	0.115	0.095	0.094	0.067	0.069
	M(a)	0.390	0.387	0.383	0.380	0.377	0.362	0.332	0.306	0.281	0.258
	M(b)	0.387	0.384	0.381	0.378	0.376	0.362	0.335	0.311	0.288	0.267
A-PARCH	D	0.337	0.328	0.294	0.291	0.287	0.212	0.196	0.181	0.154	0.152
	M	0.421	0.418	0.415	0.412	0.409	0.395	0.368	0.343	0.320	0.298
AVGARCH	D	0.343	0.338	0.330	0.314	0.316	0.258	0.249	0.230	0.207	0.200
	M	0.506	0.504	0.502	0.500	0.498	0.488	0.469	0.450	0.433	0.416

D = Autocorrelations estimated from the S&P 500 daily return series.
M = Autocorrelations computed from the estimated model.
M(a) = Autocorrelations computed from the estimated model by reducing the estimate of α_1 until the stationarity condition is satisfied ($\hat{\gamma}_4 = 0.9999$).
M(b) = Autocorrelations computed from the estimated model by reducing the estimate of β_1 until the stationarity condition is satisfied ($\hat{\gamma}_4 = 0.9999$).

tonically increasing function of both α_1 and β_1, and the autocorrelations converge to an asymptote as the fourth moment vanishes. In order to obtain an approximation to an asymptotic autocorrelation function of squares we decrease the estimates of these parameters in turn such that the fourth moment just exists ($\gamma_4 = 0.9999$) for the two obtained parameter combinations. This yields approximations to two extreme asymptotic autocorrelation functions that, however, lie close to each other; the remaining ones may be obtained by reducing both parameters in size simultaneously until $\gamma_4 < 1$. Note that one of the asymptotic values for the first-order autocorrelation together with the corresponding autocorrelations for the AVGARCH and A-PARCH models also appear in Figure 2.

It is seen from Table 2 that for this GARCH(1, 1) model, the discrepancy between the asymptotic autocorrelation functions and the autocorrelations estimated directly from the data is large. For the AVGARCH(1, 1) model, there is also a large discrepancy between the high autocorrelations obtained from the model and those estimated from the data. The gap between the two is much smaller for the power ARCH model. Interestingly enough, the model-based autocorrelations seem to decay at a slower rate up to 50 lags than the direct ones although the decay rate of the model-based autocorrelations is just exponential. Nevertheless, even this comparison shows that the extra parameters in the A-PARCH(1, 1) model seem to have considerably improved the correspondence between stylized facts in the data on the one hand and the model on the other. Finally, Figure 2 shows that, even with series of 500,000 observations, the autocorrelation estimates obtained by simulation are underestimates of the true values. This agrees with He and Teräsvirta (1999b) who recently observed the same phenomenon.

5 Conclusions

In this paper we demonstrate how the A-PARCH model, at least after a slight modification, may also be viewed as a standard GARCH model for observations that have been transformed by a sign-preserving power transformation implied by the (modified) A-PARCH parameterization. This insight is important in deriving results concerning moments of the process. We have derived an existence condition for certain fractional moment of interest in A-PARCH models and the analytical expression for this moment when it exists. These results may in turn be used for drawing conclusions about the existence of integer moments on the basis of estimated models and for deriving autocorrelation functions of power-transformed observations. Furthermore, we have shown that there exists a value of the heteroskedasticity parameter such that it *ceteris paribus* minimizes the first-order autocorrelation of squares of the power-transformed series.

The empirical example shows that the two extra parameters, δ and ϕ, are useful in reproducing a stylized fact in the data, namely, the first-order autocorrelation $\rho_1(|\varepsilon_t|^d, |\varepsilon_{t-1}|^d)$ as a function of d. On the other hand, it seems that the autocorrelations of the estimated A-PARCH model do not peak for d close to unity as do the autocorrelations estimated directly from the S&P 500 return series.

The results on moments and the autocorrelation function generalize to higher-order A-PARCH processes by applying the results in He and Teräsvirta (1999a) to the present situation. As such a generalization involves tedious notation and because the first-order case is by far the most popular one in practice, we have chosen not to discuss higher-order A-PARCH processes in this paper. They are needed if the first few autocorrelations in the observed autocorrelation function of absolute values or squares do not fit into the general exponential decay pattern of the autocorrelations. This possibility has recently been discussed in He and Teräsvirta (1999c) in the context of the standard GARCH process (see also Nelson and Cao, 1992), and their results pertain to the present situation.

Appendix Proofs

Proof of Theorem 2. Suppose first that $\delta > 1$ and compare (16) with (17). In this case, $\phi_\delta > 2$, and $(\phi_{2\delta}\nu_{2\delta} - \frac{1}{2}\phi_\delta^2\nu_\delta^2)/(\nu_{2\delta} - \nu_\delta^2) > 2$ implies that $\rho_1^*(\delta) > \rho_1^\circ(\delta)$. When $\delta = 1$, $\phi_\delta = 2$ and $(\phi_{2\delta}\nu_{2\delta} - \frac{1}{2}\phi_\delta^2\nu_\delta^2)/(\nu_{2\delta} - \nu_\delta^2) > 2$. This proves

(20). When $0 < \delta < 1$, extra conditions are needed for $\rho_1^*(\delta) > \rho_1^o(\delta)$. The moment γ_δ should be sufficiently large so that the numerator on the right side of (16) is dominated by γ_δ. This is because $1 < \phi_\delta < 2$ and $(\phi_{2\delta}\nu_{2\delta} - \frac{1}{2}\phi_\delta^2\nu_\delta^2)/(\nu_{2\delta} - \nu_\delta^2) > 2$. (For example, from $\gamma_\delta \geq 0.8$ it already follows that $\rho_1^*(\delta) > \rho_1^o(\delta)$. In practice, (21) tends to hold for $0 < \delta < 1$ because the estimated $\widehat{\gamma}_\delta$ is usually quite close to unity.) ∎

Proof of Property 3.1. Let $\rho_1(\delta) = u/v$ where $u = \alpha_1(1 - \beta_1^2)\nu_\delta - \alpha_1^2\beta_1\nu_\delta^2$ and $v = (1 - \beta_1^2) - 2\alpha_1\beta_1\nu_\delta$ from (16). It follows that $\rho_1(\delta)$ is continuous and twice differentiable on I_δ. The first derivative $\rho_1'(\delta) = (u'v - uv')/v^2$, where u' and v' are the first order derivatives with respect to δ.

First we show that there exists a unique $\delta_0 \in I_\delta$ such that $\rho_1'(\delta_0) = 0$. Set

$$u'v - uv'$$
$$= \alpha_1(1 - \beta_1^2)^2\nu_\delta' - 2\alpha_1^2\beta_1(1 - \beta_1^2)\nu_\delta\nu_\delta' + 2\alpha_1^3\beta_1^2\nu_\delta^2\nu_\delta' = 0, \tag{A.1}$$

where ν_δ' is a first derivative of ν_δ with respect to δ. From (A.1) it follows that either (i) $\nu_\delta' = 0$, or (ii) $2\alpha_1^2\beta_1^2\nu_\delta^2 - 2\alpha_1\beta_1(1 - \beta_1^2)\nu_\delta - (1 - \beta_1^2)^2 = 0$. If (ii) holds, then $\nu_\delta = (1 - \beta_1^2)(1 \pm \sqrt{3})/2\alpha_1\beta_1$. Consider $\nu_d = (1 - \beta_1^2)(1 - \sqrt{3})/2\alpha_1\beta_1$. This implies $\nu_\delta < 0$, which is not possible. Alternatively, the solution $\nu_\delta = (1 - \beta_1^2)(1 + \sqrt{3})/2\alpha_1\beta_1$. Then $2\alpha_1\beta_1\nu_\delta < 1 - \beta_1^2$, which violates the moment condition $\gamma_{2\delta} < 1$. Thus $\nu_{\delta_0}' = 0$. Assume there exists $\delta_0 \in I_\delta$ such that $\nu_{\delta_0}' = 0$. Then $\rho_1'(\delta_0) = 0$.

Second, we show that the second derivative $\rho_1''(\delta_0) > 0$. Write $\rho_1''(\delta) = [(u''v - uv'')v - 2(u'v - uv')v']/v^3$. It suffices to show that $u''v - uv'' > 0$ at $\delta = \delta_0$. From (4) we have $1 - \beta_1^2 > \delta_1^2\nu_\delta + 2\alpha_1\beta_1\nu_\delta$ so that

$$u''v - uv''\big|_{\delta=\delta_0}$$
$$= \alpha_1\nu_{\delta_0}''[(1 - \beta_1^2)^2 + 2\alpha_1\beta_1(1 - \beta_1^2)\nu_{\delta_0} - 6\alpha_1^2\beta_1^2\nu_{\delta_0}^2]$$
$$> \alpha_1\nu_{\delta_0}''[\alpha_1^4\nu_{2\delta_0}^2 + 6\alpha_1^3\beta_1\nu_{\delta_0}\nu_{2\delta_0} + 2\alpha_1^2\beta_1^2\nu_{\delta_0}^2]$$
$$> 0. \quad ∎ \tag{A.2}$$

References

Bollerslev, T. (1986). "Generalized autoregressive conditional heteroskedasticity." *Journal of Econometrics*, 31: 307–27.

Bollerslev, T., R. F. Engle and D. B. Nelson (1994). "ARCH models." In R. F. Engle and D. L. McFadden (eds.), *Handbook of Econometrics*, vol. 4, pp. 2959–3038. Amsterdam: Elsevier.

Ding, Z. and C. W. J. Granger (1996). "Modeling volatility persistence of speculative returns: a new approach." *Journal of Econometrics*, 73: 185–215.

Ding, Z., C. W. J. Granger, and R. F. Engle (1993). "A long memory property of stock market returns and a new model." *Journal of Empirical Finance*, 1: 83–106.

Granger, C. W. J. and Z. Ding (1995a). "Some properties of absolute returns: an alternative measure of risk." *Annales d'économie et de statistique*, 40: 67–95.

Granger, C. W. J. and Z. Ding (1995b). "Stylized facts on the temporal and distributional properties of daily data from speculative markets." Department of Economics, University of California, San Diego, unpublished paper.

Granger, C. W. J. and Z. Ding (1996). "Varieties of long memory models." *Journal of Econometrics*, 73: 61–77.

Granger, C. W. J. and O. Morgenstern (1963). "Spectral analysis of New York stock market prices." *Kyklos*, 17: 1–27.

Granger, C. W. J. and O. Morgenstern (1970). *Predictability of stock market prices*. New York: Academic Press.

Guégan, D. (1994). *Séries chronologiques non linéaires à temps discret.* Paris: Economica.

He, C. and T. Teräsvirta (1999a). "Fourth moment structure of the GARCH(p, q) process." *Econometric Theory*, forthcoming.

He, C. and T. Teräsvirta (1999b). "Properties of moments of a family of GARCH processes." *Journal of Econometrics*, forthcoming.

He, C. and T. Teräsvirta (1999c). "Properties of the autocorrelation function of squared observations for second order GARCH process under two sets of parameter constraints." *Journal of Time Series Analysis*, 20: 23–30.

McDonald, J. B. and W. K. Newey (1988). "Partially adaptive estimation of regression models via the generalized t distribution." *Econometric Theory*, 4: 428–57.

Nelson, D. B. and C. Q. Cao (1992). "Inequality constraints in the univariate GARCH model." *Journal of Business and Economic Statistics*, 10: 229–35.

Schwert, G. W. (1989). "Why does stock market volatility change over time?" *Journal of Finance*, 45: 1129–55.

Taylor, S. (1986). *Modelling Financial Time Series.* New York: Wiley.

20
A Long-Run and Short-Run Component Model of Stock Return Volatility

ROBERT F. ENGLE AND GARY G. J. LEE

1 Introduction

An overriding theme in Clive Granger's long and insightful career inventing time series analysis for economists, has been the study of long and short memory forecasting models. The most famous venue for this was the research on unit roots, fractional integration and cointegration in the mean of a time series. In less well known but very influential work on second moments, Granger applied ideas of persistence and causality to variance processes. See for example Ding and Granger (1996), Ding, Granger, and Engle (1993) and Engle, Granger, and Robins (1986). In these papers, evidence was presented showing that volatilities were highly persistent, possibly requiring a long memory or fractionally integrated process. Many researchers have followed this strategy and now there is a substantial literature on FIGARCH, or fractionally integrated GARCH models. See for example Baillie and Bollerslev (1994) and Bollerslev and Mikkelsen (1996).

In this paper a different approach is taken. The long memory behavior of the volatility process is modeled as the sum of two conventional models where one has nearly a unit root, and the other has a much more rapid time decay. This two component structure extends the rich and complicated dynamics of French, Schwert and Stambaugh (1987), Chou (1988), Nelson (1989, 1990b), Pagan and Schwert (1990), and Engle, Bollerslev, and Nelson (1994), among others. By labeling these as permanent and transitory volatility components, substantial intuition is achieved and several natural hypotheses can be tested.

The decomposition of stock return volatility can also be motivated by examining the term structure of implied volatilities derived from market prices of traded stock options with a range of option expirations. It is well observed

We have benefited greatly from the comment of John Conlisk, Clive Granger, Wouter Den Haan, Bruce Lehmann and Alex Kane. Of course, all remaining errors are solely our responsibility. The authors gratefully acknowledge NSF support in grants SES–91–22056, SBR–9422575, and SBR–9730062.

that there are two dominant scenarios describing the implied volatility term structure movement in equity, foreign exchange and interest rate derivatives markets. The dominant effect is the parallel movement of implied volatilities of various maturities. However, the interesting second feature is that the amplitude is much greater for the short maturities. The volatility of short-term volatility is much greater than for long horizon volatility. In fact, the term structure of implied volatilities can change slope within a short period of time as the short volatilities move from abnormally low to abnormally high. For such a model of implieds, see Xu and Taylor (1994). This phenomenon indicates a mean-reverting property of implied volatility where short-term volatilities mean-revert more rapidly than long-term volatilities.

The decomposition of volatility into components allows tests of many economic and asset pricing hypotheses. It is likely that the persistence of jumps is different from ordinary news events. The component model allows shocks to be transitory; we investigate the impact of the October 1987 Crash on the short-run and the long-run volatility movement in the stock market. The market risk premium is shown by Merton (1980) to depend upon market volatility, an effect first estimated by French, Schwert, and Stambaugh (1987); however it is not clear whether this is better modeled by the permanent or the transitory component of volatility. Similarly, the leverage effect first addressed by Black (1976) and Christie (1982) and modeled by Nelson (1990a) may have either transitory or permanent effects.

The relationship between aggregate stock return volatility and individual stock return volatility can also be investigated within this framework. As pointed out by Black (1976), much of the movement and hence volatility of an individual stock is associated with movements in the market. Following the spirit of Schwert and Seguin (1990), and Ng, Engle and Rothschild (1992), we study the volatility components of individual stocks in conjunction with those of the market index in a CAPM or one-factor framework of the APT of Ross (1976, 1977). The one-factor setting implies that the time-varying individual stock return volatility is due either to the market factor, or to the idiosyncratic shocks, or both. Each is given a component structure to allow a flexible measurement of the persistence of stock volatilities.

The paper is arranged as follows: Section 2 introduces the component model for the conditional variance and Section 3 discusses the statistical properties of the component model. Section 4 reports estimates of the component model and tests of volatility persistence for US and Japanese index data and for large US equities. Section 5 examines the 1987 crash period and the implications of this model. Section 6 examines the long-run and the short-run structure of the "leverage effect" in the stock market. Section 7 applies the component model to a study of the relationship between risk premia and stock return volatility. Section 8 examines the volatility process of the idiosyncratic component of individual equity returns and Section 9 concludes.

2 A Volatility Component Model of Asset Returns

In financial econometrics, the conditional variance of asset returns, or the equivalent conditional standard deviation, is often used as a forward looking volatility measure for the market under consideration. The volatility component model proposed is defined as a member of the ARCH class of models originated by Engle (1982). Denote the information set containing the historical information of the time series of interest available at time $(t-1)$ as F_{t-1}, and the mathematical expectation conditional on F_{t-1} as $E[\cdot|F_{t-1}]$, or $E_{t-1}[\cdot]$. The conditional mean of an asset return series $\{r_t\}$ at time t is defined by:

$$m_t \equiv E_{t-1}[r_t] \tag{2.1}$$

and the conditional variance of $\{r_t\}$ by:

$$h_t \equiv E_{t-1}[(r_t - m_t)^2] = E_{t-1}[\varepsilon_t^2] \tag{2.2}$$

where $\varepsilon_t = (r_t - m_t)$ is the residual or unexpected return.

The popular generalized ARCH model (GARCH) developed by Bollerslev (1986), in a slightly transformed form, specifies the dynamic structure of the conditional variance as:

$$h_t = \sigma^2 + \alpha(\varepsilon_{t-1}^2 - \sigma^2) + \beta(h_{t-1} - \sigma^2) \tag{2.3}$$

where σ^2 is the unconditional variance, and $(\varepsilon_{t-1}^2 - \sigma^2)$ serves as the shock to asset return volatility. When $(\alpha + \beta) < 1$, called the mean-reverting rate or the persistent rate, the conditional variance will mean-revert to the unconditional variance at a geometric rate of $(\alpha + \beta)$. The smaller the mean-reverting rate, the less persistent the sensitivity of the volatility expectation to market shocks in the past.

With vast empirical findings in the ARCH literature about time-varying and mean-reverting volatility of equity, foreign exchange and interest rate markets, we may well question whether the long-run volatility represented by σ^2 in GARCH(1, 1), is truly constant over time.

In a more flexible specification, we replace σ^2 with the long-run volatility q_t, which is given a time series representation and allowed to evolve slowly in an autoregressive manner:

$$(h_t - q_t) = \alpha(\varepsilon_{t-1}^2 - q_{t-1}) + \beta(h_{t-1} - q_{t-1}), \tag{2.4}$$
$$q_t = \omega + \rho q_{t-1} + \varphi(\varepsilon_{t-1}^2 - h_{t-1}). \tag{2.5}$$

Equations (2.4) and (2.5) thus define the volatility component model of asset returns: the long-run (trend) volatility component q is stochastic, and the difference between the conditional variance and its trend, $(h_t - q_t)$, is called the short-run (transitory) volatility component. Rewriting these processes in an alternative form emphasizes the symmetry in the representation:

$$h_t = q_t + s_t,$$
$$s_t = (\alpha + \beta)s_{t-1} + \alpha(\varepsilon_{t-1}^2 - h_{t-1}),$$
$$q_t = \omega + \rho q_{t-1} + \phi(\varepsilon_{t-1}^2 - h_{t-1}),$$

where s is the transitory component. Notice that the volatility innovation, $(\varepsilon_{t-1}^2 - h_{t-1})$, drives both the permanent and the transitory volatility components.

The interpretation of the volatility component dynamics is straightforward. First, the short-run volatility component mean-reverts to zero at a geometric rate of $(\alpha + \beta)$ if $0 < (\alpha + \beta) < 1$. Secondly, the long-run volatility component itself evolves over time following an AR process, which, if $0 < \rho < 1$, will converge to a constant level defined by $\omega/(1 - \rho)$. Thirdly, we assume that the long-run component has a much slower mean-reverting rate than the short-run component, or in other words, the long-run component is more persistent than the short-run one, i.e., $0 < (\alpha + \beta) < \rho < 1$. This simply identifies the model since otherwise the two components would be interchangeable.

Forecasts from this model display many of its features. Define the multi-step conditional expectation of the variance and the permanent component as:

$$h_{t+k/t-1} \equiv E_{t-1}[\varepsilon_{t+k}^2], \quad q_{t+k/t-1} \equiv E_{t-1}[q_{t+k}]. \tag{2.6}$$

The forecast of the transitory volatility component is

$$(h_{t+k/t-1} - q_{t+k/t-1}) = (\alpha + \beta)^k(h_t - q_t), \tag{2.7}$$

by (2.4). The sensitivity of the transitory component forecast to volatility shocks thus becomes:

$$\partial(h_{t+k/t-1} - q_{t+k/t-1})/\partial\varepsilon_{t-1}^2 = (\alpha + \beta)^k \partial(h_t - q_t)/\partial\varepsilon_{t-1}^2 = (\alpha + \beta)^k\alpha. \tag{2.8}$$

If $0 < (\alpha + \beta) \ll 1$, the impact of volatility shocks on the short-run volatility component is short-lived.

On the other hand, the forecast of the volatility trend is:

$$q_{t+k/t-1} = \omega + \rho q_{t+k-1/t-1} + \varphi E_{t-1}[\varepsilon_{t+k-1}^2 - h_{t+k-1}]$$
$$= \omega + \rho q_{t+k-1/t-1}, \tag{2.9}$$

by (2.5) and (2.6). If $0 < \rho < 1$, the forecast in (2.9) becomes:

$$q_{t+k/t-1} = \omega/(1 - \rho) + \rho^k(q_t - \omega/(1 - \rho)), \tag{2.10}$$

which converges to a constant level of $\omega/(1 - \rho)$. The sensitivity of the long-run component forecast to volatility shocks thus becomes:

$$\partial q_{t+k/t-1} / \partial \varepsilon_{t-1}^2 = \rho^k \partial q_t / \partial \varepsilon_{t-1}^2 = \rho^k \varphi. \tag{2.11}$$

If $0 < (\alpha + \beta) < \rho \leq 1$, the impact of volatility shocks on the long-run volatility component will diminish as well but will be more persistent than that of the short-run component.

We would also expect that the immediate impact of volatility shocks on the long-run component would be smaller than that on the short-run component, or that $\alpha \geq \varphi$ by (2.8) and (2.11).

In summary we have heuristically that h_{t+k} tends to q_{t+k} as $k \to \infty$ and that $q_{t+k} \to \omega/(1-\rho)$ as $k \to \infty$ if $0 < (\alpha + \beta) < \rho \leq 1$. In this case, the contribution of the volatility component model to the literature is its decomposition of asset return volatility into long-run and short-run components, which are characterized by their different sensitivities to volatility shocks and their different mean-reversion rates.

3 Further Statistical Properties of the Component Model

3.1 The Stationarity Conditions of the Component Model

The stationarity properties of the volatility component model are closely related to the mean-reversion features we discussed in Section 2. We derive conditions for stationarity by examining the dynamic structure of the conditional variance implied by the component model. The reduced form of the conditional variance dynamics defined in (2.4) and (2.5) can be shown to be:

$$h_t = (1 - \alpha - \beta)\omega + (\alpha + \varphi)\varepsilon_{t-1}^2 + [-\varphi(\alpha+\beta) - \alpha\rho]\varepsilon_{t-2}^2$$
$$+ (\rho + \beta - \varphi)h_{t-1} + [\varphi(\alpha+\beta) - \beta\rho]h_{t-2}. \tag{3.1}$$

Obviously, the reduced form (3.1) follows a GARCH(2, 2) process. This is not surprising, but the model is not fully equivalent as not all GARCH(2, 2) processes have the component structure. Although there are five parameters in each representation, by constraining the parameters to be positive and real in the component model parameterization, there cannot be complex roots and positive variances are insured. Thus the component model is a constrained version of the GARCH(2, 2) with constraints given by a set of inequalities.

By rewriting (3.1) as an ARMA(2, 2) the stationarity conditions are immediately apparent.

$$\varepsilon_t^2 = \omega(1 - \alpha - \beta) + (\alpha + \beta + \rho)\varepsilon_{t-1}^2 - (\rho\alpha + \rho\beta)\varepsilon_{t-2}^2$$
$$+ \eta_t - (\rho + \beta - \phi)\eta_{t-1} - [\phi(\alpha+\beta) - \beta\rho]\eta_{t-2} \tag{3.2}$$

where $\eta_t = \varepsilon_t^2 - h_t$ is a Martingale difference sequence by construction. If and only if the autoregressive roots lie in the unit circle, $\{\varepsilon_t\}$ will be covariance stationary. Hence the condition that $\rho < 1$ and $(\alpha + \beta) < 1$ is sufficient.

The case with $\rho = 1$, the unit-root case, deserves special attention. Nelson (1990a) proved that, for the IGARCH(1, 1) process, the mean series $\{r_t\}$ is not a covariance stationary process, however, it may still be a strictly stationary and ergodic process. Bougerol and Picard (1992) discussed conditions for $\{r_t\}$ to be strictly stationary and ergodic for general cases of the GARCH model, but their results are limited to cases with only positive coefficients. As can be seen from (3.1), the component model implies some negative coefficients. So there is no known result in the literature which can be applied to the component model directly, but it seems that similar statistical features should hold. Sin and White (1996) show that GARCH(2, 2) is Near Epoch Dependent (NED) and therefore a mixingale. If it is a mixingale, then it satisfies a SLLN. If it satisfies a SLLN and is stationary with finite mean, then it must be ergodic.

There is a vast literature on unit-root tests for the mean process, which yields a set of non-standard testing inferences. The problem of testing for unit-roots in the conditional variance was solved for the first order case by Lumsdaine (1996), Lee and Hansen (1994) and Hong (1988) who showed that classical tests have standard asymptotic properties. So far, there is no known unit-root testing procedure for high-order conditional variance processes like the component model, although one might again conjecture that the results would be the same.

If there is a unit root in the long-run component, then forecasts of future variances grow with horizon as:

$$q_{t+k} = q_t + \omega k. \tag{3.3}$$

Commonly, the drift is small and can be ignored unless distant horizons are considered, but the use of a model with infinite variance may prove awkward if the objective is forecasting the second moment rather than simply forecasting the full conditional distribution.

3.2 Non-Negativity of the Conditional Variance in the Component Model

One concern about modeling volatility movements is that the volatility measure should remain non-negative over time. With respect to our volatility component model, this requirement for a non-negative conditional variance and its trend requires some constraints upon the parameters in (2.4) and (2.5). The following sufficient conditions are developed in the Appendix:

$$1 > \rho > (\alpha + \beta) > 0, \beta > \varphi > 0, \alpha > 0, \beta > 0, \omega > 0, \varphi > 0, \omega > 0,$$

which are compatible with the stationarity conditions discussed above.

Note that all these constraints are only sufficient conditions, not necessary ones, and that non-negativity is not required for the transitory volatility component, which can be positive or negative over time to reflect the self-correction feature of the mean-reverting volatility process towards its trend component.

4 Empirical Results of the Volatility Component Model for Stock Returns

4.1 Data Selections

We use three daily stock indices: the S&P 500 index for the period 1941:1–1991:1, the CRSP value-weighted index for the period 1973:6–1991:12, and the NIKKEI index for the period 1971:1–1991:9 to estimate the component model. To focus on the effect of the October 1987 Crash on the volatility estimates, we also use the S&P 500 index for the period 1971:1–1987:9 which excludes the crash period.

We also use fourteen daily individual stock series for the period 1973:6–1991:12 to estimate the component model. The companies include Amoco, Beth Steel, Boeing, Chevron, Dow, DuPont, Ford, General Electric (GE), Hewlett Packard (HP), IBM, Johnson & Johnson (JJ), McDonnell Douglas (MD), Merck, Upjohn. These are all large capitalization Blue Chip companies in the Dow Jones Industrials and are chosen because they are highly liquid and show little problem with non-synchronous closing prices.

4.2 Specifications of the Stock Return Process

All the daily returns of the stock indices and the individual stocks are calculated by taking the log difference of stock prices on two consecutive trading days. The treatments of the expected returns across stock indices and individual stocks, however, are quite different.

4.2.1 Expected Returns of Stock Indices

The treatments of the expected return on the S&P and the NIKKEI are simple. The expected return is assumed constant over time:

$$r_{mt} = E_{t-1}[r_{mt}] + \varepsilon_{mt} = c + \varepsilon_{mt}. \tag{4.1}$$

The reason for this simplicity is that these indices do not incorporate stock dividends and, with respect to expected returns, there is little gain in more careful specification. Also the return serial correlation is ignored assuming that it is caused by the non-synchronous trading of securities as argued by Fisher (1966) and others. In fact, the serial correlation is small and its impact on the variance equation is trivial.

For the CRSP value-weighted index which incorporates stock dividends, we adopt the ARCH-M model of Engle, Lilien and Robins (1987) to study the expected market-index excess returns. The excess return, or the *risk premium*, on the index is calculated by deducting from the daily index return, the three-month USD London Inter-Bank Offering Rate (LIBOR), which is taken as a close proxy of the risk-free rate. The excess return, is then assumed to be related to the expected return volatility represented by the conditional variance, h_{mt}, defined in (2.4) and (2.5):

$$r_{mt} = E_{t-1}[r_t] + \varepsilon_{mt} = \delta_m h_{mt} + \varepsilon_{mt}. \tag{4.2}$$

So $(\delta_m \cdot h_{mt})$ represents the expected risk premium which is, by Merton (1980), proportional to the expected stock market variance. Using the GARCH-M to describe the market risk premium has an interpretation in the CCAPM framework as well as in the CAPM as discussed in Rothschild (1986) and Engle, Ng and Rothschild (1990).

4.2.2 A One-Factor Model for Individual Stock Returns

When estimating the component model for individual stocks, the CAPM or the one-factor version of the APT model of Ross (1976, 1977) is explored. The one-factor model assumes that individual stock excess return is governed linearly by a single factor affecting the whole market:

$$r_{it} = \beta_{im} f_{mt} + \zeta_{it}, \tag{4.3}$$

where r_{it} is the excess return on the ith individual stock under consideration, ζ_{it} is the so-called "idiosyncratic" shock specific to the stock and uncorrelated with the market factor.

In our empirical studies of this one-factor model, the CRSP value-weighted index is used as the market factor proxy (and the three-month USD London Inter-Bank Offering Rate (LIBOR) as the risk-free rate proxy). So the conditional expectation of the one-factor stock return model in (4.3) can be written as:

$$
\begin{aligned}
r_{it} &= \beta_{im} E_{t-1}[r_{mt}] + (\beta_{im} \varepsilon_{mt} + \zeta_{it}) \\
&= \beta_{im} \lambda_{mt} + \varepsilon_{it},
\end{aligned}
\tag{4.4}
$$

from (4.2) where $\varepsilon_{it} = (\beta_{im} \cdot \varepsilon_{mt} + \zeta_{it})$ is the shock to the one-factor-based expectation of the excess return of individual stocks, and $\lambda_{mt} = \delta_m \cdot h_{mt}$ is the expected excess return of the market factor aforementioned.

4.3 Estimation Results of the Volatility Component Model

We assume conditional normality for the standard residual, $\varepsilon_t / h_t^{1/2}$, and estimate the component model using the Quasi-Maximum Likelihood Estimation (QMLE) procedure proposed by Engle (1982) and Bollerslev (1986). In the ARCH literature, many researchers have pointed out that there is still excess kurtosis after the residual is corrected by the ARCH specification. With the true distribution for the residual being unknown, the estimation based on QMLE at least gives consistent results asymptotically.

First, examine the autocorrelations of squared returns. Under the *i.i.d.* assumption for $\{\varepsilon_t\}$, the Ljung and Box (1978) tests for $\{\varepsilon_t^2\}$ and $\{\varepsilon_t^2/h_t\}$ each follow the χ^2 distribution. Autocorrelation in the squared residuals can be caused by ARCH, and lack of autocorrelation in the squared standardized residuals, indicates the success of ARCH modeling. As in most of the ARCH literature, there are tremendous improvements in the Ljung–Box test statistics of $\{\varepsilon_t^2/h_t\}$ over $\{\varepsilon_t^2\}$, indicating the success of the component model in capturing the typical serial correlation pattern in $\{\varepsilon_t^2\}$. To take the S&P index of 1941:1–1991:9 as an example, the Ljung–Box statistic for fifteenth order serial correlation of $\{\varepsilon_t^2/h_t\}$ is 16.93, as compared to that of 875.67 from $\{\varepsilon_t^2\}$. The 5 percent critical value of $\chi^2(15)$ is 25 indicating the success of the ARCH model.

We use the Likelihood Ratio test to show the performance of the component model over the simple GARCH(1, 1) model. The test is conservative in the sense that a likelihood ratio statistic of a GARCH(p, q) against a component model GARCH($(p + k)$, $(q + k)$) like (3.1) will have parameters unidentified under the null and a distribution with fewer than $2k$ degrees of freedom (for a discussion see Godfrey, 1978). The test shows, taking the stock indices as examples, the dominance of the component model with the LR statistics being as shown in Table 1. These are much bigger than the 5 percent critical value of a χ^2 distribution with two degrees of freedom, 5.99.

Table 1

Data set	LR statistic for component model
S&P 1941.1–1991.9	89.6
S&P 1941.1–1987.9	60.8
NIKKEI 1971.1–1991.9	57.2

Now let us concentrate on the parameter estimates of the component model. The results are reported in Table 2. First, we examine the shock impacts on the short-run and the long-run component represented by αs and φs, respectively. These estimates are significant for almost all the stock data, and αs are much larger than φs for the three indices and almost all of the individual stocks (except Chevron).

The mean-reverting parameters for the trend, ρs, are all above 0.99 for all the stock data except JJ and Merck, which are also over 0.98. For the indices, the half-lives of the permanent response to a shock are 532 and 384 days for the S&P full and pre-crash samples, 86 days for the CRSP, and 144 days for the NIKKEI. The mean-reverting parameters of the transitory component, $(\alpha + \beta)$s, are necessarily smaller than their corresponding ρs. For individual stocks, the highest $(\alpha + \beta)$ is 0.9738 for Chevron, the lowest, 0.2915 for Amoco, and a common range from 0.5 to 0.7 applies to most of the rest. For the indices,

Table 2. The volatility component model of daily returns on stock indices and individual stocks

$$r_t = c + \varepsilon_t \text{ (for S\&P, NIKKEI)} \tag{4.1}$$
$$r_t = \delta_m h_t + \varepsilon_t \text{ (for CRSP)} \tag{4.2}$$
$$r_t = \beta_m \lambda_{mt} + \varepsilon_t \text{ (for individual stocks)} \tag{4.4}$$
$$(h_t - q_t) = \alpha(\varepsilon_{t-1}^2 - q_{t-1}) + \beta(h_{t-1} - q_{t-1}) \tag{2.4}$$
$$q_t = \omega + \rho q_{t-1} + \varphi(\varepsilon_{t-1}^2 - h_{t-1}) \tag{2.5}$$

Dataset	β_m	α	β	φ	ρ
S&P 500	—	0.0894	0.7991	0.0318	0.9982
1941.1–1991.9		(0.0192)[a]	(0.0376)	(0.0058)	(0.0012)
S&P 500	—	0.0762	0.8455	0.0259	0.9987
1941.1–1987.9		(0.0105)	(0.0233)	(0.0044)	(0.0009)
NIKKEI	—	0.1815	0.5838	0.1239	0.9952
1971.1–1991.9		(0.0524)	(0.0962)	(0.0407)	(0.0099)
CRSP V-W	$\delta_m = 3.9859$	0.0692	0.8199	0.0380	0.9920
1973.6–1991.12	(2.3868)	(0.0380)	(0.0898)	(0.0146)	(0.0039)
Amoco	1.1459	0.1080	0.1835	0.0425	0.9954
	(0.6262)	(0.0730)	(0.2659)	(0.0137)	(0.0030)
Beth Steel	0.7441	0.1178	0.7000	0.0208	0.9938
	(0.7593)	(0.0282)	(0.0650)	(0.0065)	(0.0042)
Boeing	1.0148	0.0951	0.3405	0.0184	0.9951
	(0.5900)	(0.0266)	(0.1661)	(0.0053)	(0.0034)
Chevron	0.8012	0.0264	0.9474	0.0239	0.9973
	(0.6567)	(0.0121)	(0.0234)	(0.0117)	(0.0023)
Dow	1.2606	0.0644	0.6119	0.0306	0.9904
	(0.6431)	(0.0335)	(0.2258)	(0.0077)	(0.0035)
DuPont	0.4506	0.0791	0.5413	0.0229	0.9954
	(0.5429)	(0.0291)	(0.1323)	(0.0052)	(0.0027)
Ford	0.6459	0.1092	0.4070	0.0289	0.9987
	(0.5980)	(0.0267)	(0.1634)	(0.0051)	(0.0018)
GE	1.1183	0.0214	0.8785	0.0375	0.9931
	(0.6044)	(0.0181)	(0.1205)	(0.0120)	(0.0034)
HP	1.1593	0.1006	0.7545	0.0164	0.9980
	(0.7201)	(0.0257)	(0.0537)	(0.0058)	(0.0015)
IBM	0.6774	0.0686	0.6883	0.0320	0.9936
	(0.5890)	(0.0470)	(0.1493)	(0.0132)	(0.0077)
JJ	1.1361	0.1002	0.2752	0.0441	0.9876
	(0.5515)	(0.0344)	(0.1628)	(0.0091)	(0.0040)
MD	0.3642	0.1810	0.6412	0.0167	0.9996
	(0.5130)	(0.0303)	(0.0511)	(0.0056)	(0.0010)
Merck	1.0232	0.0677	0.6006	0.0373	0.9835
	(0.5385)	(0.0223)	(0.1650)	(0.0106)	(0.0060)
Upjohn	1.8454	0.0943	0.7726	0.0138	0.9954
	(0.8426)	(0.0275)	(0.0541)	(0.0051)	(0.0027)

[a] In parentheses are the robust standard errors based on Bollerslev and Wooldridge (1991).

the transitory half-lives are 6 or 8 days for the S&P, 6 days for CRSP and 3 days for the NIKKEI.

The results indicate a common pattern in which the persistence of transitory shocks is much less than permanent shocks, and the impact of transitory shocks is much greater than permanent shocks.

5 The Effect of the October 1987 Crash on Stock Market Volatility Changes

The October 1987 Crash was the largest stock market decline since the Great Depression. It had a unique impact on market volatility that we would like to investigate using the volatility component model.

To isolate the crash effect, we use two sample periods of the S&P 500 index: the period of 1941:1–1991:9 and the period of 1941:1–1987:9 since the latter excludes the October 1987 Crash period. Compared with the long period (almost fifty-one years), the crash period (actually only a couple of weeks of big fluctuations) is almost trivial. The estimation results should not differ significantly across the two sample periods if the crash effect is not dramatic.

First, we can see from Table 1 that the shock effects on both of the components turn out to be significantly larger by including the crash period in the sample set: (α, φ) are $(0.0762, 0.0259)$ for the period of 1971:1–1987:9 and $(0.0894, 0.0318)$ for the period of 1941:1–1991:9. This indicates the severity of the market fall of about 20 percent on one day. Secondly, the mean-reverting features of the volatility components are also significantly affected. By including the crash period, $(\alpha + \beta)$ changes from 0.9217 to 0.8885, although ρ does not change much, declining from 0.9987 to 0.9982. This suggests that the crash is more transient than other shocks. These ideas motivate the robust volatility model in Sakata and White (1998).

These results are consistent with market movements during the October 1987 Crash period. The volatility increase in the US stock market decayed very quickly after the crash reaching a normal level of fluctuation within just a few weeks. The findings also confirm those in Schwert (1990) and Engle and Mustafa (1992) who noted that implied volatilities also fell rapidly after the crash.

6 The Component Model with Asymmetric Structure to Shocks

Stock market volatility responds to stock price movement asymmetrically: "bad" news (negative shocks) tends to increase investors' expectation about future market volatility more than "good" news (positive shocks). This asymmetric volatility pattern, often called the "leverage effect," was first studied

Table 3. Asymmetric structure of stock return volatility to past market shocks of the S&P 500 index 1941.1–1991.9[a]

$corr1(\varepsilon_t, \varepsilon_{t+k}^2)$ $corr2(\varepsilon_t, \varepsilon_{t+k}^2/h_{t+k})$						
k	1	2	3	4	5	LB(15)
$Corr1$	−0.077	−0.079	−0.041	−0.010	−0.058	287.72
	(−1.46)[b]	(−2.02)	(−1.26)	(−0.52)	(−1.81)	
$Corr2$	−0.059	−0.043	−0.022	−0.037	−0.028	122.53
	(−4.47)	(−4.77)	(−2.04)	(−3.64)	(−3.59)	

[a] The conditional variance is defined in the component model (2.5) and (2.6).
[b] In parentheses are the standard t-statistics.

by Black (1976) and Christie (1982) who attributed it to the failure of firms to adjust their debt–equity ratio. A drop in the stock price will decrease the firm's market value and increase the debt–equity ratio, which thus increases the risk to stock investors as residual claimants. Therefore, negative shocks to the price will increase future volatility more than positive shocks.

We first examine this asymmetric pattern of stock return volatility by the correlation between the squared residual and the past residual, *correlation* $(\varepsilon_t, \varepsilon_{t+k}^2)$ (Corr1), for S&P 500 1941:1–1991:9. When $k > 0$, the correlation exhibits the "leverage effect" if it is negative. In this case, the direction of returns helps predict future volatilities. Table 3 presents the correlation for the raw data series used and also for the series, *correlation* $(\varepsilon_t, \varepsilon_{t+k}^2/h_{t+k})$ (Corr2), which is standardized by the conditional variance estimated by the component model as in Table 1. Correlation 1 shows the expected asymmetric pattern of stock return volatility judging from the overwhelmingly negative correlation values. Correlation 2 is to check whether the component model has corrected the asymmetry through the decomposition. The answer is no, since these show the same pattern as the raw data. The Ljung–Box tests significantly reject the null hypothesis of no correlation. So we need to further modify the model.

We use the treatment of Glosten, Jagannathan and Runkle (1993) to allow shocks to affect the volatility components asymmetrically. A similar treatment is originally seen in the EGARCH model of Nelson (1990b). Define a dummy variable D_t indicating the direction of the shock: $D_t = 1$ if $\varepsilon_t < 0$ and $D_t = 0$ if $\varepsilon_t > 0$. The component model with asymmetric structure can be specified as:

$$h_t = q_t + \alpha(\varepsilon_{t-1}^2 - q_{t-1}) + \delta_2(D_{t-1}\varepsilon_{t-1}^2 - 0.5q_{t-1}) + \beta(h_{t-1} - q_{t-1}), \tag{6.1}$$
$$q_t = \omega + \rho q_{t-1} + \varphi(\varepsilon_{t-1}^2 - h_{t-1}) + \delta_1(D_{t-1}\varepsilon_{t-1}^2 - 0.5h_{t-1}). \tag{6.2}$$

The factor, 0.5, reflecting the average effect of dummy variables, is based on the symmetric assumption about the return distribution. The shock effects of the asymmetric component model (6.1) and (6.2) with respect to "bad" news and "good" news thus become:

$$\partial q_t / \partial \varepsilon_{t-1}^2 = \varphi \qquad \text{if } \varepsilon_{t-1} > 0 \qquad (6.3)$$
$$\partial q_t / \partial \varepsilon_{t-1}^2 = \varphi + \delta_1 \qquad \text{if } \varepsilon_{t-1} < 0 \qquad (6.4)$$

for the trend component, and

$$\partial (h_t - q_t) / \partial \varepsilon_{t-1}^2 = \alpha \qquad \text{if } \varepsilon_{t-1} > 0 \qquad (6.5)$$
$$\partial (h_t - q_t) / \partial \varepsilon_{t-1}^2 = \alpha + \delta_2 \quad \text{if } \varepsilon_{t-1} < 0 \qquad (6.6)$$

for the transitory component. Thus δ_1 and δ_2 represent the long-run and the short-run "leverage effects" in the asymmetric component model, respectively.

Table 4 contains estimates of (6.1) and (6.2) for the S&P 500 index for the period of 1941:1–1991:9. The estimation shows a tremendous improvement in the likelihood value of the asymmetric component model over the original symmetric component model. Negative shocks predict higher volatility than positive shocks, but the effect is mainly temporary. The "leverage" term is significant in the transitory component for all the data sets, but not for the trend component. Furthermore, negative shocks dominate the effects on the transitory component and the effects of positive shocks almost vanish. The estimation results using the short sample set of the S&P 500 index and the NIKKEI index are very similar to the results listed here. Therefore, the "leverage effect" addressed by Black (1976) and Christie (1982) seems to be only a temporary behavior in the stock market. In a recent work by Gallant, Rossi and Tauchen (1993) using a non-parametric approach, the "leverage effect" is also found to be heavily damped over time.

To verify the correction by the asymmetric component model, Table 5 estimates the correlation for the series standardized by the conditional variance defined in (6.1) and (6.2). The Ljung–Box test now fails to reject the null hypothesis of no correlation. So the component model is successful in correcting

Table 4. The component model with asymmetric structure for the S&P 500 index 1941.1–1991.9[a]

$$h_t = q_t + \alpha(\varepsilon_{t-1}^2 - q_{t-1}) + \delta_2(D_{t-1}\varepsilon_{t-1}^2 - 0.5q_{t-1}) + \beta(h_{t-1} - q_{t-1}) \qquad (6.1)$$
$$q_t = \omega + \rho q_{t-1} + \varphi(\varepsilon_{t-1}^2 - h_{t-1}) + \delta_1(D_{t-1}\varepsilon_{t-1}^2 - 0.5h_{t-1}) \qquad (6.2)$$

δ_1	ϕ	δ_2	α	β
0.0006	0.0299	0.1593	−0.0054	0.8076
(0.0086)[b]	(0.0050)	(0.0220)	(0.0138)	(0.0256)

[a] The initial estimations show that ρs are very close to unit as in Table 1; for parsimonious parameterization, $\rho = 1$ is assumed for the estimation of (6.1) and (6.2).

[b] In the parenthesis are the robust standard errors based on Bollerslev and Wooldridge (1991).

Table 5. Correction for the asymmetry volatility component model (6.1) and (6.2) for the S&P 500 index[a]

$corr2(\varepsilon_t,\ \varepsilon_{t+k}^2/h_{t+k})$						
k	1	2	3	4	5	LB(15)
$Corr2$	−0.011	−0.004	−0.015	−0.009	−0.004	15.37
	(-0.98)[b]	(-0.48)	(-1.42)	(-0.99)	(-0.56)	

[a] The conditional variance is defined in the component model (6.1) and (6.2).
[b] In parentheses are the standard t-statistics.

the asymmetry of stock return volatility after introducing the "leverage" terms into the component model.

If the temporary asymmetry of stock return volatility to market shocks can be addressed by the "leverage effect," then the evidence of the long-run symmetry found here can be supported based on the same argument. The debt–equity ratio may be hard to adjust in the short run, but there is no reason that firms will not be able to adjust their capital structure over time towards some long-run "target value." Thus we would anticipate no asymmetric response of the volatility expectation to shocks in the long run. The empirical results in this section, along with the finding in Gallant, Rossi and Tauchen (1993), strongly support this hypothesis.

7 The Relationship between Expected Stock Returns and Volatility Components

Table 2 also shows the estimation result for the CRSP data of the ARCH-M model of Engle, Lilien and Robins (1987), which links the expected excess return, or the risk premium, to the volatility measured by the conditional variance defined in the component model. The ARCH-M parameter, δ_m, is statistically significant and has a value of 3.9859. The result is consistent with other empirical studies in the literature that stock returns generally support the positive correlation between the expected risk premium and the ex ante stock return volatility (see, e.g., French, Schwert and Stambaugh, 1987; Chou, 1988).

It is natural to ask how the risk premium is related to the long-run and the short-run volatility component. In response to such a question, we extend the GARCH-M specification to incorporate the volatility components:

$$r_{mt} = \delta_{mP}q_{mt} + \delta_{mT}(h_{mt} - q_{mt}) + \varepsilon_{mt}. \tag{7.1}$$

Thus δ_{mP} and δ_{mT} represent responses of the risk premium to the long-run volatility and the short-run component, respectively.

Table 6. The relationship between the risk premium and volatility components of the CRSP V-W index

$r_{mt} = \delta_{mP} \cdot q_{mt} + \delta_{mT} \cdot (h_{mt} - q_{mt}) + \varepsilon_{mt}$					(7.1)
$(h_t - q_t) = \alpha(\varepsilon_{t-1}^2 - q_{t-1}) + \beta(h_{t-1} - q_{t-1})$					(2.4)
$q_t = \omega + \rho q_{t-1} + \varphi(\varepsilon_{t-1}^2 - h_{t-1})$					(2.5)

δ_{mP}	δ_{mT}	α	β	φ	ρ
7.40	3.14	0.0704	0.8180	0.0386	0.9956
$(1.46)^a$	(6.21)	(0.0372)	(0.0880)	(0.0138)	(0.0037)

[a] In the parenthesis are the robust standard errors based on Bollerslev and Wooldridge (1991).

Table 6 contains the estimation results of the model (7.1) plus the component model (2.4) and (2.5) for the CRSP value-weighted index data used. While the volatility parameter estimates are similar to those in Table 2, the results of δ_{mP} and δ_{mT} are very interesting: δ_{mP} is highly significant but δ_{mT} is not. What is implied is that stock risk premia only respond to the long-run movement of market volatility. A recent independent study by den Hertog (1995) found the same result for long-term US and French government bonds based on a conditional variance decomposition method using the Kalman filter.

The explanation for the result may be straightforward. The conditional variance of stock returns, as a measure of the risk involved with stock investment, changes over time. However, the trend component of volatility may be viewed by investors as reflecting the risk level over a long-run horizon since the transitory component is largely driven by instant market shocks and, more importantly, dies out quite quickly as seen in Tables 1 and 3. Therefore, only the long-run movement of volatility is priced. The findings in this section may also be related to the "excessive volatility" in financial markets addressed by Shiller (1981) and others.

8 Idiosyncratic Volatility Components of Individual Stock Returns

The one-factor setting for individual stocks as in (4.4) implies that the shock to the excess return expectation of individual stocks is actually comprised of two parts, the shock due to market factor changes and the shock due to idiosyncratic noise. It also implies a similar relationship for the volatility structure:

$$E_{t-1}[\varepsilon_{it}^2] = E_{t-1}[(\beta_{im}\varepsilon_{mt} + \zeta_{it})^2] = \beta_{im}^2 E_{t-1}[\varepsilon_{mt}^2] + E_{t-1}[\zeta_{it}^2], \tag{8.1}$$

since the market shock and the idiosyncratic shock are not correlated. Therefore the success of the component model in describing individual stock volatility components as shown in Table 2 is not surprising given the evidence that the market factor volatility follows the component model. However, we wonder whether the component structure of individual stock volatility is inherited from the market factor alone, or from the idiosyncratic noise as well.

To estimate the idiosyncratic volatility of individual stocks, we need to study the idiosyncratic noise directly. Assume that the market factor information is known and exogenous to individual stocks, so that the idiosyncratic noise can be estimated from the one-factor model directly:

$$r_{it} = \beta_{im} r_{mt} + \zeta_{it}. \tag{8.2}$$

In our empirical study, the CRSP value-weighted index is again used as the market factor proxy. Also, the conditional variance of the idiosyncratic noise, ζ_{it}, is assumed to follow the component model (2.4) and (2.5). This model assumes that the only asymmetric effect is in the market factor. Probably, this is too restrictive an assumption. Table 7 contains the estimation results for the individual stock data used.

It is interesting to see that even the idiosyncratic volatilities of the individual stocks are well fitted by the component model. The statistical features of the idiosyncratic volatilities are very similar to the volatilities of the market indices and of the individual stocks shown in Table 1. The ρ estimates are well above 0.99 for all the individual stocks except Merck; $(\alpha + \beta)$s are much smaller than ρs, with the highest, 0.8514, for Upjohn and the lowest, 0.1965, for GE; and, αs are much higher than φs for all the stocks. These results imply that the long-run component of the idiosyncratic volatility of individual stocks is also highly persistent like that of the market factor, both contributing to the high persistence of individual stock return volatility. Although initially surprising, the claim is easy to motivate. News of the illness of a CEO or a pending lawsuit could be idiosyncratic and would likely affect volatility of the stock for an indefinite period. In fact, most types of firm-specific volatility shocks might reasonably be thought to be persistent.

We can also observe that the estimates of β_{im} are around one as suggested by the CAPM, but with much smaller standard errors than in Table 2. This is because the expected stock return is always hard to measure, especially for high frequency data.

Our study of the idiosyncratic volatility of individual stocks has some typical implications in assessing the pricing biases of the well-known Black–Scholes (BS) model for individual stock options. A recent study in this area by Amin and Ng (1993) compared the pricing difference between the BS model and their consumption-based equilibrium option pricing model. They found that the less persistent is the idiosyncratic volatility, the smaller the pricing bias of the BS model for individual stock options, since the stationary mean-reverting idiosyncratic component does not play an important role in the long-run movement of stock volatility. They also found that the pricing bias is smaller when the market systematic volatility component is larger. In other words, for those high-risk individual stocks, the pricing bias of the BS model

Table 7. Estimating idiosyncratic volatility components of individual stocks (1973.6–1991.12)

$$r_{it} = \hat{\beta}_m r_{mt} + \zeta_t \tag{8.2}$$
$$(h_t - q_t) = \alpha(\zeta_{t-1}^2 - q_{t-1}) + \beta(h_{t-1} - q_{t-1}) \tag{2.4}$$
$$q_t = \omega + \rho q_{t-1} + \varphi(\zeta_{t-1}^2 - h_{t-1}) \tag{2.5}$$

	β_{im}	α	β	φ	ρ
Amoco	0.9700	0.1328	0.3691	0.0301	0.9966
	(36.40)[a]	(5.96)	(3.29)	(4.80)	[1.78]
Beth Steel	1.2238	0.0981	0.6972	0.0220	0.9965
	(36.06)	(4.60)	(6.59)	(3.04)	[1.40]
Boeing	1.1914	0.1234	0.2550	0.0175	0.9951
	(21.37)	(3.47)	(1.80)	(4.03)	[2.10]
Chevron	1.0806	0.0803	0.6892	0.0204	0.9971
	(41.63)	(4.41)	(8.13)	(3.98)	[1.53]
Dow	1.3021	0.0622	0.4194	0.0296	0.9918
	(50.73)	(2.86)	(1.83)	(3.46)	[2.27]
DuPont	1.1853	0.0917	0.5397	0.0195	0.9964
	(58.51)	(4.25)	(4.15)	(3.82)	[1.50]
Ford	1.1370	0.0993	0.2166	0.0226	0.9985
	(49.20)	(4.27)	(1.19)	(4.97)	[0.94]
GE	1.2095	0.1072	0.0893	0.0418	0.9915
	(54.10)	(4.52)	(0.58)	(5.58)	[2.36]
HP	1.4042	0.0921	0.7174	0.0100	0.9989
	(34.95)	(4.58)	(10.51)	(2.15)	[0.73]
IBM	1.1115	0.1840	0.5046	0.0275	0.9925
	(44.51)	(4.49)	(5.18)	(3.09)	[2.59]
JJ	1.1262	0.1515	0.3615	0.0341	0.9927
	(19.85)	(4.72)	(3.24)	(4.36)	[2.21]
MD	0.8162	0.1531	0.6790	0.0181	0.9996
	(18.97)	(6.01)	(12.26)	(3.15)	[0.33]
Merck	1.0284	0.0958	0.5532	0.0256	0.9892
	(43.81)	(4.65)	(3.62)	(3.33)	[2.08]
Upjohn	1.1072	0.1186	0.7328	0.0106	0.9974
	(31.70)	(3.42)	(12.14)	(2.23)	[1.44]

[a] In parentheses are the robust t-statistics based on Bollerslev and Wooldridge (1991).

will be larger than those for low-risk individual stocks since the idiosyncratic volatility now plays an important role. Our study here surely can provide some reference points for judging the persistence level of the idiosyncratic volatility and the significance level of the market factor.

9 Conclusion

In this paper, the conditional variance of stock returns has been decomposed in a statistical unobserved component model to describe the long-run (trend) and the short-run (transitory) movements of stock market volatility. The empirical results for the S&P 500, the CRSP value-weighted index and the NIKKEI index and fourteen individual stocks, support the decomposition and reveal a general pattern of volatility component movement in stock markets. The long-run volatility component has a much slower mean-reverting (higher persistence) rate and the short-run component is more sensitive to market shocks. Application of the component model shows that the impact of the October 1987 Crash on volatility movements in the stock market was temporary, mainly affecting the transitory volatility component as reflected by the quick market recovery after the crash. The expected excess return or the risk premium in the stock market is found to be related only to the long-run movement of stock return volatility, which may have fundamental economic explanations. The observed "leverage effect" in the stock market is mainly a temporary behavior; the long-run volatility component shows no asymmetric response to market changes. Modeling the CRSP value-weighted index and fourteen individual stocks in a one-factor model framework, we found the market factor, represented by the index, and the idiosyncratic noise of the individual stocks both show highly persistent volatility trends contributing to the persistence of individual stock return volatility. Many other interesting issues, such as volatility co-persistence, time-varying correlation across different asset returns and its long-run forecast can be studied in a multivariate framework extended from the component model introduced in this paper.

Appendix

Conditions for Non-Negativity of the Conditional Variance in the Component Model

Nelson and Cao (1992) (NC) derived inequality constraints for general GARCH processes sufficient to ensure non-negative conditional variance. The central idea of the derivation is to express the conditional variance in terms of an infinite-order polynomial of the squared residuals and then find the conditions ensuring non-negative coefficients in the polynomial. The conditions are only sufficient, not necessary. Their results can be applied to the volatility component model:

$$(h_t - q_t) = \alpha(\varepsilon_{t-1}^2 - q_{t-1}) + \beta(h_{t-1} - q_{t-1}), \tag{2.4}$$
$$q_t = \omega + \rho q_{t-1} + \varphi(\varepsilon_{t-1}^2 - h_{t-1}), \tag{2.5}$$

to derive the corresponding sufficient conditions. We show below that the conditions:

$$1 > \rho > (\alpha + \beta) > 0,\ \beta > \varphi > 0,\ \alpha > 0,\ \beta > 0,\ \omega > 0,\ \varphi > 0,\ \omega > 0, \tag{A.1}$$

are sufficient to guarantee the non-negativity of the conditional variance.

Let us first examine the conditional variance process. Substituting (2.5) into (2.4), we have:

$$h_t = \omega + (\rho - \alpha - \beta)q_{t-1} + (\alpha + \varphi)\varepsilon_{t-1}^2 + (\beta - \varphi)h_{t-1}. \tag{A.2}$$

Equation (A.2) can be considered as a regular GARCH(1, 1) process with a time-varying intercept, $(\omega + (\rho - \alpha - \beta) \cdot q_{t-1})$. The sufficient conditions, conditional on the assumption of non-negative q_{t-1}, will be like that for the GARCH(1, 1)—that $\omega > 0$, $(\rho - \alpha - \beta) > 0$, $(\alpha + \varphi) > 0$ and $(\beta - \varphi) > 0$. These are all implied by (A.1).

Now let us examine the trend component. Substituting (2.4) into (2.5) gives:

$$\begin{aligned} q_t &= (1 - \beta)\omega + \varphi\varepsilon_{t-1}^2 - \varphi(\alpha + \beta)\varepsilon_{t-2}^2 + (\rho + \beta - \varphi)q_{t-1} \\ &\quad + [\varphi(\alpha + \beta) - \beta\rho]q_{t-2}. \end{aligned} \tag{A.3}$$

The trend also reduces to a GARCH(2, 2) process. In the following, we use the results of NC to examine whether q_t remains non-negative over time under the constraints (A.1).

First we need to examine the characteristic of the autoregressive polynomial of q_t. The roots of the autoregressive polynomial of q_t in (A.3) can be solved from:

$$Z^2 + [-(\rho + \beta - \phi)]Z + [\beta\rho - \phi(\alpha + \beta)] = 0, \tag{A.4}$$

so that

$$Z_1 = 0.5(\rho + \beta - \phi) + 0.5\Delta^{1/2}, \tag{A.5}$$
$$Z_2 = 0.5(\rho + \beta - \phi) - 0.5\Delta^{1/2}, \tag{A.6}$$

where $\Delta = (\rho + \beta - \phi)^2 - 4[\beta\rho - \phi(\alpha + \beta)]$. To ensure real roots, we require that Δ is non-negative, which is always true since:

$$\Delta = (\rho + \beta - \phi)^2 - 4[\beta\rho - \phi(\alpha + \beta)] = (\rho - \beta - \phi)^2 + 4\phi\alpha > 0. \tag{A.7}$$

So condition (19) of NC that the roots of (A.4) are real is satisfied. Also, (A.1) implies that the signs of the coefficients of the quadratic form in (A.4) are:

$$Z_1 + Z_2 = \rho + \beta - \phi > 0, \tag{A.8}$$
$$Z_1 Z_2 = \beta\rho - \phi(\alpha + \beta) > (\beta - \phi)(\alpha + \beta) > 0. \tag{A.9}$$

Consequently, the two roots are both positive with $Z_1 > Z_2 > 0$. So condition (20) of NC that the bigger root is positive is satisfied. Condition (8) of NC requires Z_1 and Z_2 lie inside the unit circle. Check the bigger root:

$$\begin{aligned} Z_1 &= 0.5(\rho + \beta - \phi) + 0.5\Delta^{1/2} < 0.5(\rho + \beta - \phi) + 0.5(\rho - \beta + \phi) \\ &= \rho < 1, \end{aligned} \tag{A.10}$$

since $\Delta = (\rho - \beta - \phi)^2 + 4\phi\alpha < (\rho - \beta - \phi)^2 + 4\phi\rho = (\rho - \beta + \phi)^2$ by (A.1). So condition (8) of NC is satisfied. Condition (9) of NC that there is no common root between the polynomial of q_t and the polynomial of ε_t^2 in (A.3) is generally satisfied. Satisfaction of the above conditions ensures that q_t can be expressed in terms of an infinite-order polynomial of ε_t^2s.

Secondly, we need to examine whether the coefficients of the infinite-order polynomial of ε_t^2 are non-negative under (A.1). For the intercept,

$$\omega^* = (1-\beta)\omega/(1-Z_1-Z_2+Z_1Z_2) > 0, \tag{A.11}$$

since

$$\begin{aligned}(1-Z_1-Z_2+Z_1Z_2) &= 1-(\rho+\beta-\phi)+[\beta\rho-\phi(\alpha+\beta)]\\ &> (1-\rho)(1-\beta)+\phi(1-\alpha-\beta) > 0,\end{aligned} \tag{A.12}$$

by (A.1). So condition (18) of NC is satisfied. Condition (21) of NC requires

$$\phi-\phi(\alpha+\beta)/Z_1 > 0. \tag{A.13}$$

By $\phi > 0$ and $Z_1 > 0$, it is the same as:

$$Z_1 > (\alpha+\beta), \tag{A.14}$$

which is also true under (A.1) since:

$$\begin{aligned}Z_1 &= 0.5(\rho+\beta-\phi)+0.5[(\rho-\beta-\phi)^2+4\phi\alpha]^{1/2}\\ &> 0.5[(\alpha+\beta)+\beta-\phi]+0.5\{[(\alpha+\beta)-\beta-\phi]^2+4\phi\alpha\}^{1/2}\\ &= 0.5[(\alpha+\beta)+\beta-\phi]+0.5(\alpha+\phi)\\ &= (\alpha+\beta).\end{aligned} \tag{A.15}$$

So condition (21) of NC is satisfied too. Finally let us check condition (22) of NC for the first three coefficients of the dynamics in the polynomial:

$$\begin{aligned}\theta_1 &= \phi > 0 && \text{(A.16)}\\ \theta_2 &= (\rho+\beta-\phi)\theta_1-(\alpha+\beta)\phi > 0 && \text{(A.17)}\\ \theta_3 &= (\rho+\beta-\phi)\theta_2+[\phi(\alpha+\beta)-\beta\rho]\theta_1 > 0. && \text{(A.18)}\end{aligned}$$

(A.16) is true obviously. (A.17) is also true:

$$\begin{aligned}\theta_2 &= (\rho+\beta-\phi)\phi-(\alpha+\beta)\phi = (\rho-\alpha-\phi)\phi > [(\alpha+\beta)-\alpha-\phi]-\alpha\\ &= (\beta-\phi)\phi > 0,\end{aligned} \tag{A.19}$$

under (A.1). For (A.18):

$$\begin{aligned}\theta_3 &= (\rho+\beta-\phi)(\rho-\alpha-\phi)\phi+[\phi(\alpha+\beta)-\beta\rho]\phi\\ &= [(\rho-\phi)^2-\alpha\rho-\alpha\beta+2\alpha\phi]\phi\\ &> [(\rho-\phi)(\alpha+\beta-\phi)-\alpha\rho-\alpha\beta+2\alpha\phi]\phi\\ &= [(\rho-\alpha-\phi)(\beta-\phi)]\phi > 0,\end{aligned} \tag{A.20}$$

by (A.1). So condition (22) of NC is satisfied.

All the conditions in Nelson and Cao (1992) for (A.3) are satisfied by the inequalities in (A.1). Therefore, the permanent component is non-negative which in turn ensures non-negativity of the conditional variance.

References

Amin, K. I. and V. K. Ng (1993), "Option Valuation with Systematic Stochastic Volatility," *Journal of Finance*, 48(3): 881–910.

Baillie, R. T. and T. Bollerslev (1994), "Long Memory in the Forward Premium," *Journal of International Money and Finance*, 13: 565–71.

Beveridge, S. and C. R. Nelson (1981), "A New Approach to Decomposition of Economic Time Series into Permanent and Transitory Components with Particular Attention to Measurement of the Business Cycle," *Journal of Monetary Economics*, 7: 151–74.

Black, F. (1976), "Studies of Stock Price Volatility Changes," in *Proceedings of the 1976 Meeting of the Business and Economics Statistics Section, American Statistical Association*, 177–181.

Bollerslev, T. (1986), "Generalized Autoregressive Conditional Heteroskedasticity," *Journal of Econometrics*, 31: 307–27.

Bollerslev, T. and H. O. Mikkelsen (1996), "Modeling and Pricing Long Memory in Stock Market Volatility," *Journal of Econometrics*, 73: 151–84.

Bollerslev, T. and J. M. Wooldridge (1991), "Quasi Maximum Likelihood Estimation and Inference in Dynamic Models with Time Varying Covariances," *Econometric Reviews*, forthcoming.

Bougerol, P. and N. Picard (1992), "Stationarity of GARCH Processes and of Some Nonnegative Time Series," *Journal of Econometrics*, 52: 115–28.

Chou, R. Y. (1988), "Volatility Persistence and Stock Valuations: Some Empirical Evidence Using GARCH," *Journal of Applied Econometrics*, 3: 279–94.

Christie, A. A. (1982), "The Stochastic Behavior of Common Stock Variances: Value, Leverage and Interest Rate Effects," *Journal of Financial Economics*, 10: 407–32.

den Hertog, R. G. J. (1995), "Differences in Pricing between Permanent and Transitory Volatility Components: A Latent Variable Approach," *Journal of International Financial Markets, Institutions and Money*, 5(2–3): 79–95.

Dickey, D. A. and W. A. Fuller (1979), "Distribution of the Estimators for Autoregressive Time Series with a Unit Root," *Journal of American Statistical Association*, 74: 427–31.

Dickey, D. A. and W. A. Fuller (1981), "Likelihood Ratio Statistics for Autoregressive Time Series with a Unit Root," *Econometrica*, 49: 1057–72.

Ding, Z. and C. W. J. Granger (1996), "Modeling Volatility Persistence of Speculative Returns: A New Approach," *Journal of Econometrics*, 73: 185–215.

Ding, Z., C. W. J. Granger, and R. F. Engle (1993) "A Long Memory Property of Stock Market Returns and a New Model," *Journal of Empirical Finance*, 1: 83–106.

Engle, R. F. (1982), "Autoregressive Conditional Heteroscedasticity with Estimates of the Variance of U.K. Inflation," *Econometrica*, 50: 987–1008.

Engle, R. F. and T. Bollerslev (1986), "Modeling the Persistence of Conditional Variances," *Econometric Reviews*, 5: 1–50, 81–7.

Engle, R. F. and G. Gonzalez-Rivera (1991), "Semiparametric ARCH Models," *Journal of Business and Economic Statistics*, 9: 345–60.

Engle, R. F. and C. W. J. Granger (1987), "Cointegration and Error Correction: Representation, Estimation and Testing," *Econometrica*, 55: 251–76.

Engle, R. F. and C. Mustafa (1992), "Implied ARCH Models from Options Prices," *Journal of Econometrics*, 52: 289–311.

Engle, R. F., T. Bollerslev, and D. B. Nelson (1994), "ARCH Models," *The Handbook of Econometrics*, vol. 4, pp. 2961–3031

Engle, R. F., C. W. J. Granger, and R. Robins (1986) "Wholesale and Retail Prices: Bivariate Modeling with Forecastable Variances," in David Belsley and Edwin Kuh (eds.), *Model Reliability*. Cambridge, MA: MIT Press, pp. 1–17.

Engle, R. F., D. F. Hendry, and J. F. Richard (1983), "Exogeneity," *Econometrica*, 51: 277–304.

Engle, R. F., D. M. Lilien, and R. P. Robins (1987), "Estimating Time Varying Risk Premia in the Term Structure: The ARCH-M Model," *Econometrica*, 55: 391–407.

Engle, R. F., V. Ng, and M. Rothschild (1990), "Asset Pricing with a Factor ARCH Covariance Structure: Empirical estimates for Treasure Bills," *Journal of Econometrics*, 45: 213–37.

Fama, E. F. (1965), "The Behavior of Stock Market Prices," *Journal of Business*, 38: 34–105.

Fisher, L. (1966), "Some New Stock Market Indices," *Journal of Business*, 29: 191–225.

French, K. R., G. W. Schwert, and R. F. Stambaugh (1987), "Expected Stock Returns and Volatility," *Journal of Financial Economics*, 19: 3–30.

Gallant, A. R., P. E. Rossi, and G. Tauchen (1993), "Nonlinear Dynamic Structures," *Econometrica*, 61: 871–908.

Glosten, L. R., R. Jagannathan, and D. E. Runkle (1993), "On the Relation between the Expected Value and the Volatility of the Nominal Excess Return on Stocks," *Journal of Finance*, 48(5): 1779–1801.

Godfrey, L. G. (1978), "Testing for Higher Order Serial Correlation in Regression Equations when the Regressors Include Lagged Dependent Variables," *Econometrica*, 46: 1303–10.

Hong, C.-H. (1988), "The Integrated Generalized Autoregressive Conditional Heteroskedastic Model: The Process, Estimation and Monte Carlo Experiments," unpublished manuscript, Department of Economics, University of California, San Diego.

Lee, S.-W. and B. E. Hansen (1994), "Asymptotic Theory for the GARCH(1,1) Quasi-Maximum Likelihood Estimator," *Econometric Theory*, 10(1): 29–52.

Ljung, G. M. and G. E. P. Box (1978), "On a Measure of Lack of Fit in Time Series Models," *Biometrika*, 66: 67–72.

Lumsdaine, R. L. (1996), "Consistency and Asymptotic Normality of the Quasi-Maximum Likelihood Estimator in IGARCH(1,1) and Covariance Stationary GARCH(1,1) Models," *Econometrica*, 64(3): 575–96.

Malkiel, B. (1979), "The Capital Formation Problem in the United States," *Journal of Finance*, 34: 291–306.

Mandelbrot, B. (1963), "The Variation of Certain Speculative Prices," *Journal of Business*, 36: 147–65.

Merton, R. C. (1980), "On Estimating the Expected Return on the Market: An Exploratory Investigation," *Journal of Financial Economics*, 8(4): 323–61.

Merville, L. J. and D. R. Pieptea (1989), "Stock-Price Volatility, Mean-Reverting Diffusion, and Noise," *Journal of Financial Economics*, 24: 193–214.

Nelson, D. B. (1989), "Modeling Stock Market Volatility Changes," in *Proceedings of the American Statistical Association, Business and Economic Statistics Section*, 93–8.

Nelson, D. B. (1990a), "Stationarity and Persistence in the GARCH(1, 1) Model," *Econometric Theory*, 6: 318–34.

Nelson, D. B. (1990b), "Conditional Heteroskedasticity in Asset Returns: A New Approach," *Econometrica*, 59: 347–70.

Nelson, D. B. and C. Q. Cao (1992), "Inequality Constraints in the Univariate GARCH Model," *Journal of Business and Economic Statistics*, 10: 229–35.

Ng, V., R. F. Engle, and M. Rothschild (1992), "A Multi-Dynamic-Factor Model for Stock Returns," *Journal of Econometrics*, 52(1–2): 245–66.

Pagan, A. R. and G. W. Schwert (1990), "Alternative Models for Conditional Stock Volatility," *Journal of Econometrics*, 45: 267–90.

Pindyck, R. S. (1984), "Risk, Inflation and the Stock Market," *American Economic Review*, 74: 335–51.

Poterba, J. M. and L. H. Summers (1986), "The Persistence of Volatility and Stock Market Fluctuations," *American Economic Review*, 76: 1142–51.

Ross, S. A. (1976), "The Arbitrage Theory of Capital Asset Pricing," *Journal of Economic Theory*, 13: 341–60.

Ross, S. A. (1977), "The Capital Asset Pricing Model (CAPM), Short-Sale Restrictions and Related Issues," *Journal of Finance*, 32(1): 177–83.

Rothschild, M. (1986), "Asset Pricing Theories," in W. Heller, R. Starr, and D. Starrett (eds.), *Uncertainty, Information and Communication: Essays in Honor of Kenneth J. Arrow*, vol. 3. New York: Cambridge University Press.

Said, S. E. and D. A. Dickey (1984), "Testing for Unit Roots in Autoregressive-Moving Average Models of Unknown Order," *Biometrika*, 71: 1142–51.

Said, S. E. and D. A. Dickey (1985), "Hypothesis Testing in ARIMA(p,1,q) Models," *Journal of the American Statistical Association*, 80: 368–74.

Sakata, S. and H. L. White (1998), "High Breakdown Point Coditional Dispersion Estimation with Application to S&P 500 Daily Returns Volatility," *Econometrica*, 66: 529–68.

Schwert, G. W. (1990), "Stock Volatility and the Crash of '87," *Review of Financial Studies*, 3: 77–102.

Schwert, G. W. and P. J. Seguin (1990), "Heteroskedasticity in Stock Returns," *Journal of Finance*, 4: 1129–56.

Shiller, R. (1981), "Do Stock Prices Move Too Much To Be Justified by Subsequent Changes in Dividends?" *American Economic Review*, 71: 421–36.

Sin, C.-Y. and H. White (1996), "Information Criteria for Selecting Possibly Misspecified Parametric Models," *Journal of Econometrics*, 71: 207–25.

Xu, X. and S. J. Taylor (1994), "The Term Structure of Volatility Implied by Foreign Exchange Options," *Journal of Financial and Quantitative Analysis*, 29/1: 57–74.